Mastering
Microsoft®
Exchange Server
2007

Mastering
Microsoft®
Exchange Server
2007

Barry Gerber

Jim McBee

Wiley Publishing, Inc.

Acquisitions Editor: Tom Cirtin
Development Editor: Kim Wimpsett
Technical Editor: Brian Tirch
Production Editor: Martine Dardignac
Copy Editor: Judy Flynn
Production Manager: Tim Tate
Vice President and Executive Group Publisher: Richard Swadley
Vice President and Executive Publisher: Joseph B. Wikert
Vice President and Publisher: Neil Edde
Book Designers: Maureen Forys and Judy Fung
Compositor: Laserwords Private Limited, Chennai, India
Proofreader: Nancy Hanger
Indexer: Jack Lewis
Anniversary Logo Design: Richard Pacifico
Cover Designer: Ryan Sneed
Cover Image: © Pete Gardner / Digital Vision / gettyimage

For general information on our other products and services or to obtain technical support, please contact our Customer Care Department within the U.S. at (800) 762-2974, outside the U.S. at (317) 572-3993 or fax (317) 572-4002.

Wiley also publishes its books in a variety of electronic formats. Some content that appears in print may not be available in electronic books.

Library of Congress Cataloging-in-Publication Data
Gerber, Barry.
    Mastering Microsoft Exchange Server 2007 / Barry Gerber, Jim McBee.
        p.   cm.
    Includes index.
    ISBN 978-0-470-04289-2 (paper/website)
    1.   Microsoft Exchange server   2.   Client/server computing.   3.   Electronic mail systems. I. McBee, Jim.   II. Title.
    QA76.9.C55G465 2007
    005.2'768 — dc22

                                                2007009243

10 9 8 7 6 5 4 3 2 1

To Jane, my wife and best friend, for reminding me in so many ways that technology should serve and not control humanity. To my children, Margot, Karl, and Georg, for showing me both how much and how little we influence others. And to everyone who is trying to make our often harsh and nasty world a better place to live in.

To the men and women of the United States Armed Forces who bravely serve our country.

Acknowledgments

It has been just over a year since I got my hands on the Exchange Server 2007 beta 1 software. And what a year it has been. In May 2006, I began talking with Barry Gerber and Tom Cirtin (Wiley acquisitions editor) about contributing to this book.

Along the way, a lot of people have been involved in reviewing the content of this book. I hope that I am remembering everyone who has jumped in and offered advice and constructive criticism along the way. First and foremost is Devin Ganger (3Sharp); when we realized that we were going to run short on time, Devin jumped on board and developed the content for several chapters. As deadlines crunched even further, Exchange MVP Simon Butler and Outlook MVP Ben Schorr also provided content.

During the early development of the book and the first drafts of chapters, a number of Exchange gurus and administrators provided me with feedback on the book's outline, reviewed chapter content, or just answered my questions. These skilled people include William Lefkovics, Todd Hawkins, Ben Craig, Paul Robichaux, John Fullbright, Chuck Swanson, Cynthia Wang, Desmond Lee, Josh Maher, Omar Drubi, Peter O'Dowd, Rich Matheisen, Glen Scales, Bob Christian, David Elfassy, Mark Watts, Andy Schan, Nick Gillott, Vlad Mazek, Rick Taylor, Konrad Sagala, Bob Lawler, Daniel Petri, Andy David, Missy Koslosky, Mark Arnold, Pavel Nagaev, Andy Webb, Bharat Suneja, Elizabeth Owusu, Damion Jones, and Siegfried Jagott. My hat is also off to the hundreds of people I have talked to at conferences and events over the past year who have given me ideas for topics and how things can be better explained.

As with any new product, often not much public information is available prior to its release. Many people at Microsoft patiently and carefully explained new concepts to me and answered questions. These good folks include Kevin Miller, Paul Bowden, David Espinoza, Scott Schnoll, Ross Smith IV, KC Lemson, David Lemson, Jon Gollogly, Karena Lynch, Ben Winzenz, Tim McMichael, Nino Bilic, Melissa Travers, Harold Wong, and Evan Dodds.

I was also extremely lucky to be able to recommend a technical editor. The most experienced Exchange 2007 person I know outside of Microsoft is Brian Tirch. Since the Exchange 2007 beta 1 cycle, Brian has been running an Exchange 2007 organization with thousands of users.

This book gave me an opportunity to once again work with the great folks at Wiley. These include acquisitions editor Tom Cirtin, development editor Kim Wimpsett, production editor Martine Dardignac, copyeditor Judy Flynn, and proofreader Nancy Hanger. Thanks to all of you for your guidance, sense of humor, and tolerance in the face of deadlines.

Thanks to everyone for all your help. Whatever errors of fact or judgment remain are mine and mine alone.

— *Jim McBee*
— *Honolulu, Hawaii*

Contents at a Glance

Contents

Introduction

Mastering Microsoft Exchange Server 2007 is the latest in a successful series of *Mastering Exchange Server* books. Each book has helped introduce tens of thousands of readers to the concepts of Exchange and helped Exchange administrators successfully support their Exchange systems better and more accurately.

We took a step back and looked at the previous editions of the book to try to figure out how much of the previous material was still relevant. We quickly realized that the book was going to have to be almost completely rewritten since the entire administrative model of Exchange 2007 has changed. We were faced with the challenge of explaining not only a completely new management interface, but also the new Exchange Management Shell command-line interface, new server roles, and new features.

We started designing the new book almost a year before Exchange Server 2007 was to be released. Much of the book was written using beta 2 code and consequently updated once the released version was ready. In writing this book, we had a few goals for both the book and the knowledge we want to impart to the reader.

- The book is designed to help you master the basics of Exchange Server 2007. We want you to get all of the basic skills necessary to install and manage an Exchange Server 2007 system.

- The skills and tasks covered in this book should be applicable to 80 percent of all organizations running Exchange Server.

- The book should educate not only "new to product" administrators, but those "new to version" administrators that are upgrading from a previous version.

- The book should introduce you to that 20 percent feature set, such as clustering and unified messaging, that will be applicable to only certain types of organizations.

- The book should impart as much practical advice as possible given that as we write this book, Exchange Server 2007 has only been in the hands of customers for a few months.

Despite the fact that many things have changed, if you are upgrading from a previous version you will still be comfortable with the concepts and principles of operation. Exchange Server 5.5 was one of the most powerful, extensible, scalable, easy-to-use, and manageable electronic-messaging back ends on the market. Exchange 2000 Server retained all of 5.5's best features and added new ones. Exchange Server 2003 went a step further, altering interfaces that didn't quite work in the 2000 flavor and adding some great new features.

Microsoft listened to the advice of many of its customers and its internal consultants at Microsoft Consulting Services (MCS) and to Microsoft Certified Systems Engineers (MCSEs), Most Valued Professionals (MVPs), and Microsoft Certified Trainers (MCTs) to find out what was missing from earlier versions of the product and what organizations' needs were. Much of this work even started before Exchange Server 2003 was released. Here are some of the common requests, feedback, and complaints that customers frequently provided about earlier versions of Exchange Server:

◆ Simply the management interface and make it easier to script all Exchange management functions.

◆ Allow for local or remote replicas of Exchange databases.

◆ Provide better anti-spam capabilities and update anti-spam configuration data and signatures frequently.

◆ Provide better security for mobile devices and make them easier to manage.

◆ Provide better integration with voicemail and faxing solutions.

◆ Make resource scheduling and calendaring better integrated.

◆ Reduce the burden on help desks by enabling clients to be configured automatically.

Improvements to Exchange Server 2007 are not to any single component. For starters, the management interface was completely revamped. The new Exchange Management Console simplifies Exchange Server administration with a totally redesigned interface that makes finding features and components much easier. The Exchange Management Shell provides a powerful alternative to the Exchange Management Console; all administrative tasks can be performed via the Exchange Management Shell, including many advanced tasks that cannot even be performed in the graphical user interface. All mail-enabled recipient administration (mailboxes, groups, and contacts) is now performed through the Exchange Management Console utility, not the Active Directory Users and Computers utility; needless to say, this was a bit of a controversial decision. The Exchange 2000/2003 extensions for Active Directory Users and Computers no longer work reliably with Exchange Server 2007. Some features continue to work, but mail-enabled objects should not be created through Exchange System Manager, and once they have been moved to Exchange 2007 servers, they should not be managed using Exchange System Manager.

Another controversial decision was to support only x64 processor architecture. Exchange Server 2007 requires Windows 2003 SP1 x64 or Windows 2003 R2 x64. The decision to support the x64 architecture was driven by the need for more RAM in larger organizations. Exchange Server 2007 has been tested heavily in environments with up to 32GB of RAM. More RAM improves disk I/O performance dramatically.

Exchange Server 2007's tight integration with Active Directory has not changed; almost all of the Exchange configuration data and recipient e-mail attributes is still stored in the Active Directory just as it was with Exchange 2000/2003. A popular misconception is that Exchange recipient configuration is no longer in the Active Directory since the recipient management utility is no longer Active Directory Users and Computers.

To simplify installation of Exchange Server 2007 and to make it easier for organizations that split server functions across multiple servers, the setup program allows you to chose which functions (called roles) the server supports. These roles include the Mailbox server, the Client Access server, the Hub Transport server, the Unified Messaging server and the Edge Transport server. Additionally, during installation, a server can be configured as either an active clustered server or a passive cluster server. By allowing the installer to easily separate the functions of a server during installation, setup is simpler and the server is more secure because only the components necessary for that server's functions are installed.

One of the most interesting new feature sets for Exchange Server 2007 is the ability to replicate a database to another location on the same server or a remote server. The replication is based on replicating the transaction logs; once they have been completely filled to another location, the logs are replayed to a backup copy of the database. Local continuous replication allows you to replicate a copy of the database to another location on the local server and to very quickly recover from a database failure. Clustered continuous replication allows you to keep a replicated copy of the databases from the active node on the passive node of the cluster.

Although sender filtering, recipient filtering, sender ID, and real-time block list features have been retained, anti-spam capabilities have been improved with additional methods of connection filtering, such as reputation filtering. An all-new version of the Intelligent Message Filter (IMF) is now included with Exchange Server 2007 and is called the content filter. Customers with Enterprise client access licenses can get daily updates to the reputation filter and the content filter. Anti-spam components can be installed on the Hub Transport servers or they can be offloaded to dedicated Edge Transport servers in an organization's perimeter network. Enterprise client access licenses allow an organization to use Microsoft's Forefront Security for Exchange (formerly Sybari Antigen).

If you ever wanted to have better control of messages in transit, then the redesigned message transport and transport rules will have you dancing on tables. All messages are delivered through a Hub Transport server role regardless of whether they are being delivered locally or remotely. Transport rules allow you to apply conditions to messages moving through the transport (such as sender/recipient, sender/recipient group memberships, message classification, and so on) and take actions on them.

Calendaring and resource scheduling have been dramatically improved. The free/busy functions of earlier versions of Exchange have been completely replaced with a new web service. Resource mailboxes are now specific mailbox types rather than just generic mailboxes as with previous versions. The Calendar Concierge feature allows the administrator to configuration automatic resource booking options.

Outlook Web Access is better than ever with a completely revamped interface that includes improved options, better scheduling integration, and the ability to manage mobile devices via the Outlook Web Access interface.

Another new web service is the Autodiscover service; the Autodiscover service works with Outlook 2007 and Windows Mobile 6 devices automatically configure Outlook to connect to the correct Exchange resources regardless of whether the client is on the internal network or the external network.

An entirely new Exchange Server function is the Unified Messaging server role, which integrates with your Voice over IP phone system or legacy PBX via VOIP gateway. This allows Exchange Server to handle your automated call routing, inbound voicemail, and inbound faxing. Exchange users can call into the Unified Messaging server to retrieve their voicemail, have their e-mail read to them, listen to their calendar, or even move items around on their calendar.

With these and an impressive array of other features, Exchange Server 2007 can help your organization move smoothly and productively into the world of advanced, enhanced electronic messaging.

What You Need to Run Exchange Server

Exchange Server 2007 is a complex product, but the user interface has been completely revamped to make it easier to administer. All of this complexity and parallel ease of use requires an industrial-strength computer. The minimum server requirements suggested here are for testing, learning about, and evaluating the product. It's also enough for a small, noncritical installation. However, as we discuss in the book, when the server moves into critical production environments where it will be accessed by large numbers of users, you'll need to beef up its hardware and add a number of fault-tolerance capabilities. On the client side, with the broad range of clients available for Exchange, the machines in most organizations should be more than adequate.

At a minimum, to test, learn about, and evaluate Exchange Server, you need the following:

◆ Either Microsoft Exchange Server 2007 and Windows Server 2003 SP1 or Windows 2003 R2 or Microsoft Exchange Server 2007 Enterprise Edition and Windows Server 2007 Enterprise or Datacenter Edition.

◆ An AMD x64– or Intel x64–compatible processor with 2GB of RAM and two 9GB disk drives. This allows you to complete exercises involving a single Exchange server.

◆ A minimum of three additional computers in the class just described. This allows you to complete exercises involving multiple computers in multiple administrative groups and Windows Server 2003 domains.

◆ Tape backup hardware or at least one independent disk drive for backup.

◆ A local area network (preferably connected to the Internet).

◆ At least one 800MHz Pentium III or 4 or equivalent computer with 128MB of memory running Windows XP Professional for testing Outlook and other client-side functions.

During the development of this book, we used a combination of Dell Xeon-based servers, HP Athlon-based servers, and lots and lots of virtual machines using VMWare. During the development, we did not have access to 64-bit versions of VMWare, so we used the 32-bit version of Exchange Server 2007 for testing. The 32-bit version of Exchange Server 2007 can be downloaded for evaluation, classroom, lab, and testing purposes, but it is not to be used in public.

How This Book Is Organized

This book is made up of 21 chapters and an appendix, divided into seven broad topic areas. As you proceed through the book, you'll move from basic concepts to several increasingly complex levels of hands-on implementation.

This book won't work well for practitioners of the timeworn ritual of chapter hopping. We have taken great pains to write an integrated book on Windows Server 2003 and Exchange Server 2007. Unless you already have considerable experience with these products, to get the maximum value out of this book, you need to track through the chapters in order. In later chapters, you will frequently find us referring to previous chapters to get more details on a specific topic.

If you are an Exchange 2000/2003 administrator and you are ready to get started with your migration, we recommend that you pay close attention to Part 2, "Installing, Configuring, Migrating, and Scaling" (Chapters 4, 5, and 6). While you should not read just these three chapters and then start your migration, they will definitely send you on your way.

However, if you're in a hurry to get your hands dirty, start with Part 3, "Basic Exchange Server 2007 Management. Chapter 7, "Administering Exchange 2007," will introduce you to the new Exchange Management Console and the new Exchange Management Shell, and Chapter 10, "Managing Recipients," will get you rolling on managing mail-enabled recipients. As long as you're not planning to put your quickie server into production immediately, there should be no harm done. Before going into production, though, we strongly suggest that you explore other parts of this book. Here's a guide to what's in each chapter.

Part 1: Understanding and Planning

This part of the book focuses on concepts and features of Microsoft's Windows Server 2003 and Exchange Server 2007 client/server electronic messaging system. It is designed to provide you with the underlying knowledge that you'll need when you tackle Windows and Exchange Server 2007 installation, administration, and management later in this book.

Chapter 1, "Introducing Exchange Server 2007," presents some basic information about Exchange Server 2007 products, helping you optimize the value of these products in your organization. This chapter will introduce you to new features as well as features that are being de-emphasized in Exchange Server 2007.

Chapter 2, "Exchange Server 2007 Architecture," looks in some detail at the decision to move to the 64-bit architecture as well as system requirements for running Exchange Server 2007. This chapter also discusses the Exchange Server 2007 dependencies on Windows 2003 and Active Directory.

Chapter 3, "Designing a New Exchange 2007 System," covers Windows Server 2003 and Exchange 2007 system planning and design, facilitating your initial use of these complex products in your organization.

Part 2: Installation, Configuring, Migrating, and Scaling

Microsoft Exchange Server 2007 runs on top of Microsoft's Windows Server 2003. This part covers the installation of Exchange Server 2007. In previous versions, we also covered installation of Windows, but we recommend that you refer to a dedicated Window reference such as *Mastering Windows Server 2003* by Mark Minasi (Sybex, 2003).

Chapter 4, "Installing Exchange Server 2007," provides the details on Exchange Server 2007 installation, server roles, disk configuration, and basic security.

Chapter 5, "Upgrading to Exchange Server 2007," covers migrating from Exchange 2000 or Exchange 2003 to Exchange Server 2007, including prerequisites and factors to consider before starting a migration. Also included in this chapter are recommendations for migration phases, co-existence, and reasons you would need to keep older Exchange servers in production.

Chapter 6, "Scaling Upward and Outward," helps you to determine when to add an additional server and whether you should add more mailbox databases. Local continuous replication is also covered in this chapter.

Part 3: Basic Exchange Server 2007 Management

Attention shifts in this section to day-to-day Exchange Server operational tasks. Most of these tasks are carried out within the Exchange Management Console, but some can be performed only through the Exchange Management Shell.

Chapter 7, "Administering Exchange 2007," covers many of the basic administrative changes to Exchange Server 2007, including delegating permissions for users, using the Exchange Management Console, and an introduction to using the Exchange Management Shell.

Chapter 8, "Exchange Organization, Server, and Recipient Management," focuses on how to find the necessary configuration options for components that affect the entire organization, individual servers, and mail-enabled servers and lists many of the Exchange Management Shell cmdlets. Much of this chapter is covered in more detail in other chapters, but this chapter will help both new Exchange administrators as well as those upgrading from previous versions when you need to find a particular option.

Chapter 9, "Imposing Limits," covers the different types of limits (mailbox sizes, message sizes, folder sizes, connector limits) that an administrator can apply in Exchange 2007 and how to apply them.

Chapter 10, "Managing Recipients," concentrates on the Recipient Configuration work center in the Exchange Management Console and on using it to administer and manage mail-enabled recipients. This includes mailbox-enabled users, resource mailbox management, mail-enabled groups, and mail-enabled contacts.

Chapter 11, "Managing Address Lists," covers the use of the default global address list, custom address lists, offline address books, and the distribution of offline address books.

Chapter 12, "Managing Folder Content," introduces the new messaging records management features of Exchange 2007, including creating managed custom folders, defining folder content settings, and configuring managed folder mailbox policies.

Chapter 13, "Managing Messages in Transit," introduces the new transport rule feature and how to implement it. This chapter also discusses message journaling.

Chapter 14, "Public Folder Administration," introduces management of public folders and the Exchange 2007 Exchange Management Shell cmdlets necessary to manage public folder properties. Additionally, this chapter covers using the Exchange 2003 System Manager console if you want to continue to have a graphical user interface for managing public folder properties because the Exchange 2007 release-to-manufacturing version does not include one.

Part 4: Exchange Server Reliability and Availability

If you ask your users what they expect most from you as the Exchange server administrator, they will probably tell you uninterrupted messaging service. Well, and maybe that you will answer your cell phone 24/7. In this section, we discuss techniques for providing better availability for Exchange Server 2007 and for ensuring that you can recover in the event of a server failure or a disaster.

Chapter 15, "Reliability and Availability 101," introduces many of the concepts of providing better availability for Exchange Server 2007, and it includes a lot of basic tips for ensuring that your server platform is reliable and stable. There are also discussions of using Microsoft's Network Load Balancing utility and an introduction to clustering.

Chapter 16, "Backup and Disaster Recovery," includes discussions on developing a backup plan for your Exchange Server 2007 severs as well as backup procedures using the Windows Backup utility. The chapter also covers restoring mailbox databases to recovery storage groups.

Part 5: Outlook

Exchange Server is a pretty nifty little gadget. But without clients, it's nothing more than fancy technology. Although this is a book on Exchange Server, the Outlook client merits some discussion. This section is devoted to that discussion.

Chapter 17, "Supporting Outlook 2007," covers the Outlook 2007 client from an administrative perspective and includes features that are useful for the Exchange Server administrator to be aware of. This chapter includes coverage of the new Autodiscover feature as well as how to set up Exchange Server to support Autodiscover.

Part 6: Connectivity

The Connectivity section of the book covers message delivery and Exchange client connectivity.

Chapter 18, "Delivering E-mail," concentrates on the Hub Transport and Edge Transport roles within an organization. This includes configuring a Hub Transport server to send and receive e-mail directly to and from the Internet and using the Edge Transport server role to provide anti-spam functions.

Chapter 19, "Exchange Anywhere," addresses connectivity to the Exchange server from variety of clients that might be used remotely, including using Outlook Web Access, Exchange ActiveSync, and Outlook Anywhere (RPC over HTTP). This section also covers how to enable and configure these the POP3 or IMAP4 protocols on a Exchange Server 2007 Client Access server.

Part 7: Security and Tracking Activities

The final section of this book revolves around security, auditing, and tracking including improving security of each of the server roles, using the Exchange Best Practices Analyzer, enabling protocol logging, tracking messages, and using the Exchange Queue Viewer application.

Chapter 20, "Securing Exchange Server," discusses the use of firewalls, hardening Exchange server using the Security Configuration Wizard, and providing multiple layers of security for Exchange servers. This chapter also includes a discussion on publishing Outlook Web Access and other web applications using a reverse proxy server such as ISA Server.

Chapter 21, "Logging, Auditing, and Monitoring," wraps up our discussion of Exchange Server 2007. We feel particularly strongly that you should enable a fair degree of auditing and logging features in Exchange Server 2007 since these are frequently things you don't realize you need until after the fact. In this chapter, we also cover the use of the Queue Viewer and the Exchange Best Practices Analyzer.

Appendix: Cool Third-Party Applications for Exchange Server and Outlook Clients

This book's appendix takes you on a thrill ride through some of the many products that exist today to enhance and extend the reach of Exchange Server. Coverage includes applications and services that do the following:

◆ Make Exchange Server installation and administration easier.

◆ Bring faxing and document management capabilities to Exchange servers.

◆ Improve upon the backup software built into Windows/Exchange Server 2007.

◆ Provide near-line storage message archiving.

◆ Check for potential and actual internal and external security breaches.

◆ Guard Exchange servers and networks against virus attacks and spam messages.

◆ Provide messaging systems linking e-mail, telephone services, voice, and text.

◆ Improve workflow by using e-mail to connect users working on a common task.

Conventions Used in This Book

We've included many notes in this book. Generally, they are positioned below the material to which they refer. There are three kinds of notes: notes, tips, and warnings.

> **NOTE**
>
> Notes give you information pertinent to the procedure or topic being discussed.

TIP

Tips indicate practical hints that might make your work easier.

WARNING

Warnings alert you to potential problems that you might encounter while using the program.

Remember, Exchange is designed to help your organization do what it does better, more efficiently, and with greater productivity. Have fun, be productive, and prosper!

Part 1

Understanding and Planning

In this section you will learn to:

- Chapter 1: Introducing Exchange Server 2007
- Chapter 2: Exchange Server 2007 Architecture
- Chapter 3: Designing a New Exchange 2007 System

Chapter 1

Introducing Exchange Server 2007

A hint of understanding passed over the butler's stoic face when he found the bloodstained candelabra, but loyalty to the master would prevent him from saying...oh, sorry, wrong book. Let's try this again. One of the most common misconceptions that even experienced Exchange administrators are making when approaching Microsoft Exchange Server 2007 is to assume it is a "point" release. It is too bad that Microsoft has moved away from a system that more objectively identifies the significance of the release, such as v4.0, v5.0, v5.5, and so on. Now the products are named without actually including major or minor versions.

Someone simply examining the product names Exchange Server 2003 and Exchange Server 2007 might not think there have been significant changes. Although moving from Exchange 2000 or Exchange 2003 to Exchange 2007 is not quite as significant as moving from Exchange 5.5 to Exchange 2000, Exchange Server 2007 does introduce enough new features and a major shift in the administration model that it must be considered a major release.

During the year coming up to the initial release of Exchange 2007, experienced Exchange administrators have often made comments similar to this: "Exchange 2003 already has most of the features and functions that we need. How could it significantly be improved?" Clearly, Exchange 2007 offers a significant enough number of improvements that all Exchange administrators will see some of the advantages in upgrading. Many sessions have been attended at TechEd, seminars have been held, and literally hundreds of articles and blog entries have been written about Exchange 2007. Arguably, Exchange 2007 is the most anticipated release of Exchange Server ever. Certainly it is the most widely hyped. The improvements (along with the misconceptions about Exchange 2007) have been widely discussed.

We'll discuss these improvements in this chapter, but in short Exchange 2007 introduces simplified administration as well as improvements in e-mail life cycle management, scalability, the availability of services, security, and internal SharePoint portals.

Summarizing even a few of the new features in this brief introduction is difficult, but early adopters of Exchange 2007 have reported the following features to be some of the most popular and useful:

- ◆ Powerful message transport rules applied and enforced at the server

- ◆ Continuously replicated Exchange databases for both clustered servers and nonclustered servers

- ◆ Vastly improved anti-spam features

- ◆ Customizable "over quota" and nondelivery messages

- ◆ Exchange Management Shell command line and scripting interface

- ◆ Transportable databases (databases that can be restored to a different server)

◆ Improved calendaring support via calendar concierge, the Availability service, and resource mailboxes

◆ Simplified permissions model and message routing

◆ Unified messaging technology that is now an integrated part of Exchange Server 2007

This list could go on for the entire chapter, but this gives you a taste of a few of the features that Exchange administrators as well as administrators from other messaging systems are getting excited about when they talk about Exchange 2007.

In this chapter, we will cover the changes to Exchange 2007 not only to give experienced Exchange administrators the proper perspective on Exchange 2007 but also to educate newly minted Exchange administrators on just how powerful Exchange has become and some of the new features.

Topics in this chapter include the following:

◆ The evolution of e-mail

◆ The new features of Exchange 2007

◆ Features and functions being deemphasized or phased out

◆ Some common points of confusion

Do You Believe in Evolution?

If you're currently responsible for electronic messaging in your organization, no one has to tell you about the steadily expanding use of e-messaging. You know it's happening every time you check the storage space on your disk drives or need an additional tape to complete the backup of your mail server. In this section, we will discuss some of the aspects of electronic mail and the ever-changing nature of e-mail. Even experienced Exchange server administrators may want to review this section to better understand how your users and requirements are evolving.

Over the past 10 years, the number of e-mail addresses has grown significantly. The technology research company International Data Corporation (IDC) estimated that in 2002, the number of e-mailboxes worldwide was more than 500 million. As of 2006, the Radicati Group estimates that there are now more than 1.5 billion e-mail accounts worldwide, accounting for over 135 billion e-mail messages per day.

Certainly e-mail systems have come a long, long way since the first mainframe and mini-computer systems from more than 30 years ago. Even the primitive text-based systems like cc:Mail, Microsoft Mail, WordPerfect Office, and Da Vinci eMail that first appeared on local area networks in the late 1980s are almost unrecognizable ancestors when compared with a modern system based on Exchange Server 2007 and Outlook 2007.

The similarities between these systems stop at just a few basic functions, including the ability to send text messages from one individual to another individual or group. The sender and message recipients were usually always within the organization. Early e-mail systems were looked at by organizations as a luxury or an option rather than an important part of an organization's daily work processes.

Electronic messaging is now far more than e-mail. It involves the use of an underlying messaging infrastructure (addressing, routing, store-and-forward technologies, and so on) to build applications that are based on cooperative tasking, whether by humans or computers. Working in tandem with real-time interactive technologies, electronic messaging systems have already produced a set of wildly imaginative business, entertainment, and educational applications with high payoff potential. All of this action, of course, accelerates the demand for electronic messaging capabilities and services.

Microsoft's Exchange Server products have played and will continue to play a key role in electronic messaging. Exchange Server 2007 is one of the most powerful, extensible, scalable, easy-to-use, and manageable electronic messaging back ends currently on the market. Combined with Microsoft's excellent Outlook clients, Internet-based clients from Microsoft and other vendors, mobile devices that use ActiveSync, and third-party or home-grown applications, Exchange Server 2007 can help your organization move smoothly and productively into the electronic messaging future.

E-mail Is Only the Beginning

Together, Exchange Server 2007 and its clients perform a variety of messaging-based functions. These include e-mail, message routing, scheduling, and support for several types of custom applications. Certainly, e-mail is a key feature of any messaging system, and the Outlook Calendar is far better than previous versions of Microsoft's appointment and meeting-scheduling software. Outlook 2007 together with Exchange 2007 introduces even more improvements. Figures 1.1 and 1.2 show the Outlook 2007 client Inbox and Calendar in action.

FIGURE 1.1
The Outlook 2007 client Inbox

Figure 1.3 shows the new Outlook Web Access 2007 web browser client that you can use with Exchange Server 2007.

E-mail clients are exciting and sexy, but to get the most out of Exchange Server 2007, you need to throw away any preconceptions you have that messaging systems are only for e-mail and scheduling. The really exciting applications are not those that use simple e-mail or scheduling, but those that are based on the routing capabilities of messaging systems. These applications bring people and computers together for improved collaboration.

FIGURE 1.2
The Outlook 2007 client
Calendar

FIGURE 1.3
Outlook Web Access web
browser accesses mail
stored on an Exchange
Server 2007.

Message Complexity

E-mail clients such as Outlook and Outlook Web Access allow for the creation of much more
complex e-mail messages than in the past. What does "more complex" mean? Well, take as an
example the message shown in Figure 1.4. This Outlook 2007 message is formatted with fonts,
a numbered list, a substantial message signature/disclaimer, and a corporate logo in the signature; all of this is formatted using HTML or rich text so that the message is viewable by any

web-based mail system or HTML-compatible clients. Finally, the message is digitally signed and authenticated with a digital signature.

FIGURE 1.4
A typical e-mail message

The whole point of this discussion is to illustrate the changing nature of e-mail. Organizations depend far more on e-mail today than they did even five years ago, and their users send even more mail than in the past. And as you saw, messages are formatted with rich text or HTML formatting and can contain disclaimers and often digital signatures. All of these things help us to communicate more effectively.

In addition to regular e-mail messages, users are sending scheduling requests, contact items, forms-enabled e-mail messages, and more. Each of these increases the complexity of the messaging system and also an organization's dependency on it.

The message shown in Figure 1.4 has only a few hundred bytes of actual message content, including the recipient information, but it is 30KB in size. This is just to convey a few hundred bytes of information!

Integrating Voicemail, Faxing, and E-mail

E-mail systems are converging with their voicemail and faxing cousins. The concept of unified messaging is nothing new to e-mail users. For at least the past 10 years, third-party vendors have included e-mail integration tools for voicemail and network faxing solutions. However, for most organizations, integrated voicemail and faxing solutions remain the exception rather than the rule. Exchange 2007 introduces integrated voice and fax solutions as part of the base product.

Organizations with IP-based telephone systems or telephone systems with an IP gateway can now easily integrate a user's voicemail and inbound faxing with the Exchange user's mailbox. The Exchange 2007 Unified Messaging server handles the interaction between an organization's telephone system and Exchange mailboxes. Inbound voicemail is transferred in to the user's mailbox as a WMA file attachment; this message includes an Outlook form that allows the user to play the message. A short voicemail message may be anywhere from 40KB to 75KB in size, while longer voicemail messages may be 200KB to 500KB in size. One estimate that is frequently used to estimate the size of a voicemail message is around 5KB per second of message.

Inbound faxes are transferred to the user's mailbox as a message containing an Outlook form with a Group IV TIFF attachment; a single-page fax can be as small as 25KB, while multipage faxes can easily be 200KB or larger. Incorporating third-party scanning and outbound faxing products (outbound faxing is not supported out of the box with Exchange 2007) can further increase the size of a mailbox.

With Outlook Voice Access, a user can now dial in to the Exchange 2007 Unified Messaging server and access their mailbox, have e-mail read to them, have appointments read to them, and move or cancel appointments. If an appointment is changed, Outlook Voice Access will automatically notify attendees of scheduling changes; this is very useful if you are sitting in traffic on the freeway with nothing but your cell phone (using your headset of course)!

Inbound voicemail and inbound faxes will increase the demands on your Exchange server from the perspective of required disk space and possibly additional server hardware, though. This needs to be considered. Outlook Voice Access will increase the potential number of connections and usage of your Exchange mailbox servers and Unified Messaging servers.

Multiple Points of Access

For years, the only point of access for one's e-mail system was to use a Windows, Macintosh, or Unix-based client and access the e-mail system directly. In the case of Outlook and Exchange, this access was originally in the form of a MAPI client directly against the Exchange server. As Exchange has evolved, POP3 and IMAP4 access has been included in the product, then Web-based e-mail access, and finally mobile device access. Exchange Server 2007 supports additional technologies such as Web Services that can provide additional mechanisms for accessing data in mailboxes.

Outlook Web Access has evolved quickly and in Exchange 2007 bears almost no resemblance to the original version found in Exchange 5.0 in terms of features, functions, and the look of the interface.

Mobile device access was first provided to Exchange 2000 using Microsoft Mobile Information Server and then later included as part of Exchange 2003. Mobile device functionality has been further improved in Exchange 2007. User demand for integrating mobile devices with e-mail are becoming more common. The Radicati Group estimated that in 2006 there were 14 million wireless e-mail users but by 2010 that number will grow to 228 million. You can bet that your users will want to be included!

Unified Messaging and Outlook Voice Access now allow a user with nothing but a telephone to access their e-mail and calendar and even make changes via the telephone.

With all of these mechanisms for retrieving and sending e-mail, it is not unusual for users to be accessing their mailbox using more than one. In some cases, we have seen users accessing their mailbox from their desktop computer, their notebook computer (using RPC over HTTP), and their Windows Mobile device.

In medium and large organizations, the fact that users are now accessing their mailbox from more than one device and/or mechanism will affect not only hardware sizing but potentially your licensing costs.

Just a Step beyond Mail

Most e-mail administrators are familiar with *attachments* — those word-processing, spreadsheet and other files that you can attach to messages. Using attachments is a simple way to move files to the people who need to see them. They also tend to gobble up disk space extremely fast!

Sure, you could send your files on disk or tell people where on the network they can find and download them. But e-mail attachments let you make the files available to others with a click of their mouse buttons. Recipients just double-click on an icon and the attachment opens in the original application that produced it. This is true, of course, only if your correspondent has access to the application or to software that was used to create the attachment.

Using attachments offers the added advantage of putting the files and accompanying messages right in the faces of those who need to see them. This leaves less room for excuses such as "I couldn't find/open that network folder" or "The dog ate the disk."

As great as attachments can be, they have one real weakness: The minute an attachment leaves your Outbox, it's out-of-date. If you do further work on the original file, the work is not reflected in the copy that you sent to others. If someone then edits a copy of the attached file, it's totally out of sync with the original and all other copies. Getting everything synchronized again can involve tedious hours or days of manually comparing different versions and cutting and pasting them to create one master document.

Office 2003 and Office 2007 offer two neat ways to avoid this problem. First, they let you insert a link to a file. When you open the file, you're opening the file the link point to. If the file is changed, you see the changed file. Second, Office lets you attach a file to a message and set a shared folder where an updateable version of the file is stored. When the copy attached to the user's e-mail is updated, these updates can be incorporated into the shared copy of the file. This option allows broader access to the file than a link.

The use of portals such as Microsoft Office SharePoint Server is becoming increasingly common-place in organizations as they look for better ways to store, find, and manage the data that their users are producing. Both Outlook and Outlook Web Access can better integrate with SharePoint and provide an alternate location for the storage of attachments.

Mailbox Size Limits

As users have become more savvy and competent at using Outlook and the features of Exchange and e-mail messages themselves have become more complex, the need for e-mail storage has grown. Back in the days of Exchange 4.0, an organization that gave their users a 25MB mailbox was considered generous. With Exchange 2003, a typical user's mailbox now may have a storage limit of 300 to 500MB, with power users and VIPs requiring even more.

At TechEd 2006, Exchange gurus were tossing about the idea that in the future a default mailbox limit would be closer to 2GB as users start incorporating Unified Messaging features. We all see users with mailbox sizes in the gigabyte range, but is your organization prepared for a typical user with a 2GB message size limit? What sort of concerns will you face when your average user has 1 to 2GB of content (not just e-mail!) in their mailbox?

Certainly the need for more disk storage will be the first factor that organizations need to consider. However, disk storage is reasonably cheap, and many larger organizations that are supporting thousands of mailbox users on a single mailbox server usually already have more disk space than they can practically use. This is due to the fact that they require more disk spindles to accommodate the number of simultaneous I/Os per second (IOPS) that are required by a large number of users.

For more administrators with large amounts of mail storage, the primary concern they face is the ability to quickly and efficiently restore data in the event of a failure. These administrators are often faced with service-level agreements that bind them to maximum restoration times. In even the most optimal circumstances, a 300GB mailbox database will take some time to restore from backup media!

Microsoft recommends that you do not allow an Exchange mailbox database to grow larger than 100GB unless you are implementing local continuous replication. If you use local continuous replication or clustered continuous replication to keep a copy of the database ready to use in case of database corruption, do not let the mailbox database grow to larger than 200GB. If you require more than 100GB (or 200GB) of mailbox database storage, Exchange 2007 Standard Edition allows you to have up to 5 mailbox databases while Exchange 2007 Enterprise Edition allows you to have up to 50.

The solution in the past was to restrain the user community by preventing them from keeping all of the necessary mail data that they might require on the mail server. This was done by imposing low mailbox limits, implementing message archival requirements, keeping deleted items for only a few days, and keeping deleted mailboxes for only a few days.

However, as Unified Messaging data now starts to arrive in a user's mailbox and users have increasing mechanisms for accessing the data stored in their mailbox, keeping mail data around longer and longer is not only going to be a requirement of your user community, it will be one of their demands.

Off-the-Shelf Messaging-Enabled Applications

Microsoft Office enables messaging in many word-processing and spreadsheet applications. For example, when you install the Outlook client on your computer, Microsoft's Office products such as Word and Excel are enabled for electronic messaging. You can select the Routing Recipient option from the application's File ➤ Send To menu. An electronic routing slip pops up. You then add addresses to the slip from your Exchange address books or from your Outlook contacts, select the routing method you want to use, and set other attributes for the route. Finally, you add the routing slip to the document with a click of the Add Slip button and ship it off to others using options on the File ➤ Send To menu.

As you can see in Figure 1.5, a file can be routed either sequentially or all at once to each address you selected. Routing sequentially helps eliminate problems associated with multiple users editing the same file at the same time. With applications such as Microsoft Word that keep track of each person's comments and changes, once the document has been routed, the original author can read the comments and incorporate or not incorporate them as they see fit.

Although it's simple, application-based messaging can significantly improve user productivity and speed up a range of business processes.

Objects

Object insertion and linking further enhance the functionality of the Exchange messaging system. Take a close look at Figure 1.6. Yes, the message includes an Excel spreadsheet and chart. The person who sent the message simply selected Object from the Insert menu that appears on every Exchange message. Then they specified a file with an existing spreadsheet as the source of the object to be inserted into the message. The Outlook client then inserted the file into the message as an object.

The recipient can see the spreadsheet as a graphic image in the message, as shown in the figure. When they double-click the graphic image, Excel is launched inside the message, and Excel's menus and toolbars replace those of the message (see Figure 1.7). In essence, the message becomes Excel.

FIGURE 1.5
Microsoft Word 2003 includes messaging-enabled functions for sending and routing.

FIGURE 1.6
Object insertion makes it easy to create sophisticated messaging-enabled applications.

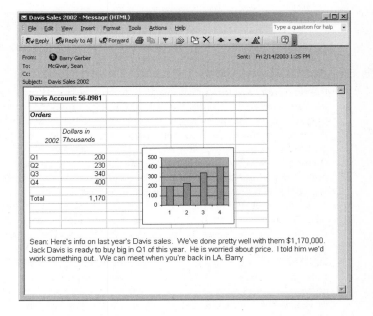

The Excel spreadsheet is fully editable. Excel must be available to a recipient for them to be able to edit the spreadsheet. Without Excel, they can only look at the spreadsheet in graphic image form, although the graphic image changes when the spreadsheet is edited in Excel.

You can also insert in a message an object that is a link to an application file. As with other kinds of object insertion, your recipient sees a graphic picture of the contents of the file and can edit the file by double-clicking the graphic picture. Links are a bit more flexible, because they allow users to work with files stored on a shared disk. With inserted objects, users work with a file embedded in the message itself.

FIGURE 1.7
Double-clicking an Excel spreadsheet object in a message enables Excel menus and toolbars.

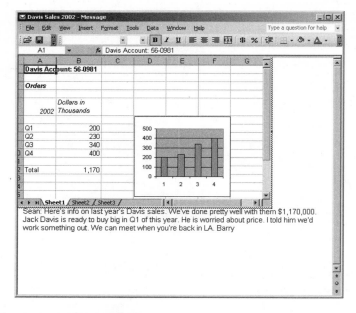

Applications Using Exchange Public Folders

Public folders are for common access to messages and files. Files can be dragged from file-access interfaces, such as Windows Explorer, and dropped into public folders. The whole concept of public folders has many organizations in a quandary as they try to figure out the best place for these collaborative applications. Increasingly, applications that were once "best suited" for a public folder are now better suited for web pages or portals such as SharePoint workspaces. Although the whole concept of public folders is being deemphasized in Exchange 2007, this release continues to support public folders and many organizations will continue to find useful applications for public folders for the foreseeable future.

You can set up sorting rules for a public folder so that items in the folder are organized by a range of attributes, such as the name of the sender or creator of the item or the date that the item was placed in the folder. Items in a public folder can be sorted by conversation threads. You can also put applications built on existing products such as Word or Excel or built with Exchange or Outlook Forms Designer, client or server scripting, or the Exchange API set into public folders. You can use public folders to replace many of the maddening paper-based processes that abound in every organization.

For easy access to items in a public folder, you can use a *folder link*. You can send a link to a folder in a message. When someone navigates to the folder and double-clicks a file, the file opens. Everyone who receives the message works with the same linked attachment, so everyone reads and can modify the same file. As with document routing, applications such as Microsoft Word can keep track of each person's changes to and comments on file contents. Of course, your users will have to learn to live with the fact that only one person can edit an application file at a time. Most modern end-user applications warn the user that someone else is using the file and allow the user to open a read-only copy of the file, which of course can't be edited.

Electronic Forms

Exchange Server 2007 continues to supports forms created with the Outlook Forms Designer (OFD). You can use OFD to build information-gathering forms containing a number of the bells and whistles that you're accustomed to in Windows applications. These include drop-down list boxes, check boxes, fill-in text forms, tab dialog controls, and radio buttons (see Figure 1.8).

FIGURE 1.8
Electronic forms turn messages into structured information-gathering tools.

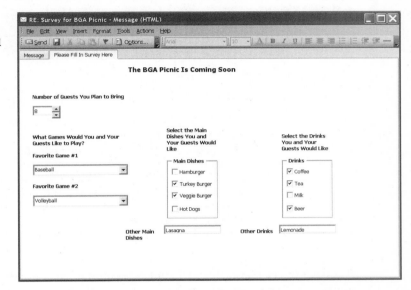

OFD, which is easy enough for nontechnical types to use, includes a variety of messaging-oriented fields and actions. For example, you can choose to include a preaddressed To field in a form so that users of the form can easily mail it off to the appropriate recipient. (The preaddressed To field for the form shown in Figure 1.8 is on the page with the tab marked Message, which is not visible in this figure.) When you've designed a form, you can make it available to all users or select users; users can access the completed form simply by selecting it while in an Outlook client.

Features! Features! Get Your New Features Here!

Reviewing the impressive list of new features and enhancements to Exchange 2007, everyone can agree that there are at least a few features that anyone can use. Customers have been asking for some of these improvements for many years, and others are new features that most customers had not even realized that they needed.

In the following sections, we will review the new features and provide a summary of what each provides. We'll discuss most of these features in more detail later in the book.

64-bit Architecture

For a long time, perhaps the most discussed (and perhaps the most controversial) enhancement to Exchange 2007 is that now Exchange 2007 server uses 64-bit extensions. Now your production servers will have to have x64 architecture–based Intel Xeon and Pentium processes or AMD64 architecture–based AMD Opteron and Athlon processors.

Although many people are thrilled with this change in the architecture, there are, no doubt, folks screaming, "What!!!?? I have to buy new hardware just to upgrade?!" A good response to this concern is that on most any messaging system upgrade, the hardware is replaced anyway. Certainly this is true for hardware that has been in production for more than three or four years. And the good news is that most server-class hardware that has been purchased since the end of 2005 or later probably already includes the x64 extensions. If you have existing hardware you want to use with Exchange 2007, confirm with your vendor that it will run Windows Server 2003 x64.

> **NOTE**
>
> There is a 32-bit version of Exchange 2007, but it is not supported in production environments. Only 64-bit Exchange is supported in production.

Is the decision to move to 64 bits a bold move? Is the Exchange team forging the way to more robust applications? Well, to a certain degree, yes, but the move to the 64-bit architecture is more out of need than forging a bold, modern path. Anyone who has supported an older version of Exchange Server with a large number of mailboxes knows that Exchange is constrained by the amount of RAM that it can access and that Exchange significantly taxes the disk I/O system.

In order to provide additional features that organizations are now requiring, such as larger mailboxes, messaging records management features, improved message content security, transport rules, unified messaging integration, and improved journaling, Exchange Server clearly needs to be able to access more physical memory. With more RAM available, Exchange caching is more efficient and thus reduces the I/O requirements that are placed on the disk subsystem.

If you are not sure if your existing hardware supports the x64 extensions, there are a number of ways that you can check this, including confirming it with the hardware vendor. If the computer is already running Windows, you can get a handy little program called CPU-Z from www.cpuid.com. Figure 1.9 shows the CPU-Z program.

FIGURE 1.9
Using CPU-Z to identify
the CPU type

Notice in the Instructions line of CPU-Z that this particular chip supports x86-64. This means this chip will support the x64 instruction sets. Intel chips will report that they support the EM64T instruction set.

Exchange Management

Exchange Server management with Exchange 2007 becomes more and more complex as administrators try to make Exchange work within their organizations particularly in larger organizations. Exchange 2000/2003 management of mail recipients was performed through the Active Directory Users and Computers console, while management of Exchange server related tasks and global recipient tasks is performed through the Exchange System Manager console. In Exchange 2007, all Exchange recipient administration tasks are now performed through the Exchange Management Console or the Exchange Management Shell.

Medium and large organizations usually develop specific needs to perform bulk changes to Exchange data, manage Exchange servers from the command line or scripts, and access or manipulate data stored in Exchange databases. Although making bulk changes or manipulating Exchange servers might seem like a simple task (after all, Windows, Active Directory, and Exchange Server are all from the same company), the truth of the matter is that it's not.

Performing bulk recipient tasks such as creating multiple mailboxes, changing many e-mail addresses, and configuring bulk properties must be performed through an application programming interface (API) or scripting interface such as Active Directory Services Interface (ADSI). Management of Exchange server properties may also need to be performed through ADSI.

Manipulation of Exchange server operations such as mounting and dismounting of databases, queue management, diagnostics logging, and tracking log management has to be handled through a number of Exchange-related APIs such as Extended Messaging Application Programming Interface (MAPI), Lightweight Directory Access Protocol (LDAP), Web Distributed Authoring and Versioning (WebDAV), CDO for Exchange Management (CDOExM), Windows Management Instrumentation (WMI), Distributed Component Object Model (DCOM), Remote Procedure Calls (RPCs), and the Internet Information Server management interface.

Finally, actually accessing or manipulating data stored in an Exchange database is also more complex than it might seem. A popular tool for Exchange 2003 administrators is the Exchange Merge (ExMerge) tool that allows data to be exported out of an Exchange mailbox and into a personal store (PST) file. Actual manipulation of data in the mailbox databases could be accomplished through MAPI, Collaborative Data Objects (CDO), Exchange Object Linking and Embedding Database (ExOLEDB) functions, or Web Distributed Authoring and Versioning (WebDAV) functions. None of these methods is either simple or trivial for nonprogrammers. Anyone that has ever tried to dismount or mount a mailbox database from a script can attest to the programming complexity involved in such a simple task.

Clearly, for any organization that is interested in customized management of Exchange (small, medium, or large organizations), Exchange 2003 and earlier versions left a lot to be desired, and required tasks could often not even be performed due to their difficulty. In the minds of many experienced Exchange administrators, this is a gaping hole in the Exchange management architecture.

With Exchange 2007, the management interface has been completely rewritten from the ground up. All management operations related to Exchange management — whether they are performed against an Exchange server, Active Directory, the Registry, or the Internet Information Server (IIS) metabase — have been broken up in to unique tasks. All Exchange tasks can be performed from the Exchange Management Shell (command-line interface); a subset of these tasks can be performed from the Exchange Management Console graphical user interface. Anything that can be performed from the Exchange Management Console can be performed via the Exchange Management Shell; there are advanced administrative tasks that can be performed only from the Exchange Management Shell.

The Exchange Management Console (shown in Figure 1.10) has been completely redesigned to make it easier to use, to better organize Exchange management tasks, to reduce the complexity, and to make administrative tasks more discoverable.

FIGURE 1.10
The new and improved Exchange Management Console

The new console is built on top of an entirely new scripting technology called PowerShell and a set of Exchange-specific extensions called the Exchange Management Shell. We will go into more details on the new management interface in Chapter 7, "Administering Exchange 2007."

Server Roles

In earlier versions of Exchange, once the Windows server was prepared to support Exchange, you simply installed an Exchange server. Then you would go about the process of customizing the Exchange configuration, configuring Internet Information Server, disabling unnecessary services, and preparing the server to assume the role you wanted it to assume, such as a mailbox server, a bridgehead server, Outlook Web Access front-end server, and so on.

Exchange 2007 officially introduces the concept of server roles at the point of setup. During the installation process, the setup program (Figure 1.11) asks the installer which roles the server will be performing.

When running setup, if you choose a custom installation, during setup you can specify the server roles by choosing from among the following options:

Mailbox Role	Supports mailboxes and public folders.
Client Access Role	Supports functions such as Outlook Web Access, Outlook Anywhere (RPC over HTTP), Windows Mobile ActiveSync, POP3, and IMAP4, and supports web services such as Autodiscover, the Availability service, and calendar sharing.

Hub Transport Role	Supports message transport functions such as delivering mail locally (to other Exchange servers in the organization) or externally (to an SMTP smart host such as an Exchange Edge Transport server).
Unified Messaging Role	Supports delivery of inbound voicemail, inbound faxing, and Outlook Voice Access features.
Edge Transport Role	Supports separate anti-spam and antivirus functions for inbound and outbound messaging. The Edge Transport server is installed on a stand-alone machine usually in a perimeter network.
Active Clustered Mailbox Role	Configures a server to support clustering as an active node. Only the Mailbox server role can be clustered. Clustered servers can be configured as part of a single copy cluster (SCC) or a clustered continuous replication (CCR) cluster.
Passive Clustered Mailbox Role	Configures a server to support clustering as a passive node. Only the Mailbox server role can be clustered.

FIGURE 1.11
Specifying server roles

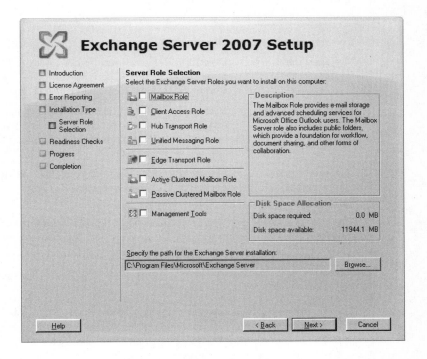

Once a roles is selected, only the components necessary for that role are installed. This reduces the overhead on machines that are dedicated to a particular task (such as a Hub Transport server); ensures that no unnecessary executables, DLLs, or services are installed; and makes creating dedicated server roles much easier. In a small organization with only one Exchange server, the same server may be assigned the Mailbox, Hub Transport, and Client Access server roles.

Improved Message and Content Control

All messaging system administrators can relate to challenges such as adequately managing the content that is stored on their mail servers, keeping business-essential information available when it is required, removing content that is no longer necessary, controlling the flow of messaging information, and preventing disclosure of information. If one or more of these challenges has been a problem for you, then Exchange 2007 has solutions.

MESSAGING RECORDS MANAGEMENT

Messaging records management (early on referred to as e-mail life cycle management) introduces to Exchange 2007 a whole new concept in the control of messaging content. Messaging records management allows administrators to more closely control the life of message content (e-mail, faxes, voicemail, calendar entries, and so on) from the moment the information is created on the Exchange server until the point at which that information no longer has business or legal value. This helps the organization to maintain important records as long as necessary but discard unnecessary information in a timely fashion. These are configured at the organization level so they will affect all Mailbox server roles.

To a certain extent, some of the features of messaging records management are distantly related to the Exchange 2000/2003 Mailbox Manager. There are a number of components to messaging records management:

Component	Function
Managed default folders	Default folders are found when an Outlook 2007 MAPI client uses its mailbox, including Calendar, Contacts, Deleted Items, Inbox, Junk E-mail, Sent Items, RSS Feeds, and so on.
Managed custom folders	Managed custom folders are folders that are created by the Exchange server administrator for users who are included in a managed folder mailbox policy. Storage limits and managed content settings can be applied to these folders.
Managed folder mailbox policies	Managed folder policies define which folders are included in a particular policy. Managed folder mailbox policies are then assigned to mailboxes.
Managed content settings	Managed content settings define retention settings and message journaling features for content such as messages, faxes, and voicemail.

> **NOTE**
>
> You can now configure message journaling based on a specific type of content or folder.

Once a user has been assigned to a managed folder mailbox policy, any additional custom folders that must be created in that user's mailbox will show up in the Managed Folders folder in the root of the user's mailbox, such as those shown in Figure 1.12.

Normally, content in these folders will be managed by the end user. Moving relevant content into these folders is their responsibility. In certain situations, managed content settings can accurately identify content types such as faxes or voicemail and can move those into the appropriate custom managed folders. A user can also build client-side rules that move content into their managed folders.

FIGURE 1.12
Managed folders assigned by the managed folder mailbox policy

MESSAGE TRANSPORT RULES

Message transport rules are quite similar to Outlook rules and are even created using a wizard similar to one used to create Outlook rules. However, these rules are quite a bit more powerful and are executed on the Hub Transport servers. Since all messages are processed by a Hub Transport server whether they are inbound, outbound, or for locally delivery, you can build powerful policies to control the messages and data that flows within your organization. Transport rules can also be defined at your organization's perimeter by using an Edge Transport server.

Every transport rule has three components: conditions, actions, and exceptions.

Although we will cover a lot more about transport rules in Chapter 13, "Managing Messages in Transit," just to give you a taste of what you can do with transport rules, it is useful to highlight some of the cool things you can do with them:

◆ Append disclaimers to outgoing messages

◆ Implement message journaling based on recipients, distribution lists, message classification, or message importance

◆ Prevent users or departments from sending e-mail to another by creating an ethical wall (aka a Chinese wall)

◆ Intercept messages based on content or text patterns using regular expressions (REGEX) found in the message subject or message body

- Apply message classifications to messages based on sender or message content

- Take action on a message with a certain attachment or attachment type or an attachment size that exceeds a specified limit

- Examine and set message headers or remove data from the message header

- Redirect, drop, or bounce messages based on certain criteria

JOURNALING

Journaling messages is the process of keeping messages from one or more senders based on long-term storage, legal, regulatory, or human resources requirements. Exchange 2000/2003 essentially had one option for message journaling. Create an additional mailbox store and move any mailboxes that must be kept to that mailbox store. Exchange 2007 has introduced a lot of new options with respect to retaining messages:

- Messages can be retained based on folder or content type using managed content settings.

- Messages can be retained using transport rules by examining sender, recipient, message priority, message classification, or message content.

- Messages can also be retained using transport rules by keeping only internal or only external messages.

- Messages can still be retained based on the journal settings on the mailbox database.

- Messages can be retained using a new hub transport feature called a journaling rule (see Figure 1.13) that allows messages to be retained based on a single sender or distribution group membership.

- Messages can be sent to an SMTP address that is external to the Exchange organization, such as a Microsoft Office SharePoint Server 2007 server or a third-party service provider.

MESSAGE CLASSIFICATIONS

Organizations that send confidential, proprietary, or classified information via e-mail often implement message classification templates. However, these client-side templates display the message classification only for the sender and the recipients; in previous versions of Exchange there was nothing within the message transport that could take action on or evaluate a classified message.

Exchange 2007 allows a message to enforce rules based on the classification of a message, such as Do Not Forward, Partner Mail, Attachment Removed, Company Confidential, Company Internal, Attorney/Client Privilege, and customized classification levels. The sender can assign the classification using Outlook 2007, Outlook Web Access 2007, or message transport rules can assign a classification based on sender, recipient, message content, importance, and so on. Figure 1.14 shows an example of a message that is being composed in Outlook Web Access and has had the built-in Attorney/Client Privilege classification assigned to it; the classification text is shown just about the address list. The server administrator can create additional classifications and customize the text strings.

FIGURE 1.13
Creating a journaling rule

FIGURE 1.14
Classifying a message using Outlook Web Access

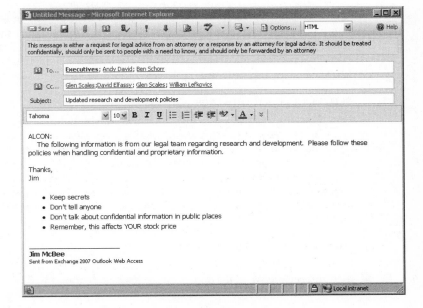

Content Storage Improvements

As we mentioned earlier, e-mail systems have evolved not only in their complexity, but in the complexity (and size!) of the messages and mailbox content being sent and stored. Users demands for improved searching and indexing of their mailboxes have stretched the limits of most server hardware. The following list includes some of the improvements with respect to data storage and recoverability:

◆ Support for recovering moved or deleted mailboxes using a recovery storage group

◆ Volume Shadow Copy restoration to recovery storage groups on alternate servers

◆ Lost log resilience that allows a database to be recovered even if the last few log files are missing

MAILBOX DATABASES

Even in a small or medium-sized organization, often mailbox size constraints are based solely on the ability to restore a certain amount of data given a specified maximum amount of time. To scale to larger mailboxes, the administrator must create more mailbox stores and storage groups. However, even Exchange Server 2003 Enterprise Edition allowed a maximum of only 4 storage groups and 20 mailbox stores.

> **NOTE**
>
> In Exchange 2000/2003, we refer to mailbox databases as *mailbox stores*. In Exchange 2007, we simply call these *mailbox databases*.

In order to allow a server to scale to support larger mailbox sizes or more mailboxes, Exchange Server 2007 Enterprise Edition allows up to 50 storage groups and 50 mailbox databases. The maximum number of mailbox databases is 50; these can be configured in 50 separate storage groups or consolidated into as few as 10 storage groups of 5 databases each. Exchange Server 2007 Standard Edition supports a maximum of 5 storage groups and 5 databases. The recommendation from Microsoft is to scale outward on storage groups so that each database has its own transaction logs.

SMALLER TRANSACTION LOGS

Experienced Exchange 2000/2003 administrators will immediately recognize an Exchange transaction log because they are always 5,120KB in size. Exchange 2007 transaction logs, however, are a bit smaller. In fact, the transaction log files are quite a bit smaller; 1,024KB to be exact.

The transaction log files are smaller because Exchange 2007 has two new high-availability features called local continuous replication and clustered continuous replication that allow log files to be copied to another location and replayed into a backup copy of their corresponding database. Reducing the log file sizes ensures that data is copied more quickly to the standby location.

IMPROVED SEARCH FEATURES

Content Indexing has been completely rewritten in Exchange 2007 so that it is far more efficient than in previous versions and is more closely integrated with the information store service. Improvements have been made so that the indexing process is throttled back during peak loads and does not affect client use of the Exchange server. By default, each mailbox database automatically has a full-text index associated with it. Messages are indexed upon arrival rather than on a fixed schedule; the index is up-to-date and immediately available to clients.

Full-text search capabilities are available from both Outlook clients as well as Outlook Web Access. Searches can be by word, phrase, or sentence, and in addition to the message bodies, attachments such as Word documents, Excel spreadsheets, text files, and HTML files can be searched.

Improved High Availability Features

One of the biggest enemies of high availability is slow restoration times. As mailbox databases get larger and larger, restore times get longer and longer. Often this is used as a rationale for limiting user's mailbox sizes to less than what they really need to do their jobs effectively.

As mentioned earlier, Exchange 2007 includes two new high-availability features called local continuous replication and clustered continuous replication. These features use a feature similar to the SQL Server log shipping technology. When a transaction log is completely filled, it is shipped (copied) to an alternate location and committed to a backup or standby copy of the database. By ensuring that there is always an update-to-date copy of the mailbox database online that is nearly complete and ready to be put in to production, downtime due to a corrupted database can be greatly reduced.

LOCAL CONTINUOUS REPLICATION

Local continuous replication (LCR) is one of the most interesting new features of Exchange 2007. It helps to ensure that an alternate copy of a mailbox database is maintained on the local server. This feature was at one time called continuous backup. The concept of LCR is illustrated in Figure 1.15. A backup copy of the production mailbox database is maintained on the local server. As the production database's transaction logs are completely filled, the transaction logs are copied to the backup location (step 1) and committed to the backup copy of the database (step 2).

FIGURE 1.15
Local continuous replication

Local disk drives

C:\ — Operating system, page file, Exchange binaries

D:\ — Exchange transaction logs (production)

①

E:\ — Exchange databases (production)

F:\ — Transaction logs (LCR copy)

②

G:\ — Exchange databases (LCR copy)

Exchange 2007 mailbox server

In the event that the production database becomes corrupted, the administrator can switch from the production database to the backup copy of the database.

CLUSTERED CONTINUOUS REPLICATION

Clustered continuous replication (CCR) is another interesting new high-availability feature of Exchange 2007. CCR introduces a whole new level of high availability and clustering to Exchange 2007. Unlike traditional single-copy clustering (SCC), in which there is only a single copy of the database, CCR not only has redundant hardware but a backup copy of the database. This backup copy of the database is kept current using replication technology similar to LCR. As transactions are committed to the production copy of a database, the log file is copied to the backup location and committed to the backup copy of the database.

CCR is implemented in the form of two-node, active-passive clustering. Quorum is maintained using a majority node set cluster; a third server acts as a "witness" by providing a file share on which the shared quorum database is located. The active node has one or more mailbox databases; the concept of CCR is illustrated in Figure 1.16. As transactions are committed to the active node's databases and transaction logs, the transaction logs are shipped (copied) to the passive node (shown in step 1).

FIGURE 1.16
Clustered continuous replication

Once the transaction log has been successfully copied to the passive node, the transactions in that log are committed to the corresponding database on the passive node (step 2). In the event of any type of failure on the active node, the passive node will automatically failover and assume responsibility for the clustered mailbox server (formerly called an Exchange virtual server).

When you're running Windows 2003, the active and passive nodes must be on the same IP subnet, but this is expected to change when the next version of Windows Server (currently code-named Longhorn Server) is released. If an organization has VLAN capability, it can conceivably place the two nodes of a CCR cluster in separate locations.

Clustered continuous replication will help to reduce the "cost of entry" for organizations wishing to move to Exchange clustering since it eliminates the need for costly shared storage such as storage area networks (SANs). Data storage for CCR clusters can be located on direct attached storage (DAS).

Improved Calendaring and Resource Management

Calendaring, resources, and out-of-office features were not as complete as most of today's sophisticated e-mail users require. Exchange 2007 and Outlook 2007 have improved each of these with new features and functions. For many of the calendaring and resource management features to work properly, Outlook 2007 is required and the Exchange 2007 Availability service must be configured on the Exchange Client Access servers.

RESOURCE MANAGEMENT

One of the biggest hurdles that messaging system managers have had to overcome with Exchange is how to manage resource calendars. In earlier versions of Exchange, a resource calendar was nothing more than a mailbox whose calendar was shared to other users or a mailbox that had scripts or event sinks that allowed for automatic acceptance and processing of meeting requests for a particular resource. Exchange 2007 introduces the concept of resource mailboxes. At mailbox creation time (see Figure 1.17), the administrator designates the type of resource that is being created (room or equipment).

FIGURE 1.17
Resource type is desig-
nated when the mailbox
is created.

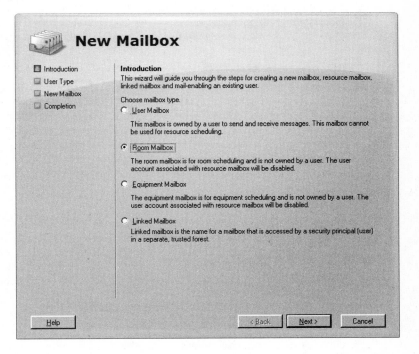

Custom properties can then be set on this resource such as room capacity or audiovisual capabilities. This information can be viewed within Outlook 2007 when a user is looking for a resource that suits the user's requirements. The Resource Booking attendant provides features that control who can book a resource, for how long, and during which hours and provides conflict information.

CALENDAR CONCIERGE

As users have become more sophisticated, their calendaring requirements have increased. The Calendar Concierge is a collection of features that allow for better management of user and resource mailboxes. The Exchange 2007 Calendar Assistant helps to keep out-of-date meeting requests from disturbing the user by ensuring that they are presented with only the most recent meeting request. The Calendar Assistant also reduces the amount of unnecessary messages relating to meeting requests, such as a Tentative response followed soon after by a Decline or Accept response. The user sees only the most recent message.

The Scheduling Assistant makes the process of scheduling a meeting using either Outlook 2007 or Outlook Web Access much simpler and recommends best meeting times based on requested attendees.

AVAILABILITY SERVICE

Earlier versions of Exchange used a system public folder for publishing a user's free/busy information. Periodically, the Outlook client had to connect to this public folder and update the user's free/busy times. Exchange 2007 introduces a new web service that runs on the Client Access server role and provides an interface to all users' free and busy times. Only Outlook 2007 clients are able to use this new web service, so the Availability service ensures that free and busy times published by older clients are accessible via the web service and free and busy times published by Outlook 2007 are available via the system public folder.

OUT-OF-OFFICE ASSISTANT

A number of improvements have been made to the simple Out-of-Office Assistant that was used by earlier versions of Outlook and Exchange. One of the most requested features for Out-of-Office is the ability to allow a user to schedule when their Out-of-Office (OOF) message starts being generated and when it stops. Other features include allowing users to select an internal and an external OOF message and to send an OOF message to only recipients that are in their own Contacts.

Additional administrative control is now possible with OOF messages to restrict which domains an OOF message is sent to and disable some users' ability to configure OOF messages.

AUTODISCOVER

One of the most time-consuming things that an Exchange administrator has to do is to help configure Outlook clients to connect to the Exchange server. In the past, profiles had to be created via scripting or profile utilities. Exchange 2007 introduces a feature called Autodiscover that makes configuration of Outlook 2007 profiles much simpler. Once the user provides their name and their e-mail address (see Figure 1.18), Outlook 2007 automatically discovers the correct server and updates the server if the mailbox moves (even if the original server is no longer online).

New and Improved Outlook Web Access

Those of us who gushed when we saw the Outlook Web Access interface in Exchange 2003 thought a web interface could not get much better. For Outlook Web Access in Exchange 2007, the Exchange team started over from scratch to build a much more functional interface than ever before. Here are some of the new features in Outlook Web Access 2007:

◆ Ability to browse the global address list (GAL)

◆ Document access on internal file shares and Windows SharePoint services

◆ The ability to manage and remotely wipe Windows mobile devices

◆ Improved meeting booking features

◆ Ability to perform full-text searches on mailbox content

◆ Selectable message format (HTML or plain text) when composing a message

◆ Ability to set out-of-office messages, define them as internal or external, and schedule when they start

◆ Manage voicemail features such as their greeting, reset their voicemail PIN, and turn on missed call notifications

FIGURE 1.18
Configuring Outlook
2007 for Autodiscover

Edge Transport Services

The amount of spam and viruses that some organizations receive is staggering. Even small organizations are receiving tens of thousands of pieces of spam, dozens of viruses, and hundreds of thousands of dictionary spamming attacks each week. Some organizations estimate that as much as 90 percent of all inbound e-mail is spam or other unwanted content. Keeping as much of this unwanted content away from your Exchange servers as possible is important. A common practice for messaging administrators is to employ additional layers of message hygiene and security. The first layer is usually some type of appliance or third-party SMTP software package that is installed in the organization's perimeter network. The problem with these third-party utilities is that the administrator has to become an expert on an additional technology.

Microsoft's solution to this dilemma is the Edge Transport server. The Edge Transport server is a stand-alone message transport server that is managed using the Exchange Management

Shell (EMS) and the same basic management console that is used to manage Exchange 2007. A server functioning in an Edge Transport should not be a member of the organization's internal Active Directory.

Functions such as transport rules are identical to those that run on an Exchange 2007 Hub Transport server. Content filtering (formerly referred to as the Intelligent Message Filter, or IMF) and Microsoft Forefront Security for Exchange are implemented on the Edge Transport server.

An example of how an organization might deploy an Edge Transport server is shown in Figure 1.19. Inbound e-mail is first delivered to the Edge Transport servers that are located in the organization's perimeter network where it is inspected by the content filter, Forefront Security for Exchange, and any message transport rules. The inbound message is then sent on to the internal Hub Transport servers. Additionally, the Exchange 2007 Hub Transport servers are configured to deliver mail leaving the organization to the Edge Transport servers rather than configuring them to deliver mail directly to the Internet.

FIGURE 1.19
Deploying an Edge Transport server

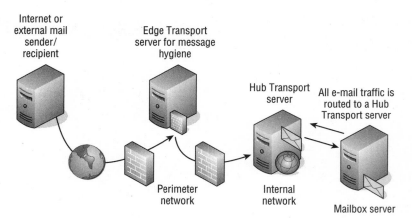

The Edge Transport server is a fully functional SMTP message hygiene system with many of the same features that are found in expensive message hygiene software packages and appliances. The following features are included:

◆ Per-user safe-sender and blocked sender lists are replicated from the user's mailbox out to the Edge Transport server.

◆ Recipient filtering is enabled when valid recipients are synchronized to the Edge Transport server's local Active Directory Application Mode (ADAM) database.

◆ Integrated Microsoft content filter is included for spam detection. Spam can be rejected, deleted, quarantined, or delivered to the user's Junk E-mail folder.

◆ Multitier quarantine allows messages that are highly likely to be spam to be quarantined in the perimeter network while maintaining a separate quarantine inside the network for messages that are still tagged as spam but with a lower Spam Confidence Level (SCL).

◆ Microsoft Forefront Security for Exchange Server (formerly known as Antigen) is available for the Edge Transport server when Enterprise client access licenses are used.

◆ Daily content filter and virus signature updates are available for organizations using Microsoft Forefront Security for Exchange Server.

- Real-time block lists (RBLs) and IP Reputation Service allow an IP address to be checked to see if it is a known source of spam.

- Sender ID filters allow for the verification of the mail server that sent a message and whether it is allowed to send mail for the message sender.

- Sender reputation filters allow a sender to be temporarily placed on a block list based on characteristics of mail coming from that sender, such as message content, Sender ID verification, and sender behavior.

Unified Messaging

The concept of unified messaging means that information from multiple sources is all accessed in a single location. This concept is by no means a new one; third-party vendors have had fax and voicemail gateways for most major e-mail systems. The Exchange 2007 Unified Messaging server role represents Microsoft's entrance into this market.

The Unified Messaging server role functions as just another Exchange server in your organization, but this role includes components that allow IP-based phone systems and IP/PBX (public branch exchange) gateways to interface directly with Exchange over the network. This is provided the IP phone system or IP/PBX can communicate using Session Initiated Protocol (SIP) over TCP or Real-Time Transport Protocol (RTP) for voice communication or T.38 protocol for real-time facsimile transport.

When the Exchange 2007 Unified Messaging role is integrated with an IP-based phone system or a PBX with an IP/PBX gateway, the following additional functions may be possible:

- Inbound voicemail is delivered directly to the user's mailbox.

- Inbound faxes are delivered directly to the user's mailbox.

- Users can call in to the phone system and have their e-mail read to them, listen to their schedule, or move appointments around on their schedule and notify attendees.

- Users can call in to the phone system and look up users from the global address list.

New Programming Interfaces

Much of the underlying infrastructure of Exchange 2007 has been completely rewritten. As a result, many of the application programming interfaces (APIs) used to access Exchange data and to manage Exchange components have been replaced with new APIs.

EXCHANGE MANAGEMENT

Management of Exchange-related components and recipient objects is now performed with the new management API. All operations that can be performed have been defined as tasks. The management API provides access to all management functions via the Exchange Management Shell tasks, also known as cmdlets (pronounced "command-lets"). The Exchange Management Shell is a set of extensions for the Windows PowerShell. Exchange management functionality can be extended and accessed via managed code and custom scripts can integrate with and use .NET objects.

TRANSPORT AGENTS

All messages and message content traveling through the message transport system (on a Hub Transport server or Edge Transport server) can be manipulated using transport agents. Transport agents are written using managed code. They replace Exchange 2000/2003 transport sinks.

EXCHANGE MANAGED APIS

Exchange Managed APIs extend the Microsoft .NET Framework by providing classes and data structures that allow custom programs to access and manipulate different parts of e-mail message content. Functions include accessing MIME content; filtering e-mail body content; converting message content between plain-text, HTML, and RTF formats; and reading or writing calendar items.

WEB SERVICES

One of the most exciting new APIs is the Web Services API. Web Services allows developers to write applications that can remotely access mailboxes, folders, and message content. Many of the new Exchange services — such as the Autodiscover service, Availability service, and Messaging Records Management — use the Web Services API. Services can be developed that can send notifications to client applications and provide synchronization of mailbox folders and items. The Web Services API provides these features:

- Ability to manage folders in a user mailbox, including creating, deleting, copying, changing, searching, viewing, and moving folders

- Ability to manage messages in a user mailbox, including creating, deleting, copying, changing, searching, viewing, moving, and sending messages as well as accessing message content

- Ability to enumerate distribution group memberships

Now, Where Did That Go?

As new and better functions and APIs have been introduced, naturally some functions are no longer emphasized or no longer supported. There has been a lot of confusion surrounding what will continue to be supported in Exchange 2007 and what will no longer work. The phrase "no longer supported" itself tends to also generate a lot of confusion because a function may actually continue to work because it has not truly been removed. These functions and APIs fall in to two unique categories: functions that have been deemphasized and functions that are no longer available.

Deemphasized Functions

When Microsoft says that in Exchange 2007 certain functions or APIs are no longer emphasized, this means that it will not continue to enhance these features. They will continue to be supported, and if there are bugs with these features, the bugs will be fixed. However, if something is being deemphasized, then the writing is on the wall; you should consider replacing your use of this technology with something else.

The following is a list of some of the APIs and functions that are being deemphasized:

- Public folders are still supported in Exchange 2007, but their use is being deemphasized as newer collaborative technologies have been introduced, such as SharePoint and other portal technologies.

- Collaborative Data Objects technologies such as CDOSYS, CDO 1.2.1, and CDOExM are being deemphasized. Applications using these APIs will continue to work but they should be rewritten using the Transport Agents API or Exchange Web Services API.

◆ Functions provided by Exchange WebDAV extensions are now provided by the Web Services API.

◆ The Exchange Object Linking and Embedding Database (ExOLEDB) API functionality is now provided via the Web Services API.

Features No Longer Included

Some features and APIs have been completely removed from the Exchange 2007 product. If you require any of these features or APIs, you will need to keep an Exchange 2000 or Exchange 2003 server in operation:

◆ Exchange 5.5 interoperability is no longer available. You cannot install an Exchange 2007 server until your Exchange organization is in native Exchange 2000/2003 mode.

◆ Mail recipient management using the Active Directory Users and Computers console extensions no longer works. All recipient management must be performed through the Exchange Management Console. There are a few exceptions, of course, but using the Exchange Management Console or the Exchange Management Shell is preferred. This will also keep you from accidentally doing something that is not supported.

◆ Administrative groups are no longer available. All permissions delegation is handled either on a server-by-server basis or at the organization level.

◆ Outlook Mobile Access, the lightweight browser-based access for WAP-based mobile phones, is not available. Nor are Exchange ActiveSync Always Up-to-Date notifications.

◆ Non-MAPI public folder hierarchies are no longer available.

◆ Public folder access via NNTP, IMAP4, and Outlook Web Access is no longer available.

◆ Network News Transport Protocol (NNTP) features have been cut from Exchange 2007 completely.

◆ The Exchange Management Console cannot be used to perform management of public folder properties. This must continue to be performed through the Exchange 2000/2003 Exchange System Manager console. Public folder management using the Exchange Management Console should be included in Exchange Server 2007 Service Pack 1.

◆ Routing groups and routing group connectors are no longer required. In a native Exchange 2007 organization, the message routing topology is determined using the Active Directory sites in which the Exchange servers are located. Message delivery between Exchange 2007 servers in different Active Directory sites is handled automatically.

◆ Mailbox databases no longer have a streaming database file (STM file). All mail, regardless of its original source, is stored in the EDB database file.

◆ The Recipient Update Service functionality has been replaced. E-mail proxy addresses and address list membership is set on a mail recipient object at the time of creation. These can be updated from the Exchange Management Shell.

◆ X.400 connectors are no longer available.

◆ ExMerge can no longer be run from the Exchange 2007 server console; it can continue to be run against Exchange 2007 mailboxes, but it must be run from a computer with Outlook installed.

◆ On two-node clusters, active-active clustering cannot be configured. Exchange 2007 requires active-passive clustering on two-node clusters.

◆ Transport event sinks no longer work. You must keep Exchange 2000/2003 Server for software that uses this functionality or update the code to use transport agents.

◆ Functionality for applications built from Workflow Designer and CDO for Workflow is not available. Applications built using these APIs should be replaced with applications built using Windows Workflow Services (WWS).

◆ Collaborative Data Objects for Exchange Management (CDOExM) is not available. Applications or scripts using CDOExM should be rewritten to use the new Exchange management APIs or Exchange Management Shell cmdlets.

◆ The Exchange Queue Viewer API has been cut from Exchange 2007. Applications that use this API should be rewritten using the new Exchange management APIs.

◆ Exchange Windows Management Instrumentation (WMI) classes have been discontinued. Applications that use Exchange WMI should be rewritten using the Exchange management APIs.

◆ The Exchange Event Service is no longer available. Applications should be rewritten to use the Web Services API instead.

◆ The Exchange Installable File System (ExIFS) is no longer available; this was commonly also referred to as the M: drive in Exchange 2000. This functionality can be duplicated writing applications using the Web Services API.

◆ POP3 and IMAP4 configuration is now performed through Exchange Management Shell tasks rather than the graphical user interface.

◆ The Exchange 2000/2003 Recipient Update Service (RUS) is no longer required to stamp mail-enabled objects with e-mail address and address list information. This information is now associated with mail-enabled objects when the object is created.

◆ X.400 connectivity is no longer included with Exchange 2007; this functionality is available from a third party.

Clearing Up Some Confusion

We mentioned earlier that Exchange has certainly been hyped a lot during the design and beta testing process. This has generated a lot of buzz in the information technology (IT) industry, but this buzz has also generated a lot of confusion and some misinformation. We want to take this opportunity to clear up some of this confusion by answering some of the more common questions that have generated misconceptions about Exchange 2007.

Do I have to have three or four separate servers to run each of the server roles?　A single server can host all four primary server roles (Mailbox, Client Access, Hub Transport, and Unified Messaging) except in the case of clustered mailbox servers. The Client Access, Hub Transport, and Unified Messaging server roles cannot be on the clustered mailbox server. The Edge Transport role must be installed on a separate server. The active clustered mailbox and passive clustered mailbox server roles must be on separate servers.

Is there a 32-bit version of Exchange?　Yes, there is an evaluation, testing, and lab version of Exchange 2007 that is a 32-bit version. This version must not be used in production.

Is Microsoft Forefront Security for Exchange included with Exchange 2007? Forefront Security for Exchange (formerly known as Sybari Antigen) is included with Exchange 2007 if you have purchased Exchange Enterprise Client Access Licenses (CALs).

Is the Edge Transport server required? No, Edge Transport servers are not required. You can use any third-party message hygiene system in your perimeter network or you can direct inbound and outbound mail through your hub transport servers or both.

Is Exchange 2007 using a SQL database for mailboxes and public folders? Although there has been debate for years about using SQL Server for the Exchange databases, Exchange 2007 uses the Extensible Storage Engine (ESE), also known as the JET database engine.

Is Exchange Management Shell knowledge required? Do I have to learn scripting? Most common administrative tasks can be performed through the Exchange Management Console graphical interface. Command-line management and scripting for Exchange 2007 has been greatly improved through the use of the Exchange Management Shell. Many tasks are simplified or more powerful through the Exchange Management Shell, but it is not necessary to learn scripting in order to start working with Exchange 2007. We strongly encourage you to get know many of the powerful features of the EMS as you get comfortable with Exchange 2007. A number of advanced administration tasks do not have a graphical user interface option.

What is happening with public folders? The use of public folders with Exchange 2007 is still available and supported, but their use is being deemphasized as newer collaborative technologies such as websites and portals have become commonplace. We urge you to examine your public folder applications with an eye toward migrating them to systems such as Microsoft Office SharePoint Server 2007.

Is there still 32KB a limitation on folder rules? For power users, the 32KB limit on the size of rules for a folder was a serious annoyance. This limit is no longer a constraint for Outlook 2007 users whose mailbox is on an Exchange 2007 mailbox server.

Is local continuous replication (LCR) and clustered continuous replication (CCR) the same as mailbox replication? LCR and CCR do not replicate individual mailboxes but rather an entire mailbox database. The administrator selects an entire storage group (which must contain only a single database); Exchange replicates the data to a backup copy of the mailbox database by copying the transaction logs as they are filled.

Do I need to use every Exchange 2007 server role to have a functional Exchange 2007 system? In order to build a completely functional Exchange 2007 system, you need the Mailbox, Hub Transport, and Client Access server roles. These can all reside on the same physical server.

Can I run 32-bit applications with the 64-bit version of Exchange 2007? Most 32-bit Windows applications will generally run on Windows 2003 x64, but applications that integrate with Exchange (such as message hygiene or backup applications) should be 64-bit.

Summary

For most organizations, no single feature of Exchange 2007 may justify an upgrade. However, once you start looking at a combined list of improvements to Exchange 2007, then the upgrade or replacement of an existing messaging system is compelling. For many organizations, the new high-availability features such as LCR and CCR will be the most important, and for others, improvements in calendaring and Outlook Web Access will be.

All in all, this latest generation of Exchange Server packs a big punch and will be a welcome addition to any organization. The following is a short list of the features that we find the most compelling:

- Improved performance because of more available RAM
- The ability to support users' demands for larger mailboxes
- Improved high-availability functions such as CCR and LCR
- Unified messaging integration
- Improved Outlook Web Access
- Automatic configuration of Outlook 2007 profiles
- Message transport rules and the Hub Transport role

Chapter 2

Exchange Server 2007 Architecture

What separates a good Exchange Server administrator or implementer from a great one? Well, certainly there are a lot of factors, including an eye for details, patience with users, and knowledge of Exchange. However, truly effective Exchange Server 2007 planning, deployment, administration, performance optimization, and troubleshooting depend at least partially on understanding what is going on behind the scenes. This includes knowledge of the Exchange Server architecture, installation options, database configuration, and server roles.

In this chapter, we will introduce you to some of the basics of Exchange Server architecture and how you can make some of the right decisions early in your Exchange Server deployments. Certainly understanding what Exchange Server 2007 requires of its underlying operating system is a good start. And it's important to understand the differences between Exchange Server 2007 editions and client access licenses so you can pick the edition with the features and scalability that your organization requires.

A lot of changes have occurred for Exchange 2007 from the perspective of architecture and the choices that are available to the Exchange designer, implementer, or administrator. Although we introduced a lot of these concepts in Chapter 1, we will go in to more depth on the architectural changes in this chapter.

Topics in this chapter include the following:

◆ Exchange 2007 requirements

◆ How to plan for disk space

◆ The move to 64-bit Windows

◆ Active Directory and Exchange Server

◆ The basics of a client/server system

Exchange Server 2007 Requirements

To properly support Exchange 2007, you need to make sure the hardware you are using meets certain minimum requirements. This is certainly true if you are expecting Exchange 2007 to perform as expected and you expect to run in an environment supported by Microsoft. The hardware and software requirements are a bit more complex than they were for previous generations of Exchange.

Hardware Requirements

In the past, Microsoft has made recommendations for hardware based on the absolute minimums required to run Exchange Server. Now, however, the recommendations are much more practical for real-world deployments. The goal is optimal performance, and the recommendations are now made with consideration for supporting applications that often run in concert with Exchange Server, such as antivirus, anti-spam, archiving, management, monitoring, and reporting software.

PROCESSORS

The requirement for 64-bit processors is the first big change for Exchange 2007. The processor should be at least an 800MHz processor, though you will certainly benefit from processors faster than 2GHz or dual-core processors. The processor must be either an Intel Xeon or Intel Pentium x64 processor that supports the Intel Extended Memory 64 Technology (EM64T) or an AMD Opteron or Athlon 64-bit processor that supports the AMD64 platform. The Intel Itanium IA64 processor family is not supported. Table 2.1 shows the processor recommendations from Microsoft for different Exchange Server 2007 roles.

TABLE 2.1:   Processor Recommendations Based on Server Role

EXCHANGE 2007 SERVER ROLE	MINIMUM	RECOMMENDED	RECOMMENDED MAXIMUM
Edge Transport	1 × processor core	2 × processor cores	4 × processor cores
Hub Transport	1 × processor core	4 × processor cores	4 × processor cores
Client Access	1 × processor core	4 × processor cores	4 × processor cores
Unified Messaging	1 × processor core	4 × processor cores	4 × processor cores
Mailbox	1 × processor core	4 × processor cores	8 × processor cores
Multiple server roles (combinations of Hub Transport, Client Access, Unified Messaging, and Mailbox server roles)	1 × processor core	4 × processor cores	4 × processor cores

You may have noticed in Table 2.1 that for some server roles, the maximum number of processors or processor cores is less than the maximum that Windows can actually support. Most all multithreaded applications will reach a point of diminishing returns when more processors are added, so it may not be worth it to add the maximum number of processors that Windows supports.

In environments that scale past a few hundred mailboxes, certainly dual- or quad-processor systems will be put to good use. For organizations that deploy Exchange Server in a combination of roles to different physical machines, you will almost always benefit from a dual-processor or dual-core processor system.

PHYSICAL MEMORY

As we have mentioned previously, the advantage that Exchange 2007 really gets out of the 64-bit architecture is the ability to access more physical memory. Additional physical memory improves caching, reduces the disk I/O profile, and allows for the addition of more features.

Microsoft is recommending a minimum of 1GB of RAM in each Exchange 2007 server or 2GB for each server supporting the Mailbox server role. This will, of course, depend on the roles that the server is supporting. Table 2.2 shows the minimum recommended memory for each of the server roles.

TABLE 2.2: Minimum and Recommended RAM for Exchange Server 2007 Roles

SERVER ROLE	MINIMUM	RECOMMENDATION	MAXIMUM
Mailbox	2GB	2GB base memory plus per mailbox calculation.	32GB
Hub Transport	1GB	1GB per CPU core	16GB
Client Access	1GB	1GB per CPU core	4GB
Unified Messaging	1GB	1GB minimum plus 512MB for each additional CPU core	4GB
Edge Transport	1GB	1GB per CPU core	16GB
Multiple roles	2GB	4GB for combination Hub Transport, Client Access, and Unified Messaging plus the per-mailbox calculation	8GB

Once you have calculated the minimum amount of RAM that you require for the server, if you are configuring a mailbox server, you will need to add some additional RAM for each mailbox. This will depend on your user community's estimated load profile. Table 2.3 shows the additional memory required based on the number of mailboxes supported.

TABLE 2.3: Additional Memory Factor for Mailbox Servers

USER PROFILE	MAILBOX MEMORY RECOMMENDATION
Light	Add 2MB per mailbox
Average	Add 3.5MB per mailbox
Heavy	Add 5MB per mailbox

TIP

If you are curious what constitutes light, average, and heavy users, these are defined later in this chapter in Table 2.5.

So for example, a server handling a Mailbox server role should have 2GB of memory plus the additional RAM per mailbox shown in Table 2.3. If the Mailbox server is supporting 1,000 mailboxes and it is estimated that 500 of the users are average (1.75GB of RAM) and 500 are heavy users (2.5GB of RAM), the server should have about 6.3GB of RAM. For good measure, we would recommend going with 8GB of RAM so that there is additional RAM just in case it is required. Seasoned administrators of previous versions of Exchange will immediately notice that restrictions on usable physical memory no longer apply to Exchange 2007.

Remember that these RAM estimates are just that, estimates. Additional factors may require more or less RAM (usually more) than the calculations and recommendations here. For example, antivirus and anti-spam software on Mailbox servers can place a significant burden on RAM.

An alternate way to size memory for Mailbox servers is to estimate the amount of RAM required based on the number of storage groups. This method is calculated to ensure that each storage group (and mailbox database) that is in use is allocated sufficient memory for database caching. Table 2.4 shows the minimum memory recommendations based on storage groups.

TABLE 2.4:   Minimum RAM Recommendations Based on Storage Groups

NUMBER OF STORAGE GROUPS	MINIMUM RAM REQUIRED
1–4	2GB
5–8	4GB
9–12	6GB
13–16	8GB
17–20	10GB
21–24	12GB
25–28	14GB
29–32	16GB
33–36	18GB
37–40	20GB
41–44	22GB
45–38	24GB
49–50	26GB

If you calculate two different minimum recommendations for RAM, we strongly encourage you to use the larger of the two calculations. Up to 32GB, Exchange 2007 Mailbox servers will always benefit from additional performance. Of course, 32GB of RAM may not be required on a Mailbox server that is supporting only 200 mailboxes, so approach RAM sizing with a certain cautious exuberance.

OPTICAL MEDIA

Exchange Server 2007 ships only on DVD media. Although installing from a network share does work, it is generally a good idea to ensure that your servers have DVD drives available rather than CD-ROM drives. If your servers do not have DVD drives, you can still copy the Exchange software across the network or install from a network share folder.

FILE SYSTEM

The FAT and FAT32 file systems are not supported. All disks must be formatted using the NTFS file system.

DISK SPACE

Exchange Server 2007 is certainly not the first edition of Exchange for which administrators or designers have improperly sized the amount of available disk space. More than a few times, we have seen administrators scrambling for more disk space, adding additional hard drives, moving databases and transaction logs around, or begging the storage area network (SAN) administrator for more disk space. This is so important, in fact, that we are dedicating an entire section to this in Chapter 3, "Designing a New Exchange 2007 System."

For now, let's just leave the disk requirements at the utmost basics. We recommend that each system disk on an Exchange Server have at least 10GB of free disk space prior to the installation of Exchange 2007. The actual recommendation from Microsoft is 1.2GB disk space free and 200MB of free space on the system disk, but that is a bare minimum. The amount of disk space that each of the servers will actually require will depend on the server role, the number of users you support, mailbox limits, and leaving room to grow.

Operating System Requirements

There are a few requirements for the Windows Server operating system. For the release to manufacturing (RTM) version of Exchange 2007, the only version of Windows Server that can be used is the Windows Server 2003 x64 SP1 (or later) or Windows Server 2003 x64 R2 family. Windows 2003 with the Multilingual User Interface (MUI) pack can also be used.

Exchange 2007 can be installed on either the Standard Edition or Enterprise Edition of Windows Server 2003. Windows 2003 Enterprise Edition is required if you will be installing clustered mailbox servers.

At some point in the future, Microsoft will include support for Exchange 2007 to run on top of the new Windows Server operating system that is currently code-named Longhorn. This will be in the time frame of Exchange 2007 Service Pack 1. Do not try to install Exchange 2007 on Longhorn Server in production until you have specific instructions from Microsoft as to how to support it.

The following list includes other requirements for preparing the Windows server to run Exchange 2007:

◆ Install the Microsoft .NET Framework v2.0.

◆ Install the Windows PowerShell. The released version can be downloaded from http://preview.tinyurl.com/e5x2t.

◆ Install Microsoft Management Console 3.0. You can find more information and download links in Microsoft Knowledge Base article 907265, "MMC 3.0 update is available for Windows Server 2003 and for Windows XP."

> **NOTE**
>
> Unlike with previous versions of Exchange, the Internet Information Server components Network News Transfer Protocol (NNTP) and Simple Mail Transfer Protocol (SMTP) should not be installed.

All additional applications that you run on an Exchange 2007 server should be 64-bit applications. Although Windows x64 supports 32-bit applications in WOW64 emulation provided the applications' kernel mode components are 64-bit, it remains to be seen whether mixing and matching 32-bit and 64-bit applications on an Exchange 2007 server is a good idea. Many of us still remember poorly performing and unstable 16-bit Windows applications that adversely affected Windows NT 4.0, so this may potentially be true with 32-bit Windows applications on Windows 64-bit.

The 64-bit versions of Windowssupport applications in WOW64 to support Exchange. The only requirement is that kernel mode components of those applications have to work, so those have to be x64. The main application can be 32 bit running in WOW64. In our opinion, any third-party tools and utilities that run on an Exchange 2007 server should be 64-bit versions.

The Move to 64-Bit Architecture

The move to a 64-bit architecture has been a controversial decision on the part of Microsoft, but in our opinion this certainly makes a lot of sense. Additional accessible memory is the number one reason for moving to the 64-bit architecture. Exchange 2003 Server quickly becomes short on RAM available for caching and other Exchange operations. Microsoft could not add too many additional server-side features to Exchange 2007 without getting around this constraint.

Although the 32-bit architecture certainly leaves a lot of room to grow when fewer mailboxes per server are supported, servers with more mailboxes begin to hit limitations. Microsoft was faced with a decision to support both 32-bit and 64-bit versions of Exchange or to require everyone to move to the 64-bit version. Supporting two different processors' architectures for the same product is both more difficult and more costly than supporting a single version. This is certainly the case with Microsoft, but it is true to a certain degree for the customer as well. As third-party products are released, as fixes are released, and as customizations or tweaks are documented, there will be more possible choices for processors, editions, and operating systems and the customer's support responsibilities will become more difficult.

ROOM TO GROW

For servers supporting larger numbers of mailboxes, the Exchange team had clearly exceeded the limits of the 32-bit architecture with Exchange 2003. Adding additional server-side processes such as messaging records management, improved calendaring and scheduling, transport rules, Unified Messaging services, integration with Windows Rights Management Services, and other new features would not have been possible without additional room to grow.

IMPROVED CACHING AND REDUCED I/O PROFILES

Even on a server with only a few hundred mailboxes, Exchange Server 2000/2003 quickly reaches the maximum amount of RAM available for caching (1.2GB maximum). As more and more users vie for the same physical memory for caching, Exchange Server quickly becomes constrained by the amount of I/O (input output) operations that the Exchange server's disk subsystem can support.

Hundreds of pages of material have been written on the concept of optimizing Exchange Server for maximizing performance by improving I/O performance with Exchange, and we certainly can't do the concept justice in just a few paragraphs, but understanding the basic input/output per second (IOPS) requirements of users is helpful. Microsoft and hardware vendors have done much research on I/O requirements based on the mailbox size and the average load that each user places on the server. Table 2.5 shows the estimated IOPS given a user type and an estimated mailbox size for Exchange 2003. IOPS requirements climb as the number of messages sent and received increases and as the mailbox size increases.

TABLE 2.5: User Profile, Mailbox Size, and Estimated IOPS for Exchange 2003

USER TYPE	DATABASE VOLUME IOPS	MESSAGES SENT/RECEIVED PER DAY	MAILBOX SIZE
Light	.5	20 sent/50 received	50MB
Average	.75	30 sent/75 received	100MB
Heavy	1.0	40 sent/100 received	200MB
Large	1.5	60 sent/150 received	500MB

For an Exchange 2003 server that is supporting 3,000 heavy mailbox users, the disk subsystem would have to support at least 3,000 IOPS. In order to meet this requirement, the disk subsystem may have too many additional disks; thus, the disk subsystem may have far more disk space than is actually necessary in order to support the IOPS profile. Failure to plan for sufficient IOPS capacity on the disk subsystem will significantly hurt performance.

The 64-bit architectural improvements to Exchange 2007 allow the operating system and Exchange Server 2007 to access more physical memory. With additional physical memory available for caching, disk I/O is significantly reduced. Microsoft estimates that I/O requirements are reduced by approximately 70 percent provided the Exchange 2007 server has the recommended amount of RAM. Table 2.6 shows the estimated IOPS requirements for Exchange 2007 Mailbox servers. Please keep in mind that these are estimates and may change over time. These numbers are also calculated when the Mailbox server is configured with more than the recommended amount of RAM.

TABLE 2.6: User Profile, Mailbox Size, and Estimated IOPS for Exchange 2007

USER TYPE	DATABASE VOLUME IOPS	MESSAGES SENT/RECEIVED PER DAY	MAILBOX SIZE
Light	.14	20 sent/50 received	50MB
Average	.20	30 sent/75 received	100MB
Heavy	.27	40 sent/100 received	200MB
Large	.41	60 sent/150 received	500MB

With this significant improvement in caching Exchange data, the Extensible Storage Engine (ESE) database engine needs to read and write from the disk less frequently and thus reduces the IOPS requirements. When the IOPS requirements are reduced, fewer disks are required to support the I/O load.

Active Directory and Exchange Server 2007

Active Directory is a grand repository for information about such objects as users, domains, computers, domain controllers, groups, contacts, and shared resources (such as files and printers).

Active Directory lets you log into very large domains and use resources across the domain with ease. All objects in Active Directory are protected by a security system based on Kerberos, an industry-standard secret-key encryption network authentication protocol developed at the Massachusetts Institute of Technology. (For more on Kerberos, see `http://web.mit.edu/kerberos/www/`.)

Windows Server controls who can see each object in Active Directory, what attributes each user can see, and what actions a user can perform on an object. The Windows Active Directory permissions model is richer and more complex under the hood than directory services permissions in earlier versions of Windows such as Windows NT 4, but it's quite easy to manage at the user interface level.

Exchange Depends on Active Directory

Exchange Server 2007, like Exchange 2000/2003, depends entirely on a healthy and functioning Active Directory and the availability of Domain Name Service (DNS) services. In order for Exchange servers to properly locate domain controllers and global catalogs, DNS must accurately resolve domain controller and global catalog service location records and host information as well as information about Active Directory sites. Exchange must retrieve configuration and recipient information from Active Directory as well; if either DNS or Active Directory does not respond to an Exchange 2007 server's queries, clients will not be able to authenticate, address lookups will not occur, and e-mail will not flow.

Almost the entire Exchange 2007 configuration is stored in the Active Directory; this information is stored in a partition of the Active Directory called the Configuration partition. The Configuration partition (Figure 2.1) is replicated to all domain controllers in the entire forest, not just the domain in which the Exchange server is installed.

FIGURE 2.1
Viewing the configuration from ADSI Edit

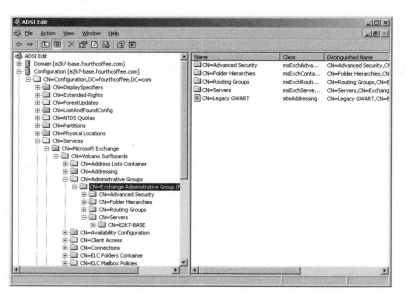

The information you see in Figure 2.1 represents the Exchange 2007 configuration as viewed using the Windows 2003 Support Tools utility ADSI Edit. This is a very primitive view of the Exchange configuration in much the same way that REGEDIT gives you an inside look at the Windows Registry. Actually configuring Exchange properties is much easier (and safer!) to do when you use the Exchange Management Console (EMC) or the Exchange Management Shell (EMS). You should only use ADSI Edit to manipulate your Exchange organization's configuration when you have specific guidance from Microsoft or a trustworthy source.

When an Exchange server starts running services such as the Microsoft Exchange System Attendant, the Microsoft Exchange Active Directory Topology service determines in which Active Directory site the Exchange server is located and then locates all domain controllers and global catalog servers in that site. Exchange Server then reads its configuration from Active Directory; this would include determining which roles that server supports, the mailbox databases to mount, and more.

When Exchange 2007 Hub Transport server is routing messages to Exchange recipients, t it must query a global catalog server in order to determine properties of the recipient such as proxy addresses, home mailbox server, and mailbox restrictions. Figure 2.2 shows the E-mail Addresses property page of a mailbox recipient; mail recipients are managed through the Exchange Management Console (EMC).

FIGURE 2.2
E-mail Addresses
properties

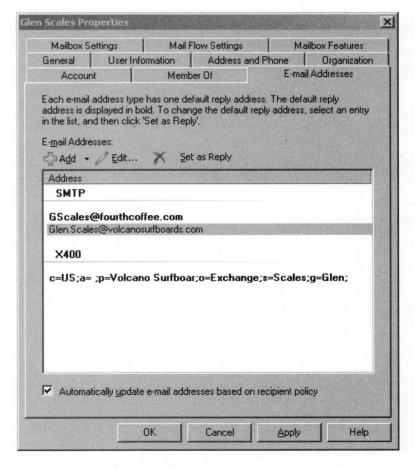

All recipient information is stored in the Active Directory, so information regarding e-mail addresses, home server, mailbox limits, message size limits, and so on are found in the Active Directory. Exchange server must retrieve this information from an Active Directory global catalog server. Exchange server is dependent on the availability and health of domain controllers and global catalog servers; if Active Directory resources are not available, Exchange will not function.

Active Directory Site Membership

Exchange Server 2007 is an Active-Directory-site-aware application. Exchange 2007 uses Active Directory site information for a couple of purposes.

Exchange 2007 servers automatically learn the Active Directory topology and determine in which Active Directory site each Exchange 2007 server is located. Exchange Server uses the IP subnets to locate the sites; if the subnet information is incomplete or incorrect, Exchange Server will not be able to correctly determine site membership and mail may not be delivered properly.

Different Exchange Server 2007 server roles use the Active Directory site information in different ways:

◆ All Exchange 2007 server roles use the site architecture to locate domain controllers and global catalog servers closest to them from the network's perspective.

◆ Hub Transport servers determine the remote Hub Transport servers names in other Active Directory sites to which they need to transmit messages intended for remote Mailbox servers.

◆ Mailbox servers determine which Hub Transport servers are in their own site so they can notify those servers that they have messages that must be transferred.

◆ Unified Messaging servers submit voicemail messages and faxes to Hub Transport servers in their own site for routing to Mailbox servers. Unified Messaging servers do not transfer voicemail and fax messages directly to a Mailbox server.

◆ Client Access servers look for site information in order to determine if they are located in the same Active Directory site mailboxes that they are being asked to provide access to. If not, the Client Access server refers the client to a Client Access server that is in the same site as the required Mailbox server.

◆ Exchange Server refers Outlook 2000, 2002, and 2003 clients to global catalog servers that are in the same site as the Exchange server for global address list lookups.

If there are weaknesses in your Active Directory site design, Exchange 2007 will certainly expose them. You should ensure that for Active Directory forests with more than one Active Directory site, subnets are properly defined and associated with the appropriate site.

> **WARNING**
>
> Active Directory IP subnet information must be correct. If it's not, Exchange components might not function properly and messages might not be delivered.

Domain Controllers and Global Catalog Servers

The simplest way to describe the Exchange 2007 requirements for Active Directory is to say that all domain controllers should be running (at a minimum) Windows 2003 Service Pack 1 or later, each domain should be at Windows 2003 domain functional level, and the forest should be at Windows 2003 functional level. Although that is the best case scenario, it might not be practical and it is not correct. The following are the actual minimum requirements for Windows 2003 domain controllers and Active Directory:

◆ Each Active Directory site that has Exchange 2007 servers must have at least one Windows 2003 Service Pack 1 or later global catalog server. For redundancy, an additional global catalog server should be available. The recommended ratio of Exchange servers to global catalog servers is based on the number of CPUs; that ratio is 4:1. For each quad processor Exchange server, a single processor global catalog server should be available in the site, but that may not take in to consideration redundancy requirements.

◆ Each domain that will host Exchange 2007 servers or mail-enabled recipients must be at a minimum Windows 2000 native functional level.

◆ If you are supporting the Exchange 2007 Outlook Web Access browsable global address list, you must use Windows 2003 Service Pack 1 or later global catalog servers.

◆ The schema master flexible single master of operations role must be hosted on a domain controller running Windows 2003 Service Pack 1 or later.

◆ If you have Exchange organizations in multiple forests and require forest-to-forest trusts, then all forests involved in forest-to-forests trusts must be at Windows 2003 forest functional mode.

Tips for Healthy Interaction with Active Directory

Any experienced Exchange administrator will tell you that a healthy Active Directory goes a long way toward ensuring that Exchange Server is healthy and trouble free. We have learned a number of lessons (sometimes the hard way) over the years and can offer some useful tips for ensuring that Active Directory provides consistent and reliable directory services to Exchange.

◆ Even in small and medium-sized organizations, redundant domain controllers and global catalog servers help ensure higher availability.

◆ In large organizations, each Active Directory site that hosts Exchange servers should have at least two domain controllers that host the global catalog server role.

◆ In large organizations with many thousands of mailboxes, implementing dedicated domain controller/global catalog server sites that are exclusively for use by Exchange servers will ensure that Exchange does not interfere with Active Directory's other functions (such as authenticating users) and vice versa.

◆ All clients and member servers should have a primary DNS server and a secondary DNS server address configured.

◆ In large organizations, clients and member servers should have a primary, secondary, and tertiary DNS server IP addresses configured.

◆ Either Windows 2003 32-bit or 64-bit can be used for domain controllers and global catalog servers, but if the Active Directory database (NTDS.DIT) exceeds 1GB, then better performance will be achieved with 64-bit Windows 2003. For organizations with NTDS.DIT files larger than a few hundred megabytes, separating the database transaction logs to a RAID 1 volume array and the NTDS.DIT database file to a RAID 5 array can also improve performance.

◆ Installing the DNS service on all domain controllers and using Active Directory–integrated DNS zones on all domain controllers in the forest will improve the reliability of DNS and therefore Active Directory. If you have more than two domain controllers/DNS servers in your organizations, all domain controllers and member servers should be configured with a primary DNS server, a secondary DNS server, and a tertiary DNS server.

Exchange Editions

When you plan to purchase Exchange 2007, you need to make sure you purchase the correct edition of Exchange server and purchase the client access licenses to license the features that you will require. Table 2.7 lists some of the features that are included with Exchange 2007 Standard Edition and Enterprise Edition.

TABLE 2.7:   Exchange 2007 Standard Edition versus Enterprise Edition

FEATURE	STANDARD	ENTERPRISE
Maximum database size	16TB (unlimited)	16TB (unlimited)
Maximum number of storage groups	5	50
Supports Recovery Storage Group	✓	✓
Number of databases	5	50
Supports Client Access server role	✓	✓
Supports single-copy clustered Mailbox servers		✓
Supports clustered continuous replication Mailbox servers		✓
Supports Edge Transport role	✓	✓
Supports Hub Transport role	✓	✓
Supports local continuous replication	✓	✓
Supports Mailbox role	✓	✓
Supports Unified Messaging role	✓	✓

In the past, you only had a single option when purchasing Exchange Server client access licenses (CALs). Exchange 2007 introduces the Exchange Enterprise CAL and Exchange Standard CAL. Either can be used against either Exchange Server Enterprise Edition or Exchange Server Standard Edition. The choice for which CAL you require will depend on which premium features of Exchange Server 2007 you are going to require.

The Exchange Enterprise CAL adds additional features above and beyond the Exchange Standard CAL. The Exchange Standard CAL provides your users with the ability to use Exchange features such as accessing their mailbox from a MAPI client, Outlook Web Access, ActiveSync devices, and Outlook Anywhere (RPC over HTTP). The Exchange Enterprise CAL includes the following additional functions:

◆ Unified Messaging services

◆ Microsoft Forefront Security for Exchange Server

◆ Advanced compliance capabilities such as per-user and per-distribution group journaling

◆ Messaging records management features

◆ Anti-spam and antivirus protection using Microsoft Exchange Hosted Filtering Services as an external service provider

Standard client access licenses must be purchased for each mailbox that is accessed on your system. If you have users that use multiple devices (Outlook, Outlook Web Access, Windows Mobile, ActiveSync, Outlook Anywhere) to access their mailbox and their total percentage of time accessing their mailbox from their primary device is less than 80 percent, then you must purchase an additional CAL for each user.

If you use Exchange Enterprise CALs for all of your users, then you get to use all of the features available for Enterprise CALs. However, if you purchase Enterprise CALs only for a subset of your users that require a feature such as Unified Messaging and Journaling and also choose to use Forefront Security for Exchange, then the remainder of the users must be licensed separately for Forefront Security for Exchange.

Server Roles

The best way to think of Exchange 2007 server roles is to think of a server that has the necessary software and configuration to perform only a specific set of functions. This makes installing servers with dedicated functions much easier. Dedicated server roles are also more secure because only the necessary software is installed, thus reducing the attack surface.

The concept of server roles is not really new. In Exchange 2000/2003, to build a server for handling Internet messaging or inter-routing group messaging, you would install Exchange Server, flag the machine as a front-end server (optionally), and disable services such as the web service. To configure a machine as an Outlook Web Access or ActiveSync server, you would install Exchange, flag the Exchange server as a front-end server, and disable the information store and SMTP services. With Exchange 2007, the server roles are assigned when Setup is run.

Server Roles Overview

Exchange 2007 has made the assignment of specific server roles simpler by allowing the server roles to be designated at installation time. When you group together and install only the necessary services for a specific function, server installation is simpler and more secure and the server has less overhead. There are five basic server roles:

◆ Mailbox

◆ Client Access

◆ Hub Transport

◆ Unified Messaging

◆ Edge Transport

The Mailbox server role can be installed as a clustered mailbox server. In small and medium-size organizations, a single physical server will usually host more than one server role except in the case of the Edge Transport role. Edge Transport must run on its own server.

MAILBOX SERVER ROLE

The Mailbox server role is responsible for mailbox and public folder databases and for allowing direct connectivity from MAPI/RPC clients. Clients such as Outlook 2003 or Outlook 2007 using MAPI/RPC will connect directly to the MAPI interface on the Mailbox server role. The Hub Transport and Client Access server roles are required for a fully functioning e-mail environment, but they do not necessarily have to be on the same physical server.

The Mailbox server role must exist on its own physical server if it is being installed as part of a clustered mailbox server environment. In that case, the Hub Transport, Client Access, and Unified Messaging server roles must be on separate physical hardware. A server handling a mailbox server role will typically be configured with significantly more RAM, hard disk space, and processor capacity than the other server roles.

High-availability options for Mailbox servers include local continuous replication, single copy clusters, and clustered continuous replication.

Local Continuous Replication

Local continuous replication (LCR) is a new technology for Exchange 2007. LCR is designed so that a production copy of a database can be synchronized and have a backup copy always ready to be put in to production if the primary copy becomes corrupted; the administrator initiates the switch over to the backup copy of the database. LCR is configured storage group by storage group, and each storage group can have only a single database in it.

When a server is configured to support LCR, an additional set of local disks should be allocated for the LCR transaction logs and for the backup copy of the database. These disks can be directly attached to the server or attached via storage area network (SAN) or Internet small computer systems interface (iSCSI). As transaction logs are completely filled and closed on the production copy of the database, they are copied to the backup location and committed to the backup copy of the database.

> **NOTE**
>
> Local continuous replication is resource intensive since transaction logs are being copied and replayed to backup copies of a database.

Clustered Continuous Replication

Clustered continuous replication (CCR) is also a new technology for Exchange Server 2007. This technology is similar to LCR in that as transaction logs are filled, they are copied to a backup location and committed to a backup (or passive) copy of the database. However, with CCR, the implementation is in the form of a two-node active-passive cluster. When Windows 2003 clustering services are used, both the active and passive nodes must reside on the same IP subnet. The backup location is on the passive node; the transaction log files are pulled to the passive node and committed to the database on the passive node.

If the primary node of the cluster fails, the passive node automatically comes online and takes over handling the clustered mailbox server. Unlike Microsoft's previous implementation of Exchange clustering (single-copy clusters), there is not a single copy of the database and transaction logs that is shared by all nodes of the cluster.

Single-Copy Clusters

A Single-copy cluster (SCC) is the same technology that existed in earlier versions of Exchange. An active node of the cluster owns shared disks (usually on a storage area network or on network attached storage, or NAS). The cluster can consist of from two to eight nodes, but there must always be at least one passive node. There is only a single copy of the database and transaction log files, and they are located on the shared storage.

If an active node of the cluster fails, then one of the passive nodes will take ownership of the shared disks and database, mount the shared database, and start servicing clients for that particular clustered mailbox server (CMS); the CMS was formerly known as an Exchange virtual server (EVS) in previous Exchange cluster implementations.

CLIENT ACCESS SERVER ROLE

The Client Access server is considered a middle-tier server; this server role handles communications between non-MAPI clients and the Mailbox server role. In order to have a fully functioning e-mail environment, the Client Access server role must be functioning. The following are some of the functions of the Client Access server role supports:

◆ Outlook Web Access clients

◆ ActiveSync-enabled mobile devices

◆ Outlook Anywhere (RPC over HTTP) clients

◆ POP3 and IMAP4 clients

◆ Offline Address Book Web distribution

◆ Web services such as Autodiscover and the Availability service

◆ Web Services that require access to user mailboxes

The Client Access server accepts connections from these clients via HTTP, POP3, or IMAP4 and then passes requests on to the Mailbox server via MAPI over RPC. Each Active Directory site that contains a Mailbox server role must also contain at least one Client Access server.

High-availability options for the Client Access server role include implementing some type of network load-balancing solution such as the Cisco Local Director or Windows Network Load Balancing. The Client Access role cannot be configured on a clustered mailbox server.

HUB TRANSPORT SERVER ROLE

The Hub Transport server role is responsible for all message delivery regardless of whether the message is being delivered from one mailbox to another in the same mailbox database, a Mailbox server in the same Active Directory site, a server in a remote Active Directory site, or outside of the organization. At least one Hub Transport server role is required in each Active Directory site that contains a Mailbox server.

For internal mail routing, Exchange Server 2007 will automatically load-balance and fail over if more than one Hub Transport server exists in an Active Directory site. For redundancy in inbound SMTP mail from outside the organization, you have a couple of options. If inbound mail is coming directly into the Hub Transport servers, multiple MX records or network load balancing are good solutions. If mail is coming into a perimeter network solution such as Edge Transport or a third-party SMTP gateway, configure these solutions to use multiple internal Hub Transport servers.

For smaller organizations with a single server Exchange implementation, the Hub Transport server can perform most of the message hygiene functions performed by the Edge Transport server role to connect Exchange to outside world. However, separating message hygiene functions to a separate server role located on the perimeter network is more secure.

UNIFIED MESSAGING ROLE

The Unified Message server role is considered a middle-tier system and is an entirely new concept for Exchange 2007. This server role integrates voicemail and inbound faxing with Exchange mailboxes. The Unified Messaging server requires an IP-based telephone switch or a traditional PBX-to-IP gateway (PBX stands for public branch exchange). The following functions are handled by the Unified Messaging server role:

◆ Provides voicemail for users of the IP-based phone system or through the PBX-to-IP gateway including voicemail greetings and options. Inbound voicemail is recorded as a WMA file and stored as a message in a user's Inbox.

◆ Accepts inbound faxes that are designated for specific mailboxes, converts the fax to a TIFF file, and stores that message in a user's Inbox.

◆ Allows a user to dial in to the Unified Messaging server to retrieve voicemail, listen to e-mail messages, review their calendar, or change appointments.

◆ Provides voice menus and prompting call menus acting as an auto-attendant system.

EDGE TRANSPORT ROLE

The Edge Transport server role is an entirely new role. In the past, Exchange servers could be implemented as an additional tier of message hygiene protection. However, there are a number of reasons that you might not want to use Exchange servers as perimeter message hygiene systems:

◆ In order to process delivery reports, nondelivery reports, and address rewrites, the information store service must be running and the default mailbox database must be mounted.

◆ Placing an Exchange 2000/2003 server in the perimeter network requires many ports to be opened on the firewall from the perimeter network to the internal network.

◆ Allowing inbound e-mail directly to an Exchange server could jeopardize both Exchange and Active Directory.

For these reasons, a server role was developed that has many of the advantages of an Exchange 2007 server but can be made much more secure since it can run in the perimeter network as a stand-alone computer and does not require Active Directory membership. The following are some of the characteristics of the Edge Transport server role:

◆ The Edge Transport server role should be deployed in the perimeter network.

◆ It can be managed with Exchange Management Shell scripts and the Exchange Management Console in much the same way a regular Exchange server is managed.

◆ The only components required to run the Edge Transport role are the message transport system and an instance of the Active Directory Application Mode (ADAM) database.

- ◆ Features such as transport rules can be implemented in the perimeter network and provide message policy enforcement for messages entering or leaving the organization that is separate from that provided on the internal network.

- ◆ Connectivity between internal Hub Transport servers and Edge Transport servers can be authenticated and the data stream encrypted.

- ◆ The content filter functionality and other anti-spam and message security tools are built in, as is the ability to add third-party content filtering/message hygiene tools.

- ◆ Microsoft Forefront Security for Exchange Server can be employed on the Edge Transport server role for virus detection and quarantine.

For medium and large organizations, higher availability comes in the form of installing multiple Edge Transport servers and providing load balancing either using multiple DNS mail exchanger (MX) records, network load balancing, DNS round robin, or failover using multiple Internet connections.

Microsoft and Deployment Planning

Early in the Exchange 2007 life cycle, Microsoft defined some new terminologies, acronyms, and organization types that are used when designing and deploying an Exchange 2007 organization for businesses of different sizes. We felt it important to define these terms here so that there will be less confusion when reading both this book and the Microsoft documentation.

Using some of these terms, Microsoft has attempted to more clearly standardize design methodologies and approaches to deployment of Exchange in order to simplify Exchange operations.

The first of these terms is *Service Delivery Location (SDL)*. The SDL is essentially the location of your servers. In a small organization, the SDL may be a secured and environmentally controlled closet within your own facility or it could be operated by a service provider or located at a colocation site. In a medium-size or large organization, an SDL may be distributed through many data centers in dozens or hundreds of locations throughout the world or it could be a consolidated, centralized data center with hundreds of servers servicing clients worldwide.

This brings us to the location of the actual clients, or the *Client Service Location (CSL)*. This is the location from which your clients access the services you are providing. In a small organization, the CSL may be on the same physical LAN as the SDL, while larger organizations may see the CSL span countries, continents, or the entire world.

To simplify deployment concepts, Microsoft has defined four types of organization models representing topologies in which Exchange 2007 may be deployed. These are the simple, standard, large, and complex organization types. There is no exact formula for figuring out exactly which organization type might describe your organization. The physical distribution of your user community, your organization's high-availability requirements, your organization's fault tolerance requirements, the volume of data that your users process, and other factors will all influence the organization model that you choose or a variation on these models that you choose to create yourself.

TIP

It's important to understand that there might not be an organization model that describes your organization exactly.

SIMPLE EXCHANGE ORGANIZATIONS

A simple Exchange organization is well suited for organizations with under approximately 200 mailboxes. Please note that "200 mailboxes" is somewhat arbitrary since organizations with either more or fewer mailboxes may fit in to this category depending on their user community, requirements, and messaging load. The simple organization has a single Exchange 2007 server that is running on the same physical machine as the organization's domain controller. The Exchange 2007 server handles the Mailbox, Hub Transport, Client Access, and Unified Messaging roles. The optional Edge Transport server role must still be on a separate physical server and should be located in the perimeter network.

In a simple Exchange organization, the users and the Exchange server are usually located in the same physical location, but that is not fixed rule. Even small organizations have telecommuters and users that access their organization using mobile technologies. Although the SDL is usually in the same location as the users, an emerging trend is for even smaller organizations to locate their server resources in a colocation site that provides Internet connectivity, power conditioning, backup power, air cooling, and physical security services. Another trend is to outsource the messaging functions entirely.

NOTE

Organizations considering a single-server deployment that fits the simple Exchange organization model should consider a Microsoft Windows Small Business Server deployment. All of the components are tested together much more thoroughly (such as running Exchange Server on a domain controller).

Providing multiple layers of message hygiene and security for simple Exchange organizations would come in the form of a reverse proxy to handle inbound HTTP requests and an Edge Transport server in the organization's perimeter network. Figure 2.3 shows a simple Exchange

FIGURE 2.3
Protecting a simple
Exchange organization

organization that is separated from the Internet using Microsoft ISA server and a perimeter network.

Microsoft also offers an additional service called Exchange Hosted Filtering that allows organizations to direct their inbound mail to Microsoft's servers. The Hosted Filtering service inspects mail for viruses and spam and then passes the mail on to your servers. If you have purchased Enterprise client access licenses for all of your users, then this service is included.

Inbound SMTP mail from the Internet is directed to the Edge Transport server, which is located in the perimeter/DMZ network. Inbound e-mail is inspected in the perimeter network for viruses or spam and message transport rules can enforce organizational policies on messages arriving from the Internet.

Inbound Outlook Web Access, ActiveSync, and Outlook RPC over HTTP connections terminate at the Microsoft ISA Server 2006 firewall; ISA Server acts as a reverse proxy, inspecting the inbound HTTP requests and then passing them on to the internal Exchange 2007 server's client access components.

STANDARD EXCHANGE ORGANIZATIONS

The standard Exchange model is by far the most common and flexible of the four Exchange server organization models. It will also be the organizational model most commonly found in organizations with from a few hundred to potentially tens of thousands of mailboxes. An organization will choose the standard Exchange model if any one of the following is true:

◆ Need to support more than approximately 200 mailboxes

◆ Require dedicated Exchange servers

◆ May need to split Exchange server roles among multiple physical servers

◆ Require dedicated domain controllers

◆ Need to support clustered mailbox servers

◆ Need to support more than one service delivery location (SDL)

◆ Require more scalability or infrastructure fault tolerance than the simple Exchange model can support

The standard Exchange organization is more scalable than the simple Exchange organization. Exchange servers are usually installed as member servers rather than on a domain controller. Exchange servers may span multiple Active Directory sites and server roles may be dedicated to specific physical servers rather than a single physical server. In this model, a single Active Directory forest is also required.

A standard Exchange organization with between a few hundred and a few thousand mailboxes might look like the one in Figure 2.4. In Figure 2.4, this organization has only a single SDL and requires high availability and redundancy. The Mailbox server is clustered to provide high availability for the mailbox databases while the Client Access and Hub Transport roles are both installed on two physical servers. By combining these two roles on two servers, the organization can provide better availability for message transport and web clients.

The organization could scale to as many as five Active Directory sites with Exchange 2007 servers and multiple Internet access points but still be considered a standard organization. The number of mailboxes is somewhat less of a factor here than the organization's needs. A company that places greater importance on its messaging needs and availability will find itself with dedicated servers and Exchange servers installed as member servers. When designing an Exchange organization for a company that meets this profile, the administrator will have to take into consideration the business needs, budget constraints, and availability requirements of the organization.

FIGURE 2.4
A standard Exchange organization

LARGE EXCHANGE ORGANIZATIONS

Large Exchange organizations are the most scalable of the Exchange organizational models; they allow an Exchange organization to support tens of thousands or hundreds of thousands of mailboxes. A large Exchange organization can have the same characteristics a standard Exchange organization has plus the following:

◆ More than five Active Directory sites and multiple SDLs

◆ Multiple CSLs

◆ Multiple Active Directory domains within a single Active Directory forest

Although the large Exchange organization is certainly more scalable than the standard Exchange organization, the skills required to manage and build a standard Exchange organization do transfer upward to the large Exchange organization.

COMPLEX EXCHANGE ORGANIZATIONS

Complex Exchange 2007 organizations represent increasing complexity of Exchange 2007 in businesses that might have multiple Active Directory forests and resource forests or that host multiple companies within the same Exchange organization. In addition to the scalable features of a standard or large Exchange organization, the following are some of the characteristics of a complex organization:

◆ Multiple Active Directory forests with recipient replication using tools such as Microsoft Identity Integration services

◆ Multiple-organization support or support for multiple subsidiaries or business units in a single Exchange organization

◆ Integration with external Exchange organizations such as when a new business unit has been acquired but not merged in to a single organization

◆ Public folders, free and busy information, or shared calendaring between multiple organizations all using Exchange Server 2007

Size is often not the determining factor when designing and deploying a complex Exchange organization. In some cases, due to business requirements, even an organization with fewer than 1,000 mailboxes may find itself requiring multiple forests or other situations that require a complex Exchange organizational design.

Combining or Splitting Server Roles

A common question with respect to Exchange 2007 and server roles is, When should server roles be split across multiple physical machines? With few exceptions, there is not a rule that says that server roles should be split across multiple pieces of hardware. However, even for a smaller organization, the need for high availability will drive the need for multiple Exchange 2007 servers. The only server role that can be installed on a clustered mailbox server is the Mailbox role. This means an environment that requires clustering of the Mailbox server role will require the other server roles (Hub Transport and Client Access) to be located on separate physical server.

In a small environment, the Hub Transport and Client Access roles can exist on the same physical server. In a medium-sized environment that requires high availability of the Client Access and Hub Transport servers, two Windows servers could be installed and load-balanced. Both of those servers could then host the Client Access and Hub Transport server roles.

What are some other reasons multiple Exchange servers might be required? The justification for additional hardware will be different from one organization to the next and will often depend on the organization's size, but here are a few:

◆ Server load is too great for a single machine. For example, a server supporting 1,000 mailboxes may be using local continuous replication and thus have an IO profile that precludes having additional disk-intensive, processor-intensive, or Active Directory–intensive roles.

◆ Redundancy in message routing is required and thus multiple servers with the Hub Transport role are required.

◆ Redundancy when providing Web Services or Internet access to messaging data requires multiple Client Access servers.

◆ Simplifying server recovery and rebuilds may require placing different server roles on different physical servers.

Major Components

The services and components that you find on an Exchange 2007 server will vary depending on which roles are installed for that server. Figure 2.5 shows some of the Exchange 2007 services that are found in the services console.

FIGURE 2.5
Common Exchange
Server 2007 services

If you are an experienced Exchange 2000/2003 administrator, you will also find that many of the services and executables are not recognizable. Exchange 2000/2003 has fewer core components and they were all installed on any Exchange server that you built. The Exchange 2007 components are shown in Table 2.8.

TABLE 2.8: Exchange 2007 Components

SERVICE NAME/ SHORT SERVICE NAME	EXECUTABLE NAME	FUNCTION
Microsoft Exchange Active Directory Topology/ MSExchangeADTopology	MSExchangeADTopology Service.exe	Provides Exchange Server 2007 with Active Directory site, domain controller, and global catalog server information. This component is found on all Exchange 2007 server roles except the Edge Transport.
Microsoft Exchange ADAM/ ADAM_MSExchange	Dsamain.exe	This is the ADAM instance that holds the Edge Transport server role's configuration, recipient information, safe sender lists, and blocked sender lists. This service is only found on the Edge Transport role.

TABLE 2.8:   Exchange 2007 Components *(CONTINUED)*

SERVICE NAME/ SHORT SERVICE NAME	EXECUTABLE NAME	FUNCTION
Microsoft Exchange Anti-spam Update/ MSExchange AntispamUpdate	`Microsoft.Exchange .AntispamUpdateSvc .exe`	This service provides updates for the content filter service. This service is found on the Edge Transport and Hub Transport server roles.
Microsoft Exchange Credential Service/ EdgeCredentialSvc	`EdgeCredentialSvc .exe`	This service monitors credential changes for the ADAM database and updates the Edge Transport server. This service is found only on the Edge Transport server role.
Microsoft Exchange EdgeSync/ MSExchangeEdgeSync	`Microsoft.Exchange .EdgeSyncSvc.exe`	Handles synchronization of recipient and hub transport information to Edge Transport servers in the perimeter network. The EdgeSync process synchronizes to the Edge Transport server's ADAM database; the synchronization is a push synchronization from the Hub Transport role out to the Edge Transport server. This component is found on Exchange 2007 Hub Transport server roles.
Microsoft Exchange File Distribution/ MSExchangeFDS	`MSExchangeFDS.exe`	The File Distribution Service handles distribution of offline address books on Client Access servers and custom Unified Messaging prompts on UM servers. It is found on Exchange 2007 Client Access and Unified Messaging server roles.
Microsoft Exchange IMAP4/ MSExchangeIMAP4	`Microsoft.Exchange .Imap4Service.exe`	Provides IMAP4 client connectivity and is found on Exchange 2007 Client Access server roles. This service is set to manual by default and must be enabled to support IMAP4 clients.
Microsoft Exchange Information Store/MSExchangeIS	`Store.exe`	The information store service runs the database engine and provides client access for MAPI clients as well as access to mailboxes for connections from Client Access and Hub Transport servers. This service is only found on Exchange 2007 servers with the Mailbox server role. This service also consumes the most RAM of any of the Exchange 2007 services.
Microsoft Exchange Mail Submission Service/ MSExchangeMail Submission	`MSExchangeMail Submission.exe`	Handles notifying Hub Transport servers that a message is waiting to be retrieved from a local database. This service attempts to distribute the message delivery load if multiple Hub Transport servers are found. This service is found on the Exchange 2007 Mailbox server role.

(CONTINUED)

TABLE 2.8: Exchange 2007 Components *(CONTINUED)*

SERVICE NAME/ SHORT SERVICE NAME	EXECUTABLE NAME	FUNCTION
Microsoft Exchange Mailbox Assistants/ MSExchangeMailbox Assistants	`Microsoft.Exchange .InfoWorker .Assistants.exe`	The Mailbox Assistants service handles calendaring functionality such as Calendar Assistant, Resource Booking Assistant, Out-of-Office Assistant, and the Managed Folder Mailbox Assistant. This service is found only on Exchange 2007 Mailbox servers.
Microsoft Exchange Monitoring/ MSExchangeMonitoring	`Microsoft.Exchange .Monitoring.exe`	Provides an interface for applications to use Exchange 2007 monitoring tasks. This service is found on all Exchange 2007 server roles.
Microsoft Exchange POP3/MSExchangePOP3	`Microsoft.Exchange .Pop3Service.exe`	Provides POP3 client connectivity and is found on Exchange 2007 Client Access server roles. This service is set to manual by default and must be enabled to support POP3 clients.
Microsoft Exchange Replication Service/ MSExchangeRepl	`Microsoft.Exchange .Cluster .ReplayService.exe`	This service handles copying log files from their original location to the backup log location on Exchange 2007 Mailbox servers that have the local continuous replication or clustered continuous replication functions enabled. This service is found only on Exchange 2007 Mailbox server roles.
Microsoft Exchange Search Indexer/ MSExchangeSearch	`Microsoft.Exchange. Search. ExSearch.exe`	The Microsoft Exchange Search Indexer provides content to the Microsoft Search (Exchange Server) service for full-text indexing. This service is found only on Mailbox server roles
Microsoft Exchange Service Host/ MSExchangeServiceHost	`Microsoft.Exchange. ServiceHost.exe`	This service handles the configuration of RPC virtual directories and Registry information necessary to support OutlookAnywhere (RPC over HTTP). This service is found on Exchange Mailbox and Client Access server roles.
Microsoft Exchange Speech Engine/MSS	`MSSService .SpeechService.exe`	The Speech Engine service provides the speech processing capabilities that are used by Unified Messaging services. This service is found only on Unified Messaging server roles.
Microsoft Exchange System Attendant/ MSExchangeSA	`Mad.exe`	This service provides monitoring and directory lookup services for Exchange server. This service is found only on Mailbox server roles.
Microsoft Exchange Transport/ MSExchangeTransport	`MSExchangeTransport .exe`	This service provides the SMTP transport functions. Mail will not flow at all if this service is halted. This service is found on all Exchange 2007 Hub Transport and Edge Transport server roles.

TABLE 2.8: Exchange 2007 Components *(CONTINUED)*

SERVICE NAME/ SHORT SERVICE NAME	EXECUTABLE NAME	FUNCTION
Microsoft Exchange Transport Log Search/ MSExchangeTransport LogSearch	MSExchange TransportLog Search.exe	Provides the ability to search the Exchange message transport logs. This service is found on all Exchange 2007 Mailbox, Hub Transport, and Edge Transport server roles.
Microsoft Exchange Unified Messaging/ MSExchangeUM	umservice.exe	The Unified Messaging service handles access to user's mailbox via Outlook Voice Access, the creation of voicemail messages, and the creation of fax messages. This service is found only on the Unified Messaging server role.
Microsoft Search (Exchange)/ MSFTESQL-Exchange	Msftesql.exe	This Search service creates full-text indexes on mailbox content. This service is found only on the Exchange 2007 Mailbox server role.
World Wide Web Publishing Service	svchost.exe/ inetinfo	A component of Internet Information Services that is required on all Exchange 2007 Client Access server roles in order to provide access to web services. This service is required on Exchange 2007 Mailbox servers if you will be managing public folders using Exchange System Manager or PFDAVAdmin.

Depending on the server's role(s), you will see many of these executables in the Windows Task Manager (shown in Figure 2.6). One frequently misunderstood service is the Microsoft Exchange Information Store service, or `store.exe`. By design this service will attempt to allocate as much physical memory as possible. On a server with 32GB of physical memory, it may not be unusual to see this service using 80 to 90 percent of that RAM.

Databases and Database Sizing

Exchange 2007 includes a number of noteworthy improvements with respect to the Exchange mailbox and public folder databases. Although Exchange databases still uses the Extensible Storage Engine (ESE), aka Jet database engine, rather than a SQL Server database, improvements allow greater scalability. The following are some of the changes that have been designed to improve scalability, improve performance, and make replication of data more feasible:

◆ The 64-bit version of the ESE database engine can access far more RAM for caching than previous versions.

◆ Each Exchange Server 2007 Enterprise Edition server supports up to 50 storage groups.

◆ Each Exchange Server 2007 Enterprise Edition server supports up to 50 databases.

◆ The database page size has been increased from 4KB (in previous editions) to 8KB in Exchange 2007 to improve read and write performance.

◆ Transaction log files are now 1MB in size rather than 5MB; this allows data to be replicated to a backup database location (in the case of LCR or CCR) much more quickly.

◆ The streaming store (STM) file found in previous versions of Exchange has been removed. Each Exchange database consists of a single EDB database file in which all content is stored.

FIGURE 2.6
Exchange 2007 services in Task Manager

We talked earlier about calculating the amount of disk space that you may require for Exchange Server 2007 mailbox servers. In Chapter 1, we reviewed the changing nature of e-mail and messaging technologies and emphasized that mail storage requirements are greater than ever. We always recommended planning for more disk space and e-mail capacity than you think you will require.

However, more e-mail storage means including in your Exchange server design a maximum size for each database. Why specify a maximum size for your database? As you saw earlier, specifying a maximum size gives you guidelines for distribution mailboxes and the maximum number of databases that your server must support. In general, there are a number of good reasons for limiting the maximum size of each database. Here are some thoughts and pointers on calculating maximum database size:

◆ Maximum database size when using streaming backups and restores should be around 50GB to 100GB.

◆ When using LCR as the primary database restoration mechanism, databases can be allowed to grow to 200GB.

◆ Always take into consideration the restoration time when calculating maximum database size and ensure that you can restore within a timeline specified by your service level agreement (SLA).

◆ Restoring from streaming tape backups can take significantly longer than restoring from backups on disk.

◆ Larger databases take longer for online maintenance procedures to run. Microsoft recommends online maintenance at least once every two weeks on each database for best performance.

One popular reason for limiting the size of a database or maximum mailbox sizes is the length of time it takes to restore a server. On one hand, this represents good planning, but often mail administrators wield that excuse like a sword in order to keep their user storage limits lower. An Exchange administrator commented one time that "keeping mailboxes smaller is easier on us," meaning the IT department.

Storage limits and maximum mailbox sizes are all fine and good, but limits should not be set for the sake of IT. You should set limits that allow users to effectively do their jobs and to access the information they need to access, but you should also consider the needs of operations, archiving, and budgeting. Also keep in mind that the default mailbox limit for mailbox databases is 2GB unless you change it, so make sure when you create new mailboxes databases that you also configure the correct limits. See more about establishing limits in Chapter 9, "Imposing Limits and Why."

Message Routing

In earlier versions of Exchange (2000 and 2003), if more than physical or geographic location existed, the Exchange servers could be broken up based on their physical location. The architecture of message routing is based on routing groups. By placing Exchange servers in different routing groups, the administrator can control messaging traffic between those locations and can more accurately focus public folder connectivity by Outlook clients. In almost all situations, the servers located in routing groups correspond to the location of an Active Directory site, though not all Active Directory sites might actually have an Exchange server.

Exchange 2007 simplifies the management of the physical layout of Exchange by eliminating the need for routing groups and relying on the Active Directory site architecture instead. Servers with the Hub Transport role accept messages from Mailbox servers, determine the location of the destination mailbox database, and deliver the message to a Hub Transport server in the remote Active Directory site.

Message Routing and the Hub Transport Server

The Hub Transport server role is at the center of the message transport architecture. The Hub Transport server maintains Send and Receive connectors that are responsible for receiving mail from the Internet, sending mail to the Internet, sending mail to remote Hub Transport servers, and receiving mail from remote Hub Transport servers. All messages must be processed by the Hub Transport system regardless of whether they will be delivered to a local mailbox or a remote recipient.

NOTE

In Exchange 2000/2003 there was the concept of SMTP virtual servers, which could either send or receive SMTP mail. Send connectors are responsible for outbound SMTP mail only and Receive connectors are responsible for inbound mail only. One big advantage of this is separation of logging.

The message transport architecture and dependencies are illustrated in Figure 2.7. Messages enter the Exchange 2007 message transport system through one of three possible mechanisms: a message can be submitted to the Hub Transport via SMTP, a Mailbox server's store driver, or the file system's Pickup folder on the Hub Transport server. The Hub Transport relies on Active Directory for configuration, topology, and recipient information and thus must have access to domain controllers and global catalog servers.

FIGURE 2.7
Basics of the Hub Transport architecture

Once a message is submitted to the Hub Transport system, it enters the message queuing system where the message Categorizer reviews it and determines how to deliver it. There are five possible queues that can be found on a Hub Transport server:

◆ The *submission queue* is the queue in which messages are placed when they enter the Hub Transport server (via SMTP, store driver, or pickup folder). The categorizer processes the messages as they arrive in this queue. The submission queue is also called the categorizer queue or the submit queue.

◆ The *poison message queue* is the queue in which messages are placed if there is a problem that prevents the message from being categorized.

◆ The *unreachable domain queue* is the queue in which messages are placed if there is no route available.

◆ *Local delivery queues* are queues in which messages are placed if they are to be delivered to a Mailbox server in the same Active Directory site.

◆ *Remote delivery queues* are queues in which messages are placed to be delivered to remote Hub Transport servers or outside of the organization. The remote delivery queue is the only type of queue available on the Edge Transport server role.

The Categorizer component is the Hub Transport component that watches the submission queue. As messages arrive in the submission queue, the Categorizer picks them up and processes them. The following are some of the steps involved in message categorization:

◆ Expand any distribution lists, if applicable, by querying the global catalog.

◆ Resolve recipient addresses to determine which recipients are local, remote, or outside of the organization.

◆ Apply message transport rules to the message.

◆ Split the message into multiple parts if the message is going to local and remote recipients; this process is called bifurcation.

◆ Examine the message sender, recipients, header, body, and attachments and apply message transport rules that apply to the message.

◆ Convert the message to the appropriate message format (Summary-TNEF, MIME, or UUENCODE) depending on its destination.

◆ Determine the next "hop" for the message.

◆ Place the message in to appropriate local or remote delivery queue.

> **NOTE**
>
> With a few exceptions, such as application transport rules, the Categorizer function has not changed from Exchange 2000/2003.

Message Transport Security

One of the intentions of the design of Exchange 2007 was to make messaging more secure. One of the outcomes of this was to ensure that message content is secured as it is being transmitted from one server to another. This includes authenticated connections and encrypting the data as it crosses the network. Figure 2.8 shows the possible places a message may be passed across the network and how protection is or may be implemented.

FIGURE 2.8
Security when messages are being transmitted

As messages are transmitted via MAPI over RPC between Mailbox servers and Hub Transport servers, RPC encryption is automatically used. When a message is transmitted from one Hub Transport server to another, the Hub Transport servers authenticate using Kerberos and the data stream is encrypted using Transport Layer Security (TLS). When messages are transmitted from a Hub Transport server to an Edge Transport server, mutual authentication using certificates is used and messages can be encrypted using TLS. Optionally, an organization that is sending messages to another organization also using Edge Transport services can configure authenticated connections and TLS encryption to these remote organizations. Messaging security and Edge Transport is going to be covered in more detail in Chapter 20, "Securing Exchange Server."

Inter Site Message Routing

In previous versions of Exchange, in order to deliver mail from one Exchange 2000/2003 routing group to another, a connector needed to be created (for example, Routing Group connector, SMTP connector, and X.400 connector). The Exchange 2007 equivalents of routing group connectors are SMTP Send and SMTP Receive connectors.

One feature that will surprise some Exchange 2000/2003 administrators is that, by default, Exchange 2007 Hub Transport servers will behave as if connectivity between them is a full mesh. In previous versions of Exchange, messages flowed only between Exchange servers with explicit routing group connectors.

Take, for example, the organization in Figure 2.9. This organization has four Active Directory sites. In three of them, there is a Mailbox server and a Hub Transport server.

FIGURE 2.9
Sample message routing architecture

The Active Directory site link architecture defines the site links as shown in Table 2.9.

TABLE 2.9:   Sample Active Directory Site Links and Costs

LINK NAME	COST
Site Link H–A	1
Site Link H–B	1
Site Link H–C	2
Site Link A–C	100
Site Link A–B	100
Site Link B–C	100

Clearly, this Active Directory design intended for all replication to go through the "hub" site known as Site H. Thus, a logical assumption would be that messages would be routed using this site link cost architecture. However, if a message originates on a Mailbox server in Site C and is intended for a recipient in Site B, the Hub Transport server will always attempt to route the message directly first. If the direct path is not available, then the message will be routed to the Hub Transport server in Site H. The site link costs are used to determine message routing paths only if the direct connection fails.

Exchange Server 2007 as a Client/Server System

The technology industry has overused the term *client/server* to the point that it is almost meaningless. To put it simply, there are two kinds of networked applications: shared-file and client/server. The typical Exchange and Outlook deployment is a client-server messaging system and always has been. However for people just getting involved in Exchange Server deployments, these concepts should be reviewed.

Shared-File Applications

Early networked applications were all based on *shared-file* systems. The network shell that let you load your word processor from a network server and also allowed you to read from and write to files stored on a server. At the time, this was the easiest and most natural way to grow networked applications.

Microsoft's first e-mail product, Mail for PC Networks, was a shared-file application. You run a Windows, OS/2, DOS, or Macintosh client application, which sends and receives messages by accessing files on a Microsoft Mail for PC Networks post office that resides on a network file server. The front-end application and your PC do all the work; the server is passive. Figure 2.10 shows a typical Microsoft Mail for PC Networks setup.

Easy as it was to develop, this architecture leads to some serious problems in today's networked computing world:

◆ Changing the underlying structure of the server file system is difficult because you have to change both the server and the client.

◆ System security is always compromised because users must have read and write permissions for the whole server file system, which includes all other users' message files. Things are so bad that in some cases a naive or malicious user can actually destroy shared-file system databases.

◆ Network traffic is high because the client application must constantly access indexes and hunt around the server's file system for user messages.

◆ Because the user workstation writes directly to shared files, the server-based files can be destroyed if workstation hardware or software stops functioning for some unexpected reason.

◆ Often the client program would open these shared files and lock them for use. This frequently prevented important data files from being backed up.

FIGURE 2.10
Microsoft Mail for PC Networks is a typical shared-file electronic messaging system.

Shared-file applications are in decline. Sure, plenty of *legacy* (that is, out-of-date) applications will probably live on for the data-processing equivalent of eternity, but client/server systems have quickly supplanted the shared-file model. This is especially true in the world of electronic messaging.

Client/Server Applications

Though they have some limitations of their own, client/server applications overcome the shortcomings of shared-file apps. So today, networked applications increasingly are based on the client/server model. The server is an active partner in client/server applications. Clients tell servers what they want done, and if security requirements are met, servers do what they are asked.

Processes running on a server find and ship data to processes running on a client. When a client process sends data, a server receives it and writes it to server-based files. Server processes can do more than simply interact with client processes. For example, they can compact data files on the server or — as they do on Exchange Server — automatically reply to incoming messages to let people know, for instance, that you're going to be out of the office for a period of time. Figure 2.11 shows how Exchange implements the client/server model.

FIGURE 2.11
Microsoft Exchange is based on the client/server model.

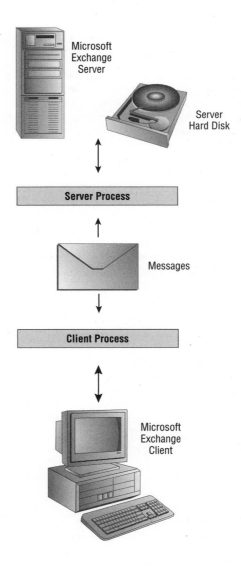

Client/server applications are strong in all the areas in which shared-file apps are weak:

◆ Changing the underlying structure of the server file system is easier than with shared-file systems because only the server processes access the file system.

◆ System security can be much tighter, again because only the server processes access the file system.

◆ Network traffic is lighter because all the work of file access is done by the server, on the server.

◆ Because server processes are the only ones that access server data, breakdowns of user workstation hardware or software are less likely to spoil data. With appropriate transaction logging features, client/server systems can even protect against server hardware or software malfunctions.

As good as the client/server model is, it does have some general drawbacks. Client/server apps require more computing horsepower, especially on the server side. With Exchange, you should plan to start with very fast Pentium or better machines, lots of RAM, and plenty of hard disk and tape backup capacity — and expect to grow from there.

Client/server applications are more complex than shared-file apps. This is partly because of the nature of the client/server model and partly because of the tendency of client/server apps to be newer and thus filled with all kinds of great capabilities that you won't find in shared-file applications. Generally, you're safe in assuming that you'll need to devote more and more sophisticated human resources to managing a client/server application than to tending to a similar one based on shared files.

The good news is that Microsoft has done a lot to reduce the management load and to make it easier for someone who isn't a computer scientist to administer an Exchange system. I've looked at many client/server messaging systems, and I can say without any doubt that Exchange is absolutely the easiest to administer, even in its slightly more complex 2007 implementation. Exchange Server 2007 includes both a graphical user interface and a management shell that organizes the processes of management very nicely. With these interfaces, you can do everything from adding users to assessing the health of your messaging system.

Summary

Microsoft Exchange Server 2007 continues to build on a solid history of messaging servers. Improvements in the architecture of Exchange 2007 allow for continued innovation, improvement, and scalability. The move to the 64-bit architecture is clearly needed to allow Exchange to be enhanced further and to reduce I/O requirements.

Server installation and configuration has been further enhanced and simplified by the introduction of server roles; the person that performs the Exchange Server installation chooses, which components are necessary for a particular server's function.

Chapter 3

Designing a New Exchange 2007 System

Whether your system will be based on a single Exchange server in a single physical location or hundreds of Exchange servers spread out over multiple locations, you need to consider a number of design issues before implementation. This chapter presents a step-by-step planning model based loosely on a process developed by Microsoft. Tracking and retracking through these steps will help your organization decide where it wants to go with electronic messaging and how it can get there with Exchange.

One of the common reasons that Exchange server deployments are slow or have many problems is that organizations don't take the time to properly gather and review all of the relevant information. We can tell you from lots of experience that this process really works. Generally, we have found that we can gather any required information and generate a fairly complex first-draft plan, complete with a most convincing executive summary, in a month or so.

WARNING

Exchange deployments often fail when all of the factors that affect Exchange and Active Directory are not considered.

This chapter isn't just about design, though. It also offers practical information about Exchange Server 2007 and how it works. For example, you'll find detailed information about Exchange's network connection options: what they do and which networking topologies and protocols support them. Information such as this is central to designing and implementing an Exchange system, and it's not found anywhere else in this book.

This is a long chapter covering a great deal of information in detail. Just as you wouldn't try to implement a complex Exchange system in one day, you shouldn't try to plow through this chapter in one hour.

NOTE

We cover installing Exchange Server 2007 as well as migrating Exchange Server 2000/2003 systems to Exchange Server 2007 in later chapters. However, even if your immediate goal is a migration, we strongly suggest you first carefully read this chapter.

Much of the information found in this chapter will be more relevant to an organization that is deploying Exchange Server for the first time, but we hope even organizations that are upgrading from Exchange 2000/2003 (or earlier) will still find some useful information in this chapter. If you are new to Exchange management and someone else designed your organization's Exchange infrastructure, this chapter may be of use to you when figuring out why some of the things are designed the way they are.

Topics in this chapter include the following:

◆ Assigning accountabilities for planning, design, and management

◆ Performing a needs assessment

◆ Planning your network configuration

◆ Rolling out the plan

Taking the Large View

This discussion builds upon a process presented by Microsoft in the Exchange documentation and other Microsoft publications, but it is far from a word-for-word regurgitation. Therefore, you should blame us — not Microsoft — if you encounter any problems from following the advice we give in this chapter. (And of course, if this stuff helps in any way, you should send the fruit baskets and such to us.)

Some of these steps include selecting an Active Directory architecture. Active Directory is widely deployed and thus some of these steps will probably be irrelevant for you. However, we hope you will find some relevance and useful information, so here, then, are the steps that we suggest you follow in designing your Exchange Server 2007 system:

1. Assign planning, design, and management responsibilities to staff.

2. Assess user needs.

3. Study your organization's geographic profile.

4. Assess your organization's network.

5. Establish naming conventions.

6. Select a Microsoft networking domain model.

7. Define your Active Directory site infrastructure

8. Define administrative responsibilities.

9. Plan message routing links.

10. Plan servers and internal connections.

11. Plan connections to other systems.

12. Validate and optimize your design.

13. Deploy a test lab or a pilot project with a small group of users.

14. Roll out the plan.

These steps fit nicely into four categories:

◆ Delegating the planning, design, and management of your Exchange 2007 system

◆ Analyzing user and technical needs

◆ Dealing with the complex tasks involved in network planning

◆ Rolling out your Exchange system

As you go through this process, we strongly recommend that you and each of your team members take copious notes and that these notes be combined to form a journal that documents the process you took to arrive at your design decisions. This is often useful later when you need to figure out why you made certain decisions.

Now let's discuss each of the steps in more detail. The following sections fully describe all the tasks of designing and setting up an Exchange 2007 system and getting all the users up and running.

Exchange Design Is Iterative, Not Linear

Throughout this chapter, remember that designing an Exchange system is not a linear process but an iterative one. You'll find yourself coming back to each of the steps to gather new information, to reinterpret information that you've already gathered, and to collect even more information based on those reinterpretations. New information will likely lead to new questions, design changes, and further iterations. Even after you've fully implemented your Exchange Server 2007 system, you'll return to steps in the design process as problems arise or as your organization changes.

Within reason, the more iterations that you go through, the better your final design will be. But take care not to use iteration as a route to procrastination. Whatever you do, start running Exchange 2007 — if only in a limited test environment — as soon as you can.

Assigning Responsibility for Planning, Design, and Management

You need to ensure that two sets of specific responsibilities are assigned to staff. First, you have to assign a set of responsibilities related mostly to planning and design. Then you have to assign a second set of responsibilities that deal with ongoing management of key aspects of your Exchange Server 2007 system when it is in place.

Assigning Responsibilities for Planning and Design

Microsoft has identified 14 different roles that must be filled in planning, designing, and, to some extent, implementing and operating an Exchange Server system. That doesn't mean that you need 14 staff members to fill these roles, but it does mean that you need to assign each of these roles to a staff member. In a very large organization (tens of thousands of users), each of these roles may well be assigned to a different staff member. If you're the only staff member responsible for Exchange, then you will hold all of these roles. Good luck! However the roles are assigned, the responsibilities for each of the roles must be covered.

Here's a list of the 14 roles and their related responsibilities.

Product manager Sets objectives, coordinates schedules, manages external relationships, and sets the budget

Program manager Has overall responsibility for Microsoft Exchange network design and implementation and specifies Exchange messaging system functional requirements

Exchange engineer Determines technical configuration of all components of Exchange servers

Testing and QA engineer   Ensures that the Exchange messaging system conforms to functional requirements and corporate standards as well as planning acceptance or sign-off testing

Operations developer   Develops procedures, policies, and programs that monitor and control the Exchange network

Technical consultant   Provides consulting services and problem resolution for internal business units

Training developer   Develops training materials and documentation for end users and technical support personnel

Rollout planner   Determines the most efficient way to roll out Exchange servers and accompanying Windows servers, minimizes deployment costs, and promotes efficient implementation

Migration planner   Determines the work needed to migrate from an existing messaging system to Exchange Server 2007

Implementation manager   Manages the implementation of Exchange servers and associated components and the implementation of all of the plans made by all of the previous roles

End-user technical support technician   Provides end-user support for Exchange-related problems and questions

Messaging transport operations engineer   Maintains, operates, and repairs the Exchange server environment after installation

Marketing and consumer relations manager   Develops and carries out the Exchange rollout marketing program (product demonstrations, newsletters, pilot site coordination, and so on)

Financial controller   Monitors financial aspects of the project and tracks expenses against budget allocations

If you've ever implemented an information systems project, these roles are likely quite familiar to you, even if you've never thought specifically or in great detail about each of them. The key point here is that you're much more likely to successfully roll out your new Exchange Server 2007 system if you ensure that each of these 14 roles is properly filled. As we go through the planning and design process, think about these roles and how you might fill them.

Assigning Responsibilities for Day-to-Day Management

When your Exchange Server 2007 system has been implemented, you need to fill seven operational roles that support your system. Again, you might assign each of these roles to a separate person or combine and assign them to one or two people. These seven roles are listed here along with the responsibilities associated with them.

Recipient administrator/user manager   Administers mail-recipient aspects of Exchange Server 2007 and possibly account administration for Windows Server 2003 Active Directory, such as creation and management of recipients (Exchange mailboxes, distribution groups, and contacts)

Organizational administrator   Administers components of Exchange Server 2007 that affect all server roles throughout the entire organization, e-mail addressing rules, messaging records management, transport rules, and so on

Server administrator   Administers selected servers or groups of servers of the Exchange Server 2007 environment

Message routing manager   Administers the message routing infrastructure, including connectivity between Active Directory sites and messages sent and received to/from the Internet

Message hygiene manager   Administers components of Exchange 2007 relating to message security, antivirus, anti-spam, content inspection, and transport rules

Public folder manager   Administers Exchange Server public folder hierarchy

Application development manager   Administers development of Exchange Server–related add-on applications

This list is based on a list of roles originally provided by Microsoft, though we have taken some liberties and separated server management roles, message hygiene, application development, and message routing into multiple categories.

As with the set of 14 roles illustrated in the preceding section, as we go through the planning and design process, think about these operational roles and how you might fill them. If you think about your own experiences or your organization's needs, you might break these roles down in to even more discrete operational responsibilities.

Performing a Needs Assessment

A needs assessment is a two-part process. First, you must understand the current state of affairs in some detail. Then, using your knowledge about what is currently in place, you must come up with an analysis of need that focuses on both keeping the best of what is and developing new approaches where required. You should perform needs assessments in each of these categories:

◆ Users

◆ Geography

◆ Data networks

You'll probably find that assessing user needs will be the most difficult because you're dealing almost exclusively with people and their perceptions of their needs and those of your organization. You should focus on the fact that, in addition to being an e-mail system, Exchange is a platform for a range of collaborative applications. You also should remember that user needs and wants have significant costs in time, money, and computer and network capacity.

A geographical needs assessment focuses on discovery of network components, servers, and users and the buildings, cities, states, and countries in which they are located. You need to know what kind of computing capacity, networking hardware, and software you have. Then you need to determine what, if any, changes must be made to ensure that everyone in your organization can participate in your Exchange system at a reasonably optimal level.

Exchange is nothing without quality network links from workstation to server and from server to server. Your network needs assessment should deal with three key issues. The first is the location and nature of your network connections, the second relates to the bandwidth on your network, and the third relates to network reliability.

Assessing User Needs

Here you're interested in who needs what, when they need it, and how you'll provide it. You'll want to get a handle on the programming, software, hardware, management information services (MIS) systems, systems support, and training resources that will be required to satisfy user needs.

Remember that Exchange is an electronic messaging package, not just an e-mail product. Users might need specific electronic-messaging-enabled applications. Depending on what users have in mind, application development can be a real resource hog. Also remember that, in some cases, hardware and software might require new workstations, not just new servers.

Be prepared to give users a clear idea of what Exchange can do. You don't need to get technical with most users; just give them a view of Exchange from the end user's perspective. Take another look at Chapter 1, "Introducing Exchange Server 2007," and Chapter 2, "Exchange Server 2007 Architecture," to see how you might organize your presentation.

Keep in mind that one of the biggest mistakes that most people make when implementing a system is to ignore or give only passing attention to this step. Knowing as much as you can about what the users require up front means that you'll have an easier time during implementation. For example, imagine that you don't know from the get-go that your organization could benefit significantly from a particular custom-programmed electronic-messaging-enabled application. You go ahead and implement Exchange as an e-mail system with only the resources such an implementation requires. You get your Exchange system up and it's perking along just fine when, maybe three months later, some user comes up with this great idea for an electronic-messaging-enabled app. Boink! Suddenly you have to tell management that you need a few programmers and maybe more hardware to implement this idea that nobody thought of four or five months ago. I'll leave the rest to your imagination.

> **NOTE**
>
> Regardless of what you find out in your user needs assessment, add a fudge factor in favor of more hardware and support personnel. Exchange has so many capabilities that you can be sure your users will find all kinds of ways to challenge whatever resources you make available. Depending on your users and their ability to get away with unplanned demands for resources, fudging by as much as 25 percent is reasonable. You can go with less fudge if your organization is particularly cost conscious and willing to adhere closely to plans.

Suffice it to say that a user needs assessment is the single most important part of the Exchange design process. Therefore, we'll cover it in more detail than the other Exchange design steps.

QUESTIONS TO ASK

You'll want to answer a number of questions during your user needs assessment. Here are the major ones:

◆ What kinds of users (for example, managers, salespeople, clerical staff, lawyers, doctors) does your organization have, and what do they think they want from the new Exchange system?

◆ What sorts of electronic messaging services are different groups of users likely to need (for example, e-mail, calendars and scheduling, public folders, specially designed applications)?

◆ Is integration with other collaborative applications such as SharePoint required?

◆ In addition to LAN access, will users need wireless LAN and/or WAN access to your Exchange system? Will this access have to be secure?

◆ Which specially designed applications can be developed by users, and which must be developed by MIS personnel?

◆ Do all users need every capability from day one, or can implementation be phased in, perhaps based on user groupings? If you are migrating from an existing messaging system, can you start by simply replacing the users' existing functionality and then adding more functionality at later a time.

◆ What client applications will be used by the users? Outlook MAPI clients? Outlook Anywhere (RPC over HTTP)? Outlook Web Access? Outlook Voice Access? POP3? IMAP4? Windows Mobile and ActiveSync devices? Other mobile access technologies such as Blackberry and GoodMail?

◆ Is your organization affected by regulatory compliance such as laws that require specialized protection for some messages or mail retention for certain types of messages?

◆ What sorts of demands will users (or groups of users) put on your Exchange servers? Much of the information in this category can be used with Microsoft's Exchange server load simulation program to predict expected server load and project server hardware and networking requirements.

   ◆ How many mailboxes will you create per server?

   ◆ How many messages will the typical user send per day?

   ◆ How many messages will the typical user receive per day?

   ◆ How frequently will users send messages to others on their server? In their own site? In each of the sites in your organization? Outside your organization? (Be sure to break this down by the different kinds of external connections you'll have.)

   ◆ How often will users read messages in their mailboxes?

   ◆ How often will users read messages in public folders?

   ◆ How often will users move messages to personal folders stored locally and on the network?

   ◆ How often will users move messages to public folders?

   ◆ How big will the messages be? What percentage will be 1KB, 2KB, 4KB, 10KB, 40KB, 60KB, 80KB, 100KB, 200KB, and so on?

◆ What level of message delivery service will users want and need? This should be stated in hours or minutes between the time a message is sent and received. You'll need to specify this for both internal and external communications. Do you have a service level agreement that specifies expected response and message delivery times.

◆ What sorts of hardware and software resources (for example, computers, mobile phones, operating systems, Exchange client access licenses) will different groups of users need to implement Exchange on the client side?

◆ What kinds of training will be required for users or groups of users? Remember to consider training for administrators as well as training for anything that affects users.

◆ What sorts of MIS resources will be required to support user needs?

Studying Your Organization's Geographic Profile

You need a list of all the geographical locations in your organization. Here you should think not only in terms of cities, states, and countries, but also in-city and even in-building locations. Start at the top and work your way down. At this point, diagrams are important. Draw maps and building layouts.

This is the time to gather information on the workstations and servers you have in each location. You'll want to know how many run each of the different kinds of operating systems in your organization. Operating systems to watch for include these:

◆ Windows Server 2003

◆ Windows 2000 Server

◆ Windows 95/98/ME/2000/XP/Vista desktop operating systems

◆ Windows CE, Windows Mobile, and ActiveSync-enabled devices

◆ Apple Macintosh

◆ Unix workstations by type of operating system

◆ Workstations used remotely

If you have hardware and software inventories for these machines, including CPU type, RAM, and free disk space, your job will be a lot easier. You can use all the information that you collect about workstations and servers to determine who's ready for Exchange and how many client access licenses you'll have to buy. Don't forget that you need to determine how many standard client access licenses you will need versus enterprise client access licenses.

As you gather information in other steps, begin to look at it in the context of your geographic profile. For example, you'll want to meld geographic information with what you find out about user needs and user groupings.

MORE ON USER WORKSTATIONS

Most user workstations are underpowered. That's a pretty strong statement, but I, Barry Gerber, stand by it. I limped along for quite some time running Windows 2000 Professional on a substandard 400MHz Pentium II workstation with 128MB of memory. Then I moved up to a 1GHz dual Pentium III processor and 768MB of RAM. When I ran Windows 2000 on my old, underpowered sleepwalker, it was all I could do to keep my word processor, a spreadsheet, and my e-mail software open at the same time. If I opened anything else, the machine started thrashing around so much between RAM and virtual memory that it slowed to a nearly useless crawl.

With my new system and Windows XP Pro, I can run word-processing programs, spreadsheet programs, and Outlook together without wasting precious time to switch among them. And I still have plenty of horsepower left for all those tasks that I used to do with paper because I couldn't bring up the applications fast enough when I needed them. At will, I can now simultaneously open — and keep open — such apps as an accounting package and Microsoft Word, Excel, Project, and Power-Point. With all that computer power, I'm also no longer reluctant to run other key programs — say, web browsers or Control Panel applets — at the drop of a hat.

Here's the bottom line: I've had my new system for less than a year. By my estimates, the productivity increase that I've experienced in that time has already paid back the cost of the system's purchase.

May be all your users don't need a dual 1GHz Pentium system with Windows XP Pro and 768MB of RAM. However, as you start assessing user needs, don't let the dismal state of your organization's stable of workstations stop you and your users from reaching for the stars as you think about potential applications for Exchange.

Assessing Your Organization's Network

In this step, you just want to know what your network looks like now. This isn't the place to get into what kinds of networking you'll need; that comes later. You need to answer three key questions here:

- What's connected to what, and how? (Okay, if you're counting, that's two questions.)
- How much bandwidth do you have on each network?
- How reliable are your networks?

WHAT'S CONNECTED TO WHAT, AND HOW?

Generally, in answering these questions, you should start at the top of your organization and work down to the domain or server level. For each link, name the following:

- Physical connection
- Networking topology
- Networking protocols running on the connection

For example, physical connection = local hardwire, networking topology = 100BaseT Ethernet, networking protocols = NetBEUI, TCP/IP, IPX/SPX, SNA. This information, especially when combined with the information you collected in steps 1, 2, and 3, will prove valuable as you start to plan for the Exchange connectivity that you'll need.

In looking at your organization's network, don't forget about connections to the outside world. Do you have connections to the Internet or trading partners?

HOW MUCH BANDWIDTH DO YOU HAVE ON EACH NETWORK?

Although bandwidth begins with network topology (type of connection), such as 100BaseT, T1, and DSL, it doesn't stop there. You need to know how much of your network topology's theoretical bandwidth is actually available.

To assess the actual bandwidth on each of your networks, you need some help from a network monitoring tool. If your networks are Windows 2003, you can try using the performance monitoring tools that come with the operating system to get a handle on traffic. For Windows 2000 and 2003, select Start Menu ➤ Programs ➤ Administrative Tools ➤ Performance.

TIP

Microsoft's built-in tools will tell you only so much about the usage of your network. Consider third-party tools when doing network assessments.

What you want here is a chart that tells you, on average, how much of a network's bandwidth is available during each of the 24 hours in a day. You'll have to take several samples to get reliable data, but it's worth it. A warning light should go on in your head if you're already using more than, say, 60 to 70 percent of the available bandwidth on any network during daytime hours and you're not already running a heavy-duty messaging system such as Exchange. With that kind of scenario, you just might have to make some changes in the network before installing Exchange. We'll talk about those changes later; for now, be sure to collect this data on available bandwidth and incorporate it into your organizational maps.

How Reliable Are Your Networks?

Having a reliable network is an important issue. Increasingly in corporate America, there is strong pressure to centralize network servers. Centralization makes good economic sense. If all network servers are in one place, one set of staff members can support and monitor them, ensuring 24-hours-a-day, 7-days-a-week uptime.

Of course, 24/7 server availability is useless if the networks that people use to get to the servers are unreliable. We've seen this scenario play itself out in several organizations: They centralize the servers, the network fails, users can't get to their now mission-critical e-mail and other data, responsible IS planners are roundly criticized, and lower-level IS personnel are even more heavily criticized or fired. Grrr!

Here's the bottom line: Don't make your users work on unreliable networks. If your networks can't come close to matching the reliability of your servers, put the servers closer to their users. The little extra that it costs to manage decentralized servers is worth the access insurance that it buys. Sure, get those networks up to par, but don't risk your Exchange implementation on centralized servers before a reliable network is in place to support them.

Planning Your Network Configuration

Although it takes but a few words to say, planning your network configuration will take you on a long and winding road. In the following sections, we will cover some of the important parts of the planning process:

- ◆ Establishing naming conventions for objects in your Exchange server hierarchy
- ◆ Selecting a Microsoft networking domain model
- ◆ Defining administrative responsibilities
- ◆ Planning servers and internal connections to them
- ◆ Planning connections to other systems such as the Internet
- ◆ Validating and optimizing your design

You need to establish naming conventions for your Exchange organization, servers, connectors, and recipients. Some of these names depend on how you name Windows 2003 objects, while others have no dependency on the operating system. The Windows 2003 domain model that you choose will significantly affect how your Exchange servers interact, especially from a security standpoint.

Recipient, Organizational, and Server administrative permissions replace administrative group security in Exchange 2000/2003 How you set their boundaries depends heavily on how you want to parcel out responsibility for Exchange server management in your organization. Active Directory sites are now used as the boundary for local message routing instead of the routing group structure used in Exchange 2000/2003 and the server-to-server communication functionality of Exchange 5.5 sites.

The servers where you install Exchange 2007 must have adequate capacity; in Chapter 2, "Exchange Server 2007 Architecture," we reviewed some of the hardware requirements for Exchange Server 2007. Even if you plan for servers of very high capacity and even though Exchange 2007 allows lots of mailboxes on a server, you may consider distributing user mailboxes across multiple servers to increase performance. You also should consider setting user storage quotas to ensure adequate disk capacity over time. In addition, you should be sure that your servers are protected against low-level and catastrophic glitches by such things as fault-tolerant hardware, uninterruptible power supplies, and a reliable backup system. Finally, you should ensure that users have adequate bandwidth to access messages and other objects on your Exchange servers.

If you need to communicate with the Internet (and most organizations do), then you will need to think about message hygiene (antivirus and anti-spam protection), perimeter network protection, how you allow SMTP mail in to your organization, and which Hub Transport server(s) will be responsible for sending and receiving Internet mail.

Finally, when key aspects of your Exchange system are in place, you need to test them to be sure that they work at all. Then you need to ensure that they work up to whatever performance and other standards you need to meet.

Okay, let's start our trip down that long and winding road.

Establishing Naming Conventions

Using naming conventions seems like such a small thing, but you will quickly change your mind if you work in an organization in which the server's IP address is easier and quicker to type (or remember!) than its name. Here you set some criteria for naming the key Exchange organizational components:

- Organization

- Servers

- Storage groups and databases

- Recipients (including users, contacts, and distribution groups)

- Exchange components

> **TIP**
>
> Note that the organization name is chosen when your first Exchange server is installed. Once it is set, it cannot be changed without removing all Exchange servers.

Your goal should be to establish a logical and consistent set of naming conventions that fit in well with your real-world organizational structure and culture.

NAMING THE ORGANIZATION AND SERVERS

Here's one easy and usually safe naming convention that you can use:

Organization The master company name, for example, Barry Gerber and Associates. Names for the Exchange organizations can be up to 256 characters long, but we strongly suggest that you keep names to around 32 characters. Organization names should be less of a factor with Exchange 2007 since the organization name does not even appear in the Exchange Management Console.

Server You can use generic naming, such as, for example, EXCHANGE01, LAXEXMB01, LAXEXCA01, and so on.

Server names are set when you install Windows Server. They are limited to a maximum of 63 characters, but you should limit them to 15 characters if pre–Windows 2000/XP clients will access them.

For most names, almost any character is permitted. However, we strongly suggest you use only the 26 uppercase and lowercase letters of the alphabet, the numerals 0 through 9, and the hyphen. Don't use spaces, underscores, or any accented letters.

When you begin to establish server names, if you are going to have more than one server in your organization, there are a couple of factors that you should take in to consideration:

◆ The naming standard should be easy to remember

◆ The naming standard should makes sense; yes it is fun to name servers after *X-Men* or *Battlestar Galactica* characters, but the naming makes absolutely no sense to anyone else.

◆ It should allow for some growth and scalability. Growth can be accomplished by including a couple of digits at the end of the name. Scalability can be accomplished by allowing for a portion of the name to identify a specific location if you have more than one location or think that you will.

◆ It should easily identify the server's function (mailbox server, domain controller, file server, and so on).

◆ In organizations with more than one location, the name should have a code that identifies the server's physical location. We are fond of airport codes or building numbers.

In an environment with more than a few servers, having some portion of the naming standard that helps to identify the role will quickly reduce frustration for everyone concerned. Table 3.1 shows some two-digit codes that can help to identify a server's role.

Although the codes in Table 3.1 are merely examples, you can expand on them or develop your own to meet your needs. Many organizations use three-digit codes to more accurately represent the function of a server.

Once you have role codes, you can begin to determine what the naming standard will look like. A favorite of ours includes a three-digit location code, server type, and a unique number; many organizations use the local airport code as the location code. Table 3.2 shows some examples of server names and how they would be decoded.

NAMING RECIPIENT MAILBOXES

Even before you get to the point of assigning mailboxes, you should consider having a standard for creating and naming user accounts. Remember that the username (the pre-Windows 2000 name) must be unique for the entire domain. The user principal name (UPN) by default consists of the user's username and the forest root domain's DNS suffix; the UPN name must be unique for the entire forest. Ideally, the username should be unique across the entire forest. Some organizations will use the employee number (if applicable), while others randomly generate characters that are appended to the end of a username.

TIP

The username does not have to be the same as the Exchange alias; the Exchange alias is used (by default) to generate SMTP e-mail addresses for the mailboxes.

TABLE 3.1:   Identifying Server Roles with Two-Digit Codes

SERVER FUNCTION	SERVER CODE
Mailbox	MB
Clustered mailbox	CM
Hub Transport	HT
Unified Messaging	UM
Client Access	CA
Edge Transport	ET
Combined functions	CF
Domain controller	DC
Cluster node	CN
File server	FS
Print server	PS
Web server	WB

TABLE 3.2:   Examples of Server Names

SERVER NAME	EXPLANATION
LAXCN01	Los Angeles cluster node 01
LAXCN02	Los Angeles cluster node 02
LAXCM01	Los Angeles clustered Mailbox server 01
LAXHT01	Los Angeles Hub Transport 01
LAXCA01	Los Angeles Client Access 02
HNLCF01	Honolulu combined function server 01
SFOMB01	San Francisco Mailbox server 01
SFOCF01	San Francisco combined function server 01

You also need some criteria for naming mailboxes. There are four key names for each Exchange mailbox:

◆ First

◆ Last

◆ Display

◆ Alias

Mailbox administrators create and modify these names in the Windows 2003 Active Directory Users and Computers Microsoft Management Console snap-in; they can also be created or modified using the Exchange Management Console.

The first and last names are entered when the user's Windows 2003 login account is created. The display name is created from the first and last name (as well as the middle initial or name, if present). The alias name is created from the user's Windows 2003 logon name, which is entered when the user's Windows 2003 account is created.

The first and last names and the display name are Windows 2003 objects that are also used by Exchange. The alias is an Exchange object that is used in forming some Exchange e-mail addresses (for example, the user's Internet address). The Exchange alias should be unique, if possible, in order to avoid conflicts with other e-mail addresses that are created.

FIGURE 3.1
Display names are created using first and last names when a user account is created.

You can change the default rules for constructing mailbox names, and you can manually change these names. In Figure 3.1, you can see the first and last names as well as the display name for an Exchange 2007 mailbox in Active Directory Users and Computers, but this information can also be displayed and modified using the Exchange Management Console.

Figure 3.2 shows the Exchange alias name for a user's mailbox; this information is only visible in the mailbox properties when using the Exchange Management Console. This is a change for Exchange 2000/2003 administrators who may be used to finding this information in Active Directory Users and Computers.

FIGURE 3.2
The alias name for an Exchange 2007 mailbox

Display Names

The Outlook client global address list shows the display name for each mailbox (see Figure 3.3). You need to decide on a convention for display names. This naming convention should account for potentially duplicate display names and allow for information in the display name that will let a user pick the correct name when there is, for example, more than one John Smith. You might even want to include department names or titles in display names so that users aren't faced with ambiguous selections, as they might be if they encountered a list of 25 recipients named John Smith. Options include *first-name-space-last-name* (as in John Smith) or *last-name-comma-space-first-name* (as in Smith, John). You may even opt for something fancier that includes the user's location, title, or department. The default is *first-name-space-last name*.

Display names can be up to 256 characters long. They are only a convenience — they're not a part of the mailbox's e-mail address. However, they are the way in which Exchange users find the people they want to communicate with, so don't scrimp when setting them up. You can also create custom address lists ordered by attributes of users. For example, you can create an address list that includes only users in a specific department.

> **TIP**
>
> Display names will directly affect your users every day. Choose the naming standard for display names carefully.

Practically speaking, display name lengths should be limited only by your users' willingness to read through lots of stuff to find the mailbox they're looking for. The length (and additional information in the display name) may also be affected by the size of the organization and how familiar your users are with their fellow e-mail recipients. Additional information in the display name (such as title or location) can make it a lot easier for a user to determine that they are selecting the right mailbox from a list of thousands.

> **TIP**
>
> Display names are also included in messages going to the Internet, so be careful about including information that might be considered sensitive, such as job title.

Full-blown arguments have sprung up around the metaphysics of choosing display name conventions. We'll leave the decision to you, although we prefer the convention *Last_Name,*

First_Name (as in Doe, Jane). In a larger organization, it is easier to find Jane Doe among a list of the Does than among a list of the Janes. If you are interested in some examples of how different display name standards would look, here are some ideas. Which of these would help you in preventing duplicate display names for your organizations?

Mark Watts	The default, first name and last name.
Elfassy, David	Last name and first name, commonly used and easy to follow.
Martha Lanoza at HQ (x54321)	Identifies first name and last name as well as the location and the user's telephone number extension.
Jones, Damion Mr. (SFO - Network Manager)	Includes location and title.
Craig, Benjamin GS-14 US Air Force	Pay grade and organization.
Maher, Joshua MAJ-US Army, Fort Irwin	Title, organization, and location.
Swanson, Chuck (Volcano Surfboards)	Includes company name (useful for mail going outside of your organization). This is also a useful standard when naming mail-enabled contacts since it allows your users to identify recipients outside of your company.
Eiler Brian CAPT N651 COMPACFLT	User's last name and first name without the comma. Includes the title, job code, and the department.

> **WARNING**
>
> Something as apparently simple as changing the default order of last and first name in display names isn't all that simple with Exchange 2007. In Exchange Server 5.5, you made the change in the Exchange Administrator program. With Windows Server 2003/Exchange Server 2007, you have to edit the Active Directory schema. Why? Display names aren't just for Exchange mailboxes anymore. They're also used whenever end users or system administrators go looking for a specific Windows 2003 user in Active Directory. That's why it's an Active Directory issue. Editing Active Directory is somewhat akin to editing the Windows Registry. It's not a job for amateurs, and it's a job that may be done by someone not directly involved in day-to-day Exchange Server 2007 management. In addition, the decision to change the display name default for an Active Directory namespace is no longer simply an Exchange Server issue. It's an organization-wide issue because these changes affect more than electronic messaging.

Alias Names

For some messaging systems, the user's mailbox is identified by an alias name, which is part of the mailbox's address. Either Exchange itself or the gateway for the foreign mail system constructs an address using the alias. For other messaging systems, the mailbox name is constructed from other information.

Figure 3.4 shows the two addresses that Exchange built for a user by default for the Internet and for X.400. The Internet addresses use the Exchange alias Andy.Schan. X.400 addresses do not use the alias. Instead, they use the full first and last name attributes of the user. Natively, Exchange

2007 does not require the X.400 address but it is generated for backward compatibility with older e-mail systems.

FIGURE 3.4
Exchange Server uses the mailbox alias or the first and last names to construct e-mail addresses.

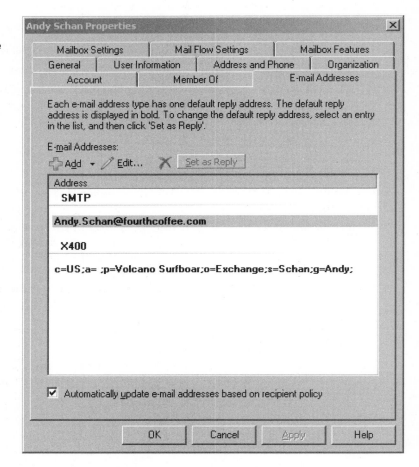

Aliases can be up to 63 characters long. That's too long, of course, because some people in foreign messaging systems will have to type in the alias as part of an electronic messaging address. Try to keep aliases short — 10 characters is long enough.

For some foreign messaging system addressing schemes, Exchange must remove illegal characters and shorten the alias to meet maximum character-length requirements. For example, underscores become question marks in X.400 addresses. You should do all you that you can to ensure that aliases are constructed using less-esoteric characters.

As with display naming, alias naming conventions are taken seriously, almost religiously. So don't be surprised if you have trouble deciding on one when you run them by "the committee."

NAMING MAIL-ENABLED GROUPS

As simple as it sounds, many organizations spend hours or days debating and deciding their display name standard for mailboxes and then give no thought to naming their mail-enabled groups. The thought actually comes once all of the mailboxes and mail-enabled groups have been created and they realize that groups are distributed throughout the global address list alphabetically just as the users are. There should be a naming standard for distribution group names just as there is with display names and alias names, and again, as with all naming standards, people can get pretty passionate about what they think is the best.

Mail-enabled groups are sorted using the group name attribute. This is configured either through Active Directory Users and Computers or through the Exchange Management Console (EMC). Figure 3.5 shows the Group Information property page of a mail-enabled group using the EMC; the group's display name is changed in the Group Name field.

FIGURE 3.5
Mail-enabled group properties as viewed through the Exchange Management Console

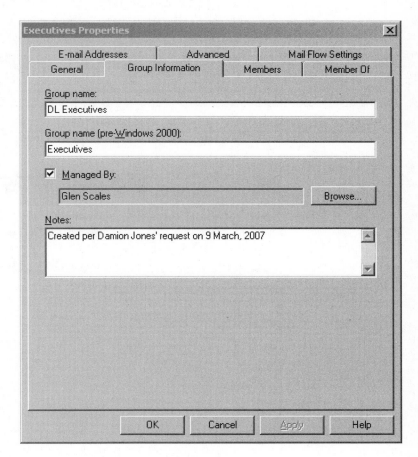

Each of us has our own preferences, but most Exchange administrators agree that there should be something in distribution group names that identifies them as mail-enabled distribution groups. Another possible idea is to include some character or character string that identifies and sorts all of the distribution groups together. Here are some examples:

_Directory Update Sales Team

$Everyone in Marketing

DL - IT Help Desk

zz Human Resources

This list illustrates three possible ways to name and sort mail-enabled groups. The first is to use a special character — such as the underscore (_), the dollar sign ($), the exclamation symbol (!), or the pound symbol (#). The advantage of these characters is that they will sort all of the mail-enabled groups to the top of the global address list. Another example is using the letters *DL* (for distribution list) in front of each mail-enabled group; this will keep all of the mail groups sorted together. Finally, you could use characters such as *zz*; this will put the mail-enabled groups together but place them all at the bottom of the global address list. The advantage of having them all at the bottom rather than at the top is that it is less likely that a user will accidentally select a group.

TIP

In Exchange 2007, all mail-enabled groups must be universal groups.

If a user just needs to see the groups in the global address list, they can also use the All Groups address list. The All Groups view shows only the objects in the directory that are mail-enabled groups.

NAMING EXCHANGE COMPONENTS

Display names for mailboxes or groups affect the end user and therefore getting them right is a pretty important task. There are, however, a number Exchange-related components or objects for which you should consider naming standards. Why? Because incorporating standards for Exchange objects will make *your* life easier and the lives of your fellow Exchange administrators.

The objects and components that we are alluding to are found in the Exchange Management Console or the Exchange Management Shell:

◆ Managed folder mailbox policies

◆ Offline address books

◆ Exchange ActiveSync mailbox policies

◆ Transport rules

◆ Edge subscriptions

◆ E-mail address policies

◆ Unified Messaging dial plans

◆ Unified Messaging policies

◆ Storage groups

◆ Send connectors

◆ Receive connectors

◆ Mailbox databases

In a small organization, naming conventions for policies and objects that are listed in the organization-wide and server configuration settings are not as necessary since you may have only a few of these. However, in a larger organization with many locations and possibly many groups of administrators, include in the name of each policy or object enough information to identify what the object does and who is responsible for it. For example, even a small organization can identify with the transport rules (shown in Figure 3.6). Once an organization has dozen or more transport rules, it can be difficult to find the rule you need to edit.

FIGURE 3.6
Managing more than a few transport rules can become difficult.

Imagine the difficulty that an organization with administrators in multiple organizations around the world would face when they have to find a specific transport rule that affects only a certain part of their user community.

Storage groups and mailbox databases are sets of objects that should have standardized names. This helps not only the person that must administer the mailbox servers but also the recipient/ mailbox administrators. A clearly defined naming standard can help when creating mailboxes or assigning mailboxes. Figure 3.7 shows the Mailbox Settings screen for the New Mailbox Wizard; note the Storage Group and Mailbox Database fields.

FIGURE 3.7
Assigning a storage group and mailbox database to a new mailbox

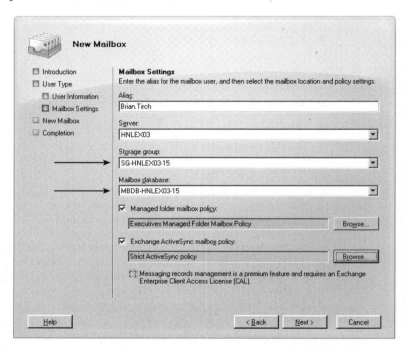

In the naming standard we are using for the storage groups and mailbox database, we include MBDB for mailbox database or SG for storage group. The name also includes the name of the server on which the database or storage group is found and a unique number for that storage group or mailbox store. Here are some examples:

SG-LAXMB01-01

SG-NYCCM01-02

MBDB-LAXMB01-01

MBDB-LAXMB01-02

MBDB-LAXMB01-02

If you have already deployed some mailbox stores or storage groups, not to worry; you can easily rename them as you will find in later chapters. We recommend that you name the database file the same as the logical database. For example, the database MBDB-HNLEX03-01 would have a database file named MBDB-HNLEX03-01.EDB.

Selecting a Microsoft Active Directory Domain Model

Active Directory is widely deployed in organizations all over the world. This section may not be relevant to your organization since you may have a fully deployed Active Directory. However, even if you are a dedicated Exchange server administrator, understanding Active Directory is important and will make it easier for you to operate and troubleshoot Exchange.

As many different options for multiple trees and child domains as you may have (and may be tempted to use), we strongly urge you to consider a single domain mode whenever possible. This is by far the simplest to deploy and administer, and administrative permissions can still be delegated for individual resource and account management. Of course, if necessary, you can create a single root domain for your user accounts and create child domains (subdomains) and control access to various network resources using this model.

Aside from certain security requirements, one of the main reasons for multi-domain Windows NT networks was the difficulty of building single domains that crossed lower-bandwidth links. Microsoft has outfitted Windows 2003 with such features as sites and site connectors to deal with this issue. Unless you must adhere to strong regulatory or security requirements, the single-root domain model really makes the most sense.

If it works for your organization, you can even use your Internet domain name for your Windows 2003 root domain. This simplifies Exchange server installation just a little, although you need to be especially careful to protect any internal resources that shouldn't be accessible on the Internet. If you want to use a separate DNS name for your Windows 2003 root domain, then by all means do so. This can also help to reduce confusion and make your DNS names a little easier to support. You can still use your Internet domain name for external Exchange messaging. We like this approach and use .local for Windows domain names and .com, .edu, and so on for Internet domain names.

TIP

Your Active Directory DNS names do not have to be the same as your Internet names and/or Internet SMTP addresses.

Defining Active Directory Sites

An Active Directory site is a collection of IP subnets that are all separated by reasonably high-speed connectivity. The definition of "high speed" is usually left up to the designer of the Active Directory, but we recommend that all of the subnets in a single Active Directory site have at least 10Mb Ethernet connectivity between each of the subnets in the site.

Since Windows 2000 was first released, Active Directory sites have been used to define replication paths between domain controllers and to help Windows clients find the closest domain controller when authenticating users. Exchange 2000/2003 servers used Active Directory sites to locate the domain controllers and global catalog servers that were closest to them on the network; they then used these domain controllers and global catalog servers for authentication, LDAP queries, and referring MAPI clients to global catalog servers.

In the past, administrators sometimes would not properly create all of the Active Directory sites for their organization or, worse, would not define all of the IP subnets properly. This would result in long login times and performance problems with Exchange because Exchange servers could be querying domain controllers and global catalog servers on the opposite side of the globe. An incorrect Active Directory site and subnet configuration is a mistake that you cannot afford to make with Exchange 2007. In addition to all of the performance problems that might occur with past versions, you may experience mail delivery failures because Exchange 2007 relies on the site architecture to properly deliver mail between Exchange servers in different sites.

> **TIP**
>
> One simple way to check for Active Directory site problems is to check on each domain controller's Netlogon.log file found in the \windows\debug folder. If you see reports of clients logging in to that domain controller from undefined subnets, then you know you have some subnets that are not fully defined with Active Directory.

If you have more than one network physical location that has domain controllers and Exchange servers, you need to get your site and subnet architecture clearly and accurately defined. This is done in the Active Directory Sites and Services management console (Figure 3.8). For each of your physical locations, you must define the IP subnets and associate those subnets with the correct Active Directory site.

FIGURE 3.8
Defining Active Directory sites and subnets

Exchange 2003 Administrative Group Boundaries

If you are planning to migrate from an Exchange 2000/2003 organization, you will retain the Exchange 2000/2003 administrative groups through the migration. If you are building a brand-new Exchange 2007 organization, you will not need to worry about administrative groups.

Administrative groups play a couple of roles in an Exchange 2000/2003 environment as well as an Exchange 2007 organization that is in the middle of a migration. First, they can be used to control administrative access to your Exchange 2000/2003 server environment. You can set permissions on an administrative group so that only certain users can manage the Exchange 2000/2003 servers and other objects in the group. In this way, you can parcel out responsibility for managing different sets of Exchange servers to different people.

The administrative group structure of your Exchange 2000/2003 environment will probably depend to some extent on the structure of your organization. If you want a particular group, such as a department, to manage its own Exchange server environment, you would create an administrative group, put the department's Exchange server(s) in the administrative group, and assign permissions to manage the group to the appropriate Windows 2003 users or group.

Once the first Exchange 2007 server is installed in to an existing environment, a new Exchange administrative group is created that holds all of the Exchange 2007 servers regardless of the permissions necessary to manage them. This is called Exchange Administrative Group (FYDI-BOHF23SPDLT); the text "FYDIBOHF23SPDLT" is a unique identifier is associated with the new administrative group name when the first Exchange 2007 server is installed to guarantee that the administrative group name is unique. The unique name for the Exchange Administrative Group (FYDIBOHF23SPDLT) administrative group's routing group is Exchange Routing Group (DWBGZMFD01QNBJR). These administrative group and routing group names are hard-coded and must not be changed.

Secret Ciphers

If you are curious about the unique identifiers DWBGZMFD01QNBJR and FYDIBOHF23SPDLT, then we will let you in a poorly kept secret. They are actually simple ciphers. Take each letter in the identifier FYDIBOHF23SPDLT and change it to the preceding letter in the alphabet and see what you get. Hint, *F* becomes *E*, *Y* becomes *X*, and so on. Conversely, with the DWBGZMFD01QNBJR identifier, take each letter in the identifier and change it to the next letter in the alphabet, so *D* becomes *E*, *W* becomes *X*. Try it and see what you get. If you are as big a fan of Exchange Server as we are, then we are sure you will agree.

Although the administrative groups do not show up in the Exchange 2007 Exchange Management Console, you can see them in the Exchange 2000/2003 Exchange System Manager console (see Figure 3.9).

FIGURE 3.9
Exchange System Manager after the first Exchange 2007 server is installed

Exchange 2003 Routing Group Boundaries

In Exchange 2000/2003, the routing groups defined the physical separation of Exchange servers; this separation was usually determined based on slow, unreliable, or non-full-time links. When defining Exchange 2000/2003 routing group boundaries, you should keep a couple of things in mind. First, Exchange 2000/2003 routing groups and Microsoft network domains are related. Second, all the Exchange servers in a routing group should have certain networking capabilities.

Routing groups have been replaced by Active Directory sites in Exchange 2007, but an organization that is going to have interoperability between Exchange 2007 and Exchange 2000/2003 will continue to see routing groups in Exchange System Manager. When the first Exchange 2007 server is installed, a new administrative group and routing group is created that will allow interoperability between Exchange 2000/2003 servers and Exchange 2007. Figure 3.10 shows a new unique routing group that is created in the new Exchange 2007 specific administrative group. This routing group will hold all Exchange 2007 servers.

FIGURE 3.10
Exchange 2007 routing group container used for interoperability with Exchange 2000/2003

Planning Your Disk Space Requirements

Disk space is one of the requirements of Exchange that most often confuses people or is not figured properly. The disk space requirements for supporting the Exchange server itself are relatively straight forward. The disk volume on which Exchange Server 2007 is installed requires approximately 1.2GB of disk space; the system disk requires another 200MB of disk space. If the Exchange server is supporting the Unified Messaging server role, plan for an additional 500MB of disk space for each Unified Messaging language pack that will be installed.

The operating system disk should also have sufficient free disk space to allow a page file that is at least the amount of RAM plus 100MB. This is to allow Windows to dump the memory in the case of an operating system crash. Exchange servers that support larger numbers of mailboxes often have dedicated spindles or partitions just for the page file.

Figure 3.11 shows a conceptual diagram of an Exchange 2007 mailbox server that is designed to support 1,000 mailboxes. In the following section we will explain the process through which we went to estimate the storage required. In some cases, we picked a typical large drive size. Mailbox servers are by far the biggest consumers of disk storage, and this is something you must plan for. You must also be prepared for growth.

We have also taken into consideration the use of local continuous replication (LCR) in Figure 3.11 and thus have allocated disk space for it. Ideally, transaction logs and the operating system are on dedicated RAID-1 spindles and the databases are on dedicated RAID-5 spindles. Even though we have labeled this figure as having local drives, you could deploy this same configuration using iSCSI or SAN disks. We estimated 72GB of space for the operating system, page file, and Exchange binaries, 146GB for the transaction log volume, and 2.6TB of space for the database volume.

FIGURE 3.11
Disk configuration for an Exchange 2007 Mailbox server

Local disk drives

C:\ — Operating system, page file, Exchange binaries RAID 1 - 72GB

D:\ — Exchange transaction logs RAID 1 – 146GB

E:\ — Exchange databases and indexes RAID 5 - 2.6TB

F:\ — LCR Exchange transaction logs RAID 1 – 146GB

G:\ — LCR Exchange databases RAID 5 - 2.6TB

Mailbox Server Storage

Exchange servers holding the Mailbox server role consume the most disk space. Where Exchange system designers often fall short in their designs is that they do not allow sufficient disk space for mail storage, transaction logs, and extra disk space. Often the disk space is not partitioned correctly, either. Here are some important points to keep in mind when planning your disk space requirements:

◆ Transaction log files should be on a separate set of physical disks (spindles) from their corresponding Exchange database files. RAID-1 or RAID-0+1 arrays provide better performance for transaction logs.

◆ Allow for at least 7 to 10 days' worth of transaction logs to be stored for each storage group. The estimated amount of transaction logs will vary dramatically from one organization to another, but a good starting point is about 5GB of transaction logs per day per 1,000 mailboxes.

◆ Allow for 10 to 15 percent white space estimates in the maximum size of each of your database files.

◆ Allow for 10 to 15 percent deleted item and deleted mailbox retention space in each database file.

◆ When planning for local continuous replication, make sure the replicated transaction logs and backup copy of the databases are on separate physical disks from the source.

◆ Allocate enough free space on the disk so that you can always make a backup copy of your largest database and still have some free disk space. A good way to calculate this is to take

110 percent of the largest database you will support since that also allows you to defragment the database using ESEUTIL if necessary.

◆ Consider additional disk space for message tracking, message transport, HTTP protocol, POP3 protocol, and IMAP4 protocol log files.

So, to use some of these points when calculating necessary disk space, here is an example for a server that will support 1,000 mailboxes. Further, we are estimating that we will provide the typical user with a "prohibit send" size warning of 500MB and a "prohibit send and receive" limit of 600MB. In any organization of 1,000 users, you have to take in to consideration that 10 percent will qualify as some type of VIP that will be allowed more mail storage than a typical user; in this case, we will allow 100 VIP users to have a "prohibit send and receive" limit of 2GB.

This gives us 540GB of mail storage requirements (600MB times 900 mailboxes) for the first 900 users plus another 200GB (2GB times 100 mailboxes) for the VIP users. This is a maximum amount of mail storage of 740GB. However, this estimate does not include estimates for deleted items in a user's mailbox and deleted mailboxes, so we want to add an additional overhead factor of about 15 percent, or about 111MB, plus an additional overhead factor of another 15 percent (another 111MB) for database "white space." The white space is the empty space that is found in the database at any given time.

So at any given time, for these 1,000 mailboxes, we can expect mail database storage (valid e-mail content, deleted data, and empty database space) to consume approximately 962GB, but since we like round numbers, let's average that up to 1,000GB, or 1TB.

In this example, let's say that we have decided the maximum database size we want to be able to back up or restore is 100GB. This means that we need to split our users' mailboxes across 10 mailbox databases and storage groups.

For the transaction logs, we estimate that we will generate approximately 5GB of transaction logs per day. We should plan for enough disk space on the transaction log disk for at least 50GB of available disk space.

Next, since full-text indexing is enabled by default, we should allow enough disk space for the full-text index files. In this case, we will estimate that the full-text index files will consume a maximum of about 5 to 10 percent of the total size of the mail data, or approximately 100GB. If we combine the full-text index files on the same disk drive as the database files, we will require approximately 1.3TB of disk space.

Finally, on this server we are planning to implement local continuous replication, so we will need to plan for a separate set of spindles for the databases (1.3TB) and the transaction logs (50GB).

Anytime there is any doubt as to how much disk space you should include, it is usually a good idea to plan for more rather than less. Although disk space is reasonably inexpensive, unless you have sophisticated storage systems, adding additional disk space can be time consuming and costly from the perspective of effort and downtime.

Planning for Growth

Growth?! You may be saying to yourself, "I just gave the typical user a maximum mailbox size of 600MB and the VIPs a maximum size of 2GB! How can my users possibly need more mailbox space?" Predicting the amount of growth you may need in the future is a very difficult task. You may not be able to foresee new organizational requirements or that you might be influenced by future laws that require specific data retention periods.

In our experience, though, mailbox limits, regardless of how rigid you plan to be, are managed by exception and by need. In the preceding example, we calculated that we would need 1.3TB of disk space for our 1,000 mailboxes. Would we partition or create a disk of exactly that size? Probably not.

Instead of carving out exactly the amount of disk space you anticipate needing, add a "fluff factor" to your calculations. We recommend doubling the anticipated amount of storage you think you will require, but this is just a wild guess. In this example, though, we might anticipate using 2.6TB of disk space if we doubled our expected requirements. Here are some factors that you may want to consider when deciding how much growth you should expect for your mailbox servers:

◆ Average annual growth in the number of employees

◆ Acquisitions, mergers, or consolidations that are planned for the foreseeable future

◆ Addition of new mail-enabled applications such as Unified Messaging features or electronic forms routing

◆ Government regulations that require some types of corporate records (including e-mail) to be retained for a number of years.

Conversely, there are potential things in your future that could actually reduce the amount of mailbox storage you require. Many organizations are now including message archival and long-term retention systems in their messaging systems. These systems archive older content out of a user's mailbox and move it to some type of external storage such as disk, SAN, NAS, optical, or tape storage. The user can still access or search for archived content, but it no longer takes up space in your Exchange server mailbox databases.

Archive systems are great for organizations that must retain much of the information in their mailboxes but want to move it to external storage. However, depending on the system, you don't want to archive everything older than five days since the user may not be able to access it via Outlook Web Access or mobile devices. Further, once the content is archived from their mailbox, it will not longer be accessible from a user's desktop search engine such as the Google Desktop or the Windows Desktop search engine. So keeping a certain amount content in the user's mailbox will always make sense.

Planning Servers and Internal Connections to Them

There's quite a bit to do in planning your servers and user links. You must decide what kinds of hardware to use for each of your Exchange servers. Then you need to think through some policies relating to storage. After that, you must figure out how to back up the servers. Then you need to make sure you've got adequate bandwidth on your local networks to keep Exchange happy; if you don't have it, you have to decide how to get it. Finally, before you go on to the next step in the Exchange design process, you must think about remote users and how you'll connect them to Exchange.

Designing Your Exchange Servers

The intricacies of Exchange Server design and fine-tuning could occupy a whole book; you'll have to experiment here. Fortunately, Microsoft doesn't leave you out in the cold when it comes to this experimentation. The company provides applications for testing the capacity of hardware you might use to run Exchange Server. These include the Exchange Server Jetstress, Exchange Load Generator, and Exchange Server Stress and Performance tools. Jetstress places load on your disk subsystem similar to an Exchange server load while the Exchange Load Generator and the Exchange Server Stress and Performance tools tests your server hardware (CPU, disk drives, RAM) and network capacity by simulating messaging loads on an Exchange 2007 server.

To begin your experimentation, install Windows Server 2003 and Exchange Server 2007. There are earlier versions of these tools (such as a tool called LoadSim) but we recommend you use the latest versions available from Microsoft. You can download these from `http://preview.tinyurl.com/37k89y`.

WARNING

Tools such as Load Generator, Stress and Performance, and Jetstress should never be run against production mail servers or in production environments.

Next, take out that set of user-demand numbers that you put together when you did your user needs assessment. Plug those numbers into LoadSim, and run it against a reasonable Exchange server machine — say, a 3GHz Pentium 4 or Xeon machine with 2GB of memory and at least two 9GB SCSI hard drives. Don't run LoadSim on your Exchange server. Instead, run it on a separate 1GHz or better Pentium-based Windows XP workstation with at least 1GB of memory. And don't try to simulate more than 200 users on one LoadSim machine. If you don't follow these guidelines, LoadSim might not be capable of generating the loads that you've asked it to and you could be led to believe that your Exchange server hardware is adequate when it's not.

In selecting servers for Exchange, our recommendation is to always go for the biggest guns that you can afford, commensurate with expected user loads. After working a while now with Windows Server 2003 and Exchange Server 2007, we have our own ideas about server sizing. A good machine would be a dual-core Intel Xeon or greater computer with 4GB of random access memory (RAM) and a hardware RAID-5 disk capacity of at least 500GB. Such a computer should be capable of handling upwards of 200 average Exchange Server 2007 users, network bandwidth willing.

In a busier environment, Exchange 2007 not only doesn't benefit from running on a domain controller, it actually suffers as it competes with Active Directory and other CPU/disk-intensive software that runs on a Windows Server 2003 domain controller.

If you had to gulp a few times after reading our recommendations for a production Exchange 2007 server, don't worry. You can get by with less horsepower, especially if you need to support fewer users.

If you do decide to go with less costly or less powerful hardware, we strongly suggest that you go with SCSI disk drives over Enhanced IDE drives or SATA drives. Enhanced IDE and SATA drives are nice and inexpensive, but for production Exchange servers, we prefer SCSI drives. They're fast and tend to be more reliable than IDE drives over the long haul. For best performance, choose ultrawide SCSI drives.

When you're comfortable with the basic design of your servers, you need to plan for uninterruptible power supplies (UPSs). We consider a UPS to be part of a server, not an add-on. UPSs are cheap, given the peace of mind that they can bring. In spite of Windows Server 2003's and Exchange Server 2007's capability of recovering from most disastrous events, you don't want to tempt fate and risk damage to your organization's precious electronic messaging data. Get enough UPSs to serve the power needs of each server, and get a UPS that comes with software to gracefully shut down your servers if power stays off for an extended period. We'll talk more about UPSs in Chapter 15, "Reliability and Availability 101."

SERVER FAULT TOLERANCE

The more fault tolerance you can build into your Exchange Server hardware, the better you and your users will sleep at night. Almost nothing is worse than losing even one user's e-mail messages. Here are a few steps that you can take to improve server fault tolerance:

◆ Look for systems with error-correcting RAM memory.

◆ On the disk side, consider multiple SCSI controllers or RAID level 5 technologies implemented in hardware.

◆ Look for computers with two or more redundant power supplies.

◆ Buy computers that let you swap out failed RAID drives and power supplies without even bringing down your system.

◆ Consider Microsoft's Windows 2003 Advanced and Datacenter Server editions, which let you set up clusters of Windows 2003/Exchange 2007 servers that are able to continue serving users even if one cluster node fails.

◆ Use load-balancing services such as the Windows Load Balancing or the Cisco Local Director to provide higher availability for Client Access and Edge Transport servers

◆ Install multiple Hub Transport servers in each Active Directory site that has Mailbox server roles for redundancy in message routing.

Setting Exchange Server Storage Policies

You need to start thinking now about how you'll manage user storage on each server. Storage management gives you more control over how much of what is stored on Exchange server disks, and it helps you remain within your server disk budget. You need to answer several disk management policy questions, including these:

◆ Do you want some or all of your users to store messages in personal folders on a workstation or networked disk drives instead of in their Exchange Server–based mailboxes? This is probably not a good idea and we recommend against using personal folders as a user's primary mail storage location.

◆ For those who will use their Exchange Server mailboxes, do you want to limit the amount of storage that they can use?

◆ Do you want to impose limits on the storage used by public folders?

◆ If you have public folders containing messages that lose value with time (for example, messages from Internet lists or Usenet news feeds), do you want Exchange to automatically delete messages from these folders based on message age?

◆ Will you implement Exchange Server's capability to save deleted messages for a designated period of time? This is a neat capability because users can recover messages that they accidentally deleted. However, all those "deleted" messages can take up lots of Exchange server disk space.

You can base your answers to most of these questions on the results of your user needs assessment, although you're bound to make adjustments as you pass through iterations of the design process. Also note that while it's tempting to force users to store messages in personal folders on local or networked disk drives to save on the Exchange server disk, you then run the risk that key user messages won't get backed up. As the ever-present "they" say, "You pays your money and you takes your chances."

Planning disk storage is important enough that we had an entire section on planning your mailbox storage requirements and disk space. Later in Chapter 9, "Imposing Limits and Why," we will further this concept by dedicating an entire chapter to how you can impose storage limits and message size limits on your users.

Backing Up Your Exchange Servers

When you know what your Exchange servers and networks will look like, you can begin thinking about backing up your servers. You need to use backup software that is especially designed for Exchange's client/server-transaction-oriented architecture. Such software enables you to back up an Exchange server's information store without shutting down Exchange processes and thus closing off user access to the server. The software communicates with Exchange's information store service to ensure that the databases that it is responsible for are fully backed up. We'll talk more about the fine points of Exchange backup in Chapter 16, "Backup and Disaster Recovery."

Windows Server 2003's own backup program has add-ons to do a proper backup of Exchange servers. Windows 2003's volume snapshot capability is a great way to get a consistent image of a disk drive while applications such as Exchange are running and online. Other Windows Server 2003 backup vendors have released add-ons that can properly back up Exchange Server 2007. Third-party vendors can also support Windows 2003's volume snapshot capability. These products add better backup scheduling, easier-to-use logs, multiple-server backup from a single instance of the backup program, quicker and easier restore of backed-up data, and disaster recovery options.

Backups can be to tape or disk or, for greater reliability, to both. Volume snapshots are best and most quickly done to disk. Do backups to tape during off-hours when backup speed is less of an issue. Be sure to include both backup disk and backup tape in your hardware/software backup resources plans.

You can back up an Exchange server either locally or over the network. When you back it up over the network, you can run the backup from a Windows 2003 server or from an Exchange 2007 server. For Exchange servers with lots of disk space (200GB or more) and slow network links to potential backup servers (less than 100Mbps), we strongly suggest that you bypass the networked server backup option and do the backup locally on and from the Exchange server itself. You have to spend some money on a backup device and software for the Exchange server, but you'll get it back in available bandwidth and faster backups. Available bandwidth means that other network-dependent tasks — and there are lots of those on a Windows 2003/Exchange 2007 network — run faster. Faster backups mean shorter periods of that awful feeling you get when important data is not yet on tape.

If you have high-speed across-the-network backup systems, just make sure that the restoration of data can occur within your service level agreement. If you do not have a service level agreement, at least confirm that the restoration of data can occur in a time that your organization will consider reasonable.

Whether you back up over the network or locally, don't skimp on backup hardware. You're going to *add* hard disk storage to your Exchange server, not take it away. Go for high-capacity 4mm, 8mm, DLT, or LTO tape backup systems. Think about tape autoloaders, those neat gizmos that give one or more tape drives automatic access to anything from a few tapes to hundreds of them. If you choose to use disk in your backup strategy, use solid RAID-5 disk-based backup systems, or if your organization has the resources and you need their special features, consider storage area networks with their sophisticated backup systems.

Don't forget those personal folders stored on user workstations. You have to decide who will be responsible for backing them up: Exchange staff, other MIS staff, or users themselves. The technology for centralized workstation backup is readily available. For example, agents for most third-party Windows Server 2003 backup products let you back up all or part of specific user workstations.

While you're at it, don't forget Windows Server 2003 backup. If you have Windows 2003 servers that don't support Exchange, you need to back them up too. You can back up a Windows 2003 server over the network, but if the servers have lots of disk space, consider the same local backup strategy that we suggested for Exchange servers. You can also consider a dedicated network just for backups. All you need is an extra Gigabit Ethernet adapter in each server and in your backup computer or computers and a gigabit hub.

Networking Your Exchange Users

When you have your server design down, you need to think about how to connect users to your Exchange servers. It's usually a no-brainer for local connections, although you want to be sure that you've got enough bandwidth to move the stuff that Exchange makes available to your users. For example, a message with a very simple embedded color screen capture is 855KB. The graphic looks impressive, and it lets you make a point that you never could have made without it. Still, you wouldn't want your recipients to get it over a 33.3Kbps or 56Kbps connection.

If you're concerned about LAN bandwidth, you can do a couple things. First, get rid of those slower networks. Dump 4Mbps Token Ring and Arcnet networks. Yes, they are still around. If you haven't already, you might also want to consider upgrading 10BaseT networks to 100BaseT. Second, segment your LANs to reduce the number of users on any segment. In this situation, you might even put multiple network adapters in your Exchange server, one for each segment or group of segments. And do take a look at faster networking technologies such as 100Mbps Ethernet, those really neat networking switches that can replace routers and significantly improve network backbone performance, and the latest switched Fast Ethernet hubs that bring switching to workstation connectivity and are quite low in price these days. Yes, any of these options will cost your organization some bucks, but they're likely to be bucks well spent. Just as with user workstations, slow technologies don't get used and the benefits of the applications that you're trying to run on top of them are lost.

Don't forget remote Exchange users. Many users need to keep in touch when they're away from the office, whether at home or on the road. Remote users can connect to their Exchange servers by way of direct or RPC over HTTP links through an Internet service provider (ISP) using dial-up or home-based DSL or cable connections. And don't forget the Internet-based POP3, IMAP4, and web browser–based client options that are supported by Exchange Server. With their lighter-weight demands on workstation resources, they could be just what the doctor ordered for your remote users.

Ideally, users with lower bandwidth connections should be using Outlook 2003 or later and the Exchange local cache mode configuration. This will provide the best possible experience for the end user.

Validating and Optimizing Your Design

Validation means ensuring that you have a system that guarantees message delivery, integrity, and security. It also means making sure the system you designed is versatile enough to handle the range of documents, messaging formats, and applications that your organization needs. *Optimization* is a balancing act in which you try to build the fastest, most stable, and most reliable systems that you can while still meeting organizational requirements and keeping costs down.

Guaranteed Delivery

Guaranteed message delivery comes with reliable Windows 2003 and Exchange 2007 servers and reliable internal and external networks. To increase the likelihood of guaranteed delivery, go for as much server fault tolerance and networking redundancy as your organization can afford. Use high-quality server and networking hardware and software inside your organization; buy outside networking services from stable, experienced, and well-established providers. Monitor the health of your networks, and be prepared to fix problems quickly. During the validation phase, send messages of all kinds through all your connections, and then check to see if they arrive intact. When problems arise, use Exchange's own message-tracking tools to catch up with wayward messages, and take advantage of Exchange's network- and system-monitoring tools to discover why a message didn't get through.

Reliability is only one side of guaranteed message delivery. You also need Exchange servers that are sufficiently fast and networks that have the bandwidth to move messages quickly enough to meet maximum delivery time parameters. If you specified that all messages should be delivered to all internal users within five minutes, for example, now's the time to see if your Exchange system is capable of performing up to spec. If not, you must either increase your permissible maximum delivery times or, depending on the source of the problem, come up with speedier servers or higher-bandwidth networks.

Message Integrity

Message integrity means that messages arrive in the same form as they were transmitted. Problems with message integrity can often be traced to mismatched binary message-part encoding and decoding. For example, a binary attachment to a message bound for the Internet is UUencoded by the sender, while the receiver expects MIME encoding. As you'll see later, there are lots of ways to set encoding parameters in Exchange to help avoid problems such as this.

Message Security

RSA encryption and public keys both work within a single Exchange organization and can be enabled to work across Exchange organizations. Exchange Server 2007 uses a number of Windows 2003–based security features to significantly enhance message security. For messages destined for foreign electronic messaging systems, Exchange Server implements a set of encryption and authentication standards: NTLM encryption, TLS encryption, SASL clear-text authentication, and Secure MIME. (More on these topics comes in Chapter 20, "Securing Exchange Server.")

You can try to validate message security on your own or with the help of a certified electronic data processing auditor. If security is important to your organization, we strongly recommend the latter.

System Versatility

Exchange's internal message formatting, along with formatting available for Internet-bound mail, means that you are able to send documents of almost any type containing virtually anything from text to last night's Letterman show. But be sure to validate that everything you need is there and works.

Exchange Server is a very popular product, so plenty of Exchange-based applications are already available from third-party vendors; many more are in development. Keep your eyes open for the latest "killer" Exchange apps.

Optimization

When you've done everything to ensure guaranteed message delivery, message integrity, and security as well as system versatility, it's time for *optimization*. You optimize your design by checking out alternatives that might help improve your Exchange system.

Optimization can also focus on reducing costs without compromising the quality of your system. For example, you might want to come up with lower-cost options for connecting Exchange routing groups or for realizing network redundancy.

Rolling Out the Plan

The specifics of your rollout will depend on the plans you've made. There are some basic processes you have to attend to in a rollout. Many of these processes are people-oriented processes, not technically oriented processes. This section focuses on the former. *Rollout* doesn't mean dropping a whole Exchange system on your organization at once. It means making Exchange available to specific systems administrators and users according to a carefully thought-out schedule. You should also go through a testing phase with specific users. Rollout to your general user population needs to be geared to your assessment of user readiness, perhaps at the departmental or subdepartmental level. Rollout also must be deeply rooted in the capacity of systems and user support staff to handle the many issues that arise during implementation of a major new software product. And, in all of this, don't forget that without information technology commitment and support, it's highly unlikely that you'll be able to smoothly pull off a successful Exchange rollout.

Start in the Right Place   You might start your rollout in the information technology (IT) department — maybe just with yourself, if you're part of IT. When you pick users, always start with users that will have the least impact until you are sure you have all the bugs worked out of the your deployment. Keep management informed of the users that will be involved in the initial rollout. Next, you might move on to samples of users based on the groupings that you uncovered in your user needs assessment or an assessment of user readiness for the change you are about to drop on them. Remember, you've been working with Exchange and its clients for a while. IT support and users might have had little exposure to it. The change you are bringing will shake their world up more than it does yours. Then move steadily onward until all users are up and running in Exchange. The key is to get Exchange out to all users as quickly as possible without crashing your organization. (Here we are referring to your *real* organization, not your Exchange organization.)

Don't Forget Design during Rollout   Remember that rollout is an integral part of the Exchange design process. As you step through your implementation plans, be ready to change your design. If something doesn't work, change it now. Don't let things pile up to the point that change becomes virtually impossible. How you schedule your rollout relative to user need and readiness as well as MIS support capacity will determine how able you are to keep up with change orders.

Pay Close Attention to Users   Whether you're in a test or production rollout phase, be sure to keep your big shot and plain old users in the loop. Get them committed to Exchange. Let them know if and when they're going to see a new e-mail client. Show them the client, just so they can see how really easy it is to use to get basic work done. Explain to them how they can use the client you plan to provide both to do what they're already doing and to get other tasks done.

This is where user training comes in. You probably already know this, but user training is both essential and a major drain on resources. Spend lots of time planning user training. Think very carefully about the amount of time and dollars you're willing to devote to user training. Training is a very specialized activity. If you don't have enough training resources in-house, consider outsourcing user training. Know that some users will get it right away and some will come back again and again seeking answers to questions that were answered both in group training and one-on-one by user support personnel. Finally, remember that your Exchange roll-out can be a great success technically, but if no one comes to the show, it will be considered a failure by your bosses or your clients and their bosses.

Stay Close to IT Staff   Keep IT staff involved and informed as well. An Exchange installation and implementation is a big deal for an IT department. Over time, just about everyone in IT will get involved with Exchange. IT staff should understand and welcome Exchange, not see it as a threat to their jobs. Train IT personnel as data-processing colleagues rather than just end users. You don't have to tell everyone in IT everything there is to know about Exchange. But be sure to talk to them about both server and client basics from a more technical perspective.

Summary

Designing a new Exchange system is neither easy nor fast. You must complete several steps and then track back to ensure that you've taken each step's impact on other steps into account. Moving through this iterative process while covering each of the steps in painstaking detail ensures that your Exchange system will function pretty much as expected from the get-go and that costly redesign is kept to a minimum.

One of the most important steps is the allocation of responsibility for very specific stages of the design and implementation process. This should be the first step in the design process. It ensures that the right people with the right skills and knowledge are in place and that they are clearly in charge of and must account for their particular piece of the design puzzle.

Needs assessments are another key to effective Exchange system design. You must perform assessments of user need, the geographic distribution of your organization and its computing and networking resources, and your data network. Needs assessments focus not only on what new resources and ideas are required, but also on what can be preserved.

Exchange Server 2007 is a network-dependent, network-intensive system. You need to establish a consistent set of conventions for naming your Exchange organization, administrative groups, servers, and recipients. You must choose a Windows 2003 networking model that fits well with your organization's geographical distribution and business structures. You must define the boundaries of Exchange administrative groups, the administrative units you use in your Exchange organization. As with domain models, geographic distribution and business structures might be key to setting these boundaries. If required, you must define boundaries for Exchange routing groups and determine how your routing groups will communicate across wide area networks.

Next, you must design your Exchange servers, paying attention to performance, storage capacity, reliability, backup, and networking users. When you've designed your Exchange Server environment, you must deal with connecting your servers to other messaging systems, both public and private. Here you must select from among available Exchange connectors and gateways. As your Exchange network becomes a reality, you must ensure, through exhaustive testing, that everything works as planned and up to whatever performance, reliability, and other standards you must adhere to.

Finally, you need to develop a plan for rolling out your Exchange system when everything is ready and has been tested. You shouldn't expect everything to be perfect on first rollout. However, if you've adhered to the design steps laid out in this chapter, your rollout experience should be a fairly pleasant one.

In the next chapter, we will talk about Exchange Server 2007 installations and then in the following chapter we will talk about upgrading from Exchange Server 2000/2003 to Exchange Server 2007. Even if you don't need to do an upgrade, we encourage you to read the next chapter. Thinking through the upgrade process will help you better understand the inner workings of Windows Server 2003 and Exchange Server 2007.

Part 2

Installing, Configuring, Migrating, and Scaling

In this section you will learn to:

◆ **Chapter 4: Installing Exchange Server 2007**

◆ **Chapter 5: Upgrading to Exchange Server 2007**

◆ **Chapter 6: Scaling Upward and Outward**

Chapter 4

Installing Exchange Server 2007

Now that you've had a chance to learn and absorb the theory behind the new Exchange 2007 architecture, you can get your hands dirty and get it installed in your organization. If you're familiar with Exchange 2003 or Exchange 2000, your first look at the Exchange 2007 installation process is going to be a mix of the familiar and the new.

The look of the graphic-mode installer has completely changed; not only is it easier to navigate, but it actually gives you useful progress indicators as it works through its many complicated tasks and actions. This improvement alone is pretty good, but the ability to perform a full installation from the command line, while never leaving text mode, turns "pretty good" into "great."

Installing an Exchange 2007 server involves the following steps:

1. Choose your Exchange 2007 roles.

2. Prepare your Windows server.

3. Perform the installation, using either the graphic- or text-mode setup options.

4. Run through the postinstallation checklists.

Listed out as a dry collection of steps, it sounds like a lot of work. It's actually pretty simple to do, and the new installation improvements allow you to automate a lot more of the work with a lot less effort than you could in previous versions of Exchange. Without further ado, let's get our hands dirty and get installing!

> **NOTE**
>
> As you read through this chapter, you'll see that it presumes you're installing a brand-new Exchange 2007 organization rather than upgrading from an existing Exchange 2003 or Exchange 2000 organization. If you're looking to upgrade, then you're going to want to read Chapter 5. Before you skip ahead, though, read through this chapter to master the mechanical steps of installing Exchange 2007. Chapter 5 won't cover them again but will instead focus on the specific issues you'll need to address in order to keep Exchange 2007 and your existing organization interoperating smoothly during your upgrade period.

Topics in this chapter include the following:

◆ Choosing roles

◆ Preparing your server

◆ Installing Exchange Server

◆ Performing postinstallation tasks

Step 0, or Before All Else. . .

Before we go any further, we'd like to introduce you to — or reacquaint you with — the single most important acronym you will ever encounter in the alphabet soup that IT professionals eat on a daily basis: RTFM, or Read The Fine Manual.

The improvements in Exchange 2007 don't just stop at the technical. Shortly after the Exchange 2003 release, the folks on the Exchange product team realized that a lot of their customers needed the kind of documentation that only the product team could deliver and have since done their best to step up to the plate to deliver thorough, usable content that actually answers the questions and solves the problems faced by people just like you. By now, they've gotten it down to a fine art; as a result, the Exchange 2007 documentation is more complete and realistic than the documentation for any previous version of Exchange.

Books such as this can help fill in the gaps and give you a good objective view of how to use Exchange 2007. Vendor documentation (whether from Microsoft or someone else) tends to make assumptions about your environment that may not be valid in order to push you toward the most recently adopted set of best practices that may not have had time to filter out into the real world but have proven their worth, and it may gloss over the pain points you're likely to hit even if you're following all of the official deployment advice. We, on the other hand, can tell you where those hidden assumptions are and how not meeting them will affect you, explain the operations of Exchange so that you can judge whether a new best practice actually makes sense in your environment, and highlight where you're going to hit trouble even when you're doing everything right.

That said, the product documentation is still an invaluable reference that should be a core part of your Exchange toolkit. Best of all, the documentation is freely downloadable from the Microsoft website, and the installer gives you links directly to the applicable downloads, which Microsoft updates on a regular basis.

We recommend that you download the Exchange documentation, browse through it, and see what kind of material it covers. Note any topics that seem especially pertinent to your organization or to issues you think are likely to be a problem for you. Read through the sections that cover those topics and see whether they make sense; if they don't, put them aside for later. There will come a day when you will read back through those sections and suddenly realize that you understand what they are saying.

Are you back with us now? Great! It's time to sit down at (or connect to) your server and get busy installing Exchange 2007.

WARNING

Even if you've decided you don't need to read the rest of the documentation, we urge you to at least read the single most critical piece of documentation: the release notes. You'll find them as a single HTML file in the installer directory, and if Microsoft follows the same practice they used during the Exchange 2007 beta period, it will give you the location from which you can download the most current version of the release notes. These are required reading, as they'll tell you about any last-minute issues, workarounds, and bugs that may impact your deployment.

Choosing Roles

Before you can reasonably expect to install Exchange 2007 on a server, you need to know what that server is going to be used for. As you remember from the section "Server Roles Overview" in Chapter 2, Exchange 2007 no longer installs the same set of binaries and services to every Exchange server (requiring you to then remove and shut down unnecessary features and services). Instead, it defines five separate roles: Edge Transport, Hub Transport, Client Access, Mailbox, and Unified Messaging.

Some of these roles are required in your organization, while others are optional. Others are required depending on how you plan to place your servers. Some roles can be colocated on the same physical server, while others must be stand-alone. You must factor a number of program dependencies, deployment best practices, and economic-driven compromises into your Exchange 2007 design. It can be overwhelming to untangle this web on your own.

Instead of leaving you to guess, we offer the following discussions to help you determine which roles you need and where you need to place them. Although we can't account for every factor, we can help you sort out the ones that are driven by Exchange 2007 requirements and which ones are under your control.

> **NOTE**
>
> One of the key factors in determining which roles can be colocated, how many servers you need with a given role, and where to locate those servers is how many users you plan to support. Unfortunately, as this book is being written, we don't yet have a lot of published real-world sizing data. This is the kind of information that is likely to be showing up on the Microsoft Exchange 2007 website in the months following the release of Exchange 2007.

Edge Transport

If you're looking at using the Edge Transport role, you have a pretty easy deployment decision: it must be installed on its own physical server and cannot be colocated with any other role. Contrary to rumors already floating around the Microsoft technical community, you will not be able to colocate the Edge Transport role and Microsoft ISA Server 2006 on the same physical server using the release to manufacturing (RTM) versions of Exchange 2007 and ISA 2006 — at least not without pulling weird tricks using virtual servers, which would be less than secure and possibly take you outside the boundaries of Microsoft-supported configuration.

> **NOTE**
>
> Why can't you install the Edge Transport role and ISA 2006 on the same server? Very simply, ISA 2006 cannot be installed on any 64-bit version of Windows Server — and if you remember, you can only run your production Exchange 2007 servers on x64 Windows Server 2003 or later. Microsoft may address this problem in future service packs, but at least for now, this is how it is.

WARNING

And don't try to fudge it by using the 32-bit version of Exchange 2007 on your Edge Transport server. That violates the licensing restrictions for Exchange and could end up costing you far more than buying a separate machine for ISA 2006 would. If that's not enough to dissuade you, the 32-bit version is a 180-day trial version; you'd have to rebuild your Edge Transport servers every six months. You also lose the automatic anti-spam definition updates (which aren't provided to 32-bit machines).

The real question is do you need to deploy the Edge Transport role? The answer is simple: you are not required to have an Edge Transport server in your organization in order to successfully use Exchange 2007, although it offers a lot of advantages that the alternatives don't. Remember that the Edge Transport role is specifically designed to be installed in your perimeter network, with no requirements for connectivity to Active Directory. In fact, Microsoft strongly recommends that you not join your Edge Transport servers to the same Active Directory forest (or forests, in a multiforest organization) that your internal Exchange servers are joined to. You can join the Edge Transport server to a management forest in your perimeter network or leave it as a stand-alone workgroup member and still get all of the new functionality without compromising your inner network security or driving your firewall administrator mad. The new Edge Subscription feature allows your Edge Transport servers to still receive all of the necessary updates they need to fully protect your organization.

TIP

The term *perimeter network* is Microsoft's preferred terminology for the network concept of the *DMZ*: a separate network segment that allows you to provide a degree of isolation between your protected internal servers and your servers (such as web servers or mail gateways) that need to accept incoming connections from untrusted hosts on the Internet. The two terms mean the same thing, but Microsoft is phasing out the use of DMZ in their documentation.

With legacy versions of Exchange, if you placed them directly in your perimeter network, you'd find that you had stepped directly into a nightmare of firewall configuration. Prior to 2007, all Exchange 2000 and 2003 servers were required to be full member servers in an Active Directory forest; in order to get them to work correctly in the perimeter, you had to poke so many holes in the firewall for the various protocols that you ended up with no real increase in protection. While this was the recommended deployment for Exchange 2000 front-end servers for a time, Microsoft eventually solved this problem by using ISA Server in the perimeter.

With the Edge Transport role, Exchange 2007 solves this problem the same way that it's solved by other edge mail router solutions, such as specialized messaging appliances or software mail applications such as Postfix, Sendmail, and Exim: place the Edge Transport server in the perimeter network without requiring it to have full access to Active Directory on the interior network. Like these other solutions, Edge is designed to do two things:

◆ Route SMTP traffic between your trusted Exchange servers and untrusted Internet hosts, using a best-practice perimeter network placement with full integration into your Exchange organization.

◆ Provide a "safe" platform for performing message hygiene functions (anti-spam, antivirus, and other forms of content inspection) in the perimeter network before your full Exchange servers (and Windows domain controllers) have to handle the extra load caused by unwanted message traffic. It also sanitizes messages going out from your organization to the Internet so that you're not contributing pollution to the Internet.

An Edge server's main advantage is that it offers most, if not all, of the same message hygiene features you can find on other solutions — if not out-of-the-box, then at least via add-ins that you can purchase or download from third-party vendors (or even develop yourself). And it does this while offering an unparalleled level of integration with your Exchange organization:

◆ Although the Edge server should never be joined to the same Active Directory forest as your Exchange org, it can be joined to a separate management forest in your perimeter network if your perimeter is large enough to incur the overhead of an additional Active Directory deployment to secure and manage.

◆ The Edge Transport role requires a Hub Transport instance in your organization, both for SMTP routing and optionally for Edge Subscription configuration. This really isn't a problem because you have to have at least one Hub Transport instances, but it may affect placement of your Hub Transport instances and Edge Transport servers to ensure good network connectivity between them.

◆ Using the Edge Subscription feature, your Hub Transport instances can be easily configured to automatically update your Edge Transport servers with the specific subset of information they need to effectively process incoming mail. Since this is a push process from Hub Transport instances to your Edge Transport servers, you don't need to open additional holes in your firewall (unlike mail router solutions that offer Exchange "integration" through LDAP lookups back into your domain controllers). Even though this step is not done as part of the install, you should consider it to be a required deployment step because you lose a lot of functionality (including the ability to manage your entire organization from inside the firewall) by not doing it.

◆ The Edge Transport server can be managed from within your organization using the Exchange Management Shell and the Exchange Management Console, just as you manage any other Exchange server. Again, this simplifies management and makes it easier to script bulk operations (although many of the common types of activities you might want to script are already automatically updated using Edge Subscriptions).

◆ An Edge Transport server comes with a host of existing anti-spam components out of the box. While some of these components can also be deployed on a Hub Transport instance, many can't. See Chapter 18, "Delivering E-mail," for more details.

◆ An Edge Transport server easily integrates with the Microsoft Forefront Security for Exchange Server, a multi-engine malware scanner developed from the Antigen line of products that Microsoft acquired from Sybari.

◆ The Exchange 2007 organization can collect some of the per-user settings from user mailboxes, such as blocked and allowed sender lists, and propagate them out to the Edge Transport server. This allows the Edge Transport server to intelligently accept and deny incoming messages based on who they're addressed to without requiring any additional work from the users or the Exchange administrators — a feature we've seen in no other message gateway solution.

> **TIP**
>
> Do remember that the Edge Transport role is designed only for SMTP traffic. It does not handle any other protocols, such as client access protocols like HTTP, POP3, IMAP, or MAPI. The Edge Transport role is purely for SMTP connections between your organization and mail servers out on the Internet.

Client Access

If you only ever plan to have MAPI users connect to your Exchange mailboxes, then you don't need to have a Client Access server in your Exchange organization.

> **TIP**
>
> The Microsoft documentation refers to the Client Access role by the abbreviation CAS. How come the abbreviation for the Client Access role isn't CA? Easy; that acronym is already used to signify *certificate authority*, a key component of a public key infrastructure. If you're using SSL or S/MIME, then you already deal with certificate authorities. Since it's common to deal with digital certificates and certificate authorities when configuring and managing Client Access servers, Microsoft wisely avoided potential confusion by not reusing the acronym.

These days, it's the rare organization that offers only MAPI access to mailboxes. While Outlook is the only full MAPI client that accesses Exchange mailboxes using MAPI Remote Procedure Calls (RPCs) protocol, it's not convenient or possible to use Outlook all the time:

◆ Microsoft's Entourage client for Mac OS X uses WebDAV (HTTP/HTTPS), as does Novell's Evolution client for Linux.

◆ Almost all other mail clients offer at least IMAP, POP3, or HTTP/HTTPS. Some of the more common ones out there are Apple Mail, Eudora, Mozilla Thunderbird; there are a vast number of others in use. Some clients will also offer NNTP access to Exchange public folders.

◆ Outlook Anywhere (the new name for RPC over HTTPS) uses HTTP or HTTPS.

◆ Exchange ActiveSync uses HTTP/HTTPS.

◆ Of course, Outlook Web Access uses HTTP/HTTPS.

> **WARNING**
>
> Exchange 2007 no longer offers Network News Transport Protocol (NNTP) access, even if you implement public folders. You must use an Exchange 2000 or 2003 server in your organization to provide NNTP support if you wish to continue offering it. NNTP access is outside the scope of this book.

Clearly, if you have any need to offer HTTP, IMAP, or POP3 access to your users, you're going to need the Client Access role in your organization. Lest you be tempted to think of it as "just" a renamed front-end Exchange server, remember that the Client Access role does not offer the capability to handle SMTP. In the Exchange 2003 world, a front-end server still had the SMTP service running by default and would frequently be used as an SMTP bridgehead as well as a front-end server, to the point that many people became confused as to what exactly a front-end server was supposed to do! With Exchange 2007, the separation is very real: the Client Access role handles client access protocols, the Hub Transport role handles SMTP. If you need to put these roles onto separate machines, you can; if you need to combine them, you can.

Now you just need to know how many Client Access servers you need and where you need to locate them. At a minimum, keep the following rules of thumb in mind:

◆ You need at least one Client Access role in every site and domain in which you have Exchange Mailbox servers.

◆ The Client Access role needs to have good network connectivity (good available bandwidth and low latency, usually a 100Mbps Ethernet connection or better) with the Mailbox servers it serves.

◆ The Client Access role is required to allow any HTTP access to mailboxes, whether from internal clients or from outside of your organization.

◆ You may wish to have one set of Client Access servers deal with external connections and another service internal clients. The POP3 and IMAP protocols allow mailbox access only; they do not provide any way for the client to submit messages back to the server. These clients must use SMTP. As a result, you may wish to colocate the Client Access and Hub Transport roles onto servers you use to handle external client access.

TIP

Although you might think you can place the Client Access role in your perimeter network to deal with traffic coming from the Internet, suddenly you're back in the middle of the firewall configuration nightmare of trying to keep a member server in the perimeter. Instead, you should keep the Client Access role in your protected network and place an ISA 2006 server (or a Blue Coat appliance, a Linux Squid proxy server, or some other equivalent reverse proxy solution) in the perimeter to accept outside connections. Your firewall administrators will thank you. Also remember that with Exchange 2007, Microsoft does not support placing Client Access role in the perimeter network. Getting this configuration to work securely means not only that you have a lot of extra work to do to secure your servers and connections, but also that you are risking going without full Microsoft product support when problems develop.

Hub Transport

Since all messages in an Exchange organization must travel through a server running the Hub Transport role you must have at least one Hub Transport role in your organization. That's the easy part. Unless you have a small organization, though, you may want to have more than one Hub Transport role to remove the single point of weakness.

> **NOTE**
>
> If you think it's inefficient for Exchange 2007 to require all messages to be handled by the Hub Transport role, you need to consider the growing role of regulatory and policy compliance. This new architecture allows Exchange to easily inspect every single message and apply policies uniformly. See Chapter 13, "Managing Messages in Transit," for more details on the new transport rule and policy features.

Depending on the level of traffic that your Mailbox servers and network have to deal with, you may want to colocate your Hub Transport and Mailbox roles on the same physical servers. Then again, you may want to have multiple Mailbox servers in each site, with only a pair of Hub Transport servers to provide the necessary message routing for the site. Regardless of where the roles are located, the Hub Transport and Mailbox roles communicate using MAPI RPCs.

As long as you meet the necessary minimum placement guidelines and take care to provide enough Hub Transport capacity close enough to your Mailbox servers to keep message traffic from getting caught in bottlenecks, you have an amazing degree of flexibility in how you actually deploy Hub Transport roles. Exchange 2007 servers running the Mailbox role will automatically discover the Hub Transport roles in your organization and attempt to use the ones in the same Active Directory site. If there are multiple Hub Transport instances in the site, the Mailbox servers will intelligently load-balance traffic between them without any extra effort on your part. If one of your Hub Transport instances becomes inaccessible, the Mailbox servers will automatically switch to another Hub Transport instances.

When deciding which physical servers to place the Hub Transport role on, keep in mind the following conditions:

◆ You need at least one Hub Transport role in every site and domain in which you have the Mailbox role. Servers running the Mailbox role can only connect to Hub Transport roles in the same site. If all of the Hub Transport instances in a site go down, Mailbox servers in that site will not be able to fail over to using a Hub Transport role in a neighboring site and all message traffic in the affected site will come to a grinding halt.

◆ If you colocate the Hub Transport role with the Mailbox role, that Mailbox instance will always try to use the local Hub Transport instance before talking to other Hub Transport instances in the site. This breaks the natural load-balancing behavior we mentioned previously and is a good reason to separate the Hub Transport and Mailbox roles in larger organizations or sites. Remember that you can't put the Hub Transport role on a cluster, so if you're going to deploy clustered Mailbox servers, you have to put the Hub Transport role on a separate server.

◆ The Hub Transport role needs to have good network connectivity (good available bandwidth and low latency, usually a 100Mbps Ethernet connection or better) with the Mailbox instances it serves.

◆ At least one Hub Transport instance is required to allow any SMTP access to your organization, whether from non-Exchange mail machines inside of your organization, from Edge Transport servers, or from some other mail routing solution that brings external mail into your organization.

◆ The Edge Transport role requires a Hub Transport instance in your organization, both for SMTP routing and optionally for Edge Subscription configuration. This really isn't a problem because you have to have at least one Hub Transport instances, but it may affect placement of your Hub Transport instances and Edge Transport servers to ensure good network connectivity between them.

◆ You may wish to have one set of Hub Transport instances to handle external connections and another to service internal clients. The POP3 and IMAP protocols allow mailbox access only; they do not provide any way for the client to submit messages back to the server. These clients must use SMTP. As a result, you may wish to colocate the Client Access and Hub Transport roles onto servers you use to handle external client access.

TIP

If you're thinking about putting a Hub Transport instance in your perimeter network, don't. As with the Client Access role, you will go through a lot of effort to make it work, complicate your firewall configuration, and end up with an unsupported Exchange configuration. Use the Edge Transport role (recommended) or some other mail gateway solution instead.

Mailbox

Strictly speaking, you aren't required to have a single Mailbox server role in your organization. Of course, the resulting organization can have no mailboxes and is pretty darn pointless. Mailbox servers are the heart and soul of Exchange; as a result, you will probably spend more time installing and configuring the Mailbox role than any other.

Users have come to depend on the ubiquitous and near-instantaneous transmission of e-mail. Ten years ago, it was not uncommon to send an e-mail and know that it would be 10 to 15 minutes at a minimum before it was spooled off of the local mail server and head out to the recipient. Today, that kind of delay is considered to be unacceptable unless there are special concerns regarding limited bandwidth or Internet connectivity. Even then, these types of concerns are considered the exception to the rule rather than the norm.

Modern e-mail users will start calling the help desk, or badgering the mail administrators, if they aren't receiving a steady stream of mail throughout the day. Imagine for a moment the reaction these same users are likely to have if they cannot access their Mailbox server. Cached copies of their mailbox in Outlook aren't going to cut it; they're going to riot. It's not surprising, therefore, that a lot of money and time is spent ensuring the high availability of Mailbox servers. Since Outlook MAPI clients connect directly to the user's Mailbox server, the user can be the first to know if something's not right on the server.

In Exchange 2007, Microsoft tries to provide for high levels of availability for all of the server roles. The Mailbox role, however, is the only one that offers options for traditional clustering solutions, now called Single Copy Clusters (SCCs). It also offers two new availability options: Clustered Continuous Replication (CCR) and local Continuous Replication (LCR). These availability options are designed to keep the mailbox data available even if the server hardware fails and are explained in more detail in Chapter 15, "Reliability and Availability 101." Because traditional clustering is only supported on the Mailbox role, you cannot colocate other roles on a clustered Mailbox server.

It should not be a surprise that the Mailbox server role storage requirements are potentially far more enormous than for the other roles. As a result, the disk configuration for your Mailbox instances is far more important than for any other role. Exchange 2000 and Exchange 2003 lived and died around their disk I/O requirements; Exchange 2007 still requires you to carefully plan, design, and test your disk subsystem, even with the I/O performance improvements provided by the 64-bit architecture.

When designing your Mailbox servers roles, here are the relevant guidelines to keep in mind:

◆ All other factors being equal, the closer your users are to their Mailbox servers, the better. This is not to downplay the impact of Outlook cached mode and server consolidation, however, because most of the time not all other factors are equal.

◆ Those other factors include but by no means are limited to the following: the overhead cost of the server hardware, the level of hardware redundancy (the failure of a single power supply or disk controller can really ruin your day), the per-server power consumption, the server room's cooling capacity, the cost of disks, the effects on backup and restore policies and SLAs, the cost of training and maintaining administrative personnel, the cost of software licensing, and the physical shelving and racking requirements.

◆ If you're planning on doing single copy clustering, your Mailbox server hardware must be on Microsoft's Cluster Hardware Compatibility List. If you're going to do clustered contin-uous replication, however, your hardware only has to be on the Windows Hardware Compatibility List, which can be significantly cheaper.

◆ The Hub Transport role needs to have good network connectivity (good available band-width and low latency, usually a 100Mbps Ethernet connection or better) with the Mailbox instances it serves.

◆ If you colocate the Hub Transport role with the Mailbox server role, that Mailbox role instance will always try to use the local Hub Transport instance before talking to other Hub Transport instances in the site. This breaks the natural load-balancing behavior we men-tioned previously and is a good reason to separate the Hub Transport and Mailbox server roles in larger organizations or sites. Remember that you can't put the Hub Transport server role on a cluster, so if you're going to deploy clustered Mailbox servers, you have to put the Hub Transport role on a separate server.

◆ The Mailbox role no longer uses the SMTP protocol to communicate with other Exchange servers in the organization. They use RPC to communicate with other roles in their site; all communications with servers in other sites take place through intermediary Hub Transport instances.

Unified Messaging

We're not going to spend a lot of time talking about the Unified Messaging role because it requires an advanced set of equipment and skills to properly implement. If you're planning to deploy this role in your organization, you will require the services of experienced telephony personnel, whether in-house or contractors.

We've heard Microsoft personnel say that you can colocate the Unified Messaging role on the same physical server as other roles as long as your organization is very small and there is plenty of extra capacity on your server. The catch is, though, determining what they mean by "very small." We have seen no specific guidance for determining how to size a Unified Messaging server and how to tell when it can safely coexist with some other server roles.

> **TIP**
>
> Unless you are hosting a handful of users — no more than 30 — on a single Exchange 2007 server that is running other roles, we highly recommend that you consider buying a separate server to use for Unified Messaging. If e-mail is mission critical, voicemail is often as critical or more so. The cost of buying separate hardware and software licenses will more than pay for itself in the trouble you save by not having your single server overloaded on a constant basis, dropping both e-mail and voicemails. If you can't afford that cost, you probably need to rethink whether your organization will truly derive any real benefit from the features the Unified Messaging role provides.

Management Tools

There is a not-so-hidden sixth role in Exchange 2007: the management tools role, consisting of the Exchange Management Shell (EMS) and the Exchange Management Console (EMC). This role is the sole exception to the "no 32-bit Exchange 2007 on your production network" rule. You are allowed to install the 32-bit version of the Exchange management tools on your administrative workstation if you're still running 32-bit version Windows XP. In fact, Microsoft has provided the 32-bit version of the Exchange 2007 management tools as a separate download from their website.

Recommended Order of Installation

Now that you've decided which roles you're installing on your servers, which order are you going to install them in? If you're deploying a combined function server, you don't have to answer this question. When you have multiple physical servers, though, you need to figure out in what order you're going to deploy them. Which servers you deploy first is determined by what roles they have installed. The official Microsoft-recommended order is as follows:

1. Directory preparation
2. Edge Transport (optional)
3. Client Access
4. Hub Transport
5. Mailbox
6. Unified Messaging (optional)

> **TIP**
>
> Remember that *before* is a relative term; if you're combining the Client Access, Hub Transport, and Mailbox roles on one server, you're following the outlined order, even if it's the first Exchange server in the organization.

We'll be honest — we think this list is good, but we're convinced that it's aimed at the organization upgrading from Exchange 2003 or 2000 to Exchange 2007. We really don't think it's the right fit for someone who is installing a brand-new Exchange 2007 organization; we recommend holding off on your Edge installation at least until after you've got an HT server in place, and possibly after you've got Mailbox servers up and running.

Why would we think that? There are a several reasons:

◆ The first is aesthetics. Microsoft's order works from the outside layers of an organization into the crunchy nougat center. Our preferred order of deployment for just about any software is to first establish the core functionality (in this case, the ability for your users to e-mail each other within your organization) and then go after the extras like Outlook Web Access ActiveSync, Unified Messaging, and Edge Transport.

◆ If you recall, the Edge Transport role requires a Hub Transport role to talk to, both for SMTP and for the Edge Subscription feature to allow centralized provisioning and configuration. You don't need to configure Edge Subscription, but then you lose nice functionality such as recipient filtering and per-user blocked/allowed sender lists — and you have to manage your Edge Transport server manually. Given our preferences, we'd rather install the Edge Transport server and be able to immediately configure the Edge Subscription as opposed to have to come back to it later.

◆ Finally, we tend to think that anyone who is installing Windows Server 2007 from scratch (as opposed to upgrading from a previous version of Exchange) is probably migrating from some other messaging system, whatever it may be. Sure, there are going to be new companies just getting started or existing companies transitioning from hosted e-mail scenarios, but the bulk of these "new" installations are already going to have an existing e-mail service. These companies probably already have some sort of messaging gateway in place, and unless that's the major pain point driving their migration to Exchange 2007, they probably want to concentrate on getting users shifted over rather than fiddling with an Edge Transport server. Their existing spam appliance or Linux mail gateway is doing a fine enough job for the time being.

There's nothing wrong with Microsoft's recommended order of installation, and you won't be doing a bad thing by following it. Just be aware that it is a recommendation, not a rule; the installer won't refuse to install the HT role until it detects a CAS in the org. If you have a good reason for altering the order to meet the needs of your organization, then by all means do it.

TIP

The only two guidelines that we hesitate to recommend violating are these: install a Hub Transport instance in the site before you install your Mailbox instances, and wait to install the Unified Messaging role until everything else is installed and mostly working. You won't be able to test mail flow without a working Hub Transport instance in the site, and Unified Messaging is complicated enough to be worth giving it all your attention.

Preparing the Windows Server

Before you actually install Exchange 2007 on your server, you have to make sure the chosen server is ready. We already covered the hardware and software requirements in previous chapters, but we'll quickly recap them here with an emphasis on the practical tasks ahead of you.

You'll need to consider the following aspects of your server before beginning the installation process:

- ◆ Operating system requirements
- ◆ Memory configuration
- ◆ Disk configuration
- ◆ Exchange prerequisites

Let's examine these in more detail.

Windows Requirements

The following Windows operating system requirements must be met before beginning Exchange 2007 installation:

- ◆ Ensure that the version of the operating system matches your intended use:
  - ◆ Production servers: Windows Server 2003 x64 Standard or Enterprise with SP1 applied, or Windows Server 2003 R2 x64 Standard or Enterprise. You can't use Web Edition or Datacenter Edition.
  - ◆ Test lab and training servers, including those in a virtual machine: Windows Server 2003 Standard or Enterprise with SP1 applied, or Windows Server 2003 R2 Standard or Enterprise. You can use either the x86 or x64 versions for test and training.
  - ◆ Clustered Mailbox servers: Windows Server 2003 x64 Enterprise with SP1 applied, or Windows Server 2003 R2 x64 Enterprise.
  - ◆ Management workstations: Windows XP Professional with SP2 applied, or Windows Vista. You can use either the x86 or x64 versions.
  - ◆ Exchange 2007 will coexist with the Multilingual User Interface Pack (MUI) installed on Windows Server 2003.

WARNING

If you are installing your test or training servers into a Microsoft virtual environment, remember that Microsoft Virtual PC and Microsoft Virtual Server only support 32-bit guest servers. This is scheduled to change sometime in the Longhorn timeframe when Microsoft makes its hypervisor technology available to support 64-bit guest servers.

WARNING

Exchange 2007 cannot be installed on Itanium processor-based systems. You also cannot install it on the Web or Datacenter Editions of Windows Server 2003 regardless of the platform.

NOTE

Microsoft has said it will support Exchange 2007 on Longhorn Server in the Exchange 2007 SP1 timeframe. It will provide detailed compatibility information at that time, so be sure to check the release notes when SP1 is released.

◆ Ensure that you have the correct components installed:

   ◆ You have installed the proper version of the Microsoft.NET Framework 2.0 for your operating system.

   ◆ If this server is hosting a CAS, you the have IIS World Wide Web Service and ASP.NET components installed. You do not need any IIS components otherwise.

> **WARNING**
>
> Unlike legacy versions of Exchange, the IIS NNTP and SMTP components are not required for Exchange 2007 and must not be installed.

◆ Ensure that any other applications running on the server are meant for the same platform. Do not mix 32-bit and 64-bit applications on production Exchange 2007 servers; use only 64-bit add-ons and plug-ins. Remove unnecessary software.

◆ It is recommended that you at least disable any server-level antivirus software on the server. We recommend that you remove it entirely; it competes with Exchange for memory and CPU, slows down disk access, and provides questionable value. If you must have antivirus software on the server, make sure it is configured to ignore all directories that Exchange uses — the binary install directory tree, transaction logs, mailbox databases, and queue databases.

◆ Disable any anti-spyware or anti-malware software you may have running, such as Windows Defender.

◆ Ensure that the server is joined to the proper domain.

◆ Verify that your network configuration is correct, that you can resolve DNS without any issues, and that you have no problems with your Active Directory connectivity. We recommend using the netdiag and dcdiag utilities in the Windows Server 2003 SP1 Support Tools, which can be downloaded from Microsoft Downloads.

◆ If you are using the ISA Firewall Client in your environment, ensure that it is properly configured and can detect and authenticate to the proper ISA server array.

◆ Ensure that you have run Windows Update or Microsoft Update and have downloaded all recommended and critical patches for your system.

Memory Configuration

The following memory configuration considerations should be addressed before beginning Exchange 2007 installation:

◆ The nice thing about running 64-bit Windows is that you don't have to worry about inserting arcane switches into your boot.ini configuration file.

◆ Ensure that you have the proper amount of RAM for your server's intended use and load. For Mailbox servers, the current sizing guideline is to have 2GB base memory plus an additional 5MB per mailbox. This ensures that you will have enough memory to cache the most frequently accessed items for all users on the server and get the full benefit of the switch to 64 bits.

Disk Configuration

The following disk configuration considerations should be addressed before beginning Exchange 2007 installation:

◆ All disk volumes used for Exchange must be NTFS formatted. No exceptions!

◆ Ensure that you have enough free disk space:

  ◆ The system volume requires 200MB. This is above and beyond any necessary space for logs and program files (if you install Exchange on the system volume).

  ◆ The system volume should allow Windows to create a page file that can hold a memory dump. This is the amount of physical RAM plus 100MB.

  ◆ The disk volume you install Exchange on requires at least 1.2GB for the binaries.

  ◆ If this server will hold the Unified Messaging role, allocate +500MB for each Unified Messaging language pack that will be installed.

◆ Transaction log files should be on a separate set of physical disks (spindles) from their corresponding Exchange database files.

◆ Allow for at least 7 to 10 days of transaction logs per storage group. One rule of thumb is 5GB of logs per day per 1,000 mailboxes.

◆ Allow for at least 10 to 15 percent white space estimates in the maximum size of each of your database files.

◆ Allow for 10 to 15 percent deleted item and deleted mailbox retention space in each mailbox database.

◆ Local continuous replication replica databases and transaction logs should be on separate physical disks from the originals.

◆ Leave sufficient free space on database disks to make an extra copy of your largest database without running out of space, such as when you're performing backups, recovering from backups, or performing troubleshooting and offline maintenance. One rule of thumb is 110 percent of the largest database you will support.

◆ Plan for full-text indexing to use approximately 25 percent of the total size of the mailbox database.

◆ Faster disks are always better than slower disks. The performance delta between 7,200RPM disks and 15,000RPM disks isn't even worth writing about.

◆ Try to use more reliable server-oriented disk technologies for your direct-attached storage, such as SAS and UltraSCSI over SATA or EIDE.

◆ Cap your maximum individual mailbox database size to allow you to backup and restore each database within the time limit specified by your service level agreement (SLA).

◆ Unlike with Exchange 2003, plan on creating one mailbox database per storage group. This improves your caching and gives you a separate set of transaction logs for each database, which means each database can truly be backed up (and restored) independently of the rest. We recommend that you create additional databases in a storage group only when you've used up all of your available storage groups. Note, however, that this will increase the number of spindles you require to maintain proper I/O and offset the savings you gain from Exchange 2007's architecture.

> **NOTE**
>
> Keep in mind the number of databases and storage groups you can have for your edition of Exchange 2007. Standard Edition restricts you to a maximum of five storage groups or databases, while Enterprise Edition gives you up to 50. So in Standard Edition, you could have a single storage group with five databases, two storage groups with some combination of five databases between them, or (best) five separate storage groups each with a single database

Exchange Prerequisites

Now that you've got the server issues out of the way, it's time to take care of the specific prerequisites that Exchange requires. If you fire up the Exchange 2007 graphic-mode installer (see the section "Graphic Installer" later in this chapter), the Setup splash page will show you the prerequisites and give you links to download them if you don't have them on your system already.

MMC UPDATE

Exchange 2007 requires the Microsoft Management Console version 3.0. This version of the MMC provides a lot of the new graphical look and feel of the EMC, but it's required because it allows Microsoft to create MMC snap-ins using managed languages in the .NET Framework.

POWERSHELL UPDATE

You will also need to install the released to manufacturing (RTM) version of the Windows Power-Shell 1.0. This is a separate product not only used by Exchange and other forthcoming applications, but also available as a stand-alone download for system administrators. Because of this, Microsoft may release minor version number updates to PowerShell. PowerShell requires the Microsoft .NET Framework 2.0, which you may have already installed. PowerShell is the basis of not only the EMS and EMC, but also the Exchange 2007 Setup utility.

WARNING

It's a good general rule to resist the temptation to upgrade PowerShell on your Exchange servers (to get the benefits of these future upgrades) unless the release notes specifically say it is compatible with your deployed version of Exchange 2007, or unless you are instructed to upgrade by a future Exchange 2007 update. PowerShell is completely entwined with Exchange 2007 and an untested upgrade could break not only Exchange Server, but the Exchange installer as well.

Installing Exchange

The time has come. You get to install Exchange 2007. But now you have to decide: graphic mode or text mode?

Graphic Installer

Most Exchange administrators are used to GUI setup wizards, and the Exchange 2007 installer (imaginatively named `setup.exe`) will be familiar territory, even if it has received a face-lift. When you run `setup.exe` without any command-line switches, you automatically start the installer as shown in Figure 4.1.

FIGURE 4.1
The Exchange 2007 setup GUI

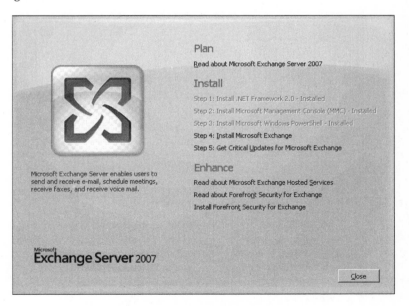

When you select the option to install Exchange, you will be taken into a typical setup process, including the display of the EULA. One thing you might notice is that the installer does not ask for a license key. When you install Exchange 2007, you have 30 days to enter a valid license key from EMS or the EMC.

You will next be asked whether you want a typical installation or a custom installation, as shown in Figure 4.2. The typical installation is suitable for a small, one-server Exchange organization; if you want to control which roles are placed on the server, you should select the custom installation.

FIGURE 4.2
Exchange 2007 setup
options

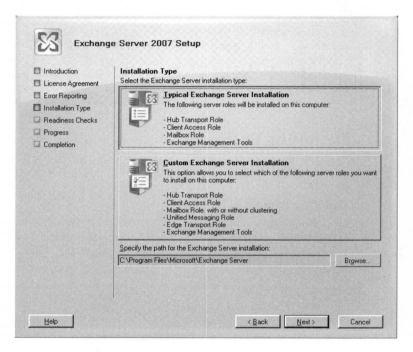

There's actually not a whole lot to customize: you are given a list of check boxes to select which roles you want to install, as show in Figure 4.3. Notice that some of them are mutually exclusive; if you check any role other than Edge Transport, the Edge Transport role will be grayed out and vice versa.

At this point, depending on what tasks you've already completed in your Exchange organization, you may be asked for further information:

◆ If this is the first Exchange server in the organization, you will be asked to provide the Exchange organization name.

◆ If an Exchange 2000/2003 organization is detected and this is the first Exchange 2007 Hub Transport instance, you will be asked to select which existing Exchange 2003 SMTP bridgehead to use as your legacy routing server. This creates the necessary routing group connectors to ensure connectivity with the Exchange 2003 servers, which are in separate administrative groups and routing groups.

◆ If this is the first Exchange 2007 Mailbox instance in the organization, you are asked if you want to support legacy Outlook clients. If you choose not to support Outlook 2003 and previous, Exchange will not install a public folder database on the Mailbox server.

FIGURE 4.3
Customizing the
installation

Finally, Exchange Setup will perform the various tasks to complete installation. If you have the necessary privileges and Setup does not detect the Exchange 2007 extensions to Active Directory, it will automatically perform the steps to configure Active Directory appropriately. Otherwise it will fail with an error and you will have to rerun the installation using an account with the proper privileges.

Setup keeps track of the status of its various tasks and provides a detailed report of its progress, as shown in Figure 4.4. Finally, it will complete the setup (assuming no errors are encountered) and give you the option of immediately launching the EMC.

Command-Line Installer

For the first time, Exchange administrators finally have a first-class text-mode installer than can be used to completely install an Exchange organization without ever once kicking off a GUI or wizard. In fact, no matter whether you use Setup in graphical or text mode, it will install over a special text-mode version of the installer Exsetup that you can later use to modify the configuration of the server (such as adding or removing roles).

FIGURE 4.4
A successful CAS
installation

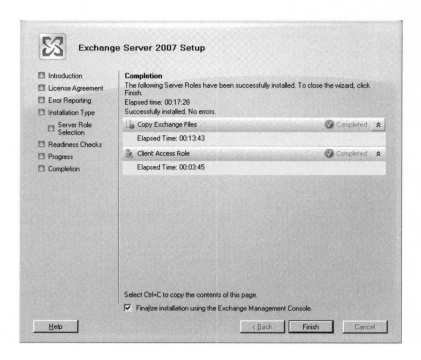

INSTALLING FOR THE FIRST TIME

When you initially install Exchange 2007 on a server, you need to run Setup from the directory where you have the installation media. Here's an example of how easy it is to install a new Mailbox server instance into an existing Exchange 2007 organization:

```
D:\>setup /m:install /r:mb

Welcome to Microsoft Exchange Server 2007 Unattended Setup

Preparing Exchange Setup

    Copying Setup Files
    ........................ COMPLETED

The following Server Roles will be installed
    Management Tools
    Mailbox Role

Performing Microsoft Exchange Server Prerequisite Check

    Mailbox Role Checks
    ........................ COMPLETED
```

```
Configuring Microsoft Exchange Server

    Copying Exchange Files
    ....................... COMPLETED

    Mailbox Role
    ....................... COMPLETED

The Microsoft Exchange Server setup operation completed
    successfully.
```

That was almost understandable, wasn't it? Now, start thinking about how convenient it would be to install 5 (or 10, or 20, or more) Exchange 2007 servers into your organization using this method.

We'll go into more detail about the various options and switches you can give to Setup in just a moment.

USING EXSETUP

In the previous examples, one of the tasks the Exchange installer performs is "copying Exchange files." Exchange is copying the necessary source files to the server's drive so that if you later decide you want to add a new role (or remove an existing one), you can do so from the local machine without requiring access to the installation media or a network share. Exchange also gives you a special copy of the installer, called Exsetup.exe.

Other than the name, Exsetup works just like Setup; the list of setup options we'll go into later work the same for both Setup and Exsetup.

By default, Exsetup is not placed in your PATH environment variable. It is located in the \bin subdirectory of the folder Exchange was installed to.

Since it is an executable, you can run it from the Start ➢ Run command, from cmd.exe, or from EMS. Here's an example of using Exsetup to remove all installed roles from a server:

```
C:\Program Files\Microsoft\Exchange Server\Bin>exsetup
    /mode:uninstall

Welcome to Microsoft Exchange Server 2007 Unattended Setup
The following Server Roles will be removed
    Hub Transport Role
    Mailbox Role
    Management Tools

Performing Microsoft Exchange Server Prerequisite Check

    Hub Transport Role Checks
    ....................... COMPLETED
    Mailbox Role Checks
    ....................... COMPLETED
```

```
Configuring Microsoft Exchange Server

  Hub Transport Server Role
  ........................ COMPLETED
  Mailbox Role
  ........................ COMPLETED
  Removing Exchange Files
  ........................ COMPLETED


The Microsoft Exchange Server setup operation completed
    successfully.
```

It's just as easy as installing!

SETUP OPTIONS

Both Setup and Exsetup look easy in the previous examples, but of course with an application as complicated as Exchange 2007, there are always a few wrinkles that may keep things from being as simple as we'd like. Let's take a closer look at the options available to us.

You can always see the complete set of Setup and Exsetup options by typing **setup /help** or **exsetup /help** at the command prompt.

Preparing Topology

The following parameters are used when manually preparing the organization for Exchange 2007:

◆ When installing Exchange 2007 into an existing Exchange 2000/2003 organization, this performs the necessary permissions for coexistence (see Chapter 5 for more details):

```
/PrepareLegacyExchangePermissions, /pl
```

◆ This option is a useful shortcut for single-domain forests; it prepares Active Directory for Exchange 2007 by performing the /PrepareSchema option on the forest and /PrepareDomain on the local domain:

```
/PrepareAD, /p
```

◆ The following extends the Active Directory schema in the forest with the necessary Exchange 2007 additions:

```
/PrepareSchema, /ps
```

◆ The following prepares the local domain for the Exchange 2007 by creating the necessary objects:

```
/PrepareDomain, /pd
```

◆ The following prepares the specified domain for the Exchange installation. This is useful for preparing specific domains in multidomain Active Directory forests when not all domain need to be prepared:

```
/PrepareDomain:<domain FQDN>, /pd:<domain FQDN>
```

◆ The following prepares all domains in the forest for the Exchange installation:

```
/PrepareAllDomains, /pad
```

Install and Uninstall

You've already seen examples of the install and uninstall modes. When you use these modes, the following switches are required. When multiple forms are listed, you can use any of them:

◆ The following specifies the operation to perform: install or uninstall. Install is the default option:

```
/mode, /m
```

◆ The following specifies which server roles to install or uninstall:

```
/roles, /role, /r
```

You can specify these roles or the abbreviations with the /role setup switch:

◆ HubTransport, HT, H

◆ ClientAccess, CA, C

◆ Mailbox, MB, M

◆ UnifiedMessaging, UM, U

◆ EdgeTransport, ET, E

◆ ManagementTools, MT, T

The following parameters are one-time options that are only required at specific points in the installation process:

◆ The following option prevents the Edge Transport Service from being started during setup on Hub Transport and Edge Transport instances:

```
/DoNotStartTransport
```

◆ The following specifies that legacy outlook clients can connect to the Exchange 2007 servers. This parameter can only be specified during the first Exchange 2007 Mailbox role installation to an organization (we'll talk more about this in Chapter 5):

```
/EnableLegacyOutlook
```

◆ When installing the first Hub Transport instance into an existing Exchange 2000/2003 organization, the following allows you to specify which existing SMTP bridgehead server to route messages to (we'll talk more about this in Chapter 5 and in Chapter 18, "Delivering E-mail"):

```
/LegacyRoutingServer
```

◆ If the organization has not already been created, you must use the following option to specify the name of the Exchange organization:

```
/OrganizationName, /on
```

The following advanced parameters provide extra control over specific role installs:

◆ The following tells Setup to configure the Edge AD/AM instance to use the specified port for LDAP connections:

```
/AdamLdapPort
```

◆ The following tells Setup to configure the Edge AD/AM instance to use the specified port for SSL connections:

```
/AdamSslPort
```

◆ This tells Setup to use a preprepared answer file that contains advanced parameters to be used. The format for the answer file is Key = Value (see the Setup help text for more details):

```
/AnswerFile /af
```

◆ We don't know why you'd want to use this, but if you want to disable error reporting, this is your option:

```
/DisableErrorReporting
```

◆ For the Client Access and Unified Messaging roles, this prevents Setup from creating self-signed certificates for SSL/TLS sessions. By default, Setup will only create these certificates if no other certificates are found (see Chapter 20 for more details):

```
/NoSelfSignedCertificates
```

Delegated Installation Options

Once your administrators have performed the topology preparation and initial installations, you may want to enable other personnel in your organization to perform additional server installs, even if they don't have the correct permissions to modify Active Directory. This is especially useful when you want to delegate the installation of branch office Exchange servers to support personnel but don't want to have to grant them domainwide permissions in Active Directory.

By using these options, you can pre-create and remove the necessary modifications for new servers in Active Directory, allowing personnel to perform the actual setup tasks:

◆ This option creates a placeholder server object so that a delegated server admin can run Exchange installation:

```
/NewProvisionedServer:<ServerName>, /nprs
```

◆ Use this option to remove the provisioned server object:

  `/RemoveProvisionedServer, /rprs`

◆ This option creates an additional set of the Exchange security groups in a separate forest:

  `/ForeignForestFQDN`

◆ This optional parameter permits the delegation of setup rights:

  `/ServerAdmin, /sa`

This parameter specifies the user or group that will be granted Server Administrator permissions. If you use this option, it can only be used with the `/NewProvisionedServer` switch.

Common Optional Parameters

The following parameters are optional and, in fact, can be used during almost every setup and Exsetup operation if desired:

◆ This option instructs Setup to use a specific DC for Active Directory reads and writes. You can specify the hostname in NetBIOS or FQDN format:

  `/DomainController, /dc`

◆ This option specifies the path to the Exchange 2007 source files, whether on a network share or distributed media:

  `/SourceDir, /s`

◆ Use this option to tell Setup where to install the Exchange Server 2007 files on the local hard drive (by default, this location is `%programfiles%\Microsoft\Exchange Server`):

  `/TargetDir, /t`

◆ Exchange updates stored in the directory specified by this option will be installed during setup:

  `/UpdatesDir, /u`

Recovering a Server

Setup and Exsetup provide a special mode to assist in the disaster recovery of an existing Exchange server. Using the *RecoverServer* mode, Setup will pull the server's configuration information from Active Directory rather than creating it as a new server. See Chapter 15 for more information.

Cluster

When you're creating clustered Mailbox servers, things are a bit different. Setup and Exsetup provide additional switches to add and remove clustered Mailbox server instances. You would use these options when working with Mailbox servers that are using the Microsoft Clustering Service, which needs be installed and configured before you install Exchange. See Chapter 15 for more details on using these setup options.

UM Language Packs

If the Unified Messaging role is installed on the server, you can use the following switches to add and remove Unified Messaging language packs:

◆ This switch adds the language packs for the specified cultures:

```
/AddUmLanguagePack
```

◆ This option removes the installed language packs:

```
/RemoveUmLanguagePack
```

Like other modes, these switches take the optional parameters /SourceDir and /UpdatesDir. Since we're not going to have coverage of the Unified Messaging role later in the book, here are a few examples:

◆ To add the German, French, and Japanese UM language packs from a network share, use this command:

```
Exsetup/AddUmLanguagePack:de-DE,fr-FR,ja-JP'
/s:\\myshare\langpacks
```

◆ To remove the German and French language packs, use this command:

```
Exsetup /RemoveUmLanguagePack:de-DE,fr-FR
```

> **NOTE**
>
> You cannot add or remove the English (en-US) language pack; it is installed as part of the core UM role.

Performing Postinstallation Tasks

Exchange 2007 is installed, but your work isn't over. There are several post-installation tasks you have left to complete.

Starting the Exchange Management Console

If you used Setup's graphic mode to install Exchange, then you were given the option to automatically start EMC when the installation was complete. Otherwise, click Start ➤ All Programs ➤ Microsoft Exchange ➤ Exchange Management Console to launch the EMC.

When you first open the EMC, you see a screen much like that shown in Figure 4.5. It contains a list of tasks that you need to accomplish in order to finalize your deployment. This list may be longer or shorter depending on which roles you have in your organization. Each task is a hyperlink that will lead you to specific instructions on how to accomplish it.

There is also a tab in the MMC that shows you additional, tasks you can do to further improve the usability of your Exchange organization, such as configuring accepted domains. You can see an example of this tab in Figure 4.6.

FIGURE 4.5
Finalizing the
deployment

FIGURE 4.6
End-to-end scenarios

Delegating Permissions

One common post-setup task is the delegation of Exchange administrative permissions. By default, Exchange 2007 includes a number of predefined administrator roles that you can use as a basis for delegating management permissions among your staff. These built-in roles are as follows:

Exchange Organization Administrator   Users and groups assigned to this role have complete access to all Exchange properties and objects organization-wide. This is the highest level of permission in Exchange 2007.

Exchange Recipient Administrator   Users and groups assigned to this role can read all of the Domain Users containers in each Exchange-prepared domain in the Active Directory forest and have write access to the Exchange properties on all user objects in those containers. They can, in short, manage the Exchange properties of any recipient in an Exchange-prepared domain. Note that they do not have the underlying Active Directory permissions to create, manage, or delete the user objects, and if you do not run /PrepareAD for a given domain, they will have no Exchange-granted access to that domain.

Exchange Server Administrator   Users and groups assigned to this role are granted the ability to administer server-specific configuration items for the server this role is associated with. This role is granular on a server-by-server basis, allowing you to finely delegate administrative permissions without the use of administrative groups.

Exchange View-Only Administrator   Just what it says; users and groups assigned to this role get to peek at organization-wide configuration settings and Domain Users containers in Exchange-prepared domains, but they can't change any settings.

You may have noticed that, by default, these permissions are set up to explicitly enforce a split-permission model between Active Directory and Exchange. This model helps large organizations enforce the difference between Active Directory administrators and Exchange administrators.

> **WARNING**
>
> The split-permission model has some subtle implications too. For example, the Exchange extensions to the Active Directory Users and Computers MMC snap-in are a thing of the past. In order to do any recipient management, you must use the Exchange tools.

Summary

Installing Exchange 2007 may at first appear to be overwhelming. The proliferation of new server roles, combined with prerequisite software and hardware configuration, gives you a lot of options and details to keep track of. However, the new command-line installer gives you back a lot of power in managing your deployment. Your design work from the previous chapter combined with the detailed coverage and recommendations in this chapter, will give you the specific guidance you need to easily determine which steps you need to take in which order.

If we had to reduce this chapter down to a single list of guidelines, here's what we'd want you to remember:

◆ Download and read the current Exchange 2007 documentation. Microsoft will be updating it on a regular basis to ensure that it stays fresh and incorporates the latest updates and real-world deployment feedback.

◆ Pay proper attention to sizing your servers.

◆ Text-mode setup is your friend.

◆ Do your Active Directory preparation before beginning to install server roles.

◆ You must have at least one Client Access and Hub Transport server instance per site.

◆ Install a Client Access and Hub Transport server instance in a given site before installing the first Mailbox server instance.

◆ Don't install an Edge Transport server until you have a Hub Transport instance in your organization.

◆ Clusters must be dedicated to the Mailbox server role only.

◆ Wait to install the Unified Messaging server until you know everything else is working.

If you take your time and test your deployment plan thoroughly, you'll have a working Exchange 2007 installation in no time!

Chapter 5

Upgrading to Exchange Server 2007

With Exchange being the number one messaging system on the market, it's quite a solid bet that there will be a lot of existing Exchange customers who will be looking at upgrading. If you're reading this chapter, whether you turned to it directly or come here by way of the previous chapter, we're guessing that you're one of those people. Before we go on, though, let's take a moment to clear up a matter of terminology and distinguish between *upgrading* and *migrating*.

Many people have different expectations about what an upgrade consists of. We're used to *in-place upgrades* where we have an existing version of the software on the computer, run the installer, and end up with the new version of the software. Previous versions of Exchange have supported an in-place upgrade process for at least one previous version back, but the Exchange 2007 upgrade process doesn't. As explained in previous chapters, the lack of support for 64-bit Windows in Exchange 2003 and the lack of support for 32-bit Windows in Exchange 2007 combine to make the upgrade process a bit more complicated. Life is not all gloom and doom, however, and this seeming complication will have its compensation in the end.

The Exchange 2007 upgrade process is what many people consider to be a *migration* — a change from one messaging system to another. That's certainly how Microsoft uses the term; although some early Exchange documentation referred to the transition from Windows NT domains and Exchange 5.5 to Active Directory and Exchange 2000 as a migration, Microsoft has settled on a more consistent usage in recent years. No Microsoft documentation will ever state it this simply, but the difference between upgrades and migration boils down to a very simple rule: if you're moving from a previous supported version of Microsoft software, it's an upgrade no matter what process you take to get there, whereas if you've moving from some other product, it's a migration.

TIP

To fully understand the difference between upgrades and migration, you must pay attention to the words *supported version*. Microsoft supports upgrades to Exchange 2007 from Exchange 2000 and Exchange 2003. If you're coming from Exchange 5.5, then you're migrating even though you're coming from a previous version of Exchange because upgrades from Exchange 5.5 aren't supported by Microsoft. You either get to upgrade to Exchange 2003 as an interim step or use third-party migration tools to move your mailboxes and data into what will effectively be a new Exchange 2007 organization.

Just to make things less straightforward, the Exchange 2007 documentation gives you two upgrade strategies: upgrade your existing organization, which Microsoft calls a *transition*, or create a new organization and move your messaging data over. Unfortunately, Microsoft has chosen to call this *migration* as well. However, be aware that this use of *migration* refers only to the act of moving your data between the two organizations!

To be consistent with Microsoft usage and minimize confusion, we'll use the term *upgrade* to refer to the process of moving from an existing Exchange 2000/2003 organization to Exchange 2007, no matter the strategy you use to get there. Actual migrations from different messaging systems (or from Exchange 5.5) are outside the scope of this book. When we do need to refer to moving data between organizations, we'll explicitly say *migration strategy*. This helps us be clear and stay consistent with the excellent documentation provided for Exchange 2007.

> **NOTE**
>
> We'll use the phrase *legacy Exchange servers* in this chapter to refer to the existing Exchange 2000 Server and Exchange Server 2003 machines in your organization. This might cause a slight bit of cognitive dissonance for those of you used to thinking of Exchange 5.5 servers as legacy servers.

Topics in this chapter include the following:

◆ What factors you need to consider before doing your upgrade

◆ The two Exchange 2007 upgrade strategies and how to tell where each is appropriate

◆ Coexisting with legacy Exchange servers

Factors to Consider Before Upgrading

Are you ready to upgrade? Not so fast! Before you pull the trigger and pop the Exchange 2007 installation media into the drive, you need to consider a few factors. Let's take some time to go over them in more detail so that your upgrade is successful.

Prerequisites

Before you can begin upgrading your Exchange organization, you have to ensure that it meets the necessary prerequisites. We've gone over some of these already in previous chapters from the context of a fresh install of Exchange 2007, but let's look at them again with a fresh eye, thinking about how your existing Exchange deployment may affect your ability to meet them.

HARDWARE AND OPERATING SYSTEM

For production use, you must have x64-compatible hardware — systems with one of the following types of processors:

◆ The Opteron processor line, made by AMD, is found in high-end servers hardware. AMD also makes Athlon 64 processors that are meant for inexpensive servers and high-end workstations.

◆ Intel offers both its Xeon and Pentium line of processors with the Extended Memory 64 Technology (EM64T) extensions. The Xeon family is typically found in high-end servers, while the Pentiums are found in low-end servers and workstations.

NOTE

The Intel Itanium processor line is not compatible with Exchange 2007. Unlike some other Microsoft restrictions, this isn't just a case of being a supported configuration; the Itanium processors are not compatible with the x64 specification and Exchange 2007 has not been compiled against the Itanium family of CPUs.

Nowadays, multi-core processors are increasingly common — both Intel and AMD. Although Windows recognizes multiple cores as separate processors when managing processes and threads, Microsoft licensing does not make a distinction between single-core and dual-core processors. This is to your benefit, because Exchange will certainly benefit from additional cores.

You can run Exchange 2007 on any of the following versions of Windows Server:

◆ Windows Server 2003 x64 Standard Edition with SP1 or later applied

◆ Windows Server 2003 x64 Enterprise Edition with SP1 or later applied

◆ Windows Server 2003 R2 x64 Standard Edition

◆ Windows Server 2003 R2 x64 Enterprise Edition

At press time, Windows Server 2003 SP2 was in the final release candidate stage and is intended to be compatible with Exchange 2007.

TIP

Windows Server 2003 Standard Edition limits you to a maximum of four CPUs. By making use of multi-core processors, you can still use the cheaper Standard Edition while maximizing your server's CPU power, which can be important for some server roles (or for servers that are hosting multiple roles). Remember, though, that if you're planning on deploying clustered mailbox servers, you can't use Windows Server 2003 Standard Edition in clusters.

If you're one of the people using prerelease versions of Windows Longhorn Server (the codename for the next generation of Windows Server), don't even think about trying to use it with Exchange 2007. You shouldn't be using prerelease versions of Windows in production (unless you're directed to by Microsoft as part of one of its special early-adopter programs). However, bitter experience has taught the folks at Microsoft that even when they clearly tell people not to do something, someone out there will do try to do it, so Microsoft has made Exchange 2007 incompatible with Longhorn. Microsoft has, however, stated that Longhorn support will be part of the Exchange 2007 SP1 timeframe. Until then, you can't install Exchange 2007 on Longhorn, nor can you have Longhorn domain controllers in any site that contains an Exchange 2007 server.

When Microsoft first began releasing the specific requirements for Exchange 2007 deployments, no single revelation drew greater attention than the requirement for 64-bit hardware. Even now, many people insist that the lack of support for 32-bit hardware will dramatically increase the final cost of upgrades to Exchange 2007. Microsoft, though, makes the argument that most of the servers sold in recent timeframes already have 64-bit support. As the x64 hardware platform (initially introduced by AMD for its Opteron and Athlon 64 processors, then supported by Intel with the EM64T extensions to its Xeon and Pentium 4 processors) is backward compatible with 32-bit hardware and operating systems, many server manufacturers switched to offering 64-bit hardware regardless of which operating system their customers order.

This doesn't mean you're completely off the hook on the hardware front, however. Even if your current Exchange 2003 servers are running on 64-bit hardware, you can't just pop the Exchange 2007 DVD in and do an in-place upgrade. Why not?

♦ Previous versions of Exchange are all 32-bit only and can't be run on Windows Server 2003 x64. Note that this is not a matter of support; Exchange 2000 and 2003 will not run on 64-bit Windows — period, end of story.

♦ You can't upgrade from Windows Server 2003 x86 to Windows Server 2003 x64. You have to perform a clean install.

♦ Remember that you can't run the 32-bit version of Exchange 2007 in production. The 32-bit version is intended for testing and training and cannot be taken out of trial mode, which means that it will cease to operate after a set number of days.

This means that to reuse existing server hardware, you're going to have to have at least one spare server and be prepared to reinstall Windows and Exchange on your servers as you go. We'll discuss this in more detail in the section "Transitioning Your Exchange Organization" later in the chapter.

ACTIVE DIRECTORY

Because Exchange 2007 continues to have such a dependence on Active Directory, you need to take a good look at the domain controllers and global catalog servers in your Active Directory forest before starting the upgrade process.

Unlike Exchange 2003, which could use domain controllers running either Windows 2000 Server with the appropriate service pack or Windows Server 2003, Exchange 2007 requires that all of the following domain controllers be running Windows Server 2003 + SP1:

♦ The schema master domain controller. This is usually the first domain controller that you installed in the forest, unless you have moved the schema master FSMO role to another domain controller.

♦ At least one global catalog server in each Active Directory site in your forest where you will be installing an Exchange 2007 server.

Our recommendation is to upgrade all your domain controllers to Windows Server 2003 + SP1, especially if you still have Windows 2000 Server domain controllers. The Active Directory improvements in Windows Server 2003 can help vastly reduce the amount of bandwidth required for Active Directory replication, and several Exchange 2007 features (such as address book browsing in OWA) rely on features in Windows Server 2003 SP1. By making sure you've upgraded all of your domain controllers, you increase the redundancy and resiliency of your Exchange/Active Directory integration.

TIP

It is extremely important that Active Directory be healthy. Exchange 2007 relies directly on your Active Directory site structure for message routing information. In previous versions of Exchange, the Active Directory site design could become decoupled from the Exchange Server routing design.

Whether you upgrade all of your domain controllers or just the minimum number, you need to list all the domains in which you will either install Exchange 2007 or create Exchange 2007 recipient objects such as users, contacts, and mail-enabled groups. For each of these domains, ensure that the domain functional level is set to either the Windows 2000 native or Windows 2003 native level. This ensures that you have no lingering Windows NT 4.0 servers acting as down-level domain controllers via the PDC emulator.

TIP

If you can't upgrade all of the domain controllers in your forest, we recommend at the very least upgrading all of the domain controllers in the sites and domains that will be hosting Exchange servers and recipient objects. Officially, you only need to have a single Windows Server 2003 SP1 global catalog server in each site, but Windows Server 2003 SP1 domain controllers offer many advantages to your organization above and beyond their benefits to Exchange Server 2007.

For Windows 2003 Active Directory forests, there is no direct requirement for the forest functional level as long as each domain that will be used for Exchange 2007 meets the per-domain requirements.

A few additional caveats exist:

◆ If you plan on using OWA and any of your domain controllers are using a non-English version of Windows, you will need to install the hotfix in Knowledge Base article 919166 on each non-English domain controller.

◆ DNS must be configured correctly. In addition, each server that you plan to install Exchange 2007 on cannot have a *disjoint namespace*; that is, the server's primary DNS suffix (set in the Computer Name tab of the computer's property sheet) must match the DNS name of the domain the server belongs to.

◆ You may want to use 64-bit Windows Server 2003 on your domain controllers for performance increases; however, this is not required.

◆ Assuming similar speeds and models of processor, you should still plan to meet the long-standing recommendation of having a ratio of Exchange processors to global catalog processors in a given site be no higher than 4:1. This helps ensure that global catalog lookups happen quickly enough to keep Exchange responding in a timely fashion.

◆ While it is supported to install Exchange 2007 on a domain controller, we really recommend that you don't do it. Such a combined server is much less resilient to service outages or configuration changes and is much harder to restore in the event of a disaster. If you do go this route, you will have to uninstall Exchange if you ever want to demote the machine from being a domain controller; you cannot run `dcpromo` once Exchange is installed.

EXCHANGE VERSION

The final prerequisite you must consider is what mode your legacy Exchange organization is in. By default, these versions of Exchange install in mixed mode even when you did not upgrade from Exchange 5.5. You must upgrade the organization to Exchange 2000 or 2003 native mode. Note that in order to do this, you must ensure the following points:

◆ No Exchange 5.5 servers remain in the organization.

◆ No legacy Exchange Site Replication Service (SRS) instances remain in the organization.

◆ No configured Connection Agreements in the Active Directory Connector (ADC) remain in the organization. In fact, if you still have the ADC in your organization and you have no more Exchange 5.5 servers or legacy Exchange SRS instances, remove the ADC from the organization.

Once you have verified that your Active Directory domains and forest and Exchange organization meet these prerequisites, you can begin the process of installing Exchange 2007 by preparing Active Directory as described in Chapter 4.

Setting the Legacy Routing Server Parameter

In Chapter 4, we briefly mentioned the /LegacyRoutingServer installation option. We'll now cover more about why it exists and what problems it solves.

When you install Exchange 2007 into an existing legacy Exchange organization, you need to address some architectural differences. We said before that Exchange 2007 doesn't use administrative groups or routing groups, and that's almost completely true. Although Exchange 2007 servers don't make use of them, the legacy Exchange servers do require them; in a mixed organization, you're going to have the administrative groups and routing groups created for the older Exchange servers. So far, so good; the Exchange 2007 servers use the new Active Directory site-based architecture and the legacy Exchange servers use the administrative groups and routing groups. Under these conditions, everything is happy until the new Exchange 2007 server tries to interact with a legacy Exchange server.

To deal with this, the Exchange 2007 installer takes several actions to ensure compatibility with legacy Exchange servers:

◆ To facilitate communication with legacy Exchange servers, the Exchange 2007 installer creates a special administrative group the first time it is run in a legacy organization. All Exchange 2007 servers are placed into this special administrative group, which is named Exchange Administrative Group (FYDIBOHF23SPDLT). The Exchange 2007 servers don't use this group, but it will show up, along with all of the Exchange 2007 servers, in the legacy Exchange System Manager.

◆ The installer also creates a special routing group for Exchange 2007 servers, named Exchange Routing Group (DWBGZMFD01QNBJR). As with the administrative group, all Exchange 2007 servers are placed into this routing group, even though they use the native Exchange 2007 and Active Directory site-based routing mechanisms; the group and servers are visible in the legacy Exchange System Manager. The only purpose of this routing group is to force the legacy Exchange servers to use a routing group connector to communicate with Exchange 2007 servers.

◆ The installer also creates a universal security group named ExchangeLegacyInterop in Active Directory. This group is used by Exchange 2007 servers to determine which legacy servers are permitted to submit messages to the default SMTP receive connectors on the Exchange 2007 Hub Transport instances. By default, these connectors require successful authentication and permit message submission only from legacy servers whose computer accounts are in this group, such as the legacy Exchange bridgehead server. We'll go into more detail in Chapter 18 about the various options for Hub Transport receive connectors.

◆ When the first Exchange 2007 Hub Transport role is installed, the installer creates a two-way routing group connector between the Exchange 2007 routing group and a user-selected legacy Exchange bridgehead server. If you use the command-line installer, you use the `/LegacyRoutingServer` switch to specify which legacy Exchange server to use. You can add additional bridgehead servers to this routing group after the installation is complete, and we'll talk about that in more detail later in the chapter. As with the administrative and routing groups, this connector is visible in the legacy Exchange System Manger.

At first these changes may seem overwhelming, especially if your current Exchange organization consists of only one or two administrative and routing groups. The thought of adding another administrative group and routing group into the mix initially strikes many people as counterintuitive; after all, the point of the move away from them is to simplify things, not clutter them up! Consider for a moment an organization that consists of the following elements:

◆ A single Active Directory forest and domain.

◆ Two sites, imaginatively named Site A and Site B.

◆ A domain controller and global catalog server in each site, for a total of four domain controllers.

◆ An Exchange 2003 organization, consisting of a separate administrative group and routing group for each site. For the sake of argument, we'll say that this administrative and routing group design is a legacy of an earlier upgrade from Exchange 5.5.

◆ Four Exchange 2003 servers in each site: two mailbox servers, a front-end server, and a bridgehead server. This makes a total of eight Exchange 2003 servers.

Now, this organization wants to install Exchange 2007. The goal is to end up with a total of six Exchange 2007 servers: one Mailbox instance, one Client Access instance, and one Hub Transport instance for each AD site. As shown in Figure 5.1, things certainly look messy while they're in the middle of their upgrade.

Very scary! They've got administrative groups, routing groups, and Active Directory structures all over the place. Even with at most a total of 18 servers to handle, tracking the multiple overlapping memberships gets ugly. Ah, but when they've completed their upgrade, things are a lot calmer, as shown in Figure 5.2. They've got their two Active Directory sites, a single deprecated Exchange administrative group, and a single deprecated Exchange routing group.

WARNING

The names of the Exchange 2007 administrative and routing groups are designed to be unique, something that is not likely to be already present in any legacy organization. Do not rename these groups!

FIGURE 5.1
Logical structures present when Exchange 2007 coexists in a legacy organization

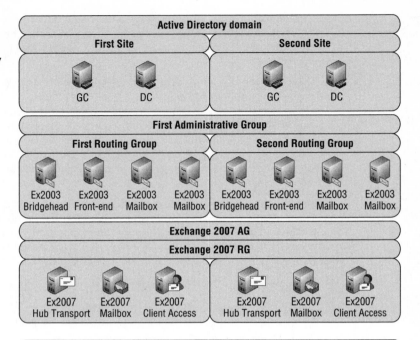

FIGURE 5.2
Logical structures simplified when only Exchange 2007 remains

---

WARNING

The Exchange 2007 administrative group and routing group are intended only for Exchange 2007 servers. Do not place legacy Exchange servers in these groups thinking that it will somehow improve interoperability or remove the need for the routing group connector. You will break mail flow because there is no other mechanism for translating between the legacy Exchange routing mechanism and the Exchange 2007 routing mechanism.

Once you've specified the legacy bridgehead server and successfully added the first Exchange 2007 Hub Transport instance into the organization, you can at a later time configure the default routing group connector with additional legacy Exchange bridgehead servers or even create new routing group connectors to simplify the message routing paths in your organization. However, you're going to have to perform these tasks from the Exchange Management Shell; you won't see the legacy routing group connectors listed in the Exchange Management Console.

To see the existing legacy routing group connectors, use the `Get-RoutingGroupConnector` cmdlet. Its output is shown in Figure 5.3.

FIGURE 5.3
Output from the Get-RoutingGroup Connector cmdlet

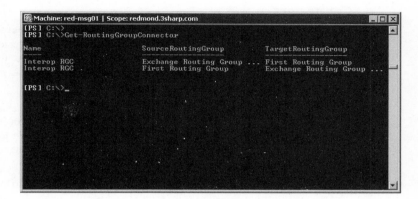

To add a new legacy bridgehead to an existing legacy routing group connector, use the `Set-RoutingGroupConnector` cmdlet. Here is an example where we are adding Exchange 2003 servers `hnlbh01.somorita.int` and `hnlbh02.somorita.int` and Exchange 2007 servers `hnlht03.somorita.int` and `hnlht04.somorita.int` to a routing group connector called E2K7 to E2K3 RGC:

```
Set-RoutingGroupConnector -Name "E2K7 to E2K3 RGC"
-SourceTransportServers "hnlht03.somorita.int",
"hnlht04.somorita.int" -TargetTransportServers
    "hnlbh01.somorita.int", "hnlbh02.somorita.int"
```

This cmdlet ensures that the legacy servers are automatically added to the ExchangeLegacy-Interop security group so that SMTP authentication will take place and messages will flow properly.

To create a new routing group connector, use the `New-RoutingGroupConnector` cmdlet. Here is an example of creating a new routing group connector called E2K7 to Hawaii RG using the Exchange 2003 server `hnlbh01.somorita.int` and the Exchange 2007 server `hnlht01.somorita.net` as bridgehead servers.

```
New-RoutingGroupConnector -Name "E2K7 to Hawaii RG"
-SourceTransportServers "hnlht01.somorita.int"
-TargetTransportServers "hnlbh01.somorita.int"
-Cost 100 -Bidirectional $True -PublicFoldersEnabled $True
```

> **WARNING**
>
> When you use the `New-RoutingGroupConnector` and `Set-RoutingGroupConnector` cmdlets to specify the TargetTransportServers and SourceTransportServers parameters, you need to specify all of the servers you wish to be bridgeheads for the connector. Each invocation of the cmdlet will overwrite the existing parameter.

Connectors

Another area for you to consider as you're getting ready to upgrade to Exchange 2007 is your connectors. In legacy Exchange organizations, you have four basic types of connectors: routing group connectors, SMTP connectors, X.400 connectors, and other foreign connectors to specialized messaging systems such as Lotus Notes and Novell GroupWise. In general, you'll want to treat these connectors in the following fashion:

Routing group connectors   Routing group connectors still exist in Exchange 2007 but are meant solely as a means of interoperation with legacy Exchange servers. They will be naturally phased out as you convert your Exchange infrastructure over to Exchange 2007, decommission your legacy Exchange servers, and remove the legacy administrative and routing groups from your organization.

SMTP connectors   SMTP connectors provide connections to external SMTP-speaking systems and the Internet; they generally aren't used within legacy Exchange forests unless you have a multiple forest configuration. In Exchange 2007, connectors are divided into receive connectors, which are configured on a per-server basis, and send connectors, which are configured and maintained throughout the organization.

As with the routing group connectors, these legacy SMTP connectors will be phased out as you move your message routing functions off of your legacy Exchange servers to your new Exchange 2007 Hub Transport and Edge Transport servers. We'll talk more about your routing and SMTP connector options, as well as tell you how to configure Exchange 2007 Hub Transport and Edge Transport SMTP connectivity to the Internet, in Chapter 18.

X.400 connectors   X.400 connectors are finally gone in Exchange 2007. With the decline and fall of X.400 as a messaging standard, almost all of the X.400 connectors used in legacy Exchange organizations today are used to connect to the MTA service in Exchange 5.5 sites. Since you can't have Exchange 5.5 sites and servers in an organization with Exchange 2007, you'll need to get these sites and connectors removed before beginning your upgrade.

If you've got a non-Exchange X.400 system that you connect to, you'll need to maintain your legacy Exchange server until you can arrange some sort of alternate connection supported natively by Exchange 2007.

Foreign connectors   Foreign connectors are dramatically different in Exchange 2007. The new foreign connectors don't try to implement a specific non-SMTP protocol; instead, they require you to define a drop directory on the Hub Transport server or network file share. When messages are routed through this connector, they will be written to the drop directory and the remote gateway software can then pick them up and process them appropriately.

If you're using the Exchange 2000 cc:Mail or MS Mail connectors, or the Exchange 2003 Group-Wise or Lotus Notes connectors can't transition to an SMTP connection, then you'll need to keep the relevant legacy Exchange servers in your organization. (Of course, if you're still using cc:Mail or MS Mail, my only question to you is *why*.)

You'll need to consider your current routing topology, especially if you've got a single routing group in your legacy organization. By default, legacy Exchange servers route messages directly out of their local SMTP virtual server. This default behavior means that, out of the box, Exchange 2000 Server and Exchange Server 2003 servers directly attempt to deliver external messages based on DNS MX record lookups instead of forwarding messages to bridgehead servers. For many small organizations, this behavior is acceptable, and as a result many Exchange administrators never get around to creating an SMTP connector and defining bridgehead servers for their organization.

When you install the first Exchange 2007 Hub Transport instance into your legacy Exchange organization, it creates its own routing group and associated routing group connector, as previously discussed. It also creates a default set of SMTP connectors that are enough to send and receive authenticated SMTP from other Exchange servers in the organization; the send connector is configured with the default SMTP address space of *. You may now find that your organization is suddenly unable to exchange mail with systems outside of your organization.

If this is the case, here's what's happened: You've failed to set an SMTP connector in your legacy Exchange organization. By installing your first Exchange 2007 Hub Transport instance, you've created a routable SMTP connector with the default address space. Your legacy Exchange servers do what they're supposed to do and allow this new SMTP connector configuration to override the SMTP virtual server configuration. Instead of attempting to send externally addressed messages directly to the MX host, the legacy Exchange servers send these messages through the brand-new routing group connector to your new Exchange 2007 Hub Transport server. Even better, the Hub Transport server only has the default connectors, which don't include the configuration necessary to allow unauthenticated traffic to and from the Internet; Exchange 2007 assumes that you'll be using the Edge Transport role to do that, and you'll have to configure it otherwise if you're not going to use the Edge Transport role. Now, all your outbound external mail starts to pile up in the Hub Transport server's queues.

Luckily, the fix for this situation is simple, and you even have three selections from which to choose:

◆ Create an outbound SMTP send connector on your Exchange 2007 Hub Transport server. This may be suboptimal in some instances, but if you're already using an external mail gateway, then you can simply configure Exchange 2007 to pass outbound mail to the appropriate smarthost. We'll cover this option in detail later in Chapter 18.

◆ Deploy an Exchange 2007 Edge Transport server to handle your outbound traffic. If you're upgrading to Exchange 2007 to take advantage of its advanced message hygiene capabilities, we recommend this option; it gets your incoming and outgoing mail going through Exchange 2007 sooner rather than later. Again, we'll talk about this configuration in depth in Chapter 18.

◆ Alternately, create an SMTP connector with the default address space in your legacy Exchange organization before you begin installing Exchange 2007. This option has the advantage that it keeps mail flow in your organization going through a known and trusted set of bridgehead servers until you have your Hub Transport and Edge Transport servers configured and tested. If you have existing legacy Exchange servers configured with mail hygiene solutions, this is probably what you're going to want to select for the short term.

> **WARNING**
>
> Don't be afraid or hesitant to continue using your legacy Exchange servers as bridgeheads to the Internet while you're working your way through your Exchange 2007 upgrade. Although we firmly believe that configuring and troubleshooting message flow and routing is much easier with Exchange 2007, you've still got a lot of material to learn and master as you begin to put Exchange 2007 into play. Choose your battles.

Legacy Exchange and Third-Party Services

Another factor you need to consider is whether you are using additional legacy Exchange services that are no longer present in Exchange 2007. We've already covered the case of the various foreign connectors that are no longer part of Exchange 2007, but those aren't the only services and features you need to watch out for.

Previous versions of Exchange included several services that are now supplied by either Windows Server 2003 components or other Microsoft applications. If your organization depends on these, you'll need to keep the appropriate legacy servers around until you can migrate or upgrade the services off the Exchange servers.

Theses services include the following:

◆ Exchange 2000 Conferencing Server

◆ Exchange 2000 Instant Messaging Server

◆ Exchange 2000 Key Management Server

◆ Exchange 2000 Chat Server

◆ Any connectors supported by the legacy Exchange servers but no longer supported by Exchange 2007, such as the X.400 connector and the GroupWise connector

If you are currently using these services and cannot (or will not) upgrade to a Exchange 2007–compatible versions, then you will need to leave the legacy Exchange servers hosting these services intact within your organization.

> **WARNING**
>
> If you are keeping legacy Exchange servers in your organization, do not forget to preserve the management consoles and tools necessary to administer the services.

You may also have third-party services that are essential to your organization. Examples of such services include, but by no means are limited to, the following:

◆ Message hygiene add-ins such as spam filters and virus scanners (both for transport and store).

◆ Fax services.

◆ Message discovery, compliance, archival, and retention solutions.

◆ Geo-clustering, mailbox snapshot, and other storage-related solutions.

◆ Transport event sinks, whether commercial or custom. A common event sink is a module to stamp disclaimers on all outbound e-mail.

◆ Conference room and shared resource booking management software.

◆ Mailbox database backup and restore agents.

Of course, there are many other possibilities. The point is that you need to ensure that these products are going to work with Exchange 2007. Some products may work directly with Exchange 2007 already, while others may require an upgrade of their own. In some cases, you may need to switch software packages if your current vendor's product isn't compatible with Exchange 2007 and you require that functionality.

NOTE

There's always the possibility that you no longer need a given third-party package because new functionality in Exchange 2007 allows you to perform the same task natively.

Choosing Your Strategy

Now that you've considered the various factors that could affect your upgrade, you need to figure out which strategy you're going to use. As we mentioned earlier, you have two main choices: *migration* or *transition*, as Microsoft calls them. Although neither option gives you the relative ease of the traditional in-place upgrade, each option has its own pros and cons. In the following sections, we'll review them briefly and then move on to a more in-depth discussion.

Comparing the Strategies

If you're like many readers, you've probably got at least some preference for your upgrade strategy already in mind. Before you set that choice in stone, though, read through this section and see whether there are any surprises (good or bad) that might allow you to address some aspect of the upgrade that you hadn't previously considered. If, on the other hand, you're not really sure which strategy would be best for you, then this section should help give you enough information to begin making a well-informed decision.

Let's start by taking a look at an overview of how the two strategies stack up. Table 5.1 lists several points of comparison between the migration and transition strategies.

For the most part, Table 5.1 speaks for itself; if any point requires more in-depth discussion, we'll address it properly during the detailed sections that follow.

MIGRATING YOUR EXCHANGE ORGANIZATION

From the overview given in Table 5.1, it may seem as if we have a grudge against upgrading to Exchange 2007 by using the migration strategy. Although we have to admit it's not our favorite strategy, we'll hasten to say that migration offers many advantages that a transition upgrade doesn't offer:

◆ It is the only realistic way to consolidate two or more separate Exchange organizations into a single organization. This kind of consolidation can happen as the result of a major reorganization inside of one company or as the result of merger or acquisitions.

TABLE 5.1:   Comparison of Exchange 2007 Upgrade Strategies

POINT OF COMPARISON	MIGRATION STRATEGY	TRANSITION STRATEGY
Tools	You will need a combination of free Microsoft tools to manage the multiple sets of data that need to be migrated (Active Directory user information and Exchange mailbox data at a minimum). These tools usually result in at least some minor information loss. Alternately, you can spend extra money to purchase and use third-party tools.	You can use the built-in tools in Exchange 2007 and Windows Server to control all aspects of the transition, from building the new servers, reconfiguring Active Directory, or moving mailbox data.
Hardware	You will usually require a significant amount of new hardware. You may not need to have a complete spare set of replacement hardware, but you'll need enough to have the basic infrastructure of your new Exchange 2007 organization in place.	You can accomplish this strategy with a minimal amount of new hardware, typically no more than one or two extra servers, as long as your existing servers are 64-bit ready. Otherwise, you will need new hardware for your Exchange 2007 servers.
Active Directory and DNS	You must create a new Active Directory forest. Typically, this means that you cannot reuse the same AD and DNS domain names (although you will be able to share the same SMTP domain names).	You can make use of your existing Active Directory and DNS deployment; however, you will first need to upgrade your existing domain controllers and global catalogs to meet the prerequisites.
User accounts	You must migrate your user accounts to the new AD forest or recreate them.	Your users will be able to use their existing accounts without any changes.
Message routing	Your SMTP domains must be split between your legacy organization and your new organization; one of them must be configured to be nonauthoritative and route to the other. This configuration may need to change during the course of the migration. Additionally, you must set up explicit external SMTP connectors between the two organizations or play tricks with name resolution.	Your organization continues to be a single entity, with full knowledge of all authoritative domains shared among all Exchange servers. Message flow between organizations can be controlled by the simple addition of bridgehead servers to the default legacy routing group connector or the creation of additional legacy routing group connectors to meet the needs of your topology.

TABLE 5.1:   Comparison of Exchange 2007 Upgrade Strategies *(CONTINUED)*

POINT OF COMPARISON	MIGRATION STRATEGY	TRANSITION STRATEGY
Outlook profiles	You will either need to create new Outlook profiles (either manually or using the tools found in the matching version of the Microsoft Office Resource Kit) or use third-party tools to migrate them over to the new organization. This may cause the loss of information.	As long as you keep the legacy mailbox servers up and running during an appropriate transition phase, Outlook will transparently update their your users' profiles to their new mailbox server the first time they open it after their mailbox is moved to Exchange 2007.
Single-instance storage	Removing mailbox information from the organization to move it breaks single-instance storage. In order to preserve it, you'll need to look at buying third-party migration tools.	The mailbox movement tools included in Exchange 2007 will preserve single-instance storage as mailbox data is moved to the new Exchange 2007 servers and storage groups.

◆ It allows you to set up a *greenfield* (a term used to denote the ideal state of implementation) deployment of Exchange 2007. No matter how conscientious you are as an admin, any real network represents the product of a number of design compromises. After a while, the weight of those compromises and workarounds add up; the design and structure of your network can reflect imperatives and inputs that no longer exist, or are no longer relevant, in your organization. It's nice to be able to wipe the slate clean, especially if that ends up being less work than trying to start with your current mess and clean it up.

◆ It permits you to move your Exchange servers out of your existing Active Directory forest and establish them in their own forest. If you're in an environment that separates administrative control between Active Directory and the Exchange organization, having a separate forest for Exchange can make it a lot easier to accomplish many of the day-to-day management tasks on your servers. (We don't know about you, but we'd much prefer to have control of the OU structure and Group Policy objects that affect our Exchange servers.) If the benefits of a multi-forest deployment outweigh the drawbacks, then this configuration may actually improve the efficiency of the split between directory/account administration and Exchange administration.

◆ It gives you the chance to easily define new policies and procedures that apply equally to everyone, from account provisioning to server naming conventions. With the importance of regulatory compliance and strong internal IT controls and auditing rising on a daily basis, this can be a strong motivator.

◆ It allows you to perform additional configuration and testing of your new organization before you move the bulk of your live data and users to it. Being able to perform additional validation, perhaps with a pilot group of users, gives you additional confidence in the strength of your design and affords you extra opportunities to spot problems and correct them while you can.

◆ It gives you the ability to ensure that the new environment is properly locked down and secured. Exchange 2007 provides support for the Security Configuration Wizard, a new tool included with Windows Server 2003 SP1 and Windows Server 2003 R2 that permits administrators to easily and automatically harden and lock down servers based on what roles they play. When this tool is combined with the ability to define and configure a fresh set of Group Policy objects, a new organization can take advantage of security technologies and techniques that might be extremely difficult to deploy in your current environment while ensuring that your Exchange 2007 servers can still communicate with your legacy Exchange servers, your Active Directory infrastructure, and your users' machines.

Now that we've said that, we should point out that a migration strategy usually involves more work, more money, or both. Sometimes, though, it's what you have to do.

Let's take a look at what a migration might look like:

1. Deploy a new Active Directory forest and root domain, as well as any additional domains. These will probably be named something different than the domains in use in our current network so that we can operate in both environments (and our users can as well). We could be using this forest as an Exchange resource forest, or we could be moving all of our servers and desktops as well. Because migrations don't happen overnight, we'll probably need some sort of forest trust between our forests so that accounts and permissions will work properly while the work is in progress. This step is outside the scope of this book.

2. Migrate a suitable set of user accounts to the new forest. Perhaps we're concentrating on one site at one time to minimize confusion; if so, we need to migrate each user account in the site to the corresponding site in the new Active Directory forest. Again, this step is outside the scope of this book.

3. Install Windows Server 2003 x64 + SP1 and Exchange 2007 on a suitable number of 64-bit servers to form the core of our new Exchange 2007 organization. We don't need to have new servers for everything, but we usually need to have at least a site's worth of equipment on hand. We'll need to configure SMTP connectors between the two organizations, and we'll need to have some sort of directory synchronization going on between the two forests so that as users get moved into the new forest, each global address list (GAL) is properly updated to ensure that internal mail is delivered to the right Exchange organization. We'll probably need to configure public folder synchronization so that free-busy data is shared between the two organizations as well.

4. Move the mailbox data for the site from the legacy Exchange mailbox servers to the new Exchange 2007 mailbox servers. We'll need to update our users' Outlook profiles so that they can get to their mailboxes, and we'll need to ensure that the GAL information is updated so that mail follows these users to their new mailbox servers. Once everything is working, we can remove the legacy Exchange servers from this site.

5. Let's not forget that we may need to join our users' desktops, as well as any other Windows member servers (such as file/print, database, and web servers) to the new forest if it isn't being used exclusively as an Exchange resource forest. This step is outside the scope of this book.

6. Continue this process one site at a time until we've moved all of our user accounts and mailbox data into the Exchange 2007 organization and have decommissioned the remaining legacy Exchange servers.

Now you can see why we consider the migration strategy to be the labor-intensive route. You don't have the luxury of accepting your existing Active Directory structure and accounts. While you can move message data over to a new organization, there's more effort involved in making sure users' profiles are properly updated; or you can rebuild your users' profiles and accept some data loss. If you're upgrading the desktop clients to Outlook 2007, you have the additional worry of whether you need to move the desktop machines into a new forest.

On the other hand, if you have an Active Directory deployment with serious structural problems (whether through years of accumulation or the results of previous mistakes), if you need to extract your Exchange servers into a separate Active Directory forest, or if there is some other reason transitioning your existing organization isn't going to work for you, then migration has a lot to offer.

Migrations require you to keep track of a lot of details and separate types of information. While you can migrate all of the important information — mailboxes, public folders, global address list data — using the freely available Microsoft tools, you'll have a harder time migrating some of the smaller details that aren't mission critical but nonetheless can add up to a very negative user experience. If the users' first experience on the new messaging system is having to reconfigure Outlook with all of their preferences, they're going to be less than happy about the experience. The cost of third-party migration tools may well prove to be a good investment that saves you time, reduces your complexity, and gains you the goodwill of your users.

TRANSITIONING YOUR EXCHANGE ORGANIZATION

The process of transitioning your legacy Exchange organization to Exchange 2007 in many ways resembles the process required to upgrade from Exchange 5.5 to Exchange 2000 or Exchange 2003. If you have experience in that particular upgrade, relax; transitioning to Exchange 2007 is much easier. You're using Active Directory, so no directory upgrade or synchronization is required. You're not multiplying the number of organizational structures required, as the transition from Exchange 5.5 sites to Exchange 2000 administrative groups and routing groups did. You're not changing from the X.400-based MTA protocol to SMTP. All you're doing is moving mailboxes and public folder information, so it's easy. Well, as easy as these projects get.

Let's take a closer look at the average transition to Exchange 2007.

An Overview of Transition

Let's imagine that we have an Exchange 2003 organization that has eight mailbox servers, two front-end servers, and two bridgehead servers that handle all SMTP traffic with the Internet. For the sake of illustration, we'll stipulate that all of our existing Exchange servers are already on 64-bit hardware; we have spares that we plan on using during the transition to keep our new hardware costs to a minimum.

In this organization, the transition process would look something like this:

1. Ensure that our organization meets all the prerequisites, including upgrading at least one Active Directory domain controller in each Active Directory site to Windows Server 2003 SP1 if they're not already at that level. We go ahead and run the Active Directory preparation to upgrade the forest schema with the Exchange 2007 extensions and to create the proper objects in the domains.

2. Install the first Exchange 2007 Client Access instance into our organization. Once it is configured, we can bring it into production use and decommission the first Exchange 2003 front-end server. We can then reuse this hardware to install the second Exchange 2007 Client Access instance and decommission the second Exchange 2003 front-end server.

3. Install the first Exchange 2007 Hub Transport instance into our organization. This instance could be on the same 64-bit machine as one of the Client Access instances (or as an intended Mailbox server) or on a separate machine; however, both the Client Access and Hub Transport roles need to exist before we install our first Exchange 2007 Mailbox instance. We also install an Exchange 2007 Edge Transport server on a separate machine. We configure the Edge Subscription connection between the Edge Transport server and the Hub Transport server and establish the send connector. We can now remove the first Exchange 2003 bridgehead server.

4. Install the second Exchange 2007 Hub Transport instance. We can either install a second Edge Transport server or live with the existing one. Once the second Hub Transport instance (and second Edge Transport server, if deployed) is in production, we reconfigure our SMTP connectors so that our Edge Transport servers are now handling all external SMTP traffic. We then retire the second Exchange 2003 bridgehead server.

5. Install Windows Server 2003 x64 + SP1 on our spare 64-bit mailbox server hardware. Install Exchange 2007 on it as the first Exchange 2007 Mailbox instance in the organization.

6. Move the mailboxes from the first Exchange 2003 mailbox server onto the first Exchange 2007 Mailbox server. Remove the first Exchange 2003 mailbox server from the organization.

7. Perform a clean install of Windows Server 2003 x64 + SP1 on this server and then install the Exchange 2007 Mailbox instance. Move the mailboxes from the second Exchange 2007 server onto this new Mailbox instance.

8. Continue the process in Step 7 one server at a time until we've moved all mailboxes onto Exchange 2007 Mailbox instances and we have no remaining Exchange 2003 mailbox servers left in the organization. At this point, we'll have the same number of spare servers we started with. If they are 64-bit machines, we can install some other Exchange 2007 role on them.

It sounds like a lot of work, but there are many people who have favored this kind of approach even in previous upgrades to Exchange. It gives you the advantage of having a clean installation of Windows to work with and allows you to ensure that the configuration of the operating system is exactly the way you want it.

Order of Installation for Exchange 2007 Roles

Microsoft makes some specific recommendations on the order in which you should install the various roles. Technically, you can install your roles in any order you like. However, following Microsoft's recommendations allows you to minimize the deployment of new server hardware and get the most reuse value from your existing servers if that's a major consideration in your upgrade plans.

NOTE

Microsoft's recommended order ensures that as each role is installed it can locate the prerequisite roles it depends on for proper function. You do not, however, need to install all instances of a particular role before beginning to deploy instances of the next role. You can always go back and install additional instances of any role as you scale up a site.

Client Access Servers

The Client Access role should be the first Exchange 2007 instance you install into a legacy Exchange organization. The reason for this is simple: once you actually have mailboxes on Exchange 2007 servers and your users attempt to access them using any protocol other than MAPI over RPC, you will need to have an Exchange 2007 Client Access instance to provide that protocol access. The Exchange 2007 Client Access role can also provide access to legacy Exchange mailboxes in much the same fashion that an Exchange 2003 front-end server provides access to both Exchange 2003 and Exchange 2000 mailbox servers. This allows you to switch client and web protocol access to Exchange 2007 and decommission your legacy front-end servers. In contrast, a legacy Exchange server cannot provide front-end or client protocol access to a server running a newer version of Exchange.

In smaller organizations, it is common to deploy the Client Access, Hub Transport, and Mailbox roles on the same physical server. In fact, this is the standard Exchange 2007 installation option when you use the GUI setup.

TIP

Upgrading the front-end servers first has long been an Exchange best practice; even when applying service packs, you always want the front-end server running the most recent version of Exchange. Although the Client Access role isn't exactly the same thing as a front-end server, this rule of thumb still applies in Exchange 2007.

WARNING

The Client Access role cannot be placed on clustered hardware. If you plan to use a clustered Mailbox server configuration, you must place this role on a separate non-clustered machine (which can of course be shared with other roles such as Hub Transport).

When you are determining the number of Client Access instances you need, remember that you must have at least one Client Access instance in each Active Directory site where you will have an Exchange 2007 mailbox. Although any Client Access instance can answer an incoming request, if the requested resource is on a Mailbox server that is not in the same site as the initial Client Access instance, it will redirect the request to an available Client Access instance in the Mailbox server's Active Directory site.

This role is mandatory in an Exchange 2007 organization — unless you never plan on using any protocol to access your mailboxes other than Outlook in MAPI over RPC mode. If you use POP3, IMAP, or any of the HTTP-based protocols (OWA, Outlook Anywhere/RPC over HTTPS, or Exchange ActiveSync), you must have the Client Access role in your organization.

Hub Transport Servers

The Hub Transport role is the next logical role to install. Under the new Exchange 2007 architecture, Mailbox servers are no longer responsible for transporting messages directly. This task is now handled by the Hub Transport role. Likewise, all SMTP traffic with other routing groups and external systems is routed through Hub Transport instances. Even if you installed Exchange 2007 Mailbox servers first, they would literally be unable to communicate with any other Exchange servers until an Exchange 2007 Hub Transport instance was installed in the same site. If multiple Hub Transport instances are available in the same site, Exchange 2007 will automatically load-balance SMTP traffic across the available instances.

In smaller organizations, it is common to deploy the Client Access, Hub Transport, and Mailbox roles on the same physical server. In fact, this is the standard Exchange 2007 installation option when you use the GUI setup.

TIP

If you are considering colocating the Hub Transport role on the same physical server as the Mailbox role, remember that Mailbox instance will always attempt to use the Hub Transport instance that is on the same physical server and only connect to other Hub Transport instances if there is a problem. This can cause problems with the automatic load balancing in a site with multiple Mailbox servers.

WARNING

The Hub Transport role cannot be placed on clustered hardware. If you plan to use a clustered Mailbox server configuration, you must place the Hub Transport role on a separate machine (which can of course be shared with other roles).

When you are planning the number of Hub Transport instances you need, remember that you must have at least one Hub Transport instance in each Active Directory site where you will have an Exchange 2007 Mailbox server. As messages are routed to recipients in the organization, the Hub Transport instance that is processing the message looks up the mailbox data in Active Directory. If the mailbox is in the same site, the Hub Transport instance will directly pass the message along; if the recipient's mailbox is in a different site, the Hub Transport instance will transmit the message to an available Hub Transport instance in the recipient's Active Directory site.

The Hub Transport role is mandatory in an Exchange 2007 organization.

Mailbox Servers

After you have suitable Client Access and Hub Transport roles in a given site, you can begin deploying the Mailbox role. Until you have mailboxes hosted on Exchange 2007, the advanced features of Exchange 2007, such as Unified Messaging, cannot be used.

The Mailbox role is the only role that can be used in a clustered configuration.

In smaller organizations, it is common to deploy the Client Access, Hub Transport, and Mailbox server roles on the same physical server. In fact, this is the standard Exchange 2007 installation option when you use the GUI setup.

> **NOTE**
>
> When moving mailboxes to Exchange 2007 Mailbox servers, only use the Exchange 2007 Exchange Management Console Mailbox Move Wizard or the Exchange Management Shell `Move-Mailbox` cmdlet. In particular, do not use the wizard in legacy versions of Exchange or you could break the mailboxes.

The Mailbox role is mandatory in an Exchange 2007 organization. Well, we suppose that technically it's not — but if you're not going to have mailboxes, why bother to upgrade?

Edge Transport Servers

The Edge Transport server role can be deployed once you have a Hub Transport instance in your organization. Since the Edge Subscription process is initiated and controlled by Hub Transport instances, and Edge Transport servers should not be part of the same Active Directory forest as the rest of the Exchange organization, there are no requirements for site affinity.

The Edge Transport role must be placed on its own physical server and cannot be colocated with any other roles.

> **NOTE**
>
> The Edge Transport role is designed to be placed in perimeter networks with limited connectivity to the internal network. Although there are no requirements for where you place the Edge Transport server, for best performance it should be placed so that it has a low-latency, high-bandwidth connection to the Internet, as well as one or more Hub Transport instances, through the appropriate firewalls.

Unified Messaging Servers

Although the Unified Messaging role is not within the scope of this book, we can make a few general observations about deploying it. This is probably the last role to deploy in your organization; it requires working Hub Transport and Mailbox instances in the organization; it also requires a Hub Transport instance to be placed in the same Active Directory site that the Unified Messaging server will be placed in. This Hub Transport instance will transmit messages created by the Unified Messaging server instance to recipient mailboxes in the organization.

Depending on the number of recipients and the hardware configuration, you can combine the Unified Messaging role with any (or all) of the Client Access, Hub Transport, or Mailbox roles on the same physical server.

The Unified Messaging role is, of course, optional.

> **NOTE**
>
> For your users to make use of the UM functionality, you must have sufficient Enterprise Client Access Licenses (CALs) for those users.

Management Consoles

As you install Exchange 2007 on your servers, you may or may not wish to install the sixth role — the management tools role. You can instead place the management tools role on a separate server or workstation and use it as a management console.

The management tools role is the only role that can be installed for production use with the 32-bit version of Exchange 2007, thus allowing you to install it on existing management consoles. In fact, Microsoft makes the 32-bit version of these tools available as a separate download from their website.

By using this version you can install the Exchange 2007 management tools on the same machines your existing legacy Exchange management tools are on. If you do choose to use the 32-bit versions of the management tools, you will need to first install the 32-bit version of the Exchange 2007 prerequisites.

> **WARNING**
>
> You cannot install the legacy Exchange System Manager on an Exchange 2007 server; legacy versions of Exchange are not supported on 64-bit Windows, and the IIS SMTP component required by the legacy System Manager would conflict with the Exchange 2007 SMTP stack.

So, why would you want to have the legacy System Manager on your Exchange 2007 management console?

◆ You still have existing legacy Exchange servers during the duration of your transition.

◆ You have legacy Exchange servers with features that are not supported in Exchange 2007. As long as you use these features, you will need to keep the legacy System Manager.

◆ You have public folders in your organization. While you can manage them using the Exchange Management Shell, it is frankly easier to do it using the System Manager. If you have a large public folder infrastructure, we would say that keeping the System Manager is mandatory — unless, of course, you don't value your sanity.

> **WARNING**
>
> In legacy versions of Exchange, the creation of user accounts and provisioning of Exchange features all took place with extensions to the Active Directory Users and Computers MMC snap-in. In Exchange 2007, you can only use the management tools to provision existing users or create new mail-enabled objects. You may be tempted to continue using Active Directory Users and Computers MMC snap-in to provision mailboxes and other recipients on your Exchange 2007 servers. However, these recipients are in "mixed mode" and cannot use most of the new Exchange 2007 features until you use the Exchange 2007 management tools to update them. When you move mailboxes to an Exchange 2007 Mailbox server using the Exchange 2007 Move Mailbox Wizard or Move-Mailbox cmdlet, the user object is automatically upgraded.

Coexistence

As you proceed with your Exchange 2007 upgrade, you will almost certainly have a period of time during which your Exchange 2007 servers will be required to coexist with legacy Exchange. During this time, there are several points you should consider:

◆ If you have multiple routing group connectors with legacy Exchange routing groups, especially so that there are multiple paths between a legacy Exchange routing group and the Exchange 2007 routing group, you must disable the propagation of link state routing. Link state routing is not used by Exchange 2007, but the presence of multiple paths can cause message routing loops in the legacy Exchange servers. The Exchange 2007 documentation contains instructions on performing this task under the topic "How to Suppress Link State Updates."

◆ Legacy Exchange servers use the X-EXCH50 SMTP extension to pass Exchange-specific properties with message data within the organization. While Exchange 2007 no longer uses this connection, any routing group connectors created with legacy routing groups in the organization are automatically configured to support this extension. If you have a multiple-forest configuration where Exchange 2007 and legacy Exchange servers are communicating but in separate forests, you will need to enable this extension manually. The Exchange 2007 documentation contains instructions on performing this task under the topic "Configuring Cross-Forest Connectors."

◆ The Edge role can be used as a smarthost for an Exchange 2003 organization without requiring the Active Directory preparation steps. However, because Edge cannot synchronize with a legacy Exchange organization, you lose much of the advanced functionality that it offers.

◆ The UM role cannot offers services for recipients whose mailboxes are on legacy Exchange servers.

Summary

Upgrades to Exchange 2007 require you to think carefully about your current Exchange organization and to identify any potential trouble spots. You must be aware of how you plan to get from your current legacy organization to the final goal of an all-Exchange 2007 organization. Are you going to use a transition strategy and upgrade the organization from within, allowing legacy Exchange and Exchange 2007 to coexist side by side for a time, or are you going to pursue the migration strategy and recreate your Exchange 2007 organization from scratch?

Whichever strategy you use, you must be aware of any special roles, applications, and add-ons you are using that will not be compatible with Exchange 2007. Although you can allow these legacy servers to be part of the organization for a while, keeping legacy servers around indefinitely may create more problems than it solves.

Chapter 6

Scaling Upward and Outward

Under what circumstances should you add an Exchange server? How do you know whether you need an additional Active Directory global catalog server? When should you add mailbox servers to a remote Active Directory site? When should you create more storage groups? Or mailbox databases? How many mailboxes should be located on a single mailbox database?

These are all questions that affect your Exchange 2007 design, deployment, and even day-to-day operations. If you don't provide sufficient resources, then the Exchange organization will not operate as effectively as it should. Sometimes the decision points for adding more servers or creating new databases are clearly defined based on your organization's requirements. Other times, however, the decision matrix for expanding your Exchange Server environment is not always cut-and-dried.

This a good topic to address in its own chapter so we can give you ideas and guidance on the factors that may affect your decision to scale upward and outward.

Topics in this chapter include the following:

◆ Deciding when to grow

◆ Performance monitoring basics

◆ Adding more mailbox storage

◆ Enabling local continuous replication

Deciding When to Grow

Do you have clear guidance that tells you when you should expand, add servers, or add capacity? Sometimes your gut instinct just tells you that it is time. But is that something you can take to your boss?

If you are lucky, you can back up your request for a new server or more capacity with tangible evidence. We will discuss both the tangible and intangible factors that may influence the need to expand your Exchange organization.

When you are trying to increase your budget, nothing impresses your boss more than having hard numbers or company policies to back up your requests (well, unless you have a PowerPoint presentation with lots of colorful clipart, charts, and graphs). And you may even be surprised to learn just what you can assign hard-core values to.

The first factors we'll discuss actually involve organizational requirements. A number of different components of organizational requirements may affect the number of servers and their placement. The first is high availability. Here are some factors that will increase the number of Exchange 2007 servers that you will require:

◆ Clustering always requires at least two servers; one server is the active mailbox server and one server is the passive server. This includes shared copy clusters as well as clustered continuous replication clusters.

◆ Other server roles cannot be installed on a clustered mailbox server. This means that other roles, such as Hub Transport, Client Access, or Unified Messaging servers, must be placed on a separate physical machine.

◆ Fault tolerance for internal message routing is achieved with multiple Hub Transport servers. Exchange 2007 will automatically load-balance between multiple Hub Transport servers in the same Active Directory site.

◆ Fault tolerance or higher availability for server roles such as Client Access or Unified Messaging is achieved with multiple servers and using a load-balancing technology (recommended) or DNS round robin (not recommended).

◆ Each Active Directory site that contains a Mailbox server must have the Hub Transport and Client Access server roles. If the Unified Messaging server role is used, the Active Directory site must have a Unified Messaging server installed in the site.

◆ Using Edge Transport services always requires an additional Windows server. Providing fault tolerance for Edge Transport server roles means installing at least two Edge Transport server roles. It is recommended that the Edge Transport servers be installed in your organization's perimeter or DMZ network.

◆ Large organizations will often create a dedicated Active Directory site containing domain controllers and global catalogs servers. These servers are then used exclusively by Exchange servers. This way Exchange does not interfere with domain controllers that are handling user and computer authentication and vice versa.

Let's not forget about supporting network infrastructure services. In a small organization, a single Windows domain controller/global catalog server/DNS server will be sufficient. However, if your organization is supporting more than a few hundred mailboxes, then the requirements for more supporting infrastructure components will increase as well. Here are some factors that may increase the number of network infrastructure services your organization requires:

◆ Some organizations split their DNS servers on to servers or appliances that are separate from the servers that support Active Directory. While we normally recommend using the Windows 2003 DNS server running on a domain controller, if you choose to move DNS to another system, make sure that you have redundancy and that all Windows servers are configured with a primary and secondary DNS server. If you want to use the Active Directory–integrated DNS zone feature of the Windows 2003 DNS server, then the DNS server must be running on a domain controller.

◆ The generic recommendation for the number of domain controllers and global catalog servers is one domain controller CPU for each four Exchange CPUs. This does not take into consideration fault tolerance for the domain controllers, so in organizations with more than 500 mailboxes, we recommend at least one redundant domain controller. That domain controller should be configured as a global catalog server.

◆ If fault tolerance is specified in your Exchange design, it should be specified in your Active Directory design. This means each Active Directory site that contains an Exchange mailbox server (and consequently Hub Transport and Client Access server roles) should contain two domain controller/global catalog servers.

◆ Remember that Outlook 2000 and later clients also use global catalog servers for global address list lookups.

Another factor that we consider a tangible factor when designing an Exchange 2007 system is recoverability and meeting service level agreements. As you will learn in Chapter 16, "Backup and Disaster Recovery," there are many types of outages and many approaches to recovering from them. Your Active Directory and Exchange designs may be subject to meeting a specific service level agreement that includes a statement defining recovery time for different types of outages:

◆ The simpler a server's configuration is, the more quickly you can rebuild it if you have to perform a bare metal restore. Bare metal restores usually require that you start over with the server build and redo everything from the operating system on up to the application and all customization that has been done to the server. While small organizations (under 500) may not be able to segment server roles on to dedicated server hardware, for large organizations this certainly can help reduce the complexity of the server. Reduced server configuration complexity assists in speeding recovery.

◆ The local continuous replication (LCR) feature of Exchange 2007 is one of its most promising features with respect to improving recoverability times. LCR allows you to keep a almost completely synchronized copy of the database ready to put into production in case the live copy of the database has corruption. At a bare minimum, this feature will require twice as much disk space (if you replicate all of your databases) as you had originally planned for. Naturally, there is additional overhead associated with keeping a synchronized copy of the database, so if you are using LCR you may not be able to support as many mailboxes on one mailbox server.

◆ The time it takes to restore a mailbox database from backup is directly proportional to the size of the database. Larger databases mean longer restoration times in the event of a single database corruption or failure. Creating more databases with fewer mailboxes can help reduce recovery time. Exchange Server 2007 Standard Edition provides you with up to 5 mailbox databases and Exchange Server 2007 Enterprise Edition provides you with up to 50. We recommend that no single database in exceed 100GB in a non-LCR environment and 200GB in an LCR environment.

◆ Potential speed of data restoration may affect the sizing of your servers. Calculate the amount of data that you will be hosting on any given mailbox server and then calculate how long it will take you to restore that data in a worst-case scenario. Is that acceptable in your environment?

Do you remember those hard numbers and graphs that prove to your boss that you have exceeded your current computing capacity? Nothing beats performance monitoring tools and reports for visually providing tangible evidence that you are exceeding your capacity. We will look at these in more detail later in this chapter, but for now here are some things that you can use performance monitoring to locate bottlenecks that would indicate insufficient resources:

◆ Performance monitoring may indicate insufficient hardware resources such as memory or disk I/O capacity on existing servers.

◆ When querying a domain controller or global catalog, performance monitoring may pinpoint bottlenecks that indicate either a performance problem or an overloaded domain controller/global catalog.

The final tangible factor in sizing servers and choosing hardware is the eighth layer of the OSI model; this is the political layer. We all frequently joke about our jobs being part politics, but in many organizations this is a reality. Here are some factors that might require a political design decision rather than a technical design decision:

◆ Satellite or regional offices require their own Exchange server hardware even in the face of consolidation.

◆ Executives or some divisions of an organization expect to be on isolated server hardware.

◆ A department feels like having their mail on a server with everyone else is not secure enough.

Monitoring Performance

Using the Windows performance monitoring tools to monitor Exchange server is a topic that could easily cover an entire chapter or even two. In this chapter, we'll cover some basic performance monitoring counters and EMS cmdlets that can help you in determining whether you have performance problems.

Performance Degradation

If all we had to worry about was measuring performance and planning for server capacity, then our jobs would be much easier. In your server design, capacity planning, and analysis, there are a number of addition factors to consider:

◆ Consolidated servers (multiple roles on a single server) can contribute to degraded server performance. On a server that supports more than 500 mailboxes as well as other functions, such as Hub Transport and Client Access server roles, ensure that transaction logs, message databases, and message queues are all on separate physical disk drives.

◆ Local continuous replication (LCR) will significantly increase the I/O requirements for mailbox servers. LCR databases and transaction logs must be on separate physical disks to ensure that performance does not suffer.

◆ LCR will place a significant burden on the server's CPU — by some estimates, as much as 40 percent additional burden if all databases have an LCR copy. Consider this when calculating CPU capacity and the number of mailboxes that a single server can support.

◆ Antivirus software configured to scan mailbox databases using the Exchange Antivirus API can use significant amounts of RAM and CPU capacity.

◆ Antivirus applications on Hub Transport servers can also use quite a bit of RAM and consume some of the CPU resources.

◆ Transport rules are executed for every message that passes through a Hub Transport server. The more transport rules that are processed, the more CPU and memory overhead will be consumed by the Hub Transport server. In an organization with more than 100 transport rules, consider segmenting the Hub Transport role to its own physical hardware.

◆ Backup applications use a significant amount of resources during the backup process. Streaming backup applications use a lot of disk I/O time when backing up data in mailbox databases. Volume shadow copy backups of production databases will also impact perceived response time for users who are working during the backups. Perform streaming backups during the off-hours or implement LCR and then volume shadow copy backups of the LCR databases rather than the production databases.

◆ Implementing Secure Sockets Layer (SSL) on Client Access servers is essential for providing better security for web applications such as Outlook Anywhere, Outlook Web Access, and ActiveSync. However, SSL will introduce approximately a 25 percent CPU overhead on the Client Access server.

◆ EdgeSync can place a larger load on a Hub Transport server if it is run frequently. EdgeSync requires internal connectivity to both Active Directory and mailbox servers.

◆ Running scheduled tasks such as updating address lists and e-mail address lists can generate additional disk utilization as well as CPU activity and Active Directory queries.

Exchange Management Shell Cmdlets

Exchange 2007 has a few cmdlets that are useful when testing or measuring potential performance problems. The first is the `Test-MAPIConnectivity` cmdlet. It allows you to test MAPI connectivity to a mailbox you specify. For example, if you want to test MAPI connectivity for a mailbox named Suriya.Supatanasakul, you would type this:

```
Test-MAPIConnectivity Suriya.Supatanasakul

MailboxServer    Database          Result    Latency(MS) Error
-------------    --------          ------    ----------- -----
HNLEX03          Mailbox Database  Success        20
```

The mailbox test will access the mailbox store on which the mailbox is located and access the mailbox to ensure that it can be accessed. The output tells you whether or not that test was successful and how much latency was measured. The latency should usually be less than 200 milliseconds. Higher latencies could indicate a network problem or that the server is not responding to RPC requests quickly enough.

If you do not specify a mailbox name, the cmdlet will access all of the system mailboxes on the local server and report latency for each of those mailbox databases:

```
[PS] C:\>Test-MAPIConnectivity

MailboxServer    Database          Result    Latency(MS) Error
-------------    --------          ------    ----------- -----
HNLEX03          Engineering Mail  Success        58
HNLEX03          Mailbox Database  Success        18
```

Another useful testing tool for measuring server response time is the `Test-Mailflow` cmdlet. Without any parameters, the `Test-Mailflow` cmdlet will send mail to the local system mailbox:

```
Test-Mailflow

TestMailflowResult    MessageLatencyTime         IsRemoteTest
------------------    ------------------         ------------
Success               00:00:01.6388565                  False
```

The `MessageLatencyTime` column indicates (in seconds) how long it took to deliver a message. Within the same Active Directory site (or within the same server), this should take no longer than 2 or 3 seconds. By sending a test message (to a system mailbox by default), the `Test-Mailflow` cmdlet tests not only the Mailbox server's responsiveness, but also how well the Hub Transport server is responding as well as the efficiency of Active Directory queries. Each of these places can be a bottleneck when a message is sent.

However, you can specify a source server and a specific target server using the `-TargetMailboxServer` parameter. Here is an example:

```
Test-Mailflow hnlex01 -TargetMailboxServer hnlex03

TestMailflowResult      MessageLatencyTime              IsRemoteTest
------------------      ------------------              ------------
Success                 00:00:02.8396133                        True
```

For tests that indicate a message latency time of greater than 3 to 5 seconds within the same Active Directory site or greater than 10 seconds between Active Directory sites, you should begin to look for potential bottlenecks such as insufficient Hub Transport server capacity, low system resources (low memory, not enough disk I/O capacity) on the mailbox server, and bottlenecks when Active Directory is queried.

If you want to test responsiveness of Outlook Web Access, there is also a `Test-OwaConnectivity` cmdlet that can prove useful. However, that cmdlet requires a that Client Access server (CAS) test user be created; the `New-TestCasConnectivityUser.ps1` script (included with the Exchange 2007 scripts) will create this user for you.

Performance Monitoring as a Work of Art

There is a lot more to performance monitoring than just adding a few counters to a chart or report and then making some conclusions based on what you see. Getting an accurate picture of the performance and bottlenecks is something between a science and an art form. Before we jump in to the actual mechanics of performance monitoring, we would like to cover just a few basic and important tips:

◆ When monitoring, take averages over a period of hours (usually during the busiest part of the day).

◆ Avoid the temptation to look at a small snapshot of performance and making load-balancing situations. Spikes or lulls in usage will not represent your average performance.

◆ Don't run performance monitoring against a server you have just rebooted. Sometimes a server may take a few days to settle in to a typical performance profile.

◆ Always develop a performance baseline for a system so that you know what counter values are "normal" for a particular usage profile. Remember, though, that this will change over time as usage increases, more features are used, or more users are added to the system.

Now let's look at some of the basics of using the System Monitor application and what you can find when you use the Performance Monitor console and the System Monitor object. Figure 6.1 shows the Add Counters dialog box from the System Monitor tool. Counters are the meat and potatoes of what you are looking for when you use the System Monitor tool in the Performance Monitor console. However, we want to look a little more closely at this interface.

At the top of the Add Counters interface is the option to specify which computer you are actually looking at. You can either specify the local computer or you can monitor another computer across the network. This means you don't actually have to be sitting on the console of the computer you want to monitor.

The Performance Object drop-down list allows you to select a specific performance object or object category. Different software components will add additional performance monitor objects to a server; this is also true of Exchange Server 2007 roles. Different server roles will add additional performance objects and this will explain why you will see different performance objects on different servers.

Some performance objects have multiple instances. A good example is the Processor object. You will have a _Total instance that represents all of the processes combined and you will have individual processor numbers (starting from 0). This means that you could monitor the performance of an individual CPU on a multiprocessor system.

Finally we get to the counters list. The counters are what actually provide us with data about the components of Windows and Exchange. In Figure 6.1, you see that the performance object that is selected is the Processor object; possible counters for that particular object include the percentage of idle time (%Idle Time), the percentage of time the CPU is running privileged threads (%Privileged Time), and the percentage of time the processor is doing real work (%Processor Time). Each object will have unique counters. Some of these counters report actual, measured data while others (such as the processor counters) may report on data measured in a percentage (0 to 100).

When performance monitor data is displayed, there are two views you'll find useful. The first is the chart view; the chart view is probably the most common (see Figure 6.2).

FIGURE 6.2

Using the chart view of the System Monitor

The chart view is best for spotting trends; by default it provides only 100 seconds of historical information, but the sample interval can be changed on the System Monitor property page (shown in Figure 6.3). If you are trying to gather information over a period of time (say, for an entire morning), you would definitely want to change the sample interval. For example, if you wanted the chart to include three hours worth of information, you would change the sample interval to about 77 seconds.

The Performance Monitor console can also record activity over a period of time using the Counter Logs feature. You can schedule the Performance Monitor to start at a specific time (such as 8:30 in the morning), record the objects and counters you desire, and then stop at a specific time. You can then use the recorded Performance Monitor counters to review activity in a chart (or report) over time.

The report view of the System Monitor is not as spiffy-looking as the chart view, but it provides you with a much easier way to look at actual numbers as opposed to trends. If the data source you are viewing is current activity, then the values shown on the report view will be the average of the previous recorded value and the current recorded value. If the data source is a previously recorded log file, then the report view shows you the average over the life span of the log file. The System Monitor view in Figure 6.4 shows the report view. When looking at live data, the report view is helpful for looking at a specific piece of information at a certain point in time. Remember that when you're looking at performance statistics and analyzing bottlenecks, a particular point in time is not as useful as looking at averages over a period of time, such as when the server is busiest.

The report view is helpful in seeing information that is static or that does not change much over time.

FIGURE 6.3
Changing System
Monitor properties

FIGURE 6.4
Using the report view of
System Monitor

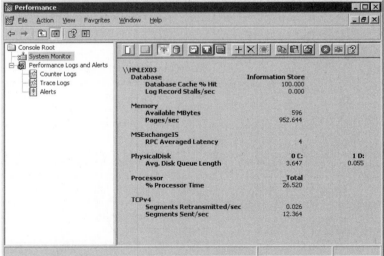

Performance Monitor Counters

As we mentioned earlier, a full discussion of performance monitoring and Exchange 2007 could consume several chapters. Indeed, once Exchange 2007 is installed on a server (depending on the roles selected), nearly 70 different Performance Monitor objects are created; that says nothing of the actual counters and instances of each of these objects!

In this section, we'll look at some of the counters that may help you to understand when a server has exceeded its capacity. Let's start with some basic operating system objects and counters; these are pretty universal when it comes to performance monitoring, so you may have seen them before. The recommendations that we are making for minimum or maximum thresholds are based on our own experiences and may not agree with "official" Microsoft documentation. Some of the basic operating system counters are shown in Table 6.1. These can help you decide if you need to add more capacity to an existing server or to add an additional server.

While we can't easily come up with performance counters that will help you in every situation, the ones in Table 6.1 are generic enough to help you get started and to help you in deciding if you have a specific type of bottleneck.

TABLE 6.1: Operating System Performance Counters and Recommended Thresholds

OBJECT/COUNTER	RECOMMENDED VALUES
Processor/ %Processor Time	This is the total percentage of time that the server's CPU is doing useful work (as opposed to idle threads). Examine this counter over a period of typical usage rather than worrying about spikes in activity. The average value of the %Processor Time should usually be less than 70%. If CPU activity is excessive, examine other counters to make sure the server does not need memory or additional disk capacity before deciding you need additional CPU capacity. If the server is truly CPU bound, then the solution may be to move some Exchange roles or mailboxes to an additional Mailbox server. If a server does appear to have a CPU bottleneck, you can use the Process object's %Processor Time counter to isolate which process is using the most CPU time; for this counter, select the process instances you are interested in monitoring.
Memory/Available MBytes	Shows the total amount of unused RAM. All versions of Exchange Server love physical memory. Exchange Server 2007 can consume just about as much memory as you can throw at it. This additional memory will improve performance by allowing more and more data to be cached in RAM, thus reducing dependencies on disk I/O. If you see the Available MBytes counter reporting that there is less than 10% of the total amount of RAM available, you should consider adding additional RAM.
Memory/Pages/sec	The Pages/sec counter indicates the number of times per second that Windows goes to the page file to store or retrieve information that is in virtual memory. Paging can harm performance since disk access is significantly slower than RAM access. Specific maximum recommended paging values for the Pages/sec counter may vary widely depending on who is making the recommendation. In general, we consider sustained values of more than 10 pages/sec to be excessive. Additional physical RAM is usually the answer to reducing paging, though faster hard disks to support the page file may also provide better throughput for paging.

TABLE 6.1:   Operating System Performance Counters and Recommended
Thresholds *(CONTINUED)*

OBJECT/COUNTER	RECOMMENDED VALUES
TCPv4/Segments Retransmitted/sec	This counter shows the number of TCP segments that have had to be retransmitted each second. If you find that the value of this counter is greater than 5% of the total TCPv4/Segments Sent/sec counter, then you may have network problems such as routers that are congested or switching problems. Each of these things can cause dropped or lost packets. Always check your network card configurations to make sure they are connected and make sure your network drivers are up-to-date, but this problem is almost always related to the physical infrastructure of your network.
Database/Database Cache % Hits	This is an Exchange Server–specific counter for the ESE database engine that tells you what percentage of disk requests are serviced from cache rather than from the disk. This value should be as high as possible (greater than 95%). The lower the value, the more of a disk I/O burden Exchange places on the disk subsystem. Increasing the available RAM on a server can improve the Database Cache % Hits ratio.
Database/Log Record Stalls/sec	This is an Exchange Server–specific counter for the ESE database engine that tells you if the ESE database engine is having to wait because the log buffers are full. Increasing the log buffer size may correct this, or you can increase the amount of memory in the server. Increasing the memory may reduce the amount of I/O operations that are necessary. If the server has sufficient memory, then improving the speed of the disk subsystem may be the next move. Moving transaction log file to dedicated spindles can help, as can increasing the I/O capacity of the disks that are used by the transaction logs. On servers that are hosting multiple server roles, moving roles that are disk intensive (such as the Mailbox and Hub Transport roles) to different servers can reduce the I/O load on the disk subsystem.
LogicalDisk/ %Disk Time	This counter reports how busy the disk is performing read and write operations. This is one of those counters that should be monitored over a period of typical activity. This value should not exceed 75% average utilization during this time. If disk usage is excessive, adding physical memory or additional disk I/O capacity can help, as can moving data or transaction logs off to other physical disks.
LogicalDisk/Avg. Disk Queue Length	The average disk queue length is the number of requests waiting in the disk queue to either be written to the disks or read from the disk. This is another value that should be monitored over a period of average activity rather than looking at a single point in time. The value should not be more than 2 over a sustained period of activity. Larger values may indicate that the disk subsystem is not able to keep up with the disk I/O requirements. If disk usage is excessive, adding physical memory or additional disk I/O capacity can help, as can moving data or transaction logs off to other physical disks.
MSExchangeIS/RPC Averaged Latency	The RPC Averaged Latency counter reports the latency of remote procedure calls that are serviced by the information store. The value is the average if the RPC latency of the last 1,024 RPC packets; the value displayed is in milliseconds. In general, it should not exceed 50 milliseconds. Insufficient server resources can often cause this value to be too high, but it is more frequently due to network problems.

(CONTINUED)

TABLE 6.1: Operating System Performance Counters and Recommended Thresholds *(CONTINUED)*

OBJECT/COUNTER	RECOMMENDED VALUES
MSExchangeIS/RPC Requests	The RPC Requests counter reports the number of remote procedure call requests that are currently being serviced by the information store. The information store service can service a maximum of 100 requests and this value should usually not exceed 30 requests. Insufficient Exchange Server resources (either memory or I/O capacity) usually contribute to the server accumulating RPC requests. If RPC requests are not being serviced in a timely manner, the RPC Averaged Latency counter value will also increase.
Network Interface/Bytes Total/sec	Bytes Total per second indicates the total data transfer rate of the network adapter. For 100MB network adapters, this value should be below approximately 6MB/second. For 1GB network adapters, this value should be below 60MB/second. If these values are exceeded, it may indicate that the network is a bottleneck or the server is under too much load. Installing additional servers and moving mailboxes or server roles may alleviate this condition. Upgrade to 1GB adapters and switches for the network segment that hosts the Exchange servers with only 100MB network adapters. Additional network adapters can also alleviate performance problems by locating clients on one network segment and Active Directory resources on a different network segment.
MSExchange ADAccess Domain Controllers/LDAP Read Time	The LDAP read time is the time (in milliseconds) that it takes to send an LDAP query and receive a response. For this counter, there are multiple instances (each a separate domain controller). The value of this counter should stay below 50ms on average. If it is higher than this on a sustained basis, you have a domain controller bottleneck. Adding additional domain controllers, adding additional memory to existing domain controllers, or replacing 32-bit Windows domain controllers with 64-bit domain controllers may help. Of course, poor network performance can also cause this counter to be high; local domain controllers are always preferred to domain controllers in another Active Directory site.
MSExchange ADAccess Domain Controllers/LDAP Search Time	The LDAP search time is the amount of time (in milliseconds) that it takes to send an LDAP search to a domain controller and then receive a response. Performance characteristics for this counter are the same as the LDAP Read time mentioned earlier.

Adding More Mailbox Storage

A common way to improve the scalability of mailbox servers is to add additional storage groups and mailbox databases. While this might not improve overall server performance or a user's perceived response time, it allows you to break up the amount of data you are storing and place it across multiple smaller mailbox databases. In turn, this allows you to support larger mailboxes. Keep in mind as you increase the number of mailboxes that each Mailbox server supports, increasing the amount of RAM will help improve performance and reduce the disk I/O profile.

When creating additional mailbox databases, you should plan to place each storage group's transaction logs on separate disk spindles from the database files. This can help improve performance as well as recoverability.

In the following section, we will show you how first create a new storage group and then create a database in that storage group.

Managing Storage Groups

Creating a new storage group is a simple process in either the Exchange Management Console (EMC) or the Exchange Management Shell (EMS). Storage groups for each Mailbox server role are created and managed from within the EMC within the Mailbox subcontainer of the Server Configuration work center. Figure 6.5 shows the Mailbox subcontainer of the Server Configuration work center along with the Database Management work pane.

FIGURE 6.5
Managing storage groups and mailbox databases using the Exchange Management Console

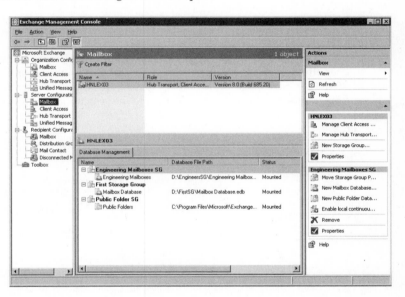

All EMC-based storage group, mailbox database, and public folder database management is performed through the Database Management pane. However, the Database Management pane is shown below the Results pane only if you have selected the Mailbox subcontainer. The EMC Actions pane is the on the right side of the EMC interface and gives you access to the following storage group management tasks:

◆ Creating a new storage group

◆ Moving existing storage group files

◆ Creating a database (mailbox or public folder) within the storage group

◆ Enabling local continuous replication

You can also retrieve a list of storage groups using the `Get-StorageGroup` EMS cmdlet. Here is an example:

```
[PS] C:\>Get-StorageGroup

Name                      Server      Replicated    Recovery
----                      ------      ----------    --------
First Storage Group       HNLEX03     None          False
Public Folder SG          HNLEX03     None          False
Engineering Mailboxes SG  HNLEX03     None          False
Executives SG             HNLEX03     None          False
```

We could have narrowed the scope of that query using the `Where` cmdlet so that only the storage groups from a specific server are listed. Here is an example that lists only the storage groups on server HNLEX03:

```
Get-StorageGroup | where {$_.Server -eq "HNLEX03"}
```

To create a new storage group, chose the New Storage Group task from the Actions pane to run the New Storage Group Wizard. The wizard is quite simple and has only two pages; the New Storage Group page (shown in Figure 6.6) prompts for the name of the storage group, the path to the transaction log files, and the path to the system files.

FIGURE 6.6
Creating a new storage group using the Exchange Management Console

You can also enable local continuous replication when you create the storage group, but we will come back and do that later. Notice also in Figure 6.6 that we are selecting the default location for the transaction logs and system files. We will come back and move them later.

When you click the New button on the New Storage Group Wizard, the task is executed and the new storage group is created; the EMS cmdlet that is executed is the `New-StorageGroup` cmdlet. The Completion page shows the EMS command that was executed to create this storage group:

```
New-StorageGroup -Server 'HNLEX03' -Name 'Executives SG'
-LogFolderPath 'C:\Program Files\Microsoft\Exchange
    Server\Mailbox\Executives SG' -SystemFolderPath
'C:\Program Files\Microsoft\Exchange Server\Mailbox\Executives SG'
```

Now that the storage group is created, the first thing you should do is move the transaction log and system files to an alternate path. This can also be accomplished via the EMC or the EMS. In the EMC, you just need to select the storage group you want to move and then choose the Move Storage Group Path task from the Actions pane. The Introduction page of the Move Storage Group Path task is shown in Figure 6.7.

FIGURE 6.7
Moving a storage group's transaction logs and system files

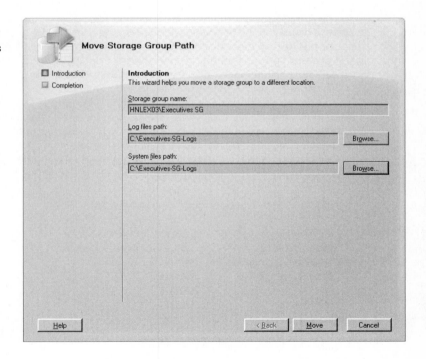

The only information that is required to move the storage group is the new location of the log files path and/or the system files path. When you click the Move button, the task is executed. The EMS cmdlet `Move-StorageGroupPath` sets the storage group's path *and* moves the existing system and/or log files. The following command was executed:

```
move-StorageGroupPath -Identity 'HNLEX03\Executives SG'
-LogFolderPath 'C:\Executives-SG-Logs'
-SystemFolderPath 'C:\Executives-SG-Logs'
```

However, if no mailbox stores have been created and mounted in the storage group, then there will be no system or transaction log files. The wizard will actually tell you this if it does not find any files. Therefore, you would need to run a slightly modified version of the cmdlet since the files do not need to be moved. You would need to include the -ConfigurationOnly switch in the command line:

```
Move-StorageGroupPath 'HNLEX03\Executives SG'
-LogFolderPath 'C:\Executives-SG-Logs' -SystemFolderPath
   'C:\Executives-SG-Logs' -ConfigurationOnly -Confirm:$False
```

You can view the properties of the storage group by selecting it in the Database Management work pane and then selecting the Properties task on the Actions pane. In this case there are two Properties tasks on the Actions pane, so select the one in the storage group portion of the pane.

The storage group properties are shown in Figure 6.8. From here you can change the storage group's display name or enable circular logging. Circular logging tells the Exchange database engine not to keep more than a few of the previous transaction log files. Enabling circular logging will prevent up-to-the minute recoverability of databases from a restore since there will not be enough transaction logs available after the most recent backup.

The storage group's properties also include the transaction log path, the system files path, the log file prefix, and the date on which the storage group was last modified. The log file prefix is used when creating log files for this storage group; this is a system-assigned value and cannot be changed. In the case of the storage group shown in Figure 6.8, the log file prefix is E03; a sample log filename would look like this: E03000011A0.log.

You can also retrieve the storage group's properties using the Get-StorageGroup cmdlet. The following example shows all of the properties of the Executives SG storage group:

```
[PS] C:\>Get-StorageGroup "Executives SG" | FL

LogFolderPath          : c:\executives-SG-Logs
SystemFolderPath       : c:\executives-sg-Logs
CircularLoggingEnabled : False
ZeroDatabasePages      : False
LogFilePrefix          : E03
LogFileSize            : 1024
RecoveryEnabled        : True
OnlineDefragEnabled    : True
IndexCheckingEnabled   : True
EventLogSourceID       : MSExchangeIS
LogCheckpointDepth     : 20971520
CommitDefault          : False
DatabaseExtensionSize  : 256
PageFragment           : 8
PageTempDBMinimum      : 0
```

```
Server                  : HNLEX03
ServerName              : HNLEX03
CopyLogFolderPath       :
CopySystemFolderPath    :
Recovery                : False
Name                    : Executives SG
Replicated              : None
HasLocalCopy            : False
MinAdminVersion         : -2147453113
AdminDisplayName        :
ExchangeVersion         : 0.1 (8.0.535.0)
DistinguishedName       : CN=Executives
    SG,CN=InformationStore,CN=HNLEX03,CN=Servers,
CN=Exchange Administrative Group (FYDIBOHF23SPDLT),
CN=Administrative Groups,CN=Volcano Surfboards,
CN=Microsoft Exchange,CN=Services,CN=Configuration,
DC=volcanosurfboards,DC=com
Identity                : HNLEX03\Executives SG
Guid                    : 772e9d5a-0b82-4cdc-867b-8922ed55215f
ObjectCategory          : volcanosurfboards.com/Configuration/
Schema/ms-Exch-Storage-Group
ObjectClass             : {top, container, msExchStorageGroup}
WhenChanged             : 12/6/2006 7:35:13 PM
WhenCreated             : 12/6/2006 7:13:46 PM
OriginatingServer       : HNLDC01.volcanosurfboards.com
IsValid                 : True
```

Many of these values can be changed by the Set-StorageGroup cmdlet. If you want to enable circular logging, you would type this command:

```
Set-StorageGroup "Executives SG" -CircularLoggingEnabled:$True
```

Managing Mailbox Databases

Now that we have created a storage group, we can create a new database in it. While both Exchange Server 2007 Standard Edition and Enterprise Edition allow up to five mailbox databases in a storage group, we are going to limit our examples to a single mailbox database per storage group. This is the Microsoft recommendation, and one mailbox database per storage group is also a requirement of local continuous replication.

You can view the current mailbox database for each server using the EMC, or you can use the Get-MailboxDatabase cmdlet to list all of the mailbox databases in the entire organization:

```
Get-MailboxDatabase
```

Name	Server	StorageGroup	Recovery
Mailbox Database	HNLEX03	First Storage Group	False
Engineering Mailb...	HNLEX03	Engineering Mailb...	False
Executives	HNLEX03	Executives SG	False

FIGURE 6.8
Viewing a storage
group's properties

Of course, you can narrow the scope of this output to just a specific server or a specific storage group using the Where cmdlet. Here are two examples:

```
Get-MailboxDatabase | Where {$_.Server -eq "HNLEX03"}
Get-MailboxDatabase | Where {$_.StorageGroupName -eq "Executives SG"}
```

TIP

When creating a new mailbox database, name the database something that is standardized and descriptive. Making sure the filename matches the display name of the database will ensure that it is easier to manage.

To create a new mailbox database, highlight the storage group in which you want the mailbox database to be created and select the New Mailbox Database task from the Actions pane. This launches the New Mailbox Database Wizard that is shown in Figure 6.9. All that is required to create a new mailbox database is to provide the name; the path will automatically be completed and the database's EDB file will be put in the same path as the transaction logs.

FIGURE 6.9
Creating a new
mailbox database
using the Exchange
Management Console

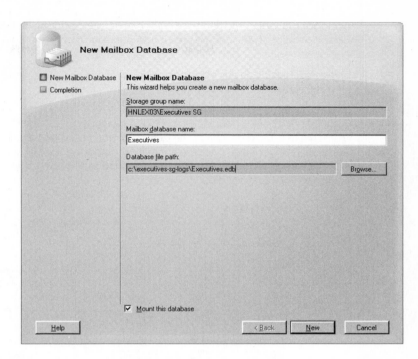

Ideally, you should click the Browse button and select a correct location for the mailbox database now, but we will show you how to move the mailbox database here shortly.

NOTE

Exchange 2000/2003 administrators may notice that the database has only an EDB file. Exchange 2007 does not have an STM file; each Exchange 2007 database consists of a single EDB file.

The wizard will also mount the database once the wizard creates the configuration for the database. This will initialize a new empty database file. The resulting commands are as follows; the New-MailboxDatabase cmdlet is used in the command to create the database and the Mount-Database cmdlet is used in the command to mount the database:

```
New-MailboxDatabase -StorageGroup 'CN=Executives
    SG,CN=InformationStore,CN=HNLEX03,CN=Servers,
CN=Exchange Administrative Group (FYDIBOHF23SPDLT),
CN=Administrative Groups,CN=Volcano Surfboards,
CN=Microsoft Exchange,CN=Services,CN=Configuration,
DC=volcanosurfboards,DC=com' -Name 'Executives'
-EdbFilePath 'c:\executives-sg-logs\Executives.edb'

Mount-Database -Identity 'CN=Executives,CN=Executives
    SG,CN=InformationStore,CN=HNLEX03,CN=Servers,
CN=Exchange Administrative Group (FYDIBOHF23SPDLT),
CN=Administrative Groups,CN=Volcano Surfboards,CN=Microsoft
    Exchange,CN=Services,CN=Configuration,DC=volcanosurfboards,DC=com'
```

Notice that when the database was created, the distinguished name of the storage group was used. However, if the storage group and database names were unique, you could also specify these commands:

```
New-MailboxDatabase -StorageGroup 'Executives SG' -Name 'Executives'
-EdbFilePath 'c:\executives-sg-logs\Executives.edb'

Mount-Database 'Executives'
```

We created the database in the default path so we could illustrate the process of moving it. Using the EMC, we can move the database by choosing the Move Database Path task in the Actions pane. The only thing that needs to be provided in the Move Database Path Wizard is the new location of the database file.

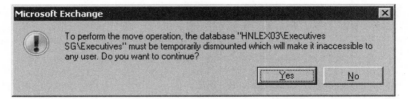

When you specify that you are about to move the database, you are warned that the database will be dismounted while the files are being copied and that it will be inaccessible.

The amount of time that it takes to move the database file will depend both on the size of the database file and the speed of the disk subsystem. Once the file is moved, the Completion page of the Move Database Path Wizard will show the EMS command that was used to move the database file. Here is an example:

```
Move-DatabasePath -Identity 'HNLEX03\Executives SG\Executives'
    -EdbFilePath 'D:\Executives-SG-DB\Executives.edb'
```

Now let's look at some of the properties of a mailbox database. Figure 6.10 shows the General property tab of the mailbox database property page. At the top is the display name of the mailbox database. From here, you can rename the database if you need to conform to a new database naming standard. The path to the database is shown, but you cannot change the path here; you must use the `Move-MailboxDatabase` cmdlet or the Move Database Path task. The database copy path is set when you configure local continuous replication.

FIGURE 6.10
General property page of
a mailbox database

There is a lot of dynamic information on the General property page of a mailbox database as well. This includes:

◆ The last full backup indicates the last time a full or normal backup was run using an Exchange API–based backup solution. Transaction logs would have also been purged at that time.

◆ The last incremental backup indicates the last time an incremental backup was run. This backup type will back up the storage group's transaction logs and then it purges them.

◆ The status indicates if the database is mounted or dismounted.

◆ The Modified field shows the date and time the database properties in Active Directory were last changed.

The Journal Recipient option allows you to specify a journaling recipient for all mailboxes located on this mailbox database. If this is enabled, a copy of any message or delivery receipt sent or received by a mailbox on this system will be sent to the journal mailbox.

The Maintenance Schedule drop-down list (or Customize button) allows you to specify when online maintenance is scheduled for this particular database. Online maintenance includes purging deleted items permanently from the mailbox database, purging deleted mailboxes permanently from the database, verifying that mailboxes on the database are all connected to an Active

Directory account, cleaning up unused folder views, and rearranging white space. Online maintenance must complete periodically, otherwise the database will be come less and less efficient and the database file will continue to grow since the deleted items and mailboxes will never be completely purged.

The Do Not Mount This Database at Startup check box allows the administrator to prevent the database from being mounted after the information store service is restarted. This might be useful when the administrator wants to make the mailbox databases available one or two at a time rather than all at once.

The This Database Can Be Overwritten by a Restore check box is used when you must restore a database file from an offline backup. An offline backup occurs when the database file itself is backed up, such as making a file copy of the database file. This has no effect when restoring a database backup that was made from an online backup.

The next tab on a mailbox database property page is the Limits property page. We will look at different ways to establish limits on mailbox database in Chapter 9, "Imposing Limits and Why," but let's do a quick review here (see Figure 6.11).

The Storage Limits section allows you to specify the amount of storage that the mailbox is allowed to have. What you see in Figure 6.11 are the storage limit defaults; administrators of previous versions will be surprised to learn that newly created mailbox databases have defaults. *Everyone* will be surprised to see the actual default values:

◆ Issue Warning at (KB) is set to 1,991,680KB. When a mailbox reaches this limit, the user will be sent an e-mail message that informs them that they have reached a limit on their mailbox and they should clean up some data in it.

◆ Prohibit Send at (KB) is set to 2,097,152KB. Once the mailbox hits this limit, user will be unable to send new messages or reply to existing messages. Both Outlook and Outlook Web Access will inform the user if they try to send a message and they are over this limit.

◆ Prohibit Send and Receive at (KB) is set to 2,411,520KB. When a mailbox exceeds this limit, the mailbox is closed or disabled. Even though the user can access the mailbox, the server will not allow the user to send new messages or reply to existing messages. In addition, the mailbox will not receive any incoming mail from other Exchange users or from outside of the organization.

Outlook Web Access has a neat new feature that will inform the user of how close they are to their limit or if they are over their limit. Simply move your mouse pointer over the top of the mailbox in the folder listing pane of Outlook Web Access and you will see a pop-up box similar to one of the ones shown here.

FIGURE 6.11
Setting limits on a
mailbox database

The limit that you see in this message is the Prohibit Send at (KB) limit, not the Prohibit Send and Receive at (KB) limit.

The Warning Message Interval drop-down list is the interval at which Exchange generates a warning message informing users that they are over their Issue Warning limit. By default, this is sent once daily at 1:00 a.m. local time. You can customize this to another time, but be careful. The Schedule dialog box (shown in Figure 6.12) has a detail view option of either 1 hour or 15 minutes.

When using any schedule box that has a 1 hour and a 15 minute view, switch to the 15 minute view to set a schedule. If you select an entire hour, then whatever process you are scheduling will run four times per hour. In this case, if you select an entire hour, a warning message will be sent to all mailboxes over their warning limit four times per hour. The users would *not* be amused. An example of the warning message is shown in Figure 6.13.

The Deletion Settings section of the Limits tab allows you to configure how long the server will retain deleted items for this mailbox and how long the server will retain a mailbox once it is deleted. The Keep Deleted Items for (Days) options specifies how many days the Exchange server will keep items that have been deleted either from the Deleted Items folder or via a hard delete (Shift+Delete) from another folder. Once a message has been in the deleted item cache for longer than this period (14 days by default for Exchange 2007), the user will no longer be able to retrieve the message using the Outlook Recover Deleted Items feature.

FIGURE 6.12
Using the Customize
Schedule dialog box

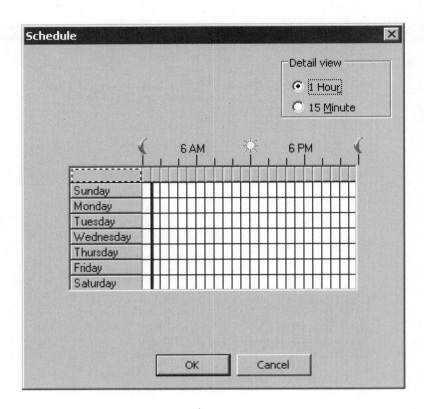

FIGURE 6.13
Warning message a user
receives when their
mailbox exceeds the
Prohibit Send at (KB)
limit

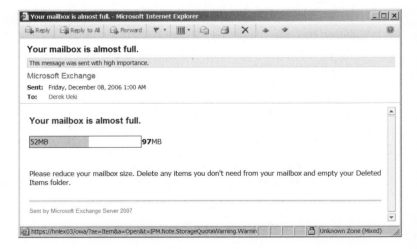

The Keep Deleted Mailboxes for (Days) option specifies how long the mailbox database will keep a deleted mailbox before it is permanently purged. The default is 30 days and that is reasonable for most organizations. A mailbox can be recovered using the EMC's Disconnected Mailbox feature or via the EMS `Connect-Mailbox` cmdlet.

The Do Not Permanently Delete Items Until the Database Has Been Backed Up check box tells the server that it should not permanently purge an item or a mailbox until the mailbox database has been backed up. This ensures that a copy of the deleted item or deleted mailbox could be recovered from backup media if necessary.

The Client Settings tab of a mailbox store (shown in Figure 6.14) allows the administrator to specify two configuration settings that affect the mailboxes on this store. The first is the Default Public Folder Database setting; this field contains the name of the public folder database that MAPI clients should connect to first when retrieving information about public folder hierarchy or content.

FIGURE 6.14
Client Settings properties of a mailbox database

The other setting affects clients that work in offline mode or local cache mode. This is the Offline Address Book setting; here you specify which offline address book (OAB) a MAPI client should download. The default is the default offline address book; this OAB contains the default global address list and is sufficient for most small and medium-sized businesses.

The properties we have just examined using the graphical user interface can also be examined using the Get-MailboxDatabase cmdlet. The following is an example of retrieving mailbox database properties and sending them to a formatted list:

```
Get-MailboxDatabase "Executives" | FL

JournalRecipient              :
MailboxRetention              : 30.00:00:00
OfflineAddressBook            : \Default Offline Address List
OriginalDatabase              :
PublicFolderDatabase          : HNLEX03\Public Folder SG\Public Folders
ProhibitSendReceiveQuota      : 2355MB
Recovery                      : False
ProhibitSendQuota             : 2GB
IndexEnabled                  : True
AdministrativeGroup           : Exchange Administrative Group (FYDIBOHF23SPDLT)
AllowFileRestore              : False
BackupInProgress              :
CopyEdbFilePath               :
DatabaseCreated               : True
Description                   :
EdbFilePath                   : D:\Executives-SG-DB\Executives.edb
ExchangeLegacyDN              : /o=Volcano Surfboards/ou=Exchange Administrative
   Group (FYDIBOHF23SPDLT)/cn=Configuration/cn=Servers
/cn=HNLEX03/cn=Microsoft Private MDB
HasLocalCopy                  : False
DeletedItemRetention          : 14.00:00:00
LastFullBackup                :
LastIncrementalBackup         :
MaintenanceSchedule           : {Sun.1:00 AM-Sun.5:00 AM, Mon.1:00 AM-Mon.5:00AM,
Tue.1:00 AM-Tue.5:00 AM, Wed.1:00 AM-Wed.5:00 AM, Thu.1:00 AM-Thu.5:00 AM,
Fri.1:00 AM-Fri.5:00 AM, Sat.1:00 AM-Sat.5:00 AM}
MountAtStartup                : True
Mounted                       :
Organization                  : Volcano Surfboards
QuotaNotificationSchedule     : {Sun.1:00 AM-Sun.1:15 AM, Mon.1:00 AM-Mon.1:15AM,
Tue.1:00 AM-Tue.1:15 AM, Wed.1:00 AM-Wed.1:15 AM, Thu.1:00 AM-Thu.1:15 AM,
Fri.1:00 AM-Fri.1:15 AM, Sat.1:00 AM-Sat.1:15 AM}
RetainDeletedItemsUntilBackup : False
Server                        : HNLEX03
ServerName                    : HNLEX03
StorageGroup                  : HNLEX03\Executives SG
StorageGroupName              : Executives SG
IssueWarningQuota             : 1945MB
EventHistoryRetentionPeriod   : 7.00:00:00
Name                          : Executives
MinAdminVersion               : -2147453113
AdminDisplayName              : Executives
ExchangeVersion               : 0.1 (8.0.535.0)
```

```
DistinguishedName             : CN=Executives,CN=Executives SG,
CN=InformationStore,CN=HNLEX03,CN=Servers,CN=Exchange
Administrative Group (FYDIBOHF23SPDLT),CN=Administrative Groups,
CN=Volcano Surfboards,CN=Microsoft Exchange,CN=Services,
CN=Configuration,DC=volcanosurfboards,DC=com
Identity                      : HNLEX03\Executives SG\Executives
Guid                          : 99c3570b-d19b-493b-aec6-4da1b2c3bbb3
ObjectCategory                : volcanosurfboards.com/Configuration/Schema/
ms-Exch-Private-MDB
ObjectClass                   : {top, msExchMDB, msExchPrivateMDB}
WhenChanged                   : 12/6/2006 8:32:31 PM
WhenCreated                   : 12/6/2006 8:27:15 PM
OriginatingServer             : HNLDC01.volcanosurfboards.com
IsValid                       : True
```

Not all of these properties that you see in the output of the Get-MailboxDatabase cmdlet can be changed, of course. The mailbox database location must be changed using the Move-MailboxDatabase cmdlet and some of these are system properties.

The properties that you are able to change can be changed through the EMS using the Set-MailboxDatabase cmdlet. For example, to change the Prohibit Send At (KB) quota to 100MB, you would type this:

```
Set-MailboxDatabase "Executives" -ProhibitSendQuota:100MB
```

Local Continuous Replication

Local continuous replication (LCR) is one of the most promising features of Exchange 2007. The key point of LCR is to allow you to have a nearly completely replicated copy of the current database on the local server. In a situation where the production database is no longer functioning, the administrator can switch from the production database to the LCR database.

LCR is enabled on a per-storage group basis and the storage group cannot have more than one mailbox or public folder database. When first enabled, LCR creates a seeded copy of the current database; at the point of creation, the LCR database that was seeded will be the same as the production database. As transactions are committed to the production database, the transaction logs are filled. When a transaction log fills up, LCR copies the transaction log file to the LCR transaction log location for that particular storage group. The log is then replayed into the LCR copy of the database; Microsoft calls the LCR database the "passive" copy of the database. At any given time, the LCR database should be within one transaction log of being completely synchronized. If the database is dismounted, the LCR database becomes fully synchronized.

TIP

Local continuous replication is one of the reasons that the Exchange database transaction log file size was reduced from 5MB to 1MB. This ensures that transactions are committed to the LCR database more quickly.

The advantage of this is that it reduces the amount of time necessary to restore a database from backup to practically no time at all. This will allow you to safely support larger and larger database sizes and still maintain good recoverability and recover times. Still, supporting LCR is not a license to have 5TB mailbox databases since you still have to worry about a situation in which you might have to completely rebuild the server or the entire disk subsystem. Databases still have to be backed up to an alternate media even if you do have LCR copies. Further, the database size show not be so large that nightly online maintenance cannot be completed at least once every week.

Microsoft recommends mailbox databases of no more than 100GB without LCR and mailbox databases of up to 200GB with LCR.

> **TIP**
>
> Local continuous replication provides you with a locally backed-up copy of databases. If the entire server fails or must be rebuilt, you still have to restore data from an alternate media. Keep this in mind when planning for database sizes.

One additional possible advantage to using LCR is that you can streamline your backup process. Streaming backups and volume shadow copy (VSS) backups of production databases can adversely affect performance during the backup windows. Backup windows have to be precisely calculated in order to ensure that online maintenance is completed at least once week for each database.

An alternate backup approach for Exchange is to use LCR to keep a completely synchronized copy of the production database and then to use a VSS backup of the LCR database. As long as the LCR copy of the database is on different spindles from the production database, the VSS back should not noticeably affect the I/O on the production database disk.

Requirements for Local Continuous Replication

There are some requirements that you need to plan for when you implement LCR. These include ensuring that you have adequate server capacity and that your storage groups are configured properly. Here are some tips when planning to implement LCR:

◆ Implementing LCR will generally increase the amount of CPU and memory capacity on a server by at least 30 to 40 percent. Do not implement LCR on a server that is already on the border of having performance problems. Move mailboxes or server roles to another server to lighten the load on a mailbox server on which you are planning to enable LCR.

◆ For the best level of recoverability and performance, LCR databases and transaction logs should be on separate physical disks or separate logical units (LUNS if you using a SAN) from the production databases and logs.

◆ Sufficient disk capacity must exist for LCR databases and transaction logs. If you have 500GB of available disk space for the production databases, your LCR database will need to be the same size. The disks that host the LCR databases and transaction logs should be capable of the same I/O capacity as the production databases.

◆ On heavily loaded mailbox servers, you may run out of drive letter capacity when adding LCR databases and transaction logs. Volume mount points can be used in this instance.

◆ Storage groups can have no more than one mailbox or public folder database each.

◆ Only one public folder database in an entire Exchange organization can be replicated with LCR. The LCR solution for organizations with more than one public folder database is to use public folder replication.

◆ It is more efficient to start using LCR immediately after you create a storage group and mailbox database. Enabling LCR for an existing storage group and database will take longer if the database file size is large.

If you can't meet the prerequisites for LCR, then you should look at improving the capacity of your server resources and configuration prior to starting. If a server is not configured with the proper capacity, you will find that you make performance problems worse.

Configuring Local Continuous Replication

Configuring LCR is pretty simple to do and it can be done via the Exchange Management Console (EMC) or the Exchange Management Shell (EMS). We will take you through a configuration of LCR using the EMC and then cover the necessary EMS steps to accomplish the same tasks.

To enable a storage group to use LCR via the EMC, you can use a wizard. In the EMC, locate the storage group in the Server Configuration work center and under the Mailbox subcontainer. Highlight the server name in the Results pane and then locate the storage group in the Work pane. Select the Enable Local Continuous Replication task in the Actions pane; this runs the Enable Storage Group Local Continuous Replication Wizard. The Introduction page of this wizard is shown in Figure 6.15.

FIGURE 6.15

Starting the Enable Storage Group Local Continuous Replication Wizard

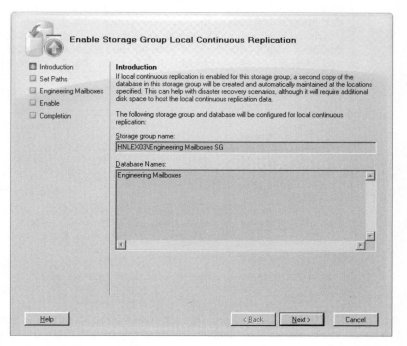

All you have to do on the Introduction page of the wizard is confirm the storage group name and confirm that there is only a single database in the storage group. The database list is labeled "Database Names," but the wizard will stop you later if the storage group has more than one database.

Just like creating a storage group, you must define the location of the transaction log files and the system files. On the Set Paths page (shown in Figure 6.16), you must specify the LCR paths for the transaction logs and system files. Ideally, these paths should be on a separate physical disk from the original transaction logs, the original database, and the LCR database.

FIGURE 6.16
Specifying LCR paths
for transaction logs and
system paths

The screen capture shown in Figure 6.17 shows the Engineering Mailboxes page of the Enable Storage Group Local Continuous Replication Wizard. This page is unique to the database contained in the storage group you have selected and thus will usually be different depending on the database that appears in the Database Names field.

On the Engineering Mailboxes page, the only thing you can specify is the location of the LCR database. Ideally, like the LCR path for the system and transaction log files, this should path should be on a separate physical disk from the original database and transaction log files as well as the LCR transaction log and system files.

The Enable page of the wizard simply shows the configuration summary of what tasks are about to be performed.

Once the Enable button is clicked on the Enable page, the Enable-DatabaseCopy and Enable-StorageGroup copy cmdlets are used to enable LCR for this storage group and database. The following are the commands that are actually executed by the wizard:

```
Enable-DatabaseCopy -Identity 'HNLEX03\Engineering Mailboxes
    SG\Engineering Mailboxes'
-CopyEdbFilePath 'D:\Engineers-Mailboxes-LCR\Engineering Mailboxes.edb'

Enable-StorageGroupCopy -Identity 'CN=Engineering Mailboxes SG,CN=InformationStore,
CN=HNLEX03,CN=Servers,CN=Exchange Administrative Group (FYDIBOHF23SPDLT),
```

```
CN=Administrative Groups,CN=Volcano Surfboards,CN=Microsoft Exchange,CN=Services,
CN=Configuration,DC=volcanosurfboards,DC=com'
-CopyLogFolderPath 'D:\EngineersSG-LCR'
-CopySystemFolderPath 'D:\EngineersSG-LCR'
```

FIGURE 6.17
Specifying a path for the
LCR database

Notice that the fully qualified distinguished name was used in the `Enable-StorageGroupCopy` command to identify the storage group name. To help you disseminate and decode what was done, here is a summary of the configuration parameters used to enable LCR for the storage group and database:

Storage group name	Engineering Mailboxes SG
Database name	Engineering Mailboxes
LCR transaction logs path	`D:\EngineersSG-LCR`
LCR system files path	`D:\EngineersSG-LCR`
LCR database path	`D:\Engineers-Mailboxes-LCR`

Managing Local Continuous Replication

Once LCR is enabled for a storage group, there are a few management tasks that you may need to perform. Management tasks for LCR include checking the health of a storage group's replication, suspending replication, resuming replication, and resynchronizing (aka reseeding) the entire database.

HEALTH CHECKS

Now that storage group replication is enabled, you can confirm that it is working in a number of different ways. The first is just to look at the listing of storage groups and databases names in the Work pane. Notice for the Engineering Mailboxes SG that the value in the Copy Status column is Healthy.

Here are the possible status values you may see in the Copy Status column (or in the SummaryCopyStatus property when you use the EMS cmdlet):

◆ **Healthy** means that LCR is working normally and data is replicating and being committed to the LCR copy of the database.

◆ **Disabled** means that LCR is not configured.

◆ **Suspended** means that an operator has temporarily stopped replication.

◆ **Seeding** means that the production database is being copied to the LCR location.

◆ **Failed** means that something has failed during the replication process and there may be problems with the configuration, logs, or database. Consult the event logs.

◆ **Not Supported** means that the current configuration does not support or allow LCR.

Using the EMS cmdlet `Get-StorageGroupCopyStatus`, you can retrieve more useful and detailed information about the LCR status of a particular storage group. Here is an example:

```
Get-StorageGroupCopyStatus "Engineering Mailboxes SG" | Format-List
```

```
Identity                      : HNLEX03\Engineering Mailboxes SG
StorageGroupName              : Engineering Mailboxes SG
SummaryCopyStatus             : Healthy
CCRTargetNode                 :
Failed                        : False
FailedMessage                 :
Seeding                       : False
Suspend                       : False
SuspendComment                :
CopyQueueLength               : 2
ReplayQueueLength             : 9
LatestAvailableLogTime        : 12/10/2006 11:39:27 PM
LastCopyNotificationedLogTime : 12/10/2006 11:39:27 PM
LastCopiedLogTime             : 12/10/2006 11:39:26 PM
LastInspectedLogTime          : 12/10/2006 11:38:45 PM
LastReplayedLogTime           : 12/10/2006 11:33:18 PM
LastLogGenerated              : 1768
LastLogCopyNotified           : 1768
LastLogCopied                 : 1767
LastLogInspected              : 1766
LastLogReplayed               : 1757
LatestFullBackupTime          : 11/25/2006 12:05:57 PM
LatestIncrementalBackupTime   : 12/4/2006 8:46:09 PM
SnapshotBackup                : False
IsValid                       : True
ObjectState                   : Unchanged
```

SUSPENDING AND RESUMING REPLICATION

There is really not much that you need to do to an LCR database once it is replicating. If you have to do maintenance on the disk on which LCR is running or if you want to stop all replication, you can highlight the storage group that is running LCR and click Suspend Local Continuous Replication in the Actions pane. When you choose to suspend LCR, you are prompted for a reason. Simply type a reason and click Yes.

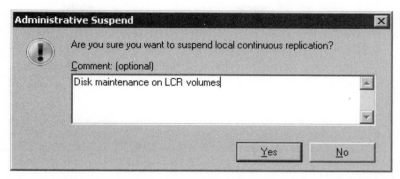

To resume LCR on the storage group, select the storage group and then click Resume Local Continuous Replication in the Actions pane. You will be prompted to confirm that this is what you want to do and you will see the reason that LCR was suspended previously.

You can accomplish the same thing using the Suspend-StorageGroupCopy and Resume-StorageGroupCopy cmdlets:

```
Suspend-StorageGroupCopy "Engineering Mailboxes SG" -SuspendComment "LC
R disk maintenance on December 12" -Confirm:$False
```

Once LCR is suspended, you can confirm it also using the Get-StorageGroupCopyStatus cmdlet, as you can see in this example:

```
get-storagegroupcopystatus "Engineering Mailboxes SG" |
FL Identity,StorageGroupName,SummaryCopyStatus,SuspendComment

Identity            : HNLEX03\Engineering Mailboxes SG
StorageGroupName    : Engineering Mailboxes SG
SummaryCopyStatus   : Suspended
SuspendComment      : LCR disk maintenance on December 12
```

The Application event log will contain event ID 2083 from the MSExchangeRepl service indicating that replication for the storage group has been suspended:

```
Event Type: Information
Event Source: MSExchangeRepl
```

```
Event Category: Action
Event ID: 2083
Date: 12/10/2006
Time: 11:50:58 PM
Computer: HNLEX03
Description:
Replication for storage group HNLEX03\Engineering Mailboxes SG has been suspended.
```

TIP

If you suspend LCR during busy times for your server, expect to have a lot of logs that need to be replayed when you resume LCR.

When you are ready to resume LCR for that storage group, you can use the `Resume-StorageGroupCopy` cmdlet:

```
Resume-StorageGroupCopy "Engineering Mailboxes SG"
```

The `Resume-StorageGroupCopy` cmdlet starts the log files copying and replaying once again and it clears the `SuspendComment` property. When LCR is restarted, you will see the following event information in the Application event log:

```
Event Type: Information
Event Source: MSExchangeRepl
Event Category: Action
Event ID: 2084
Date: 12/11/2006
Time: 8:04:24 AM
Computer: HNLEX03
Description:
Replication for storage group HNLEX03\Engineering Mailboxes SG has been resumed.
```

You will also see events in the event log indicating that the log files have started copying (event ID 2114) and log files have started replying (event ID 2115). These are normal and expected:

```
Event Type: Information
Event Source: MSExchangeRepl
Event Category: Service
Event ID: 2115
Date: 12/11/2006
Time: 8:05:08 AM
Computer: HNLEX03
Description:
The replication instance for storage group Engineering Mailboxes SG
has started replaying logfiles. Logfiles up to generation 1788
have been replayed.
```

RESYNCHRONIZING LOCAL CONTINUOUS REPLICATION

Under some circumstances, it may be come necessary to resynchronize the database or to manually resume replication. This operation is also called reseeding. This may be necessary if you created an LCR database before the original database was created, if you have performed an offline defragmentation of the original database, if the LCR database gets deleted, or if the LCR database becomes corrupted.

The only way to resynchronize the database is to use the EMS cmdlet `Update-StorageGroupCopy`. Prior to running this cmdlet, you should suspend LCR for the storage group that you are working on and then delete the LCR files (database and transaction log files) unless you are planning to use the `-DeleteExistingFiles` parameter. Here is an example:

```
Update-StorageGroupCopy "Engineering Mailboxes SG" -DeleteExistingFiles

Confirm
Continuous replication seeding found an obsolete checkpoint
'D:\EngineersSG-LCR\E02.chk' file for storage group copy 'Engineering
 Mailboxes  SG'. The checkpoint file will be deleted, and then the
 database will be seeded if you confirm now.
[Y] Yes  [A] Yes to All  [N] No  [L] No to All  [S] Suspend  [?] Help
(default is "Y"):y

Confirm
Continuous replication seeding found an existing target database
'D:\Engineers-Mailboxes-LCR\Engineering Mailboxes.edb' for storage
 group copy 'Engineering Mailboxes SG'. This target database will
be deleted, before seeding starts, if you confirm.
[Y] Yes  [A] Yes to All  [N] No  [L] No to All  [S] Suspend  [?] Help
(default is "Y"):y
```

This operation can take a fairly significant amount of time if the production database is large. Remember that it is making a copy of the production database. If you do this during a period when the load on the Exchange server is typical, you may affect your end users' response times when they are using the server. We recommend you perform this operation during off-hours or periods of low usage.

Recovery Using Local Continuous Replication

The reason you put LCR into operation in the first place is to allow you to very quickly bring online a backup copy of the database. You would only need to do this if the production database has become corrupted. Database corruption is a tough topic to try to address in just a few lines, but we should state clearly here that as long as the production database is on a separate physical disk from the transaction logs, the LCR transaction logs, and the LCR copy of the database, the corruption should not extend to the LCR copy of the database.

How will you know that your production database is corrupted? We can think of a couple of situations:

◆ Normal or full backups of the production database fail. Online backups of the database using Exchange-aware backup software will perform a page-by-page check of the database as it backs it up. If a page-level error is detected, the backup halts, the error is logged to the backup log, and the error is logged to the Application event log.

◆ If corruption is detected during normal operations (for example, if the database engine reads a page of data that is corrupted), Exchange confirms that the page in the database is bad and logs an event to the Event Viewer.

◆ The database will not mount or reports errors when you try to mount it.

FIGURE 6.18
Errors found when Exchange Server reads a corrupted page from the database

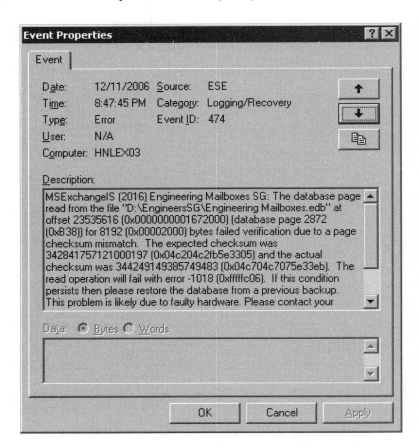

Monitoring for potential errors in your production databases is something you should do regularly, or you should configure your monitoring system to monitor for specific errors in either the Application event log (such as the one shown in Figure 6.18) or the backup logs such as the one shown here:

```
Backup started on 12/11/2006 at 8:47 PM.
The 'Microsoft Information Store' returned 'Error returned from an
ESE function call (d).
' from a call to 'HrESEBackupRead()' additional data '-'The 'Microsoft
 Information Store' returned 'Error returned from an ESE function call
```

```
(d).
' from a call to 'HrESEBackupRead()' additional data '-'
The operation was ended.
Backup completed on 12/11/2006 at 8:47 PM.
Directories: 0
```

Note in the case of the error shown in Figure 6.18 that the database was mounted and functioning. The error did not interfere with the normal functioning of the database but was rather a single page in the database that could not be read properly. This error was probably due to the disk subsystem, device driver, or firmware. It is unlikely that the problem would extend to the LCR copy of the database.

If you realize that your production database is corrupted, you can manually switch the LCR database into production. This is done using the `Restore-StorageGroupCopy` cmdlet. Before we do an example, let's look at the current location of the live database and logs as well as the locations of the LCR files. Here are two quick ways to retrieve this information using the EMS:

```
[PS] C:\>Get-StorageGroup "Engineering Mailboxes SG" | FL name,*path*

Name                  : Engineering Mailboxes SG
LogFolderPath         : D:\EngineersSG
SystemFolderPath      : D:\EngineersSG
CopyLogFolderPath     : D:\EngineersSG-LCR
CopySystemFolderPath  : D:\EngineersSG-LCR


[PS] C:\>Get-MailboxDatabase "Engineering Mailboxes" | FL name,*path*

Name            : Engineering Mailboxes
CopyEdbFilePath : D:\Engineers-Mailboxes-LCR\Engineering Mailboxes.edb
EdbFilePath     : D:\EngineersSG\Engineering Mailboxes.edb
```

There are two steps to switching over to using an LCR database instead of the original production database. The production database must be dismounted and then the LCR database/log locations are swapped out. There are two approaches to "swapping out" the database. The first (and desired) approach is to copy the LCR database to the production database location. Here is an example:

```
[PS] C:\>Dismount-Database "engineering mailboxes" -Confirm:$False
[PS] C:\>Restore-StorageGroupCopy "Engineering Mailboxes SG"
      Base name: e02
      Log file: D:\EngineersSG\E0200000774.log
      Csv file: D:\EngineersSG-LCR\IgnoredLogs\q5cfbb2m.koe

      Base name: e02
      Log file: D:\EngineersSG-LCR\E0200000774.log
      Csv file: D:\EngineersSG-LCR\IgnoredLogs\5p52d1ni.kxz

Integrity check passed for log file: D:\EngineersSG-LCR\inspector\E0200000775.log
Integrity check passed for log file: D:\EngineersSG-LCR\inspector\E0200000776.log
```

```
Integrity check passed for log file: D:\EngineersSG-LCR\inspector\E0200000777.log
Integrity check passed for log file: D:\EngineersSG-LCR\inspector\E0200000778.log
Integrity check passed for log file: D:\EngineersSG-LCR\inspector\E0200000779.log
Integrity check passed for log file: D:\EngineersSG-LCR\inspector\E02.log
WARNING: Restore-StorageGroupCopy on Engineering Mailboxes SG was successful.
All logs were successfully copied.
```

Once this is executed, you must manually copy it into the production location. You can do this by just copying the files, or if the paths are the same but the drive letters are unique, you could simply reassign the drive letters. For example, if the production database is on D:\EngineeringMailboxes and the LCR database is on E:\EngineeringMailboxes, you could simply tell the server that the D: drive is now the E: drive. The advantage to this approach is that the documented locations of all of the database and storage group files remains the same. The downside to this is that the *only* Exchange data that could be on the D: and E: drives in this example would be that one database that is being swapped out.

The other way to swap out the database files is simply to swap out the locations; this is done with the Restore-StorageGroupCopy cmdlet and the -ReplaceLocations option. Here is an example:

```
[PS] C:\>Restore-StorageGroupCopy "Engineering Mailboxes SG" -ReplaceLocations
     Base name: e02
     Log file: D:\EngineersSG\E020000001F.log
     Csv file: D:\EngineersSG-LCR\IgnoredLogs\raobyk4o.lqt

     Base name: e02
     Log file: D:\EngineersSG-LCR\E020000001F.log
     Csv file: D:\EngineersSG-LCR\IgnoredLogs\hosrmoec.5v1

Integrity check passed for log file: D:\EngineersSG-LCR\inspector\E02.log
WARNING: The Restore-StorageGroupCopy operation for storage group copy
Engineering Mailboxes SG was successful, and production paths
were updated. All logs were successfully copied.
```

The database can now be remounted, but it is now in use in a different location. We can confirm this with the Get-StorageGroup and the Get-MailboxDatabase cmdlets. Notice also that LCR has been disabled for this storage group after the Restore-StorageGroupCopy cmdlet was run:

```
[PS] C:\>Get-StorageGroup "Engineering Mailboxes SG" | FL Name,*path*,HasLocalCopy

Name                   : Engineering Mailboxes SG
LogFolderPath          : D:\EngineersSG-LCR
SystemFolderPath       : D:\EngineersSG-LCR
CopyLogFolderPath      :
CopySystemFolderPath   :
HasLocalCopy           : False

[PS] C:\>Get-MailboxDatabase "Engineering Mailboxes" | fl Name,HasLocalCopy,*path*
```

```
Name            : Engineering Mailboxes
HasLocalCopy    : False
CopyEdbFilePath :
EdbFilePath     : D:\Engineers-Mailboxes-LCR\Engineering Mailboxes.edb
```

The Microsoft online documentation makes a very good point that if you use the
−ReplaceLocations parameter, you should make an effort to update your documentation to
reflect the new database location or move the database back to the original location. Otherwise,
your documentation will now be out-of-date and other administrators may be confused as to why
the production databases are in folders that have *LCR* in their name.

Summary

Scaling upward and outward is a necessary evil for organizations with more than a few hundred
users. While a single machine can easily support all the necessary server roles for a few hundred
mailboxes, if it is not properly configured, it may experience performance problems. Recognizing
potential performance bottleneck points and how to correct them is an essential skill for Exchange
administrators.

As more mailboxes are supported on a single Exchange Mailbox server, scaling the server
upward to support more storage is also an important configuration item. Creating more storage
groups and mailbox databases will help you to support larger mailboxes and more data while
preventing any single database from growing too large.

Local continuous replication is a new feature of Exchange 2007 that also allows you to grow
and scale your organization. This feature allows you to support larger mailboxes but still have
low recoverability times for mailbox databases. By allowing important mailbox databases (or all
mailbox databases) to be configured to use LCR, you can have a nearly perfectly synchronized
copy of the production database that can be swapped in to production in a moment's notice.

Part 3

Basic Exchange Server 2007 Management

In this section you will learn to:

Chapter 7

Administering Exchange 2007

Administrators of Exchange 2000/2003 in both small and large organizations always end up hearing the same complaints when it comes to managing an Exchange 2000/2003 organization. The following are some of the common complaints administrators reported hearing:

◆ Finding the right object or configuration task within Exchange System Manager is difficult because the object or task is often buried many levels deep.

◆ The Exchange System Manager is poorly designed and often objects are found in the tree view and tree objects are found in the management pane.

◆ Management of Exchange servers and mail recipients through scripting is very difficult.

◆ Bulk management of recipient objects is difficult.

◆ There are too many different APIs for managing Exchange-related configuration data and mailbox data.

The new Exchange 2007 administrative architecture is designed to be much more administrator friendly whether you prefer to work from the graphical user interface or from the command line. The Exchange Management Console has been greatly improved and the new Exchange Management Shell will keep command-line enthusiasts and Unix administrators very happy.

Topics in this chapter include the following:

◆ The new administrative architecture

◆ The Exchange Management Console

◆ Assigning administrative permissions

◆ Basics of the Exchange Management Shell

Understanding the New Administrative Architecture

The Exchange 2003 administrative architecture has many shortcomings. The most noticeable is that automating or scripting most administrative tasks is difficult, to say the least. An administrator may need to understand two or more scripting interfaces or application programming interfaces (APIs), such as Active Directory Services Interface (ADSI), Collaborative Data Objects (CDOs), CDO for Exchange, CDO for Exchange Management, Exchange Windows Management Instrumentation (WMI) classes, and others.

While the Exchange 2000/2003 Exchange System Manager (ESM) console (shown in Figure 7.1) is not the most difficult interface to use in the world, administrators frequently complain that it is difficult to actually find the objects that might need to be configured and the tasks that can be performed against each object.

FIGURE 7.1
Exchange System
Manager console for
Exchange 2000/2003

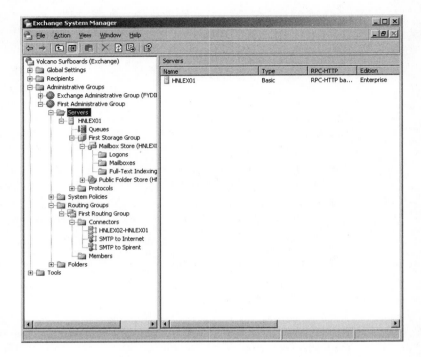

A common complaint among Exchange administrators is that the ESM interface objects are often buried seven or eight levels deep in the ESM hierarchy. Administrators also complain that leaf objects appear in the tree pane and tree objects appear in the results pane of the interface.

While some of the configuration tasks are performed directly against the Active Directory and can be duplicated with an ADSI script, other tasks are performed against the Registry, Exchange components, the file system, or indirectly against Internet Information Server (IIS) components. Thus, many of the tasks that are performed in the ESM become extremely difficult to automate or script.

The need for a better and more consistent interface for managing Exchange server objects, Exchange tasks, and mail recipients had to be developed. The management interface had to be capable of managing a combination of Active Directory objects (Exchange configuration and recipient information), Registry settings, file system components, IIS components, Windows services, and Exchange components. The new interface had to provide a consistent interface for managing Exchange and allow for easier scripting and command-line management.

About the same time the Exchange team started working on a new management interface, the Windows team was designing a new shell and scripting interface for Windows. This shell (originally code named Monad) is called the Windows PowerShell. The PowerShell is a completely redesigned command-line interface (CLI) for Windows that may eventually replace the traditional command prompt that we are all used to.

The Exchange team decided to provide access to the Exchange management functions through the Windows PowerShell. All objects that would need to be manipulated by an Exchange server administrator were defined (such as mailboxes, mailbox databases, distribution groups, etc.) and then the actions that might be taken against these objects were defined (such as enable, set, get, mount, test, etc.).

From the objects that would need to be manipulated, and the actions that would need to be performed on these objects, a series of tasks (or actions) were defined. This is the underlying Exchange administrative model as shown in Figure 7.2.

FIGURE 7.2
Exchange 2007 administrative architecture

Exchange tasks are given access to differing types of data and components relating to Exchange through the Exchange Management API. These tasks, or cmdlets (pronounced "command-lets"), can be accessed via the Windows PowerShell and the Exchange Management Shell (EMS) or through the Exchange Management Console (EMC). EMC interacts with the EMS tasks through the WinForms and PowerShell data providers. All of the EMS tasks are exposed as .NET classes and could also be accessed and used through applications written with the .NET Framework.

Installing the Administrative Tools

You will want to install the administrative tools on your desktop computer so that you do not have to be continually logging on to an Exchange server's console in order to administer Exchange Server 2007. If you are migrating, you may also want to provide access to manage Exchange

2000/2003 servers from desktop workstations. The catch is that the two management interfaces cannot be on the same machine.

> **TIP**
>
> All Exchange 2007 server roles can be managed remotely except the Edge Transport server role. The Edge Transport role must be managed from that server's console.

Installing the Exchange 2007 Management Tools

One of the nice things about Exchange 2007's setup program is that you can easily install all of the components necessary to manage Exchange Server 2007. That is the good news; the better news is that if you have the 32-bit version of Exchange 2007, you can install the Exchange management tools on Windows XP 32-bit or Windows 2003 32-bit. The Exchange management tools include the Exchange Management Shell, the Exchange Help file, the Exchange Best Practices Analyzer tool, and the Exchange Troubleshooting Assistant tool.

Just don't be tempted to install the 32-bit version of Exchange Server 2007 in production since the server components are intended only for testing, evaluation, training, and lab purposes and are not supported in production.

To start the installation, you will first need to meet some prerequisites. For each of the prerequisite pieces of software, there is a 32-bit and a 64-bit version, so the prerequisites depend on which version of Windows you are using:

1. If the workstation on which you are planning to install the Exchange 2007 management tools has the Exchange 2003 System Manager, remove it.

2. Ensure that the computer on which you are installing the Exchange management tools has at least 500MB of free disk space and that the disk is formatted as NTFS, has 512MB of RAM, and an 1.0GHz processor or greater.

3. Install the IIS common files.

4. If it's not already installed, install the .NET Framework 2.0 and ensure that you have any updates and patches.

5. Install Microsoft Management Console (MMC) 3.0 if it's not already installed.

6. Install the Windows PowerShell (`http://preview.tinyurl.com/e5x2t`).

7. Once you have met the prerequisites, run the Exchange 2007 setup program.

8. On Introduction screen of Exchange Server 2007 Setup Wizard, click Next.

9. Accept the license agreement and click Next.

10. Select Yes or No to error reporting and click Next.

11. On the Installation Type screen, select Custom Exchange Server Installation, specify the installation path if necessary, and click Next.

12. On the Server Role Selection screen (shown in Figure 7.3), select Management Tools and click Next.

13. Once the readiness checks have completed successfully, click Install.

14. Click Finish on the Completion screen.

FIGURE 7.3
Installing the Exchange 2007 Management Tools

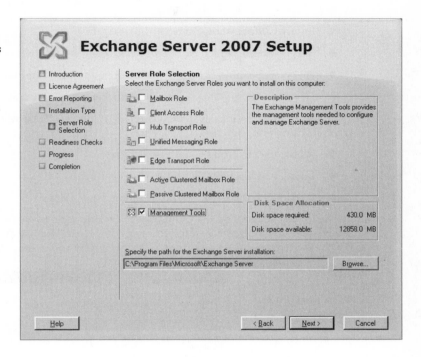

Installing the Exchange 2003 Management Tools

> **NOTE**
>
> The Exchange 2003 management tools will be required for a couple of different reasons; unfortunately you cannot install them on an Exchange 2007 server. First and foremost, if you are running Exchange 2000/2003 servers, you will need to manage those servers from the Exchange System Manager for Exchange 2000/2003. Second, you will need to install the Exchange System Manager if you will be managing public folders through the graphical user interface.

Exchange 2003 management tools cannot be installed on an Exchange 2007 server. You must use the Exchange 2003 management tools from a computer other than your Exchange 2007 servers.

If you need to manage public folders through the Exchange System Manager (ESM), any Exchange 2007 mailbox server that contains a public folder database must also have the World Wide Web Publishing Service installed. ESM uses the WebDAV interface to manage the public folder structure. The Exchange 2003 management tools are 32-bit tools only, so you should install them only on Windows XP/2003 32-bit operating systems.

To install on Windows 2003, here are the recommended prerequisites:

◆ Domain membership in the forest in which Exchange Server is installed

◆ Windows 2003 SP1 or later

◆ Internet Information Services (IIS) snap-in

◆ SMTP service (which can be disabled after installation)

◆ WWW Publishing Service (which can be disabled after installation)

◆ Windows Server 2003 Administration Tools Pack (adminpak.msi)

To install the Exchange system management tools on Windows XP Professional, here are the recommended prerequisites:

◆ Windows XP Professional Service Pack 2

◆ Internet Information Services (IIS) snap-in

◆ Windows Server 2003 Administration Tools Pack

During installation, on the Component Selection screen (shown in Figure 7.4), ensure that the action type next to the Microsoft Exchange component is set to Custom and that it's set to Install next to the Microsoft Exchange System Management Tools component.

FIGURE 7.4
Installing the
Exchange 2003 system
management tools

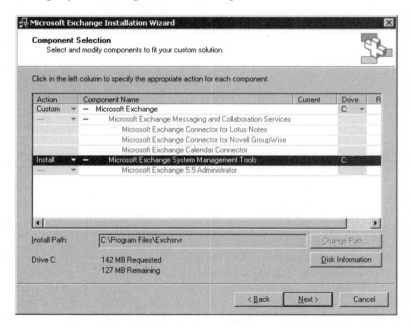

Once you have completed the installation, we recommend that you apply the latest Exchange 2003 service pack.

Exploring the Exchange Management Console

Now that you know how to install the Exchange 2007 management tools, let's take a look at the console layout, wizards, and new features. We think that you will be impressed once you have some time to get to know it. We are particularly impressed with the ease of use, how quickly you can find the exact tasks you need, and the ability to save your configuration.

There have been many improvements to reduce the complexity of the console tree, to make objects more discoverable, and to separate objects that can be configured from the tree and tree containers.

Console Layout

Let's start by taking a look at the console as a whole and then we will dissect it in to its various components or parts. Figure 7.5 shows the Exchange Management Console (EMC) with the four major components, or panes.

FIGURE 7.5
Introducing the Exchange 2007 Management Console

Notice that the default console is broken up in to four separate sections, or panes. These are the navigation tree pane, the work pane, the Results pane, and the Actions pane.

NAVIGATION TREE

The console navigation tree is one of the biggest improvements in the Exchange 2007 EMC. Unlike the Exchange 2003 System Manager, the EMC contains only static data and containers; there is no dynamic data or objects that must be configured in the navigation tree. The EMC navigation tree is a maximum of only three levels deep and by default contains only four work centers. A view of just the navigation tree is shown in Figure 7.6.

The work centers you see in Figure 7.6 show the different types of configuration data or operations that an administrator may be required to manage. Later in this chapter, we will show you

FIGURE 7.6
Exchange Management
Console navigation tree

how to break the console up so that an administrator can only see a particular work center. The Exchange 2007 work centers are as follows:

Work Center	Description
Organization Configuration	Contains objects and properties related to the configuration of the entire Exchange 2007 organization. These objects and properties affect all servers and recipients.
Server Configuration	Contains the server objects that can be configured individually, such as mailbox databases, Outlook Web Access virtual directories, SMTP receive connectors, and Unified Messaging components.
Recipient Configuration	Contains the recipient data for all mail-enabled objects in the organization, including mail-enabled users, mail-enabled contacts, and mail-enabled groups. In Exchange 2000/2003, this information was managed through Active Directory Users and Computers.
Toolbox	A launching pad for additional tools or consoles, including the Exchange Best Practices Analyzer, the Queue Viewer, the Mail Flow Troubleshooter and tools for database recovery management and message tracking.

Also note in Figure 7.6 that the Organization, Server, and Recipient Configuration work centers include containers that help to categorize the types of objects found in them.

RESULTS PANE

The Results pane of the EMC will be different depending on which work center object and subcontainer is highlighted in the navigation tree. For example, if you highlight the Recipient

Configuration object in the tree, the Results pane will show all mail-enabled recipients (users, contacts, groups). A view of the entire Recipient Configuration container is shown in Figure 7.7.

FIGURE 7.7
General view of the Recipient Configuration work center

However, the console layout will change and the scope of what is displayed in the Results pane will be different if you select the Mailbox subcontainer that is found under the Recipient Configuration object. Figure 7.8 shows the view of the Recipient Configuration Results pane when the Mailbox subcontainer is selected. As you would expect, the Results pane contains only user and resource mailboxes.

You can further restrict the scope of what is displayed in the Results pane by applying a filter. At the very top of the Results pane is a Create Filter button; you can use this option to create expressions that define or restrict the scope of what is displayed in the Results pane. While filters can be defined for any result in the Results pane, we are using the example once again of mail-enabled recipients. To create a filter, click the Create Filter button and the filter options will appear at the top of the Results pane.

The leftmost part of the filter defines the attribute on which you want to filter. Attributes on which you can build a filter include ActiveSync Mailbox Policy, Alias (Exchange alias), City, Company, Custom Attributes 1–15, Database (mailbox database), Department, Display Name, E-Mail Address, External E-mail Address, First Name, Last Name, Managed By, Mailbox Folder Mailbox Policy, Name, Office, Recipient Type Details, Server (home mailbox server), State or Province, UM Enabled, User Logon Name (pre-Windows 2000), and User Principal Name (UPN).

The middle option defines the operator for the attribute you are filtering; operators include Equals, Does Not Equal, Contains, Does Not Contain, Starts With, Ends With, Is Present, and Is

FIGURE 7.8
Mailbox-specific view
of the Recipient
Configuration work
center

Not Present. The actual operators you see will be based on the attribute on which you are building the filter.

Finally, the rightmost portion is where you enter the data for which you are building the filter. The preceding screen shot shows that we have created a filter that displays only mail-enabled users whose city is Honolulu. We can click the Add Expression button and add additional expressions to further filter the information that is displayed in the Results pane. In this example, we have further restricted the filter using two expressions so that it shows only recipients whose city is Honolulu and whose department is Viper Pilots.

This filter will only be in effect for the Mailbox container since that is the subcontainer on which we created it; if we select the entire Recipient Configuration work center or the Distribution Group, Mail Contact, or Disconnected Mailbox subcontainers, the filter does not apply.

Certain types of attributes, such as the ActiveSync Mailbox Policy, Managed Folder Mailbox Policy, and the Unified Messaging Mailbox Policy, will include a Browse button that allows you to browse the directory for the specific policy for which you want to set the filter. When you choose the Recipient Type Details attribute, the last field is converted to a drop-down list and you can select the specific type of recipient you are looking for. The recipient types include Dynamic Distribution Group, User Mailbox, Legacy Mailbox (a mailbox located on Exchange 2000/2003), Linked Mailbox, Shared Mailbox, Room Mailbox, Equipment Mailbox, Mail Contact, Mail User, Mail Universal Distribution Group, Mail Universal Security Group, and Mail Non-Universal Group.

WORK PANE

Some Results panes list objects that require more than just a single set of property pages. Objects such as Exchange servers have property pages, but also objects under the server, such as storage groups and mailbox databases. Server objects require an additional pane under the Results pane called the Work pane. In Figure 7.9, we have selected the Mailbox subcontainer found under the Server Configuration work center. Notice that there is a new pane below the Results pane; this is the Work pane.

FIGURE 7.9
Server objects include a Work pane.

Since we have selected the Mailbox subcontainer, the Results pane lists only servers that hold the Mailbox server role. Since the Mailbox subcontainer is highlighted, the work pane will have property pages (in this case, only one property page) related to mailbox server management. Notice that the Work pane has a Database Management property page that contains the storage groups for the highlighted server in the Results pane as well as the mailbox and public folder databases. Since the Mailbox subcontainer has been highlighted, you will see only the Mailbox-server-related properties in the Work pane.

If you select the Client Access subcontainer in the Server Configuration work center, the Work pane shows only the properties related to the Client Access server that you have selected in the Results pane. Figure 7.10 shows the Work pane if the Client Access subcontainer is selected.

FIGURE 7.10
Work pane property pages and objects when the Client Access server subcontainer is selected

ACTIONS PANE

The Actions pane is the most dynamic of the panes found in the Exchange Management Console. It is also arguably the biggest change found in the EMC interface. Any change of a selected object in the navigation tree, the Results pane, or the work pane will change the Actions pane in one way or another. The Actions pane consists of the tasks or actions that are available for the selected object. As different objects are selected in the navigation tree, Results pane, or work pane, the Actions pane will change. The addition of the Actions pane is a result of Exchange administrators reporting to Microsoft that they have difficulty finding out what the available tasks for a particular object are.

Figure 7.11 is a good example of the Actions pane. In this example, the Server Configuration's Mailbox subcontainer is selected, in the Results pane a mailbox server is selected, and in the work pane, a storage group called First Storage Group is selected.

Notice that the Actions pane has a Mailbox section, a section for the specific Exchange server that we are working on (E2K7-BASE), and a section for the storage group that we have selected (First Storage Group). The actions that are available against the server (E2K7-BASE) are to view its properties, to create a new storage group, and to change the management view to another role (Manage Hub Transport Rule or Manage Client Access Role). These actions are available because this server supports all three roles (Mailbox, Client Access, and Hub Transport).

Finally, the actions available in the First Storage Group section include moving the selected storage group's files, creating a new mailbox or public folder database, enabling local continuous replication, deleting the storage group, and viewing the storage group's properties.

FIGURE 7.11
Corresponding actions available based on selected objects

The object First Storage Group was also the most recent object selected in the interface, so the actions found in the Actions pane for this object will correspond with the actions found on the context (right-click) menu and on the Action pull-down menu.

One final example of Action menu tasks are the actions that are available when the Mailbox subcontainer under the Recipient Configuration navigation tree object is highlighted.

Figure 7.12 shows the Actions pane for the Mailbox subcontainer. Notice that the Actions pane has two sections; the first section shows the actions available for the Mailboxes subcontainer. This includes modifying the maximum number of mailboxes returned, setting view options, and creating a new mailbox.

FIGURE 7.12
Actions pane for Recipient Configuration Mailboxes subcontainer

The second section shows actions for a specific mailbox because we have selected the mailbox Damion Jones. From here, we can disable the mailbox, remove the mailbox from the account, move the mailbox to another database, enable Unified Messaging, or view the user and mailbox properties. You may be wondering if this is the only information we will cover on recipient management. Don't worry; we just want you to become familiar with the console right now. In Chapter 10, we will cover in depth recipient management, including managing mailboxes, contacts, and groups.

Exchange Management Console Customization

The new Microsoft Management Console v3.0 is much more flexible and customizable than earlier versions. This means that you will be able customize your Exchange Management Console even further and create specialized consoles for tasks such as recipient management.

CUSTOMIZING THE CONSOLE VIEW

There may be features or views of the EMC that you simply don't need in order to complete your daily tasks. Many of the console components (such as the tree, toolbar, status bar, and Actions pane) can be removed from the default view. From within your console, select View ➤ Customize to see the Customize View dialog box shown in Figure 7.13.

FIGURE 7.13
Customizing the
components shown
in the Exchange
Management Console

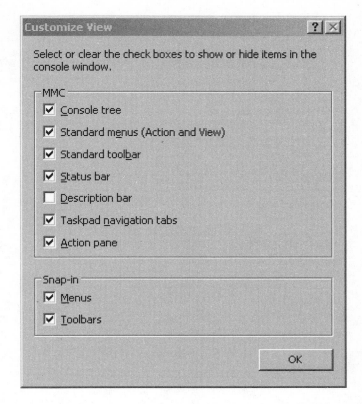

If you are creating a scaled-back EMC console for a junior or delegated administrator, restricting or removing some of the console features may be helpful in order to create a more simplified interface. From the Customize View dialog box, you can enable or disable the following components from the console view:

◆ The navigation tree

◆ MMC-specific Action and View menus

◆ MMC-specific toolbars

◆ The MMC status bar

◆ The MMC description bar

◆ Taskpad navigation tabs (if creating taskpads)

◆ The Actions pane

◆ Exchange Management Console — specific menus

◆ Exchange Management Console — specific toolbars

For an experienced administrator, there will probably not be a need to restrict these features, but as you will see in the following example, you can certainly make the console simpler by removing some of the unnecessary features.

CREATING A RECIPIENT MANAGEMENT CONSOLE

Even with earlier versions of the Microsoft Management Console (MMC), there was a lot of flexibility in creating and customizing the views that are available to the administrator. The Exchange 2007 EMC is even more customizable. Consoles can be scaled back and restricted so that only specific functions are available. In a medium-size or large organization, an excellent example of this would be the need to create a management console that allows the user to manage only recipients.

In the example we are going to show you, we are creating a console that allows the person using it to manage mailbox objects only. The end result of this customization is shown in Figure 7.14.

FIGURE 7.14
Customized recipient management console

So, how did we scale back a full-blown EMC to just mailbox management features? It's pretty easy once you know of a few of the tricks. Follow these steps to create a customized MMC that can be used just for mailbox management; you can do variations of these steps to create other types of consoles, too.

1. Run `mmc.exe` to create an empty console window.

2. From the menu, select File ➢ Add/Remove Snap-in.

3. Click the Add button, scroll through the list of available snap-ins until you find Exchange Server 2007and select it, click Add, and then click Close.

4. Click the OK button.

5. In the console tree, expand the Microsoft Exchange Management Console and then expand the Recipient Configuration work center.

6. Right-click on the Recipients Configuration container and choose Modify Recipient Scope to see the Recipient Scope dialog box. In the console shown in Figure 7.14, we had restricted the scope of the view to a single OU; you do this by selecting the View All Recipients in Specified Organizational Unit radio button and then specifying the domain name and OU name. This step will be optional if you do not need to filter by domain or OU.

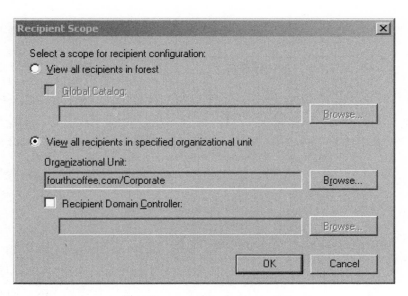

7. Right-click on the Mailbox subcontainer under the Recipient Configuration work center and choose New Window from Here. This creates a window with just the mail-enabled recipients.

8. From the View menu, choose Add/Remove Columns, remove Recipient Type Details from the Displayed columns list since we know that everything in this list will be a mailbox. Add City and move it up to just under Alias. Click OK.

9. Now we can remove some of the unnecessary components of the console from the view. From the menu, select View ➤ Customize. This will display the Customize View dialog box. Ensure that the only check box that is enabled is the Action Pane check box; the rest of the console components are unnecessary for this specific console. Click OK when finished.

10. In the MMC, select File ➢ Options, and then in the Console Mode drop-down list, select User Mode - Limited Access, Single Window. Click OK.

11. In the MMC, select File ➢ Save As and give the MMC file a name such as `MailboxRecipientManagement.msc`.

12. If you have any other MMC windows open within the MMC you are creating, you will see a prompt that says, "You chose to display a single window interface when this console opens in user mode, but you have more than one window open. The user can view only the currently active window. Are you sure you want to display a single window interface when this console opens in user mode?" Simply answer Yes at this prompt.

Congratulations. You have just created a simplified EMC that will allow the user of this console to manage just mailbox recipients. You can use this MSC file from any computer on which the Exchange 2007 Management Tools have been installed provided the user has been delegated the appropriate permissions to manage the user objects in Active Directory and they have been delegated recipient administration permissions to Exchange 2007.

Toolbox Work Center

The Toolbox work center that is found in the Exchange 2007 EMC is a new concept for Exchange management tools. The Toolbox work center from a default installation of Exchange 2007 is shown in Figure 7.15.

FIGURE 7.15
The Toolbox work
center of the Exchange
Management Console

The tools that are found in the Toolbox are not directly integrated with the Exchange Management Console, but rather the Toolbox provides links to these external tools. As new or updated tools are released by Microsoft, the Toolbox can be updated. The following tools are found in the Toolbox:

◆ The very popular Exchange Best Practices Analyzer (BPA) tool, which analyzes your Exchange configuration and makes recommendations for configuration and security improvements based on Microsoft and industry best practices.

◆ The Database Recovery Management tool helps guide Exchange administrators through the process of performing disaster recoveries of various server roles.

◆ The Database Troubleshooter tool helps an Exchange administrator determine why mailbox databases will not mount or why transaction log files will not replay.

◆ The Mail Flow Troubleshooter helps diagnose problems relating to messages being transferred between Mailbox, Hub Transport, and Edge Transport servers.

◆ The Message Tracking tool allows you to track a message's progress through an Exchange organization and see which Exchange components have processed the message.

◆ The Queue Viewer allows you to view the message queues on Hub Transport servers.

◆ The Performance Monitor tool is a Windows tool that helps analyze and troubleshoot Windows performance. When you launch the tool from the EMC Toolbox work center, it includes common performance counters related to Exchange servers.

◆ The Performance Troubleshooter analyzes a server and looks at common factors that could hurt performance, such as memory and disk configuration, and makes recommendations to improve them.

Finalize Deployment Tips

If you highlight the Microsoft Exchange portion of the EMC's navigation tree, two property pages appear in the Results pane. These are the Finalize Deployment and End-to-end Scenario pages; the Finalize Deployment page is shown in Figure 7.16.

The information on the Finalize Deployment and End-to-end Scenario property pages provide links to tips and help on the topics shown. These tips and help topics are provide to give administrators quick reference to things they must commonly configure. For example, if you click the Create a postmaster mailbox task, the steps necessary to create a postmaster address are displayed.

Here are some other tasks you'll find in the Finalize Deployment page:

◆ Enter the Exchange Server product key. The product key is required to keep using the 32-bit evaluation edition longer than 120 days and it is required to use the Exchange Server 2007 Enterprise Edition features with the 64-bit version. See Chapter 4 for more information.

◆ Running the Exchange Best Practices Analyzer helps you to find potential configuration problems and tune your configuration to Microsoft's recommendations.

◆ Creating offline address books for Outlook 2007 clients involves creating offline address book virtual directories on Client Access servers. This allows these clients to download the offline address book and use a local copy.

◆ Creating offline address books for Outlook 2003 and earlier clients involves designating that the offline address books be created for older clients and that they are replicated to public folder servers that are near the client computers.

FIGURE 7.16
Finalize Deployment
tips in the Exchange
Management Console.

- Configuring SSL for Client Access servers helps to secure Web client connectivity to Exchange. Each Client Access server includes a self-signed certificate, but these should be replaced with certificates that were signed by a trusted certificate authority.

- Configuring Exchange ActiveSync (including defining ActiveSync policies) if users will be using Windows Mobile– or ActiveSync-enabled devices.

- Configure a list of domains for which your Exchange organization will accept e-mail (on the Accepted Domains list). This tells Exchange which domains are internal or for which you must relay mail.

- Configuring an EdgeSync subscription so that you can synchronize recipient, safe sender, and block sender lists to an Edge Transport server.

- Configuring Unified Messaging that allows a user's mailbox to accept inbound faxing or inbound voice mail.

Wizards and Things

There have been a lot of additional improvements in the graphical user interface in an effort to make it more intuitive and easy to use. This includes making the wizards easier to use, providing indications that a wizard is working, showing problems where information is incorrect or missing, and giving the user the ability to view or block information.

Most wizards also include an option on most screens that allows you to type Ctrl + C and copy the contents of the wizards on to the Clipboard. This is very useful if you need to quickly document what you are doing or if you need to paste this information into Notepad or some other editor. Most of the wizards also show the Exchange Management Shell command that was used to perform the task the wizard performed. You can use this information to create scripts and one-line commands for future use.

CONFIRMATION DIALOG BOXES

EMC wizards now include a confirmation page that allows administrators to confirm that the actions that they selected are really what they want to do. Figure 7.17 shows the confirmation screen for the Move Mailbox Wizard.

FIGURE 7.17
Confirmation screen for the Move Mailbox Wizard

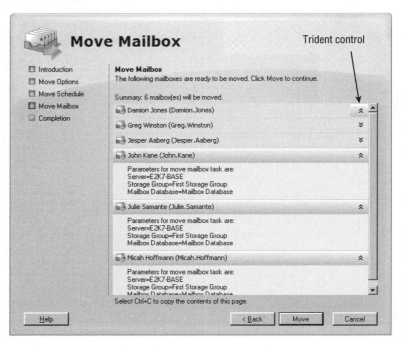

Confirmation dialog boxes and progress dialog boxes also include a new control called a trident control. We have included on Figure 7.17 a pointer to a trident control; they look like double *v* either facing upward or downward. By clicking on these controls, you can expand the line for more information or collapse the line for less information.

PROGRESS DIALOG BOXES

Progress dialog boxes have been enhanced so that they give the administrator a better feel for "something is happening." Figure 7.18 shows the new progress dialog box for the Move Mailbox Wizard. Notice at the end of each of the status lines there is a trident control that allows you to display more information or to collapse each line so that less information is shown.

COMPLETION AND MANAGEMENT SHELL TASKS

If you are trying to learn the Exchange Management Shell (EMS) but find yourself continually having to look up how to do something, don't feel bad; you are not alone. The designers of the EMC wanted to help you along a little bit even when you're managing objects from the graphical user interface (GUI). When you run a wizard, the wizard's completion screen includes the EMS cmdlets required to complete the task that you just executed via the GUI.

An excellent example of this is the Move Mailbox Wizard that we have been looking at in previous screen captures. Figure 7.19 shows the completion screen for the mailboxes that were moved.

FIGURE 7.18
Move Mailbox Wizard
progress screen

FIGURE 7.19
Move Mailbox Wizard
Completion screen and
EMS cmdlets

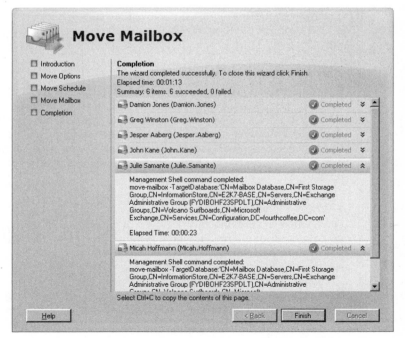

Notice that the first mailbox that was moved *and* has a full completion report is the mailbox for Julie Samante; we collapsed the trident controls for the other mailboxes. The Completion dialog box includes the EMS command necessary to move Julie Samante's mailbox to another mailbox database. The Completion screen also gives you the option to type CTRL + C and copy the text contents of the screen in to the computer's paste buffer; you can then paste that text in to Notepad or some other program. Here you can see where we have copied the results of the command on the Completion screen so that we can reused the command:

```
move-mailbox -TargetDatabase:'CN=Mailbox Database,CN=First Storage
  Group,CN=InformationStore,CN=E2K7-BASE,CN=Servers,CN=Exchange
Administrative Group (FYDIBOHF23SPDLT),CN=Administrative Groups,
CN=Volcano Surfboards,CN=Microsoft
Exchange,CN=Services,CN=Configuration,
DC=fourthcoffee,DC=com'
```

Although we are not quite ready to start teaching you the EMS cmdlets, we will tell you that this command was created using the absolute most unique name of the mailbox database. That is the distinguished name of the mailbox object, or CN = Mailbox Database, CN = First Storage Group, CN = InformationStore, CN = E2K7-BASE, CN = Servers, CN = Exchange Administrative Group (FYDIBOHF23SPDLT), CN = Administrative Groups, CN = Volcano Surfboards, CN = Microsoft Exchange, CN = Services, CN = Configuration, DC = fourthcoffee, DC = com. If there was only a single mailbox database called Mailbox Database in your entire organization, you could have moved Julie's mailbox by typing this:

```
Move-mailbox "Julie Samante" -TargetDatabase:"Mailbox Database"
```

However, the distinguished name of the mailbox store was used in order to guarantee uniqueness. As you start to learn the EMS, you will find there are usually multiple ways to accomplish the same task.

SCHEDULE DIALOG BOXES

The Move Mailbox Wizard also has a schedule option; the ability to schedule mailbox moves first came about in Exchange 2003, but since that time the wizard options have changed just a bit. Figure 7.20 shows the new schedule options. Now you can specify the start time and then specify the maximum running time as opposed to the time at which the moves should stop if they are not completed. Anyone who has ever had to wait around until after hours to move mailboxes when running Exchange 2000 or Exchange 5.5 will tell you what a handy feature this is. Schedule your mailboxes to move and then go home!

ERROR NOTIFICATIONS

Often when you are doing something in a graphical user interface, you get an error message but you can't quickly figure out where you made the error. The Exchange 2007 EMC helps to point you to the error more quickly by not only showing a pop-up error but also including a warning icon next to the offending property.

In Figure 7.21, we are creating a mail-enabled contact. We tried to save the contact without first entering a valid external address; the EMC shows us an error indicating that the proxy address cannot be empty, but also a small red and white exclamation point shows up next to the External E-Mail Address field. We have circled this exclamation point to make it a little more clear on the screen capture.

FIGURE 7.20
The Move Schedule page of the Move Mailbox Wizard

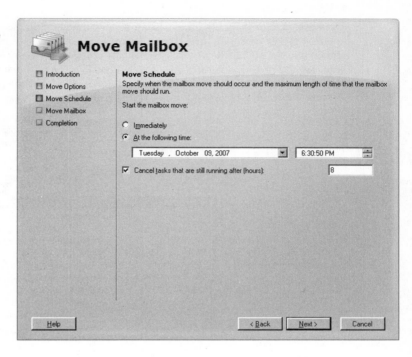

FIGURE 7.21
Improved error controls

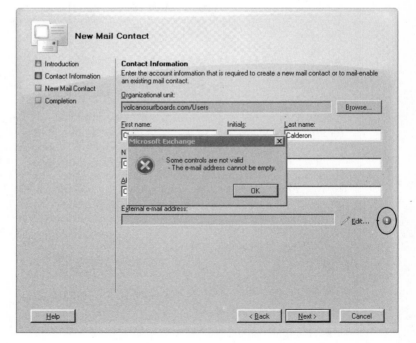

OBJECT PICKERS

When assigning a mailbox to an existing user or mail-enabling a universal group, you will use an object picker when you browse the Active Directory. In the simplest format, the object picker (shown in Figure 7.22) allows you to scroll through the list of user accounts in the Active Directory. Note that the object picker includes a Recipient Type Details column (User or Mailbox User), which may make the interface more difficult to use than it really needs to be by mixing up users who don't have mailboxes and those who already have mailboxes.

FIGURE 7.22
Selecting objects from
Active Directory

However, the object picker has some nice features. First, it automatically filters the list of users from the Active Directory so that only users without a mailbox or an e-mail address will appear. Second, you can enter part of the name for which you are searching in the Search box and click the Find Now button. If you do a little exploring, though, you will find an option under the View menu called Enable Column Filtering. Column filtering is (also shown in Figure 7.22) allows you to specify a filter for any of the columns. The filter is similar to the Results pane filtering option; you can specify that the data in the column meets a certain criteria. The filter options are as follows:

◆ Column Contains

◆ Column Does Not Contain

◆ Column Starts With

◆ Column Ends With

◆ Column Is Exactly

◆ Column Is Not

Delegating Administrative Permissions

In earlier versions of Exchange, administrative permissions were delegated via sites or administrative groups. If you are interoperating with Exchange 2000/2003, permissions for Exchange 2000/2003 administrative tasks will still be delegated via administrative groups. However, permission delegation has been simplified and made more flexible for Exchange 2007.

> **NOTE**
>
> Active Directory administrative permissions and Exchange 2007 administrative permissions are split by design. This allows for more administrative flexibility.

An important consideration to keep in mind is that just because you have been delegated Exchange 2007 permissions does not automatically make you an administrator of Windows 2003 servers on which Exchange server is operating, nor does it make you an Active Directory administrator.

Exchange 2007 Administrative Roles

Before we look at Exchange 2007 administrative roles, we should quickly review the Exchange 2000/2003 administrative roles. This will help administrators who are making the transition from Exchange 2000/2003 organizations to Exchange 2007 better understand the changes. Exchange 2003 offered three types of administrative roles, as shown in Table 7.1.

TABLE 7.1:   Exchange 2003 Administrative Roles

ROLE	PERMISSIONS
Exchange View Only Administrator	Gives users or groups that have been assigned this role the ability to view the Exchange organization and server configuration. Mailbox administrators required this role in order to enumerate Exchange server names, storage groups, and mailbox store names.
Exchange Administrator	Gives users or groups that have been assigned this role the ability to manage (create/change/delete) Exchange objects at either the organization level or within a specific administrative group, depending on where the role was delegated.
Exchange Full Administrator	Gives users or groups all of the permissions that the Exchange Administrator role has but also the ability to change permissions on objects.

Although these worked well for some organizations, the roles could only be assigned to an entire administrative group or the entire organization. For medium-size and large organizations where administrative tasks are sometimes very granular, the people assigned these roles may not necessarily have the specific permissions they need or they might have too many permissions. For example, if one group was responsible for managing all bridgehead servers and mail transport functions, the organization's bridgehead servers would have to all be in the same administrative group. If all servers (bridgehead, Outlook Web Access, and Mailbox servers) were in the same administrative groups, the management permissions would have to be assigned to all of the servers manually. Further, the administrative permissions for the organization and each administrative group had to be delegated once Exchange Server was installed.

Exchange 2007 has improved the Exchange administrative model by defining three types of administrative roles:

The *Exchange Recipient Administrator* role has the permissions to modify Exchange-related properties (e-mail addresses, home server, Client Access server, and Unified Messaging) of mail-enabled objects such as users, contacts, and groups. This role grants only read and write permissions to Exchange properties only for objects found in the Users container in each domain in which Exchange 2007 PrepareDomain has been run. For additional management permissions, an administrator would have to be delegated Active Directory permissions to manage objects in an OU, given membership in the Account Operators group, or be a member of Domain Admins. If a user or group is delegated the Exchange Recipient Administrator role, that user or group will have these permissions for the entire organization.

The *Exchange Server Administrator* role can be delegated permissions to one or more individual Exchange 2007 servers regardless of the roles that server maintains. Someone with these permissions can manage any configuration data for that particular server, has the Exchange View Only Administrator role, and will be made a member of the computer's local Administrators group. This role allows medium and large organizations to delegate permissions for Exchange management more precisely.

FIGURE 7.23
Delegating
Exchange 2007
administrative roles

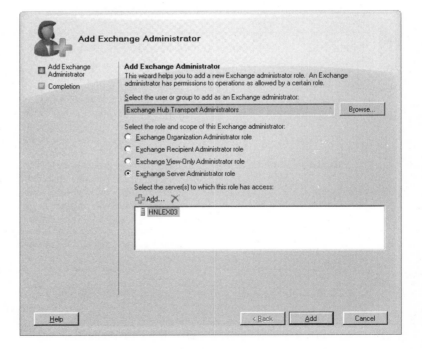

The *Exchange Organization Administrator* role provides the permissions necessary to manage the organization-wide properties of Exchange 2007, including connectors, global settings, accepted e-mail domains, transport rules, Unified Messaging properties, ActiveSync policies, managed folders, and messaging records management policies. This role is by far the most powerful of the three Exchange 2007 roles.

The *Exchange View-Only Administrator* role allows an administrator to view the Exchange configuration, but they cannot make any changes.

Most organizations will not need to do this, but these permissions can be delegated at the Organization Configuration level of the EMC navigation tree. Simply select the Organization Configuration work center and choose the Add Delegate action; this will display the Add Delegate Wizard. In Figure 7.23, we are delegating the Exchange Server Administrator role for just a single Exchange server (called HNLEX03) to a group called Exchange Hub Transport Administrators.

Exchange 2007 Built-In Administrative Groups

Now that we have explained the administrative roles that you *could* use to delegate permissions, we will tell you that you probably don't need to do any delegation yourself. For small or medium-size organizations, you will probably not need to delegate additional roles for your users and groups. This is because when the first Exchange 2007 server is installed, some preconfigured groups are created for you. In most organizations, these groups will be sufficient for assigning the permissions you need for different types of administrators.

These universal security groups are created in an organizational unit (OU) called Microsoft Exchange Security Groups, which is found in the forest root domain. Figure 7.24 shows the Microsoft Exchange Security Groups organizational unit and the groups that are created in that container.

FIGURE 7.24
Prebuilt Windows security groups for managing Exchange 2007

We recommend you use these built-in groups when assigning the necessary permissions to your administrators. The following are the built-in Windows security groups and the permissions they assign to their members:

Exchange Organization Administrators provides members with the permissions necessary to manage all Exchange properties for the entire organization.

Exchange Recipient Administrators provides members with the permissions necessary to manage mail-enabled objects (including assigning mailboxes to users and mail-enabling contacts and groups.)

Exchange Servers provides the permissions necessary for Exchange servers to interact with each other was well as with the Active Directory. Each Exchange 2007 server's computer account will automatically be assigned membership in this group. Administrators do not need to belong to this group.

Exchange View-Only Administrators provides the permissions necessary to read Exchange configuration data from the Active Directory and read access to mail-enabled objects.

Exchange2003Interop provides permissions necessary for interoperability with Exchange 2003.

Exchange Management Shell Primer

Depending on whom you ask, some experienced Exchange administrators will tell you that the Exchange Management Shell (EMS) is the best improvement that has been introduced for Exchange 2007. Is knowledge of the EMS required? Some administrators will manage their Exchange servers for years and rarely use the EMS, while others will use it daily. However, we think it is safe to say that at least limited knowledge of the EMS will be required by all administrators.

As we stated earlier in the chapter, the intent of the EMS was to provide a consistent interface for performing management tasks for Exchange 2007 servers, whether the tasks are automation tasks, writing scripts, or extending the management capabilities. Tasks or operations that once required multiple programming APIs and hundreds of lines of scripting can now be accomplished in a single command.

The Exchange Management Shell is a set of Exchange-specific extensions to the Windows PowerShell. In this section, we want to introduce you to the PowerShell as well as the EMS and to do so without overwhelming you. Introducing a concept like the PowerShell or the EMS in just a few pages is difficult, but we hope to give you a basic idea of some of the capabilities and encourage you to learn more.

In total, there are about 350 Exchange-related cmdlets that you can use in the EMS; the goal is to cover all Exchange-related administrative tasks. You will find cmdlets that manipulate other data in the Active Directory (such as cmdlets for managing user accounts) and manipulating Exchange-related data in the Registry or Internet Information Services, but the cmdlets will manipulate or manage only data related to Exchange. The Exchange team is expecting other internal Microsoft teams such as the Active Directory and Internet Information Server teams to provide their own extensions to the management shell.

Command Syntax

The problem with a lot of scripting languages and command shells is that as they get more complex and powerful, the command syntax gets more and more cryptic. The Windows PowerShell and the EMS seek to make using the command-line interface and scripting more intuitive. To this end, most of the PowerShell and EMS cmdlets consist of two components, a verb and a noun.

JUST IN CASE

The PowerShell cmdlets and the EMS extensions for the PowerShell are case not case sensitive. That means that you can type everything in uppercase, type everything in lowercase, or mix and match the case of the letters in your commands. For readability and per suggestions from folks on the Exchange team at Microsoft, we are using Pascal casing in this book. When you use Pascal casing, the first letter of each word is in uppercase, whether the cmdlet consists of one word or more than one word. All other letters in the cmdlet are in lowercase. So the cmdlet that is used to retrieve mailbox statistics is written as `Get-MailboxStatistics`. We are writing them this way merely for readability, though.

VERBS AND NOUNS

The verb identifies the action that is being taken and the noun indicates the object on which the action is being taken. The verb always comes first and the verb and noun are separated by a hyphen such as `Get-Mailbox`. Table 7.2 shows some of the common verbs that are found when using the EMS; some of these are specific to the EMS, but most are generic Windows PowerShell verbs.

TABLE 7.2:   Common EMS Cmdlet Verbs

VERB	DESCRIPTION
Get	Get is the probably the most common verb that you will use. Get retrieves information about the specified object and outputs information about the object.
Set	Set is probably the second most common verb that you will use. Set allows you to update properties of the object specified in the noun.
New	New creates new instances of the object specified in the noun.
Enable	Enable activates or enables a configuration on the object specified, such as enabling an existing user account.
Remove	Remove deletes an instance of the object specified in the noun.
Disable	Disable disables or deactivates the object specified in the noun. An example of this is removing a mailbox from an existing user (but not deleting the user account).
Mount	Mount is used to mount an Exchange 2007 mailbox or public folder database.
Dismount	Dismount is used to dismount an Exchange 2007 mailbox or public folder database.
Move	Move can be used to move mailboxes to other mailbox database.
Test	Test performs diagnostics tests against the object specified by the noun and the identity option.

TABLE 7.3:   Commonly Used EMS Nouns

NOUN	DESCRIPTION
ActiveSyncMailboxPolicy	Properties of ActiveSync policies that can be assigned to mailbox
CASMailbox	Properties of a mailbox relating to client features, such as OWA and MAPI properties
ClientAccessServer	Properties specific to an Exchange Client Access server role
DistributionGroup	Properties relating to mail-enabled distribution groups
DynamicDistributionGroup	Properties relating to a dynamic distribution group
EmailAddressPolicy	Properties relating to the policies that are used to define e-mail addresses
ExchangeServer	Properties related to Exchange servers
Mailbox	Properties related to user mailboxes
MailboxDatabase	Properties related to mailbox databases
MailboxServer	Properties specific to an Exchange Mailbox server role
MailContact	Properties relating to mail-enabled contact objects
MailPublicFolder	Properties relating to mail-enabled public folder objects
MailUser	Properties related to a user that has an e-mail address but not a mailbox
ReceiveConnector	Properties relating to Receive connectors
SendConnector	Properties relating to Send connectors
StorageGroup	Properties relating to storage groups
TransportServer	Properties specific to an Exchange Hub Transport server role
UMMailbox	Properties relating to Unified Messaging
UMServer	Properties specific to an Exchange Unified Messaging server role
User	Properties related to user objects

The actual nouns that are used in conjunction with these verbs are too numerous to mention in even a few pages of text. Table 7.3 shows a list of some of the more common nouns; not to worry, though, later in this chapter we will show you how to use the online help to find more of the cmdlets that you need. The nouns in Table 7.3 can be used in conjunction with verbs such as the ones found in 7.2 to manipulate the properties of Exchange-related objects. Not all verbs work with all nouns, though.

One important thing to keep in mind with cmdlets is that they are not individual executables but rather .NET classes that are only accessible from within the PowerShell and only if the Exchange extensions to PowerShell are loaded.

IDENTITY

For cmdlets that require input, usually the first parameter provided is the -Identity parameter. For example, if you want to retrieve information about a mailbox called Clayton Kamiya in the Corporate organizational unit (OU), you would type this:

```
Get-Mailbox -Identity 'fourthcoffee.com/Corporate/Clayton Kamiya'
```

However, you will quickly find that the identity parameter is not required. And, if your aliases or account names are unique, even the domain and organizational unit information is not required. For example, this command would yield the exact same results:

```
Get-Mailbox 'fourthcoffee.com/Corporate/Clayton Kamiya'
```

We can drop the domain and the OU name and as long as there is only one Clayton Kamiya in the Active Directory, this cmdlet will yield the exact same result:

```
Get-Mailbox 'Clayton Kamiya'
```

> **TIP**
>
> Anytime the identity you are using has a space in it, you must use quotes. Either single or double quotes will work as long as you are consistent.

So the point is if you find that the identity parameter is not required, don't be concerned because it is by design. As you will find shortly, the input can even be piped in from another cmdlet's output.

If you are not sure what input can be specified for the identity parameter, you can easily look this information up either in the Exchange online help or using the EMS command-line help (more on this later in this chapter). For now, let's look at one small piece of the Get-Mailbox help screen:

```
    -Identity <MailboxIdParameter>
        The Identity parameter identifies the mailbox. You can use one
of the following values:
        * GUID
        * Distinguished name (DN)
        * Domain\Account
```

```
* User principal name (UPN)
* LegacyExchangeDN
* SmtpAddress
* Alias

Required?                    false
Position?                    1
Default value
Accept pipeline input?       True
Accept wildcard characters?  True
```

From here, you can see that the identity parameter will take the mailbox GUID, the user's distinguished name, the domain name and account, the UPN name, the legacy Exchange distinguished name, the SMTP address, or the Exchange alias. And, of course you can pipe in input from the output of other cmdlets.

CMDLET VS. COMMAND

You will notice us sometimes using *command* and sometimes using *cmdlet* when talking about the PowerShell. There is a subtle difference. A cmdlet is the verb-noun combination that performs a specific task. For example, `Get-Mailbox` is a cmdlet. A complete command is the cmdlet along with any necessary options that the task might require. The command necessary to retrieve information about a specific mailbox looks like this:

```
Get-Mailbox "Mark Watts"
```

POWERSHELL VS. EXCHANGE MANAGEMENT SHELL

When we talk about generic Windows PowerShell functions such as `Get-User` or `Get-Event`, we refer to those as PowerShell functions. The Exchange Management Shell (EMS) is a series of extensions or additional functions that are added to PowerShell. These include functions such `Get-Mailbox` and `Mount-Database` that are specific to Exchange Server 2007. The Exchange Management Shell extensions always include the generic PowerShell functions.

MISSING EXCHANGE MANAGEMENT SHELL CMDLETS AND FUNCTIONS?

A pretty common problem with new PowerShell and EMS users is that they open up the PowerShell and try to use Exchange specific cmdlets or use Exchange specific help. By default, the Exchange snap-ins are not loaded when you load the generic Windows PowerShell. You should run the Exchange Management Shell shortcut in the Microsoft Exchange Server 2007 start menu folder to get the correct EMS extensions.

However, from a generic Windows PowerShell command line on an machine that has the Exchange management tools installed, you can type `Add-PSSnapin *exchange*` and load the Exchange specific snap-ins.

CMDLET PARAMETERS

PowerShell and EMS cmdlets also support a number of command-line parameters that are useful. Table 7.4 shows some of the parameters that cmdlets accept; not all cmdlets will accept all of these parameters — parameters are usually optional — and of course, some of these will not be relevant to some of the cmdlets you will use.

TABLE 7.4:   PowerShell Cmdlet Parameters

PARAMETER	DESCRIPTION
-Identity	Specifies a unique object on which the cmdlet is going to act. The Identity parameter is a positional parameter, which means that it does not necessarily have to be on the command line; PowerShell will prompt you for the identity if it is not specified. As we noted previously, in most cases you do not need to specify the -Identity parameter, just the unique object name.
-Whatif	Tells the cmdlet to simulate the action that it would normally perform but not actually make the change.
-Confirm	Asks the cmdlet to prompt for confirmation prior to starting the action. This option type is a Boolean, so you need to include either $True or $False. Some cmdlets (such as Move-Mailbox) do this by default, so you could specify -Confirm:$false if you did not want the confirmation to occur.
-Validate	Validate will check the prerequisites of the cmdlet to verify that it will run correctly and let you know.
-Credential	Allows you to specify alternate credentials when running a PowerShell command.
-DomainController	Allows you to specify the FQDN of a specific domain controller that you want to perform a PowerShell task against.
-ResultSize	Allows you to specify a maximum number of results when working with Get- cmdlets.
-SortBy	Allows you to specify a sorting criteria when outputting data that is usually the result of a Get- cmdlet.
-Verbose	Instructs Get- cmdlets to return more information about their execution and possibly more data will be output.
-Debug	Instructs the cmdlet to output more information and to proceed step-by-step through the process of performing a task. Debug returns more information that than a typical administrator needs to perform daily tasks.

If you are piping output of one cmdlet in to another, the parameters must be within the cmdlet that you want them to affect.

TAB COMPLETION

In order to be descriptive and helpful, some of the cmdlets are actually pretty long. Consider if you had to type Get-DistributionGroupMember several times! However, the PowerShell includes a feature called tab completion. If you type part of a command and then press the Tab key, PowerShell will complete the cmdlet with the first matching cmdlet it can find. For example, if you type Get-Distri and press Tab, PowerShell will automatically fill out Get-DistributionGroup. If you press Tab again, PowerShell will move on to the next matching cmdlet, in this case Get-DistributionGroupMember.

The Tab completion feature also works for cmdlet parameters. If you type a cmdlet followed by a space and a hyphen, such as Get-Mailbox -, and then press Tab, you will cycle through all of the parameters for that particular cmdlet.

Object Oriented

The PowerShell is even more flexible because the output of commands is not text based but rather object based. The PowerShell uses an object model that is based on the Microsoft .NET Framework. PowerShell cmdlets accept and return structured data. Don't let the terms *object model* and *object oriented* scare you, though. This is really quite simple. For example, Figure 7.25 shows the output of the Get-Mailbox cmdlet.

FIGURE 7.25
Output of the
Get-Mailbox cmdlet

What you see on the screen is text, but to the PowerShell it is really a list of objects. You can manipulate the output to see the properties you want, filter the output, or pipe the output (the objects) to another cmdlet.

FILTERING OUTPUT

In Figure 7.25, you can see that the cmdlet we used (Get-Mailbox) output every mailbox in the entire organization. There are a number of ways that you can filter or narrow the scope of the output that are you looking for from a specific cmdlet. In the case of Get-Mailbox and other cmdlets, you can specify just the identity of the mailbox that you are looking for.

PowerShell includes two options that can be used specifically for filtering the output. These are the `where` and the `filter` clauses. The `where` clause can be used on most any cmdlet and `filter` is applied at the client. The `filter` clause is only available on a subset of the commands since the filter is applied by the server:

```
Get-Mailbox | where {$_.MaxSendSize -gt 25000000}
```

The output of the `Get-Mailbox` cmdlet is piped to the `where` clause that filters the output. In this case, the output is any mailbox whose `MaxSendSize` parameter is greater than 25000000 bytes. Did you notice `$_.MaxSendSize` the portion of the where statement? The `$_` portion represents the object that is being piped to the `where` clause, and the `.MaxSendSize` represents the `MaxSendSize` property of that object.

For nonprogrammers, this might seem a little difficult at first, but we promise it gets much easier as you go along. The operators are also simple to remember. Table 7.5 shows a list of common operators that can be used in clauses such as `where`.

TABLE 7.5:   Shell Values and Operators

SHELL VALUE	OPERATOR	FUNCTION
-eq	Equals	The object.property value must match exactly the specified value.
-ne	Not equals	The object.property value must not match the specified value.
-gt	Greater than	The greater than works when the object.property value is an integer.
-ge	Greater than or equal to	The greater than or equal to works when the object.property value is an integer.
-lt	Less than	The less than works when the object.property value is an integer.
-le	Less than or equal to	The less than or equal to works when the object.property value is an integer.
-like	Contains	Contains is used when the object.property value is a text string. The matching string can either match exactly or contain wildcards (*) at the beginning or end.
-notlike	Does not contain	Does not contain is used when the object.property value is a text string and you want to see if the values do not match the string. The matching string can contain wildcards (*) at the beginning or end.

FORMATTING OUTPUT

If you look at the output of the `Get-Mailbox` cmdlet shown in Figure 7.25, you might be tempted to think that the output capabilities of the PowerShell is limited, but this is far from the truth. The output shown in Figure 7.25 was the default output for the `Get-Mailbox` cmdlet. The programmer decided that the output should be in a formatted table with the name, alias, home server, and prohibit send quota properties as columns. However, you can select the properties you want by merely piping the output of the `Get-Mailbox` cmdlet to either the `Format-Table` (FT for short) or `Select` cmdlet. For example, in Figure 7.26, you can see that we used the following cmdlets:

```
Get-Mailbox | FT Name,ProhibitSendquota,ProhibitSendReceiveQuota
```

FIGURE 7.26
Outputting to a formatted table

The output of the `Get-Mailbox` cmdlet was directed to the `Format-Table` (or FT) cmdlet; the result was columns for the name, prohibit send, and prohibit send and receive quota limits.

You may be wondering how you can learn all of the properties of an object. The default output of the `Get-Mailbox` cmdlet, for example, is probably not the most useful for your organization. We will go into more detail on getting help in the PowerShell and Exchange Management Shell a bit later, but here is a simple trick to see all of the properties of an object: direct the output the results of a `Get-` cmdlet to the `Format-List` (FL for short) cmdlet instead of the default `Format-Table` output.

When you direct the output of a cmdlet such as `Get-Mailbox` to the `Format-List` cmdlet, you will see *all* of the properties for that object. Figure 7.27 shows an example where we have directed the output of a `Get-Mailbox` cmdlet to the FL (`Format-List`) cmdlet. The command we have used is `Get-Mailbox ''Clayton Kamiya'' | Format-List`.

Outputting data to the screen is great, but it doesn't help you with reports. You can also output data to CSV and XML files. There are two cmdlets that make this easy to do; the `Export-Csv` and `Export-Clixml` cmdlets. Simply direct the output you want sent to a file and these cmdlets will take care of it. Let's use the same example we used previously, where we want a report of all mailboxes and their prohibit send and prohibit send and receive limits. However, we cannot use the `Format-Table` cmdlet in this instance. We have to use the `Select-Object` or just `Select` cmdlet to specify the output since we will be directing this to another cmdlet. Here is an example of the `Get-Mailbox` cmdlet when used with the `Select` command:

```
Get-Mailbox | Select Name, ProhibitSendQuota, ProhibitSendReceiveQuota
```

FIGURE 7.27
Outputting to a formatted list

The output is shown here:

Name	ProhibitSendQuota	ProhibitSendReceiveQuota
Missy Kosloksy	unlimited	unlimited
Sueko Miura	unlimited	unlimited
Daniel Petri	unlimited	unlimited
Matt Paleafei	unlimited	unlimited
Shawn Harbert	550000KB	575000KB
William Lefkovics	unlimited	unlimited
Dan Holme	unlimited	unlimited
Todd Hawkins	unlimited	unlimited
Karen Floyd	unlimited	unlimited
Jason Serino	unlimited	unlimited

To direct this output to the C:\report.csv file, we simply pipe it to the Export-Csv cmdlet as shown here:

```
Get-Mailbox | Select Name, ProhibitSendQuota, ProhibitSendReceiveQuota
 | Export-CSV c:\report.csv
```

If you want to export the report to an XML file, simply use the Export-Xml cmdlet instead of Export-CSV.

Finally, just as when working with the DOS prompt, you can redirect output of a command to a text file. To send the output of Get-Mailbox to the file C:\mailboxes.txt, you would type this:

```
Get-Mailbox > c:\mailboxes.txt
```

DIRECTING OUTPUT TO OTHER CMDLETS

You have already seen a couple of examples where we used the pipe symbol (|) to direct the output of one command to be the input of the next command, such as Get-Mailbox | FT. We can do this because the output of PowerShell commands consists of objects, not just text. Unlike with other shells or scripting languages, we don't have to use string commands or variables to pass data from one command to another. The result is that you can use a single line to perform a query and complex task, something that might have required hundreds of lines of programming in the past.

One of our favorite examples would be making specific changes to a group of people's mailboxes. Let's say that we need to ensure that all executives in our organization are able to send and receive a message that up to 50MB in size rather than the default 10MB. Earlier we showed you how you could get the properties of the mailbox that you were interested in, such as the MaxSendSize and MaxReceiveSize properties.

First, let's use the Get-DistributionGroupMember cmdlet to retrieve the members of the Executives distribution group. Here are the results of typing Get-DistributionGroupMember ''executives'':

```
Get-DistributionGroupMember "executives"
Name                                       RecipientType
----                                       -------------
Mark Watts                                 MailboxUser
David Elfassy                              MailboxUser
Brian Tirch                                MailboxUser
Paul Robichaux                             MailboxUser
Devin Ganger                               MailboxUser
Julie Samante                              MailboxUser
Todd Hawkins                               MailboxUser
```

Remember that while we see the text listing of the group members, what is actually output are objects representing each of the members. Now let's pipe the output of that cmdlet to the Set-Mailbox cmdlet and do some real work! To change the maximum incoming and outgoing message size for the members of the Executives group, we would type this:

```
Get-DistributionGroupMember "executives" | Set-Mailbox
-MaxSendSize:50MB -MaxReceiveSize:50MB
```

Notice that the `Set-Mailbox` cmdlet did not require any input since it will take as input the objects that are output from `Get-DistributionGroupMember`. When you run these two commands, there will be no output unless you have specified other options. But, you can easily check the results by requesting the membership of the Executives group, pipe that to the `Get-Mailbox` cmdlet, and then pipe that output to the `Format-Table` cmdlet:

```
Get-DistributionGroupMember "Executives" | Get-Mailbox |
FT Name,MaxSendSize,MaxReceiveSize
```

Name	MaxSendSize	MaxReceiveSize
Mark Watts	50MB	50MB
David Elfassy	50MB	50MB
Brian Tirch	50MB	50MB
Paul Robichaux	50MB	50MB
Devin Ganger	50MB	50MB
Julie Samante	50MB	50MB
Todd Hawkins	50MB	50MB

Pretty cool, eh? After just a few minutes working with the PowerShell and the EMS extensions, we hope that you will be as pleased with their ease of use as we are. We will leave you with one more example of piping and hopefully this will be an example that you can use in the future. We will do a report of the mailbox statistics using the `Get-MailboxStatistics` cmdlet and will narrow the focus of the output so that the system mailboxes are not included. We will limit the output by using the `Where` command clause, choose the properties to output using the `Select` command, and finally pipe that output to the `Export-Csv` cmdlet:

```
Get-MailboxStatistics | Where {$_.DisplayName -notlike "System*"} |
  Select DisplayName,ItemCount,TotalItemSize,StorageLimitStatus |
  Export-Csv c:\StorStats.csv
```

Getting Help

We have shown you a few simple yet powerful examples of how to use the PowerShell and the EMS. Once you dig in and start using the EMS, you will need some references to help you figure out all of the syntax and properties of each of the cmdlets. A great starting place for just reading about the cmdlets is in the Microsoft Exchange Server 2007 help file. The help file documents how to do most common operations both through the graphical user interface and through the EMS. Figure 7.28 shows the online help for how to create a new mailbox. After the procedures for creating the mailbox through the GUI are shown, you will see the procedures for using the EMS.

After the example that is shown for creating the mailbox, you see a link to the `New-Mailbox` cmdlet that will take you to much more detailed information on that specific cmdlet. The `New-Mailbox` help topic (shown in Figure 7.29) will provide you with a great amount of detail about the use of the cmdlet. We strongly recommend you take advantage of the Exchange help file that is included with Exchange Server. In fact, you might want to even copy the file and save it to your workstation. The filename is `ExchHelp.chm`.

Information is also available on the cmdlets from within the PowerShell. For a good starting point, you can just type the `help` command and this will give you a good overview of using the

FIGURE 7.28
Referring to the online help for creating a new mailbox

FIGURE 7.29
Online help for creating a new mailbox using the Exchange Management Shell

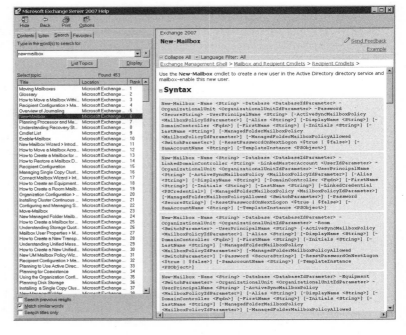

PowerShell and how to get more help. Table 7.6 shows a list of some common methods of getting help on PowerShell and Exchange Management Shell cmdlets.

TABLE 7.6: Different Methods of Getting Help within the EMS

ACTION	DESCRIPTION
Help	Provides generic PowerShell help information.
Help *keyword*	Lists all cmdlets that contain the keyword. For example, if you want to find all cmdlets that work with mailboxes, you would type **help *mailbox***.
Get-Command *keyword*	Lists all cmdlets and files (such as help files) that contain the keyword.
Get-Command	Lists all cmdlets (including all PowerShell extensions currently loaded such as the EMS cmdlets).
Get-Excommand	Lists all Exchange cmdlets.
Get-PSommand	Lists all PowerShell cmdlets.
Help *cmdlet* or Get-Help *cmdlet*	List online help for the specified cmdlet and pauses between each screen. Provide multiple views of the online help (such as detailed, full, examples, and default).
Cmdlet -?	Lists online help for the specified cmdlet.

When you're working with help within the PowerShell, help topics are displayed based on the view of help that you request. In other words, you can't just type **Get-Help CmdletName** and see everything about the specified cmdlet. The **Get-Help** cmdlet includes four possible views of help for each cmdlet. Table 7.7 explains the four primary views plus the parameters view.

The full option for **Get-Help** includes in its output each parameter's metadata:

Required?	Is the parameter required? This is either true or false
Position?	Specifies the position of the parameter. If the position is "named," then the parameter name has to be included in the parameter list. Most parameters are named parameters. However, the Identity parameter is "1," which means that it is always the first parameter and the -Identity tag is not required.
Default value	For most parameters this is blank, but it specifies what a value will be for a parameter if nothing else is specified.
Accept Pipeline Input?	Specifies if the parameter will accept input that is piped in from another cmdlet. The value is either true or false.
Accept wildcard characters?	Specifies if the parameter accepts wildcard characters such as the asterisk or question mark. This is either true or false.

TABLE 7.7:   Possible Output Views for the Get-Help Cmdlet

VIEW OPTION	EXPLANATION
Default	The default view lists the minimum amount of information to describe the function of the cmdlet and show its syntax.
Example	The example view includes a synopsis of the cmdlet and some examples of its usage.
Detailed	The detailed view shows more details on a cmdlet, including parameters and parameter descriptions.
Full	The full view shows all the details available on a cmdlet, including a synopsis of the cmdlet, a detailed description, parameter descriptions, parameter metadata, and examples.
Parameters	The parameters view allows you to specify a parameter and get help on the usage of just that particular parameter.

Still not clear about what each view gives you? Perhaps Table 7.8 can shed some further light on the issue. This table shows you the different sections that are output when using each view option.

TABLE 7.8:   Information Output for Each Get-Help View

	DEFAULT VIEW	EXAMPLE VIEW	DETAILED VIEW	FULL VIEW
Synopsis	✓	✓	✓	✓
Detailed description	✓		✓	✓
Syntax	✓		✓	✓
Parameters			✓	✓
Parameter metadata				✓
Input type				✓
Return type				✓
Errors				✓
Notes				✓
Examples		✓	✓	✓

To use these parameters, you type would use the following `Get-Help` cmdlet by the view option. For example, to see the example view for `Get-Mailbox`, you would type this:

```
Get-Help Get-Mailbox -Example
```

Let's look at a couple of more detailed examples for the `Get-MailboxStatistics` cmdlet. We are choosing a cmdlet (`Get-MailboxStatistics`) that we feel is pretty representative of the EMS cmdlets but also does not have a huge amount of help information. We feel it is important for administrators to understand the available online help options. First, let's look at the default view. We can type just `Get-Help Get-MailboxStatistics`, the -Default option is not necessary:

```
Get-Help Get-MailboxStatistics -Default

NAME
    Get-MailboxStatistics

SYNOPSIS
    Use the Get-MailboxStatistics cmdlet to obtain information about a
mailbox, such as the size of the mailbox, the number of messages it
contains, and the last time it was accessed.

SYNTAX
    Get-MailboxStatistics [-Identity <GeneralMailboxIdParameter>] [-
    DomainController <Fqdn>] [<CommonParameters>]

    Get-MailboxStatistics -Database <DatabaseIdParameter>
[-DomainController <Fqdn>] [<CommonParameters>]

    Get-MailboxStatistics -Server <ServerIdParameter>
[-DomainController <Fqdn>] [<CommonParameters>]


DETAILED DESCRIPTION
    To run the Get-MailboxStatistics cmdlet on a computer that has any
server role installed, except the Edge Transport server role, you must
log on by using a domain account that has the permissions assigned to
the Exchange Server Administrators group. The account must also be a
member of the local Administrators group on that computer.

    On Mailbox servers only, you can use the Get-MailboxStatistics
cmdlet without parameters. In this case, the cmdlet will return the
statistics for all mailboxes on all databases on the local server.


RELATED LINKS
```

REMARKS
>   For more information, type: "get-help Get-MailboxStatistics -
> detailed".
>   For technical information, type: "get-help Get-MailboxStatistics -
> full".

This view (as you could have predicted from Table 7.8) includes the synopsis, syntax, and detailed description sections. Let's change our approach and look at the example view:

```
Get-Help Get-MailboxStatistics -Examples
```

NAME
>   Get-MailboxStatistics

SYNOPSIS
>   Use the Get-MailboxStatistics cmdlet to obtain information about a
> mailbox, such as the size of the mailbox, the number of messages it
> contains, and the last time it was accessed.

```
    Get-MailboxStatistics
    Get-MailboxStatistics -Server MailboxServer01
    Get-MailboxStatistics -Identity contoso\chris
    Get-MailboxStatistics -Database "Mailbox Database"
    Get-MailboxStatistics | Where {$_.DisconnectDate -ne $null}
```

The example view does not have as much data, but a lot of techies learn by looking at examples, so we find this view particularly useful. Next let's look at the detailed view; since this view includes the parameters, it will have quite a bit more information:

```
Get-Help Get-MailboxStatistics -Detailed
```

NAME
>   Get-MailboxStatistics

SYNOPSIS
>   Use the Get-MailboxStatistics cmdlet to obtain information about a
> mailbox, such as the size of the mailbox, the number of messages it
> contains, and the last time it was accessed.

SYNTAX
>   Get-MailboxStatistics [-Identity <GeneralMailboxIdParameter>]
> [-DomainController <Fqdn>] [<CommonParameters>]
>
>   Get-MailboxStatistics -Database <DatabaseIdParameter>
> [-DomainController <Fqdn>] [<CommonParameters>]

```
Get-MailboxStatistics -Server <ServerIdParameter>
[-DomainController <Fqdn>] [<CommonParameters>]
```

DETAILED DESCRIPTION
   To run the Get-MailboxStatistics cmdlet on a computer that has any
server role installed, except the Edge Transport server role, you must
log on by using a domain account that has the permissions assigned to
the Exchange Serv Administrators group. The account must also be a
member of the local Administrators group on that computer.

   On Mailbox servers only, you can use the Get-MailboxStatistics
cmdlet without parameters. In this case, the cmdlet will return the
statistics for all mailboxes on all databases on the local server.

PARAMETERS
   -Database <DatabaseIdParameter>
      The Database parameter specifies the name of the mailbox
database. When you specify a value for the Database parameter, the
Exchange Management Shell returns statistics for all the mailboxes
on the database specified.
      You can use the following values:
      * Server\StorageGroup\Database
      * Server\Database
      * Database
      This parameter accepts pipeline input from the Get-
   MailboxDatabase cmdlet.

   -Server <ServerIdParameter>
      The Server parameter specifies the server from which you want
   to obtain mailbox statistics. You can use one of the following values:
      * Fully qualified domain name (FQDN)
      * NetBIOS name

      When you specify a value for the Server parameter, the command
returns statistics for all the mailboxes on all the databases,
including recovery databases, on the specified server. If you do not
specify this parameter, the command returns logon statistics for the
local server.
      This parameter accepts pipeline input from the Get-
ExchangeServer and Get-MailboxServer cmdlets.

   -DomainController <Fqdn>
      To specify the fully qualified domain name (FQDN) of the domain
controller that retrieves data from the Active Directory directory
service, include the DomainController parameter in the command.
```
```

```
-Identity <GeneralMailboxIdParameter>
        The Identity parameter specifies a mailbox. When you specify a
value for the Identity parameter, the command looks up the mailbox that
is specified in the Identity parameter, connects to the server where
the mailbox resides, and returns the statistics for the mailbox. You
can use one
         of the following values:
        * GUID
        * Distinguished name (DN)
        * Domain\Account
        * User principal name (UPN)
        * Legacy Exchange DN
        * SmtpAddress
        * Alias
        This parameter accepts pipeline input from the Get-Mailbox
    cmdlet.


    <CommonParameters>
        This cmdlet supports the common parameters: -Verbose, -Debug,
        -ErrorAction, -ErrorVariable, and -OutVariable. For more
information,type, "get-help about_commonparameters".

    Get-MailboxStatistics
    Get-MailboxStatistics -Server MailboxServer01
    Get-MailboxStatistics -Identity contoso\chris
    Get-MailboxStatistics -Database "Mailbox Database"
    Get-MailboxStatistics | Where {$_.DisconnectDate -ne $null}

REMARKS
    For more information, type: "get-help Get-MailboxStatistics -
    detailed".
    For technical information, type: "get-help Get-MailboxStatistics -
    full".
```

Naturally, the full view is going to contain a little bit more information than the detailed view.
The full view includes the metadata for each parameter as well as examples:

```
Get-Help Get-MailboxStatistics -Full

NAME
    Get-MailboxStatistics

SYNOPSIS
    Use the Get-MailboxStatistics cmdlet to obtain information about a
    mailbox, such as the size of the mailbox, the number of messages it
    contains, and the last time it was accessed.
```

SYNTAX
    Get-MailboxStatistics [-Identity <GeneralMailboxIdParameter>]
[-DomainController <Fqdn>] [<CommonParameters>]

    Get-MailboxStatistics -Database <DatabaseIdParameter>
[-DomainController <Fqdn>] [<CommonParameters>]

    Get-MailboxStatistics -Server <ServerIdParameter> [-
DomainController <Fqdn>] [<CommonParameters>]

DETAILED DESCRIPTION
    To run the Get-MailboxStatistics cmdlet on a computer that has any
server role installed, except the Edge Transport server role, you must
log on by using a domain account that has the permissions assigned to
the Exchange Server Administrators group. The account must also be a
member of the local Administrators group on that computer.
    On Mailbox servers only, you can use the Get-MailboxStatistics
cmdlet without parameters. In this case, the cmdlet will return the
statistics for all mailboxes on all databases on the local server.

PARAMETERS
    -Database <DatabaseIdParameter>
        The Database parameter specifies the name of the mailbox
database. When you specify a value for the Database parameter, the
Exchange Management Shell returns statistics for all the mailboxes
on the database specified.
        You can use the following values:
        * Server\StorageGroup\Database
        * Server\Database
        * Database

        This parameter accepts pipeline input from the Get-
    MailboxDatabase cmdlet.

        Required?   true
        Position?   Named
        Default value
        Accept pipeline input?   True
        Accept wildcard characters? false

    -Server <ServerIdParameter>
        The Server parameter specifies the server from which you want
to obtain mailbox statistics. You can use one of the following values:
        * Fully qualified domain name (FQDN)
        * NetBIOS name

When you specify a value for the Server parameter, the command
returns statistics for all the mailboxes on all the databases, including
recovery databases, on the specified server. If you do not specify
this parameter, the command returns logon statistics for the local
server.
This parameter accepts pipeline input from the Get-
ExchangeServer and Get-MailboxServer cmdlets.

Required?	true
Position?	Named
Default value	
Accept pipeline input?	True
Accept wildcard characters?	false

-DomainController <Fqdn>
To specify the fully qualified domain name (FQDN) of the domain
controller that retrieves data from the Active Directory directory
service, include the DomainController parameter in the command.

Required?	false
Position?	Named
Default value	
Accept pipeline input?	False
Accept wildcard characters?	false

-Identity <GeneralMailboxIdParameter>
The Identity parameter specifies a mailbox. When you specify a
value for the Identity parameter, the command looks up the mailbox
that is specified in the Identity parameter, connects to the server
where the mailbox resides, and returns the statistics for the mailbox.
You can use one
of the following values:
* GUID
* Distinguished name (DN)
* Domain\Account
* User principal name (UPN)
* Legacy Exchange DN
* SmtpAddress
* Alias
This parameter accepts pipeline input from the Get-Mailbox
cmdlet.

Required?	false
Position?	1
Default value	
Accept pipeline input?	True
Accept wildcard characters?	false

```
    <CommonParameters>
        This cmdlet supports the common parameters: -Verbose, -Debug,
        -ErrorAction, -ErrorVariable, and -OutVariable. For more
    information, type, "get-help about_commonparameters".

INPUT TYPE

RETURN TYPE

TERMINATING ERRORS
    (Category: )

    Type:
    Target Object Type:
    Suggested Action:

NON-TERMINATING ERRORS
    (Category: )

    Type:
    Target Object Type:
    Suggested Action:

    Get-MailboxStatistics
    Get-MailboxStatistics -Server MailboxServer01
    Get-MailboxStatistics -Identity contoso\chris
    Get-MailboxStatistics -Database "Mailbox Database"
    Get-MailboxStatistics | Where {$_.DisconnectDate -ne $null}

RELATED LINKS
```

Yes, that is a lot of text for examples of one cmdlet, but we hope that these examples will make it easier for you to quickly learn the capabilities of all cmdlets and how you can use them.

The EMS help system also gives you some options with respect to getting help on parameters. For example, here is an example if you want help on just the -**Database** parameter of the Get-MailboxStatistics cmdlet:

```
Get-Help Get-MailboxStatistics -Parameter Database

-Database <DatabaseIdParameter>
    The Database parameter specifies the name of the mailbox database.
When you specify a value for the Database parameter, the Exchange
Management Shell returns statistics for all the mailboxes on the
database specified.

    You can use the following values:
    * Server\StorageGroup\Database
    * Server\Database
    * Database
```

```
This parameter accepts pipeline input from the Get-MailboxDatabase
cmdlet.

Required?                   true
Position?                   Named
Default value
Accept pipeline input?      True
Accept wildcard characters? false
```

The parameters option also accepts the asterisk (*) wildcard. Here is an example where we want to see help on all of the parameters that contain SCLQuarantine:

```
Get-Help Set-Mailbox -Parameter *SCLQuarantine*

-SCLQuarantineEnabled <Nullable>
    The SCLQuarantineEnabled parameter specifies whether messages that
meet the spam confidence level threshold specified by the
SCLQuarantineThreshold parameter will be quarantined. If a message is
quarantined, it is sent to the quarantine mailbox where the messaging
administrator can review it. You can use the following values:
    * $true
    * $false
    * $null

Required?                   false
Position?                   Named
Default value               Null
Accept pipeline input?      False
Accept wildcard characters? false


-SCLQuarantineThreshold <Nullable>
    The SCLQuarantineThreshold parameter specifies the spam confidence
level at which a message will be quarantined, if the SCLQuarantineEnabled
parameteris set to $true.
    You must specify an integer between 0 and 9 inclusive.

Required?                   false
Position?                   Named
Default value               Null
Accept pipeline input?      False
Accept wildcard characters? false
```

Summary

Exchange 2007 administration has definitely changed. Organizations that have become dependent on delegating mailbox administration through Active Directory Users and Computers will surely experience some growing pains as they transition their mail-recipient administrators back to the Exchange Management Console. To add insult to injury, the Exchange Management Console has been completely revamped and has a completely new look and feel. Finally, more complex administrative tasks will often have to be performed through the Exchange Management Shell.

That is the bad news. Well, not *really* bad news since the new Exchange Management Console is very intuitive and makes Exchange management much easier. The ability to create custom consoles that provide administrators with only the tasks necessary to do their jobs, such as managing mailboxes, will simplify mail recipient administration rather than make it more difficult.

The PowerShell and the Exchange Management Shell extensions may seem complex and intimidating at first, but they are nowhere near as complex as other command-line interfaces, including other Windows CLIs. In just a few hours, you will be using the PowerShell and the EMS like an old pro.

After a few days of using the new Exchange 2007 administrative tools, you will wonder how you ever did your job without them.

Chapter 8

Exchange Organization, Server, and Recipient Management

The Exchange organization configuration is stored in a number of different places. First and foremost, most of the Exchange configuration information is stored in the Active Directory's configuration partition, but you will also find Exchange-related configuration information in the Internet Information Server (IIS) metabase as well as the Windows Registry.

The administrative tools such as the Exchange Management Console (EMC) and the Exchange Management Shell (EMS) hide the complexity of accessing, viewing, and updating this configuration information.

Whether you are just getting started with Exchange server as an e-mail platform or you are an experienced Exchange administrator, you may have a bit of trouble finding the right place to make a configuration change. Microsoft has tried hard to make the management interface simpler and more intuitive, but the fact remains that sometimes finding the right object is a little difficult.

> **NOTE**
>
> This chapter should serve as an introduction to where the settings for different objects are located. You can find more information about configuring most of these in other places in the book.

In this chapter we hope to provide you with more insight into finding the right place to make configuration changes. For experienced Exchange 2000/2003 administrators, we will be providing some parallels to where you will find some of the configuration tasks that you used to perform in the Exchange System Manager.

Topics in this chapter include the following:

◆ Active Directory storage of configuration data

◆ Exchange organization-wide configuration

◆ Server-by-server configuration

◆ Recipient management tools

Understanding the Active Directory Configuration Partition

Let's first take a quick look at where the configuration data is stored in the Active Directory. Most of the Exchange configuration is stored in the Active Directory configuration partition. The configuration partition is a piece of the Active Directory database that is replicated to all domain controllers in the entire forest. This partition stores information about Active Directory partitions, configuration, sites, display specifiers, and more.

When the first Exchange server is installed into an Active Directory forest, new configuration data is stored in this partition. The Exchange-related information is stored in the CN=Services, CN=Microsoft Exchange container. Figure 8.1 shows the container as seen in the Windows 2003 support tool ADSIEdit.

FIGURE 8.1
Viewing the Exchange 2007 configuration data using ADSIEdit

You can also use the Exchange management tools to organize and present the information you see in Figure 8.1, but in a friendlier and more manageable format. It is unusual to actually edit the information in the Active Directory configuration partition, but it is useful to know where the configuration data is located.

Managing Organization-Wide Configuration Parameters

Let's start with a view of the configuration options and parameters that affect the entire Exchange organization (every server and every object). For Exchange 2000/2003 administrators, these are the same types of things you would find under the Global Settings and Recipients containers in Exchange System Manager.

NOTE

Parameters and objects found in the Organization Configuration work center affect every server and mail-enabled recipient in the organization.

Setting the Junk E-mail Folder Threshold

You use the `Get-OrganizationConfig` and `Set-OrganizationConfig` cmdlets to view the organization configuration and set organization configuration parameters. For the organization configuration, there is one important parameter that will be of use to many administrators; this is the `SCLJunkThreshold` parameter. This is set to by default to a value of 4. If messages are processed by the Content Filter (formerly known as the Microsoft Exchange Intelligent Message Filter) and are determined to have a value of 4 or higher, they will be placed in the user's Junk E-mail folder.

Setting Message Size and Recipient Count Limit

Message sizes can be set in a lot of places; size limits can be configured for the entire organization, a specific connector, or an individual mailbox. However, to set them globally, you must set them from the EMS. The `Get-TransportConfig` and the `Set-TransportConfig` cmdlets have the `-MaxReceiveSize`, `-MaxSendSize`, and `-MaxRecipientEnvelopeLimit` parameters, which control the maximum incoming message size, the maximum outgoing message size, and the maximum number of recipients per message. For more information on these, see Chapter 9, "Imposing Limits."

Configuring Administrative Permissions

When the first Exchange 2007 server is installed in to the Active Directory forest, a container called Microsoft Exchange Security Groups (shown in Figure 8.2) is created in the root domain. For most organizations, making a user a member of one of these groups will suffice when delegating the necessary permissions to manage the Exchange organization, Exchange recipients, or Exchange servers.

FIGURE 8.2
Active Directory security groups

In larger organizations, custom permissions may need to be delegated or assigned based on the organization's requirements. Additional or custom permissions can be delegated using the EMC. Figure 8.3 shows the EMC with the Organization Configuration work center selected.

Exchange administrative permissions can also be viewed, assigned, and removed using the EMS cmdlets `Get-ExchangeAdministrator`, `Add-ExchangeAdministrator`, and `Remove-ExchangeAdministrator`.

FIGURE 8.3
Using the Exchange
Management Console
to assign permissions

You can find more information about administrative permissions in Chapter 7, "Administering Exchange 2007."

Configuring Messaging Records Management

Messaging records management is a combination of a new set of features for Exchange Server 2007 and the Exchange 2000/2003 mailbox manager features. Messaging records management allows you to create custom folders in a user's mailbox and manage the content in both the default folders as well as the custom folders. Management and configuration of messaging records management components is performed in the EMC under the Organization Configuration work center and under the Mailbox subcontainer.

The Mailbox subcontainer of the Organization Configuration work center is shown in Figure 8.4. The Managed Custom Folders tab in the results pane allows you to create additional managed custom folders and assign managed content settings to them.

FIGURE 8.4
Managing message
records management
settings

From the Managed Default Folders tab in the results pane, you can assign managed content settings to default folders such as the Inbox, Deleted Items, and Sent Items.

The final component of message records management (at least from the organization's perspective) is the creation of managed folder mailbox policies. These policies specify which folders are assigned to a mailbox. The mailbox is then assigned policies found on the Managed Folder Mailbox Policies tab.

If you are inclined to manage messaging records management components from the command line, here are some of the cmdlets you can use:

Cmdlet	Description
Start-ManagedFolderAssistant	Starts the managed folder assistant on a Mailbox server
Stop-ManagedFolderAssistant	Stops the managed folder assistant on a Mailbox server
New-ManagedFolder	Creates a new managed custom or default folder
New-ManagedFolderMailboxPolicy	Defines a new managed folder mailbox policy
New-ManagedContentSettings	Creates a new managed content settings object in the specified managed folder
Get-ManagedFolder	Retrieves a list of managed folders or the properties of an individual managed folder if it is specified in the command line
Get-ManagedFolderMailboxPolicy	Retrieves a list of managed folder mailbox policies or the properties of an individual managed folder mailbox policy if it is specified in the command line
Get-ManagedContentSettings	Retrieves all of the managed content setting objects or the properties of an individual content settings object if it is specified
Set-ManagedFolder	Sets properties on a managed folder
Set-ManagedFolderMailboxPolicy	Sets the properties on a managed folder mailbox policy
Set-ManagedContentSettings	Sets the properties on a managed content settings object
Remove-ManagedFolder	Removes an existing managed folder
Remove-ManagedFolderMailboxPolicy	Removes a managed folder mailbox policy
Remove-ManagedContentSettings	Removes a managed content settings object

You can find more information about messaging records management in Chapter 12, "Managing Folder Content."

Managing Address Lists

There are a couple of different types of address lists that can be created and managed in Exchange 2007. These include the custom address lists, offline address books, and global address lists.

Address lists were found in the Exchange 2000/2003 Exchange System Manager console under Recipients\All Address Lists and are also called custom address lists. Exchange 2007 includes the default address lists All Users, All Rooms, All Groups, and All Contacts. These address lists, as well as new ones, are managed from the Mailbox subfolder of the Organization Configuration work center. Figure 8.5 shows the Address Lists tab.

FIGURE 8.5
Address lists when
viewed from the
Exchange Management
Console

Offline address books are managed from the Offline Address Book tab in the results pane of the Mailbox subfolder. Figure 8.6 shows the Offline Address Book tab.

Global address list management is not configured from the Exchange Management Console but instead through the EMS. The following are the EMS cmdlets for managing custom address lists, offline address books, and global address lists:

Cmdlet	Description
New-AddressList	Creates a new custom address list.
New-GlobalAddressList	Creates a new global address list.
New-OfflineAddressBook	Creates a new offline address book.
Get-AddressList	Retrieves a listing of the existing address lists or the properties of a specific address list.
Get-GlobalAddressList	Retrieves a listing of the existing global address lists or the properties of a specific global address list.
Get-OfflineAddressBook	Retrieves a listing of the existing offline address book or the properties of a specific offline address book.
Set-AddressList	Sets the properties of an existing address list.
Set-GlobalAddressList	Sets the properties of an existing global address list.
Set-OfflineAddressBook	Sets the properties of an existing offline address book.
Remove-AddressList	Removes an existing address list.
Remove-GlobalAddressList	Removes an existing global address list.
Remove-OfflineAddressBook	Removes an existing offline address book.
Update-AddressList	Updates the membership of an address list. Anytime address list membership criteria is changed, this should be run.
Update-GlobalAddressList	Updates the membership of a global address list. Anytime global address list membership is changed, this should be run.

Update-OfflineAddressBook	Updates the offline address book information that is distributed to offline clients. This should be run on a regular basis.
Move-AddressList	Moves an address list from one address list container to another.
Move-OfflineAddressBook	Changes the offline address book generation server for an offline address book.

FIGURE 8.6
Offline address book management viewed from the Exchange Management Console

You can learn more information about creating and managing the different types of address lists in Chapter 11.

Setting ActiveSync Policies

Exchange 2007 allows you to support more than one ActiveSync policy for Windows Mobile devices. These are configured globally in the Client Access subcontainer of the Organization Configuration work center of the EMC. The Exchange ActiveSync Mailbox Policies tab is shown in Figure 8.7 with the General property page of one of the policies. In Exchange 2003, you can find these settings under Global Settings\Mobile Services.

From an ActiveSync Mailbox policy, you can define maximum attachment sizes, SharePoint and Windows file share access, password complexity, and device encryption requirements. Once a policy is defined, it must be assigned to the user accounts/mailboxes on which it must be enforced.

Cmdlet	Description
New-ActiveSyncMailboxPolicy	Creates a new ActiveSync mailbox policy
Remove-ActiveSyncMailboxPolicy	Deletes an existing ActiveSync mailbox policy
Set-ActiveSyncMailboxPolicy	Sets the properties of the specified ActiveSync mailbox policy
Get-ActiveSyncMailboxPolicy	Retrieves a list of ActiveSync mailbox policies or properties of an individual mailbox policy if the policy name is specified

You can find more information about Exchange ActiveSync mailbox policies in Chapter 19, "Exchange Anywhere."

FIGURE 8.7
Managing ActiveSync
Mailbox policies
using the Exchange
Management Console

Removing or Wiping ActiveSync Devices

ActiveSync devices can be removed or disassociated with Exchange 2007 if the device is no longer used or it needs to be completely reset and rebuilt. You may also need to initiate a remote wipe of a device if the device is lost or stolen. You can use the following EMS cmdlets to manage these features:

Cmdlet	Description
Get-ActiveSyncDeviceStatistics	Lists the statistics of a specific ActiveSync device when you specify the mailbox name that the device is synchronizing with
Clear-ActiveSyncDevice	Initiates a remote wipe-out of the ActiveSync device the next time it connects to a Client Access server to synchronize
Remove-ActiveSyncDevice	Removes an ActiveSync device partnership

Managing Outbound Message Formats

When Exchange delivers a message to the Internet, it uses the format specified in the Remote Domains list. Different domains can use different outbound message formats, too. There is more to remote domain configuration than just message formats, though. A remote domain configuration includes:

◆ Out-of-Office message types to be delivered

◆ Outbound message character sets

◆ Whether or not automatic replies, automatic forwards, delivery reports, and non-delivery reports are generated to the specified domain

The default format is used for all outbound SMTP mail to all external domains and is configured in the Remote Domains tab in the Exchange Management Console under the Hub Transport section of the Organization Configuration work center. The Remote Domains tab is shown in Figure 8.8 as well as the General property page of the default message format. In Exchange 2000/2003, you can find this information in the Global Settings\Internet Message Defaults container.

FIGURE 8.8
Managing Internet message formats using the Exchange Management Console

If you are inclined to manage these settings from the EMS, here are the EMS cmdlets for managing remote domain message formats:

Cmdlet	Description
Get-RemoteDomain	Retrieves a list of existing remote domains or the properties of a specific remote domain object
New-RemoteDomain	Creates a new remote domain object
Set-RemoteDomain	Sets the properties of a remote domain object
Remove-RemoteDomain	Deletes an existing remote domain object

Configuring SMTP Accepted Domains

Exchange 2007 (like Exchange 2000/2003) must be configured with a list of SMTP domains that it will accept either as internal domains or to be relayed on to another SMTP system. In Exchange 2000/2003, this function was combined with recipient policies so that e-mail addresses could also be automatically generated if the policy applied to any recipients. This function has been broken out into the accepted domains feature; accepted domains are defined using the EMC by locating the Organization Configuration work center and viewing the Hub Transport subcontainer. The accepted domain list is found on the Accepted Domains tab. Figure 8.9 shows the Accepted Domains tab as well as the properties of one of the accepted domains.

FIGURE 8.9
Accepted domains properties in the Exchange Management Console

You can manage accepted domains using the EMS command shell also. The following are some of the relevant cmdlets:

Cmdlet	Description
Get-AcceptedDomain	Retrieves a list of accepted domains or the properties of the specified accepted domain
New-AcceptedDomain	Creates a new accepted domain
Set-AcceptedDomain	Sets the accepted domain properties
Remove-AcceptedDomain	Removes an accepted domain

An accepted domain can be configured so that e-mail is always delivered to the internal Exchange organization (an authoritative domain), a domain in which your Exchange organization has mail-enabled contacts (an internal relay domain), or a domain in which you relay all mail externally (an external relay domain.) You can learn more about configuring and using the accepted domains feature in Chapter 10, "Managing Recipients."

Generating and Assigning E-mail Addresses

E-mail address policies are responsible for generating e-mail addresses for mail-enabled recipients (mailboxes, groups, contacts, etc.). In Exchange 2000/2003, e-mail addresses were defined using a recipient policy so e-mail address policies are somewhat similar to an Exchange 2000/2003 recipient policy. One difference is that in Exchange 2000/2003, the recipient policy defined not only e-mail addresses that were generated for mail-enabled recipients but also which SMTP domains were accepted.

Figure 8.10 shows the E-mail Addresses Policies tab of the Hub Transport results pane and the Edit E-mail Address Policy Wizard. The E-mail Addresses Policy Wizard can be launched to create a new e-mail address policy or edit an existing one.

FIGURE 8.10
Editing an e-mail
address policy using the
Exchange Management
Console

Once a policy is created, it must be applied to the mail-enabled objects. The policy is applied based on its conditions; conditions of a policy include including recipients based on department name, company name, state, or a custom attribute. The administrator can apply the policy immediately after creation either by clicking the Apply button on the Actions pane or by running an EMS cmdlet. The following cmdlets apply to e-mail address policies:

Cmdlet	Description
Get-EmailAddressPolicy	Retrieves a list of the e-mail address policies or the properties of a specified e-mail address policy.
Set-EmailAddressPolicy	Sets the properties of an e-mail address policy.
New-EmailAddressPolicy	Creates a new e-mail address policy.
Remove-EmailAddressPolicy	Removes an existing e-mail address policy.
Update-EmailAddressPolicy	Applies the policy based on the conditions specified when the policy was created. The policy must be applied before affected users be assigned e-mail e-mail addresses that the policy specified.

You can learn more about creating and managing e-mail address policies by referring to Chapter 10, "Managing Recipients."

Managing Transport Rules

Transport rules are a new feature of Exchange 2007. They allow you to specify conditions under which a certain action will be applied to a message. An example of this would be applying an "Attorney / Client Privilege" classification label (the action) to any message sent by a member of the legal time group (the condition).

Transport rules are created and managed under the Transport Rules tab of the Hub Transport rules pane (found under the Organization Configuration work center.) Transport rules are edited and created using the Edit Transport Rule Wizard. Figure 8.11 shows the Transport Rules tab as well as the Actions page of the wizard.

FIGURE 8.11
Editing a transport rule using the Exchange Management Console

The following are the EMS cmdlets that can be used to create and manage transport rules:

Cmdlet	Description
Get-TransportRule	Retrieves a list of transport rules or the properties of a specific transport rule
Set-TransportRule	Sets the properties of a transport rule
New-TransportRule	Creates a new transport rule
Remove-TransportRule	Deletes a transport rule
Disable-TransportRule	Disables a transport rule so that Hub Transport servers will not process that particular rule
Enable-TransportRule	Enables a transport rule that was previously disabled
Get-TransportRulePredicate	Lists the transport rule conditions
Get-TransportRuleAction	Lists the transport rule actions

We have devoted an entire chapter to creating, managing, and using transport rules. Please see Chapter 13, "Managing Messages in Transit."

Managing Journaling

Journaling is a feature that has been in Exchange since the Exchange 5.5 days. In previous versions of Exchange, though, you could only configure journaling for all mailboxes on an entire mailbox database. This feature still exists, of course, and can be used if that is the way you have configured journaling to work in your organization. You must locate the mailbox database that contains the mailboxes for which you want to keep journaled copies of sent and received e-mail. On the General property page (shown in Figure 8.12) of that mailbox database, you specify the journal recipient.

FIGURE 8.12
Configuring journaling for an entire mailbox database

You can read more about properties of mailbox databases in Chapter 6: "Scaling Upward and Outward."

Exchange 2007 introduced a couple of new approaches to journaling. You can now configure journaling with an organization-wide journaling feature found in the Journaling tab of the Organization Configuration work center's Hub Transport subcontainer. Figure 8.13 shows this tab and a journaling rule's General property page.

If you are so inclined, here are the EMS cmdlets you can use for managing journal rules:

Cmdlet	Description
Get-JournalRule	Retrieves a list of journal rules or just the properties of a specified journal rule
Set-JournalRule	Sets the properties of a journal rule
New-JournalRule	Creates a new journal rule

`Remove-JournalRule`	Deletes a journal rule
`Enable-JournalRule`	Enables a journal rule that was disabled
`Disable-JournalRule`	Disables the specified journal rule

FIGURE 8.13
Creating a journaling rule

Journaling can also be achieved by creating transport rules that will forward a message to a journaling mailbox if certain conditions are met. Messaging records management introduces an additional way that messages can be journaled, though this feature requires user participation, so this approach can also be thought of as an archival or retention feature. On a managed content setting, you can configure the properties of a folder within a user's mailbox so that when a message is placed there, a copy of it is sent to a separate e-mail address. Figure 8.14 shows the Journaling property page of a managed content setting.

Managed content settings and messaging records management are discussed in more detail in Chapter 12, "Managing Folder Content."

Managing Outbound E-mail to External SMTP Domains

The Send connector is the component that you configure to send outbound SMTP mail to external SMTP domains. It is the equivalent of the Exchange 2000/2003 SMTP Connector and is defined under the Organization Configuration work center of the EMC and is found in the Hub Transport results pane under the Send Connectors tab. The Source Server properties of a Send connector as well as the Send Connectors tab is shown in Figure 8.15.

The EMS cmdlets necessary to create and manage a Send connector are as follows:

Cmdlet	Description
`Get-SendConnector`	Retrieve a list of the existing Send connectors or properties of a specified Send connector

Set-SendConnector	Sets Send connector properties
New-SendConnector	Creates a new Send connector
Remove-SendConnector	Deletes a Send connector

For more information on connectivity and Send connectors, see Chapter 18, ''Delivering E-mail.''

FIGURE 8.14
Assigning journaling settings to a managed content setting

FIGURE 8.15
Properties of a Send connector as shown in the Exchange Management Console

Managing Edge Transport Subscriptions

Another new feature of Exchange Server 2007 is the Edge Transport server role. In order to properly use the Edge Transport server role, you must configure an Edge Subscription. These are created and managed under the Edge Subscription tab of the Hub Transport results pane. The Edge Subscriptions tab and the New Edge Subscription Wizard are shown in Figure 8.16.

FIGURE 8.16
Creating a new Edge Subscription using the Exchange Management Console

You might find a number of Edge Transport–related EMS cmdlets useful; these include the following:

Cmdlet	Description
Get-EdgeSubscriptions	Lists the current Edge Subscriptions and their properties
New-EdgeSubscription	Creates a new Edge Subscription
Remove-EdgeSubscription	Deletes an Edge Subscription
Start-EdgeSynchronization	Starts an immediate EdgeSync session
Stop-EdgeSynchronization	Stops an EdgeSync session
Test-EdgeSynchronization	Tests the specified Edge Transport server's subscription to ensure that the Edge Transport servers have current and accurate synchronized data.

To learn more about anti-spam features and the Edge Transport server role, refer to Chapter 18, "Delivering E-mail."

Configuring Exchange Server Anti-spam Features

There are a lot of possible ways to protect your organization from spam. You could have a managed provider than handles your spam services, or you could use a third-party appliance or software. You could use an Edge Transport server, or you could accept mail directly from the Internet to your Hub Transport servers.

If your Hub Transport servers are responsible for accepting mail directly from the Internet, you can install the anti-spam agents on the Hub Transport servers. Figure 8.17 shows the Anti-spam tab for the organization-wide Hub Transport settings.

FIGURE 8.17
Anti-spam configuration using the Exchange Management Console

If you have been exploring the Exchange Management Console interface, you may be surprised to see that Anti-spam tab. It is not there by default; you must run the C:\Program Files\Microsoft\ exchange server\scripts\Install-AntispamAgents.ps1 PowerShell script in order to install the necessary transport agents and to reveal this tab on the interface. Installing the anti-spam agent enables quite a few additional EMS cmdlets. These cmdlets will work on a Hub Transport server that has had the anti-spam agents installed and they will also work on an Edge Transport server:

Cmdlet	Description
Get-ContentFilterConfig	Views the Content Filter configuration
Set-ConfigFilterConfig	Sets the Content Filter configuration
Get-ContentFilterPhrase	Views the Content Filter's list of phrases and words that are always considered spam or never considered spam
Set-ContentFilterPhrase	Adds words or phrases to the Content Filter phrase list
Get-IPAllowListProvider	Reviews the IP Allow List provider configuration
Set-IPAllowListProvider	Sets the IP Allow List provider configuration
Add-IPAllowListProvider	Adds an IP Allow List provider
Remove-IPAllowListProvider	Removes an IP Allow List provider
Get-IPAllowListConfig	Views the IP Allow List configuration
Set-IPAllowListConfig	Sets the IP Allow List configuration

`Get-IPAllowListEntry`	Views the entries in the IP Allow List
`Add-IPAllowListEntry`	Adds entries to the IP Allow List
`Remove-IPAllowListEntry`	Removes an entry from the IP Allow List
`Test-IPAllowListProvider`	Tests an IP Allow List provider
`Get-IPAllowListProvidersConfig`	Views the configuration of the IP Allow List Providers
`Set-IPAllowListProvidersConfig`	Sets the configuration of the IP Allow List providers
`Test-IPBLockListProvider`	Tests the specified IP Block List provider
`Get-IPBlockListConfig`	Views the IP Block List configuration
`Set-IPBlockListConfig`	Sets the IP Block List configuration
`Get-IPBlockListProvider`	Views the IP Block List providers currently configured
`Set-IPBlockListProvider`	Sets the configuration of an IP Block List provider
`Add-IPBlockListProvider`	Adds a new IP Block List provider
`Remove-IPBlockListProvider`	Removes an IP Block List provider
`Get-IPBlockListProvidersConfig`	Views the configuration of an IP Block List provider
`Set-IPBlockListProvidersConfig`	Sets the configuration of an IP Block List provider
`Add-IPBlockListEntry`	Adds an IP address to the IP Block List
`Remove-IPBlockListEntry`	Removes an IP address from the IP Block List
`Get-IPBlockListEntry`	Views the IP Block List entries
`Get-RecipientFilterConfig`	Views the Recipient Filter configuration
`Set-RecipientFitlerConfig`	Sets the Recipient Filter configuration
`Get-SenderReputationConfig`	Views the Sender Reputation configuration
`Set- SenderReputationConfig`	Configures the Sender Reputation configuration
`Get-SenderIdConfig`	Views the Sender ID configuration
`Set-SenderIdConfig`	Sets the Sender ID configuration
`Test-SenderId`	Tests the Sender ID configuration
`Get-SenderFilterConfig`	Views the Sender Filter configuration
`Set-SenderFilterConfig`	Sets the Sender Filter configuration
`Disable-AntispamUpdates`	Prevents the servers from downloading anti-spam system updates automatically
`Enable-AntispamUpdates`	Enables automatic download and installation of anti-spam updates
`Get-AntispamUpdates`	Views the configuration of the anti-spam updates system and retrieve updates

For more information on using the Exchange 2007 anti-spam features and the Edge Transport server role, see Chapter 18, "Delivering E-mail."

Performing Server-by-Server Configuration

Now that you have looked at some of the configuration properties that you might need to use when configuring your Exchange Server 2007 organization, we'll shift gears and look at some of the things you can do for each server. In the following sections, we will be focusing on the properties and objects found within the Server Configuration work center of the Exchange Management Console.

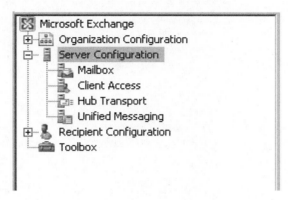

Entering a Product Key

If you are using Exchange 2007 without entering a product key, you will be dutifully notified each time you run the Exchange Management Console. In the results pane, select the server that needs a license key (this is the server with the small paper symbol and the blue and white exclamation mark icon). You should see the Enter Product Key task on the Actions pane. Figure 8.18 shows an example.

FIGURE 8.18
The Exchange
Management Console
showing an unlicensed
server

If you are looking at an unlicensed server using the 32-bit version of the Exchange Management Console, the Enter Product Key task will not appear on the Actions pane. You must use the `Set-ExchangeServer -ProductKey` command. You can also use this command to enter an updated product key number.

Managing Server Properties

If you select each of the subcontainers under the Server Configuration work center, highlight a server in the results pane, and then display the properties, you will see a slightly different set of property pages. However, if you highlight the Server Configuration container itself, all of the servers show up in the results pane. If you display the properties of a server in the results pane now, you will see all of the property pages for all of the server roles that are installed. Figure 8.19 shows the properties for an Exchange Server 2007 server that has all four server roles (Mailbox, Client Access, Hub Transport, and Unified Messaging) installed.

FIGURE 8.19
Properties of an
Exchange 2007 server

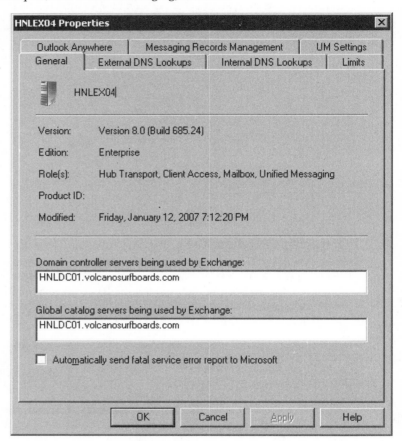

Upon further investigation, though, you will find that these properties are all viewed and set with different EMS cmdlets, depending on the server roles that are installed. The following are the cmdlets you would use for setting Exchange server properties:

Cmdlet	Description
Get-ExchangeServer	Views Exchange server properties that are shared by all server roles
Set-ExchangeServer	Sets Exchange server properties that are shared by all server roles
Get-TransportServer	Lists the Hub Transport servers and views Hub Transport server properties

Set-TransportServer	Sets Hub Transport server properties
Get-MailboxServer	Lists all of the Mailbox servers and views Mailbox server properties
Set-MailboxServer	Sets Mailbox server properties
Get-ClientAccessServer	Lists all of the Client Access servers and views Client Access server properties
Set-ClientAccessServer	Sets Client Access server properties
Get-UMServer	Lists all of the Unified Messaging servers and views Unified Messaging server properties
Set-UMServer	Sets Unified Messaging server properties
Enable-UMServer	Enables a Unified Messaging server to process voicemail, faxes, and call routing
Disable-UMServer	Disables a Unified Message server so that it will not process voicemail, faxes, or route calls
Get-ClusteredMailboxServer	Retrieves a list of clustered Mailbox servers
Move-ClusteredMailboxServer	Moves a clustered Mailbox server to a passive clustered node
Start-ClusteredMailboxServer	Starts clustered Mailbox server services
Stop-ClusteredMailboxServer	Stops clustered Mailbox server services

Managing Mailbox and Public Folder Databases

If you highlight the Mailbox subcontainer of the Exchange Management Console, the results pane will show you all servers that host the Mailbox server role and the work pane (below the results pane) will show you the storage groups, mailbox databases, and public folder databases. Figure 8.20 shows this view of the EMC.

FIGURE 8.20
Managing storage groups, mailbox databases, and public folder databases

There are quite a few tasks that can be defined within this view of the EMC with respect to storage groups, mailbox databases, and public folder databases:

◆ Creating and deleting storage groups

◆ Creating and deleting mailbox and public folder databases

◆ Configuring or moving file locations for storage groups and databases

◆ Mounting or dismounting databases

◆ Configuring database maintenance schedules

◆ Enabling, suspending, and resuming local continuous replication

◆ Establishing storage limits for mailboxes and public folders supported on a particular database

◆ Configuring deleted item and deleted mailbox retention times

◆ Enabling mailbox database journaling

◆ Setting default public folder databases and offline address books

There are also quite a few EMS cmdlets that can be used for managing storage groups, mailbox databases, and public folder databases. Let's look first at a list of the cmdlets that are used to manage storage group properties:

Cmdlet	Description
New-StorageGroup	Creates a new storage group
Move-StorageGroup	Moves transaction logs or system files to another location.
Get-StorageGroup	Retrieves a list of storage groups or storage group properties
Set-StorageGroup	Sets a storage group's properties
Remove-StorageGroup	Deletes a storage group
Enable-StorageGroupCopy	Enables local continuous replication for a storage group
Disable-StorageGroupCopy	Disables local continuous replication for a storage group
Suspend-StorageGroupCopy	Temporarily suspends local continuous replication
Update-StorageGroupCopy	Instructs local continuous replication to reestablish local continuous replication
Resume-StorageGroupCopy	Starts local continuous replication after it was previously suspended
Restore-StorageGroupCopy	Switches the local continuous replication database for the production copy
Get-StorageGroupCopyStatus	Views the status of local continuous replication

The following cmdlets can be used to manage mailbox and public folder databases:

Cmdlet	Description
New-MailboxDatabase	Creates a new mailbox database
Get-MailboxDatabase	Retrieves a list of mailbox databases or properties of mailbox databases
Set-MailboxDatabase	Sets the properties of a mailbox database
Remove-MailboxDatabase	Deletes a mailbox database
Clean-MailboxDatabase	Disconnects mailboxes on the specified mailbox database if the mailbox has been deleted in Active Directory
New-PublicFolderDatabase	Creates a new public folder database
Get-PublicFolderDatabase	Retrieves a list of public folder databases or public databases
Set-PublicFolderDatabase	Sets the properties of a public folder database
Remove-PublicFolderDatabase	Deletes a public folder database
Mount-Database	Mounts the specified mailbox or public folder database
Dismount-Database	Dismounts the specified pubic folder database
Move-DatabasePath	Moves public folder or mailbox database files to another location
Enable-DatabaseCopy	Enables local continuous replication for the specified database

If you are looking for additional information on creating and managing mailbox databases as well as managing local continuous replication, see Chapter 6, "Scaling Upward and Outward."

Managing Client Access Server Properties

The Client Access server role has a lot of functions in an organization that is using Outlook 2007, Outlook Anywhere (RPC over HTTP), Outlook Web Access, or ActiveSync technologies. When you select the Client Access subcontainer of the Server Configuration work center, the results pane shows the servers that host that particular server role. The work pane shows tabs for Outlook Web Access, Exchange ActiveSync, and Offline Address Book distribution. Figure 8.21 shows the Client Access subcontainer of the EMC.

While some organizations may be able to use the default configuration of Exchange 2007, other organizations will need to perform some changes or do some customizing. You can configure the following options through the Client Access subcontainer:

◆ Enabling or disabling Outlook Anywhere

◆ Managing internal and external URLs for Outlook Web Access, offline address books, Outlook Anywhere, and Exchange ActiveSync

◆ Managing authentication options for Outlook Web Access

◆ Managing segmentation options for Outlook Web Access

◆ Managing POP3 and IMAP4 options

◆ Configuring file and SharePoint servers that can be accessed remotely by Outlook Web Access and ActiveSync users

FIGURE 8.21
Managing Client Access server properties

With this many possible Client Access server-related tasks, naturally there are a lot of EMS cmdlets. Some Exchange 2007 components such as POP3, IMAP4, and Autodiscover settings cannot be managed through a graphical user interface, and so you must use the EMS. The following list includes some of the Client Access server role cmdlets:

Cmdlet	Description
Get-OutlookAnywhere	Retrieves the Outlook Anywhere configuration
Set-OutlookAnywhere	Sets the Outlook Anywhere configuration
Enable-OutlookAnywhere	Enables Outlook Anywhere support for a Client Access server
Disable-OutlookAnywhere	Disables Outlook Anywhere support for a Client Access server
Get-OwaVirtualDirectory	Retrieves a list of the OWA virtual directories and the OWA virtual directory properties
Set-OwaVirtualDirectory	Sets OWA virtual directory properties
New-OwaVirtualDirectory	Creates a new OWA virtual directory
Remove-OwaVirtualDirectory	Deletes an OWA virtual directory
Test-OwaConnectivity	Tests OWA connectivity
New-ActiveSyncVirtualDirectory	Creates a new Exchange ActiveSync virtual directory
Set-ActiveSyncVirtualDirectory	Sets ActiveSync virtual directory properties
Get-ActiveSyncVirtualDirectory	Retrieves a list of the ActiveSync virtual directories and ActiveSync virtual directory properties

Remove-ActiveSyncVirtualDirectory	Deletes an ActiveSync virtual directory
Test-ActiveSyncConnectivity	Tests Exchange ActiveSync connectivity
Export-ActiveSyncLog	Exports ActiveSync usage information from the IIS log files
Get-OABVirtualDirectory	Retrieves offline address book virtual directory information and properties
New-OABVirtualDirectory	Creates a new offline address book virtual directory
Remove-OABVirtualDirectory	Deletes an offline address book virtual directory
Set-OABVirtualDirectory	Sets the properties of an offline address book virtual directory
Get-AutodiscoverVirtualDirectory	Retrieves a list of Autodiscover virtual directories and their properties
Set-AutodiscoverVirtualDirectory	Sets Autodiscover virtual directory properties
Remove-AutodiscoverVirtualDirectory	Deletes an Autodiscover virtual directory
New-AutodiscoverVirtualDirectory	Creates a new Autodiscover virtual directory
Get-POPSettings	Retrieves the POP3 configuration for a Client Access server
Set-POPSettings	Sets the POP3 configuration
Get-IMAPSettings	Retrieves the IMAP4 configuration for a Client Access server
Set-IMAPSettings	Sets the IMAP4 configuration

You can find more information about enabling Outlook Anywhere, Outlook Web Access, POP3, and IMAP4 in Chapter 19, "Exchange Anywhere."

Managing Receive Connectors

Receive connectors are defined for each Hub Transport server role in your organization. By default there are two Receive connectors configured for each Hub Transport server; these are the default and client receive connects. You can see the Receive Connectors tab in the work pane when you select the Hub Transport subcontainer of the Server Configuration work center in the EMC; an example is shown in Figure 8.22.

If you want to manage the receive connectors from the EMS, here are the cmdlets you can use:

Cmdlet	Description
Get-ReceiveConnector	Retrieves a list of Receive connector and their properties
Set-ReceiveConnector	Sets the properties of a Receive connector
New-ReceiveConnector	Creates a new Receive connector
Remove-ReceiveConnector	Deletes a Receive connector

FIGURE 8.22
Managing Hub Transport
properties and Receive
connectors

You can find more information about managing Receive connectors as well as e-mail connectivity in Chapter 18, "Delivering E-mail."

Recipient Administration

In Chapter 10, "Managing Recipients," we will go in to a lot more detail on recipient administration. For now, we want to introduce the Recipient Configuration work center of the Exchange Management Console and the show you many of the recipient management EMS cmdlets. Recipients management is most easily performed using the Recipient Configuration work center of the EMC (see Figure 8.23).

FIGURE 8.23
Managing Exchange
2007 recipients
using the Exchange
Management Console

For many medium and large businesses, the EMS will prove most useful for managing mail-enabled recipients. For that reason, we wanted to provide a fairly comprehensive list of the EMS cmdlets available. In the following sections, we will review the management of each type of recipient and provide you with a list of the EMS cmdlets that can be use for each.

Mailbox Management

If you select the Mailboxes subcontainer of the Recipient Configuration work center of the EMC, you can see just the mailbox-enabled users in the organization. This could potentially be a pretty big list, so you can apply filters to narrow the scope of the list to just what you want to see. From here, you can select the properties of a mailbox (such as those shown in Figure 8.24).

FIGURE 8.24
Managing a mailbox's properties using the Exchange Management Console

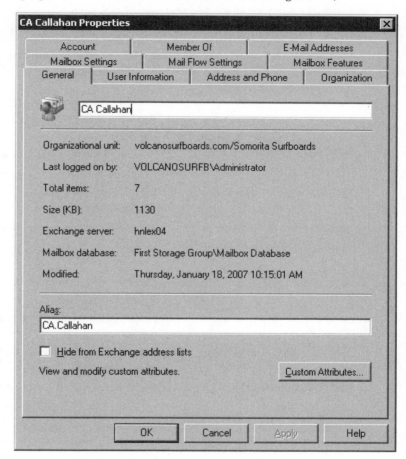

The mailbox properties you see in Figure 8.24 include attributes of the user account that are not really Exchange specific. For example, you can change information such as telephone numbers, department, web page, address, manager, and office location. There are quite a few tasks and actions you can perform against a mailbox and not all of them can be performed via the graphical user interface. The following list includes some of these tasks:

◆ Managing user account attributes such as phone, address, and organization properties

◆ Moving mailboxes to another mailbox store (or even another Exchange organization)

◆ Assigning storage limits, messages size limits, recipient limits, and deleted item retention settings for a mailbox

◆ Defining message delivery restrictions and e-mail forwarding options

◆ Enabling web service features such as ActiveSync and Outlook Web Access as well as enabling or disabling MAPI connectivity

◆ Assigning ActiveSync and messaging records management policies to a mailbox

◆ Managing permissions that other users have to a mailbox

◆ Managing the ActiveSync devices associated with a mailbox

Let's take a look the cmdlets that are used to manage mailboxes and user accounts:

Cmdlet	Description
Get-User	Retrieves account information about a user in the Active Directory
Set-User	Sets the properties of a user account
Get-Mailbox	Retrieves mailboxes and properties of mailboxes
Get-MailboxStatistics	Retrieves mailbox storage statistics for a mailbox database or a specified mailbox
Get-MailboxFolderStatistics	Retrieves mailbox folder statistics for a specified mailbox
Get-MailboxCalendarSettings	Retrieves the Calendar Attendant settings for the specified mailbox
Get-UMMailbox	Retrieves the Unified Messaging properties for the specified mailbox
Get-CASMailbox	Retrieves the Client Access server properties for a specified mailbox
Get-MailboxPermissions	Retrieves the permissions that are assigned or inherited for the specified mailbox
Get-UMMailboxPIN	Retrieves a Unified Messaging PIN for the specified mailbox
Move-Mailbox	Moves a mailbox from one mailbox database to another
Connect-Mailbox	Reconnects an existing user account to a mailbox that was previously deleted
Enable-UMMailbox	Enables a mailbox to support Unified Messaging
Restore-Mailbox	Copies mailbox data from a recovery storage group to the production mailbox location
Export-Mailbox	Exports mailbox content to an alternate location
Remove-ActiveSyncDevice	Removes an ActiveSync device that is associated with the specified mailbox
Clear-ActiveSyncDevice	Performs a remote wipeout of the specified ActiveSync device the next time it connects
Get-ActiveSyncDeviceStatistics	Retrieves usages statistics and device information about the specified ActiveSync device

`New-Mailbox`	Creates a new user account and mailbox
`Enable-Mailbox`	Enables an existing user so that it has a mailbox
`Remove-Mailbox`	Deletes the specified user account and mailbox
`Disable-Mailbox`	Removes a mailbox from the specified user but does not delete the use account
`Set-Mailbox`	Sets mailbox properties
`Set-UMMailbox`	Sets Unified Messaging–related properties on a mailbox
`Set-CASMailbox`	Sets Client Access server–related properties on a mailbox
`Add-MailboxPermission`	Adds permissions to a mailbox
`Remove-MailboxPermission`	Removes permissions from a mailbox
`Set-UMMailboxPIN`	Sets the Unified Messaging PIN for a mailbox
`Disable-UMMailbox`	Disable a mailbox's UM features so that it no longer supports Unified Messaging
`New-MailUser`	Creates a new user account and associates an external e-mail address with that user
`Enable-MailUser`	Associates an external e-mail address with an existing user account
`Remove-MailUser`	Removes a mail-enabled user account from the directory
`Disable-MailUser`	Removes an external e-mail address that is associated with a user
`Get-MailUser`	Retrieves a list of mail-enabled users or properties of mail-enabled users
`Set-MailUser`	Sets properties of a mail-enabled user account

Mail-Enabled Group Management

Mail-enabled groups are managed from the Distribution Group subcontainer of the Recipient Configuration work center. From here you can create new Active Directory groups, mail-enable existing groups, and edit the properties of existing groups. One of the more common tasks an administrator performs on mail-enabled groups is to add or remove members. Figure 8.25 shows the Members property page of a mail-enabled group.

Here is a list of tasks you may need to perform on mail-enabled groups:

◆ Managing group membership

◆ Configuring messaging restrictions such as maximum message size and who can send mail to a group

◆ Specifying if a group can receive anonymous messages

◆ Assigning additional SMTP addresses for a group

◆ Configuring an expansion server

◆ Configuring delivery report behavior

FIGURE 8.25
Managing the
membership of a
mail-enabled group

If you want to manage mail-enabled groups from the EMS, here are some of the cmdlets available:

Cmdlet	Description
Set-Group	Manages the properties of a security or distribution group
Get-Group	Retrieves a list of security and distribution groups (regardless of mail-enabled status) in the Active Directory
Enable-DistributionGroup	Mail-enables an existing group in the Active Directory
Disable-DistributionGroup	Disables the mail features of an existing group but does not delete it
New-DistributionGroup	Creates a new group in the Active Directory and mail-enables it
Remove-DistributionGroup	Deletes a mail-enabled group from the Active Directory

Set-DistributionGroup	Sets the properties of a mail-enabled group
Get-DistributionGroup	Retrieves a list of mail-enabled groups or the properties of specified mail-enabled groups
Add-DistributionGroupMember	Adds a user to a mail-enabled group
Get-DistributionGroupMember	Retrieves the membership of a mail-enabled group
Remove-DistributionGroupMember	Removes a member from a mail-enabled group
New-DynamicDistributionGroup	Creates a new dynamic distribution group
Set-DynamicDistributionGroup	Sets the properties of a dynamic distribution group
Get-DynamicDistributionGroup	Retrieves a list of dynamic distribution groups or the properties of a specific dynamic distribution group
Remove-DynamicDistributionGroup	Deletes a dynamic distribution group

For more information on mail-enabled group management, see Chapter 10, "Managing Recipients."

Mail-Enabled Contact Management

Mail-enabled contacts appear in the Exchange global address list, but they do not need to be security principals. You can use the EMC to create and manage enabled contacts in the Mail Contacts subcontainer of the Recipient Configuration work center. Figure 8.26 shows the E-Mail Addresses property page of a mail-enabled contact. This page includes the e-mail addresses that will be accepted for this recipient as well as the external e-mail address of the recipient (the address to which the message will be forwarded).

Mail-enabled contacts can be managed from the EMS as well as the EMC. Here are the EMS cmdlets you can use for managing mail-enabled contacts:

Cmdlet	Description
Get-Contact	Retrieves the contacts from the Active Directory or retrieves the properties of specified contacts
Set-Contact	Sets the properties of a contact in the Active Directory
Enable-MailContact	Mail-enables an existing Active Directory contact
Disable-MailContact	Disables the mail attributes for an Active Directory contact but does not delete the contact
Remove-MailContact	Deletes a mail-enabled contact from the Active Directory
Get-MailContact	Retrieves a list of the mail-enabled contacts in the Active Directory or the properties of specified contacts
Set-MailContact	Sets the properties of a mail-enabled contact

You can find more information on creating and managing mail-enabled contacts in Chapter 10, "Managing Recipients."

FIGURE 8.26
Managing a
mail-enabled contact's
e-mail addresses

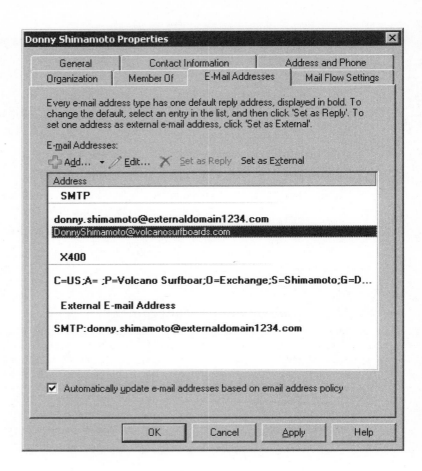

Public Folder Management

One thing that tends to confuse experienced Exchange 2000/2003 administrators is that there is not an Exchange Server 2007–based graphical user interface for managing public folders. This means that either you have to keep a copy of the Exchange 2003 System Manager program running or you have to manage the public folder properties entirely from the Exchange Management Shell. Here is a list of the EMS cmdlets that can be used to manage public folders:

Cmdlet	Description
Remove- PublicFolderClientPermissions	Removes client permissions from a public folder
Add- PublicFolderClientPermissions	Adds client permissions to a public folder
Get- PublicFolderClientPermissions	Retrieves a list of client permissions for a public folder
Get- PublicFolderAdministrativePermissions	Retrieves the public folder administrative permissions

Add-PublicFolderAdministrativePermissions	Adds administrative permissions to a public folder
Remove-PublicFolderAdministrativePermissions	Removes administrative permissions from a public folder
New-PublicFolder	Creates a new public folder
Remove-PublicFolder	Deletes a public folder
Get-PublicFolder	Retrieves public folders or the properties of specified public folder properties
Set-PublicFolder	Sets public folder properties
Enable-MailPublicFolder	Mail-enables a public folder
Disable-MailPublicFolder	Disables mail properties of a public folder
Get-MailPublicFolder	Retrieves a list of mail-enabled public folders or properties of a mail-enabled public folder
Set-MailPublicFolder	Sets mail-enabled public folder properties
Update-PublicFolder	Forces an update of public folder content
Update-PublicFolderHierarchy	Forces an update of the public folder hierarchy
Get-PublicFolderStatistics	Retrieves public folder statistics

You can find more information about public folder man in Chapter 14, "Public Folder Administration."

Summary

Even for experienced Exchange administrators, the new management interfaces can be a bit intimidating. It helps to know where to find the objects you need and the tasks that you most frequently perform.

In this chapter we reviewed where the configuration data is stored for Exchange server; this is a special partition of the Active Directory called the configuration partition. We also looked at the different work centers of the Exchange Management Console and the types of tasks that can be performed in each.

In the Organization Configuration work center, you perform configuration tasks that affect the entire organization. These objects found in the Organization Configuration work center have the potential to affect every server and mail recipient in the entire Exchange organization.

In the Server Configuration work center you can perform tasks that affect specific Exchange servers and server roles. Finally, the Recipient Configuration work center allows you to manage mail-enabled recipients (users, groups, contacts).

Chapter 9

Imposing Limits

Imposing limits on users and mailboxes seems like a strange topic to which to dedicate an entire chapter. We feel this is an important topic because even in mature messaging environments (organizations that have had Exchange or some other client-server messaging system deployed for 10+ years), limits are often not imposed.

Mail administrators often cringe at the prospect of imposing limits on their users, certainly their VIP users. Imposing limits is a touchy subject, even with IT and company management, who may often feel that they are necessary but should not apply to them.

So why is this an important topic? Simple. You need to be configuring your organization for predictable operations. Every morning when you wake up and go to work, you need to have some assurances that, provided nothing terrible has happened, your mail system is in pretty much the same state it was in when you left it the day before. This not only helps with ongoing operations, it makes it easier to recognize when something has gone wrong.

Ensuring that your Exchange system is operating in a predictable fashion with respect to mailbox or message limitations mean that you do not exceed your designed disk capacity and you don't flood your network connections with messages that are too large. Operating predictably certainly does not stop at mailbox limits, but for purpose of this chapter, we will limit the scope to just predicting disk space usage and network usage.

Another important factor to consider when assigning limits for your users is that limits help prevent abuse of the mail system, such as a user sending a message to the entire Everyone distribution group advertising their garage sale or a user sending out a message with a 200MB attachment.

More and more organizations are faced with state, provincial, or federal government regulations. For example, users may be required to keep historical information available, which would in turn affect the limits you imposed on their mailboxes.

Failure to define and properly establish messaging system limits can have adverse or even catastrophic effects on your daily operations. This is very true of mailbox limits. More than a few Exchange administrators have came to work one morning only to discover that they are out of disk space on the database disk drive. Why? They were not on top of the mailbox growth and it caught them by surprise. Dealing with a server whose mailbox databases are dismounted because you are out of disk space is almost as difficult as facing management to explain why you are out of disk space and why you have to buy more.

NOTE

The ultimate decision about limits and enforcement is usually "above our pay grade." Management has to understand why limits are necessary and what appropriate limits might be for your organization. Management must balance functionality, organizational requirements, and availability.

Although we certainly can't help you with your "political" issues, we can help you determine the right place to apply limits and maybe even suggest some appropriate limits. In this chapter, we will discuss a number of different approaches to applying messaging system limits.

Topics in this chapter include the following:

◆ Applying mailbox-by-mailbox mail storage limits

◆ Applying mailbox limits for an entire mailbox database

◆ Applying message size limits

◆ Applying limits to public folders

Typical Limits

Way back in Chapter 1, "Introducing Exchange Server 2007," we talked some about the changing nature of e-mail and how message sizes and mailbox content has changed. Later, in Chapter 3, "Designing a New Exchange 2007 System," we included a section called "Planning Your Disk Space Requirements." In that section, we took you through a planning exercise to figure out roughly how much disk space you will require given maximum mailbox sizes.

NOTE

Regardless of what we may tell you are typical limits, you must find the right balance for your own organization. That balance may be far above or below the limits we recommend.

If your organization has not set mailbox limits or message size limits, then your first challenge is to figure out what those actually need to be. If you currently have limits in place, then you need to determine if they are effective. Let's first look at mailbox storage limits. A question we are frequently asked is, "What is typical for the industry?"

Unfortunately, there is no set guideline for what "the industry" is doing with respect to mailbox limits. In the Exchange 2003 time frame, these limits are commonplace:

Issue warning	250MB
Prohibit send	275MB
Prohibit send and receive	300MB
Maximum outgoing message size	10MB (the default)
Maximum incoming message size	10MB (the default)

We have had individuals in some large corporations and European organizations report to us that the following limits are more commonplace. Notice that the message sizes are higher, but the mailbox limits are a bit lower:

Issue warning	150MB
Prohibit send	200MB
Prohibit send and receive	300MB
Maximum outgoing message size	20MB
Maximum incoming message size	20MB

Some organizations look at these limits and wish they could provide their users with as much mailbox space, while other organizations see these limits as clearly insufficient for their messaging needs. Exchange 2007 has not yet been in use long enough to see any clearly defined trends, but here are limits that we are using for planning capacity for a typical organization:

Issue warning	500MB
Prohibit send	550MB
Prohibit send and receive	600MB
Maximum outgoing message size	10MB
Maximum incoming message size	10MB

These limits have to be carefully balanced with available disk space, backup and restore resources, and users' needs.

> **TIP**
>
> If your users require lots of mailbox space for official business reasons, you should find a way to support that requirement.

As we mentioned in an earlier chapter, some people at Microsoft are already hinting that a 2GB mailbox limit will become commonplace. Indeed, the default Exchange 2007 mailbox database limits are as follows:

Issue warning	1,945MB
Prohibit send	2,048MB
Prohibit send and receive	2,355MB

While most of us would personally love to have a 2GB mailbox on our corporate mail server, there are a number of factors that you should consider when setting limits.

> **TIP**
>
> The default mailbox storage limits for mailbox databases is now 2GB. Please keep this in mind when creating a mailbox database. This may be far higher than you want for your users.

Once you have evaluated some of these factors and decided if you need to raise your limits, you need to find a way to effectively increase your technological capacity to support these limits. This includes larger disks, faster backup/restore capabilities, and larger backup/restore capabilities, and it could include additional technologies such as archival solutions. The following list includes some of the factors you need to consider:

◆ Is there a business reason for giving users more mail storage? Consider the cost of a user trying to find information that at one time was in their mailbox and is now gone.

◆ Evaluate your current limits (if you have them). Do you users have to delete/archive mail frequently in order to stay under their prescribed limit? Do they require e-mail that they have deleted or archived?

◆ Consider your VIPs, executives, and other heavy messaging users: Do they need more or less space than a typical user? A heavy messaging user may not necessarily be a VIP. In some organizations, the salespeople, engineers, architects, or paralegals may be the heaviest users of messaging technologies.

◆ Do you have an e-mail archival system in place that automatically moves older mail out of a user's folders or managed folders and stores that data in a long-term storage repository? Centralized repositories may actually reduce mailbox space requirements since data can be retained for much longer periods of time without actually impacting the mailbox database. However, retention periods for the content in a user's mailbox will still depend on allowing the user to access that data via Outlook, Outlook Web Access, Outlook using RPC over HTTP, or Windows Mobile devices. Depending on the archival system, older messages might not be accessible from all devices or locations, so this should be considered when planning for retention times.

◆ Basic mailbox content includes e-mail messages, appointments, contacts, tasks, and journaling information. What other technologies are you employing that would increase the average size of a mailbox?

  ◆ Integrated faxing? How many faxes would your users need to retain?

  ◆ Integrated voicemail? How many voicemail messages would your users need to retain?

  ◆ Forms routing and workflow? Would a historical record of forms processed (expense reports, purchase requests, travel approval, etc.) need to be retained by the sender as well as other people in the forms routing process?

◆ Are you faced with regulatory requirements that require the retention of certain types of information for a long period of time?

◆ Could larger mailbox sizes expose you to potential denial-of-service attacks where someone sends lots of large messages to your users until all mailboxes and possibly the database or transaction log disk are filled?

These are just some of the factors that may affect your decisions with respect to assigning mailbox limits. Just when you think you are out of the woods with respect to this decision, you have another decision to make. What about message size limits?

The default message size limit for both incoming and outgoing messages is 10MB; this limit has not changed since Exchange 2003. This value is not just an arbitrary or nice round number; it is based on Microsoft's best practices and feedback from many customers. We often find this limit to be insufficient in many environments where large attachments are used. Regardless of whether or not it is a good practice to send a 50MB file through e-mail, sometimes it is just not possible for users to easily transfer large attachments between organizations. If your organization requires the transfer of large files, always try to find an alterative such as using portals, websites, FTP servers, or instant messaging.

NOTE

Just because you raise your organization's outgoing message size limit does not necessarily mean that a remote organization will be able receive messages as large as your users can send.

So what are some factors to take in to consideration when planning for a maximum message size? This is not as clear-cut and easy to handle as mailbox size limits, but here are some things to think about:

◆ Do your users need to transmit large file attachments?

◆ Do you have a mechanism to prevent "large attachment" abuse such as preventing MPG, WMA, WMV, and MP3 files from being sent via e-mail, if those file types are considered inappropriate in your organization?

◆ Is there an alternative to sending or receiving large attachments, such as allowing internal users to post content to a SharePoint portal page; using extranet pages, intranet solutions, or instant messaging; or providing external users with an alternative way to send you large files?

◆ Can large content be automatically compressed by some client-side utility, thus reducing attachment sizes?

◆ If large message sizes are allowed, can your network links and Internet connection handle the capacity?

Setting Mailbox Storage Limits

Limiting the amount of content that is stored in a user's mailbox is pretty easy to do. In many respects, it is no different than handling limits was in Exchange 4.0. Limits can be applied to all mailboxes in a mailbox database, or the mailbox database limits can be overridden on a mailbox-by-mailbox basis.

One difference between Exchange 2000/2003 and Exchange 2007, though, is that there is no longer the concept of a Mailbox Store Policy. The mailbox store policy allowed an administrator to apply limits to mailbox databases as a group rather than individually. Instead you will either have to apply limits manually or use Exchange Management Shell (EMS) tasks.

There are a number of properties that you will find on a Limits property page of a mailbox database. Table 9.1 discusses these properties and what the options mean. If you have used earlier versions of Exchange, you are already familiar with these options and their effect on mailboxes.

TABLE 9.1:   Exchange Mailbox Database Limits

OPTION	EXPLANATION
Issue Warning At (KB)	Specifies the limit at which the user is sent a warning e-mail message indicating that they are nearing their mail storage limit. The default is 1,991,680KB.
Prohibit Send At (KB)	Specifies the limit at which the user is no longer able to send or reply to e-mail. The user must reduce the amount of data in their mailbox before they can send new messages or reply to existing messages. The default is 2,097,152KB.
Prohibit Send and Receive At (KB)	Specifies the limit above which the mailbox will reject mail as well as not allow the user to send messages or reply to existing messages. The default is 2,411,520KB.
Warning Message Interval	Specifies the time of day when e-mail messages are sent to users that are over their Issue Warning At (KB) limit. By default this is done at 1:00 a.m., but it can be changed. Be careful about selecting the Customize button; if you select an entire hour, the warning message will be sent four times that hour.
Keep Deleted Items For (Days)	Specifies how long to keep an item once it has been emptied from the Deleted Items folder or has been hard deleted. During this period, Outlook or Outlook Web Access users can recover items they deleted. When the specified time period is over, the message is permanently deleted and the space it consumed is reused. Deleted items are permanently purged during the online maintenance process. The default is 14 days.
Keep Deleted Mailboxes For (Days)	Specifies how long to keep a mailbox in a delete state before permanently deleting it. During this period, an administrator can reconnect a mailbox to an Active Directory user account that does not have a mailbox assigned to it. Once this limit has passed, deleted mailboxes cannot be recovered. Deleted mailboxes are permanently purged during the online maintenance process. The default is 30 days.
Do Not Permanently Delete Mailboxes and Items Until the Mailbox Database Has Been Backed Up.	Tells the information store to not permanently delete an item or a mailbox even if it is past its deleted retention time unless an online backup of the store has been made. Do not select this check box if you are performing offline backups, using a non-Exchange-aware backup, or performing backups only of the local continuous replication copy of the database.

Mailbox Database Limits

Establishing limits on a mailbox database is a simple process. The settings are found on the Limits property page of each mailbox database. The Limits property page for the mailbox database named Viper Pilots is shown in Figure 9.1; the values in Figure 9.1 are the defaults for a newly created mailbox database. Notice that the Prohibit Send and Receive At (KB) limit is 2,411,520KB (about 2.4GB!); this clearly reflects Microsoft's expectation that the typical user will require more mail content storage.

FIGURE 9.1
Default mailbox
database Limits
properties

FIGURE 9.1
Default mailbox
database Limits
properties

You can also set this limit using the EMS and the Set-MailboxDatabase cmdlet. For example, suppose you want to set the following limits on the Executives mailbox database:

Issue Warning	750MB
Prohibit Send	775MB
Prohibit Send and Receive	800MB

The following command will accomplish this:

```
Set-MailboxDatabase "Executives" -IssueWarningQuota:750MB
-ProhibitSendQuota:775MB -ProhibitSendReceiveQuota:800MB
```

While this command will not output any results, you can confirm that the command was successful by using the Get-MailboxDatabase cmdlet. One way to check this is to pipe the output to the format-list cmdlet:

```
Get-MailboxDatabase "Executives" | fl name, issuewarningquota,
prohibitsendquota,prohibitsendreceivequota
```

```
Name                     : Executives
IssueWarningQuota        : 750MB
ProhibitSendQuota        : 775MB
ProhibitSendReceiveQuota : 800MB
```

You can also output the data to the `format-table` cmdlet and view the same data in a slightly different format:

```
Get-MailboxDatabase "Executives" | ft name,issuewarningquota,
prohibitsendquota,prohibitsendreceivequota

Name        IssueWarningQuota   ProhibitSendQuota ProhibitSendReceiveQuota
----        -----------------   ----------------- ------------------------
Executives  750MB               775MB             800MB
```

If you want to set default limits for an entire server, you can also use the EMS. First you need to generate a list of all of the mailbox stores on the desired server. For a server called E2K7-01, you can do this with the following command:

```
Get-MailboxDataase | where {$_.server -like "E2K7-01"}
```

This command will output a list of objects. You can pipe those objects to the same `Set-MailboxDatabase` cmdlet we just showed you. The final command would look like this:

```
Get-MailboxDatabase | where {$_.server -like "E2K7-01"} |
Set-MailboxDatabase -IssueWarningQuota:750MB
-ProhibitSendQuota:775MB -ProhibitSendReceiveQuota:800MB
```

Note also that each limit must be higher than the one before it. For example, `Prohibit-SendQuota` must be higher than `IssueWarningQuota` and `ProhibitSendReceiveQuota` must be higher than `ProhibitSendQuota`. If you make a mistake, the EMS is smart enough to check these limits and warn you.

NOTE

The Exchange 2003 extensions to Active Directory Users and Computers would allow you to set a smaller send quota than the warning quota. Exchange 2007 checks this and will not even allow you to move a mailbox on to an Exchange 2007 server unless the limits are all ordered correctly. The warning quota must be smaller than the send quota and the send quota must be smaller than the send/receive quota.

Here is an example where we accidentally set `ProhibitSendReceiveQuota` smaller than `IssueWarningQuota`:

```
Set-MailboxDatabase "Executives" -IssueWarningQuota:750MB
-ProhibitSendQuota:775MB -ProhibitSendReceiveQuota:500MB
Set-MailboxDatabase : The value of property 'ProhibitSendQuota'
```

```
must be less than or equal to that of property
'ProhibitSendReceiveQuota'. ProhibitSendQuota:
'775MB', ProhibitSendReceiveQuota: '500MB'.
At line:1 char:20 + Set-MailboxDatabase  <<<<
"Executives" -IssueWarningQuota:750MB -ProhibitSendQuota:775MB
-ProhibitSendReceiveQuota:500MB
```

Mailbox-by-Mailbox Limits

By default, a mailbox's storage limits will be the same as the mailbox database limits. Individual mailbox size limits can be overridden on a mailbox-by-mailbox basis by using the Exchange Management Console. Locate the mailbox on which you want to apply limits in the Recipients work center, view the properties of the mailbox, select the Mailbox Settings property page, and double-click the Storage Quotas option. The Storage Quotas property page for an individual mailbox is shown in Figure 9.2.

FIGURE 9.2
Individual mailbox
storage quotas

The storage quotas for an individual mailbox can also be set through the EMS by using the Set-Mailbox cmdlet. For example, if we want to use an EMS command to set the same limits shown in Figure 9.2 for a mailbox whose alias is Omar.Droubi, we would use the following cmdlet.

```
Set-Mailbox "omar.droubi" -UseDatabaseQuotaDefaults $False
-IssueWarningQuota:250000KB -ProhibitSendQuota:275000KB
-ProhibitSendReceiveQuota:300000KB
```

Note that the option -UseDatabaseQuotaDefaults must be set to $False, otherwise Exchange will not recognize that these limits have been overridden. This is the same as clearing the Use Mailbox Database Defaults check box in the user's Storage Quota's properties.

This command will not output any results to the EMS, but you can check your work using the Get-Mailbox cmdlet. Since the names of all of the properties of the mailbox include the word *quota*, you can use the Select-Object (or just Select) cmdlet and a wildcard to specify the properties you are viewing. The command and the results are shown here:

```
[MSH] C:\>get-mailbox omar.droubi | select-object name,*quota*

Name                         : Omar Droubi
ProhibitSendQuota            : 275000KB
ProhibitSendReceiveQuota     : 300000KB
UseDatabaseQuotaDefaults     : False
IssueWarningQuota            : 250000KB
RulesQuota                   : 64KB
```

Notice in this command that we set the mailbox size limits in KB rather than MB; bytes, KB, MB, or GB will work.

It's probably going to take you longer to set a single mailbox storage quota using the EMS than it would using the EMC, but you can use the skills you learn configuring a single mailbox to configure multiple mailboxes. Let's use the members of our executive team in an example. They are dispersed throughout many servers in our organization. They are, however, all members of a distribution group called Executives. We would use the Get-DistributionGroupMember cmdlet to retrieve all of the members of the Executives group and we would pipe that to the Set-Mailbox cmdlet. Here is an example:

```
Get-DistributionGroupMember "Executives" | Set-Mailbox
-UseDatabaseQuotaDefaults $False -IssueWarning:250000KB
-ProhibitSendQuota:275000KB -ProhibitSendReceiveQuota:300000KB
```

We can even run this command as a scheduled task to ensure that the members of Executives always have set the limits that we want them to have.

Message Size Limits

In most organizations, letting users send or receive messages with no limits on sizes can result in abuse of the messaging system. Before you know it, users might be sending 1GB MPEG files back and forth to one another. However, the other side of this equation is that there are actually situations in which large messages need to be sent in order to simplify file transfers.

There are a number of ways we can limit large message transfers or prevent users from sending unauthorized large files. This includes applying global message size limits, limiting message sizes of typical users, limiting message sizes sent via send and receive connectors, and even stopping messages using transport rules.

Applying Global Message Size Limits

Exchange 2007 limits the maximum size of incoming and outgoing messages that a user can send to 10MB. This value has been determined based on analysis of many large customers' environments as well as best practices. The global message transport values are not visible via the EMC and must be viewed using the EMS cmdlet `Get-TransportConfig`. Here is an output of the `Get-TransportConfig` cmdlet with no parameters or formatting options:

```
Get-TransportConfig

ClearCategories                 : True
GenerateCopyOfDSNFor            : {}
InternalSMTPServers             : {192.168.254.19, 192.168.254.102}
JournalingReportNdrTo           : <>
MaxDumpsterSizePerStorageGroup  : 18MB
MaxDumpsterTime                 : 7.00:00:00
MaxReceiveSize                  : 10MB
MaxRecipientEnvelopeLimit       : unlimited
MaxSendSize                     : 10MB
TLSReceiveDomainSecureList      : {}
TLSSendDomainSecureList         : {}
VerifySecureSubmitEnabled       : False
VoicemailJournalingEnabled      : True
Xexch50Enabled                  : True
```

You can use the `Set-TransportConfig` cmdlet to change these properties. Let's say that you want to change the default size of 10MB for inbound (`MaxReceiveSize`) and outbound (`MaxSendSize`) messages to 25MB; you would use the following cmdlet to do this:

```
Set-TransportConfig -MaxReceiveSize:25MB -MaxSendSize:25MB
```

Applying Message Size Limits Mailbox by Mailbox

You can also limit the maximum message size sent or received by an individual mailbox. The easiest way to do this for a single mailbox is to use the EMC and locate the mailbox you wish to change in the Recipient Configuration work center. On the mailbox's Mail Flow Settings property page, you need to locate the Message Size Restrictions option, highlight that option, and click the Properties button. This will display the Message Size Restrictions dialog box shown in Figure 9.3.

FIGURE 9.3
Applying message size restrictions for a single mailbox

In the example in Figure 9.3, we have limited this one user to a maximum sending and receiving message size of 5MB. This is useful if you have to override the message size limits of a single mailbox. However, in a larger organization, you may have large groups of people that require their limits be different than the global defaults. Once again, the EMS comes to the rescue.

Let's say that we have a mail-enabled group called Undergraduate Students and we want to override the default limits and restrict their maximum incoming and outgoing message sizes to 5MB. We need to use the Get-DistributionGroupMember cmdlet to retrieve the objects that are members of that particular distribution group. We will pipe the output of that cmdlet to the Set-Mailbox cmdlet. Here is an example that will accomplish this task:

```
Get-DistributionGroupMember "Undergraduate Students" | Set-Mailbox
-MaxSendSize:5MB -MaxReceiveSize:5MB
```

That was pretty simple to do! Now if one of our users attempts to send a message larger than the permitted size, they will receive a non-delivery report indicating that the message could not be delivered. An example of such as message is shown in Figure 9.4.

FIGURE 9.4
Non-delivery report indicating that a message is too large to be delivered

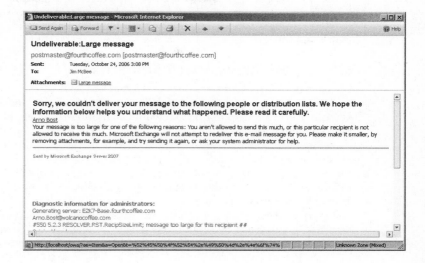

Restricting Internet Message Sizes

You might also want to restrict the size of messages that are sent to or received from the Internet. By default, your global default limits will be used for Internet-bound messages and messages received from the Internet. However, you can specify message size restrictions on the connectors that are used to send and receive messages into your organization from outside of the organization. The maximum message sizes that a send or receive connector can process are not configurable through the EMC; you must use the EMS. For receive connectors that are used to accept inbound mail from the Internet, you can change the default limit (10MB) by using the `Set-ReceiveConnector` cmdlet.

You can also use the `Get-ReceiveConnector` cmdlet to retrieve information about the receive connectors limits. Here is an example in which the receive connectors are enumerated:

```
Get-ReceiveConnector  | FT name,*size*
```

Name	MaxHeaderSize	MaxMessageSize	SizeEnabled
Default HNLHT01	64KB	10MB	True
Client HNLHT01	64KB	10MB	True

To change the maximum message size (`MaxMessageSize`) property on the receive connector called Default HNLHT01, you would use the following command:

```
Set-ReceiveConnector "Default HNLHT01" -MaxMessageSize:5MB
```

You can change the send connector size limits (MaxMessageSize) in the exact same way using the Set-SendConnector cmdlet.

While having the ability to tune the send and receive connectors is a good feature, if you have implemented additional SMTP message hygiene security using an SMTP gateway or the Exchange Edge Transport server, you should restrict inbound message sizes at that point instead. This will prevent messages that are larger than your Internet limits to actually even reach the Exchange Hub Transport servers.

Limiting Maximum Attachment Sizes

We have not introduced transport rules yet in this book other than just to mention that they exist and that they are applied by the Hub Transport server role. However, there is a condition that you can use on a transport rule that would be useful in catching messages with attachments larger than you will permit.

Let's consider as an example a situation in which an organization's information policy does not allow messages that are received from the Internet to have any single attachment larger than 5MB. You can define a transport rule that will catch these messages and drop them. Transport rules are found in the Transport Rule section of the Organization Configuration work center under the Hub Transport subcontainer.

When you launch the New Transport Rule Wizard, on the Conditions page (shown in Figure 9.5), you select two conditions. The first condition is "from users inside or outside the corporation" and the second is "when the size of any attachment is greater than or equal to limit."

FIGURE 9.5
Defining a condition that will reject messages with attachments larger than 5MB

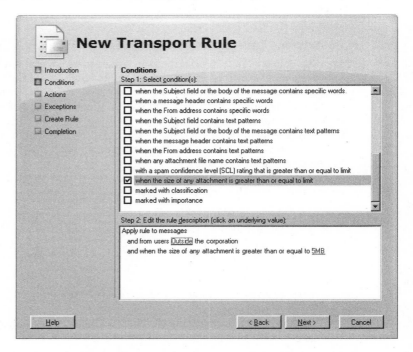

Once these are selected and show up in the Step 2: Edit the Rule Description box, you need to ensure that the rule applies to messages sent from outside the corporation by clicking the value that looks like a hyperlink. This value defaults to Inside. You also need to click on the attachment size value and change that to the maximum attachment size; the default value is 0KB.

On the Actions page, you can then select the action(s) to take when the condition is met. These actions might include just dropping the message or returning an undeliverable report back to the sender informing them of the problem. An example of this is shown in Figure 9.6.

FIGURE 9.6
Defining an action to send back a customized report of undeliverable mail message

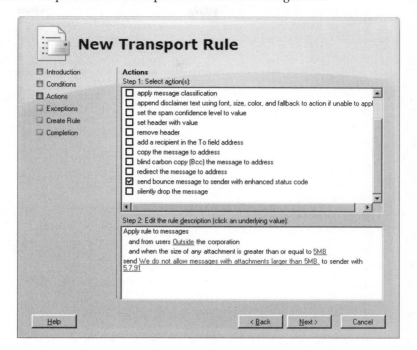

Recipient Limits

Another useful configuration property is the ability to restrict the maximum number of recipients per e-mail message. This is useful when helping to prevent misuse of the mail system. After all, the typical user in your organization probably does not need to send messages to all 100,000 users in your global address list, right?

Like Exchange 2003, by default Exchange 2007 restricts the maximum number of recipients to 5,000. That will include all recipients in the To, Cc, and Bcc lines of the message as well as the total number of members of a distribution lists that are included in the address lines. So if a user addresses a message to a distribution group that has 5,001 members, the message will be returned with an non-delivery report. Figure 9.7 shows an example of the undeliverable report that was sent to a user who tried to send to a distribution group that has more members than the user is permitted to send to.

In most organizations (especially large ones), typical users probably do not need to send to 5,000 recipients. We recommend finding a more reasonable value that would apply globally (such as 50, 100, or 250, for example) and then override the recipients limit for users that would need to send to more than the global limit. If you want to view the current maximum recipients limit, here is an example of how you would do that:

```
Get-TransportConfig | FL MaxRecipientEnvelopeLimit

MaxRecipientEnvelopeLimit : 5000
```

FIGURE 9.7
Report of undeliverable
mail issued when
recipient limit is reached

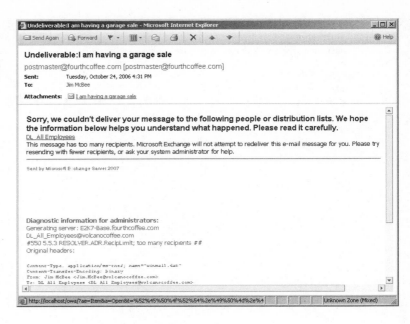

To change the transport limit to 250, you would type this:

```
Set-TransportConfig -MaxRecipientEnvelopeLimit:250
```

Once the global limit is set, you can override it on a mailbox-by-mailbox basis using the EMC. Locate the user's mailbox in the Recipient Configuration work center, display the properties of the mailbox, view the Mail Flow Settings property page, and double-click the Delivery Options selection to see the Delivery Options dialog box (shown in Figure 9.8). Enable the check box next to Maximum Recipients and then provide the maximum number of recipients in the text box.

Once this value is overridden, this mailbox will be able to send messages with more recipients than the global defaults (if the global default is smaller) or fewer than the global defaults (if the global default is larger).

If you need to do this in bulk, you can use the EMS. Like many other bulk operations that are applied to a group of objects, you need some method of finding these objects. In this example, we will assume we have a distribution group called E-Mail Entire Company. We will use the `Get-DistributionGroupMember` and the `Set-Mailbox` cmdlets to accomplish this. The following command will set all members of the E-Mail Entire Company distribution group's `RecipientLimits` property to 10,000.

```
Get-DistributionGroupMember "E-Mail Entire Company" |
Set-Mailbox -RecipientLimits:10000
```

That was pretty simple, wasn't it? Once you know just a few of the basic functions in the PowerShell and the EMS, you can start to do things that would have been very difficult in Exchange 2000/2003. You can even create a PowerShell script and schedule it to run periodically and ensure that the limit is always enforced.

FIGURE 9.8
Overriding the
maximum number of
recipients for a single
mailbox

Managed Folder Limits

Exchange 2007 introduces a new concept called managed folders. Managed folders allow the administrator to define retention policies for default folders such as Deleted Items, Inbox, and Journal as well as create custom folders for users. The users can use these folders to organize their mailboxes based on their organization's e-mail retention policies. We will cover managed folders in more details in Chapter 12, "Managing Folder Content," when we cover messaging records management. However, there is a nice feature of managed folders that is useful when establishing limits.

There is a category of managed folders called Managed Custom Folders that consists of folders that the administrator can define and have automatically created (using a managed folder mailbox policy). The managed custom folders are found in the Mailbox subcontainer of the Organization Configuration work center under the Managed Custom Folders tab. The Managed Custom Folders tab of the results pane is shown in Figure 9.9.

You can define the maximum amount of storage that a folder and all of its subfolders can have if the folder was created by a managed folder mailbox policy. However, the limit must be defined when the managed custom folder is created in the mailbox so it must exist in the policy when it is assigned to the mailbox. The administrator cannot change the limits on the policy once it is assigned.

Let's look at an example. Suppose we want to create a folder for faxes in the Managed Folders section of a user's mailbox. We will rely on the user to move faxes in to this folder, but we want to

FIGURE 9.9
The Managed Custom
Folders tab of the
results pane

make sure that the amount of content that is in this folder (and all of its subfolders) never exceeds 50MB. When viewing the properties of the Faxes folder (shown in Figure 9.10), we can click the Storage Limit (KB) for This Folder and Its Subfolders check box and specify a maximum folder size.

FIGURE 9.10
Specifying a limit for a
custom folder

If you are inclined to do things through the EMS, you could use the following EMS command to accomplish the same thing.

```
Set-ManagedFolder "Faxes" -StorageQuota:50MB
```

Public Folder Limits

Just as mailbox limits can help you to control growth of mailbox database and prevent abuse, assigning limits to public folders can be equally important in controlling public folder growth. There are a couple of different types of limits you can set with respect to public folders. These include the default limits for the public folder database and individual folder limits.

Defining Limits per Database

Each public folder database has default storage limits that are established and affect all public folders that have a replica on it. The public folder database Limits property page is shown in Figure 9.11. If you are an experienced Exchange 2000/2003 administrator, you may note that there are default limits in Exchange 2007 where none existed previously.

FIGURE 9.11
Default public folder database limits

The properties that are found on the Limits property page affect all public folder instances on the database. Table 9.2 describes these properties.

TABLE 9.2:   Limits Property Page

PROPERTY	DESCRIPTION
Issue Warning At (KB)	Sends a warning message to the folder owner and folder contacts informing them that the folder has reached is storage limit. The default is 1,945MB.
Prohibit Post At (KB)	When the folder content exceeds this size, messages can no longer be delivered to this folder (if the folder is mail enabled) and users cannot post to this folder. The default is 2GB.
Maximum Item Size (KB)	Specifies the largest message size that can be delivered to this folder (if mail enabled) or the largest item that can be posted to this folder. The default it is 10MB.
Keep Deleted Items For (Days)	Specifies the how long deleted folders will be retained before they are permanently purged. During this time, the folder owner can undelete items that were accidentally (or intentionally) deleted. The default interval is 14 days.

If you are a fond of the EMC, you can also retrieve this information from the PowerShell. In the following example, the public folder database is called Public Folder Database and the server is HNLEX02 and we are piping the output of the `Get-PublicFolderDatabase` to the `Format-List` cmdlet:

```
Get-PublicFolderDatabase "HNLEX02\Public Folder Database" |
Format-List Name,MaxItemSize,IssueWarningQuota,
ProhibitPostQuota,ItemRetention

Name               : Public Folder Database
MaxItemSize        : 10MB
IssueWarningQuota  : 1945MB
ProhibitPostQuota  : 2GB
ItemRetention      : 14.00:00:00
```

If you want to change one of these limits using the EMS (for example setting the `MaxItemSize` to 15MB), you would type this command:

```
Set-PublicFolderDatabase "HNLEX02\Public Folder Database"
-MaxItemSize:15MB
```

Defining Folder-by-Folder Limits

You can also define folder-by-folder limits. These limits override the default limits specified on a public folder database. The Exchange 2007 EMC does not provide an interface for managing individual public folder properties, so you will have to have an Exchange 2003 System Manager console installed somewhere within your organization. Unfortunately, you cannot install the

Exchange System Manager from Exchange 2003 on an Exchange 2007 server or any machine with the Exchange Management Console. See Chapter 4, "Installing Exchange Server 2007," for more information on installing and using the Exchange System Manager with Exchange 2007.

To manage individual public folder limits, you need to locate the Folders container in an Exchange administrative group. Once you have found the Folders container, you can browse the public folders, locate the folder you wish to set limits on, and display that folder's properties. Figure 9.12 shows the Limits property page of a folder called Research Documents.

FIGURE 9.12
Limits property page of the Research Documents folder

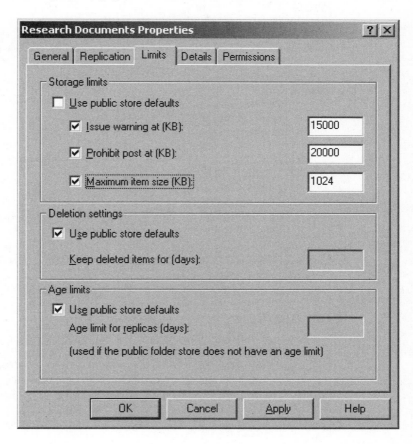

Notice in Figure 9.12 that we have cleared the Use Public Store Defaults check box and have provided our own limits (Issue Warning, Prohibit Post, and Maximum Item Size) for this particular public folder.

If you do not have an Exchange System Manager console installed anywhere in your organization, you can still manage individual public folder properties using the Exchange Management Shell. For example, here we retrieve the properties of a public folder called Somorita Surfboards:

```
C:\>get-publicfolder "\Somorita Surfboards" | FL

AgeLimit                        : 30.00:00:00
EntryId                         : 000000001A447390AA6611CD9BC800AA002FC45A030037
```

```
C54B179C6AC547BE6A36965D18C96700000001C1690000
HasSubFolders                        : True
HiddenFromAddressListsEnabled        : True
LocalReplicaAgeLimit                 :
MailEnabled                          : False
MaxItemSize                          : 4MB
Name                                 : Somorita Surfboards
ParentPath                           : \
PerUserReadStateEnabled              : True
PostStorageQuota                     : 65000KB
Replicas                             : {Public Folders, Public Folder Store (HNLEX01)}
ReplicationSchedule                  : {}
RetainDeletedItemsFor                : 15.00:00:00
StorageQuota                         : 50000KB
UseDatabaseAgeDefaults               : False
UseDatabaseQuotaDefaults             : False
UseDatabaseReplicationSchedule       : True
UseDatabaseRetentionDefaults         : False
Identity                             : \Somorita Surfboards
IsValid                              : True
OriginatingServer                    : hnlex03
```

To set the prohibit post limit (PostStorageQuota) and the issue warning quota (StorageQuota) using the EMS, here is the command you would type:

```
Set-PublicFolder "\Somorita Surfboards" -PostStorageQuota:95MB
-StorageQuota:80MB
```

Summary

When you start thinking about the number of places where you can define limits for an Exchange user, you'll see that there are quite a few. However, planning for realistic and effective limits are important for your organization. Effectively limiting mailbox sizes, public folder sizes, and message sizes can help you to predict the growth of your mail storage requirements and prevent you from exceeding the storage you have available for Exchange content. Effective limits are an important part of proactive troubleshooting because they limit potential abuse of the mail system by preventing users from sending or receiving content that is too large.

Chapter 10

Managing Recipients

Depending on your organization, recipient management will consume the vast majority of Exchange administration time. In a larger organization with lots of changes, new users, and users leaving the organization, recipient administration will probably be handled by a person or team that is separate from the person that actually manages the Exchange Server infrastructure (message routing, backups, server maintenance, and so on).

The process of recipient management involves handling anything that affects mail-enabled recipients. A mail-enabled recipient is anything to which you can send an e-mail message or that has an e-mail address. Mail-enabled recipients include the following:

- Mail-enabled user accounts
- Mail-enabled universal groups
- Mail-enabled contacts
- Mail-enabled public folders
- Resource mailboxes

In this chapter, we will discuss how to create and manage mail-enabled recipients. We'll also examine Exchange address lists and how e-mail addresses get defined.

Topics in this chapter include the following:

- Defining e-mail address policies
- Establishing mailboxes for user accounts
- Creating mail-enabled groups
- Creating mail-enabled contacts
- Managing resource mailboxes

Defining E-Mail Addresses

Before we get in to the discussion of how to create mail-enabled users, groups, or contacts, we'll first discuss how these objects get their e-mail addresses. Those of you who are familiar with Exchange 2000/2003 probably remember that e-mail addresses were defined by a recipient policy. Once the recipient policy was defined, the Microsoft Exchange System Attendant's Recipient Update Service (RUS) would establish e-mail addresses for any mail-enabled recipient at some point in the future (hopefully just a minute or two).

This process is just a bit different in Exchange 2007. E-mail addresses are generated for the object at the time the mail-enabled recipient is created and they are generated by an Exchange Management Shell (EMC) task or the Exchange Management Console (EMC). Recipient policies from Exchange 2000/2003 have been broken up in to two separate concepts: the e-mail domains that your organization will accept mail for and the e-mail address policies for your users. For addresses that will be assigned to mailboxes on your Exchange 2007 servers, you define both an accepted domain and an e-mail address policy.

Accepted Domains

An accepted domain is an SMTP domain name (aka SMTP name space) that your Exchange 2007 servers will accept mail for and either deliver to Exchange 2007 mailboxes or relay on to internal or external SMTP mail servers. If you are in the middle of a migration from Exchange 2000/2003, then the accepted domains list will include the SMTP domains for your Exchange 2000/2003 mailboxes. Accepted domains must be defined for all e-mail addresses that will be routed into or by your Exchange 2007 servers.

NOTE

Most small and medium-sized organizations will have only a single accepted domain.

Accepted domains are found within the Organization Configuration work center under the Hub Transport subcontainer. When you choose the Accepted Domains tab in the results pane, you will see a list of the accepted domains that have been defined for your organization, such as those shown in Figure 10.1.

FIGURE 10.1
List of accepted domains

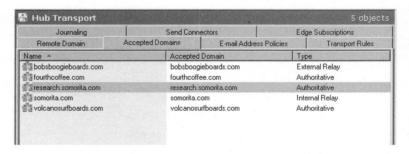

When Exchange 2007 is first installed, a single accepted domain is automatically created and given a name. This is the name of the Active Directory forest root domain; for many organizations this will not be correct since the naming convention for Active Directory names and SMTP domain names are different.

Accepted domains are simple to create and require little input. To create a new accepted domain using the EMC, double-click the New Accepted Domain task in the Actions menu to see the New Accepted Domain wizard (shown in Figure 10.2). You only need to provide a descriptive name for the accepted domain, the SMTP domain name, and how the message should be treated when it is accepted by Exchange 2007.

You can also manage accepted domains using the following EMS cmdlets: `New-AcceptedDomain`, `Set-AcceptedDomain`, `Get-AcceptedDomain`, and `Remove-AcceptedDomain`.

The only tricky thing about defining an accepted domain is that you must define how Exchange is to treat a message for it. There three types of domains you can choose when creating an accepted domain:

◆ Authoritative domains are SMTP domains for which you accept the inbound message and deliver it to an internal mailbox within your Exchange organization.

◆ Internal relay domains are SMTP domains for which your Exchange server will accept inbound SMTP mail. The Exchange server must have mail-enabled contacts that specify forwarding addresses for users in those domains. The Exchange server then relays the message onward to another internal mail system. Internal relay domains are used when two Exchange organizations are doing global address list synchronization.

◆ External relay domains are SMTP domains for which your Exchange organization will accept inbound SMTP mail but then relays that mail onward to an external SMTP mail server that is usually outside of the organization's boundaries. If Edge Transport servers are used, the Edge Transport server handles external relay domains.

FIGURE 10.2
Creating a new accepted domain

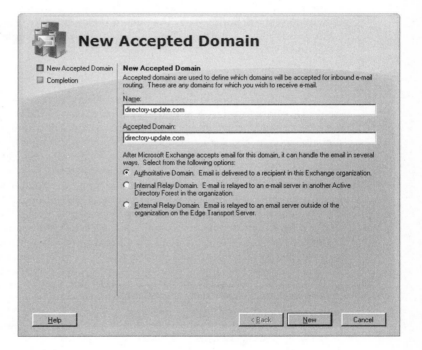

E-mail Address Policies

Exchange e-mail address policies are the configuration objects that are used by Exchange management tasks when new mail objects are created. Each policy's conditions are examined to see if the policy's conditions apply to the object that is being created; if the policy's conditions apply, then the new mail-enabled object's e-mail address policies are generated based on the e-mail address generation rules.

Using the EMC, e-mail address policies are found in the Organization Configuration work center under the Hub Transport subcontainer. Once you have highlighted the Hub Transport subcontainer, select the E-mail Address Policies tab to see a list of the e-mail address policies in the organization. In Figure 10.3, we have only two e-mail address policies.

FIGURE 10.3
The e-mail address policies for an Exchange 2007 organization

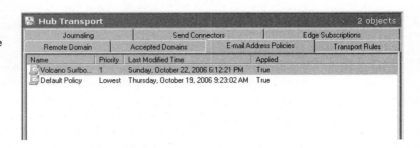

By default, a newly created Exchange 2007 organization has only a single e-mail address policy called the default policy. The default policy is the lowest-priority policy and applies if no other policies above it apply. This is just like having multiple recipient policies in Exchange 2007.

Changing an Existing Policy

The e-mail address generation rule uses the object's Exchange alias and the domain name of the Active Directory forest root. Suppose we want to change the default SMTP domain name that is on the default policy to something else. A good example of when this is relevant is when the default domain name for the Active Directory forest root is different than the public domain name used for SMTP and you need to fix this. Further, we want all e-mail addresses to be generated using the first name, followed by a period, then the last name, and then the domain name.

First, you need to define an accepted domain; if the default accepted domain is not correct for your organization, then you need to create a new accepted domain because Exchange 2007 does not allow you to change the accepted domain. Let's say that you Active Directory forest root is called `fourthcoffee.com` but your public SMTP domain is `volcanocoffee.com`. First, under the Accepted Domains tab of the Organization Configuration work center's Hub Transport subcontainer, create a new authoritative accepted domain for `volcanocoffee.com`.

Next you need to change the default e-mail address policy so that it uses the new domain name and generates an address using the *firstname.lastname* format, such as `josh.maher@volcanocoffee.com`. Locate the Default Policy in the Organization Configuration work center (found under the Hub Transport subcontainer by clicking the E-mail Address Policies tab), highlight the default policy, and click the Edit task in the Actions pane. Click Next until you reach the E-mail Addresses page (shown in Figure 10.4).

Notice in Figure 10.4, the only e-mail address that is generated is `@fourthcoffee.com`. Highlight `@fourthcoffee.com` and click the Edit button to see the SMTP E-mail Address dialog box (shown in Figure 10.5). Notice by default that the E-Mail Address Local Part check box is not checked. This means that the object's Exchange alias will be used when creating the SMTP address. You want to change that, so enable the E-Mail Address Local Part check box; once it's enabled, you will be able to select the First name.last name (john.smith) radio button.

Next, change the e-mail address domain found in the drop-down list at the bottom of the page. Once you have clicked OK in the SMTP E-mail Address dialog box, the e-mail address generation rules will have changed.

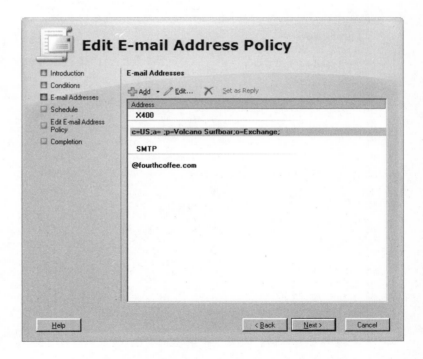

FIGURE 10.4
E-mail addresses properties of an e-mail address policy

You have now modified the Default Policy and you need to click Next on the E-Mail Addresses page to finish the modification. Next you will see the Schedule (see Figure 10.6) page of the wizard. This might be a bit confusing at first since on the surface it doesn't seem like there is anything to schedule. However, remember that in Exchange 2000/2003, the Exchange Recipient

FIGURE 10.5
Changing how the SMTP
address is generated

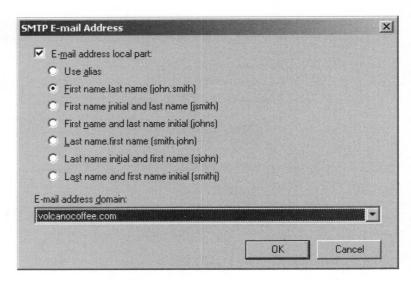

FIGURE 10.6
Scheduling an update to
the e-mail address policy

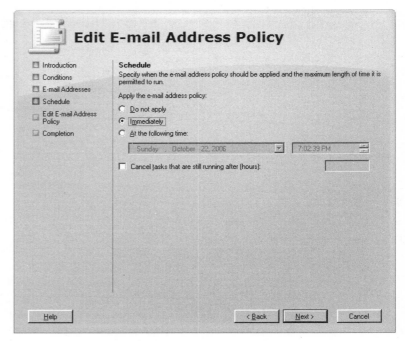

Update Service (RUS) took care of adding SMTP addresses to mail-enabled objects. There is
no such equivalence for Exchange 2007 mail-enabled recipients. Thus, some process or task
has to be kicked off that will do this. If you choose Immediately, this will kick off the Update-
EmailAddressPolicy cmdlet with the -Identity:'Default Policy' option and immediately
update any e-mail addresses.

If you don't choose Immediately, you have additional options:

◆ Do Not Apply skips the Update-EmailAddressPolicy cmdlet phase altogether. If you have just updated the default policy, you can always run the Update-EmailAddressPolicy "Default Policy" commandfrom the EMS at a later point.

◆ At the Following Time allows you to schedule the Update-EmailAddressPolicy cmdlet to run later. This is useful if you know that it will have to update thousands of mail-enabled objects in your Active Directory and you don't want it affecting usage during the business day. This option, when selected, allows you to specify that the task be canceled if it is still running after a certain number of hours.

One thing that we do want to point out is what happens to existing e-mail addresses once you change to a new default address. Figure 10.7 shows the E-mail Addresses property page for the mailbox of a user whose address was updated; notice that this user has two e-mail addresses now. He has the old e-mail address LBenjamin@fourthcoffee.com and his newly created SMTP address Lee.Benjamin@volcanocoffee.com. The process of updating e-mail addresses never removes existing addresses; it creates the new address and makes it the Reply To address.

FIGURE 10.7
Newly created SMTP address for existing user

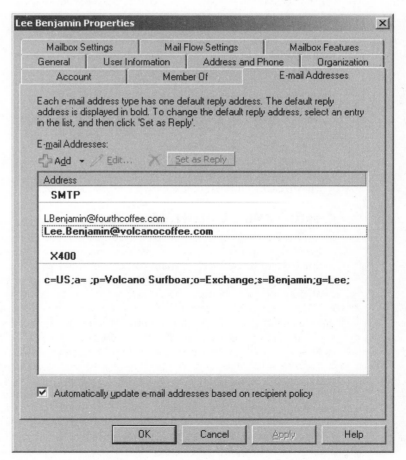

While our example was done entirely in the graphical user interface, you could use the EMS to perform the same steps. The EMS cmdlets you would need to use to create, delete, modify, and update e-mail address policies are shown in Table 10.1.

TABLE 10.1: EMS Cmdlets Used to Manipulate E-mail Address Policies

EMS CMDLET	DESCRIPTION
New-EmailAddressPolicy	Creates a new e-mail address policy
Set-EmailAddressPolicy	Changes properties of the e-mail address policy specified
Update-EmailAddressPolicy	Updates mail-enabled objects in the Active Directory if the conditions of the policy specified apply to those objects
Get-EmailAddressPolicy	Retrieves a list of e-mail address policies and their properties
Remove-EmailAddressPolicy	Deletes the specified e-mail address policy

Finally, of course, if you want to see the e-mail addresses that have been applied to a mail-enabled object, you can also use an EMS cmdlet to retrieve that information. You would use Get-Mailbox, Get-MailContact, or Get-DistributionGroup. To retrieve the e-mail addresses for a mailbox whose alias is Julie.Samante, you could type the following command and see output similar to this:

```
Get-Mailbox "julie.samante" | FL DisplayName,EmailAddresses
```

```
DisplayName    : Julie Samante
EmailAddresses : {smtp:Julie.Samante@fourthcoffee.com,
SMTP:Julie.Samante@volcanocoffee.com, X400:c=US;a=
;p=Volcano Surfboar;o=Exchange;s=Samante;g=Julie;}
```

Creating a New E-mail Address Policy

If you have a small or medium-sized organization, you probably support only a single SMTP domain for your users. However, even companies with a handful of mailboxes can sometimes require two or three SMTP domain names. Let's take as an example an organization that has two divisions, each of which requires its own unique SMTP addresses.

Previously, you changed the default policy for an organization so that all users would get an SMTP address of @volcanocoffee.com. However, we will now extend that example a bit further. Let's say that this organization has another division called Volcano Surfboards and their SMTP domain is @volcanosurfboards.com. Anyone whose company attribute contains "Volcano Surfboards" in Active Directory should have an SMTP address of *firstname.lastname* @volcanosurfboards.com. The first thing you need to do is define this as an accepted domain, and the volcanosurfboards.com accepted domain must be authoritative. If you don't define the accepted domain, you cannot define the e-mail address policy. Next, you want to create the e-mail address policy. In the EMC, select the Hub Transport subcontainer of the Organization Configuration work center, and then select the E-mail Address Policies tab in the results pane.

To create a new e-mail address policy, click the New E-mail Address Policy task in the Actions pane. On the first page (see Figure 10.8) of the New E-mail Address Policy Wizard, you will be prompted for the name of the policy and what type of objects this policy applies to.

FIGURE 10.8
Naming the e-mail
address policy and
defining the objects to
which it applies

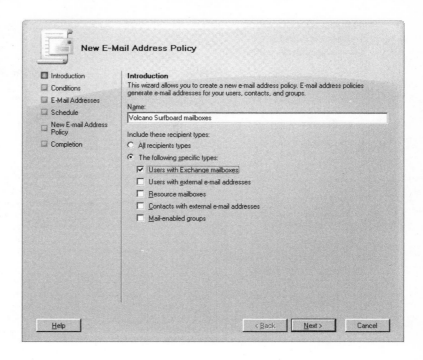

In this example, the policy is being created for the Volcano Surfboards company users and we want the policy to apply only to mailboxes, so you will provide that information on the screen shown in Figure 10.8. When you have provided this information, click Next to move on through the wizard.

The next screen is where you define the conditions under which this policy will be applied. There are two steps to the Conditions page. First, you need to narrow the scope to a specific condition, such as the State or Province attribute, Department attribute, or Company name attribute of the object. Second, you need to provide values for the attributes you have selected.

In our example, we want this policy to apply to anyone whose company name attribute contains Volcano Surfboards. Figure 10.9 shows the Conditions page after we filled in the necessary information.

Once you select the condition Recipient Is in a Company, that option shows up in the Step 2 portion of the dialog as Users with Exchange mailboxes in the *specified* Company(s). The word *specified* appears very much like a hyperlink; it is blue and underlined. If you click on that link, the dialog box appears that allows you to edit or specify one or more company names.

FIGURE 10.9
Defining conditions for
an e-mail address policy

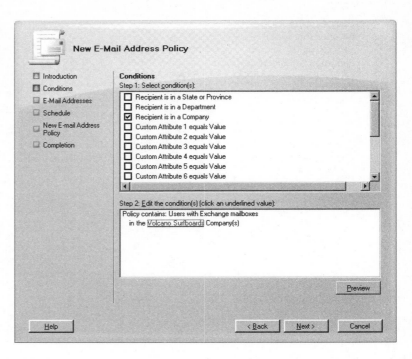

When you have entered the necessary company information (in this case, just a single company called Volcano Surfboards), you can click OK to close the Specify Company dialog box. You can verify that the conditions are defined correctly by clicking the Preview button on the Conditions page of the wizard. The Preview button displays the E-mail Address Policy Preview dialog box; you should see users with mailboxes and whose company name is Volcano Surfboards. This dialog box is shown in Figure 10.10.

The Preview button is also helpful in confirming that attributes are being entered correctly in Active Directory. The administrator may not recognize if everyone in a 10,000-user company exists in the Preview window, but hopefully it will give them an idea that the information is being entered correctly. In this case, if a user's company name does not contain exactly *Volcano Surfboards*, then the policy conditions will not be met and the user's mailbox will have the e-mail addresses from the default policy.

The next step is to define the STMP address or addresses that will be generated when the conditions of this policy apply. The default action for the Add button is to create a new SMTP address, but if you need to create a custom address, click the drop-down arrow to the left of the Add button to see a list that provides the option to create a Custom Address type.

On the E-mail Addresses page, you need to click the Add button to create a new SMTP address. You will then see the SMTP E-mail Address dialog box; select the domain (in this example, volcanosurfboards.com) from the E-mail Address Domain drop-down list and click the First name.last name (john.smith) radio button option.

FIGURE 10.10
The E-mail Address
Policy Preview
dialog box helps to
confirm that the policy
conditions are correct.

If you have not yet created an accepted domain for volcanosurfboards.com, it will not show up in the drop-down list.

The next page of the New E-mail Address Policy wizard is the Schedule page; if you want the addresses to appear immediately, you must click the Immediately radio button and click Next. If there are many thousands of addresses to be created, you may want to schedule the task to run during off-hours. Once you click Next on the Schedule page, you will see the summary page. Here you can see the tasks that will be performed once you click the New button.

The final phase of e-mail address policy creation is the Completion page. While there are no actual operations or input required here (other than clicking the Finish button), this page is useful because it provides you with the cmdlets and commands that were used to perform this particular task. In the case of creating a new e-mail address policy, the task used two cmdlets (New-EmailAddressPolicy and Update-EmailAddressPolicy). The Completion page is shown in Figure 10.11.

FIGURE 10.11
Completion page of the New E-mail Address Policy Wizard

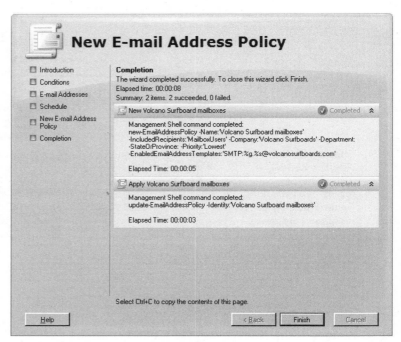

Managing Mailboxes

In some organizations a single Exchange administrator is responsible for all management tasks, while in others the tasks are broken up across different levels of administrators. In medium-sized and large organizations, recipient management such as mailbox management is separated from other day-to-day Exchange administrative tasks. This is partially because mailbox management often falls into the category of user account administration and partially because mailbox administration in larger organizations is fairly time consuming. Managing mailboxes involves the following tasks:

◆ Assigning mailboxes to users

◆ Updating Exchange-related properties of a user account

◆ Deleting mailboxes

◆ Creating and managing shared resources

◆ Moving mailboxes across different mailbox databases

In the following sections, we will cover how to accomplish these tasks. Although we will mostly focus on using the EMC, we will show you how to accomplish the same tasks using the EMS. There are certain tasks that you will only be able to accomplish using the EMS.

Managing User Mailboxes

In this first section on mailbox management, we will tackle the most common tasks: creating, managing, and deleting mailboxes associated with a real user account. Don't confuse user mailboxes with mailboxes that are associated with a resource such as a conference room or an overhead projector; user and resource mailboxes are almost identical, but we will cover resource mailboxes later in this chapter.

The Exchange Management Console (EMC) allows you to associate a mailbox with an existing user in Active Directory, or you can actually create the user account (if you have the necessary permissions).

The rules for mailbox ownership and associating an account with a mailbox have not changed since Exchange 2000. There are a couple of important things to keep in mind with respect to user account and mailbox management:

◆ A user account can own only a single mailbox.

◆ A user account can be given permissions to other mailboxes.

◆ Each mailbox must be associated with a user account that is in the same Active Directory forest as the Exchange server.

◆ A single user account from another Active Directory forest can own a mailbox, but a user account in the Exchange server's home forest must still exist and be associated with the mailbox.

ASSIGNING A MAILBOX TO AN EXISTING USER USING THE EMC

Let's start with a very common task, assigning a mailbox to an existing user. You may also hear this process referred to as "mailbox-enabling" a user or simply creating a mailbox. In this example, we have a user in Active Directory whose account is Bharat.Suneja and his unique location is fourthcoffee.com/Corporate/Bharat Suneja. To assign this user a mailbox, we must use either the EMS or the EMC; remember that extensions for Active Directory Users and Computers from Exchange 2000/2003 do not work for Exchange 2007.

Launch the EMC and navigate to the Mailboxes subcontainer of the Recipient Configuration work center. From here, click the New Mailbox task on the Actions pane. This will launch the New Mailbox Wizard. The very first screen in this wizard (shown in Figure 10.12) introduces some entirely new concepts for administrators of previous versions of Exchange. This first screen asks you to define what type of mailbox you are creating.

We have four possible choices for mailbox types; for all of them, there *must* be a user account in the same Active Directory as the Exchange servers are located.

User Mailbox	This is the most common type of mailbox that most administrators will create. Assigns a mailbox to an existing user account in the same Active Directory forest in which the Exchange server is located.

Room Mailbox	Creates a disabled user account and assigns a mailbox to that user. The `ResourceType` property of the mailbox is set to `Room`, the `RecipientTypeDetails` property is set to `ConferenceRoomMailbox`, and the `IsResource` property is set to `True`.
Equipment Mailbox	Creates a disabled user account and assigns a mailbox to that user. The `ResourceType` property of that mailbox is set to `Equipment`, the `RecipientTypeDetails` property is set to `EquipmentMailbox`, and the `IsResource` property is set to `True`.
Linked Mailbox	Creates a disabled user account, assigns it a mailbox, and prompts the administrator to provide a user account in a separate, trusted forest. The account in the other forest is considered the owner of this mailbox and has the Associated External Account permissions to the mailbox. This is used in organizations that install Exchange in a resource forest.

FIGURE 10.12
Defining the type of
mailbox to be created

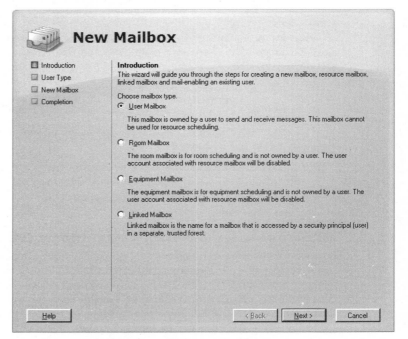

In this first example, we are creating a simple mailbox-enabled user account, so you would choose the User Mailbox radio button and then click the Next button. On the next screen, you are asked whether you are creating a new user account or using an existing user account.

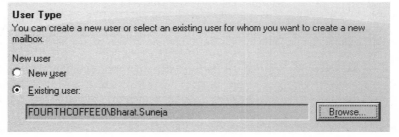

When you select the Browse button, you are presented with the Select User dialog box. From here, you can narrow down the scope of your search using the Search option. Note that only enabled user accounts that do not have a mailbox show up in this list.

After you select from the Active Directory a user that does not already have a mailbox assigned to it, the Mailbox Settings page allows you to define the mailbox database on which the mailbox will be hosted. Most of the information requested on the Mailbox Settings page (shown in Figure 10.13) will look familiar to Exchange 2000/2003 administrators.

From the Mailbox Settings page, you specify the following information:

Alias	The alias is used to generate the default SMTP addresses as well as other internal Exchange functions such as the legacy Exchange distinguished name. The alias defaults to be the same as the user account name, but it can be changed if you need it to conform to another standard.
Server	The server drop-down list specifies the mailbox server on which the mailbox will be located. Only servers that have the mailbox server role assigned to them will appear in the drop-down list.
Storage Group	This drop-down list shows a list of storage groups that are located on the mailbox server selected in the Server drop-down list.
Mailbox Database	This drop-down list will consist of mailbox databases found in the storage group that was selected in the Storage Group drop-down list.
Managed Folder Mailbox policy	The Managed Folder Mailbox Policy selection allows you to define which managed folder policy affects this particular mailbox. Once this has been assigned, the next time the Messaging Records Management process is run, the managed folders specified by this policy will be created.

Exchange ActiveSync   The Exchange ActiveSync mailbox policy defines the ActiveSync
Mailbox Policy   parameters for the user.

FIGURE 10.13
Assigning a mailbox to
a server, storage group,
and mailbox database

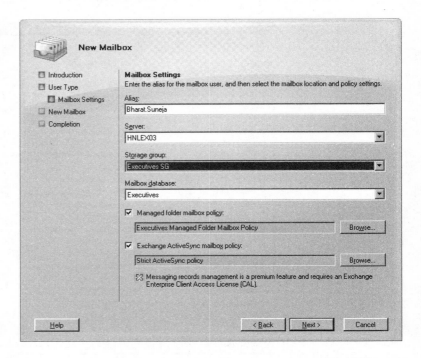

The next screen provides the configuration summary. Here you can review the configuration of the mailbox you are creating/assigning.

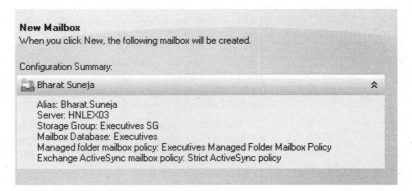

When you are convinced that the parameters for the mailbox you are creating are correct, you can click the New button. The EMC console then launches an EMS cmdlet that actually enables the mailbox in the Active Directory. The last page of the wizard is the Completion page, which tells you if the operation was successful or not and shows you the cmdlet and options that were used to perform the operation. Figure 10.14 shows the Completion screen for the mailbox we just created.

FIGURE 10.14
Successfully
completing the
assignment of a mailbox
to an existing user

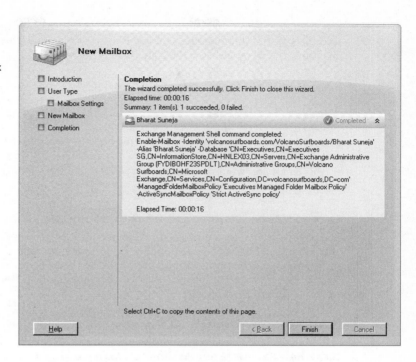

Notice that the Completion screen also allows you to copy the output of the screen to the paste buffer so that you could then paste that output in to a text editor. If you are just learning the PowerShell and the EMS, this makes it simple to learn what cmdlets do and how to use them. That is helpful if you want to mail-enable user accounts using the EMS.

Assigning a Mailbox to a User from the EMS

In a larger organization, you will probably want to streamline or script the creation of new mailboxes and/or user accounts. The EMS allows you to do this easily. For now, though, let's look at the example we just completed from the EMC graphical user interface. We enabled a mailbox for an existing user, assigned that user a mailbox on the Executives mailbox database, assigned that user the Executives Mailbox Policy, and the Standard user ActiveSync Policy. The exact cmdlet that was executed is as follows:

```
Enable-Mailbox -Identity 'volcanosurfboards.com/VolcanoSurfboards/Bharat Suneja'
-Alias 'Bharat.Suneja' -Database 'CN=Executives,CN=Executives
 SG,CN=InformationStore,CN=HNLEX03,CN=Servers,CN=Exchange
Administrative Group (FYDIBOHF23SPDLT),CN=Administrative
Groups,CN=Volcano Surfboards,CN=Microsoft Exchange,CN=Services,
CN=Configuration,DC=volcanosurfboards,DC=com'
-ManagedFolderMailboxPolicy 'Executives Managed Folder Mailbox Policy'
 -ActiveSyncMailboxPolicy 'Strict ActiveSync policy'
```

The Exchange Management Console created this command and used object names to identify the user and the home mailbox database in very explicit terms. However, we want to show you another example and simplify it just a bit. In this case, we have another existing user whose account is Kevin.Miller and he is in the FourthCoffee Active Directory domain. We will simplify this command as much as possible and here is the result:

```
Enable-Mailbox fourthcoffee\Kevin.Miller -Alias:Kevin.Miller -Database:Executives

Name              Alias            Server          ProhibitSendQuota
----              -----            ------          -----------------
Kevin Miller      Kevin.Miller     HNLEX03         unlimited
```

This command works because there is only a single mailbox database in the entire organization called Executives.

ASSIGNING PERMISSIONS TO A MAILBOX USING THE EMS

On some occasions, you may need to assign a user the permission necessary to access another user's mailbox. This was easy enough to do in Exchange 2000/2003 using Active Directory Users and Computers. However, in Exchange 2007, this must be done using the EMS cmdlet Add-MailboxPermission. In this example, we are assigning user Derek.Ueki permissions to access the Paul.Moriguchi mailbox:

```
Add-MailboxPermission Paul.Moriguchi -User Derek.Ueki -AccessRights FullAccess
```

CREATING A NEW USER AND ASSIGNING A MAILBOX USING THE EMC

Previously, you saw that the EMC's New Mailbox Wizard would allow you to create a new user account at the same time you enable the mailbox. It is true that the new EMC has some rudimentary user creating and management tasks. On the User Type page of the New Mailbox Wizard, if you select the New User radio button and click Next, you are prompted for the user account information on a screen called the User Information screen (shown in Figure 10.15).

On the User Information screen, you provide some basic account information such as the first name, middle initial, last name, UPN name, pre–Windows 2000 account name, and the password. You must also specify the organizational unit (OU) in which the user account will be created, and, of course, you must have the Active Directory permissions necessary to create user accounts in that OU.

The rest of the wizard is exactly the same as if you were enabling a mailbox for an existing user. On the Completion property page, though, you will notice some small differences in the cmdlet and the cmdlet's parameters. To create a user named Andy.Webb in the VolcanoSurfboards OU and assign his mailbox to the Engineering Mailboxes mailbox database, here is the command that the EMC performed.

```
New-Mailbox -Name 'Andy Webb' -Alias 'Andy.Webb'
-OrganizationalUnit 'volcanosurfboards.com/VolcanoSurfboards'
-UserPrincipalName 'Andy.Webb@volcanosurfboards.com'
-SamAccountName 'Andy.Webb' -FirstName 'Andy' -Initials ''
-LastName 'Webb' -Password 'System.Security.SecureString'
-ResetPasswordOnNextLogon $True -Database 'CN=Engineering
 Mailboxes,CN=Engineering Mailboxes SG,CN=InformationStore,
CN=HNLEX03,CN=Servers,CN=Exchange Administrative Group
```

```
(FYDIBOHF23SPDLT),CN=Administrative Groups,CN=Volcano
 Surfboards,CN=Microsoft Exchange,CN=Services,
CN=Configuration,DC=volcanosurfboards,DC=com'
-ManagedFolderMailboxPolicy 'Executives Managed Folder
Mailbox Policy' -ActiveSyncMailboxPolicy 'Strict ActiveSync policy'
```

FIGURE 10.15
Creating a user account
from the Exchange
Management Console

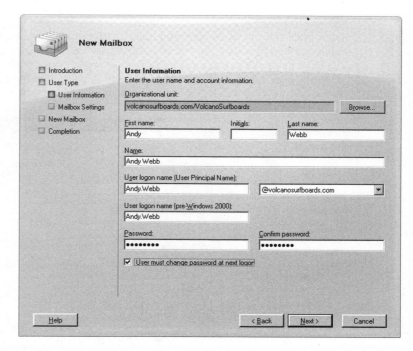

Since the Executives mailbox store is unique for the Exchange organization, we could have shortened this command as follows if we were running it from the EMS:

```
New-Mailbox -Name:'Andy Webb' -Alias:'Andy.Webb'
-OrganizationalUnit:'volcanosurfboards.com/VolcanoSurfboards'
-Database:CN=Engineering Mailboxes
-UserPrincipalName:'Andy.Webb@volcanosurfboards.com'
-SamAccountName:'Andy.Webb' -FirstName:'Andy' -Initials:''
-LastName:'Webb' -Password:'System.Security.SecureString'
-ResetPasswordOnNextLogon:$True
```

Notice that the cmdlet is not Enable-Mailbox as it was in the previous example; the Enable-Mailbox cmdlet is used to assign a mailbox to an existing user account. The cmdlet used is the New-Mailbox; this cmdlet has options for creating the user account as well as enabling the mailbox. Notice there is an -OrganizationalUnit parameter that allows you to specify the domain and the OU name in canonical name format such as volcanosurfboards.com/VolcanoSurfboards.

The New-Mailbox cmdlet also has parameters for setting the password, pre–Windows 2000 account name, and UPN name.

MANAGING USER AND MAILBOX PROPERTIES

Many of the user account properties that can be managed through the Active Directory Users and Computers console can now also be managed through the EMC or the EMS. Naturally, using the EMC is a little easier than using the command line, but the EMS is much more flexible and powerful once you learn how to use it.

Using the Exchange Management Console

Let's start with managing user and mailbox properties using the EMC. We want to take a look at a few of the things that you can do and some of the user's property pages. Let's start by taking a look at the mailbox's general information property page shown in Figure 10.16. The General property page has some interesting information on it, including the user ID of the last person to access the mailbox, the mailbox size, the home Exchange server, and the mailbox store name.

FIGURE 10.16
General information property page for a mailbox

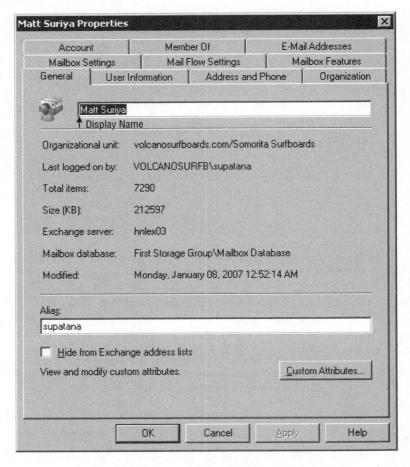

On the General property page is also the Hide From Exchange Address Lists check box that allows you to hide the mailbox from address lists such as the global address list and the Custom Attributes button that allows you to access all 15 custom attributes (aka extension attributes).

The field that is not clearly labeled (so we labeled in Figure 10.16) is the Display Name field. The display name is what users see in the global address list.

The next property page of interest is the E-mail Addresses property page (shown in Figure 10.17). From the E-mail Addresses property page, you can manage the SMTP addresses (and other address types) that are assigned to this particular mailbox. Notice in Figure 10.17 that this user has multiple SMTP addresses that can be used to send messages to this mailbox.

FIGURE 10.17
E-mail address properties of a mailbox

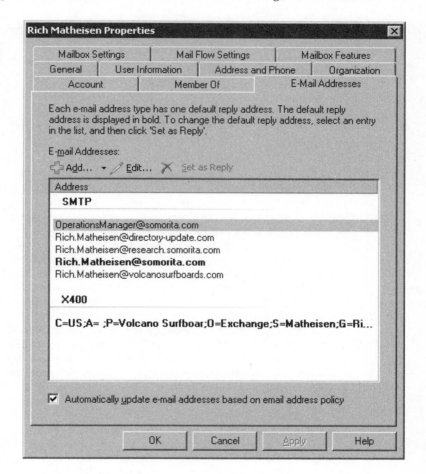

Regardless of how many e-mail addresses are assigned to this mailbox, when an Exchange user clicks the reply button to reply to a message sent to any of these addresses, the Set as Reply address is the one that is always used as the Reply To address. In Figure 10.17, this is the address shown in bold. This can be changed by selecting another address and clicking the Set as Reply button.

E-mail addresses are generated by an e-mail address policy, as we discussed earlier in the chapter. If a policy that affects this mailbox is updated and reapplied, additional e-mail addresses will be created. If a policy that affects the default SMTP address is changed, the e-mail address policy can change a user's primary e-mail address. However, the user will retain the previous

SMTP addresses. However, if you clear the Automatically Update E-mail Addresses Based on Recipient Policy check box, then any changes to the e-mail address policy that affects this mailbox will not be made.

On the Mailbox Settings property page, there are two configuration items that are of interest. These are the Messaging Records Management and Storage Quotas options. These two sets of options are shown side-by-side in Figure 10.18. Storage Quotas allow the administrator to override mailbox database limits.

FIGURE 10.18
Storage Quotas and Messaging Records Management options are found on the Mailbox Settings property page.

The Messaging Records Management options allow you to specify the managed folder mailbox policy that affects this particular mailbox. In addition to defining which policy you use, you can specify an exception time during which no action will be taken on items in this mailbox that might ordinarily be deleted, archived, expired, or moved.

The Mail Flow Settings property page of the mailbox shows mailbox settings that most experienced Exchange administrators will already be familiar with. They are now just located in slightly different places. The properties found under the Mail Flow Settings property page are grouped into Delivery Options, Message Size Restrictions, and Message Delivery Restrictions sections. You merely need to highlight one of them and then click the Properties button to see them.

The Delivery Options properties (shown in Figure 10.19) include a couple of important options. The first is the Send on Behalf permission; this allows anyone that has been assigned this permission to send a message on behalf of this user. For example, in Figure 10.19, user William Lefkovics can now send a message on behalf of this mailbox. When the message arrives, it will say it is from William Lefkovics on behalf of Rich Matheisen. This implies, at least, a tacit authorization on the part of Rich Matheisen that the message should have been sent by William Lefkovics.

Also on the Delivery Options page is the option to deliver messages to an alternate recipient. The recipient that you specify must be a mailbox in your organization or a mail-enabled contact that you find within your global address list. If you select a mail-enabled contact that you have created in your global address list, this would let you forward all of this user's mail to an external mail system. That can be useful if someone has left the organization and wants to keep getting their mail. It could also be a disaster if that person has left your organization and went to work for a competitor, so use this feature with caution.

If the Deliver Message to Both Forwarding Address and Mailbox check box is enabled, then the message is delivered both places. This is useful when "the boss" wants their assistant to receive all of their mail but they wants to see the mail as well.

Finally, the bottom part of the Delivery Options box allows you to specify the maximum number of recipients to which this person can send a message. The global default is 5,000, but some organizations want to reduce this and then allow only the VIPs to send messages to large numbers of users.

FIGURE 10.19
A mailbox's delivery
options

The Message Size Restrictions options allow you to specify the maximum size of messages the user can send or receive. If these are not specified, the user is limited by the global defaults or the connector defaults.

The final selection of settings that are found on the Mail Flow Settings property page is Message Delivery Restrictions. From the Message Delivery Restrictions options, you can restrict who is allowed to send mail to this particular mailbox. For example, if this is a VIP, you might want to restrict who can send to this mailbox to only a subset of users within the organization. Conversely, you could configure a mailbox to reject mail from a specific set of users. Figure 10.20 shows the

Message Delivery Restrictions settings for a VIP mailbox; the VIP wants to receive mail only from the other members of the Executives group, the Finance and Accounting group, and their assistants.

FIGURE 10.20
Restricting who can send mail to a mailbox

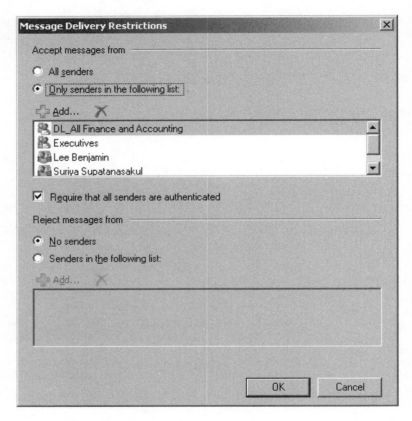

If you select the Require That All Senders Are Authenticated check box, this will cut down on the spam that mailbox receives, but it also means that no anonymous Internet mail will be received. By default, all mail received from the Internet is received anonymously.

If you have spent a lot of time troubleshooting non-delivery reports and error messages that your users have received in the past, you will be happy to hear that the Exchange team has worked hard to make the error messages more descriptive and helpful. In the case in which a user sends a message to someone they are not allowed to send to, they receive a non-delivery report message in return. Figure 10.21 shows an example.

The final property page of interest to e-mail administrators is the Mailbox Features property page (shown in Figure 10.22). On this property page, you can enable or disable additional features of the mailbox such as Outlook Web Access, Exchange ActiveSync, Unified Messaging, and MAPI access.

The Exchange ActiveSync selection has a Properties option that allows you to configure the Exchange ActiveSync policy for this user. You can now disable MAPI clients as well. The Unified Messaging option allows you to specify the user's Unified Messaging properties if you have Unified Messaging server roles installed.

FIGURE 10.21
Non-delivery report message sent when sender is not authorized to send to the intended recipient

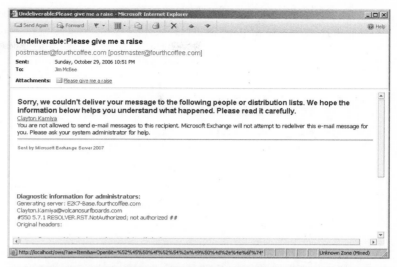

FIGURE 10.22
Mailbox features property page

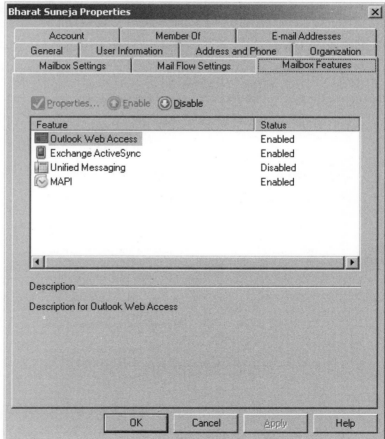

Using the Exchange Management Shell to Manage User Properties

You can also manage mailbox and user properties from the EMS. There are two cmdlets that you will need to know about in order to manage most of the properties. These are the Set-User and Set-Mailbox cmdlets. Let's start with the Set-User cmdlet and an example. Let's say that we want to update user Stan.Reimer's mobile phone number. We would type this:

```
Set-User Stan.Reimer -MobilePhone "(808) 555-1234"
```

The Set-User cmdlet has quite a few useful parameters. Table 10.2 lists many of these options. You can retrieve these from within the EMS by typing Set-User -? or Help Set-User.

TABLE 10.2:   Set-User cmdlet Parameters

PARAMETER	FUNCTION
PostalCode	Sets the zip or postal code.
Manager	Sets the name of the user's manager; input value must be a distinguished name canonical name format such as fourthcoffee.com/Corporate/Ben Craig.
DisplayName	Updates the user's display name, which appears in the global address list.
MobilePhone	Sets the mobile/cell phone number.
City	Sets the city or locality name.
FirstName	Specifies the given or first name.
LastName	Specifies the surname or last name.
Company	Sets the company name.
Department	Sets the department name.
Fax	Specifies the facsimile telephone number.
HomePhone	Sets the home phone number.
Phone	Sets the business phone number.
StateOrProvince	Sets the state or province.
StreetAddress	Sets the street address.
Title	Sets the title or job function.

You can retrieve the list of properties for `Set-User` by using the `Get-User` cmdlet, specifying a username, and then piping the output to the `Format-List` cmdlet. Here is an example:

```
Get-User vlad.mazek | Format-List
```

```
Id                    : fourthcoffee.com/Users/Vlad Mazek
IsValid               : True
Item                  :
DistinguishedName     : CN=Vlad Mazek,CN=Users,DC=fourthcoffee,DC=com
Guid                  : 08834c78-6fd7-4705-baed-54759df1dc26
Identity              : fourthcoffee.com/Users/Vlad Mazek
Name                  : Vlad Mazek
ObjectCategory        : fourthcoffee.com/Configuration/Schema/Person
ObjectCategoryName    : user
ObjectClass           : {top, person, organizationalPerson, user}
ObjectState           : Unchanged
OriginatingServer     : E2K7-Base.fourthcoffee.com
Schema                : Microsoft.Exchange.Data.Directory.Management.UserSchema
WhenChanged           : 11/5/2006 6:34:21 AM
WhenCreated           : 11/5/2006 6:31:18 AM
SamAccountName        : Vlad.Mazek
Sid                   : S-1-5-21-313647035-3844660503-1830646060-1170
SidHistory            : {}
IsSecurityPrincipal   : True
UserPrincipalName     : Vlad.Mazek@fourthcoffee.com
Assistant             :
Company               : Own Web Now Corporation
Department            : Information Security
DirectReports         : {}
Fax                   : (808) 555-4300
HomePhone             : (808) 555-1022
Initials              :
FirstName             : Vlad
LastName              : Mazek
City                  : Honolulu
Manager               : fourthcoffee.com/Corporate/Andy Webb
MobilePhone           : (808) 555-4100
Office                : Honolulu
OtherFax              : {}
OtherHomePhone        : {}
Pager                 : (808) 555-4321
Phone                 : (808) 555-1234
PostalCode            : 96816
PostOfficeBox         : {}
```

```
StateOrProvince         : Hawaii
StreetAddress           : 7019 Kalakaua Avenue
                          Suite 2001
Title                   : Operations Manager
DisplayName             : Vlad Mazek
Notes                   : Created on Nov 5, 2006 per Mark Watts - Work Order BR-549
RecipientType           : MailboxUser
RecipientTypeDetails    : MailboxUser
SimpleDisplayName       : Vlad M
WebPage                 : http://ownwebnow.com
```

> **TIP**
>
> If you pipe the properties of an object to the Format-List (FL) cmdlet, this gives you a very handy way to see all of the property names as well as their current values.

Not only does the `Get-User` cmdlet allow you to view this information about a user account, it also allows you to see all of the property names. For example, if you did not know what the property name was for the State, you can look in the output listing and see that it is `StateOrProvince`. You could then change the user's state by typing the following EMS command:

```
Set-User vlad.mazek -StateOrProvince "Florida"
```

Using the Exchange Management Shell to Manage Mailbox Properties

The `Set-User` and the `Get-User` cmdlets helped us with non-Exchange-specific properties of a user account, but the `Set-Mailbox` and the `Get-Mailbox` cmdlets will help us to set the properties of mail-enabled user account. In fact, you have already seen these cmdlets earlier in this book when we talked about setting mailbox storage limits. Let's take a quick look at some ways you can use these cmdlets. For example, if you want to change the user Cheyne.Manalo's rules quota, you would type this:

```
Set-Mailbox cheyne.manalo -RulesQuota:128KB
```

There are a lot of properties that you can set through the EMS and the `Set-Mailbox` cmdlet. A few of the more useful ones are found in Table 10.3.

Table 10.3 shows you just a few of the parameters that can be used by the `Set-Mailbox` cmdlet or that can be viewed using the `Get-Mailbox` cmdlet. If you want to look up these parameters, from the EMS you can type `Set-Mailbox -?`, or you can type `Help Set-Mailbox`. As we showed you previously with `Get-User`, you can pipe the output for a mailbox to the `Format-List` (or `fl`) cmdlet and see all of the properties for that mailbox. Here is an example:

```
Get-Mailbox "Cheyne Manalo" | FL

Database                        : HNLEX03\First Storage Group\Mailbox Database
DeletedItemFlags                : RetainUntilBackupOrCustomPeriod
UseDatabaseRetentionDefaults    : False
```

```
RetainDeletedItemsUntilBackup      : True
DeliverToMailboxAndForward         : True
RetentionHoldEnabled               : True
EndDateForRetentionHold            : 1/31/2007 2:01:32 PM
StartDateForRetentionHold          : 1/11/2007 2:01:32 PM
ManagedFolderMailboxPolicy         : Executives Managed Folder Mailbox Policy
ExchangeGuid                       : 5febe951-905a-4171-9b3b-d8bcfb8a728d
ExchangeSecurityDescriptor         : System.Security.AccessControl.
RawSecurityDescriptor
ExchangeUserAccountControl         : None
ExternalOofOptions                 : External
ForwardingAddress                  : volcanosurfboards.com/VolcanoSurfboards/To
                                     dd Hawkins
RetainDeletedItemsFor              : 30.00:00:00
IsMailboxEnabled                   : True
Languages                          : {}
OfflineAddressBook                 :
ProhibitSendQuota                  : 150000KB
ProhibitSendReceiveQuota           : 200000KB
ProtocolSettings                   : {HTTP§0§1§§§§§, POP3§1§0§1§ISO-
8859-1§1§§§, IMAP4§0§1§4§ISO-8859-1§0§1§0§0}
RecipientLimits                    : 150
UserAccountControl                 : NormalAccount
IsResource                         : False
IsLinked                           : False
IsShared                           : False
LinkedMasterAccount                :
ResourceCapacity                   :
ResourceCustom                     : {}
ResourceType                       :
SamAccountName                     : CManalo
SCLDeleteThreshold                 :
SCLDeleteEnabled                   :
SCLRejectThreshold                 :
SCLRejectEnabled                   :
SCLQuarantineThreshold             :
SCLQuarantineEnabled               :
SCLJunkThreshold                   : 4
SCLJunkEnabled                     : True
AntispamBypassEnabled              : False
ServerLegacyDN                     : /o=Volcano Surfboards/ou=Exchange
    Administrative Group (FYDIBOHF23SPDLT)/cn=Configuration/cn=Servers/cn=HNLEX03
ServerName                         : hnlex03
UseDatabaseQuotaDefaults           : False
IssueWarningQuota                  : 125000KB
RulesQuota                         : 64KB
Office                             :
UserPrincipalName                  : CManalo@volcanosurfboards.com
```

```
        UMEnabled                          : False
        MaxSafeSenders                     :
        MaxBlockedSenders                  :
        Extensions                         : {}
        AcceptMessagesOnlyFrom             : {}
        AcceptMessagesOnlyFromDLMembers    : {}
        AddressListMembership              : {Engineering, Default Global
        Address List, All Users}
        Alias                              : CManolo
        OrganizationalUnit                 : volcanosurfboards.com/VolcanoSurfboards
        CustomAttribute1                   : Angelina
        CustomAttribute10                  :
        CustomAttribute11                  :
        CustomAttribute12                  :
        CustomAttribute13                  :
        CustomAttribute14                  :
        CustomAttribute15                  :
        CustomAttribute2                   : Delta SkyMiles Member
        CustomAttribute3                   : 987654321
        CustomAttribute4                   : D.O.B. March 9, 1982
        CustomAttribute5                   :
        CustomAttribute6                   :
        CustomAttribute7                   :
        CustomAttribute8                   :
        CustomAttribute9                   :
        DisplayName                        : Cheyne Manalo
        EmailAddresses                     : {smtp:Cheyne@volcanosurfboards.com,
           X400:C=US;A=;P=Volcano
Surfboar;O=Exchange;S=Manolo;G=Cheyne;, smtp:CManolo@directory-update.com,
X500:/o=Volcano Surfboards/ou=First Administrative Group/cn=Recipients/cn=CManolo,
smtp:CManolo@research.somorita.com, SMTP:CManolo@somorita.com,
 smtp:CManolo@volcanosurfboards.com}
        GrantSendOnBehalfTo                : {Andy Webb, Bharat Suneja,
Bthaworn Thaweeaphiradeemaitree, Paul Moriguchi, Don Nguyen, Nathan Nakanishi}
        HiddenFromAddressListsEnabled      : False
        LegacyExchangeDN                   : /o=Volcano Surfboards/ou=First
Administrative Group/cn=Recipients/cn=CManolo
        MaxSendSize                        : 20MB
        MaxReceiveSize                     : 10MB
        PoliciesIncluded                   : {}
        PoliciesExcluded                   : {{26491cfc-9e50-4857-861b-0cb8df22b5d7}}
        EmailAddressPolicyEnabled          : False
        PrimarySmtpAddress                 : CManolo@somorita.com
        RecipientType                      : UserMailbox
        RecipientTypeDetails               : UserMailbox
        RejectMessagesFrom                 : {Roberry Carter, Pavel Nagaev, Townley Matt}
        RejectMessagesFromDLMembers        : {}
        RequireSenderAuthenticationEnabled : False
```

```
SimpleDisplayName              :
UMDtmfMap                      : {}
WindowsEmailAddress            : CManolo@somorita.com
IsValid                        : True
OriginatingServer              : HNLDC01.volcanosurfboards.com
ExchangeVersion                : 0.1 (8.0.535.0)
Name                           : Cheyne Manalo
DistinguishedName              : CN=Cheyne Manalo,
OU=VolcanoSurfboards,DC=volcanosurfboards,DC=com
Identity                       : volcanosurfboards.com/VolcanoSurfboards/
Cheyne Manalo
Guid                           : 2565735d-c19b-4c88-9242-075eaa8e8fee
ObjectCategory                 : volcanosurfboards.com/Configuration/
Schema/Person
ObjectClass                    : {top, person, organizationalPerson, user}
WhenChanged                    : 1/11/2007 2:06:16 PM
WhenCreated                    : 12/12/2005 9:10:28 AM
```

TABLE 10.3:   Set-Mailbox Properties

PARAMETER	FUNCTION
RulesQuota	Specifies the maximum amount of rules a user can have in a folder. Note that having more than 32KB of rules per folder requires the Outlook 2007 client.
SCLDeleteThreshold	Specifies the SCL (spam confidence level) value at and above which messages flagged as spam should be deleted.
SCLDeleteEnabled	Specifies if messages above the value of SCLDeleteThreshold property should be deleted. There are additional SCL threshold options that are not listed in this table.
RecipientLimits	Specifies the maximum number of recipients per message that a user can send to.
EmailAddressPolicy Enabled	Specifies whether or not this mailbox should have its e-mail addresses updated by e-mail address policies.
MaxSendSize	Specifies the maximum size for messages that can be sent by this mailbox.
MaxReceiveSize	Specifies the maximum size for messages that can be received in to this mailbox.
ForwardingAddress	Specifies an address to which mail sent to this mailbox will be forwarded. The value must be in canonical name format such as volcanosurfboards.com/Corporate/Mike Brown.

(CONTINUED)

TABLE 10.3: Set-Mailbox Properties *(CONTINUED)*

PARAMETER	FUNCTION
HiddenFromAddress ListsEnabled	If set to True, this mailbox will not appear in any of the Exchange address lists. The default is False.
CustomAttribute1	Specifies the value for Custom Attribute 1 (aka Extension Attribute 1). There are 15 custom attributes that can be set through the EMS; simply change 1 to 2, 3, and so on.
ProhibitSendQuota	Specifies the mailbox size above which the user will not be able to send any new messages.
ProhibitSendReceive Quota	Specifies the mailbox size above which the mailbox will reject new mail and the user will not be able to send any messages.
IssueWarningQuota	Specifies the mailbox size above which the user will receive a warning message indicating they are over their mailbox quota.
AntispamBypassEnabled	If set to True, this specifies that this mailbox should not have its mail filtered by the Exchange 2007 content filtering component on the Edge Transport or Hub Transport server. The default is False.
UseDatabaseQuota Defaults	If set to False, then the mailbox uses the storage quotas set on the mailbox. If set to True (the default), then the mailbox uses the mailbox storage quotas that are defined for the mailbox database on which the mailbox is located.

When you look at these properties, please keep in mind that not all properties can be modified, even using the EMS. Many of these properties are system properties and are either created or managed by the system.

Managing Resource Mailboxes

Finally with Exchange 2007 and Outlook 2007, the client and the server know the different between a regular user mailbox and a resource mailbox. Exchange 2007 allows us to define two different types of resource mailboxes: room and equipment mailboxes. We will first look at some of the basic features that allow you to define a resource mailbox and then we will show you some of the more advanced features of Exchange 2007 and Outlook 2007, such as advanced calendaring.

To assign an administrator the permissions necessary to create, manage, and delete resource mailboxes, make that administrator a member of the Exchange Recipient Administrators group. This administrator will also require permissions to whichever Active Directory organizational unit will hold the disabled user accounts.

CREATING AND DEFINING RESOURCE MAILBOX PROPERTIES

Let's start with a simple example of defining a room resource mailbox. Let's say we want to create a conference room resource that will be called Conference Room 1103. Just as with creating a user account, you launch the New Mailbox Wizard, but on the Introduction page you choose the Room Mailbox radio button.

⦿ R<u>o</u>om Mailbox

The room mailbox is for room scheduling and is not owned by a user. The user account associated with resource mailbox will be disabled.

Everything else about creating a room mailbox resource is exactly the same as creating a user mailbox. If the user account does not yet exist in Active Directory, specify that you are creating a new user, and then on the Mailbox Information page, provide the user account information (shown in Figure 10.23). Notice that the user is being created in an OU called Resources; that is an OU we created to hold resource user accounts.

FIGURE 10.23
Defining user information for a conference room mailbox

Notice also in Figure 10.23 that we specified a first name and a last name. This is not really necessary, but we consider it a good practice. When you have completed the New Mailbox Wizard, a disabled user account is created. Right now, the resource user and the resource user's mailbox look almost identical to a regular user mailbox. The icons are slightly different for the room and equipment mailboxes. The room mailbox icon includes a small door and the equipment mailbox includes a small projector screen.

Clayton Kamiya	Clayton.Kamiya	Mailbox User	Clayton.Kamiya@volca
Conference Room 1001	CR1001	Conference Room Mailbox	CR1001@volcanocoffe
Conference Room 1102	ConfRoom1102	Conference Room Mailbox	ConfRoom1102@volca
Conference Room 1103	CR1103	Conference Room Mailbox	ConferenceRoom.1103
Damion Jones	Damion.Jones	Mailbox User	Damion.Jones@volcan
David Elfassy	David.Elfassy	Mailbox User	David.Elfassy@volcan
Devin Ganger	Devin.Ganger	Mailbox User	Devin.Ganger@volcan
Elizabeth Owusu	Elizabeth.Owusu	Mailbox User	Elizabeth.Owusu@volc
EQUIP - Panasonic 50" Plasma TV #1	EQUIP-PANASO50	Equipment Mailbox	EQUIP-PANASO50@v
ExportMailbox	ExportMailbox	Mailbox User	ExportMailbox@volcan

But what really defines these as resources instead of just mailboxes? With Exchange 2007, there are some additional Active Directory attributes that can be assigned to a user account that defines a resource account as opposed to a regular mailbox. These attributes include the `RecipientType`, `RecipientTypeDetails`, `ResourceType`, `ResourceCapacity`, and `ResourceCustom` properties. Let's look at the resource-specific properties of the room resource we just created using the `Get-Mailbox` cmdlet. Here is the command and the output:

```
Get-Mailbox "conference room 1103" | FL Name,RecipientType,RecipientTypeDetails,
ResourceType, ResourceCapacity, ResourceCustom
Name                 : Conference Room 1103
RecipientType        : MailboxUser
RecipientTypeDetails : ConferenceRoomMailbox
ResourceType         : Room
ResourceCapacity     :
ResourceCustom       : {Room}
```

The following are the details of what you can expect to see for these properties when creating resource mailboxes:

◆ The `RecipientType` property for mailboxes (resource or regular) is always set to `MailboxUser`.

◆ The `RecipientTypeDetails` property will be set to either `ConferenceRoomMailbox` or `EquipmentMailbox`.

◆ The `ResourceType` property will be set to either `Room` or `Equipment`.

◆ The `ResourceCapacity` property is used to define room capacity (for example, the number of people that can sit in the room).

◆ The `ResourceCustom` property is used to define additional properties for this resource mailbox.

What these properties of the user account (and mailbox) do is set some features that define this mailbox as a resource mailbox. These special features enable Outlook 2007 and Outlook Web Access 2007 to recognize resource mailboxes and to differentiate a regular mailbox from an end user mailbox. Figure 10.24 shows the All Rooms view of the Outlook Web Access 2007 Address Book; this allows you to view just the conference room resources.

Enabling the client to separately view room resources makes choosing room resources simpler because it eliminates the necessity to browse the entire global address list.

DEFINING ADVANCED RESOURCE MAILBOX FEATURES

What you have seen so far with respect to resource mailboxes is not all that different from earlier versions of Exchange and Outlook. It's just that now have the ability to better sort the address list. However, Exchange 2007 actually enables a few additional features on the mailbox that make it even easier to find the room resource you need. You probably noticed the properties `ResourceCapacity` and `ResourceCustom`. What good is scheduling a conference room if you don't schedule one that will hold all of the attendees? The `ResourceCapacity` property allows you to define in Active Directory the capacity of a specific room resource.

FIGURE 10.24
Viewing just the room resources in the Address Book

Resource capacity is defined from the EMS using the `Set-Mailbox` cmdlet. Let's say we want to define the room capacity of Conference Room 1103 to 15. We would type this:

```
Set-Mailbox "Conference Room 1103" -ResourceCapacity 15
```

Before we look at how you would utilize this information, let's also look at the `ResourceCustom` property. What good is finding a conference room with a certain capacity if we can't find one with all of the tools or resources we need for a particular meeting? In many organizations, conference rooms are equipped with televisions, DVD players, and more. These things can be defined in the `ResourceCustom` property.

If we want to take advantage of this, the first thing we need to do is to define the types of properties in the property schema. Resource property schema properties are defined using the `Set-ResourceConfig` cmdlet, and you can view the current properties using the `Get-ResourceConfig` cmdlet. The property in which we are interested is the `ResourcePropertySchema`. Here is an example of retrieving the current value:

```
Get-ResourceConfig | Format-List Name,ResourcePropertySchema


Name                   : Resource Schema
ResourcePropertySchema : {Room/TV, Room/AV}
```

Each time you run the `Set-ResourceConfig` cmdlet, it replaces the existing value with the new value, so if you want to keep the existing properties, make sure you include the existing properties in the `Set-ResourceConfig` command line. Let's say, for example, that we want to define an additional type of resource property that some of the conference rooms have available. In this example, some of the conference rooms have massage chairs; to add an additional resource property of massage chair, we would type this command:

```
Set-ResourceConfig -ResourcePropertySchema ("Room/TV", "Room/AV",
"Room/Minibar")
```

Once the resource property schema includes a TV, A/V resources, and a Minibar, we can assign them as resources of a particular conference room. For room resource objects, this can be done on the Resource Information property page of the mailbox object.

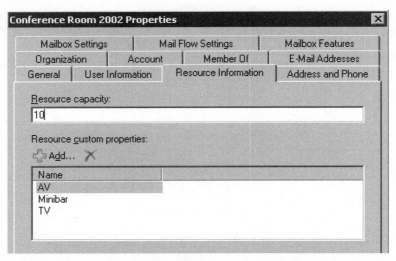

We can also set the custom resource properties via the EMS. For example, if Conference Room 1103 has TV and massage chair resources and a capacity of eight people, we would type this:

```
Set-Mailbox -Identity "Conference Room 1103" -ResourceCustom
   ("TV","Minibar")
-ResourceCapacity 8
```

This sets both the custom resource properties and the resource capacity at the same time. If you want to verify this for this particular resource, you could type this:

```
Get-Mailbox "conference room 1103" | FL Name,*resource*

Name              : Conference Room 1103
IsResource        : True
ResourceCapacity  : 8
ResourceCustom    : {MassageChairs, TV, Room}
ResourceType      : Room
```

Note in the preceding example that we did not include the -Identity parameter in the Get-Mailbox options. This was intentional so that we could show you that you that it is optional; also note that the resource's display name, Conference Room 1103, is in lowercase. The cmdlets and the parameters are not usually case sensitive, either.

Once you have defined a resource with specific properties, such as the custom properties and the capacity, the properties will show up in Outlook and Outlook Web Access when you browse for room resources. Figure 10.25 shows the Select Rooms list box in Outlook 2007. Notice that the room capacity and the room's custom resources show up in this list.

FIGURE 10.25

Browsing for room resources. Note the Capacity and Description columns.

DEFINING RESOURCE SCHEDULING POLICIES

One of the more annoying things about creating resources in earlier versions of Exchange was that you had to be creative in figuring out a way to get a resource to automatically accept scheduled appointments. There were scripts, special procedures, and third-party tools that you could use to handle automatic booking, but often even a combination of tools and software did not meet your needs.

Exchange 2007 introduces a new way to define the features of a resource mailbox, including how a resource is automatically booked and who can book a particular resource. Options such as who can book a room or equipment resource as well as time limits for booking the resource are part of the resource's calendar scheduling policy. These settings can be defined in one of two ways; the simplest way to define a resource's calendar scheduling policy is to use Outlook Web Access. You must first enable the room resource mailbox account since it will be created as a disabled user account, make sure you have the password, and then open the mailbox using Outlook Web Access. Once you have opened the mailbox in Outlook Web Access, click the Options button in the OWA interface, scroll down the options on the left pane, and choose the Resource Settings option. This option does not appear for a regular mailbox. The entire list of options is a little too big for one screen capture, so we are breaking it up into smaller screens so that we can describe each of the options; we will summarize them for you in Table 10.4. Figure 10.26 shows the Resource Scheduling Options section.

The Resource Scheduling Options section allows you to define some of the basics of how the resource will automatically accept schedule requests, whether or not it will accept recurring requests, whether or not it will even automatically process requests, and how to handle conflicting requests.

The next section in Resource Settings is Resource Scheduling Permissions; these are shown in Figure 10.27. By default, Everyone is allowed to submit schedule requests to a resource and these request will be automatically processed based on the rules defined in the Resource Scheduling Options section.

Notice that in Figure 10.27, we have changed the auto-accept permissions for this room resource just a bit (after all, it does have massage chairs). This room can only be scheduled automatically by members of the Executives group; VIPs and user Mark Arnold can automatically schedule meetings for the resource *and* submit manual requests if the resource is unavailable. Note that permissions include whether or not manual requests are automatically sent to delegates of this resource; delegates cannot be defined through this interface. Resource delegates must be defined using the EMS cmdlet `Set-MailboxCalendarSettings`. For example, if we want to assign user Simon.Butler as a delegate of this mailbox, we would type the following command:

```
Set-MailboxCalendarSettings "Conference Room 1103" -ResourceDelegates Simon.Bulter
```

FIGURE 10.26
A resource mailbox's
Resource Scheduling
Options section

Resource Scheduling Options

☑ Automatically process meeting requests and cancellations
  ☑ Disable Reminders
  Maximum number of days: `180`
  ☑ Always decline if end date is beyond this limit
  ☑ Limit meeting duration
  Maximum allowed minutes: `1440`
☐ Allow scheduling only during working hours
☐ Allow conflicts
☑ Allow recurring meetings
  Allow up to this number of individual conflicts: `0`
  Allow up to this percentage of individual conflicts: `0`

FIGURE 10.27
Defining room resource
scheduling permissions

Resource Scheduling Permissions

Specify users and groups which have permissions to schedule this resource by sending a meeting request
These users can schedule automatically if the resource is available:
○ Everyone
◉ Select Users and Groups: Executives
These users can submit a request for manual approval if the resource is available:
○ Everyone
◉ Select Users and Groups: VIPs; Mark Arnold
These users can schedule automatically if the resource is available and submit a request for manual approval if the resource is unavailable:
○ Everyone
◉ Select Users and Groups: VIPs; Mark Arnold
For requests requiring approval:
  ☑ Always forward to delegates
  ☑ Always tentatively accept these requests

The final two sections of Resource Scheduling are the Resource Privacy Options and Response Message sections; these are shown in Figure 10.28. Resource Privacy Options settings define how the automatic responses will format responses to meeting requests and if the original resource schedule request meeting will be deleted or not.

FIGURE 10.28
Resource Privacy
Options and Response
Message options

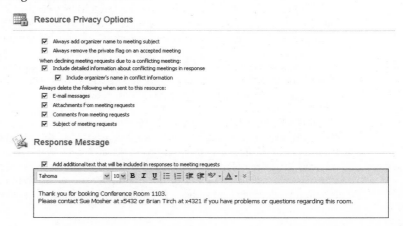

Resource Privacy Options

☑ Always add organizer name to meeting subject
☑ Always remove the private flag on an accepted meeting
When declining meeting requests due to a conflicting meeting:
☑ Include detailed information about conflicting meetings in response
  ☑ Include organizer's name in conflict information
Always delete the following when sent to this resource:
☑ E-mail messages
☑ Attachments from meeting requests
☑ Comments from meeting requests
☑ Subject of meeting requests

Response Message

☑ Add additional text that will be included in responses to meeting requests

| Tahoma | 10 | **B** *I* U̲ | ... |

Thank you for booking Conference Room 1103.
Please contact Sue Mosher at x5432 or Brian Tirch at x4321 if you have problems or questions regarding this room.

The Response Message section allows you to define a customized response that will be returned to users that request this resource. This can be useful in telling users who owns a particular resource or for sending back a reply as to the rules of usage for a resource.

We mentioned that you could define the resource properties in two ways; the second way is using the `Set-MailboxCalendarSettings` cmdlet. We have created Table 10.4 to describe the Outlook Web Access Resource Scheduling options and the corresponding parameters for the `Set-MailboxCalendarSettings` cmdlet. There will be EMS cmdlet parameters that are not available via the graphical user interface.

TABLE 10.4:   Resource Scheduling Parameters

FUNCTION	OWA SETTING	EMS CMDLET PARAMETERS
Process meeting requests automatically.	Automatically Process Meeting Requests and Cancellations	-AutomateBooking (default is $False).
Specify automatic processing options.		-AutomateProcessing
		Options:
		None—Disables all automatic processing
		AutoUpdate—Requests automatically processed by the Calendar Attendant on the server
		AutoAccept—Requests automatically processed by the mailbox.
Do not show reminders for meetings in the resource mailbox.	Disable Reminders	-DisableReminders (Set to $True or $False)
Specify a default reminder time for meeting requests.		-DefaultReminderTime
Specify from the present day the maximum booking window in which the resource can be booked. Default is 180 days.	Maximum Number of Days	-BookingWindowInDays
Specify if recurring meetings that continue to recur after maximum number of days will be rejected.		-EnforceSchedulingHorizon (Set to $True or $False)

(CONTINUED)

TABLE 10.4: Resource Scheduling Parameters *(CONTINUED)*

FUNCTION	OWA SETTING	EMS CMDLET PARAMETERS
Specify the maximum length of a meeting request. The default is 180 minutes.	Maximum Allowed Minutes	-MaximumDurationInMinutes
Specify that a resource can only be scheduled during working hours. These days and times are defined for each resource mailbox in the Calendar Options ➢ Calendar Work Week section of the OWA options.	Allow Scheduling Only During Working Hours	-ScheduleOnlyDuringWork Hours (Set to $True or $False)
Specifies if conflicts should be allowed.	Allow Conflicts	-AllowConflicts (Set to $True or $False)
Specify if recurring meetings will be allowed.	Allow Recurring Meetings	-AllowRecurringMeetings
If conflicts are allowed, specify the maximum number of conflicts that can be scheduled before a meeting request will be declined.	Allow Up to This Number of Individual Conflicts	-MaximumConflictInstances
If the number of meeting requests (for recurring meetings) conflicting with already scheduled meetings exceeds this percentage, decline the meeting requests.	Allow Up to This Percentage of Individual Conflicts	-ConflictPercentageAllowed
Display pending meeting requests as free in the Free and Busy times.		-TentativePendingApproval (Set to $True or $False)
Specify that the resource mailbox send organizer information when a meeting request is declined due to a conflict.		-OrganizerInfo (Set to $True or $False)
Define a list of users and mail-enabled groups that can book this resource automatically if it is available. This booking is done by sending a meeting request message.	These Users Can Schedule Automatically If the Resource Is Available	-BookInPolicy (Specifies list of users or groups allowed to automatically book. The AllBookInPolicy option must be set to False.)
		-AllBookInPolicy (If true, allows Everyone to automatically schedule meeting requests via a meeting request message.

TABLE 10.4:   Resource Scheduling Parameters *(CONTINUED)*

FUNCTION	OWA SETTING	EMS CMDLET PARAMETERS
Define a list of users or mail-enabled groups that can manually submit a request to schedule the room resource if it is available. This booking is done by sending a meeting request message.	These Users Can Submit a Request for Manual Approval If the Resource Is Available	`-RequestInPolicy` (Specifies a list of users or groups that are allowed to send meeting requests for the resource delegate to approve or decline.) `-AllRequestInPolicy` (If set to `True`, meeting requests can be sent to this mailbox by anyone. If set to `False`, the list of users or groups specified by the `-RequestInPolicy` list determines who can send meeting requests to this resource.)
Define a list of users or mail-enabled groups that can automatically schedule a room resource if the resource is available and submit a request for manual approval if the resource is already booked. This booking is done by sending a meeting request message.	These Users Can Schedule Automatically If the Resource Is Available and Submit a Request for Manual Approval If the Resource Is Unavailable	`-RequestOutOfPolicy` (Specifies users or groups that can have their schedule requests automatically approved if the resource is available and have the request approved manually if there is a conflict. The `-AllRequestOutOfPolicy` option must be set to `False` for this option to work.) `-AllRequestOutOfPolicy` (If set to `True`, meeting requests from everyone will be approved if the resource is available and sent to the resource mailbox delegate for approval if a conflict is occurs.)
Send approval requests to resource mailbox delegates if they require approval.	Always Forward to Delegates	`-ForwardRequestsToDelegates`
Accept schedule requests tentatively even if they require approval by the resource mailbox delegate.	Always Tentatively Accept These Requests	`-AddNewRequestsTentatively`
Accept schedule requests from senders outside of the Exchange organization.		`-ProcessExternalMeeting Messages`

(CONTINUED)

TABLE 10.4: Resource Scheduling Parameters *(CONTINUED)*

FUNCTION	OWA SETTING	EMS CMDLET PARAMETERS
Specify delegates of this resource.		-ResourceDelegates
Specify if organizer's name should be included on the meeting subject in the room resource mailbox.	Always Add Organizer Name to Meeting Subject	-AddOrganizerToSubject (Set to $True or $False)
Specify that the private flag is removed, if included, on accepted meetings.	Always Remove the Private Flag on Accepted Meeting	-RemovePrivateProperty (Set to $True or $False)
Specify if meeting request information should be included in message when a declined message is returned to the user.	Include Detailed Information about Conflicting Messages in Response	-EnableResponseDetails(Set to $True or $False)
Specify if the organizer's name should be included in a message when a meeting request is declined.	Include Organizer's Name in Conflict Information	-AddOrganizerToSubject (Set to $True or $False)
Automatically delete e-mail messages that are sent to the resource mailbox.	Always Delete the Following When Sent to This Resource: E-mail Messages	-DeleteNonCalendarItems (Set to $True or $False)
Automatically delete attachments from e-mail messages sent to the resource mailbox.	Always Delete the Following When Sent to This Resource: Attachments from Meeting Requests	-DeleteAttachments (Set to $True or $False)
Automatically delete comments from meeting request messages.	Always Delete the Following When Sent to This Resource: Comments from Meeting Requests	-DeleteComments (Set to $True or $False)
Automatically delete subject of meeting requests.	Always Delete the Following When Sent to This Resource: Subject of Meeting Requests	-DeleteSubject (Set to $True or $False)

Now that you have seen the settings and how you can implement them using Outlook Web Access, let's take a look at them from the EMS using the Get-MailboxCalendarSettings cmdlet:

```
Get-MailboxCalendarSettings "Conference Room 1103" | FL

TestFields                              : {BookInPolicyRecipients,
```

```
    BookInPolicy, RequestInPolicy, RequestOutOfPolicy,
RequestInPolicyRecipients, RequestOutOfPolicyRecipients}
AutomateProcessing                   : AutoUpdate
AllowConflicts                       : False
BookingWindowInDays                  : 180
MaximumDurationInMinutes             : 1440
AllowRecurringMeetings               : True
EnforceSchedulingHorizon             : True
ScheduleOnlyDuringWorkHours          : False
ConflictPercentageAllowed            : 0
MaximumConflictInstances             : 0
ForwardRequestsToDelegates           : True
DeleteAttachments                    : True
DeleteComments                       : True
RemovePrivateProperty                : True
DeleteSubject                        : True
DisableReminders                     : True
AddOrganizerToSubject                : True
DeleteNonCalendarItems               : True
TentativePendingApproval             : True
EnableResponseDetails                : True
OrganizerInfo                        : True
ResourceDelegates                    : {Simon Butler}
RequestOutOfPolicy                   :
AllRequestOutOfPolicy                : False
BookInPolicy                         :
AllBookInPolicy                      : True
RequestInPolicy                      :
AllRequestInPolicy                   : False
AddAdditionalResponse                : False
AdditionalResponse                   :
RemoveOldMeetingMessages             : True
AddNewRequestsTentatively            : True
ProcessExternalMeetingMessages       : False
DefaultReminderTime                  : 15
RemoveForwardedMeetingNotifications  : False
Identity                             : volcanosurfboards.com/Users/
Conference Room 1103
```

Moving Mailboxes

Moving mailboxes from one mailbox database to another is a pretty common task for most Exchange administrators. Often mailbox databases need to be "smoothed" out because too many large mailboxes are created on a single mailbox database. You may also need to decommission a server and thus move all of the mailboxes off of that server.

Mailboxes should usually be moved after a user's work hours. The mailbox can be moved while the user is working in it, but at the end of the move the user will be informed that they must close and reopen Outlook.

Consequently, we recommend that you move mailboxes during off-hours to minimize disruption to users; a user can leave Outlook open while the mailbox is being moved, though.

Mailbox move operations are certainly not instantaneous and can be quite lengthy depending on a number of factors, including bandwidth between servers, server speed, available RAM, and disk I/O. For typical servers on LAN-speed network segments, we estimate you can move from 500 MB per hour to 1.5GB per hour. Your results may vary. Depending on your Active Directory infrastructure and replication times, an Outlook Web Access user might not be able to reconnect to their mailbox for up to 15 minutes since the home mailbox attribute must replicate to all domain controllers.

As with all Exchange management tasks, you can perform move mailbox operations using the Exchange Management Console or the Exchange Management Shell.

MOVING MAILBOXES USING THE EXCHANGE MANAGEMENT CONSOLE

Mailboxes can be moved via the GUI using the Exchange Management Console (EMC). To move mailboxes using the EMC, open up the Recipient Configuration work center of the EMC and select the Mailboxes subcontainer. From within here, you can select one or more mailboxes and then select the Move Mailbox task from the Actions pane.

This launches the Move Mailbox Wizard. An experienced Exchange 2000/2003 administrator will recognize most all of the options in the wizard. The most important is found on the Introduction page (see Figure 10.29). From the Introduction page you define the destination for the mailboxes you are about to move. This includes the server, storage group, and mailbox database; you must select them in this order so that the drop-down lists display the appropriate destination storage groups and databases.

Once you have selected the destination mailbox database and clicked Next, the Move Options wizard page is displayed. On this screen you can specify whether or not to ignore corrupted messages and continue with the move mailbox operation.

Move Options
Specify how you would like to handle corrupted messages in a mailbox.

If corrupted messages are found:

○ Skip the mailbox.

● Skip the corrupted messages.

Maximum number of messages to skip: [2]

If the maximum number of corrupted messages is exceeded, the mailbox
will not be moved.

Normally mailboxes don't have corrupted messages (otherwise your telephone will be ring-ing), but occasionally the properties of a message gets corrupted. If a mailbox has more than the maximum number of corrupted messages specified, then that particular mailbox will be skipped.

FIGURE 10.29
Defining the server, storage group, and mailbox database

Move Mailbox

Introduction
Move Options
Move Schedule
Move Mailbox
Completion

Introduction
This wizard helps you move selected mailboxes to a different server or to a different mailbox database on the same server.

Specify the destination by selecting the target server, target storage group, and target mailbox database.

Server:
E2K7-BASE

Storage group:
SG-LAXMB01-15

Mailbox database:
MBDB-LAXMB01-15

Help   < Back   Next >   Cancel

On the next page of the wizard is the Move Schedule options. From the Move Schedule page you can define whether the move operation starts immediately or at some point in the future. The Cancel Tasks That Are Still Running After (Hours) option allows you to specify that mailboxes that have not yet been moved after the number of hours specified will not be processed. In the options shown in the following screen shot, we have selected that mailbox moves will not start until 8:00 in the evening and will run for a maximum of 10 hours (if not completed prior to this).

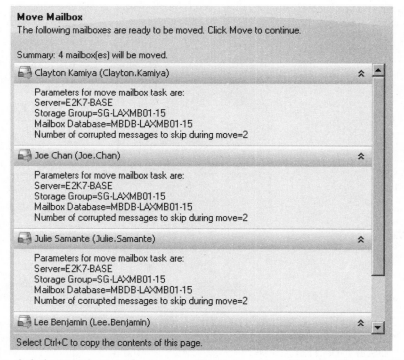

The next page is a confirmation page that allows you to review the mailboxes you are above to move as well as the destination server, storage group, and mailbox database. When you are confident you are moving all of the mailboxes you are supposed to move, you can click the Next button.

Once you click the Next button, the move mailbox operation will begin. The move mailbox task will move up to four mailboxes simultaneously. When moving mailboxes using the GUI, you see animated status bars indicating that the operation is still in progress as well as the elapsed time. An example of this is shown in Figure 10.30, where you can see completed mailbox moves as well as mailbox moves that are still in progress.

After all of the mailboxes have been moved, the final screen shows you a summary of which mailboxes were moved, the total elapsed time, and any other relevant statistics. As with many

FIGURE 10.30
Mailbox move
operations

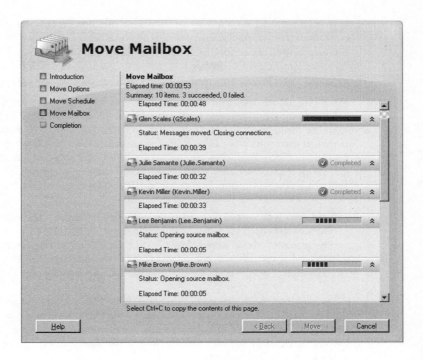

other wizards in the EMC, the actual Exchange Management Shell (EMS) command that was necessary to move the mailbox is included in the report. In the following screen capture we have collapsed a few of the trident controls so that you can see more of the summary page. Notice for mailbox David Elfassy the EMS cmdlet move-mailbox and the parameters that were used to move the mailbox.

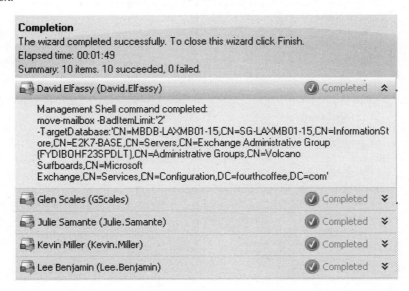

If you want to keep a copy of the move mailbox report, you can use the Ctrl + C keyboard combination to copy the information on the Completion page to the Clipboard. Once you are finished with the Completion page, just click Finish to close it.

MOVING MAILBOXES USING THE EXCHANGE MANAGEMENT SHELL

We have just showed you how easy it is to move mailboxes using the EMC; you just select the mailbox you want to move and click Next through the wizard to specify any other options, and then the EMC generates the necessary cmdlet to move the mailbox or mailboxes selected. In the previous example, one of the mailboxes moved was a mailbox for user David Elfassy. We selected that his mailbox should be moved to a mailbox database called MBDB-LAXMB01-15 in a storage group called SG-LAXMB01-15 and on a server called E2K7-BASE. The EMS generated the following command parameters for the `Move-Mailbox` cmdlet:

```
move-mailbox -BadItemLimit:'2' -TargetDatabase:'CN=MBDB-LAXMB01-15,
CN=SG-LAXMB01-15,CN=InformationStore,CN=E2K7-BASE,
CN=Servers,CN=Exchange Administrative Group (FYDIBOHF23SPDLT),
CN=Administrative Groups,CN=Volcano Surfboards,CN=Microsoft
Exchange,CN=Services,CN=Configuration,DC=fourthcoffee,DC=com'
```

Notice that the actual object that was to be moved was not included in the cmdlet; the way that the object information was passed to the `Move-Mailbox` cmdlet made this unnecessary. From the EMS, we could have shortened this command quite a bit if the target database name (MBDB-LAXMB01-15) was unique across the organization. We could have typed the following and seen the following output:

```
[MSH] C:\>Move-Mailbox david.elfassy -targetdatabase "mbdb-laxmb01-15"

Confirm
Are you sure you want to perform this action?
Moving mailbox: David Elfassy (David.Elfassy@volcanosurfboards.com) to
    Database:
E2K7-BASE\SG-LAXMB01-15\MBDB-LAXMB01-15. The operation can take a long
 time and the mailbox will be inaccessible until the move is complete [Y] Yes   [A]
Yes to All   [N] No   [L] No to All   [S] Suspend   [?] Help (default is
"Y"): y

Identity                        : fourthcoffee.com/Corporate/David Elfassy
DistinguishedName               : CN=David Elfassy,OU=Corporate,
DC=fourthcoffee,DC=com
DisplayName                     : David Elfassy
Alias                           : David.Elfassy
LegacyExchangeDN                : /o=Volcano Surfboards/ou=Exchange
Administrative Group (FYDIBOHF23SPDLT)/cn=Recipients/cn=David.Elfassy
PrimarySmtpAddress              : David.Elfassy@volcanosurfboards.com
SourceServer                    : E2K7-Base.fourthcoffee.com
```

```
SourceDatabase                       : E2K7-BASE\First Storage
   Group\Executives
SourceGlobalCatalog                  : E2K7-Base.fourthcoffee.com
TargetGlobalCatalog                  : E2K7-Base.fourthcoffee.com
TargetDomainController               : E2K7-Base.fourthcoffee.com
TargetMailbox                        :
TargetServer                         : E2K7-Base.fourthcoffee.com
TargetDatabase                       : E2K7-BASE\SG-LAXMB01-15\MBDB-LAXMB01-15
MailboxSize                          : 11KB
IsResourceMailbox                    : False
SIDUsedInMatch                       :
SMTPProxies                          :
SourceManager                        :
SourceDirectReports                  :
SourcePublicDelegates                :
SourcePublicDelegatesBL              :
MatchedTargetNTAccountDN             :
IsMatchedNTAccountMailboxEnabled     :
MatchedContactsDNList                :
TargetNTAccountDNToCreate            :
TargetManager                        :
TargetDirectReports                  :
TargetPublicDelegates                :
TargetPublicDelegatesBL              :
Options                              : Default
SourceForestCredential               :
TargetForestCredential               :
TargetFolder                         :
RsgMailboxGuid                       :
RsgMailboxLegacyExchangeDN           :
RsgMailboxDisplayName                :
RsgDatabaseGuid                      :
MoveType                             : IntraOrg
MoveStage                            : Completed
StartTime                            : 11/12/2006 4:02:41 PM
EndTime                              : 11/12/2006 4:03:03 PM
StatusCode                           : 0
StatusMessage                        : This mailbox has been moved to the
   target database.
```

If we had wanted to include the bad item count, we could have included the parameter
-BadItemLimit:'2' in the command. Notice that when we typed in the command, we had to
confirm that we wanted the mailbox to be moved. To avoid the confirmation prompt, we could
have included in the command line -Confirm:$False and the cmdlet would not have prompted
us. So that command line would look like this:

```
Move-Mailbox david.elfassy -TargetDatabase "mbdb-laxmb01-15"
-Confirm:$False -BadItemLimit:"2"
```

There are a few other tricks that may prove useful for you when you are using the Move-Mailbox cmdlet. Let's look at a couple of quick examples. In this first example, we want to move everyone that is a member of the Executives group to the mailbox database called Executives on the server E2K7MB01. We would type this command, which uses the Get-DistributionGroupMember cmdlet to enumerate the membership of the Executives group, and we pipe that output to the Move-Mailbox cmdlet:

```
Get-DistributionGroupMember "Executives" | Move-Mailbox
-TargetDatabase "E2K7MB01\Executives" -Confirm:$False
```

Another useful use of cmdlets would be to enumerate everyone whose mailbox is located on one mailbox database and then move them to another database. We need to use the Get-Mailbox cmdlet and narrow down the scope of the search using the Where cmdlet so that we only output the objects for mailboxes located on a specific database.

```
Get-Mailbox | Where {$_.database -like "E2K7-Base\VIP\VIP Mailboxes"}
| Move-Mailbox -TargetDatabase "Executives" -Confirm:$False
```

With a little creativity, you can probably figure out a number of other ways to accomplish this task or tasks similar to this.

Retrieving Mailbox Statistics

Frequently Exchange mailbox administrators need to run a report and list the amount of storage that each mailbox is consuming. With previous versions of Exchange, this information was available via the GUI, but now it is available via the EMS cmdlet Get-MailboxStatistics. Here is an example of using this cmdlet without any parameters:

```
[MSH] C:\>Get-MailboxStatistics

DisplayName               ItemCount   StorageLimitStatus   LastLogonTime
-----------               ---------   ------------------   -------------
Microsoft System Attendant   0            BelowLimit       11/11/2006 2:10:23 PM
Kevin Miller                 6                             10/24/2006 2:40:31 AM
Suriya Supatanasakul         3                             10/24/2006 2:40:31 AM
Micah Hoffmann               2            BelowLimit       10/24/2006 2:42:06 AM
Andy David                   2            BelowLimit       10/24/2006 2:40:30 AM
Jenn Long                   10            BelowLimit       10/24/2006 2:40:31 AM
SystemMailbox{F4A7C474-FE  402            BelowLimit
E5-46EA-A886-C1D8393E27F}
```

Not a real attractive report, is it? And this report includes all mailboxes, including the system mailbox and system attendant mailboxes. We will show you how to exclude these from the report as well as provide more useful information. There a few useful properties that are part of the objects that output when you use the Get-MailboxStatistcs cmdlet. These can be used to constrain the output that is sent to the screen (or a file) as well as the output if you redirect this information to a file. Table 10.5 shows some of the properties of the objects that are output when you use the Get-MailboxStatistcs cmdlet.

TABLE 10.5:   Properties of Objects Output Using Get-MailboxStatistics

PROPERTY	DESCRIPTION
DisplayName	Name of the mailbox.
ItemCount	Total number of items stored in the entire mailbox.
TotalItemSize	Total size of all of the items in the mailbox except for items in the deleted item cache.
TotalDeletedItemsSize	Total size of items that are in the deleted item cache.
StorageLimitStatus	Status of the mailbox storage limits; the limits you may see are as follows: – BelowLimit - Mailbox is below all limits. – IssueWarning - Mailbox storage is above the issue warning limit. – ProhibitSend - Mailbox is above the prohibit send limit. – MailboxDisabled - Mailbox is over the prohibit send and receive limit.
Database	Name of the database on which the mailbox is located in the format of *ServerName\StorageGroupName\DatabaseName*, such as E2K7MB01\VIP SG\VIP Mailboxes.
ServerName	Name of the mailbox server.
LastLogoffTime	Date and time of the last time someone logged off of the mailbox.
LastLogonTime	Date and time of the last time someone logged on to the mailbox.
LastLoggedOnUserAccount	Domain name and username of the last person to access the mailbox.
DisconnectDate	Date and time when the mailbox was deleted or disconnected.

So, perhaps we only want to look a mailbox report that includes the display name, total size of the mailbox, the total number of items, and the storage limit status. Further, we are going to include the where clause and filter out any mailboxes whose name contains the word *system*. The following example shows what this would look like:

```
Get-MailboxStatistics | where {$_.displayname -notlike "*System*"}
| ft displayname, @{expression={$_.totalitemsize.value.ToKB()};
width=20;label="Mailbox Size(kb)"},ItemCount,StorageLimitStatus

DisplayName          Mailbox Size(kb)     ItemCount StorageLimitStatus
-----------          ----------------     --------- ------------------
Lee Desmond                    331221          1410 IssueWarning
EQUIP - Panas...                   10             3 BelowLimit
```

```
Finance Journ...              3            1 BelowLimit
Elizabeth Owusu          958376        84325 MailboxDisabled
Damion Jones                 10            3 BelowLimit
Andy Schan                21468         3112 BelowLimit
Paul Robichaux                5            2 BelowLimit
David Elfassy            183714         8713 ProhibitSend
Conference Ro...            375           72 BelowLimit
Andy Webb                539985        47444 IssueWarning
Manfred Estrada           83837          163 BelowLimit
Devin Ganger               7548           94 BelowLimit
```

Did you notice that we threw in some new features of the PowerShell? This includes taking the output and reformatting it using the Expression feature. We can redirect the output to a text file using the > character and a filename:

```
C:\>Get-MailboxStatistics | where {$_.displayname -notlike "*Sys
tem*"} | ft displayname, @{expression={$_.totalitemsize.value.ToKB()};
width=20;label="Mailbox Size(kb)"},ItemCount,StorageLimitStatus
> c:\MailboxReport.txt
```

We could also pipe the output to either the Export-Csv or Export-Clixml cmdlet and send the data to a comma-separated value or XML file.

Deleting Mailboxes

Deleting mailboxes might not seem like such a complicated task until you look at the Actions pane once you have selected a mailbox in the Recipient Configuration work center. There are a couple of options with respect to deleting a mailbox, including simply disconnecting the mailbox from a user account, deleting both the account and the mailbox, and purging a previously deleted mailbox.

In the section of the Actions pane that reflects the mailbox that is currently selected in the results pane, you will see both a Disable and a Remove option.

Both the Remove and the Disable option will delete the mailbox; it's just how they go about doing it that is the difference.

DELETING THE MAILBOX BUT NOT THE USER

If you choose the Disable option, the mailbox is disconnected from the user account but the user account remains in Active Directory. This is the equivalent of using the EMS cmdlet `Disable-Mailbox`. For example, to remove a mailbox from an existing user, you could type this:

```
Disable-Mailbox damion.jones -Confirm:$False
```

All this does is to disconnect the mailbox from the user account; the user account remains in Active Directory. After the deleted mailbox recovery time expires, the mailbox will be permanently removed from the mailbox database.

DELETING BOTH THE USER AND THE MAILBOX

If you choose the Remove option, the mailbox is disconnected from the user account *and* the user account is deleted from the Active Directory. You can also accomplish this from the EMS using the `Remove-Mailbox` cmdlet. Here is an example:

```
Remove-Mailbox cheyne.manalo
```

This command will prompt you to ensure that you really want to remove the mailbox; you can avoid the confirmation prompt by including the `-Confirm:$False` parameter. If you want to delete the mailbox and the account and prevent the mailbox from being recovered, you can include the `-Permanent:$True` parameter. Here is another example that automatically confirms the deletion and permanently removes the mailbox:

```
Remove-Mailbox jonathan.long -Permanent:$True -Confirm:$False
```

PERMANENTLY PURGING A MAILBOX

By default, after the deleted mailbox recovery time has expired, the mailbox will be permanently purged from the mailbox database. If you have already deleted the mailbox and want to permanently purge the mailbox from the mailbox database, you can also do that, but it requires two lines. The first line is going to set a variable that retrieves the mailbox object for a mailbox whose display name is Martha Lanoza. The second line uses that variable along with the `MailboxGuid` property of that mailbox to remove that mailbox from the VIP Mailboxes database. Here are the two commands that would need to be executed:

```
$Temp = Get-MailboxStatistics | Where {$_.DisplayName -eq 'Martha Lanoza'}
Remove-Mailbox -Database "VIP Mailboxes" -StoreMailboxIdentity $Temp.MailboxGuid
```

This example assumes there would only be a single mailbox whose display name is Martha Lanoza and that there is only a single mailbox database named VIP Mailboxes. With a little creativity, you can permanently purge mailboxes in other ways, but this is a very basic EMS method of doing this.

Reconnecting a Deleted Mailbox

Exchange Server allows you to "undelete" a mailbox that you may have accidentally disconnected from a user account. The simplest way to do this is to use the EMC. In the Recipient Configuration work center you will find the Disconnected Mailbox subcontainer (shown in Figure 10.31).

Click the Connect to Server task in the Actions pane to see a mailbox listing; otherwise, deleted mailboxes may not show up in the results pane.

TIP

When you first view disconnected mailboxes, make sure you click the Connect to Server task on the Actions menu.

The disconnected mailbox listing you see in Figure 10.31 is a list of the mailboxes on the mailbox server to which we are currently connected. You can view other mailbox servers by choosing the Connect to Server option in the Actions pane.

FIGURE 10.31
Reconnecting mailboxes that have been deleted

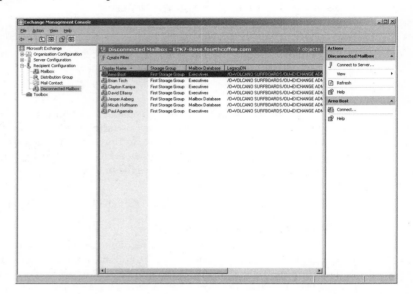

You could generate the same list using the `Get-MailboxStastics` command and filter based on viewing only objects whose `DisconnectDate` property contains data:

```
Get-MailboxStatistics | Where {$_.DisconnectDate -ne $null}
| FT DisplayName,DisconnectDate
```

```
DisplayName                          DisconnectDate
-----------                          --------------
Micah Hoffmann                       12/10/2006 3:13:37 AM
David Elfassy                        12/02/2006 3:13:23 AM
Paul Agamata                         11/25/2006 3:13:55 AM
Brian Tirch                          11/20/2006 3:13:47 AM
Clayton Kamiya                       11/16/2006 3:13:01 AM
```

If you have removed one of these mailboxes from its user account accidentally, you can still reconnect it back to a user account. In the EMC's Disconnected Mailbox subcontainer, highlight the mailbox that you want to reconnect and choose the Connect task on the Actions pane. This will launch the Connect Mailbox Wizard (shown in Figure 10.32); the main page of the Connect Mailbox Wizard looks a lot like the main page of the New Mailbox Wizard.

FIGURE 10.32
Starting the Connect Mailbox Wizard

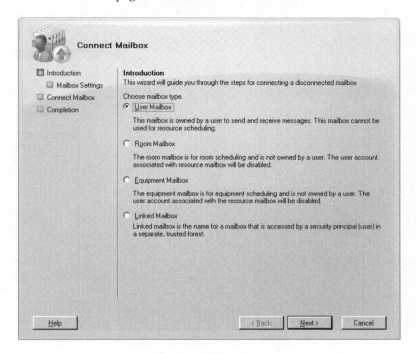

From the Connect Mailbox screen you are asked what type of mailbox you are connecting. Choices include a user mailbox, room resource mailbox, equipment resource mailbox, and a linked mailbox.

TIP

Deleted mailboxes can only be connected to a user account that does not have a mailbox already associated with it.

On the Mailbox Settings page of the Connect Mailbox Wizard (shown in Figure 10.33), you must select the user account to which you want to connect this mailbox. The user account must not already have a mailbox associated with it. There are two different ways that you can locate the user account. If you choose the Matching User radio button and then click the Browse button, the EMC will make its "best guess" at finding the right user account in the Active Directory.

If you choose the Existing User radio button and then click the Browse button, you will be presented with a browse list of all users in the Active Directory. This list will include users that have been mailbox-enabled and those that do not have mailboxes. If you select a user that already has a mailbox, you will see an error indicating that.

Regardless of whether you use the Matching User or the Existing User selection, the Exchange Alias value will be displayed and you can override it if necessary.

FIGURE 10.33
Assigning a deleted
mailbox to a user
account that does not
currently have a mailbox

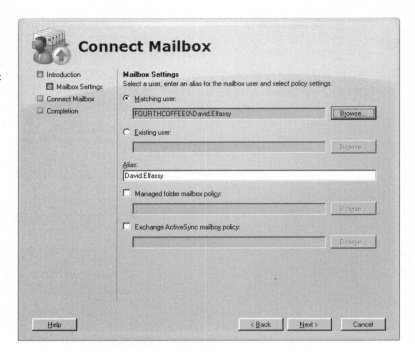

Note that you may also specify a managed folder mailbox policy and an ActiveSync policy for this mailbox. These can always be assigned later, but you have the option of re-assigning them at the time when you are reconnecting the mailbox to the account.

To do the same task using the EMS, you use the Connect-Mailbox cmdlet. This cmdlet takes as an identifier for the mailbox you are trying to connect the unique mailbox GUID, the display name, or the legacy Exchange distinguished name. The display name of the mailbox is by far the easiest to use. You also must provide the name of the database on which the mailbox is located and the user account to which you are connecting the account.

Before we do this, let's take a quick look at another iteration of the Get-MailboxStatistics cmdlet and how we can enumerate the information we need to reconnect a mailbox. In this output, we are displaying just the database name and the display name:

```
Get-MailboxStatistics | Where {$_.DisconnectDate -ne $null}
| FT DisplayName,Database

DisplayName                      Database
-----------                      --------
Aran Hoffmann                    E2K7-BASE\VIPs SG\VIPs
Paul Agamata                     E2K7-BASE\Execs SG\Executives
Donny Shimamoto                  E2K7-BASE\Execs SG\Executives
Clayton Kamiya                   E2K7-BASE\Execs SG\Executives
```

We have accidentally deleted user Clayton Kamiya's mailbox from the Executives mailbox database; this user also had a managed folder policy and an ActiveSync policy. To reconnect this user's mailbox to user account volcanosurf\Clayton.Kamiya, here is the command we would execute:

```
Connect-Mailbox "Clayton Kamiya" -Database:"Executives"
-User:"volcanosurf\Clayton.Kamiya" -Alias:"Clayton.Kamiya"
-MobileMailboxPolicy:"Standard User ActiveSync Policy"
-ManagedFolderMailboxPolicy:"All Employees"
```

Managing Mail-Enabled Groups

If your organization is like most organizations today, you make significant use of mail groups. You may refer to these as mail-enabled groups, distribution groups, or distribution lists. The official term for a mail group, though, is *mail-enabled group*. Like mail-enabled users, mail-enabled groups are Active Directory groups but they have been assigned mail properties. Within Active Directory, there are two basic types of groups:

◆ Security groups are groups that can be assigned permissions to resources or rights to perform certain tasks. Security groups can be mail-enabled and be used for addressing mail by Exchange Server recipients.

◆ Distribution groups are groups that are not security principals; they have no security identifier and thus cannot be assigned any rights or permissions. Distribution groups are intended for use with a mail system that integrates with Active Directory, such as Exchange Server. There is a subset of distribution groups called a query-based distribution groups (QBDGs); a QBDG's membership list is dynamic based on some criteria the administrator defines.

When you create a new group using the Active Directory Users and Computers interface, you will also notice that you must provide a scope for the group in addition to defining the group type.

All groups that will be utilized by Exchange 2007 must be set to the Universal scope. This tells Active Directory that the membership list attribute for that group should be replicated to all global catalog servers in the organization. In previous versions of Exchange, you could mail-enable a global or domain local group. However, this could cause mail delivery problems in organizations that have multiple Active Directory domains.

TIP

Only universal groups should be used as mail-enabled groups in Exchange 2007.

EXCHANGE 2007 AND GLOBAL OR DOMAIN LOCAL GROUPS

By default, the only type of group that you can mail-enable using the Exchange Management Console is a universal group. However, if you have migrated from Exchange 2000/2003, you may have domain local or global groups that have been mail-enabled previously. The recipient type is a MailEnabledNonUniversalGroup. We recommend that you convert each of these domain local and global groups to a universal group. This will ensure that you do not have group expansion problems in multi-domain environments.

Creating and Managing Mail-Enabled Groups

Let's first go through the process of defining a mail-enabled group and look at the steps necessary to do so. Groups can be created or mail-enabled using the EMC and the EMS command shell.

One consideration you think about when creating group names is that you should consider a standard for mail-enabled group display names. This will allow them to all be grouped together in the global address list.

USING THE EXCHANGE MANAGEMENT CONSOLE TO MANAGE GROUPS

The simplest way to create and manage mail-enabled groups is to use the EMC graphical interface. Previously, in Active Directory, we created a group called IT Operations; the group's scope is universal and the type is a security group. However, just using Active Directory Users and Computers will not define any mail attributes.

Creating Mail-Enabled Groups

To create a mail-enabled, open the EMC, navigate to the Recipient Configuration work center, and then find the Distribution Group subcontainer. Click the New Distribution Group task in the Actions pane to launch the New Distribution Group Wizard. The first screen in the wizard is the Introduction page, which prompts you to either create a new group or choose an existing group.

Introduction
This wizard will guide you through the steps for creating a new distribution group or mail-enable an existing group.

Create a Distribution Group for:
- ○ New group
- ● Existing group

IT Operations [Browse...]

Since the group we want to mail-enable is already in the Active Directory, choose the Existing Group radio button and then click the Browse button to locate and select the group. The only group types that will appear in the Select Group dialog box will be groups that are universal groups and have not already been mail-enabled.

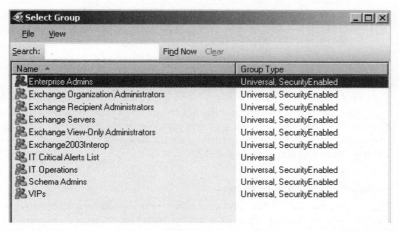

Once you have clicked Next on the Introduction page, the next page you see is the Group Information page. The Group Information page will ask you to provide the display name for the group as well as the alias. By default, the alias is used to define the SMTP e-mail address for the group and should not have any spaces in it.

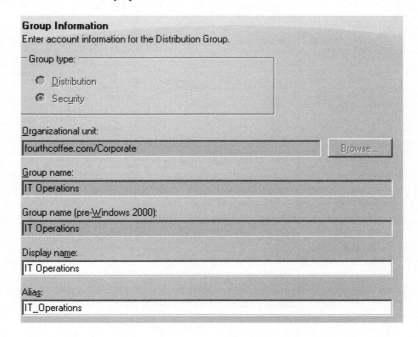

When you click Next on the Group Information page, you will see the confirmation page that allows you to verify the actions you are about to take. When you are sure that you have defined everything you need to define, you can click the New button and the group you have selected will be mail-enabled.

The resulting EMS command that performed the action is as follows:

```
Enable-DistributionGroup -Identity:'fourthcoffee.com/Corporate/IT Operations'
-DisplayName:'IT Operations' -Alias:'IT_Operations'
```

The New Distribution Group Wizard can also be used to create new mail-enabled groups as well as to mail-enable existing ones. If you choose to create a new group on the Introduction page, then you have a few additional pieces of information you must provide on the Group Information page, including the group type (distribution or security), the OU in which the group will be created, the group's name, the group's pre–Windows 2000 name, the display name, and the alias. The EMS command that is executed uses the `New-DistributionGroup` cmdlet rather than the `Enable-DistributionGroup` cmdlet.

Managing Mail-Enabled Groups

There are some additional properties that you should be aware of when you are creating mail-enabled groups. Let's start with the Mail Flow Settings property page; on the Mail Flow Settings property page, there are two different components you can configure: Message Size Restrictions and Message Delivery Restrictions. If you select the Message Size Restrictions option and click the Properties button, you will see the Message Size Restrictions dialog box. Notice that we have restricted the maximum message size for this particular group to 100KB; this can help prevent misuse of distribution groups or the accidental distribution of large files.

The Message Delivery Restrictions dialog box (shown in Figure 10.34) has a little more information. If you have looked at the message delivery restrictions for a single mailbox, you are already familiar with these settings and concepts. In the example in Figure 10.34, we have restricted who is allowed to send mail to this group. You can specify individuals and other groups. We recommend you always restrict who is allowed to send mail to large groups or groups that contain VIPs. This will help prevent accidents and keep unwanted mail content from your VIPs.

You may also note that there is a Require That All Senders Are Authenticated check box. For mail-enabled groups, this box is checked by default. We recommend that you keep it set this way; after all, you probably don't want spammers or external sales people to start sending mail to your `Everyone@company.com` or `Executives@company.com` addresses.

The E-Mail Addresses property page (Figure 10.35) shows the e-mail addresses that can be used to address a message to the group. From here, you can edit or add e-mail addresses that are used for a particular group.

FIGURE 10.34
A distribution group's
Message Delivery
Restrictions dialog box

If a distribution list is used entirely within your organization, the Reply To address will not be particularly important. However, if you use lists both internally and externally, then the reply address is the address that will be seen externally. For example, if someone sends messages to your HelpDesk@company.com address and then your internal users reply to that message and courtesy copy (Cc) the distribution group, then what ever address is the reply to address is what is seen externally.

The final property page we want to take a look at is the Advanced property page. There are several properties here that you should be aware of, and you should know what they may mean to your organization and users. The Advanced property page is shown in Figure 10.36. The first property is the Simple Display Name field. By default, when a message is sent from a recipient, the recipient's display name is included; in some organizations the display name can be quite long. Exchange also allows non-ASCII characters (Unicode characters) to be included in the display name. If you are connecting to older mail systems that do not support long display names or Unicode characters, you can include a simple display name that consists only of ASCII characters.

Message *expansion* is the process of enumerating the members of a mail-enabled group and figuring out where each member is either within your organization or externally. Expansion of large mail-enabled groups can be a pretty intensive process for a Hub Transport server as well as the Active Directory global catalog server that it is using.

FIGURE 10.35
E-mail address
properties of a
mail-enabled group

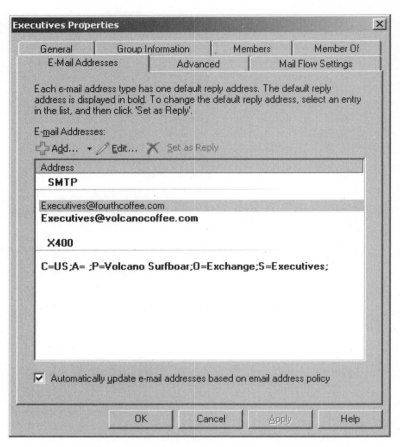

The Expansion Server drop-down list provides you with a listing of all of the Hub Transport servers in your organization. By default, Expansion Server is set to Any Server in the Organization. This means that the first Exchange Hub Transport server that receives the message is either responsible for expanding the mail-enabled group or sending it on to another Hub Transport server to expand the group. In some environments, you may want to manually specify which Hub Transport server handles expansion.

An example of this might be a mail-enabled group called Executives; you know that all members of the Executives group are in the headquarters office and thus you could designate a Hub Transport server in the headquarters office to be responsible for expansion. Unfortunately, if that Hub Transport server is down (or taken offline permanently), there is no fault tolerance in manual expansion configuration. We recommend that you keep the default settings and allow Exchange to perform manual expansion.

TIP

We recommend that you avoid using expansion servers. Allow Exchange to determine the appropriate place to expand the group's membership.

FIGURE 10.36
Advanced properties of
a mail-enabled group

The Hide Group from Exchange Address Lists check box (unchecked by default) allows you to prevent a mail-enabled group from being displayed in the address lists. This might be useful for specialized groups that are used just for mail distribution by an automated system or for users that know the SMTP address.

The Send Out-of-Office Message to Originator check box allows you to specify if an out-of-office message will be sent to the sender of a message if someone's out-of-office rule is enabled. This option is unchecked by default. For small or departmental mail-enabled groups, it might be useful to turn it on, but for large or company-wide distribution groups, you should probably leave this disabled.

If messages are not properly delivered to the intended recipients of a message sent to a mail-enabled group, you can control how the delivery reports are generated. There are three options:

◆ Send Delivery Reports to Group Manager will send the delivery reports to the person listed as the manager on the group's properties.

◆ Send Delivery Reports to Message Originator sends the delivery report back to the message sender.

◆ Do Not Send Delivery Reports prevents delivery reports from being sent to anyone.

Creating Dynamic Distribution Groups

Do you have a problem keeping your distribution groups up-to-date? Dynamic distribution groups (DDGs) may be the answer you have been looking for. Mail is sent to users in a DDG based on one or more criteria, such as organizational unit, city, department, and so on. As a user's Active Directory properties are changed or updated, the DDG membership changes automatically.

DDGs are created a little differently than a regular mail-enabled group since you have to define the filter settings and the conditions of the group. In the Distribution Group subcontainer of the Recipient Configuration work center, you can launch the New Dynamic Distribution Group Wizard by clicking the New Dynamic Distribution Group task in the Actions pane. The Introduction page of the wizard shows some typical information required for creating a new group object. This page requires that you specify the organizational unit in which you want the object created, the display name (Name), and the Exchange alias of the group.

Introduction
This wizard guides you through the steps for creating a new dynamic distribution group.

Organizational unit:

    fourthcoffee.com/Corporate   Browse...

Name:

    Everyone in Honolulu

Alias:

    EveryoneinHonolulu

Once you have specified the information necessary on the Introduction page, click Next. The next page, Filter Settings, allows you to specify which recipient container (or the entire domain) you want to apply to the filter and which types of recipients.

Filter Settings
Configure the filter that is used to select recipients for this dynamic distribution group.

Select the recipient container where you want to apply this filter.

    fourthcoffee.com/Corporate   Browse

Include these recipient types:

○ All recipients types

⦿ The following specific types:

   ☑ Users with Exchange mailboxes

   ☑ Users with external e-mail addresses

   ☐ Resource mailboxes

   ☐ Contacts with external e-mail addresses

   ☑ Mail-enabled groups

The following recipient types can be included in the filter settings:

◆ All types of recipients

◆ Mailbox-enabled user accounts (Users with Exchange Mailboxes)

◆ Mail-enabled user accounts (Users with External E-mail Addresses)

◆ Resource mailboxes (Room and equipment)

◆ Contacts with external e-mail addresses

◆ Mail-enabled groups

After selecting the recipient type and OU scope for the DDG and clicking Next, you will be able to further refine the scope of the group membership on the Conditions page. In the example shown in Figure 10.37, we have selected all users whose state or province is Hawaii.

FIGURE 10.37
Narrowing the membership of a dynamic distribution group

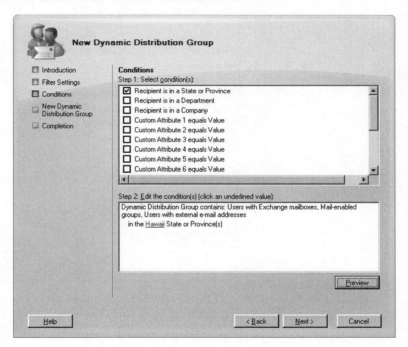

The Conditions page of the DDG allows you to specify the following attributes for inclusion in the DDG:

◆ State or province

◆ Department

◆ Company

◆ Custom attribute 1 through 15

Using DDGs will help emphasize the importance of having accurate information in Active Directory. Looking back to the example in Figure 10.37, when the account was created, if there were users who misspelled their state name or used an abbreviation rather than spelling it out, the DDG would not reflect everyone we wanted it to reflect.

The Preview button on the Conditions property page is helpful in confirming that your scope and conditions are defined properly. By clicking this button, you will see the Dynamic Distribution Group Preview dialog box. From here, you should verify that the membership appears to be what you expected.

The next screen after the Conditions screen is the New Dynamic Distribution Group screen where you confirm the configuration properties. When you are sure that the properties are correct, click the New button. As with most wizards in the EMC, the Completion screen will include the EMS command that was executed:

```
New-DynamicDistributionGroup -Name 'Everyone in Honolulu'
-IncludedRecipients 'MailboxUsers, MailGroups, MailUsers'
-ConditionalStateOrProvince 'Hawaii' -OrganizationalUnit
'fourthcoffee.com/Corporate' -Alias 'EveryoneinHonolulu'
-RecipientContainer 'fourthcoffee.com/Corporate'
```

For DDGs that are already created, you can edit or redefine the conditions and the scope of the group on the Filter and Conditions property pages. Examples of these are shown in Figure 10.38.

FIGURE 10.38
Dynamic
distribution group Filter
and Conditions property
pages

USING THE EXCHANGE MANAGEMENT SHELL TO MANAGE GROUPS

If you are just getting started with Exchange 2007 and the EMS, then managing groups is going to be a little tougher using the EMS than it will be if you use the EMC. However, we want to review the cmdlets that are available for managing and manipulating mail-enabled groups so that as you learn more about the EMS, you will have these cmdlets in your management arsenal. Table 10.6 lists the EMS cmdlets that you can use to manage groups and mail-enabled groups.

Creating Distribution Groups Using the EMS

For our purposes in this chapter, we are going to focus on only a few of the cmdlets listed in Table 10.6 and some of the more common properties that can be used with them. The best way to illustrate them is to use some examples. In the first example, let's say that we already have a universal group in the Corporate OU in Active Directory. The group is called Raptor Pilots.

Since the group already exists in the Active Directory, you'll use the Enable-DistributionGroup cmdlet. You need to assign the group an Exchange alias (the –Alias property) and you need to assign it a display name (-DisplayName). The following is an example of a command that would accomplish this:

```
Enable-DistributionGroup "Raptor Pilots" -DisplayName:"Raptor Pilots" -
Alias:"raptorpilots"
```

You could have accomplished the exact same thing (provided the group name Raptor Pilots is unique) by removing the domain and the -Identity parameter and typing this:

```
Enable-DistributionGroup "Raptor Pilots" -DisplayName:"Raptor Pilots" -
    Alias:"raptorpilots"
```

If the group did not exist in Active Directory and you wanted to create it in addition to mail-enabling it, you could have used the New-DistributionGroup cmdlet. This example would create

TABLE 10.6:   EMS and PowerShell Cmdlets for Group Management

CMDLET	FUNCTION
Get-Group	Retrieves information about all Active Directory groups. This is a built-in PowerShell cmdlet; it is not added with the EMS.
Set-Group	Sets information about an Active Directory group; this will work for any Active Directory group, not just mail-enabled ones. This is a built-in PowerShell cmdlet; it is not added with the EMS.
Get-DistributionGroup	Retrieves information related to mail-enabled groups.
Set-DistributionGroup	Sets properties of mail-enabled groups.
New-DistributionGroup	Creates a new group in Active Directory and mail-enables that group.
Enable-DistributionGroup	Mail-enables an existing group that was previously created in Active Directory.
Disable-DistributionGroup	Removes mail attributes from a mail-enabled group but does not remove the group from the Active Directory.
Remove-DistributionGroup	Deletes the mail attributes of a mail-enabled group and removes the group from the Active Directory.
Get-DistributionGroup Member	Retrieves membership list information from a mail-enabled group.
Add-DistributionGroup Member	Adds members to a mail-enabled group.
Remove-DistributionGroup Member	Removes members from a mail-enabled group.
Get-DynamicDistribution Group	Retrieves information about a dynamic distribution group.
Set-DynamicDistribution Group	Sets properties for dynamic distribution groups.
New-DynamicDistribution Group	Creates a new dynamic distribution group.
Remove-DynamicDistribution Group	Removes mail properties from a dynamic distribution group and deletes the group from the Active Directory.

the Raptor Pilots group in the Corporate OU; the -OrganizationalUnit properties is required. Notice that the -SamAccountName property is required if the group will be a security group.:

```
new-DistributionGroup -Name:'Raptor Pilots' -Type:'Distribution'
-OrganizationalUnit:'fourthcoffee.com/Corporate'
-SamAccountName:'RaptorPilots' -DisplayName:'Raptor Pilots'
-Alias:'Raptor Pilots'
```

To add members to that group, you use the Add-DistributionGroupMember cmdlet. Conversely, you can use the Remove-DistributionGroupMember cmdlet to remove members. For example, if you want to add user Elizabeth.Owusu to this group, you would type this:

```
Add-DistributionGroupMember "Raptor Pilots" -Member "elizabeth.owusu"
```

To enumerate the members of this group, you would use the Get-DistributionListMember cmdlet. Here is an example and the resulting output:

```
[PS] C:\>Get-DistributionGroupMember "raptor pilots"

Name                                RecipientType
----                                -------------
Jim McBee                           UserMailbox
Elizabeth Owusu                     UserMailbox
Clayton Kamiya                      UserMailbox
```

There are a lot of properties that you can set for a mail-enabled group, as you probably recall from seeing what you can set through the graphical user interface. To update properties of a group from the EMS, you use the Set-DistributionGroup cmdlet. Table 10.7 lists some of the more common properties that you can define for a mail-enabled group.

TABLE 10.7: Common Mail-Enabled Group Properties

PROPERTY	FUNCTION
Alias	Sets the Exchange alias for the group. By default, the alias is used when SMTP addresses are generated.
CustomAttribute1 through CustomAttribute15	Sets 1 of the 15 custom attributes (aka extension attributes).
DisplayName	Sets the display name of the mail-enabled group; the display name is what is visible in address lists.
HiddenFromAddressLists Enabled	Sets whether or not the group will be displayed in address lists. The default is that the objects are visible. You can set this to $True and it will hide the lists.
MaxReceiveSize	Sets the maximum size message that can be sent to the group.

Finally, if you no longer need this group, you can use Remove-Group to get rid of it completely (including the group object in Active Directory) or Disable-Group to simply remove the mail attributes from it.

You can also view the group's properties using the EMS cmdlet Get-DistributionGroup. This cmdlet lets you view the properties of the group. Many of these you can modify using the

Set-DistributionGroup cmdlet. Here is an example of viewing a mail-enabled universal group:

```
Get-DistributionGroup "Executives" | FL

GroupType                         : Universal
SamAccountName                    : Executives
ExpansionServer                   : /o=Volcano Surfboards/ou=Exchange
  Administrative
Group(FYDIBOHF23SPDLT)/cn=Configuration/cn=Servers/cn=HNLEX03
ReportToManagerEnabled            : False
ReportToOriginatorEnabled         : True
SendOofMessageToOriginatorEnabled : False
AcceptMessagesOnlyFrom            : {}
AcceptMessagesOnlyFromDLMembers   : {}
AddressListMembership             : {Default Global Address List, All Groups}
Alias                             : Executives
OrganizationalUnit                : volcanosurfboards.com/Users
CustomAttribute1                  :
CustomAttribute10                 :
CustomAttribute11                 :
CustomAttribute12                 :
CustomAttribute13                 :
CustomAttribute14                 :
CustomAttribute15                 :
CustomAttribute2                  :
CustomAttribute3                  :
CustomAttribute4                  :
CustomAttribute5                  :
CustomAttribute6                  :
CustomAttribute7                  :
CustomAttribute8                  :
CustomAttribute9                  :
DisplayName                       : Executives
EmailAddresses                    :
    {smtp:Executives@volcanosurfboards.com,
     smtp:Executives@research.somorita.com,
  smtp:Executives@directory-update.com,
  X400:C=US;A= ;P=Volcano Surfboar;O=Exchange;S=Executives;,
   SMTP:Executives@somorita.com}
GrantSendOnBehalfTo               : {}
HiddenFromAddressListsEnabled     : False
LegacyExchangeDN                  : /o=Volcano Surfboards/ou=First
    Administrative Group/cn=Recipients/cn=Executives
MaxSendSize                       : unlimited
MaxReceiveSize                    : unlimited
PoliciesIncluded                  : {{5AB9DF03-4F43-491F-B77A-1D5DFD5E3410},
{26491CFC-9E50-4857-861B-0CB8DF22B5D7}}
```

```
PoliciesExcluded                       : {}
EmailAddressPolicyEnabled              : True
PrimarySmtpAddress                     : Executives@somorita.com
RecipientType                          : MailUniversalDistributionGroup
RecipientTypeDetails                   : MailUniversalDistributionGroup
RejectMessagesFrom                     : {}
RejectMessagesFromDLMembers            : {}
RequireSenderAuthenticationEnabled     : False
SimpleDisplayName                      :
UMDtmfMap                              : {}
WindowsEmailAddress                    : Executives@somorita.com
IsValid                                : True
OriginatingServer                      : HNLDC01.volcanosurfboards.com
ExchangeVersion                        : 0.1 (8.0.535.0)
Name                                   : Executives
DistinguishedName                      : CN=Executives,CN=Users,
DC=volcanosurfboard,DC=com
Identity                               : volcanosurfboards.com/Users/Executives
Guid                                   : 801ea663-4763-44f7-bb21-54a297918cf0
ObjectCategory                         : volcanosurfboards.com/Configuration/
Schema/Group
ObjectClass                            : {top, group}
WhenChanged                            : 12/9/2006 12:41:21 PM
WhenCreated                            : 11/27/2006 8:38:44 AM
```

Creating Dynamic Distribution Groups Using the EMS

Let's now look at an example where we create and manage a dynamic distribution group using the EMS. Let's say that we have a group we need to create called Everyone who's on the West Coast and consists of just mailbox-enabled users. We want to create the Active Directory object in the fourthcoffee.com domain and in the Corporate organizational unit. Further, let's say that the maximum receive size should be only 75KB.

To create this DDG, you would use the following cmdlet:

```
New-DynamicDistributionGroup -Name "Everyone on the West Coast"
-IncludedRecipients 'MailboxUsers'
-ConditionalStateOrProvince 'California, Oregon, Washington'
-OrganizationalUnit 'fourthcoffee.com/Corporate'
-Alias 'EveryoneOnWestCoast'
-RecipientContainer 'fourthcoffee.com/Corporate'
```

After you get the group created, you have to use the Set-DynamicDistributionGroup cmdlet to update the maximum receive message size like so:

```
New-DynamicDistributionGroup -Name "Everyone on the West Coast"
-MaxReceiveSize 75KB
```

Dynamic distribution groups have a few additional property types that can be viewed using the EMS. Here is the output of the EMS and some of the additional properties that are found when using a dynamic distribution group:

```
Get-DynamicDistributionGroup "Everyone in Organization"
| FL Name,*Recipient*,Conditional*

Name                      : Everyone in Organization
RecipientContainer        : volcanosurfboards.com/Somorita Surfboards
RecipientFilter           :
LdapRecipientFilter       : (&(!cn=SystemMailbox{*})
(& (mailnickname=*) (|(&(objectCategory=person)(objectClass=user)(!(homeMDB=*))
(!(msExchHomeServerName=*)))(&(objectCategory=person)
(objectClass=user)(|(homeMDB=*)(msExchHomeServerName=*))) )))
IncludedRecipients        :
RecipientFilterType       : Legacy
RecipientType             : DynamicDistributionGroup
RecipientTypeDetails      : DynamicDistributionGroup
ConditionalDepartment     :
ConditionalCompany        :
ConditionalStateOrProvince :
ConditionalCustomAttribute1  :
ConditionalCustomAttribute2  :
ConditionalCustomAttribute3  :
ConditionalCustomAttribute4  :
ConditionalCustomAttribute5  :
ConditionalCustomAttribute6  :
ConditionalCustomAttribute7  :
ConditionalCustomAttribute8  :
ConditionalCustomAttribute9  :
ConditionalCustomAttribute10 :
ConditionalCustomAttribute11 :
ConditionalCustomAttribute12 :
ConditionalCustomAttribute13 :
ConditionalCustomAttribute14 :
ConditionalCustomAttribute15 :
```

Managing Contacts

Many organizations like to have the contacts that their users use frequently located in their address lists rather than having users add them to their individual contacts folders. This is the intention of the mail-enabled contact, or what we called in Exchange 5.5 and earlier a custom recipient. Mail-enabled contacts appear in your organization's address lists, but the contact directs their e-mail to an external mail system. Almost always these external contact's e-mail addresses are SMTP, so we are going to limit our discussion to that type of contact.

A contact object can be created in Active Directory, but it will not be mail-enabled and thus will not appear in the Exchange address lists. This is contrary to the way this was done in Exchange 2000/2003 where you could mail-enable a contact using the Active Directory Users and Computers extensions.

Creating a contact object in Active Directory is really simple and requires minimal information; you can simply create a new contact and specify the contact's name information.

However, you may notice that there was no e-mail address information that you provided when you created a contact in Active Directory. If you look at the contact's information (shown in Figure 10.39), you will see an e-mail property, but Exchange will not include the contact information in the address lists with just this information populated.

To properly mail-enable a contact for use with Exchange, you must use the EMC or the EMS tools.

Managing Mail-Enabled Contacts Using the Exchange Management Console

Let's start by examining how we would create and manage a mail-enabled contact using the EMC. In the Recipient Configuration work center of the EMC you will find the Mail Contact subcontainer. If you highlight this container, you will see two new tasks on the Actions pane. These are the New Mail Contact and the New Mail User tasks.

FIGURE 10.39
Contact information in
the Active Directory

The mail contact is an object that appears in the Active Directory and Exchange address lists but is not a security principal. You cannot put the mail contact into any security groups and assign it any permissions since it does not have a security identifier. This type of contact is useful when you are enabling contacts that will appear in your address lists but never need any sort of permissions in your organization.

The mail user is a user account in your organization but not one for which you host a mailbox. An example of this might be if you need to create a user account for an accounting auditor that will be working at one of your workstations for a few months; you want that person to appear in your Exchange address lists, but their mailbox is hosted somewhere else. This is also called a mail-enabled user. The easiest way to think of this is that you are *not* responsible for a mail-enabled user's mail storage, but you are responsible for a mailbox-enabled user's e-mail storage. The mailbox-enabled user is the type of mailbox we were covering earlier in this chapter.

Let's look at creating a mail-enabled contact. Simply click the New Mail Contact selection in the Actions pane to launch the New Mail Contact Wizard. The Introduction screen asks you if you want to create a new contact or mail-enable an existing contact in the Active Directory. In this example, we will mail-enable an existing contact, so choose the Existing Contact radio button and then click the Browse button to locate this contact in the Active Directory. On the next page (the Contact Information page), all you really have to provide is the external e-mail address. You cannot proceed if the object does not have an external e-mail address.

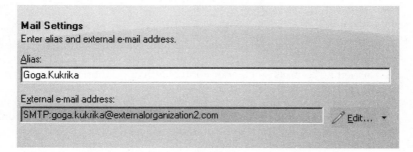

Contact Information

Enter the account information that is required to create a new mail contact or to mail-enable an existing mail contact.

O̲rganizational unit:

fourthcoffee.com/Corporate

Browse...

F̲irst name:

Andrew

Initial̲s:

Last name:

Riehemann

N̲ame:

Andrew Riehemann

A̲lias:

AndrewRiehemann

E̲xternal e-mail address:

SMTP:andrew.riehemann@externalorganization.com

⁄ E̲dit... ▾

After you confirm that this is what you want to do, the Completion screen will show you the EMS command that was used to enable this object:

```
Enable-MailContact -Identity 'fourthcoffee.com/Corporate/Andrew Riehemann'
-ExternalEmailAddress 'SMTP:andrew.riehemann@externalorganization.com'
-Alias 'AndrewRiehemann'
```

Before we go on to look at the mail-related properties of a contact, let's look at the creation of a mail-enabled user. In a similar example, you already have created an existing user account in the Active Directory. You run the New Mail User Wizard and select an existing user. On the Mail Settings property page, all you need to specify is the External E-mail Address properties.

Mail Settings

Enter alias and external e-mail address.

A̲lias:

Goga.Kukrika

E̲xternal e-mail address:

SMTP:goga.kukrika@externalorganization2.com

⁄ E̲dit... ▾

Once you confirm that the information is correct and click the New button, the command will complete and the Completion page will show the EMS command that was used to create the object:

```
Enable-MailUser -Identity 'fourthcoffee.com/Corporate/Goga Kukrika'
-Alias 'Goga.Kukrika'
-ExternalEmailAddress 'SMTP:goga.kukrika@externalorganization2.com'
```

With respect to the properties of a mail-enabled contact or a mail-enabled user, there is little that you have not already seen in this chapter, so we won't bore you with a lot of repetition. The General property page of the object does have something you may not have seen yet, though. Notice in Figure 10.40 that there is a Use MAPI Rich Text Format drop-down list.

FIGURE 10.40
Contact object's General properties

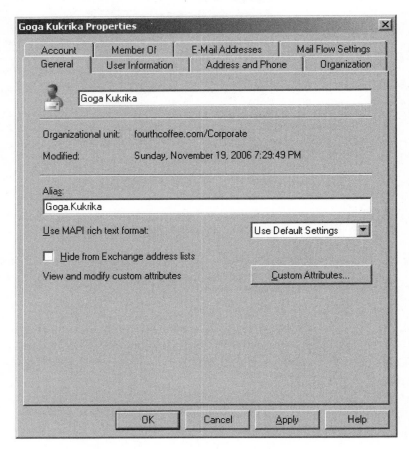

This setting controls whether or not the Exchange Hub Transport server will convert the message to a MIME or UUENCODE message when it leaves your organization. By default, all mail leaving your organization is converted into an Internet-standards-based format; this is almost always MIME. In some cases, this may strip out some formatting or features that users who use Word as their e-mail editor have put into the message. For just any old recipient on the Internet, this is fine because there is no guarantee that they have a mail client that can read those messages. However, if you know for sure that the recipient will have a mail reader on the other side that is capable of reading a rich-text formatted message (Outlook, for example), then you can send the message to the recipient in that format. You have three possible settings for this drop-down list.

◆ Use Default Settings means that the message will be sent this way if the user specified that this recipient should receive mail in rich text formatting in their address book or if you have defined Remote Domains settings for your Hub Transport servers.

◆ Always means that regardless of the user's address book settings, if the message is in rich text formatting it will be sent to this recipient.

◆ Never means that regardless of the user's address book settings, the message will always be converted to an Internet-standards message.

If someone sends a rich-text message and the recipient is not able to read it, they will see attachments named winmail.dat or a MIME attachment called application/tnef.

Managing Mail-Enabled Contacts Using the Exchange Management Shell

Once you get proficient at the EMC, as with many other tasks, you may want to try your hand at creating mail-enabled contacts or mail-enabled users from the EMS instead of the GUI. Table 10.8 shows the cmdlets that can be used to manipulate mail-enabled contacts and users.

TABLE 10.8: Exchange Management Shell Cmdlets for Mail-Enabled Contacts and Users

CMDLET	EXPLANATION
New-MailContact	Creates a new contact in Active Directory and mail-enables that contact
Enable-MailContact	Mail-enables a previously existing contact
Set-MailContact	Sets mail properties for a mail-enabled contact
Get-MailContact	Retrieves properties of a mail-enabled contact
Remove-MailContact	Removes the mail properties from a contact and deletes that contact from the Active Directory
Disable-MailContact	Removes the mail properties from a contact
New-MailUser	Creates a new user in Active Directory and mail-enables that user
Enable-MailUser	Mail-enables a previously existing user
Set-MailUser	Sets mail properties for a mail-enabled user
Get-MailUser	Retrieves properties of a mail-enabled user
Remove-MailUser	Removes the mail properties from a user and deletes that user from the Active Directory
Disable-MailUser	Removes the mail properties from a user

The best way to learn how to use the EMS to create contact and mail-enabled users is to look at some examples. Let's say a user named Russ Kaufmann is a contractor that works in your company sometimes. He requires a desk and a company logon, so you have already created his Russ.Kaufmann account in the forthcoffee.com Active Directory; the account is in an OU called Corporate. You want Russ to appear in the address lists, but he should receive his e-mail at an external address: Russ.Kaufmann@RussClusteringGuru.com. Here is the command you would use to mail-enable his user account. In this example, we are using his common name attribute instead of his username:

```
Enable-MailUser "Russ Kaufmann" -Alias 'Russ.Kaufmann'
-ExternalEmailAddress 'SMTP:Russ.Kaufmann@RussClusteringGuru.com'
```

Let's extend this example now to a mail-enabled contact. You have a contact that you want to appear in your address lists, but this contact does not need to be a security principal in your Active Directory. The contact does not yet exist, so you will create a mail-enabled contact in the Corporate OU for contact Rod Fournier whose external address will be Rod.Fournier@RodClusteringGuru .com:

```
New-MailContact -ExternalEmailAddress 'SMTP:Rod.Fournier@RodClusteringGuru.com'
-Name 'Rod Fournier' -Alias 'RodFournier'
-OrganizationalUnit 'fourthcoffee.com/Corporate'
-FirstName 'Rod' -Initials " -LastName 'Fournier'
```

When setting properties for the mail contact and mail user objects, there are some useful properties to know about. Table 10.9 shows some of the more common properties that these two object types share.

TABLE 10.9: Useful Properties That Can Be Used by the Mail Contact and Mail User Objects

PROPERTY	EXPLANATION
Alias	Set the object's Exchange alias.
CustomAttribute1 Through CustomAttribute10	Set custom attributes 1 through 10; these are also known as the extension attributes.
DisplayName	Sets the display name of the object.
ExternalEmailAddress	Sets the address that is to be used to deliver mail externally to a the user or contact.
HiddenFromAddressLists Enabled	Specifies if the object is hidden from address lists or not. The default is $False, but it can be set to $True.
MaxSendSize	Sets the maximum size of a message that can be sent to this recipient.

Summary

Recipient management is one of the core functions of many Exchange administrators. Short of some daily monitoring and running your backups, recipient management will be the task that consumes most of your Exchange bandwidth. Day-to-day recipient management includes the following:

◆ Mailbox management

◆ Resource mailbox management

◆ Mail-enabled group management

◆ Contact management

As you get started with Exchange 2007, you will probably be more dependent on the Exchange Management Console for recipient management. Most all tasks you will need to perform can be performed through the graphical user interface. As you get more comfortable with the GUI, though, we urge you to start learning more about the Exchange Management Shell. Combining some of the EMS cmdlets with PowerShell scripting capabilities can help to speed up many of the common tasks that you perform, such as bulk recipient creation and management.

Chapter 11

Managing Address Lists

Over the past 20 years, LAN-based and host-based e-mail systems have become more complex and have offered more and more features. One of the features that has become indispensable is an address book of mailboxes to which you might commonly send mail. The address book provides you with a view into the mail system's directory service database. In an Exchange environment, we refer to this address book as the global address list and the directory service is the Active Directory.

In most cases, the global address list is a comprehensive listing of all mail-enabled objects in your Active Directory. However, there are system objects (such as system mailboxes) as well as hidden objects that will not appear in the global address list (GAL), but most user mailboxes, resource mailboxes, mail-enabled users, mail-enabled contacts, and mail-enabled groups will appear in the GAL. If you have mail-enabled public folders that are not hidden, they will also appear in the GAL.

The GAL is seen by Exchange clients through a number of different mechanisms. Probably the least commonly used method is through a direct LDAP query. The most common methods to view information in the Exchange GAL are using either an Outlook MAPI client and using Outlook Web Access. For many organizations, the GAL is used not only for addressing e-mail but for looking up information about other users in the organization, such as address, title, and telephone numbers. Figure 11.1 shows an example of the Outlook 2007 address book when viewing the GAL.

Note that the GAL shown in Figure 11.1 is probably not very useful for the organization's company white pages or company directory. There is not much additional information on the mailboxes and contacts; even the title and business phone number are missing for most mail-enabled objects.

For mobile users or users that work offline, you can build a subset of the information that is found in the main GAL that can be more easily downloaded and viewed offline. These are called offline address books.

In many small and medium-sized businesses, the default listing of the GAL, the default address lists, and the default offline address book will prove to be sufficient. However, other organizations may find a need to customize these.

NOTE

Any changes you make, such adding a new address list or creating new global address lists, will not appear until the user closes their mail client and re-opens it. Since these objects are all stored in the Active Directory, waiting for the Active Directory to replicate to all global catalog servers may also slow the availability of new address lists.

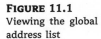

FIGURE 11.1
Viewing the global address list

Topics in this chapter include the following:

◆ Defining additional global address lists

◆ Creating custom address lists

◆ Customizing offline address books

Managing Global Address Lists

The global address list, by its very definition, is a list of all mail-enabled objects in the entire directory (in our case, the Active Directory). You can create multiple global address lists for your organization, but your users see only one. They cannot pick and choose which GAL they see in Outlook or Outlook Web Access.

Most small and medium-sized businesses will never need more than the default global address list. In fact, organizations with tens of thousands of mailboxes often never need more than a single GAL. So why is there a feature that lets you create more than one GAL? An organization might need more than one GAL for a couple of reasons:

◆ The Exchange organization is hosting more than one company or subsidiary, but users only need to see a subset of the entire organization.

◆ The Exchange organization is a hosting environment that runs many companies, but users in each company should see only the other users in their companies.

Creating Global Address Lists

Creating multiple global addresses lists and defining the permissions for them is a little beyond the job scope for the typical reader of this book, but we want to cover some of the basics nonetheless. If you are sure you do not need custom GALs, then you can safely skip this section of the chapter.

So now you may be asking, If there are multiple global address lists in a single Exchange organization and if a user cannot select which one they are viewing, then how do you use them? The client (Outlook or Outlook Web Access) selects which GAL you see based on one of three criteria. The GAL is selected in this order:

1. The GAL to which the user has permissions is selected first.

2. If the user has permissions to more than one GAL, the GAL to which the user is a member is selected.

3. If the user has permissions to more than one GAL and is a member of more than one GAL, the largest GAL is selected.

You create and manage GALs entirely through the EMS. Therefore, you should be aware of the EMS cmdlets that manipulate GAL objects. If you have been studying the EMS cmdlets in much detail, then you probably already know the verb portion of the cmdlet and just need the noun. Table 11.1 shows the cmdlets that are used to manage GAL objects.

TABLE 11.1:   Cmdlets Used to Manage Global Address List Objects

CMDLET	EXPLANATION
New-GlobalAddressList	Creates a new global address list object
Get-GlobalAddressList	Retrieves a list of GAL objects or properties of a specific GAL
Set-GlobalAddressList	Sets properties of existing GAL objects
Update-GlobalAddressList	Updates recipients in the Active Directory so that they appear in this GAL if applicable
Remove-GlobalAddressList	Deletes a GAL object

If you want to retrieve a list of all the GAL objects, you can use Get-GlobalAddressList and see these results:

```
Get-GlobalAddressList | Format-Table Name
Name
----
Default Global Address List
```

The real meat and potatoes of the GAL is the query, or filter, that is used to construct the membership list. There are a couple of properties of GAL objects that allow you to define the query that is used to construct the list. You can define a custom LDAP query, a recipient filter, or address list conditional properties. One conditional property of a GAL is the

ConditionalCompany property. Let's do the Get-GlobalAddressList query again, but this time include these properties in a formatted list:

```
Get-GlobalAddressList | Format-List Name,RecipientFilter,LdapRecipientFilter,
ConditionalCompany

Name                 : Default Global Address List
RecipientFilter      : (Alias -ne $null -and (ObjectClass -eq 'user' -or
   ObjectClass -eq 'contact' -or ObjectClass -eq 'msExchSystemMailbox'
-or ObjectClass -eq 'msExchDynamicDistributionList'
-or ObjectClass -eq 'group' -or ObjectClass -eq 'publicFolder'))
LdapRecipientFilter : (&(mailNickname=*)(|(objectClass=user)(objectClass=contact)
(objectClass=msExchSystemMailbox)(objectClass=msExchDynamicDistributionList)
(objectClass=group)(objectClass=publicFolder)))
ConditionalCompany   :
```

First notice that the ConditionalCompany property was empty for this particular GAL. The LdapRecipientFilter property contains the filter that would be used if this GAL was being used by an Exchange 2000/2003 Recipient Update Service and maps to the Active Directory attribute purportedSearch. The RecipientFilter property is used by Exchange 2007 to apply membership to address lists; for you Active Directory fanatics out there, this property maps to the msExchQueryFilter attribute of the GAL object.

Let's take apart that RecipientFilter before we go any further and see what listing it is really generating. Inside of the inner set of parentheses, notice that the filter applies to any type of ObjectClass that is equal to (-eq) user, contact, system mailbox, dynamic distribution list, group, or public folder. This is almost every type of object in the domain, right? The filter narrows it down a little further by saying that the Alias property (the Exchange alias) must not be null. This means that the objects in question must be mail-enabled. Got all of that? Don't worry if it is a little fuzzy; creating multiple GALs is a very advanced topic and requires some practice.

Let's use an example now to further illustrate the concepts and practices of implementing more than one GAL. In this example, our company has just purchased a new company (Scully Surfboards) and has moved all of their mailboxes over to our organization's Exchange servers. However, the users from the company we just purchased are a little finicky and don't like seeing *anyone* in their global address list but their own little branch of the company. Granted, we could just give them their own Active Directory and Exchange server, but that might be a waste of hardware, software, and human resources. So we will create a GAL called Scully Surfboards. Here is the command:

```
New-GlobalAddressList -Name "Scully Surfboards"
```

All this command does is create a new GAL called Scully Surfboards; we did not even use any of the RecipientFilter or conditional filter properties. Let's say that we want anyone whose company name attribute is equal to Scully Surfboards to be in this GAL. We need to modify this GAL using the Set-GlobalAddressList cmdlet. The cmdlet needs to set the -ConditionalCompany property and it needs to set the -IncludedRecipients property. Since this list will *only* contain mailbox-enabled users, the -IncludedRecipients property only needs to have MailboxUsers. The following command will accomplish this:

```
Set-GlobalAddressList "Scully Surfboards" -ConditionalCompany "Scully
Surfboards" -IncludedRecipients "MailboxUsers"
```

Now let's take a look at some of the properties that were created for this new GAL object.

```
Get-GlobalAddressList "Scully Surfboards" | Format-List
    Name,RecipientFilter,LdapRecipientFilter,RecipientFilterApplied,
IncludedRecipients,ConditionalCompany

Name                   : Scully Surfboards
RecipientFilter        : (RecipientType -eq 'UserMailbox' -and Company
-eq Scully Surfboards')
LdapRecipientFilter    : (&(objectClass=user)(objectCategory=person)
(mailNickname=*)(msExchHomeServerName=*)(company=Scully Surfboards))
RecipientFilterApplied : False
IncludedRecipients     : MailboxUsers
ConditionalCompany     : {Scully Surfboards}
```

Notice that the `RecipientFilter` and `LdapRecipientFilter` properties were automatically generated even though we used a "precanned" filter.

Applying Global Address Lists to Mail Objects

In the previous example, we created a new GAL called Scully Surfboards. In an Exchange 2000/2003 environment, eventually anyone whose company name was equal to Scully Surfboards appear in this GAL. That was because there was a process called the Recipient Update Service (RUS) that took care of little housekeeping tasks like adding recipients to addresses lists. Many people that are new to Exchange may think that this sort of thing just magically happens, but there has to be some "back end" process that actually handles this.

Anyone that has fought RUS problems with earlier versions of Exchange will be happy to know that the RUS is no longer responsible for this task. Actually, the RUS has been retired from Exchange active duty permanently. When a new mailbox-enabled user is created by the Exchange Management Console, the cmdlet that creates the user evaluates each of the address lists available. The `RecipientFilter` and `LdapRecipientFilter` properties of an address list are examined to determine if the user being created should be included in that that particular address list. If the user should be included in the address list, that user's `showInAddressBook` attribute in Active Directory will include that particular address list name.

Intuitively, you might think that each time an address list is displayed, the query or filter is simply executed once again. It turns out that enumerating members of an address list is much more efficient if the address list information is stored with the mail-enabled object. Figure 11.2 shows the `showInAddressBook` attribute for a newly created mailbox-enabled user whose company attribute contained Scully Surfboards; the object was viewed using the ADSIEdit utility.

The value was stored in this attribute as the distinguished name of the GAL; in this example that name is as follows:

```
CN=Scully Surfboards,CN=All Global Address Lists,CN=Address Lists
    Container,CN=Volcano Surfboards,CN=Microsoft Exchange,CN=Services,
CN=Configuration,DC=volcanosurfboards,DC=com
```

That takes care of mail-enabled recipients that are created *after* the GAL is created. But what about mail-enabled recipients that are already in the Active Directory or ones whose company name is changed after they are created? This is the job of the `Update-GlobalAddressList` cmdlet.

FIGURE 11.2
Viewing an
mail-enabled object's
showInAddressBook
attribute

If you know that GAL is out-of-date or not showing everyone it should, here is how you could update this:

```
Update-GlobalAddressList "Scully Surfboards"
```

If you wanted to update all of your recipients and all of the GAL objects, you could run these two cmdlets:

```
Get-GlobalAddressList | Update-GlobalAddressList
```

In an earlier EMS cmdlet, we showed you the properties of the Scully Surfboards address list. This included a property called RecipientFilterApplied. This property was set to False. Once we actually use the Update-GlobalAddressList to apply this address list to recipients, this will change to True. Here is an example:

```
Get-GlobalAddressList "Scully Surfboards" | FL Name,RecipientFilterApplied
Name               : Scully Surfboards
RecipientFilterApplied : True
```

However, RecipientFilterApplied automatically goes back to False if we make any changes to any of its properties.

Applying Permissions to Global Address Lists

Thus far we have created a global address list called Scully Surfboards and made sure that anyone whose company name attribute is equal to Scully Surfboards will be included in it. However, when a user who is included in that address list logs on to Outlook or Outlook Web Access, they are going to be sorely disappointed because they will still see the default global address list. Why is that? Well, we have not yet changed the permissions on the default global address list, so the client continues to choose that one because it is the largest.

We now need to expand our example just a bit so that we can restrict who has permissions to which address lists. We need to do this with Active Directory security groups, and to do it right we need to create two security groups. We will define a group called View the Big GAL and a group called View the Scully Surfboards GAL. We will add the appropriate users to each security group; if a user is a member of both security groups, they will see the largest of the two GALs when they use Outlook.

The easiest way to edit the permissions on the GAL objects is to use the ADSIEdit utility from the Windows 2003 Support Tools. You will need to open ADSIEdit, browse down through the Configuration partition to Services, Microsoft Exchange, *Organization Name*, Address Lists Container, and All Global Address Lists. This is shown in Figure 11.3.

FIGURE 11.3
Using ADSIEdit to manage the permissions on a global address list

In Figure 11.3, we are looking at the Security properties of the Scully Surfboards GAL object. Notice that Authenticated Users has the Read and Open Address List permissions. Clear the Read and Open Address List check boxes in the Allow column for Authenticated Users; don't check the Deny permissions since that will override the permissions you are about to assign. Now add the View the Scully Surfboards GAL group to this list and assign that group Read and Open Address List permissions in the Allow column.

Now we need to do the same thing to the default global address list group; we must add the View the Big GAL group and allow that group Read and Open Address List permissions and we must clear the Read and Open Address List permissions from the Authenticated Users group.

This may seem like a bit of hassle to set up, but once you have started down this configuration path, it is easy to add additional GALs and to assign them permissions in the same way. One potential stumbling block that you will have to cross when you are creating multiple global address lists is that the default global address list allows authenticated users to access it. You must clear the Allow permissions for the Authenticated Users group; this will ensure that users do not see the default GAL in Outlook.

Managing Address Lists

In an organization with hundreds, thousands, or tens of thousands of mail-enabled objects in its default global address list or custom global address lists, actually finding someone or sorting based on a certain criteria (such as department) can be overwhelming. Unlike multiple global address lists (which may be of use only in very specific circumstances), address lists can help users in even small or medium-sized organizations find or sort parts of the global address list.

TIP

Address lists are a great way to allow users to view a subset of the global address list.

The function of an address list is to help a user narrow the scope of the recipients in the GAL so that they see a subset of their entire address book. Examples might be viewing everyone in a specific department, state, or company. Contrary to popular misconception, you do not address e-mail to an address list; people often think of address books when they mean mail-enabled groups. Address lists allow a user to see a subset of the global address list; the user chooses which of these address lists they want to view from within the Outlook address book. Figure 11.4 shows the Outlook address book and the drop-down list that exposes the address lists available.

Figure 11.4 shows the address lists that are created by default for Exchange 2007. They have very simple filters and can be helpful for your users in basic ways, but if you find them unnecessary, you can always delete them and create more useful address lists. Table 11.2 lists the default address lists and what they contain.

FIGURE 11.4
Viewing the available address lists from within Outlook

TABLE 11.2:   Address Lists Built In to Exchange 2007

LIST NAME	EXPLANATION
All Contacts	All mail-enabled contact objects and mail-enabled users
All Groups	All mail-enabled groups and dynamic distribution groups
All Rooms	All conference room resource mailboxes
All Users	All mailbox-enabled users

Available address lists can be viewed and managed using the EMC or via the EMS. These are found in the Organization Configuration work center under the Mailbox subcontainer. Figure 11.5 shows the Address Lists container and the Actions pane from the Organization Configuration work center.

FIGURE 11.5
Viewing the address lists using the Exchange Management Console

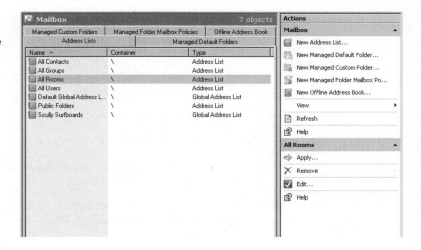

As you have probably guessed by now, you can also enumerate the address lists using the Get-AddressList cmdlet. In this chapter, we are going to stick mostly to the EMC when creating and managing address lists. However, so that you have these cmdlets in your arsenal, we are including the address list cmdlets in Table 11.3; you will find that the nouns in these cmdlets are almost identical to the ones used for managing global address lists.

Let's go through a simple example of creating a couple of new address lists. In this example, users want to be able to sort and view the global address list based on departments within the company. The first thing you need to do is to create an empty address list; this is really simple to do. When you launch the New Address List Wizard, the Introduction screen prompts you for the types of recipients. Simply specify a name for the address list and select None as the type of recipients to include. In this example, we are creating a root container for address lists called Departments.

Introduction

This wizard allows you to create a new address list. Address lists display a subset of recipients in an organization based on properties of the recipient.

Name:

Departments

Container:

\

Browse

Include these recipient types:
- (•) None
- ( ) All recipients types

TABLE 11.3: EMS Cmdlets for Manipulating Address Lists

CMDLET	EXPLANATION
New-AddressList	Creates a new address list
Set-AddressList	Sets address list properties
Get-AddressList	Retrieves address lists
Move-AddressList	Moves an address list from one container to another
Update-AddressList	Updates recipients of the specified address list so that they are now shown in the specified address list
Remove-AddressList	Deletes an address list from the directory

When this task runs, the following command is used:

```
New-AddressList -Name 'Departments' -Container '\' -IncludedRecipients 'None'
```

Now that we have a Departments container in the root of the address lists, we want to actually create an address list and specify that it should contain only people from a certain department. So we run the New Address List Wizard once again. This time on the Introduction page, you can specify that it should contain All Recipient Types or you can specify specific recipient types (mailbox-enabled users, mail-enabled users, mail-enabled contacts, and so on). You also have to select the container in which you want this address list to reside. This address list will contain mailboxes from the Engineering department, so you want this list to appear under the Departments container previously created.

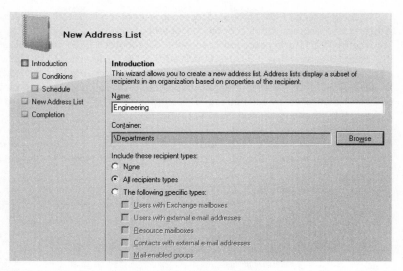

Next you find the Conditions screen. Setting the conditions is much like setting the conditions or filter for a dynamic distribution group. In our example, we are going to select the Recipient Is in a Department check box in Step 1. In Step 2, we must click the underlined text and specify the department name.

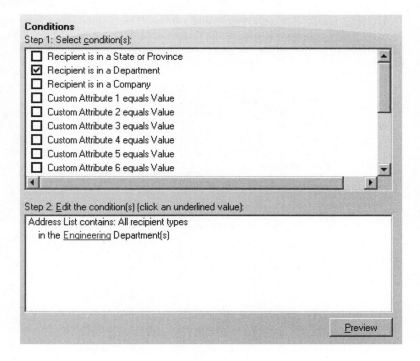

The next screen of the New Address List Wizard is the Schedule screen. In the Global Address List section of this chapter, we talked about the fact that address lists are not generated "on-the-fly" each time you want to see who is a member. Each mail-enabled object has an attribute in Active Directory that indicates which address lists they should be shown in; this multi-valued attribute is called the **showInAddressBook** attribute. Address lists get populated in this attribute for each object that matches the query by some process. In the case of global address lists, this process is kicked off by the **Update-GlobalAddressList** cmdlet; for address lists, this process is kicked off by the **Update-AddressList** cmdlet.

The Schedule page asks you when should this process be kicked off. Ideally, you run it immediately, but if you know that the address list is very large (say thousands of mail-enabled objects), then you might want to defer the process until a quieter period for your network.

Schedule
Specify when the address list should be applied and the maximum length of time it is permitted to run.

Apply the address list:

◉ Immediately

○ At the following time:

| Tuesday , November 21, 2006 | ▼ | 10:01:32 PM | ⇕ |

☐ Cancel tasks that are still running after (hours):

The next screen is merely confirming what will be applied or performed when you click the New button. It is confirming the following information: A new address list called Engineering will be created in the \Departments container. This address list will contain all types of mail-enabled recipients whose department is equal to Engineering.

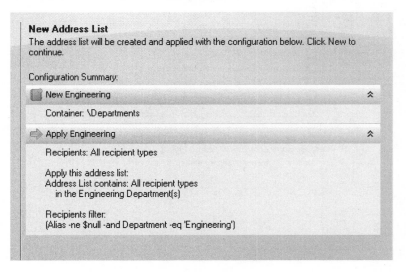

New Address List
The address list will be created and applied with the configuration below. Click New to continue.

Configuration Summary:

🔲 New Engineering   ⌃

  Container: \Departments

➡ Apply Engineering   ⌃

  Recipients: All recipient types

  Apply this address list:
  Address List contains: All recipient types
   in the Engineering Department(s)

  Recipients filter:
  (Alias -ne $null -and Department -eq 'Engineering')

When you click the New button, two commands are actually executed. The first creates the specified address list. The second updates any recipients that meet the conditions of the address list:

```
New-AddressList -Name 'Engineering' -Container '\Departments'
-IncludedRecipients 'AllRecipients' -ConditionalDepartment 'Engineering'

Update-AddressList -Identity '\Departments\Engineering'
```

If you want to view information about this newly created address list, you can use the Get-AddressList cmdlet to retrieve it. The following lines show some of the properties of the newly created address list. We have intentionally cut some of the lines out to shorten the amount of text we are showing you here. If you try this yourself, you will see more properties.

```
Get-AddressList "Engineering" | FL

Container                    : \Departments
DisplayName                  : Engineering
Name                         : Engineering
RecipientFilter              : (Alias -ne $null -and Department
                               -eq 'Engineering')
LdapRecipientFilter          : (&(mailNickname=*)(department=Engineering))
LastUpdatedRecipientFilter   : (Alias -ne $null -and Department -eq '
                               Engineering')
RecipientFilterApplied       : True
IncludedRecipients           : AllRecipients
ConditionalDepartment        : {Engineering}
ConditionalCompany           : {}
ConditionalStateOrProvince   : {}
ConditionalCustomAttribute1  :
ConditionalCustomAttribute2  :
ConditionalCustomAttribute3  :
RecipientFilterType          : Precanned
IsValid                      : True
OriginatingServer            : HNLDC01.volcanosurfboards.com
DistinguishedName            : CN=Engineering,CN=Departments,CN=All Address Lists,
CN=Address Lists Container,CN=Volcano Surfboards,CN=Microsoft Exchange,
CN=Services,CN=Configuration,DC=volcanosurfboards,DC=com
Identity                     : \Departments\Engineering
```

If a user account is mailbox-enabled and their department is equal to Engineering, then they will automatically be included in the Engineering address list. However, if an account is mailbox-enabled and then the department attribute is later changed to Engineering, the Update-AddressList cmdlet will need to be run. In this case, the command would be as follows:

```
Update-AddressList "Engineering"
```

You could also run the following cmdlet and update all of the address lists in the organization:

```
Get-AddressList | Update-AddressList
```

If you have a large global address list, take great care in running this frequently. However, if there are a lot of changes within your organization that cause changes to attributes that are conditions of address lists, you might want to schedule those cmdlets to run every night.

The result of this operation is that when you view the global address list in Outlook or Outlook Web Access, there is a new Engineering address list. Figure 11.6 shows an example of this address book that, when viewed, shows only the members of the Engineering department. This can be useful when you need to select addresses for users only in a certain department.

FIGURE 11.6
Viewing the Engineering address list

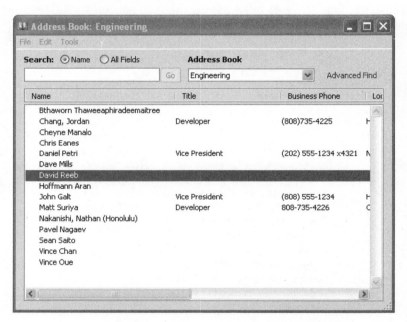

A fairly common question among users is whether they can choose a different address list than the global address list. Many users prefer to see only the users in their particular department, for example. It is possible for the user to set their own default address list. This is done when you launch the address book and choose Tools ➢ Options. The Addressing page (shown in Figure 11.7) has a drop-down list option called Show This Address List First; from here the user can select any of the address lists available to them.

If an address list does not appear for a user, the user may need to close Outlook and reopen it. If the user is working in local cache mode, they may need to download the latest offline address book or wait for the newest offline address book to be generated.

Managing Offline Address Books

The offline address book allows Outlook users to work in Outlook even while disconnected from the Exchange server and still have access to the organization's address lists. The administrator of the Exchange organization can define what is contained in an offline address book. All versions

FIGURE 11.7
Changing the default
address list

of Outlook have the ability to download an offline address book even though the format and the method of distribution has changed over the years.

Outlook 2003 and earlier clients retrieve their offline address book (OAB) files from a system public folder called OFFLINE ADDRESS BOOK. In the OFFLINE ADDRESS BOOK folder structure, you will see subfolders for differing versions of Outlook. Starting with Outlook 2007, the Outlook client can download the OAB files from either the OFFLINE ADDRESS BOOK public folder or a Web Service distribution point on an Exchange Client Access server.

With a default installation of Exchange 2007, there is automatically an offline address book created called the default offline address book. You can manage it or create additional offline address books using the Exchange Management Console. The Mailbox subcontainer of the Organization Configuration work center includes an Offline Address Book tab in the results pane; this is shown in Figure 11.8.

Managing the Default Offline Address Book

In most cases and organizations, the default offline address book will be sufficient. Even an organization with tens of thousands of users can fit compactly in to offline address book files. Unless you have a very specific need for assigning users an offline address book that is different than your global address list, you probably do not need to make changes to address lists included with the default offline address book. The configuration of the default offline address book includes the organization's default global address list. You can modify the address lists that are contained in the default offline address book on the Address Lists property page (see Figure 11.9).

FIGURE 11.8
Managing offline address books using the Exchange Management Console

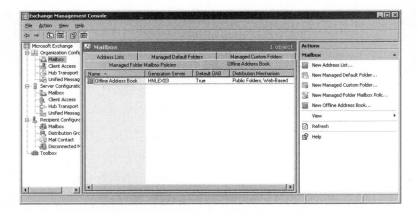

FIGURE 11.9
Configuring the address lists that an offline address book contains

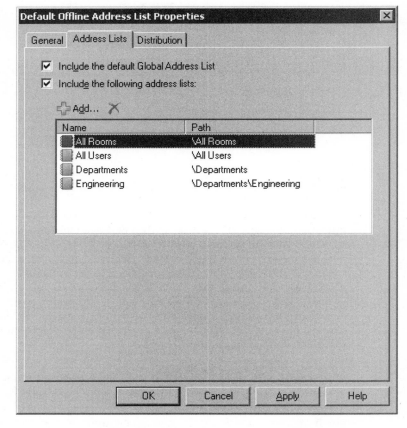

The Include the Default Global Address List check box configures the offline address book to include the entire global address list. You can also check the Include the Following Address Lists check box and add additional address lists that should be included in the offline address book.

The Distribution property page (shown in Figure 11.10) allows you to configure which clients and offline address book versions you are going to support. For each of the older Outlook versions, a public folder is created. In a large organization, you would want to ensure that those folders are replicated to public folder servers in each major location in your network.

FIGURE 11.10
Offline address book
Distribution properties

The Distribution Points section allows you to specify if you will be distributing the offline address book via a public folder. You do this by ensuring that the Enable Public Folder Distribution check box is checked.

TIP

Public folder distribution of the offline address books is required for Outlook 2003 and earlier clients.

For Outlook 2007 clients, you can click the Enable Web-Based Distribution check box and provide OAB paths. Outlook 2007 clients locate the Web distribution points using the Autodiscover service. In a larger organization with more than one Active Directory site that contains Exchange servers, an Exchange Client Access server role in each site should be configured to host an OAB virtual directory, and then that path should be included in the list of virtual directories that host each offline address book.

The OAB virtual directory paths are defined on each Client Access server role in the Server Configuration work center under the Client Access subcontainer. For each Client Access server role, there is a Offline Address Book Distribution property page in the work pane. Here you will find the OAB virtual directory; by default you will see the one for the default website (shown in Figure 11.11).

FIGURE 11.11
OAB virtual directory for the default website

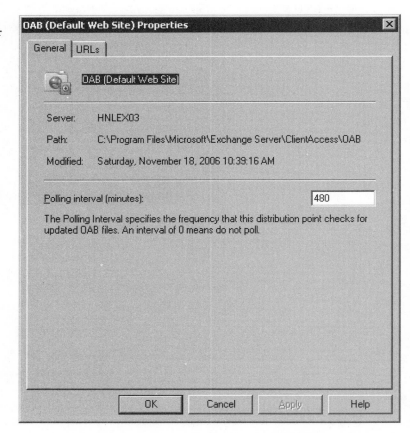

There is not really a lot you can configure for the OAB virtual directory. On the General property page, you can configure the polling interval for that particular virtual directory. The polling interval specifies how often the Client Access server will check for updated OAB files. The default is every 480 minutes, but you can force the OAB files to be updated using the Update-FileDistributionService cmdlet. To update the OAB files on server HNLEX03, you would type this:

```
Update-FileDistributionService HNLEX03 -Type "OAB"
```

The URLs property page allows you to configure the internal and external URLs that the clients use to connect to the OAB distribution points.

Creating an Offline Address Book

In this example, we have decided that we are going to assign certain users a smaller offline address book. We don't want them to see the entire global address list, but rather just the Engineering department. This type of scenario might be useful in a hosting environment or if your company has multiple subsidiaries or business units hosted in a single Exchange organization.

The easiest way to create new offline address book is using the EMC. Simply choose the New Offline Address Book task from the Actions pane to see the New Offline Address Book Wizard. On the Introduction page, you must define the name of the offline address book, the server that will be responsible for rebuilding it, if it should contain the default global address list, and if it should contain additional address lists. In our case, we want the Engineering Department OAB to include only the Engineering address list.

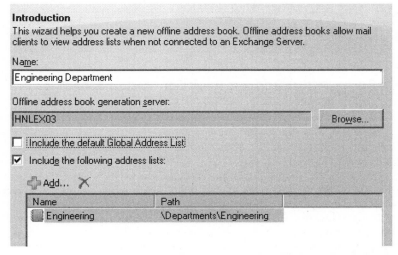

When you click Next, you see the Distribution Points page, in which you define whether you want to distribute the OAB via OAB virtual directories on the Client Access servers (Outlook

2007 only), via a public folder (Outlook 2007 and earlier versions), or both. If you select Enable Web-based Distribution, then make sure you include an OAB virtual directory on a Client Access server in each Active Directory site.

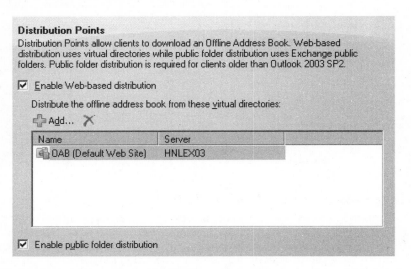

When you click New, the EMC creates the necessary EMS command to generate the new OAB and executes the command. Here is the command that was executed to generate this OAB:

```
New-OfflineAddressBook -Name 'Engineering Department'
-Server 'HNLEX03' -AddressLists '\Departments\Engineering'
-PublicFolderDistributionEnabled $true -VirtualDirectories
'HNLEX03\OAB (Default Web Site)'
```

Note that unless you specify otherwise, all Outlook versions are supported when the offline address book is created.

Defining Offline Address Book Generation Schedules

By default, the content in an offline address book public folder is generated once per day (at 5:00 a.m. local time). For an organization with tens of thousands of mail-enabled objects in its address lists, this can be pretty CPU intensive for the server doing the generation. The update schedule is defined on the General property page of each offline address book; this property page is shown in Figure 11.12.

We wanted to breach this subject because Outlook 2003 or 2007 in local cache mode only downloads the address book approximately once every 24 hours. If you create new mail-enabled objects or make changes to existing objects at 9:00 in the morning, for example, those changes will not be incorporated into the offline address book until the next day. The client then might not download the changes for another day. This often raises support questions.

In organizations with less than 5,000 mail-enabled objects, we recommend that you rebuild your offline address book two or three times per day. This increases the likelihood that new changes will be downloaded more quickly to clients that are in local cache mode. For larger organizations, you have to balance the load that the rebuild places on your Exchange servers and global catalog servers with the luxury of having more up-to-date information.

Assigning Offline Address Books

By default, all users are assigned the default offline address book. Address books are assigned based on the mailbox database on which the user's mailbox is located. The Client Settings property page is shown here. To change the offline address book that the users whose mailboxes are on this database use, click the Browse button next to the Offline Address Book box and select the correct OAB.

We could have used the following EMS command to accomplish the same thing:

```
Set-MailboxDatabase "Engineering Mailboxes"
-OfflineAddressBook "Engineering Department"
```

Managing Offline Address Books Using the Exchange Management Shell

There are a number of EMS cmdlets used for managing offline address books. While OAB management is not something that you do every day, knowledge of these cmdlets may come in handy, so we decided to include them. Table 11.4 contains the EMS cmdlets for use with OABs.

TABLE 11.4:   Exchange Management Shell Cmdlets Used to Manage Offline Address Books

CMDLET	EXPLANATION
New-OfflineAddressBook	Creates a new offline address book
Set-OfflineAddressBook	Sets the properties of an existing offline address book
Get-OfflineAddressBook	Retrieves a list of offline address books or the individual properties a specified offline address book
Update-OfflineAddressBook	Updates the offline address book contents for public-folder-based OABs
Update-FileDistributionService	Updates the offline address book content for web-based offline address book clients
Remove-OfflineAddressBook	Deletes an offline address book
New-OABVirtualDirectory	Creates a new OAB virtual directory on a Client Access server
Set-OABVirtualDirectory	Sets the properties on an existing OAB virtual directory
Get-OABVirtualDirectory	Retrieves a list offline address book virtual directories or the properties of one or more OAB virtual directories
Remove-OABVirtualDirectory	Deletes an OAB virtual directory

We have intentionally kept the information about using the EMS to manage offline address books fairly light in this book since most of the common tasks can easily be accomplished using the EMC. Good online help is available for these cmdlets, though, if you decide you want to be brave and experiment with the EMS when creating or managing OABs.

Summary

Managing address lists is a task that usually occurs when you are initially rolling out your Exchange organization. Indeed, creating multiple global address lists is something the typical

Exchange administrator never has to do. Creating multiple Exchange global address lists is a more common task within organizations with hundreds of thousands of users or organizations that provide hosting services to multiple companies or their own organization's subsidiaries.

Address lists provide users with a useful way to sort or view only a subset of the global address list information. As you learn more about how your user community works and what their needs are, you may find that additional address lists are a good addition at any point in your Exchange deployment.

Finally, offline address books are another component that you typically do not manage on a day-to-day basis. These are the sort of Exchange components that you "set and forget"; once they are configured, you usually do not need to make too many changes. Just make sure when you configure them that you understand the delay that some users may experience in seeing new changes to the address lists.

Chapter 12

Managing Folder Content

Over the years, we have seen many different approaches to managing users' mailbox content and purging older mailbox content. The need to control mailbox content and size is often due to limited disk space for mailbox databases but it may also be due to company security policies or regulatory compliance.

Seasoned Exchange Server administrators are probably familiar with the Exchange 2000/2003 Mailbox Manager function. Heck, you may even be familiar with the Exchange 5.5 Mailbox Cleanup Agent. These tools gave the administrator some control over how long content was kept in a user's mailbox folder. The administrator could configure these tools to delete information in a mailbox if it was older than the specified number of days or larger than a specified size.

Many organizations are now employing archival solutions that will remove content from users' mailboxes and store it on long-term storage such as tape, optical, network attached storage (NAS), or storage area networks (SANs). In some cases, archival solutions are put in place merely to reduce the size of the Exchange databases but still allow users long-term access to their old mail data. In other cases, an organization is required to keep certain types of message content such as financial data, official company communications, and healthcare-related data.

Mailbox archiving has raised new issues and challenges for the Exchange administrator as well as the archive system administrator. There are certainly messages that users or departments will want to keep for a long time, but probably not every message in the user's Inbox. There has to be some method of determining which messages should be retained or archived, such as moving important messages to special folders.

Organizations that are concerned about meeting regulatory requirements with respect to message archiving and long term retention of certain types of messages may also be interested in keeping a journaled copy of messages.

In this chapter, we are going to cover some of the new features of Exchange 2007 with respect to messaging records management, and we'll discuss how features included in the Exchange 2000/2003 Mailbox Manager function are now included with Exchange 2007.

Topics in this chapter include the following:

- ◆ Basics of messaging records management
- ◆ Managing default folders
- ◆ Creating and managing custom folders
- ◆ Assigning managed folder mailbox policies
- ◆ Configuring Exchange 2007 servers to supporting messaging records management

Understanding the Basics of Messaging Records Management

Before we dive in to how you would actually set up and implement messaging records management, let's discuss some of the basics. This includes some possible usage scenarios, what the user would see, and the basics of getting started.

First and foremost, let's get some terminology out of the way. Messaging records management encompasses management of e-mail content "at rest." This means that we are managing the content while it is sitting in a folder within someone's mailbox. Don't get this concept confused with transport rules, which we will discuss in more details in Chapter 13, "Managing Messages in Transit." Also, if you see or hear the term *e-mail lifecycle management*, remember that this term was used during the Exchange 2007 beta testing process; the correct term is *messaging records management*.

Further, messaging records management does not include "important message pixie dust." A popular misconception is that content that should be retained will automatically be moved to the appropriate managed folder. Messages do not get organized automatically. Users must participate in messaging records management by moving their relevant content into the appropriate managed folders.

User Participation

First and foremost, it is essential to understand that there are two different perspectives on what we can implement with messaging records management. There are certain things that we can do without the user's intervention, such as purging mail in their existing folders or moving mail to a message archive.

NOTE

Users must participate in messaging records management.

However, the real mission of messaging records management is to get the user to participate in the process. This means that we use the messaging records management process to create custom folders in the user's mailbox, but it is up to the user to determine which types of message belong in which folder. Figure 12.1 shows a set of custom folders that are created in a folder called Managed Folders. These are called managed custom folders.

The administrator decides what the managed custom folder names will be and assigns a managed folder mailbox policy to the mailbox to ensure that the folders are created. There are additional things that the administrator can do with these folders, but for now we will stick with the basics.

The users are trained to categorize their mailbox content based on the folders you make available to them. This will allow the administrator to then purge folders such as the Inbox or Sent Items every 60, 90, or 180 days without worrying about purging important information. You can specifically archive the data that you find in Managed Folders or you can leave it on the server for a longer period of time based on the users' needs or the organization's requirements.

The most important thing to realize is, as we mentioned previously, the user must participate in the process.

FIGURE 12.1
Custom managed folders
created by a managed
folder mailbox policy

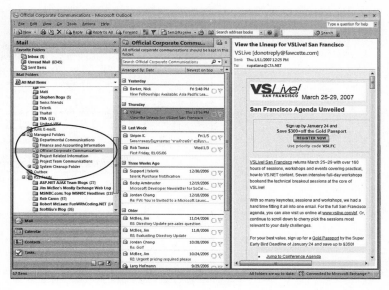

Possible Scenarios

After you finish reading this chapter, you will probably find a lot of potentially useful scenarios for messaging records management. This is true even if your organization does not perform mailbox archiving or has to deal with regulatory compliance. So, what are some possible uses for messaging records management?

◆ Creating custom folders that are used by users to categorize or organize information that must be retained

◆ Defining content settings that purge certain types of content from either custom folders or the default folders

◆ Defining for managed custom folders content settings that automatically journal specified content types (or all content types) that are moved into the folder

◆ Defining content settings for managed default folders

◆ Defining maximum folder sizes for managed custom folders

◆ Using managed content settings to expire items in a folder so they are eligible for archiving

These are just a few of the possible uses for messaging records management.

Getting Started with Messaging Records Management

Messaging records management folders, content settings, and policies can be defined in the Exchange Management Console (EMC) or the Exchange Management Shell (EMS). For most of the actions we will be describing, we will show you the EMC interface but we will follow up with EMS commands as necessary. The messaging records management content settings, policies, and folders are found in the Organization Configuration work center of the EMC under the Mailbox subcontainer. This work center is shown in Figure 12.2. You can see the Managed Default Folders tab in the results pane.

FIGURE 12.2
Viewing the messaging
records management
components in the
Exchange Management
Console

There is not one single dialog box or wizard involved in setting up messaging records management. There are a couple of steps involved in getting started. We are going to go in to more details later in the chapter on how to do each of these steps, but let's start with a basic outline of how you would get started with a policy:

1. Create managed custom folders (if applicable).

2. Define managed content settings for the managed custom folders.

3. Optionally create managed content settings for default folders.

4. Create managed folder mailbox policies that include managed custom folders and/or managed default folders.

5. Assign the managed folder mailbox polices to users.

6. Configure the mailbox servers to run the managed folder assistant on a schedule.

Managing Default Folders

Let's start by talking about a mailbox's default folders; these are the folders that are automatically created by the Outlook client the first time the mailbox is accessed. The default folders list can be found under the Managed Default Folders tab in the results pane shown in Figure 12.2.

Existing Default Folders

The Managed Default Folder list is static; you cannot create additional default folders either through the EMC or the EMS. The following is a list of the folders that are considered default folders:

◆ Calendar

◆ Contacts

◆ Deleted Items

- ◆ Drafts

- ◆ Entire Mailbox

- ◆ Inbox

- ◆ Journal

- ◆ Junk E-mail

- ◆ Notes

- ◆ Outbox

- ◆ RSS Feeds

- ◆ Sent Items

- ◆ Sync Issues

- ◆ Tasks

Depending on the client version you are using, you may not see all of these folders. For example, if you have never used the Outlook 2007 client against your mailbox, you will not see the Rss Feeds folder in your mailbox.

Creating Managed Content Settings

While we cannot define new default folders, we can manage the content in the existing folders. Managed content settings can be defined for each folder (or the entire mailbox). In many ways, the managed content settings can be used in the same way that the Exchange 2000/2003 Mailbox Manager functions could be used.

When creating a managed content setting, you must define what type of content it will be affecting; this means that you specify the message type. Table 12.1 shows the message types that you can define for managed content settings; this table includes the `MessageClass` property that would be used when creating managed content settings via the EMS and the `New-ManagedContentSettings` cmdlet.

You can optionally specify a retention period for items that meet the conditions of the message content setting. The retention period is specified in days and the retention period starts from one of two points:

- ◆ The When Delivered, End Date for Calendar and Recurring Tasks selection allows you to specify that the starting point for the retention cycle is when the message arrives in the mailbox. Alternately, if the item is a calendar entry or recurring task, the retention cycle starts at the end date of the item.

- ◆ The When Item Is Moved to the Folder selection specifies that the retention date starts when the item is first placed into the folder.

Once the retention period expires, you have to take an action on any items that meet your criteria. Table 12.2 shows a list of the possible actions you can take on an item at the end of the retention period. The table also includes the `RetentionAction` value that would be used if you were creating managed content settings from the EMS instead of the EMC.

An additional option you have available when you are creating a managed content setting is to automatically journal a copy of the message to a mailbox or external location. We will look at an example of journaling using the managed content settings.

TABLE 12.1:   Managed Content Settings Message Types

MESSAGE TYPE	MESSAGECLASS	EXPLANATION
All Message Content	*	All content types in the folder
Calendar Items	IPM.Appointment	Entries found on a calendar
Contacts	IPM.Contact	Contact items
Documents	IPM.Document	Message content that has been set as a document
Faxes	IPM.Note.Microsoft.Fax	Faxes generated by the Exchange 2007 Unified Messaging server role or compatible applications
Journal Items	IPM.Activity	Journal items
Meeting Requests, Responses, and Cancellations	IPM.Schedule	Schedule requests, responses to schedule requests, cancellations, etc.
Missed Calls	IPM.Note.Microsoft .Missed.Voice	Notices of telephone calls missed when using Exchange 2007 Unified Messaging
Notes	IPM.StickyNote	Note items usually found in the Outlook Notes folder
Posts	IPM.Post	Post item types
RSS Items	IPM.Post.RSS	RSS feed data in the Outlook 2007 client RSS Feeds folder
Tasks	IPM.Task	Task items
Voice Mail	IPM.Note.Microsoft .Voicemail	Voicemail messages generated by the Exchange 2007 Unified Messaging server or equivalent software

If you want to use the EMS to see the managed content settings that you have created, here is an example of using the Get-ManagedContentSettings cmdlet:

```
Get-ManagedContentSettings

Name                      MessageClass           ManagedFolderName
----                      ------------           -----------------
Message archival          *                      Official Corporate
   Com...
Purge the Deleted Item... *                      Deleted Items
```

```
Move items older than ... *                         Inbox
Move items older than ... *                         Sent Items
Move Faxes              IPM.Note.Microsoft.Fax*      Inbox
Move Voice Mail         IPM.Note.Microsoft.Voi...    Inbox
```

There are a number of cmdlets that you can use from within the EMS to create or manipulate managed content settings. These are shown in Table 12.3.

TABLE 12.2: Actions That Can Be Taken on Items at the End of the Retention Period

ACTION	RetentionAction	EXPLANATION
Move to the Deleted Items Folder	MoveToDeletedItems	Moves the item to the Deleted Items folder; this setting is not valid if you are trying to create a managed content setting in the Deleted Items folder.
Move to a Managed Custom Folder	MoveToFolder	Moves the item to a managed custom folder that you specify.
Delete and Allow Recovery	DeleteAndAllowRecovery	Deletes the item, but allows a user to undelete the item before the item is removed from the deleted item cache.
Permanently Delete	PermanentlyDelete	Deletes the item and does not allow it to be recovered from the deleted item cache.
Mark as Past Retention Limit	MarkAsPastRetentionLimit	Marks the item as past the retention limit but takes no further action. At this point, message archival software could take over and archive just the messages that are past their retention limit.

TABLE 12.3: Exchange Management Shell Cmdlets for Manipulating Managed Content Settings

CMDLET	EXPLANATION
New-ManagedContentSettings	Creates a new managed content setting
Set-ManagedContentSettings	Changes the properties of an existing managed content setting object
Get-ManagedContentSettings	Retrieves managed content settings
Remove-ManagedContentSettings	Deletes a managed content setting object

Let's now look at some practical examples of managed content settings.

KEEPING THE DELETED ITEMS FOLDER CLEAN

One pet peeve of many Exchange administrators we know is that users will delete messages from their Inbox or Sent Items folder, but they never actually empty the Deleted Items folder. It is not uncommon to find hundreds of megabytes of message content in a user's Deleted Items folder. Let's go through an example of a case where we want to ensure that nothing older than 14 days is kept in the Deleted Items folder but make sure the user can recover the deleted message from the deleted item cache after we empty their Deleted Items folder.

To do this through the EMC, locate the Deleted Items folder in the Managed Default Folder list and select it. On the Actions pane, select New Managed Content Settings, which will launch the New Managed Content Settings Wizard (shown in Figure 12.3). On the Introduction screen of the wizard, you specify the name of the managed content settings item, the type of message content it will apply to (in this case, all message content), the length of retention, when the retention period starts, and the action to take.

FIGURE 12.3
Configuring a managed content setting to delete items that have been in the Deleted Items folder longer than 14 days

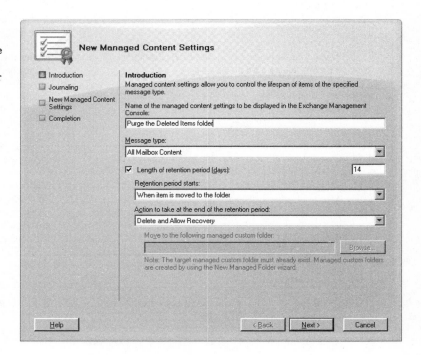

If you want to delete an item from a folder after a specified number of days, choose the When Delivered, End Date for Calendar and Recurring Tasks option in the Retention Period (Days) drop-down list. There is a bug in the release to manufacturing (RTM) version of Exchange that may prevent items from being deleted if you choose When Item Is Moved to the Folder option. Undoubtedly this will be corrected in later fixes and service packs, but be aware of this if you are an early adopter.

Since there is not a managed custom folder involved, the option to specify a managed custom folder is not available. Once you click Next, you move to the Journaling page in the wizard, but we do not need anything from that page for this particular managed content setting. The New Managed Content Settings page allows you to review what you are about to configure and then you click New. Like most EMC wizards, the Completion screen will include the EMS command that was actually executed to complete this task. The following is the EMS command that was necessary to define this managed content setting:

```
New-ManagedContentSettings -Name 'Purge the Deleted Items folder'
-FolderName 'Deleted Items' -RetentionAction 'DeleteAndAllowRecovery'
-AddressForJournaling $null -AgeLimitForRetention '14.00:00:00'
-JournalingEnabled $false -MessageFormatForJournaling 'UseTnef'
-RetentionEnabled $true -LabelForJournaling '' -MessageClass '*'
-MoveToDestinationFolder $null -TriggerForRetention 'WhenMoved'
```

Note that while we have defined the managed content setting to this particular folder, it will not yet apply to anyone's mailbox, nor will any server actually enforce this content setting. We will cover the managed folder mailbox policies and scheduling the managed folder assistant later in this chapter.

MOVING CONTENT TO AN ALTERNATE LOCATION

A good use of managed content settings is to move content to an alternate location. In this example, we will mimic one of the functions of the Exchange 2000/2003 Mailbox Manager. It had the ability to move mail that was nearly ready to be deleted from the system in to a System Cleanup folder. Mail could then be purged from the System Cleanup folder after it had been in that folder for a specified number of days.

In this example, we have already created a managed custom folder. We are going to create a managed content setting that moves all items in the Inbox folder in to the System Cleanup folder. Launch the New Managed Content Settings Wizard in exactly the same way as we did in the previous example except that this time select the Inbox. Specify a retention period of 180 days, specify that the action to take is Move to a Managed Custom Folder, and then select the System Cleanup folder. The Introduction page of the New Managed Content Settings Wizard is shown in Figure 12.4.

FIGURE 12.4
Moving content from the Inbox to the System Cleanup folder

Introduction
Managed content settings allow you to control the lifespan of items of the specified message type.

Name of the managed content settings to be displayed in the Exchange Management Console:

`Move items older than 180 days to the System Cleanup Folder`

Message type:

`All Mailbox Content`

☑ Length of retention period (days): `180`

Retention period starts:

`When delivered, end date for calendar and recurring tasks`

Action to take at the end of the retention period:

`Move to a Managed Custom Folder`

Move to the following managed custom folder:

`System Cleanup Folder` `Browse...`

Note: The target managed custom folder must already exist. Managed custom folders are created by using the New Managed Folder wizard.

The resulting EMS command that created this managed content setting is very similar to the one we used to purge the Deleted Items folder:

```
New-ManagedContentSettings -Name 'Move items older than 180 days
to the System Cleanup Folder' -FolderName 'Inbox'
-RetentionAction 'MoveToFolder' -AddressForJournaling $null
-AgeLimitForRetention '180.00:00:00' -JournalingEnabled $false
-MessageFormatForJournaling 'UseTnef' -RetentionEnabled $true
-LabelForJournaling '' -MessageClass '*'
-MoveToDestinationFolder 'System Cleanup Folder'
-TriggerForRetention 'WhenDelivered'
```

If we now want to move items in the Sent Items folder that are older than 180 days into the System Cleanup folder, we can make a few modifications to the managed content settings. The only one that is required is the -FolderName parameter; its value must be changed to 'Sent Items':

```
New-ManagedContentSettings -Name 'Move items older than 180 days
to the System Cleanup Folder' -FolderName 'Sent Items'
-RetentionAction 'MoveToFolder' -AddressForJournaling $null
-AgeLimitForRetention '180.00:00:00' -MessageClass '*'
-MoveToDestinationFolder 'System Cleanup Folder'
-TriggerForRetention 'WhenDelivered'
```

Since we did not require the journaling settings, we can remove those from the New-ManagedContentSettings command line.

Creating and Managing Custom Folders

Managed custom folders are folders that you define as the administrator and then assign to users' mailboxes. As you saw in Figure 12.1, the managed custom folders are created in the user's mailbox in the Managed Folders folder. Creating a managed custom folder is very simple. While you are viewing the Managed Custom Folders tab, simply click the New Managed Custom Folder task in the Actions pane. Figure 12.5 shows the New Managed Custom Folder Wizard.

There are only two pages for this wizard. The Introduction page asks that you provide a name for the folder, the display name that is shown in Outlook, and a comment that is shown in Outlook. Optionally, you can specify a maximum amount of space that the managed custom folder can contain. The EMS command that was used to generate this managed custom folder is as follows:

```
New-ManagedFolder -Name 'Project Team Communications'
-FolderName 'Project Team Communications' -StorageQuota '25000KB'
-Comment 'Place information in this folder related to your internal
 project time communications.  This information will be retained in
 your mailbox for 360 days from the date it was originally moved to
 this folder.'
```

The command that you enter for the folder is useful in helping users to know what the folder is supposed to be for. This comment will be displayed at the top of the listing of messages in the folder if you are using Outlook 2007. This information is not displayed with earlier versions.

FIGURE 12.5
Creating a new managed custom folder

The storage quota option is useful if you are planning to restrict content for each of the managed folders. Once a user reaches the storage quota maximum for this folder, the folder name will turn red and the user will see a dialog box informing them that their mailbox needs to be cleaned up. This dialog box (shown in Figure 12.6) is displayed only if you are using Outlook 2007 as the client.

The only problem with the dialog box shown in Figure 12.6 is that it does not tell the user which folder is over its limit.

FIGURE 12.6
The user is prompted to clean up their mailbox if a managed custom folder is over its size limit.

The Get-ManagedFolder cmdlet allows you to retrieve a list of both the managed custom folders and the default folders.

```
Get-ManagedFolder | Format-Table Name,Description
```

Name	Description
Calendar	ManagedDefaultFolder
Contacts	ManagedDefaultFolder
Deleted Items	ManagedDefaultFolder
Drafts	ManagedDefaultFolder
Inbox	ManagedDefaultFolder
Junk Email	ManagedDefaultFolder
Journal	ManagedDefaultFolder
Notes	ManagedDefaultFolder
Outbox	ManagedDefaultFolder
Sent Items	ManagedDefaultFolder
Tasks	ManagedDefaultFolder
Entire Mailbox	ManagedDefaultFolder
Rss Feeds	ManagedDefaultFolder
Sync Issues	ManagedDefaultFolder
Official Corporate Communications	ManagedCustomFolder
Project Related Information	ManagedCustomFolder

```
Finance and Accounting Information          ManagedCustomFolder
Departmental Communications                 ManagedCustomFolder
System Cleanup Folder                       ManagedCustomFolder
Project Team Communications                 ManagedCustomFolder
```

If you are a fan of the EMS, Table 12.4 shows the cmdlets that can be used for creating and managing managed custom folders.

TABLE 12.4:   Managed Folder Exchange Management Shell Cmdlets

CMDLET	EXPLANATION
New-ManagedFolder	Creates a new managed custom folder
Set-ManagedFolder	Sets properties for an existing managed custom folder
Get-ManagedFolder	Retrieves a list of the managed folders in the organization
Remove-ManagedFolder	Deletes a managed custom folder.

Managed Folder Mailbox Policies

Creating managed custom folders and defining managed content settings are just part of the equation when implementing messaging records management. Now we actually have to assign those folders to mailboxes. Assigning folders to mailboxes is done with the managed folder mailbox policy. Once you have created a managed folder mailbox policy, you can assign the policy to one or more mailboxes.

Creating Managed Folder Mailbox Policies

Managed folder mailbox policies are found in the Mailboxes subcontainer of the Organization Configuration work center. You find them under the Managed Folder Mailbox Policies (yes, say that three times fast!) tab; by default there are no managed folder mailbox policies. In a small organization, you may need only a single managed folder mailbox policy, while larger organizations may have many policies. The policies assign different managed folders or managed content settings to different users based on their departments, job functions, or company division.

A managed folder mailbox policy has very few properties. When you launch the New Managed Folder Mailbox Policy Wizard, you are asked to provide a name for the policy, and you must provide the folders (both custom and default) that will be managed by this policy. Figure 12.7 shows the New Mailbox Policy page of this wizard.

Note that the folders that are linked with this policy include both custom and default folders. A folder can be linked with more than one policy. The resulting EMS command that is executed to create this policy is as follows:

```
New-ManagedFolderMailboxPolicy -Name 'Executives Managed Folder Mailbox Policy'
-ManagedFolderLinks 'Inbox','Finance and Accounting Information',
'Official Corporate Communications','Deleted Items','Departmental
   Communications', 'Sent Items','Journal','System Cleanup Folder'
```

FIGURE 12.7
Creating a managed
folder mailbox policy

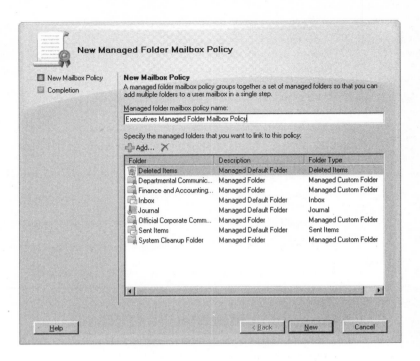

Assigning Managed Folder Mailbox Policies to Users

After a managed folder mailbox policy is defined, the next step is to assign it to a user. This can be done in one of two ways. You can assign the policy to a user during account creation; Figure 12.8 shows the Mailbox Settings page of the New Mailbox Wizard. You can check the Managed Folder Mailbox Policy check box and then browse for a listing of available managed folder mailbox policies in the organization.

If your organization is supporting Outlook 2003 or earlier clients, you will see a warning dialog box informing you that not all of the managed folder features may be available to the user. This dialog box appears whenever you assign a managed folder mailbox policy to a user account.

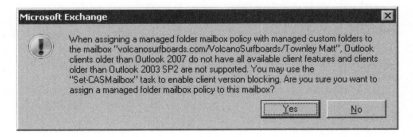

FIGURE 12.8
Assigning a managed
folder mailbox policy at
account creation

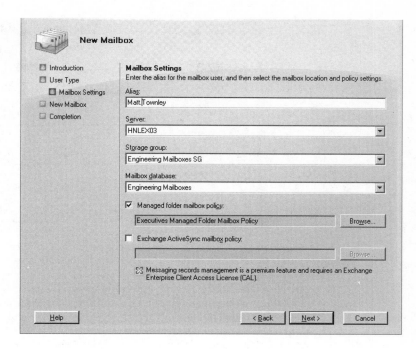

If you are using the Exchange Management Shell, you will notice an additional option in the
`Enable-Mailbox` or `New-Mailbox` command line. This option is `-ManagedFolderMailboxPolicy`
and it sets the `managedfoldermailboxpolicy` property on the mailbox. Here is an example
of an EMS command that would enable a mailbox and set the managed folder mailbox
policy:

```
Enable-Mailbox -Identity
    'volcanosurfboards.com/VolcanoSurfboards/Townley Matt'
-Alias 'Matt.Townley' -Database 'Engineering Mailboxes
-ManagedFolderMailboxPolicy 'Executives Managed Folder
Mailbox Policy'
```

If someone created an account without defining the managed folder mailbox policy, it can be
defined using the EMC. Locate the mailbox in the Recipient Configuration work center, display
the mailbox's properties, go to the Mailbox Settings property page, select Messaging Records
Management, and click the Properties button. This will display the Messaging Records
Management properties for that mailbox.

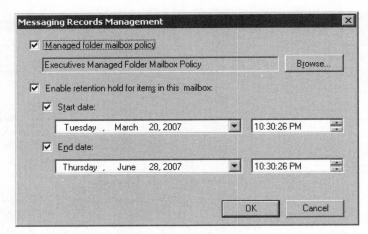

From the Messaging Records Management properties, you can define which managed folder mailbox policy is assigned, and you can optionally specify a period of time during which the policy does not apply to the particular mailbox.

If the mailbox previously existed, you could assign the policy using the EMS. For example, if you want to assign user supatana to the Executives Managed Folder Mailbox Policy, you would type the following EMS cmdlet:

```
Set-Mailbox "Supatana" -ManagedFolderMailboxPolicy "Executives Managed
Folder Mailbox Policy"
```

Actually, if you know what you have to assign a group of mailboxes to a specific policy, it is much easier to do using the EMS. For example, if you want to assign everyone in the Executives group to a managed folder mailbox policy, you can use a single EMS command to accomplish this. Before we show you the command, let's take apart the pieces.

First we want to enumerate the objects that are members of the Executives distribution group. We would use the `Get-DistributionGroupMember` cmdlet. Here is what that would look like:

```
Get-DistributionGroupMember "Executives"


Name                             RecipientType
----                             -------------
Saso Erdeljanov                  UserMailbox
Jordan Chang                     UserMailbox
Don Nguyen                       UserMailbox
Goga Kukrika                     UserMailbox
Pavel Nagaev                     UserMailbox
George Cue                       UserMailbox
Julie Samante                    UserMailbox
Chris Eanes                      UserMailbox
Bthaworn Thaweeaphiradeemaitree  UserMailbox
```

```
Cheyne Manalo                          UserMailbox
Jason Sherry                           UserMailbox
Konrad Sagala                          UserMailbox
```

Remember that when you retrieve information using the PowerShell, what is actually output is the objects; we can pipe those objects to other cmdlets. We want to pipe this command to the Set-Mailbox cmdlet in order to assign the ManagedFolderMailboxPolicy property:

```
Get-DistributionGroupMember "Executives" | Set-Mailbox
-ManagedFolderMailboxPolicy "Executives Managed Folder Mailbox Policy"
```

Another useful thing you can do from the EMS is to list the mailboxes that are already assigned to a particular policy. We just need to implement the Where cmdlet and filter only the objects whose ManagedFolderMailboxPolicy property starts with Default. Here is an example:

```
Get-Mailbox | Where {$_.ManagedFolderMailboxPolicy -like "*Default*"}
| FT Name,managed*
```

```
Name                      ManagedFolderMailboxPolicy
----                      --------------------------
Nathan Nakanishi          Default Managed Folder Mailbox Policy
Lily Ebrahimi             Default Managed Folder Mailbox Policy
Aran Hoffmann             Default Managed Folder Mailbox Policy
Ryan Tung                 Default Managed Folder Mailbox Policy
```

Enabling on the Mailbox Server

The final piece of enabling messaging records management is to configure the mailbox servers to actually schedule and run the managed folder assistant. Managed custom folders do not get created, nor do the content settings get enforced, unless the managed folder assistant is run. Each Exchange server that has the Mailbox role assigned to it has a Messaging Records Management property page. From this property page, you can define a schedule on which the managed folder assistant runs.

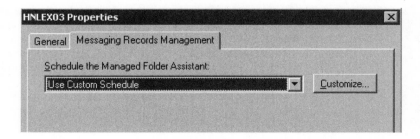

When you click the Customize button, you are presented with a schedule dialog box. The Detail View radio buttons allow you to specify if you are looking at the schedule in 15-minute increments or 1-hour increments.

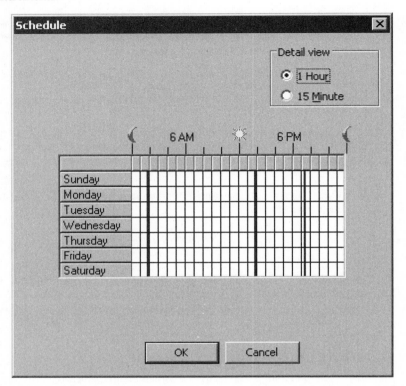

As with other schedule dialog boxes that have a 1-hour view and a 15-minute view, be very careful when selecting a schedule. If you use the 1-hour view and select an entire hour block, then the managed folder assistant will run four times per hour. We recommend that you select the 15-minute view and then schedule times in 15-minute intervals. Further, unless you have a business reason to run this more frequently, we recommend that you schedule the managed folder assistant to run no more than two or three times per day.

If you want to kick off the managed folder assistant manually, there is a cmdlet that lets you do this: the Start-ManagedFolderAssistant cmdlet. If will create any custom folders that need to be created and manage any folder content that is now eligible to be managed by messaging records management. This cmdlet is useful to know if you have just assigned a new policy to a group of users and want to make sure that any custom folders that need to be created are created immediately.

If you run Start-ManagedFolderAssistant from the EMS on a mailbox server, no parameters are necessary. However, if you want to run it on a remote mailbox server, you would type this:

```
Start-ManagedFolderAssistant hnlex03
```

You can also run the managed folder assistant against a specific mailbox, as in this example:

```
Start-ManagedFolderAssistant -Mailbox Suriya.Supatanasakul
```

Summary

Messaging records management starts with some of the features found in the Exchange 2000/2003 Mailbox Manager, such as the ability to automatically delete older content found in users' mailboxes, and then extends them further to make Exchange 2007 more friendly in environments that have third-party message archival systems as well as organizations that are required to follow government or organizational regulations.

Managed custom folders allow the administrator to specify folders in each user's mailbox that can be used for organizing and categorizing official or unofficial communications. User participation is a key factor in ensuring that these folders are successful.

The managed content setting feature allows administrators to actually control, move, and delete the content that is found in either the default Exchange folders or the managed custom folders that the administrator has created.

Chapter 13

Managing Messages in Transit

As you may have noticed by now, in spite of the extra features it offers, Exchange provides messaging as its core functionality. Messaging systems have been part of the business environment for years — long enough for the novelty of electronic messaging to wear off and for it to become a staple of the office. E-mail is now ubiquitous; right or wrong, your users think of it in the same class as utilities such as electricity, telephone service, and water. Because of this perception, the majority of messaging administrators must now deal with issues such as regulatory compliance that once were the province of a only few types of businesses.

Legacy versions of Exchange were not equipped with the tools and technology to allow administrators to effectively deal with these sorts of issues out of the box. Electronic discovery, regulatory compliance, long-term message data archival, and effective retention policies — the basic Exchange architecture was designed without these needs in mind (not that any of the common messaging systems competing with Exchange were, so it's not as if Exchange was particularly bad at dealing with them either). Yet in the modern world of messaging, they are very real problems that the majority of administrators must face to some degree. The solution has traditionally been the implementation of expensive, complicated, third-party software suites.

When setting the design goals for Exchange 2007, Microsoft wanted to ensure that it was better adapted for modern needs and problems. Wisely, the product team didn't try to become compliance experts and bake every possible needed feature into the product; if they had, we'd be seeing the first delivery sometime around 2014. Instead, they concentrated on building in key functionality and features that would make it easier for third parties to continue to develop and test Exchange 2007–compatible solutions. Software that is easier to write and test is less expensive, more trustworthy, and ultimately easier to deploy and use — all wins for you, the Exchange administrator.

In this chapter, we'll cover three of the key changes in Exchange 2007 that, while not being full-featured compliance solutions, will make it much easier for you and third-party applications to manage archival, compliance, retention, and discovery activities.

Topics in this chapter include the following:

◆ Message classifications

◆ Transport rules

◆ Message journaling

Introducing the New Exchange 2007 Transport Architecture

In all versions of Exchange from 4.0 through 2003, the message store was an integral part of the message routing and transport architecture. This is in large part because of its use of the MAPI protocol, in which the client's main point of contact with the messaging system is the MAPI session to their mailbox server. This store-centric architecture made it possible for Exchange to perform certain tasks very quickly and efficiently, but it also made it more difficult to consistently do the types of tasks necessary to meet regulatory requirements. The new role-based architecture in Exchange 2007 is a direct answer to many of these difficulties.

To illustrate the problem, take the typically common requirement in many businesses of ensuring that messaging policies are applied to all messages in the organization. In legacy Exchange, if you send a message to another user whose mailbox is on the same server your mailbox is on, the message would never pass through a transport component. The code for the message store becomes more complex in order to deal with the necessity of having to apply policies at this level, third-party developers have to find ways to hook into this process, and the mailbox server runs more and more code that has nothing to do with the basic task a mailbox server is supposed to handle (which is storing and retrieving messages in the most efficient manner possible).

In contrast, the new distinction between transport servers (two different kinds, in fact: Hub Transport and Edge Transport) and mailbox servers permits the mailbox servers to run only the code that deals with storage and disk I/O. If a message is submitted for delivery, the mailbox server doesn't have to try to figure out exactly what to do with it; instead, it hands it off to a local HT role in the site. The HT server can figure out which policies apply, which recipients need to get a copy of it, and whether any special actions need to be taken. Every message is now handled consistently, the code is cleaner and more efficient, and third-party applications have a well-defined set of interfaces to hook into without having to account for a ton of screwy special edge cases.

TIP

Yes, you read that correctly. Every single message you send in Exchange passes through a Hub Transport server, even when you're sending it to another mailbox in your storage database. Although this might seem inefficient at first glance, the reality is that the resulting benefits make this a great design change.

We'll cover three new capabilities in Exchange 2007 in detail in this chapter:

◆ *Message classifications* are annotations to an e-mail message that mark it as belonging to a designated category of information that Exchange and Outlook may need to treat in a special fashion. These annotations are exposed as properties of the message, allowing clients to display them visually for the users as well as permitting them to be exposed to the rules engine for automated processing. As an example, all messages with certain keywords can be classified as being confidential.

◆ *Transport rules* are server-side rules that allow you to create and apply messaging policies throughout the entire Exchange Server 2007 organization. They come in two varieties: hub transport rules, which are intended to be used for compliance enforcement and policy application activities, and edge transport rules, which are designed to help protect your organization from viruses and other external threats.

◆ *Message journaling* is the process of capturing complete copies and histories of specified messages within your organization. Journaled message reports are generated and sent to specified recipients, which can be within the Exchange organization or some external entity. Journaling may not be exciting or useful by itself, but it's one of the main ways to get messaging data into an external archival system.

You'll examine each of these technologies in more detail in this chapter.

Setting Up Message Classifications

At their heart, message classifications are simply a label that is set on certain messages. This label in turn allows other software such as Outlook and Outlook Web Access (OWA) to display a visual warning for the user and, optionally, take special action when processing the message with mailbox rules.

Message classifications consist of three properties:

◆ The *display name* determines how the classification is to be displayed in the client user interface and is scanned by the mailbox rules engine.

◆ The *sender description* allows the client interface to tell the sender the purpose of this classification if isn't clear from the display name alone.

◆ The *recipient description* allows the client interface to tell the recipient the purpose of this classification.

Figure 13.1 illustrates how Outlook 2007 displays a message classification on a message; the additional colored field that says "Please treat this as Confidential" illustrates the Confidential classificiation.

FIGURE 13.1

A message classification displayed in Outlook 2007

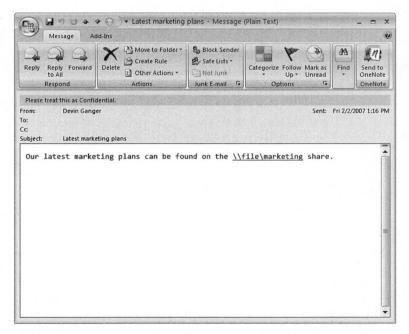

Figure 13.2 shows a user selecting a classification to apply to a message they are sending in OWA.

Out of the box, Exchange 2007 comes with four message classifications: A/C Privileged, Attachment Removed, Company Confidential, and Company Internal. By default, these classifications are informational only; no associated rules enforce them, and their purpose is simply to be

FIGURE 13.2
Applying a message classification in OWA

displayed to recipients. You can modify these default classifications, and create new ones, to suit your business needs. No GUI exists for creating and managing classifications; you must use the EMS. However, once they are created, you can use the GUI Transport Rule Wizard (covered later in this chapter in the section "Creating New Rules with the Exchange Management Console") to apply them using transport rules.

In addition to the basic classification properties, you can optionally set some other properties:

◆ You may specify the precedence, which determines the order that a given classification is applied to a message if multiple classifications are set. You have nine values (Highest, Higher, High, MediumHigh, Medium, MediumLow, Low, Lower, and Lowest) from which to choose.

◆ You may specify whether a given classification should be retained on the message if it is forwarded or replied to; some classifications, such as Attachment Removed, would make little sense when applied to a forwarded copy of a message or to its replies.

◆ You may create localized versions of message classifications if you are working in a multilingual organization.

TIP

By default, OWA supports the display and manual selection of message classifications. To use them in Outlook 2007, you must manually deploy them, which we will cover in "Deploying Message Classifications" later in this chapter. Advanced users can control permissions on message classifications and thus restrict the use of some classifications to a subset of users. See the Exchange 2007 help topic "Deploying Message Classifications" for instructions if you need this capability.

Modifying and Creating Message Classifications

To create new classifications or customize the properties of existing classifications, you must use the Get-MessageClassification and Set-MessageClassification cmdlets in the Exchange Management Shell.

Get-MessageClassification   This cmdlet shows you the existing message classifications in your organization:

```
Get-MessageClassification
```

Set-MessageClassification   This cmdlet modifies the properties of an existing classification. The following example takes an existing classification named NewMC, sets its precedence to High, and sets the RetainClassificationEnabled property so that the classification will be retained across forwards and replies:

```
Set-MessageClassification -Identity NewMC
 -DisplayPrecedence High -RetainClassificationEnabled $True
```

New-MessageClassification   This cmdlet creates a new message classification in your organization, configuring it on your Exchange 2007 servers and registering it in Active Directory:

```
New-MessageClassification -Name NewMC -DisplayName "New Classification"
 -RecipientDescription "This is what the recipient will see when viewing
 the message" -SenderDescription "This is what the sender will see when
 selecting the classification"
```

> **TIP**
>
> If you need to create localized versions of your new classification, see the Exchange 2007 help topic "How to Create Localized Versions of Message Classifications" for instructions.

Deploying Message Classifications

When you create or modify classifications, they are automatically visible to OWA users. In what is a particularly painful oversight, the same is not true for Outlook 2007 users. If you want your Outlook 2007 users to benefit from message classifications, you have two tasks to complete:

1. Export the message classifications from Exchange 2007 to an XML file.

2. Import the XML file into the Outlook 2007 configuration.

> **WARNING**
>
> These steps must be performed every time you add new classifications or modify display properties of existing classifications. Just to make it even more annoying, these tasks are completely manual.

We'll now cover these steps in greater detail.

EXPORTING CLASSIFICATIONS FROM EXCHANGE

If you're looking for an EMS cmdlet to export all of your classifications, stop. You have to use EMS, but no built-in cmdlet exists to perform this task. Instead, you need to navigate to the Scripts subdirectory of the folder you installed Exchange 2007 to (by default, this folder is located at `C:\Program Files\Microsoft\Exchange Server\Scripts`). Microsoft has provided several useful and complex EMS scripts in this folder; the one we want is named `Export-OutlookClassification.ps1`.

The syntax for exporting a classification is a bit tricky, so let's look at an example. In this example, we want to export the `Default\ExACPrivileged` and `Default\ExPartnerMail` classifications. To do this, we use the following EMS command to export these classifications to the C:\MC.XML:

```
"Default\ExACPrivileged","Default\ExPartnerMail" | Get-MessageClassification |
./Export-OutlookClassifciation.ps1 > C:\MC.XML
```

Note that the quotes are necessary around the classification names.

> **NOTE**
>
> If this file is out of sync with the actual classifications specified in Exchange, Outlook will not display the classifications that are missing from the file. It will, however, retain them if they can be retained, and they will still be on the messages (and can be viewed in OWA). Once the file is updated, they will become visible to the user.

IMPORTING CLASSIFICATIONS IN OUTLOOK

This task has two parts: creating the necessary Registry entries and copying over the XML file you just created in the previous step. Once you're created the Registry settings on a given client, you don't need to keep setting them when you update the classifications XML file.

Copying the XML File

Copying the file over is simple; you can do it manually, via a batch script, or through your existing desktop management solution. If you are going to be changing the classifications on a regular basis, you might want to think about configuring some sort of automated deployment system to minimize the need for manual involvement. Outlook reads the file in when it starts, so if the file is updated while Outlook is open, it will not use the updated information until it is next restarted.

> **TIP**
>
> You might consider the use of a logon script to ensure that the latest copy of the classifications XML file is pushed out to your clients. If you've deployed Microsoft Systems Management Server (or some third-party equivalent) in your environment, you can also use that mechanism.

Creating the Registry Entries

The following Registry key and values must be created on all Outlook 2007 computers whose users have mailboxes on Exchange 2007 servers and who are going to be sending message classifications. Until these Registry entries are created, classifications will not be displayed in Outlook, even though they exist on messages.

In the HKCU\Software\Microsoft\Office\12.0\Common key, first create a new key named Policy. Within this new key, create the following values:

```
"AdminClassificationPath"="C:\Path\To\Filename.xml"
"EnableClassifications"=dword:00000001
"TrustClassifications"=dword:00000001
```

You should set the values of these keys accordingly:

◆ AdminClassificationPath is the full path and filename of the XML file you copied from the export process. While this path can be on a network share, this could break for laptop users or other users who lose network connectivity. The file is small, so there's no harm in copying it to the local hard drive.

◆ EnableClassifications allows you to toggle whether message classifications are read and honored in Outlook 2007 on a per-user basis. The value of 1 enables classifications, while the value of 0 disables them.

◆ TrustClassifications allows you to toggle whether Outlook actually trusts classifications on messages that are sent to users on legacy Exchange mailbox servers. The value of 1 enables trust, 0 disables it. Microsoft recommends that you only enable this value for mailboxes on Exchange 2007 servers.

TIP

The Office 2007 Customization Tool, now part of the Office installer, allows you to specify additional Registry keys that will be installed when Office is installed on a machine. If you want to ensure that message classification support is universally deployed and supported in your organization, you might wish to include these Registry settings in your configuration when creating your installation scripts.

Setting Up Transport Rules

The two flavors of transport rules give you, the messaging administrator, the ability to define and automatically enforce messaging policies within your organization. In Exchange 2007, transport rules are enforced on the Hub Transport and Edge Transport roles. You create and manage them in both the Exchange Management Console and the Exchange Management Shell.

Although you use the same processes to create and manage the rules on both roles, the actual actions you can take, and the way the rules are stored, are different. Transport rules are very similar to mailbox rules, but they are applied at the server level to all traffic that goes through that server.

Like mailbox rules, transport rules have three parts:

◆ *Conditions* identify the message properties that trigger the application of the rule to a given message. If you define no conditions, then the rule will apply to all messages.

◆ *Exceptions* identify message properties that exempt a given message from being processed by the rule even if it matches the defined conditions. Exceptions are optional.

◆ *Actions* modify the properties or delivery of messages that match the conditions without matching the exceptions defined by the rule. There must be at least one action, but you can have multiple actions in a given rule.

Transport rules on a Hub Transport server are defined and stored in Active Directory; each Hub Transport server in the organization sees the entire set of defined rules and attempts to match them against all messages. This allows you to define a single, consistent set of message policies throughout your organization. You can define a total of 1,000 transport rules in your organization. That may seem like a lot, but in large enterprises, you often need hundreds of transport rules to fully define the automated policy restrictions required.

Since rules are stored in Active Directory, modifications to your transport rules are subject to your normal AD replication. Depending on your site topology, it may take some time before your current changes propagate fully throughout your organization.

WARNING

If you have legacy Exchange servers in your organization; they will not make use of your transport rules. If acting as bridgeheads, these servers may represent a significant loophole in your messaging policy enforcement. Likewise, legacy Exchange mailbox servers do not pass all messages through a Hub Transport server, so you may notice that some policies are not applied evenly until all mailboxes are on Exchange 2007 servers.

In contrast, transport rules for Edge Transport servers are defined on a per-server basis and stored in the local ADAM database on the Edge Transport server. Thus, while you have no propagation delays to worry about, you do have to manually maintain a consistent set of rules on your Edge Transport servers or have some interesting discrepancies to track down at a later date.

TIP

If you have multiple Edge Transport servers, we recommend using an EMS script to manage your transport rule configurations. Not only can you easily reuse this script on each Edge Transport server to maintain consistency, but the script makes great documentation on what your current configuration is.

Selecting Conditions and Exceptions

Since conditions and exceptions are both involved in identifying whether a given message should be processed by the rule, it should be no surprise that they give you the same set of options.

Which options you get depends on whether you're creating the rule on a Hub Transport or Edge Transport server. The Exchange 2007 help files contain detailed descriptions of how each of these conditions and exceptions are defined and applied, but this should help you get an idea of what types of selection criteria you have available at your fingertips.

HUB TRANSPORT CONDITIONS AND EXCEPTIONS

You can select the following conditions on Hub Transport servers:

◆ From people

◆ From a member of distribution list

◆ From users inside or outside the organization

◆ Sent to people

◆ Sent to a member of distribution list

◆ Sent to users inside or outside the organization

◆ Between members of distribution list and distribution list

◆ When any of the recipients in the To field is people

◆ When any of the recipients in the To field is a member of distribution list

◆ When any of the recipients in the Cc field is people

◆ When any of the recipients in the Cc field is a member of distribution list

◆ When any of the recipients in the To or Cc fields are people

◆ When any of the recipients in the To or Cc fields is a member of distribution list

◆ When the Subject field contains specific words

◆ When the Subject field or the body of the message contains specific words

◆ When a message header contains specific words

◆ When the From address contains specific words

◆ When the Subject field contains text patterns

◆ When the Subject field or the body of the message contains text patterns

◆ When the message header contains text patterns

◆ When the From address contains text patterns

◆ When any attachment file name contains text patterns

◆ With a spam confidence level (SCL) rating that is greater or equal to limit

◆ When the size of any attachment is greater than or equal to limit

◆ Marked with classification

◆ Marked with importance

EDGE TRANSPORT CONDITIONS AND EXCEPTIONS

You can select the following conditions on Edge Transport servers:

◆ When the Subject field contains specific words

◆ When the Subject field or the body of the message contains specific words

◆ When a message header contains specific words

◆ When the From address contains specific words

◆ When any recipient address contains specific words

◆ When the Subject field contains text patterns

◆ When the Subject field or the body of the message contains text patterns

◆ When the message header contains text patterns

◆ When the From address contains text patterns

◆ When text patterns in any of recipient address

◆ With a spam confidence level (SCL) rating that is greater than or equal to limit

◆ When the size of any attachment is greater than or equal to limit

◆ From users inside or outside the organization

> **NOTE**
>
> Several condition and exceptions allow you to specify text patterns, which Exchange will then attempt to match against the specified fields. These patterns are known as regular expressions; see the Exchange 2007 help topic "Regular Expressions in Transport Rules" for more details and examples.

Selecting Actions

As with conditions and exceptions, your choice of possible actions depends on whether you're creating the rule on a Hub Transport server or an Edge Transport server. The Exchange 2007 help files contain detailed descriptions of how each of these actions is defined and applied.

HUB TRANSPORT ACTIONS

You can select the following actions on Hub Transport servers:

◆ Log an event with message

◆ Prepend the subject with string

◆ Apply message classification

◆ Append disclaimer text using font, size, color, with separator, and fallback to action if unable to apply

◆ Set the spam confidence level to value

◆ Set header with value

◆ Remove header

◆ Add a recipient in the To field addresses

◆ Copy message to addresses

◆ Blind copy (Bcc) the message to addresses

◆ Redirect message to addresses

◆ Send bounce message to sender with enhanced status code

◆ Silently drop the message

> **NOTE**
>
> One disappointing lack in the Hub Transport transport rule actions is the ability to designate that a matching message must be delivered to a location in the destination mailbox. Such an action would be extremely useful in conjunction with the Managed Folders functionality described in Chapter 12, "Managing Folder Content;" it would allow the messaging administrators to automatically file certain messages (perhaps those with a specified classification) into known locations such as a managed custom folder.

EDGE TRANSPORT ACTIONS

You can select the following actions on Edge Transport servers:

◆ Log an event with message

◆ Prepend the subject with string

◆ Set the spam confidence level to value

◆ Set header with value

◆ Remove header

◆ Add a recipient in the To field addresses

◆ Copy the message to addresses

◆ Blind carbon copy (Bcc) the message to addresses

◆ Drop connection

◆ Redirect the message to addresses

◆ Put message in quarantine

◆ Reject the message with status code and response

◆ Silently drop the message

Creating New Rules with the Exchange Management Console

To create a new transport rule on your HT servers using the EMC, launch the EMC. Navigate to Exchange Organization\Organization Configuration\Hub Transport in the left-hand pane, then select the Transport Rules tab in the middle pane. Click the New Transport Rule task in the pane on the right to start the New Transport Rule Wizard.

Figure 13.3 shows the Introduction screen of the wizard. Here you provide the name and optional description of the new rule, as well as select whether the rule will be enabled once it is created. The name field is required. Click Next to continue.

FIGURE 13.3
New Transport Rule Wizard Introduction screen

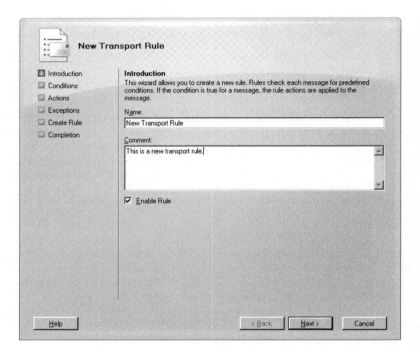

Figure 13.4 shows the Conditions screen. The default condition is Apply to Messages, which will match all messages. If you want to narrow down which messages will be affected, select the check boxes of one or more conditions; they will be added to the lower text field.

To fill in the values of the conditions, click on the underlined blue text fields and select the results from the selection dialogs that are opened. Once you are satisfied with the selections, click OK to close the selection dialogs. Click Next to continue.

Figure 13.5 shows the Actions screen. There are no default actions. Select the check boxes of one or more actions; they will be added to the lower text field.

To fill in the values of the actions, click on the underlined blue text fields and select the results from the selection dialogs that are opened. Once you are satisfied with the selections, click OK to close the selection dialogs. Click Next to continue.

Figure 13.6 shows the Exceptions screen. There are no default exceptions. If you wish to create an exception, select the check boxes of one or more exceptions; they will be added to the lower text field.

FIGURE 13.4
New Transport Rule
Wizard Conditions
screen

FIGURE 13.5
New Transport Rule
Wizard Actions screen

FIGURE 13.6
New Transport Rule
Wizard Exceptions
screen

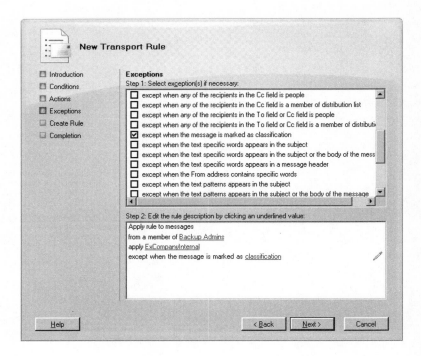

FIGURE 13.7
New Transport Rule
Wizard Create Rule
screen

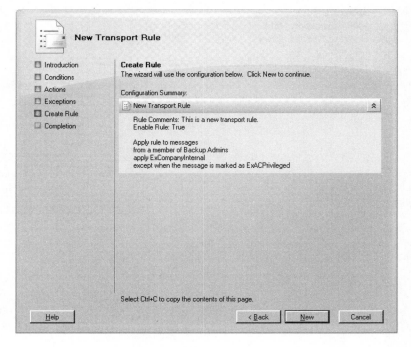

To fill in the values of the exceptions, click on the underlined blue text fields and select the results from the selection dialogs that are opened. Once you are satisfied with the selections, click OK to close the selection dialogs. Click Next to continue.

Figure 13.7 shows the Create Rule screen. This screen gives you a summary of the rule that will be created. If you are happy with it, click New to create the rule.

The transport rule is now created in Active Directory and will be replicated to all HT servers in your organization. The results of the operation, including the EMS command line used to create the rule, will be shown on the Completion screen, as shown in Figure 13.8.

FIGURE 13.8
New Transport Rule
Wizard Completion
screen

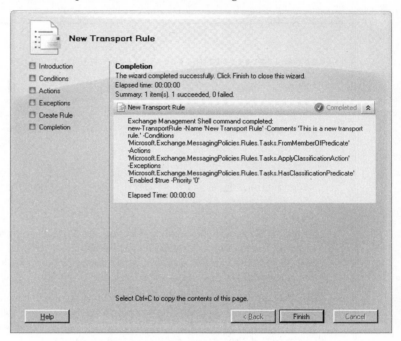

To create a new transport rule on your ET server using the EMC, launch the EMC on your ET server. Follow the same steps as for creating a new HT transport rule.

Creating New Rules with the Exchange Management Shell

The following Exchange Management Shell commands let you add, change, remove, enable, or disable transport rules that are used by the Transport Rules agent on a Hub Transport server or an Edge Transport server:

Get-TransportRule   This cmdlet shows you the existing transport rules in your organization (if run on an HT server) or Edge server (if run on an ET server):

```
Get-TransportRule
```

Enable-TransportRule   This cmdlet sets an existing transport rule as enabled, which means it will be applied to messages:

```
Enable-TransportRule -Identity MyTransportRule
```

Disable-TransportRule This cmdlet sets an existing transport rule as disabled, which means that it will still be present in the configuration but will not be applied to messages:

```
Disable-TransportRule -Identity MyTransportRule
```

> **TIP**
>
> The `Disable-TransportRule` cmdlet is useful for troubleshooting problems with transport rules.

Remove-TransportRule This cmdlet allows you to delete an existing transport rule:

```
Remove-TransportRule -Identity TransportRuleToDelete
```

Set-TransportRule This cmdlet allows you to modify the parameters of an existing transport rule:

```
$Condition = Get-TransportRulePredicate FromMemberOf
$Condition.Addresses = @((Get-DistributionGroup "Sales Group"))
Set-TransportRule -Identity FromSales -Condition @($condition)
```

To make this cmdlet manageable, we made use of variables to create the condition *from a member of distribution list* and fill its Addresses property with the *Sales Group* distribution list. We then pass the variable into the `Set-TransportRule` cmdlet, modifying the condition of the *FromSales* rule.

New-TransportRule This cmdlet allows you to create a new transport rule. Creating a new rule from the EMS is beyond the scope of this book, but it follows the same principles as the `Set-TransportRule` example. From the EMS, issue the following command for a full description of the cmdlet, including examples:

```
Help New-TransportRule -full
```

Introducing Journaling

A lot of people confuse *journaling*, which is the process of capturing a set of communications for future use, with *archiving*, which is the practice of removing less frequently accessed message data from the message store in favor of a secondary storage location. Archival is all about getting stuff out of your mailboxes, usually older and bulkier messages and attachments, so you can reduce the performance hit on your comparatively expensive mailbox server storage systems and reduce your backup windows. Journaling is record keeping; you're defining a set of users whose traffic you must keep track of, and Exchange dutifully captures faithful copies of every message they send or receive.

As we stated before, journaling is one of the main strategies that compliance and archival vendors use to get messaging data into their solutions.

> **NOTE**
>
> Archival solutions are outside the scope of this book; Exchange 2007 offers no native archival abilities.

Although you may not have any explicit applicable regulatory language that forces you to implement journaling, it can often be one of the easier ways to meet what requirements you do have. As compliance becomes more of an issue, the ability to quickly and easily put your hands on complete and accurate records of messaging communications will become critical.

Legacy Exchange offered rudimentary journaling; Exchange 2003 offered the ability to do envelope journaling, which finally captured sufficient information to be of general use. The base journaling mechanism used by Exchange 2007 is envelope journaling, which captures all recipient information (even Bcc: headers and forwards). However, you have two options for journaling:

◆ *Standard journaling* (per-mailbox database journaling) uses the Journaling agent on HT servers to journal all messages sent to and from recipients and senders whose mailboxes are homed on specified mailbox databases. also called per-mailbox database journaling.

◆ *Premium journaling* (per-recipient journaling) also uses the Journaling agent on HT servers, but it's more granular. It offers you the ability to design journaling rules for groups or even specific users if need be.

> **NOTE**
>
> You must have an Exchange Enterprise Client Access License (CAL) to use premium journaling.

Implementing Journaling

The Journaling agent, present on your Hub Transport servers, is responsible for detecting whether a given message falls under your journaling rules. When you use standard journaling, you enable it for an entire mailbox database. Any messages sent to or by recipients whose mailboxes are located on a journal-enabled database will be detected by the Journaling agent and copies will be sent to a designated *journal recipient*. This journal recipient can be another recipient in the Exchange organization — if it is an Exchange mailbox it must be dedicated to the purpose — or an SMTP address on another messaging system.

> **NOTE**
>
> Journaling to an external recipient may seem like a crazy idea at first blush. However, this allows Exchange 2007 to be used with compliance and archival solutions that are not part of the Exchange organization or even with hosted solution providers.

> **TIP**
>
> If you use an external journal recipient, you should ensure that your SMTP transport connections to the external system are fully secure and authenticated. Exchange 2007 supports the use of the TLS protocol; see Chapter 20 for details on how to configure TLS connections to specific domains and how to enable SMTP authentication.

When you use Premium journaling, you create journal rules that define a subset of the recipients in your organization. The Journaling agent on the Hub Transport server detects that the rule matches a given messages and again sends a copy of the message to the journal recipient.

Journaling rules can have three scopes, which helps the Journaling agent decide whether or not it needs to examine a given message:

◆ The Internal scope matches messages where all senders and recipients are members of the Exchange organization.

◆ The External scope matches messages where at least one sender or recipient is an external entity.

◆ The Global scope matches all messages, even those that may have already been matched by the other scopes.

> **NOTE**
>
> Premium journaling rules are stored in Active Directory and propagated to all Hub Transport servers, depending on the normal AD replication mechanism.

If you are using an internal mailbox as your journaling recipient, you should be aware that it may collect a large amount of traffic. While you can use the same mailbox for all journal reports generated in your organization, you may need to create multiple mailboxes to control mailbox size and ensure that your backup windows can be maintained. These mailboxes should be kept very secure and safe from everyday access because they may one day be material evidence in the event that your business is sued or must prove compliance to auditors.

To guard against the loss of journaling reports in the event of trouble within your Exchange organization, you can designate an *alternate journaling mailbox*. This mailbox will receive any non-delivery reports that are issued if your journaling recipient cannot be delivered to. Unfortunately, you get to configure a single alternate mailbox for your entire organization. Not only can this cause performance and mailbox size issues, your local regulations may prevent you from mixing multiple types of journal information in one mailbox.

> **NOTE**
>
> If you are using the Unified Messaging role in your organization, you may not want to journal UM-generated messages such as voicemail. On the other hand, you may be required to preserve these types of messages as well as your regular e-mail.

Reading Journal Reports

The journaling process creates a special Exchange message known as the *journal report*. This message is essentially a wrapper that contains a summary of the original message properties. It also contains a pristine copy of the original message that generated the report, neatly attached to the report. The reports are designed to be human and machine readable, allowing you to automate processing of journal reports via a third-party application as well as perform manual checks on the data.

Table 13.1 shows the fields that Exchange 2007 places in the journal report.

TABLE 13.1: Exchange 2007 Journal Report Fields

FIELD	WHAT IT CONTAINS
To	The SMTP address of a recipient in the To header or the SMTP envelope recipient. If the message was sent through a distribution list, this field contains the Expanded field. If the message was forwarded, this field contains the Forwarded field.
Cc	The SMTP address of a recipient in the Cc header or the SMTP envelope recipient. If the message was sent through a distribution list, this field contains the Expanded field. If the message was forwarded, this field contains the Forwarded field.
Bcc	The SMTP address of a recipient in the Bcc header or the SMTP envelope recipient. If the message was sent through a distribution list, this field contains the Expanded field. If the message was forwarded, this field contains the Forwarded field.
Recipient	The SMTP address of a recipient who is not a member of the Exchange 2007 organization, such as Internet recipients or recipients on legacy Exchange servers.
Sender	The sender's SMTP address, found either in the From or Sender header of the message.
On-Behalf-Of	The relevant SMTP address if the Send on Behalf Of feature was used.
Subject	The Subject header.
Message-ID	The internal Exchange Message-ID.

Depending on your routing topology and journal rule configuration, you may receive multiple journal reports for a given message. This is not an error; it reflects the fact that any given Hub Transport server may not have a complete view of the organization, depending on AD replication, recipient caching, and other factors.

Summary

The new message transport architecture of Exchange 2007 provides a wide variety of new capabilities that can make your job easier. While these new features are not going to be complete compliance solutions for any but the smallest of organizations, they provide a consistent, manageable way to establish controls across your organization.

Message classifications provide a way to visibly tag selected messages and show that they require specific treatment. On their own, they're merely advisory, but combined with transport rules and mailbox rules, they can become powerful selection criteria for managing messages and ensuring policy compliance. The catch is that while they work out of the box with OWA, using them with Outlook 2007 requires you to get your hands dirty copying files and adding Registry entries.

Transport rules give you a powerful, centralized method for creating automated policy enforcement in your environment. You can create rules on both Hub Transport and Edge Transport servers, although they serve slightly different purposes.

Journaling is still around and better than ever in Exchange 2007. In addition to journaling to mailboxes within the organization, you can now designate external recipients to send reports to. Standard journaling enables journaling on a per-database basis, while premium journaling allows you create journaling rules targeted to specific groups or even individual users.

Chapter 14

Public Folder Administration

For many companies, public folders are a major part of their Exchange Server deployments. Public folders are a powerful way to share knowledge and data throughout your organization, and they've been a staple of Exchange Server. They are a great way to share content and information with many users, and since they can be mail-enabled, they can also be an easy way for third-party application developers to hook into Exchange. Just use the MAPI libraries to connect to Exchange as a user with permissions to the specified public folder and you've got the ability to send and receive messages — and share them with multiple users — without having to do a lot of coding.

At the same time, public folder management has been a weakness in previous versions of Exchange Server:

◆ There is a distinct lack of freely available command-line tools for managing public folders and public folder stores. Some tools were available from PSS, but they weren't advertised and weren't generally supported for versions of Exchange past 5.5.

◆ The public folder support in the legacy Exchange System Manager lacked effective bulk operation support; you could not, for example, easily add a new public folder store to the replica list of a given folder and its subfolders without visiting each folder in turn or by overwriting the replica lists of the subfolders with copies of the initial folder's list.

◆ There was no easy way to export or import properties, permissions, or other settings from one public folder or server to another.

◆ The public folder replica and replication information displayed by the legacy System Manager was often incomplete, misleading, or just plain wrong.

◆ The Installable File System (IFS, or M: drive) introduced by Exchange 2000 allowed administrators to access Exchange store objects as if the store was a filesystem. Unfortunately, this allowed them to use inappropriate tools to make their management tasks "easier" and introduced a whole new category of problems that could break public folders.

Unfortunately, Microsoft's announcement that it was deemphasizing support for public folders in Exchange 2007 has caused a lot of worry and confusion. When you combine this with the lack of any GUI public folder management tools in the initial release of Exchange 2007, a lot of people have come to the conclusion that you just can't do public folders anymore. If you've got a large public folder deployment in your organization, this is obviously an area of concern for you. Be assured that public folders are alive and well, and in some ways they're even better in Exchange 2007 than they ever have been. The new EMS cmdlets for handling public folders are definitely worth the price of admission, and even the lack of built-in GUI functions are offset by the wonderful tool known as PFDAVAdmin.

Topics in this chapter include the following:

◆ Understanding how public folders are supported in Exchange 2007

◆ Understanding the limits of public folder support in Exchange 2007

◆ Managing public folders

◆ Understanding and choosing which public folder management tools are available

◆ Working with the public folder hierarchy

◆ Managing replication.

Understanding Public Folder Support in Exchange 2007

When Microsoft announced it was "deemphasizing" support for public folders in Exchange Server 2007, a lot of Exchange administrators immediately got worried. What was the future of public folders? Would Exchange Server 2007 continue to support them? If not, what would the migration path look like?

Happily, Microsoft has clarified its position on public folder support. Public folders are still fully supported in Exchange Server 2007 (and will be through 2016), although they may not be included in future releases of Exchange Server. However, Exchange Server 2007 is the first version to provide support for Microsoft Windows SharePoint Services integration as an alternative method of seamlessly sharing data within your organization and making it available to Outlook 2007 and Outlook Web Access (OWA) users.

In the meantime, you can go forward with your Exchange 2007 migration secure in the knowledge that you will be able to continue using your public folder infrastructure. You can continue to use the Exchange 2003 System Manager console to create, manage, and delete public folders, or you can use the functionality built into Exchange 2007.

Understanding Native Exchange 2007 Support

Although the Exchange Management Console (EMC) offers minimal support for public folders, Exchange 2007 provides the bulk of its built-in support via Exchange Management Shell (EMS) cmdlets. Don't worry; they're not difficult to use, even if you're not a script or command-line guru.

Before we show you how to use the new public folder cmdlets, though, we'll cover exactly what you can do in the EMC. Be warned that it isn't much: you can create and delete public folder stores on your mailbox servers and manage the basic properties of these stores. You can't view the public folder hierarchy, add or delete public folders, set folder properties, manage access permissions, or view and manage replication. To do all of those tasks, you'll need some other tool, such as Outlook to manage individual folders or EMS to deal with public folders from the server.

If you're missing the GUI and feeling left high and dry, ponder the plight of POP3, IMAP, and NNTP GUI management. Exchange 2007 includes no GUI interface for managing those protocols and EMS is the only way to go. At least with public folders, if you don't feel up to tackling EMS, you can always use the Exchange 2003 System Manager console.

Using the EMS

The EMS is built on the Windows PowerShell technology. Because it's a specialized application of PowerShell, it uses the same format as standard PowerShell cmdlets. That format is as follows:

```
verb-noun
```

By combining the noun and verb in the name of the cmdlet, each cmdlet self-describes both the type of operation it performs as well as the object it manipulates. Verbs produce a standard behavior regardless of which object they're applied to. For example, the `Get` verb will always provide a read-only list of the object's properties, while the `Set` verb will always allow you to modify those properties — even when those properties vary from object to object.

TIP

In some of the following examples, you'll see lines terminated by a backtick (') character. PowerShell uses this character for line termination; it tells the shell that the logical line of input will be continued on the next physical line. This allows you to break up long lines for display and still ensure that they work correctly when you enter them.

As a result, the same verbs and nouns tend to be used over and over again; this helps you learn your way around more quickly. Many of the properties are common across multiple objects, so you'll quickly get used to how to use them. The help page for each cmdlet lists all parameters that can be used with that cmdlet.

NOTE

As we explore the public folder cmdlets in the EMC, we'll group related cmdlets together by noun so you can see the different types of operations you can perform. It makes it a lot easier to keep related types of operations together in your mind.

PERFORMING GENERAL PUBLIC FOLDER TASKS

These cmdlets apply to the entire public folder hierarchy at once and provide broad control of your public folder infrastructure:

Get-PublicFolderStatistics   This cmdlet provides a detailed set of statistics about the public folder hierarchy on a given server:

```
Get-PublicFolderStatistics -Server "MBX01"
```

NOTE

If the -Server parameter is not specified, the cmdlet will default to displaying the statistics on the local server.

Resume-PublicFolderReplication   This cmdlet reenables all public folder content replication when it has been suspended:

```
Resume-PublicFolderReplication
```

Suspend-PublicFolderReplication   This cmdlet suspends all public folder content replication:

```
Suspend-PublicFolderReplication
```

Update-PublicFolderHierarchy   This cmdlet starts the content synchronization process for the public folder hierarchy on the specified server:

```
Update-PublicFolderHierarchy -Server "MBX01"
```

MANIPULATING INDIVIDUAL PUBLIC FOLDERS

These cmdlets are designed to work with a specific public folder:

Get-PublicFolder   This cmdlet retrieves the properties for the specified public folder. If you don't name a public folder by specifying a value for the -Identity property, it will default to the root public folder:

```
Get-PublicFolder-Identity"\Jobs\Posted"-Server"MBX01"
Get-PublicFolder-Recurse
Get-PublicFolder -Identity \NON_IPM_SUBTREE -Recurse
```

If you need to see system folders, you'll need to set the -Identity property to a value beginning with the string \NON_IPM_SUBTREE.

NOTE

By default, the Get-PublicFolder cmdlet returns the values for only a single folder. The -Recurse switch changes the behavior to report on all subfolders as well.

New-PublicFolder   This cmdlet creates a new public folder. The -Path property is required and provides the name and location of the new public folder:

```
New-PublicFolder -Identity "\Jobs\New" -Server "MBX01"
```

Remove-PublicFolder   This cmdlet deletes a public folder. The -Path property is required and provides the name and location of the public folder to be deleted:

```
Remove-PublicFolder -Identity "\Jobs\Old" -Server "MBX01"
```

NOTE

By default, the Remove-PublicFolder cmdlet removes only the named public folder. The -Recurse switch will delete all subfolders as well, which is handy for removing an entire group of folders at once.

Set-PublicFolder   This cmdlet allows you to set most of the properties for the named public folder, such as limits, replicas, replication schedules, and more:

```
Set-PublicFolder -Identity "\Jobs\Posted" -Server "MBX01"
```

> **NOTE**
>
> You cannot use the `Set-PublicFolder` cmdlet to mail-enable a public folder or to change its mail-related attributes. See the next section, "Manipulating Public Folder Mail Attributes," for the cmdlets to use for these tasks.

Update-PublicFolder   This cmdlet starts the content synchronization process for the named public folder. The `-Identity` property is required:

```
Update-PublicFolder -Identity "\Jobs\Posted"
```

MANIPULATING PUBLIC FOLDER MAIL ATTRIBUTES

These cmdlets are designed to work with a specific public folder and modify the attributes it receives when it is mail-enabled:

Disable-MailPublicFolder   This cmdlet takes an existing mail-enabled public folder and renders it mail-disabled (what a great term!):

```
Disable-MailPublicFolder -Identity "\Jobs\New"
```

Enable-MailPublicFolder   This cmdlet takes an existing public folder and renders it mail-enabled. The optional `-HiddenFromAddressListsEnabled` switch allows you to hide the folder from your address lists:

```
Enable-MailPublicFolder-Identity"\Jobs\New"
  -HiddenFromAddressListsEnabled $true -Server "MBX01"
```

> **NOTE**
>
> You set the mail-related attributes separately using the `Set-MailPublicFolder` cmdlet.

Get-MailPublicFolder   This cmdlet retrieves the mail-related properties for the specified public folder. If you don't name a public folder by specifying a value for the `-Identity` property, it will default to the root public folder:

```
Get-MailPublicFolder -Identity "\Jobs\Old" -Server "MBX01"
```

> **NOTE**
>
> You set the mail-related attributes separately.

Set-MailPublicFolder   This cmdlet allows you to set the mail-related properties for the named public folder, such as alias, e-mail addresses, send and receive sizes, permitted and prohibited senders, and so on:

```
Set-PublicFolder-Identity"\Jobs\Posted"-Server"MBX01"'
  -AliasPostedJobs-PrimarySmtpAddress "postedjobs\commatcontoso.com"
```

NOTE

Once you have set the mail-related attributes for a public folder, you must still mail-enable it using the `Enable-MailPublicFolder` cmdlet.

MANAGING PUBLIC FOLDER DATABASES

These cmdlets allow you to manage the public folder databases:

Get-PublicFolderDatabase   This cmdlet provides the functionality used by the EMC and allows you to view the properties of existing public folder databases:

```
Get-PublicFolderDatabase -Server "MBX01"
```

NOTE

The `-Identity`, `-Server`, and `-StorageGroup` parameters are not compatible with each other. Use only one of the three to narrow down your selection.

New-PublicFolderDatabase   This cmdlet allows you to create a new public folder database.

NOTE

You can see the `New-PublicFolderDatabase` cmdlet in action by using the EMC to create a new database; it will show you the exact syntax it used with the cmdlet.

Remove-PublicFolderDatabase   This cmdlet deletes an existing public folder database from the active configuration of the server:

```
Remove-PublicFolderDatabase ' -Identity "Public Folder Database"
```

NOTE

The corresponding EDB file is not deleted by the `Remove-PublicFolderDatabase` cmdlet; you have to manually remove it from the hard drive.

Set-PublicFolderDatabase   This cmdlet provides the underlying functionality used by the EMC to update the properties of existing public folder databases:

```
Set-PublicFolderDatabase'
  -Identity "PublicFolderDatabase" ' -Name "New and Improved PF Database"
```

MANAGING PUBLIC FOLDER PERMISSIONS

These cmdlets allow you to modify and monitor the permissions on your public folders. Administrative and client permissions are handled through two separate sets of nouns. The Exchange 2007 documentation contains the list of specific permissions that you can apply.

Add-PublicFolderAdministrativePermission   This cmdlet lets you add an administrative permission entry to a given public folder:

```
Add-PublicFolderAdministrativePermission -User 'Jim' -Identity "\Jobs\Posted"
  -AccessRights "ViewInformationStore, AdministerInformationStore"
```

> **NOTE**
>
> You can specify a single access right or list multiple rights at once using the syntax shown in the example for the Add-PublicFolderAdministrativePermission cmdlet.

Add-PublicFolderClientPermission   This cmdlet lets you add a client permission entry to a given public folder:

```
Add-PublicFolderClientPermission -User 'Makoto.Suzuki'
  -Identity "\Jobs\Posted" -AccessRights CreateItems
```

> **NOTE**
>
> You can specify a single access right or list multiple rights at once using the syntax shown in the example for the Add-PublicFolderAdministrativePermission cmdlet.

Get-PublicFolderAdministrativePermission   This cmdlet lets you view the administrative permission entries on a given public folder:

```
Get-PublicFolderAdministrativePermission -Identity "\Jobs\Posted"
```

Get-PublicFolderClientPermission   This cmdlet lets you view the client permission entries on a given public folder:

```
Get-PublicFolderClientPermission -Identity "\Jobs\Posted"
```

Remove-PublicFolderAdministrativePermission   This cmdlet lets you remove an administrative permission entry from a given public folder:

```
Remove-PublicFolderAdministrativePermission -User Lyle.Bullock
  -Identity "\Jobs\Posted" -AccessRights ViewInformationStore
```

> **NOTE**
>
> You can specify a single access right or list multiple rights at once using the syntax shown in the
> Remove-PublicFolderAdministrativePermission example.

Remove-PublicFolderClientPermission   This cmdlet lets you remove a client permission entry from a given public folder:

```
Remove-PublicFolderClientPermission -User Nathan.Peters'
  -Identity "\Jobs\Posted" -AccessRights CreateItems
```

> **NOTE**
>
> You can specify a single access right or list multiple rights at once using the syntax shown in the
> Remove-PublicFolderAdministrativePermission example.

USING ADDITIONAL SCRIPTS FOR COMPLICATED TASKS

While the cmdlets described in the preceding sections are certainly great for single folder operations, performing common operations on entire groups of folders starts getting sticky. Since most of us aren't scripting gurus, Exchange 2007 provides some example EMS scripts that allow you to perform more complicated server and management tasks that affect groups of folders:

◆ AddReplicaToPFRecursive.ps1 adds the specified server to the replica list for a given public folder and all folders underneath it.

◆ AddUsersToPFRecursive.ps1 allows you to grant user permissions to a folder and all folders beneath it.

◆ MoveAllReplicas.ps1 finds and replaces a server in the replica list of all public folders, including system folders.

◆ RemoveReplicaFromPFRecursive.ps1 removes the specified server from the replica list for a given public folder and all folders underneath it.

◆ ReplaceReplicaOnPFRecursive.ps1 finds and replaces a server in the replica list of a given public folder as well as all subfolders.

◆ ReplaceUserPermissionOnPFRecursive.ps1 finds and replaces one user in the permissions on a given public folder and all its subfolders with a second user; the original user permissions are not retained.

◆ `ReplaceUserWithUserOnPFRecursive.ps1` copies one user's access permissions on a given public folder and all its subfolders to a second user while retaining permissions for the first user; it's confusingly named.

◆ `RemoveReplicaFromPFRecursive.ps1` removes the given user's access permissions from the given public folder and all its subfolders.

You can find these scripts in the Scripts subfolder of the Exchange 2007 installation folder. Note that with the default Windows PowerShell configuration, you just can't click on these scripts and run them; you must invoke them from within the EMS, usually by navigating to the folder and calling them explicitly.

Using Outlook

Exchange public folders can also be created by mailbox-enabled users in their e-mail clients. We'll show you how to create a public folder using the Outlook client.

Open Outlook and make sure the folder list is displayed. Next, double-click Public Folders in the folder list, or click the plus icon just in front of Public Folders. Notice that the plus sign becomes a minus sign when a folder is expanded to show the folders within it.

You've now expanded the top-level folder for public folders, which contains two subfolders: Favorites and All Public Folders. Expand the All Public Folders folder and you'll see that it has at least one subfolder: Internet Newsgroups. If your organization uses public folders, you probably have at least one other subfolder here as well.

NOTE

If your Exchange organization has a large number of public folders, you can drag the ones that you use a lot to your Favorites subfolder. This makes them easier to find. Folders in the Favorites folder are also the only ones that are available when you work offline without a connection to your Exchange server.

To create new public folders in the folder All Public Folders, follow these steps:

1. Right-click All Public Folders, and then select New Folder from the menu that pops up. This brings up the Create New Folder dialog box (see Figure 14.1).

2. Enter a name for the folder; we've given ours the somewhat unimaginative name My New Folder.
   Note that the folder will hold e-mail and posted items. E-mail items are messages. Posted items contain a subject and text. You can post an item in a folder designed to hold posts without having to deal with messaging attributes such as whom the item is sent to. To post an item, click the down arrow near the New icon on the main Outlook window and select Post in This Folder from the drop-down menu.
   When you're done creating your folder, click OK.

If you're told that you don't have sufficient permissions to create the folder, you need to assign those permissions using one of the other Exchange public folder management tools. If you have Exchange administrative permissions, you can make this change yourself.

FIGURE 14.1
Naming a new folder

The new public folder now shows up under the All Public Folders hierarchy. If you can't see the full name of your new folder, make the Folder List pane a little wider.

Now right-click your new folder and select Properties from the pop-up menu. This brings up the Properties dialog box for the folder, shown in Figure 14.2.

We're not going to spend a lot of time with this dialog box. Among other things, mailbox owners use public folder Properties dialog boxes to do the following:

◆ Add a description for other mailbox owners who access the folder

◆ Make the folder available on the Internet

◆ Set up a default view of the folder, including grouping by such things as the subject or sender

◆ Set up some administrative rules on folder characteristics, access, and such

◆ Set permissions for using the folder

Go ahead and look around in the Properties dialog box. When you're done, click Cancel, unless you've made some changes. If you have, then click OK to save your changes.

FIGURE 14.2
The Outlook client's
Properties dialog box
for a public folder

Using the Exchange 2003 System Manager

In Exchange 5.5, you could only create public folders using an e-mail client. You couldn't create one in the Administrator program. Exchange 2003 lets you create public folders in Exchange System Manager as an Exchange administrator.

Launch the System Manager, expand the Administrative Groups node, expand the desired administrative group, and expand the Folders node. Right-click the Public Folders container and select New ➤ Public Folder from the pop-up menu to bring up the new public folder Properties dialog box.

Let's take a look at the key property pages on this dialog box.

GENERAL

You use the General property page to name your folder and enter a description. The Path field shows where the folder is located in the Public Folder hierarchy after it has been created. If Maintain Per-User Read and Unread Information for This Folder is selected, each user will see items in the folder that they have read in non-bold text. If this option is not selected, all items show in bold text for all users whether they have been read or not.

REPLICATION

This is a very important property page because it is used to manage replication of folders between this server and other Exchange servers. Replication enables you to put copies of the same folder on multiple Exchange servers. It is very useful either for local load balancing or to limit wide area network traffic and improve performance by placing copies of folders in routing groups at geographically distant sites.

LIMITS

You've seen limits property pages before. Let's look at each of the three types of limits on this page:

Storage Limits As with mailboxes, you can set thresholds at which warnings are sent and posting to the folder is prohibited. You can also set a maximum posted-item size. If you want, you can choose to use the default storage limits settings for the public folder store where the folder resides.

Deletion Setting As with mailboxes, you can set the maximum number of days that a deleted item will be kept for recovery before being totally deleted. If you deselect the Use Public Store Defaults check box, you can enter a number of days that deleted items should be retained. If you don't want items retained at all, set the number of days to 0.

Age Limits This is the number of days that an item in the folder lives before being deleted. This is a very useful tool for controlling storage usage.

When you're finished creating your public folder, click OK and admire your handiwork in the Public Folders container. You should create folders in the `Folders\Public Folders` container, not in the public folder store. The public folder store holds created folders. You create new public folders in the `Folders\Public Folders` container. Seems simple, but if we had a dollar for every time we wrongly went to the public folder store to create a new public folder, well, we'd at least be on the beach in Hawaii right now.

WARNING

In some earlier versions of Exchange, the Windows group Everyone had rights by default to create folders in the Public Folders container. This right extends to both top-level folders (folders within and, thus, just below the Public Folders container) and subfolders within top-level folders. If you want to alter this right, right-click the Public Folders container and select Properties. Use the Security tab in the Public Folders Properties dialog box to add or remove users and groups or their rights in the Public Folders container. Even if you don't want to change the default, we strongly recommend that you take a look at the Security tab. Many of the permissions on it are specific to public folders and are therefore quite different from the permissions for other types of Exchange recipients.

Using the Public Folder DAV Administration Tool

It is really unfortunate that the initial release of Exchange 2007 provides no GUI for public folder management. While the EMS cmdlets are very functional, it can take some time to master using them; in the meantime, you still have public folders to administer.

Happily, Microsoft has an outstanding freely available GUI tool, the Public Folder DAV Administrator (PFDAVAdmin.exe), that it makes available. PFDAVAdmin is a .NET application that uses WebDAV instead of MAPI to access the public folder store.

NOTE

You might now be wondering if using PFDAVAdmin is a good idea, given its reliance on WebDAV. In Exchange 2007 support for the WebDAV protocol is "deemphasized," meaning that Microsoft doesn't promise it will be around for the next major version of Exchange. But it's still here in Exchange 2007 — and it allows you to use this wonderful management tool.

PFDAVAdmin requires the .NET framework version 1.1 to be installed, which means you must maintain multiple versions of the .NET framework on your management servers and workstations.

PFDAVAdmin is a wonderfully flexible tool. At first glance, it seems to give you the ability to manage public folder permissions using a GUI that is close to the legacy Exchange System Manager. In addition to querying and setting permissions, you can add, replace, and remove individual access control entries (ACEs) across a set of folders without having to wholesale replace the access control lists (ACLs) in question. PFDAVAdmin will also notify you when an ACL is damaged or in noncanonical order (meaning that the ACEs aren't properly ordered) and allow you to fix them on more than one folder at once.

NOTE

Administrators who made use of the Installable File System (IFS) — otherwise known as the M: drive — in Exchange 2000 and 2003 would often use the Windows Explorer permission tool to modify permissions on public folders. Unfortunately, this usually causes ACEs to get written in the wrong order, causing all sorts of subtle problems. PFDAVAdmin is the easy way to fix them, if you've got to deal with them and you don't have to wait until you've got Exchange 2007 in your organization to do it! Luckily, Exchange 2007 makes the IFS go away, so once you fix the problems, they're not likely to come back.

You can also use PFDAVAdmin to do the following:

◆ Perform bulk operations on folder properties. In addition, you can do bulk search and removal operations of per-item permissions.

◆ Apply changes to your list of replicas to a folder and all subfolders without overwriting each folder's replica list (that is, add or remove specific server entries without making each folder's replica list an exact copy of your starting point).

◆ Export folder permissions on folders, public folder stores, and mailbox stores.

◆ Export and import public folder replica lists.

Microsoft makes PFDAVAdmin freely available through the Microsoft Exchange tools download website at `http://tinyurl.com/h2jvv`.

Using Other Public Folder Tools

There are a couple of additional tools that Exchange administrators have used throughout the years. While they work with legacy Exchange servers, many of them are not certified for use with Exchange 2003 (let alone Exchange 2007). However, you can still use them as long as you have legacy Exchange public folder servers in your organization. There are two in particular we'd like to mention:

◆ The PFAdmin tool (`PFAdmin.exe`) is a command-line tool for common administrative tasks. With it you can manage ACLs, manage replicas, and re-home folders. If you happen to have old product CDs laying around, you can find a copy of this tool on the BackOffice Resource Kit (BORK) 4.5 CD.

◆ The PFInfo tool (`PFInfo.exe`) is a GUI tool that provides reporting on a server's folder replicas and associated permissions. The output of this tool can even be used as input to PFAdmin, allowing you to provide a level of consistency across multiple servers.

While you might be tempted to use PFAdmin and PFInfo in your Exchange 2007 organization (especially if you're already using them), we recommend that you finally retire these tools before retiring your legacy Exchange public folder servers. The most compelling reason to use these tools with legacy Exchange servers was to provide the missing command-line and scripting capability for public folder management, and now that Exchange 2007 includes the EMS, you should really put the effort into mastering the public folder cmdlets it provides.

There is one additional legacy tool you might find of value. The Public Folder Migration Tool (`PFMigrate.wsf`) is a Visual Basic script that was introduced in the Exchange Server 2003 Deployment Tools (ExDeploy). This script was designed for one purpose: to provide a simple interface for performing bulk public folder replica transfers from Exchange 5.5 servers to Exchange 2003 servers. However, because it can handle cross-administrative group replica transfers, PFMigrate can be used to move replicas to Exchange 2007 servers. The script is downloadable from the Microsoft website as part of the latest versions of the Exchange Server 2003 ExDeploy tools.

Working with the Public Folder Hierarchy

You can create public folders in any available public folder store on any Exchange mailbox server. By default, public folder stores are not created on Exchange 2007 mailbox servers unless you specify that the server will be used with clients running Outlook 2003 and earlier. When you create a new public folder store on an Exchange 2007 mailbox server, you can create a new storage group for it or place it in a storage group that already has one or more mailbox stores in it.

A public folder hierarchy, or public folder tree, is a list of public folders and their subfolders that are stored in the default public folder stores on the Exchange servers in an Exchange organization. The hierarchy also includes the name of the server on which a copy of each folder resides. Because the hierarchy exists in Active Directory as a separate object, it does not contain any of the actual items in your various public folders. There is one organization-wide public folder hierarchy object, although in previous versions of Exchange, you could create additional public folder trees that were not visible through the Public Folder object in Outlook but could be accessed through other methods, such as NNTP.

> **NOTE**
>
> You cannot create non-visible public folder trees using the management tools in Exchange 2007; you will need to continue using the Exchange 2003 System Manager if you need to create these objects.

Replicating Public Folders

In a single Exchange server environment, the hierarchy exists and is stored on the Exchange server. In an environment with multiple public folder stores, each Exchange server that has a public folder store has a copy of the public folder hierarchy. Exchange servers work together to ensure that each Exchange server in an administrative group has an up-to-date copy of the public folder hierarchy. This process, called public folder hierarchy replication, is automatic. In Exchange 2000 and Exchange 2003, there were certain limitations with this process when replication crossed administrative and routing group boundaries. Once you've fully migrated to Exchange 2007, these limitations will be a thing of the past; all Exchange 2007 servers are in a single separate administrative group that has been created for backward compatibility with Exchange 2000 and Exchange 2003 servers in the organization.

The Exchange 2003 System Manager uses the public folder hierarchy to appropriately display public folder objects in various containers and to retrieve information about public folders, whether that information is stored in the hierarchy or on the server where the public folder physically resides. E-mail clients such as Outlook and OWA use the hierarchy to display a list of public folders available on all servers in the organization and to access items in a specific folder. Security limits associated with a given public folder, of course, limit the actual access granted to administrators and users.

> **NOTE**
>
> The public folder hierarchy also includes what are called *system folders*, such as the Schedule + Free Busy folder. We'll talk about it and the other system folders later in this chapter.

How public folders are accessed depends on the client version. By default, Outlook 2007 and Outlook Web Access clients use the new Exchange 2007 web services to determine the location of a public folder. Previous versions of Outlook will first look for a public folder on the user's public folder store, which might or might not be the same Exchange server where the user's mailbox is located. The default public folder store is configured on the General property page of the Properties dialog box for a mailbox store (see Figure 14.3).

FIGURE 14.3
The default public folder
store property of the
mailbox store

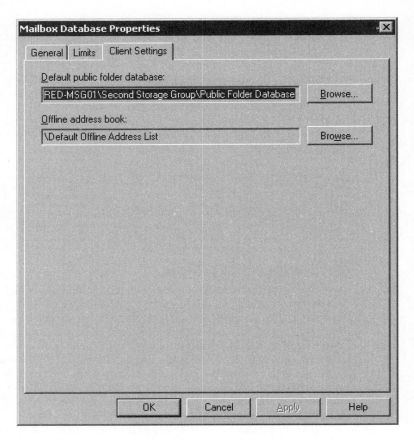

If a specific public folder doesn't exist in the default public folder store, the client is directed to a server where the public folder resides. As you can imagine, when many public folders are accessed over a lower-bandwidth network, server and network loads can get pretty heavy as users access public folders on one or a limited number of Exchange servers. If you need to, you can replicate folders on one Exchange server to other Exchange servers.

Why would you want to replicate public folders? Well, we can think of four reasons:

◆ When you need to balance public folder access loads on your Exchange servers. Having all of your users connect to a single server for all of their public folder access can quickly result in an overwhelmed server if you have a large number of users or if you have heavy public folder usage.

◆ When you have an Exchange server or group of Exchange servers separated from other servers in your organization by low-bandwidth links. In that case, you may be better off to have limited replication traffic over your links and allow users to connect to local replicas, keeping their traffic on the LAN.

◆ IMAP4 clients see folders only on the Exchange server to which they connect, including public folders. If you want an IMAP4 client to be able to see a specific public folder, you must create a replica of that folder on the IMAP4 user's mailbox server.

◆ Public folder replication is essential when you're planning to remove an Exchange server from your organization (like all those Exchange 2003 servers you're migrating away from). If the server you're removing hosts the only replica for a set of public folders and you don't want to lose those folders, you must replicate them to another Exchange server in your organization.

Now that we've whetted your appetite regarding public folder replication, we'll tackle the subject in further detail in the next section.

Managing Public Folders

All of what we said about public folders in single administrative group environments in an earlier section of this chapter ("Replicating Public Folders") applies to public folders in multi-administrative group environments. Again, remember that with Exchange 2007, you may have multiple administrative groups while you're in the process of upgrading your organization from an earlier version of Exchange, but you will end up with a single administrative group when you've finally switched completely to Exchange 2007. Until that day, though, you'll need to use the Exchange 2003 ESM to fully manage some of the complications listed in this section.

Public folder management gets to be more complex as additional administrative groups are created and connected by routing groups. Two issues come immediately to mind.

First, an Exchange organization's one and only MAPI-based default public folder tree can remain in the administrative group where it was originally created or it can be moved to another administrative group. In either case, when the default public folder tree has been moved to a new administrative group, control of its management can be delegated to a specially constituted Windows 2003 group.

WARNING

Do no delete the administrative group where the Exchange public folder hierarchy is found. Public folders will stop working.

Second, as Exchange organizations grow in size and complexity, nothing becomes more important on the public folders side than the location of public folders and replicas of public folders. You can significantly reduce network traffic and decrease folder access times by replicating heavily accessed public folders to Exchange servers in different routing groups with relatively low-bandwidth links to the Exchange servers where the public folders currently reside.

Let's take a closer look at public folder tree management and public folder replication.

ACCESSING PUBLIC FOLDERS USING THE EXCHANGE 2003 SYSTEM MANAGER

You can still create and manage public folders using the Exchange 2003 System Manager; many administrators will be more comfortable with this option than using the EMS, at least at first. For the most part, public folder management is straightforward in multiserver Exchange Server environments.

Look at Figures 14.4 and 14.5, which show the public folders on the two servers RED-EXCH01 and RED-MSG01, an Exchange 2003 server and an Exchange 2007 server, respectively.

FIGURE 14.4
Public folders on
RED-EXCH01

FIGURE 14.5
Public folders on
RED-MSG01

First, notice that RED-EXCH01 has many public folders that don't exist on RED-MSG01. This should demonstrate that by default the Public Folders container on each Exchange server contains only those folders that have replicas located in that store. So far, this is simple and makes sense; ready for the curveball?

Let's say that we want to create a new public folder on RED-MSG01. First, we need to locate the Public Folders container that holds the default public folder tree for our organization. We've selected that container in Figure 14.6.

FIGURE 14.6

The default public folder
tree container

FIGURE 14.6

The default public folder
tree container

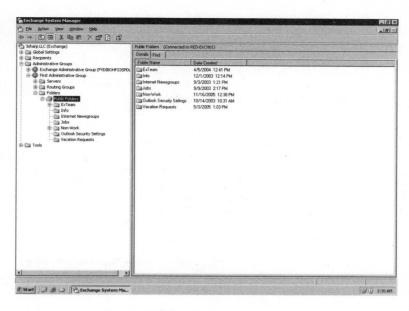

To ensure that we're working with the right public folder store, we need to right-click the
Public Folders container, select Connect To from the menu, select the appropriate public folder
store from the Select a Public Store dialog box, and click OK. See Figure 14.7.

FIGURE 14.7

Choosing a public folder
store

Now we know that we're working on the correct public folder store, and we can graphically
manage and create public folders on our Exchange 2007 server to our heart's content.

> **NOTE**
>
> You can't be sure that you're connected to the correct public folder store by the folders that are displayed in the Public Folders container. This display is based on the organization-wide public folder hierarchy, so you see all public folders in your organization regardless of what server they are stored on in the Public Folders container.

While you've still got legacy Exchange servers in your organization, you can control management access to the default public folder tree by moving that tree to an administrative group other than the one in which the tree was originally created. You should aim to move the public folder tree into the Exchange 2007 administrative group.

To do this, you must create a new Folders container in the desired administrative group and then drag and drop the default public folder tree into the new Folders container. See Figure 14.8 for an example of this being done on RED-MSG01, an Exchange 2007 mailbox server in our organization.

FIGURE 14.8
Creating a new Public Folders container on an Exchange 2007 server

For example, say we've dragged our default public folders tree from its default location to the Exchange 2007 administrative group and created a new Public Folders container just for public folder management. Delegated administrators can both view and change the properties of all public folders in the tree and create new folders in the tree. We've delegated control over our administrative group Public Folders Management to a new Windows 2003 security group PFAdmins; members of this group includes only those users we want to be able to manage the public folders in our organization. We then modify the management permissions for the Public Folders container to only allow management functions to members of the PFAdmins group.

After these changes the managers of our Exchange 2003 Los Angeles and New York administrative groups who are also members of the new security group will have full control over the public folders in their administrative groups. Managers of our Los Angeles and New York administrative groups who aren't also members of the PFAdmins security group can no longer create new public folders. That's because administrative creation of public folders can be done only on the default public folders tree, to which they no longer have access.

TIP

You can limit all administrative access to public folders in administrative groups that contain Exchange servers (Los Angeles and New York, in our case). You do this by creating an administrative group and installing Exchange servers that support only public folder stores into the new administrative group. Then you delegate control over the new administrative group to a Windows 2003 security group that includes only those Windows 2003 users whom you want to be able to manage public folders.

PERFORMING PUBLIC FOLDER REPLICATION

Technically, all copies of a public folder, including the one on the Exchange server where the folder was originally created, are called *replicas*. There's good reason for this. After a folder has been replicated, users will place items into it via the replica on their own default public folders server or on the nearest server as calculated using connector costs. So no replica of the folder can be considered a master copy. The replicas of a folder update each other on a regular basis, reinforcing the idea that there is no master copy.

You can set up replication of a public folder on either the server that will provide the folder or the server that will hold the new replica of the public folder. To replicate a folder, follow these steps:

1. Right-click the folder in either the Public Folders subcontainer of the Public Folders Store or the default public folders tree. Then select Properties from the pop-up menu. This opens the Properties dialog box for the public folder.

2. Tab over to the folder's Replication property page. In Figure 14.9, we're setting up a replication of Barry's First Public Folder from RED-EXCH01 (in our Exchange 2003 administrative group) to RED-MSG01 (in the Exchange 2007 administrative group). We clicked Add on the Replication property page to open the Select Public Store dialog box.

3. Clicking OK in the Select a Public Store dialog box adds RED-MSG01 to the list of public folder stores to which the folder's contents will be replicated. You can see this in Figure 14.10.

Let's look quickly at some of the other properties that you can set on the Replication property page. The public folder replication interval is based on a schedule that you can set. Depending on the importance of the contents of the folder and the available network bandwidth, you can accept the default Always Run, select other options from the drop-down list, or create your own custom schedule for replication of this folder.

When replication has started, the Replication Message Received field shows the latest replication status message when you click the Details button. You can give replication messages for a folder higher or lower transmission priority. Options include Not Urgent, Normal, and Urgent. Select Normal or Urgent for folders with contents of some importance to your organization; select Not Urgent for messages of lesser importance.

FIGURE 14.9
Setting up replication
of a public folder

FIGURE 14.10
Viewing the new replica
on the Exchange 2007
mailbox server

When replication has taken place, you should see the folder in the Public Folders container of the public folders store on the server on which the new replica was created. The property page will also show you whether the replication status is current or not.

That's really all there is to public folder replication. Monitoring replication is a matter of attending to the replication status of your replicas and, of course, ensuring that the connectors between your routing groups are up and running.

REPLICATING SYSTEM FOLDERS

The legacy Exchange systems use a special type of public folder to hold information used by Exchange servers and their clients. However, these system folders are normally invisible to the Exchange 2003 System Manager. To see the system folders, right-click Public Folders in the Folders container and select View System Folders.

Some of these folders must be replicated to assure smooth functioning of your Exchange system. One of these is the Schedule + Free Busy folder, which holds calendar information for every mailbox in the administrative group. If this folder isn't available to other mailbox servers, users will not be able to schedule meetings while looking at the free/busy times for people they want to invite. This folder's absence can also cause some Outlook clients to issue regular and very annoying warnings about not being able to find free busy information.

Ensure that at the very least the free/busy folder is visible across administrative groups, and if that's going to be a problem, consider replicating it. Do remember, though, that Exchange 2007 no longer requires system public folders to handle free/busy information for users on Exchange 2007 mailbox servers when dealing with newer clients (Outlook 2007 and above).

Be careful about most of the other system folders. Unless you know what you're doing, let the system replicate them.

Sometimes replication doesn't seem to be happening, even though ESM says all is well. You can push replication along in two ways. First, make sure that there is at least one item in the public folder you're replicating. Second, in the `Folders\Public Folders` subcontainer, right-click the folder you're interested in and select All Tasks ➢ Send Contents. Use the Send Contents dialog box that pops up to select the server or servers you want to synchronize and the number of days into the past that you want to resend the contents.

TIP

Don't forget that newsgroups are public folders that you can replicate like any other public folder. Everything works as it does with other public folders.

WARNING

Remember that you can't provide NNTP access to public folders from Exchange 2007 servers.

SETTING PUBLIC FOLDERS OPTIONS

While a good deal of public folder management has to do with replication and limits, there is more to public folder life. Let's take a look at some of the public folder configuration options available to you. You can use the EMS cmdlets to set these options, but we'll continue to show examples using the Exchange 2003 System Manager.

Go ahead and launch the System Manger right now and open the Properties dialog box for your chosen public folder. We'll cover at least a bit about the General, Exchange General, Exchange Advanced, Permissions, and Member Of property pages.

General

The only thing on this page that wasn't on the General property page of the dialog box that you used to create the folder is the Address List Name field. See Figure 14.11.

FIGURE 14.11
The General tab of the public folder property sheet

Before we explain this field, we need to fill you in a bit on e-mail-enabled public folders. Public folders created in the Public Folders tree — that is, inside the Public Folders container — are automatically e-mail-enabled. This means that they are assigned e-mail addresses. E-mail-enabled public folders can receive and even send messages.

You send a message from a public folder by having *Send-on-Behalf-of* or *Send-As* permissions on the folder. You can then modify the From field in an Outlook message.

NOTE

As you'll see later in this chapter, not all public folders are automatically e-mail-enabled. You can actually create additional public folder trees that are parallel to the Public Folders tree. Folders created in these trees are not automatically e-mail-enabled.

Back to the Address List Name field, you can use this field to have Exchange display a different name for the folder in Exchange's address lists than the name you gave the folder when you created it.

Exchange General

This page is very much like the Exchange General property page for a mailbox and is shown in Figure 14.12.

FIGURE 14.12
The Exchange General tab of the public folder property sheet

It has buttons for opening property pages for delivery restrictions (size of incoming and outgoing messages and from where messages will be received) and delivery options (delegate send-on-behalf-of permissions and set a forwarding address). These pages look and behave just like the same pages for a mailbox.

Exchange Advanced

The Exchange Advanced property page, shown in Figure 14.13, is similar to the same page for a mailbox.

You can use it to set a simple display name and to unhide and hide a public folder from Exchange address lists. By default, a new public folder is hidden from address lists. You must deselect Hide from Exchange Address Lists to expose it to the address lists.

The Exchange Advanced property page contains a Custom Attributes button. Click it to enter custom information for this recipient.

Permissions

The Permissions property page is shown in Figure 14.14.

This property page for a public folder includes a range of security options. These options cover client permissions, directory rights, and administrative rights. We'll cover each of these next:

Client Permissions   When you click on the Client Permissions button, you open a separate Client Permissions dialog box. You can use this dialog box to assign specific folder access rights

FIGURE 14.13
The Exchange Advanced tab of the public folder property sheet

FIGURE 14.14
The Permissions tab of the public folder property sheet

to Exchange users and distribution groups, who can then work with a public folder using their Outlook clients. For emphasis, let us restate what we just said in a somewhat different form: You grant public folder access permissions to Exchange recipients, not to Windows 2003 users and groups. Once access to a public folder is granted, Exchange recipients access the folder in their Outlook client while connected to their mailbox.

For a graphic reinforcement of this point, click Add in the Client Permissions dialog box to start adding a new user or group that will have access to this public folder. This action opens a dialog box that looks very much like the Outlook Address Book that you use to select recipients to send a message to, not the dialog box that you use to select Windows 2003 users and groups. Click Cancel to get out of the Add Users dialog box.

Because we created the public folder in Exchange System Manager while logged in as the domain administrator, Administrator is given the role of Owner. The owner of a public folder has complete control over the folder.

If a user has the correct permissions on a public folder, that user can change access permissions on the folder for other users. Permissions on a public folder can be modified in two places. They can be modified from within the Outlook client using the Permissions property page for a public folder. Permissions can also be modified using the Client Permissions dialog box that is available in Exchange System Manager.

Which of these you use depends on your security rights. If you are an Exchange user with no extraordinary permissions who is an owner of a public folder, you manage permissions for the folder in Outlook using the Permissions property page for a public folder. If you're an Exchange administrative user, you can change permissions on any public folder using the Client Permissions dialog box.

There is a group named Default that includes all Exchange recipients not separately added to the Name list box. When the folder is created, this group is automatically given the default role of Author. Note that Authors don't own the folder and can't create subfolders. Also note that Authors can edit and delete only their own folder items.

Microsoft has come up with several interesting roles — including Owner, Publishing Editor, Editor, Publishing Author, Author, Nonediting Author, Reviewer, Contributor, and Custom — each with a different combination of client permissions. We'll leave it to you to check out the specific permissions assigned to each of these roles. We'll also leave it to you to explore your options regarding public folder access permissions. Generally, the default settings work fine for most folders.

Directory Rights   Users and groups with appropriate permissions at the directory rights level can change the properties of a public folder object in Active Directory. The Directory Rights property page that pops up when you click the Directory Rights button is the same as the Security property page for other Exchange recipients. That's why public folders don't have a Security property page.

Administrative Rights   Administrative rights are permissions to manage a public folder using Exchange System Manager. Click the Administrative Rights button to open the Administrative Rights property page. Administrative permissions include rights to modify the public folder access control list and the public folder administrative access control list. These rights include permission to use the Directory Rights property page and the Administrative Rights property page, the very page that we're talking about right now. Permissions also include the right to set deleted-item retention time and space quotas for the public folder. You had the option of exercising both of these rights on the Limits page when you created your public folder earlier in this chapter.

Let us conclude this section by pointing out that administrative rights are granted to Windows 2003 users and security groups, not to Exchange recipients and distribution groups.

Member Of

We don't need to say a lot about the Member Of property page in the public folder Properties dialog box; we just want to point out that public folders, just like other Exchange recipients, can belong to security and distribution groups. When you send a message to a distribution group that includes a public folder, the message appears in the folder.

CREATING PUBLIC FOLDER STORES

Before you can create a new public folder store, you need to understand how public folder stores and what are called *public folder trees* relate to each other. You'll have a hard time using public folder stores without this knowledge.

Each public folder store is directly linked to a public folder tree. The default public folder tree on an Exchange server, Public Folders, is linked to the default public folder store, Public Folder Store (*SERVER_NAME*) on the server. A public folder store can link to only one public folder tree and vice versa. You can not link any more public folder trees to the default public folder store.

The default public folder tree and store are unique: They are the only tree and store combination that is MAPI-enabled. If you create additional public folder trees on a server, they cannot be MAPI-enabled. This means that the default public folder tree is the only one that can be accessed by MAPI-aware e-mail clients such as Outlook and IMAP4 clients.

When you look at public folders in Outlook, you're looking at the default tree defined by the mailbox store that contains your mailbox. By configuring this association at the mailbox database level, you tell Exchange from which server to access public folders replicas when a client such as Outlook opens a mailbox in your new mailbox store.

If clients such as Outlook can see only the default public folder tree on an Exchange server, of what use are additional public folder trees? Good question. The answer is simple. You can access additional public folder trees using any of the following clients:

◆ An enhanced Internet-standard Web Distributed Authoring and Versioning (WebDAV) client

◆ An Internet-standard Network News Transfer Protocol (NNTP) client

◆ Any process accessing the Exchange server through the new .NET APIs

> **WARNING**
>
> The Exchange 2003 Installable File System (IFS) is gone in Exchange 2007; while it provided another way to access additional public folder trees in Exchange 2003, you can't use it in Exchange 2007.

WebDAV clients are implemented in web browsers. Microsoft has enhanced the WebDAV Internet draft standard to allow it to work seamlessly with Exchange. WebDAV is, however, a deprecated access method in Exchange 2007.

Finally, additional public folder trees can be made available through the NNTP server protocol, which can be accessed with a Network News Transfer Protocol client such as the one in Microsoft's Outlook Express. If you require NNTP access, though, you have to have legacy servers in your organization; Exchange 2007 removes support for NNTP.

> **NOTE**
>
> Exchange 2007 does not support general purpose public folder trees. We are including information about them if you are inter-operating with Exchange 2000/2003. You must move all data in the general purpose public folder trees to the default public folder tree prior to removing Exchange 2000/2003 from your enviornment.

Now that we've addressed our public folder trees, let's create a public folder store. Before you can do so, however, you must create a public folder tree to associate it with. To create a new public folder tree, find and right-click the Folders container for your administrative group, then select New ➤ Public Folder Tree from the pop-up menu. The public folder tree Properties dialog box opens. Enter a name for the tree. We're going to call ours Demo Public Folder Tree. When you're done, click OK. You should now see your tree in the Folders container.

Now you can go ahead and create your public folder store. Right-click either your default storage group or the storage group that you created earlier in this chapter. Then select New ➤ Public Store from the pop-up menu to open the public folder store Properties dialog box. Name your new public folder store in the General property page. Next, click Browse next to the Associated Public Folder Tree field and select the public folder tree that you just created.

The Database property page looks and works exactly like the same page on the mailbox store Properties dialog box. The Limits page has a Deleted Items field, but it doesn't have a Retention field for mailboxes, for obvious reasons. Public folder stores don't hold mailboxes. The Limits page also has an additional field, Age Limits for All Folders in This Store. Use this field to set a default number of days before an item in any public folder in the store is deleted. You can override the default using the Limits page for any public folder.

When you're done creating your public folder store, click OK on the public folder store Properties dialog box. Now you should create a public folder in your new public folder tree.

MANAGING PUBLIC FOLDER STORES

Based on your experience with it when creating a public folder store, you should have no trouble using the public folder store Properties dialog box to manage your new public folder store. We won't discuss the dialog box any further here; instead, we're going to discuss three aspects of public folder store management in this section:

- ◆ Using public folder store management containers
- ◆ Mail-enabling public folders in a non-default public folder tree
- ◆ Providing access to public folders in a non-default public folder tree

Using Public Folder Store Management Containers

A public folder store has a range of subcontainers, just like a mailbox store. As with mailbox stores, these subcontainers are used for managing the store. Many of the subcontainers are used in the same way they're used for mailbox stores:

Logons Works just like the Logons subcontainer for mailbox stores.

Public Folder Instances Shows information for all public folder instances in a public folder store. This includes not only the folders in the Public Folders subcontainer, but also folders that have been replicated to this server from other Exchange servers.

Public Folders Shows resource usage and other information for all public folders in the store in a manner similar to the Mailboxes subcontainer for mailbox stores. These are folders that originated in the store or, to put it another way, that are local to the store.

Replication Status Shows progress when folders are replicating across Exchange servers.

Full-Text Indexing Works just like the same subcontainer for mailboxes. In fact, you set up full-text indexing for public folder stores exactly as you set it up for mailbox stores.

Mail-Enabling Public Folders in a Non-default Public Folder Tree

As we noted in the section "Managing Public Folders" earlier in this chapter, when you create a public folder in the default public folder store, it is automatically mail-enabled. It can send and receive messages. Public folders created in other public folder stores can send and receive e-mail messages too, but you have to mail-enable them before this is possible. Let's mail-enable the folder Test that you created earlier. To mail-enable a public folder, right-click it and select All Tasks ≻ Mail Enable from the pop-up menu.

After a few seconds, select Refresh from the Actions menu and open the Properties dialog box for the folder. The folder now has an E-Mail Addresses property page and a set of e-mail addresses to boot. Open your Outlook client and notice that the folder is in the address book. You can send messages to it. Don't close your Outlook client; we're going to use it in the next section.

Providing Access to Public Folders in a Non-default Public Folder Tree

Just to prove that non-default public folder trees are unavailable to Outlook clients, look at the public folder hierarchy in your client. You see the default public folder tree, Public Folders. However, you don't see the new tree that you just created.

Because non-default public folder trees don't support MAPI content, you can't post Exchange messages in them. However, you can send messages to them if they're mail-enabled, and you can drag and drop Exchange items such as messages from an Outlook client into them. You can also drag and drop any file that you want into them. Finally, you can right-click the folder and choose to begin creating a new file using whatever applications are supported on your computer.

WARNING

Be careful when you share a public folder or a public folder tree. Initially, the Windows 2003 group Everyone, which includes all Windows 2003 user accounts (but not anonymous connections), has a lot of control over the folder. By default, members of this group can read and add items to the folder, including subfolders. Thankfully, the group Everyone does not have delete rights by default, but you might not want it to have all of the rights granted by default. You can change Everyone's rights in the Security tab.

Summary

If you're coming new to Exchange 2007 or don't have a lot of investment in public folders in your current Exchange organization, then you probably haven't been too worried about the rumors of the demise of public folders in Exchange 2007. These rumors are fortunately not true; public folders are still supported in Exchange, even if the out-of-the box management options aren't all that we could hope for.

By concentrating its effort on providing solid support for public folder management in the Exchange Management Shell, Microsoft has finally provided the missing command-line management interface that can simplify dealing with one-off public folder management tasks. These cmdlets also make it easy to do large-scale scripted and bulk management operations.

The lack of a native GUI, however, is offset by Microsoft's continued development and support of the PFDAVAdmin tool, which provides a familiar interface for those who are used to the legacy Exchange System Manager. However, it also gives you a lot more power, providing sophisticated bulk operations and import/export capabilities that make managing large public folder deployments smoother. While you still have legacy servers in your organization, you can continue using the legacy System Manager to manage your public folder replicas.

Part 4

Exchange Server Reliability and Availability

In this section you will learn to:

◆ **Chapter 15: Reliability and Availability 101**
◆ **Chapter 16: Backup and Disaster Recovery**

Chapter 15

Reliability and Availability 101

Picking a single most important responsibility for an Exchange server administrator is tough to do. Arguably, we would have to say that the biggest responsibility is actually a tie between making sure your company's information is backed up and making sure you are providing access to that information when a user requires said data.

If you attend any Windows or networking conferences, the disaster recovery and high-availability sessions are always the ones that are standing room only. Apparently, then, providing good availability and having the ability to recover from a serious outage are universally though of as important.

In this chapter we are going to cover steps that you need to take in order to provide your users with better availability. As you will quickly learn, a lot of the things you need to do to improve the availability of Exchange are common sense and technologies that you already understand.

Experienced Exchange server administrators and consultants will tell you that some of the most important things that you do to improve availability are all procedural rather than technical. They will also tell you that much of the unplanned downtime they have been exposed to has been due to something really simple that no one thought of.

Topics in this chapter include the following:

◆ Understanding the basics of high availability

◆ Building redundancy and fault tolerance

◆ An introduction to clustering

High Availability Starts with the Basics

Too often when a consultant sets foot in a new organization that is having availability problems, the consultant starts talking about clustering, load balancing, storage area networks, replication technologies, and so on. Everyone in the room has that "deer in the headlights" look in their eyes, but all of those new technologies sure sound great!

Unfortunately, availability problems are frequently "people and process" related rather than being a technical problem. Poor documentation, insufficient training, lack of procedures, and improper preparation for supporting Exchange are the most frequent causes of downtime.

In the following sections, we will start with some of the basics of providing higher availability for your Exchange users.

BARRY GERBER ON RELIABILITY

One of the biggest issues for my clients is Exchange server disaster recovery. The first time a client brings up the subject, I tell them that disaster recovery is the last thing they should worry about. After they get up off the floor, I tell them that they should focus first on Exchange server reliability and availability, of which disaster recovery is but the last part. I go on to tell them that if they worry about the whole reliability and availability spectrum, they'll not only prepare themselves for serious non-disaster recovery scenarios, but they also might be able to avoid many of the disasters that haunt their nightly dreams.

Reliability vs. Availability

Don't sacrifice the reliability of your system just to make your availability numbers look good. In general, an hour of unplanned downtime to fix an impending problem is much more acceptable than an entire day of downtime if the impending problem actually causes a crash.

TIP

Don't sacrifice reliability for availability.

No one likes to have unplanned downtime, even if it is just for a few minutes because you need to reboot a server. An hour of unscheduled downtime in the middle of the business day is the sort of thing that users will remember for the next year. Consequently, a lot of organizations avoid unplanned downtime, even if they might be able to do something during the off-hours.

TIP

Good reliability helps you sleep at night. Good availability helps you keep your job.

Some of the tasks that might need to be performed sooner than your scheduled maintenance window will allow include things like replacing a disk drive that is running in a degraded state or swapping out a failed power supply.

Scheduled Maintenance

People don't often think about high availability and scheduled downtime at the same time. However, there will always be maintenance tasks that will require some scheduled downtime. When planning your weekly or monthly operations schedule, you need to make sure that you have a window available for maintenance. This window of time should be published to your user community and they should expect that the system may be unavailable during those times.

Scheduled downtime may be a hard sell in your organization. This is especially true if you have users that work around the clock. Still, you can make a compelling argument for this downtime window if you think about all the things you might need to do during your scheduled downtime:

- Performing server reboots
- Applying configuration changes

◆ Installing service packs and critical updates

◆ Updating firmware and the FlashBIOS

◆ Performing database maintenance such enabling or managing LCR databases

◆ Replacing power supplies, disks, UPS batteries, RAID controller batteries

◆ Reconfiguring IP addressing or networking equipment

◆ Addressing environmental issues such as air conditioning, UPS, power, and the security system

Granted, not every organization needs a weekly maintenance window, but you should ask for it anyway. You don't have to use the maintenance window if you have no maintenance to perform.

When scheduling the window, take in to consideration staffing concerns. After all, if you schedule maintenance once per week, someone knowledgeable has to be available during that time to perform the work.

Finally, when planning your scheduled downtime windows, make sure downtime during these windows do not count against your "nines."

The Quest for Nines

No respectable discussion about improving service availability is complete without a definition of "nines." Everyone is familiar with the quest to achieve 99.999 percent availability. This is a measure of the time that you are providing service (in our case, e-mail services) when compared with the time you have stated you will provide e-mail services.

If you ask your users how many "nines" you should be providing, they are undoubtedly going to tell you that you should be operating at 99.999 percent availability. What does that mean? Let's assume that you are expected to provide e-mail services 365 days per year, 24 hours per day, 7 days per week. Here is a breakdown different "nine" values and the actual amount of unplanned downtime you could actually have:

99.999   About 5.3 minutes

99.99   About 53 minutes

99.9   About 8.7 hours

99.7   About 1 day

99   About 3.7 days

Providing "five nines" is pretty hard to do; one server reboot during the business day and you have exceeded you maximum permissible downtime for the entire year. Even providing 99.99 percent availability is a hard target to meet, though this is certainly not unrealistic if you have designed in to your system redundancy, fault tolerance, and high-availability solutions.

If you were to plot on a graph the cost to implement a system on the y-axis and the desired nines on the x-axis, you will find that the cost climbs considerably as you approach (or pass) 99.999 percent availability.

For organizations that are having availability problems, we typically recommend that you first target somewhere between 99.7 and 99.9 percent availability. With good procedures, scheduled maintenance windows, hardware, and properly configured software, you can easily meet this goal even without clustering.

The Process Is Just as Important as the Technology

Some of us are just techies at heart, but information technology is more than just providing technology to our user communities. We must take into consideration a lot of other factors besides the technology, including budget, customer service, availability, documentation, responsibility, and change control. The process of running and managing information technology is becoming just as important as the technology itself.

With respect to Exchange Server, there are a number of things that we recommend you document and indoctrinate into your organization. These include creating documentation, processes, and procedures for the following:

◆ Daily and weekly maintenance

◆ Keeping documentation up-to-date

◆ Security review and audit procedures

◆ Change management and configuration control procedures

◆ Service pack and update procedures

◆ Escalation procedures and who is responsible for making decisions

◆ Information technology acceptable use and ethics policies

Building a Reliable Platform

Recommending that you build a reliable platform for Exchange may seem a bit obvious. After all, everyone wants a reliable platform. Our recommendations are meant to help you make sure that your hardware and software platform is as reliable and stable as possible.

First and foremost, when you are choosing server hardware, don't skimp when it comes to choosing the hardware you will use to support your organization's e-mail servers. You may not need the "BMW 525i" of servers, but at the very least you should be planning to buy a reliable "Honda Civic" type server. Maybe our analogy is not very good, but the point is that you need a server from a major vendor. The server hardware should have a warranty and hardware support options for replacing failed components.

When you choose components for your server (such as additional RAM, disks, disk controllers, tape devices, and so on), you should purchase these components from your server vendor. This ensures that anything that you put inside that server's case is going to be supported by the vendor. This also helps to ensure that the hardware and software integrates.

When choosing server hardware and components, make sure all components are on the Windows Server 2003 x64 Hardware Compatibility List. This is especially true if you are planning to implement clustering, volume shadow copy backups, storage area networks, or iSCSI storage. You can view the catalog of Windows Server–tested products at www.windowsservercatalog.com.

As you unbox your shiny new x64-capable server, remember that it has probably been sitting on a shelf in a warehouse for a few months or longer before it made it to your door. This means that it may well be a little out-of-date. The vendor's setup CDs are going to be out-of-date and the Windows Server 2003 R2 CD-ROM is going to be out-of-date when it comes to device drivers. There are a few things we recommend you do:

◆ Download the latest server setup CD from your hardware vendor. Use this CD to install Windows on to the server.

◆ Download any firmware and FlashBIOS updates that are relevant to the server's motherboard, backplane, network adapters, disk controllers, and so on.

◆ Confirm that you have the latest device drivers for additional hardware on your system. This includes network adapters, disk controllers, tape devices, host bus adapters, and so on.

◆ When formatting hard disks, use a 64KB allocation unit size.

◆ Confirm that you have the correct versions of any third-party software that you will be using, such as antivirus software, backup software, and storage area network (SAN) or storage management software.

◆ If your server has dual-power supplies, connect each power supply to a different UPS.

◆ As you are building your server, make sure that you have all the components you need and that they are ready to put into production. When you bring a server online for users, you want to know for sure that you don't need to come back in a few weeks and install additional software or hardware.

◆ Apply all service packs and critical updates that are available before putting the server into production.

Fault Tolerance vs. High Availability

You have probably heard as many explanations of what fault tolerance and high availability means as we have. Over the years, these two terms have been squashed together so many times that even knowledgeable people use them interchangeably. However, there is a distinct difference between fault tolerance and high availability.

Fault-tolerance features or components enable a system to offer error-free, nonstop availability in the event of a failure. Examples include mirrored disks or striping with parity volumes as well as uninterruptible power supplies (UPSs) and redundant power supplies. If a component fails that has fault tolerance, the system continues to operate without any sort of interruption in service. Clustering is not a fault tolerance solution.

High-availability solutions are things that you do in order to provide better availability for a specific service. Implementing fault tolerance is one of these things. However, while high-availability solutions promise ''better'' availability through the use of technologies such as clustering and replication, they do not offer complete tolerance from faults.

Implementing fault tolerance for disks, power supplies, and UPS systems is reasonably cost effective. However, implementing full-fledged fault-tolerance solutions for an application such as Exchange is very costly.

Complexity vs. Supportability

Do not install anything that you are not prepared to support yourself or for which you don't have someone on standby on the other end of a telephone ready to support you. We frequently see companies that have put in to production high-availability solutions, failover solutions, backup software, or procedures that are beyond their ability to support. A good example of this is a company whose vendor convinced it to install a SAN-based replication solution and a customized failover script. However, no one within the customer's organization had any experience with the SAN or the replication software or even knowledge of how the failover script worked.

No high-availability solution comes without ongoing costs. This cost may be in the form of training, additional personnel, consultant fees, or on-going maintenance costs.

We don't want to discourage you from seeking solutions that will meet your needs, but approach these solutions with realistic expectations of what they will require to support. Keep these tips in mind:

◆ Practice simplicity in any system you build or design. Even when the system is complex, keep the components and procedures as simple as possible.

◆ For any solution that you implement, ask yourself how difficult it would be to explain it for someone else to manage.

◆ Document everything!

Outlook Local Cached Mode and Perceived Downtime

If a server crashes in the woods, but no one is around to hear it, was there truly downtime? Downtime and outages are a matter of perception. If no one was affected, then no one will be calling the help desk to complain. For Outlook 2003 and 2007 users, Microsoft has included a feature that allows Outlook to keep a complete copy of the mailbox cached on the local hard disk.

By default, Outlook 2003 and 2007 enable cached Exchange mode (see Figure 15.1), but in some older Outlook profiles this may have been turned off.

FIGURE 15.1
Ensuring that cached Exchange mode is enabled

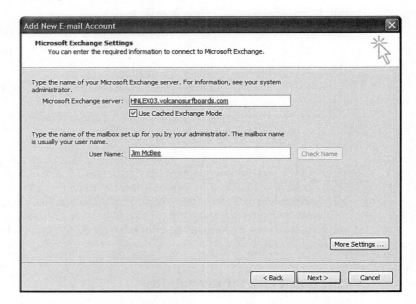

This setting won't help you with server reliability, but it can help with the user perception of those annoying little outages such as network problems or server reboots.

An Exchange server administrator can set a parameter on a user's mailbox that requires the use of cached mode. This is done using the Set-CASMailbox cmdlet. For example, if we want to require that Outlook 2003 or Outlook 2007 must be in cached Exchange mode for a certain user's mailbox, we would use this command:

```
Set-CASMailbox "Henrik.Walther" -MAPIBlockOutlookNonCachedMode $True
```

Building Redundancy

Redundant computing and networking systems can be an easy, though not always inexpensive, route to Exchange server reliability and availability. Automatic failover from a nonfunctional to a functional component is best. Even if you have to bring your system down for a short time to replace a component, with no or minimal data loss, you'll be a hero to your users. In addition to eliminating or sharply reducing downtime, redundant systems can help you avoid the pain of standard or disaster-based Exchange server recovery.

System redundancy is a complex matter. It's mostly about hardware, though a good deal of software, especially operating system software, can be involved. We are going to deal here with two areas that are essential to redundant systems: server redundancy and network redundancy.

Server Redundancy

In the following sections, we are going to talk about two basic kinds of server redundancy:

◆ Intraserver redundancy

◆ Interserver redundancy

Intraserver redundancy is all about how redundant components are installed in a single server. *Interserver redundancy* involves multiple servers that, in some form or other, mirror each other. The goal with either kind of redundancy is for good components or servers to replace bad ones as quickly as possible. Automatic replacement is highly desirable.

INTRASERVER REDUNDANCY

When you think redundancy in a server, you think about storage, power, cooling, and CPUs. Redundant disk storage and power components are the most readily available in today's servers. Tape storage has lagged behind disk storage in the area of redundancy, but it is available. Redundant cooling fans have been around for some time. Historically, Intel has not offered good support for redundant CPUs. However, the company now provides hardware for this purpose, and that hardware is finding its way into production servers.

Let's look at each aspect of server redundancy in more detail.

Redundant Storage

Redundant disk storage relies on a collection of disks to which data is written in such a way that all data continues to be available even if one of the disk drives fails. The popular acronym for this sort of set up is RAID, which stands for Redundant Array of Independent Disks.

There are several levels of RAID, one of which is not redundant. These are certainly not the only ones you will find in storage technologies. Many vendors create proprietary implementations in order to get better performance or redundancy. Here's a quick look at a few of the more common levels of RAID:

RAID 0 Raid 0 is also called striping. When data must be written to a RAID 0 disk array, the data is split into parts and each part of the data is written (striped) to a different drive in the array. RAID 0 is not redundant, but it provides the highest performance because each byte of data is written in parallel fashion, not sequentially, and there is no delay while parity data is calculated. We don't recommend implementing RAID 0 by itself in production as it provides no fault tolerance. RAID 0 is included here because RAID 0 strategies are used in another RAID design that we discuss later. RAID 0 requires a minimum of two disk drives of approximately equal size.

RAID 1   All data on a drive is mirrored to a second drive. This provides the highest reliability. Write performance is fairly slow because data must be written to both drives. Read performance can be enhanced if both drives are used when data is accessed. RAID 1 is implemented using a pairs of disks. Mirroring requires considerably more disk storage compared to RAID 5.

RAID 0 + 1   As with RAID 0, data is striped across each drive in the array. However, the array is mirrored to one or more parallel arrays. This provides the highest reliability and performance and has even higher disk storage requirements than RAID 1.

RAID 5   Data to be written to disk is broken up in to multiple blocks. Part of the data is striped to each drive in the array. However, writes include parity information that allows any data to be recovered from the remaining drives if a drive fails. RAID 5 is reliable, though performance is slower. With RAID 5, you lose the equivalent of one disk in total GB of storage. For example, a RAID 5 array of three 36GB drives gives you 72GB, not 108GB of storage. This is more efficient than RAID 1 or 0 + 1, which requires a disk for each drive mirrored, but write performance is about one-third of RAID 0 + 1 and read performance is about one-half of RAID 0 + 1.

So, which RAID level is right for you? RAID 0 + 1 is nice, but we reserve it for organizations with really demanding performance requirements such as servers with high I/O per second requirements. You compromise some with RAID 5, but it's the best price-performance-reliability option.

It should be clear how RAID works from a general redundancy/reliability perspective. Now you're probably wondering how it works to assure high availability. The answer is pretty simple. With a properly set up RAID 1, 0 + 1, or 5 system, you simply replace a failed drive and the system automatically rebuilds itself. If the system is properly configured, you can actually replace the drive while your server keeps running and supporting users. If your RAID system is really highly neat, you set up hot spares that are automatically used should a disk drive fail. A lot of this depends on the vendor of the RAID controller and whether or not the controller allows automatic rebuilds and hot spares.

BARRY GERBER ON THE VALUE OF RAID

"So, how do you know a RAID disk failed, and what do you do about it other than inserting a good drive? Most systems make entries in the Windows system event log. Many also let you know by talking to you. I'll never forget the first time a RAID 5 disk failed in one of my client's Dell servers. I got a call about a high-pitched whistling sound. They reported that they were 'going nuts from the sound.' So I had to figure out what was up as quickly as possible. I contacted Dell premium support, and within five minutes I knew it was a failed RAID drive. I used the Remote Desktop client in Windows Server 2003 to get to the computer over the Internet, using a virtual private network connection for security. Using Dell's support software for its RAID arrays, I was quickly able to shut off that horrible sound and set the server to the tasks of checking the failed drive and attempting to reinsert it into the array. Meanwhile, users were happily working away on their Exchange-based e-mail, knowing nothing about the failure. The drive recovered without a problem.

"If the failed drive was not recoverable, I would have asked my clients to remove the failed drive and insert a ready-to-go standby drive into the server. The server has three active RAID drives and three empty slots all on a hot-swap backplane. So, drive removal and insertion can be done without interrupting user access to the server. I could have also installed a fourth drive and set it up to act as a standby drive. The initial failure would then have triggered a rebuild of the array on to the standby drive. Then, at my leisure, I could come by and check the failed drive to see if it was still serviceable."

If RAID sounds like a good idea but you're worrying about costs, consider this: For most mainstream server vendors, adding a RAID controller option and a few hundred gigabytes of usable storage will increase the cost of the server by only a few thousand dollars. Figure out what a few hours (or days) of downtime and possibly a few days of lost e-mail data would cost and we think you'll conclude that the peace of mind that comes with redundant server hardware is worth the extra cost.

TIP

For the best performance, be sure to use a RAID solution that is implemented in hardware on a RAID adapter. Limited software-based RAID is available in Windows Server 2003, but you're not going to be happy with the speed of such an implementation.

RAID solutions don't necessarily have to be implemented inside a server. There is one very viable, if expensive, RAID solution that connects to your server or servers via a very high-throughput link. The technology is called a *storage area network (SAN)*. SAN devices connect to servers using fiber-optic cable. You can connect multiple servers to a SAN. Each server is connected to the SAN through one or more very high-speed switches. This provides excellent throughput between the SAN and each server. Backups also benefit from the SAN's high levels of performance. Tape units are available that connect directly to SAN fiber switches.

SANs include fairly complex storage and management software. Support is not a trivial matter, though support requirements are reduced somewhat because data can be consolidated onto one device. Minimal SAN implementations are measured in terabytes (TB) of storage. Five TB is not unusual for such an implementation. At this writing, because of their costs and complexity, SANs are being promoted by vendors for really high-end storage capacity and performance requirements. Microsoft takes the same position regarding running Exchange on SANs.

Generally, if you're going to implement a SAN solution, you'll do it in a clustered server environment. For more on server clustering, see the section, "Interserver Redundancy" later in this chapter.

WARNING

If SANs are too rich for your blood, take comfort: There are alternatives. You can buy lower-throughput, lower-capacity, external RAID, or iSCSI storage systems that attach to your server or servers using sufficiently high-speed links to support an Exchange environment. Vendors such as Network Appliance (www.netapp.com), LeftHand Networks (www.lefthandnetworks.com), Compaq (www.hp.com), and Dell (www.dell.com) offer this hardware.

If you've been tempted by network attached storage (NAS) solutions, forget it. Exchange databases must reside on a disk that is directly attached to the server. Through their switches, SANs are attached to the servers they support. NAS devices are not. It is no different than if you tried to install an Exchange information store on a disk residing on another server on your network. It doesn't work. However, if you are looking at iSCSI solutions, those are now supported.

Devices are available based on Redundant Array of Independent Tapes (RAIT) technology. Like RAID disk units, RAIT tape backup systems either mirror tapes one to one or stripe data across multiple tapes. As with disk, multitape striping can improve backup and restore performance as well as provide protection against the loss of a tape. Obviously, RAIT technology includes multiple tape drives. It is almost always implemented with tape library hardware so that tapes can be changed automatically, based on the requirements of backup software.

Redundant Power Supplies

Redundant power supplies are fairly standard in higher-end servers. Dell, IBM, and HP server-class hardware all include an additional power supply for a small incremental cost. Each power supply has its own power cord and runs all of the time. In fact, both power supplies provide power to the server at all times. Because either power supply is high enough in wattage to support the entire computer, if one power supply fails, the other is fully capable of running the computer. As with storage, system monitoring software lets you know when a power supply component has failed.

Many higher-end servers offer more than two redundant power supplies. These are designed for higher levels of system availability. They add relatively little to the cost of a server and are worth it.

Ideally, each power supply should be plugged into a different circuit. That way, the other circuit or circuits will still be there if the breaker trips on one circuit. We urge organizations that have high-availability requirements like hospitals to go a step further and ensure that one of the power supplies is plugged into an emergency circuit that is backed up by the organization's diesel-powered standby electricity-generating system. And, of course, each circuit should be plugged into an uninterruptible power supply (UPS).

Large-scale data centers will often implement two backup generators, two completely separate power grids, and two different sets of UPSs. Each server has a power supply connected to one grid and the other power supply is connected to the other.

Compaq, now a part of Hewlett Packard, offers another form of power redundancy, redundant voltage regulator modules (VRMs). In some environments, it's fine to have multiple power supplies, but if the power to your server isn't properly regulated because the computer's VRM has totally or partially failed, you'd be better off if the power had just failed. We expect that redundant VRMs will quickly become standard on higher-end servers from other manufacturers.

Redundant Cooling

Modern CPUs, RAM, and power supplies produce a lot of heat. Internal cooling fans are supposed to pull this heat out of a computer's innards and into the surrounding atmosphere. If a fan fails, components can heat to a point where they stop working or permanently fail. Redundant cooling fans help prevent this nightmare scenario. In most systems, there is an extra fan that is always running. Monitoring software lets you know when a fan fails. The system is set up so that the remaining fans can support the server until you are able to replace the failed fan.

One-for-one redundant fans are becoming more and more available. With these, each fan in a system is shadowed by an always-running matching fan. When a fan fails, monitoring software lets you know so you can replace it.

Redundant CPUs

As we mentioned earlier, redundancy has not been a strong point of Intel CPUs. Mainframe and specialty mini-computer manufacturers have offered such redundancy for years. Pushed by customers and large companies such as Microsoft, Intel now has a standard for implementation of redundant CPUs.

Each CPU lives on its own plug-in board. Each CPU has its own mirror CPU. Mirroring happens at extremely high speed. When one CPU board detects problems in the other CPU, it shuts down the CPU and takes over the task of running the server. Intel claims that these transitions are transparent to users.

System monitoring software lets you know that a CPU has been shut down. You can use management software to assess the downed CPU to see if the crash was soft (CPU is still okay and can be brought back online) or hard (time to replace the CPU board). If the board needs replacing, you can do it while the computer is running. This is another victory for hot-swappable components and high system reliability and availability.

Intel is marketing this technology for extremely high-reliability devices such as telecommunications networking. However, we expect that it will quickly find its way into higher-end corporate server systems.

NOTE

While they don't fall into the category of redundancy because they don't use backup hardware, error-correcting code (ECC) memory and registered memory deserve brief mention here. ECC memory includes parity information that allows it to correct a single bit error in an 8-bits of memory. It can also detect, but not correct, an error in 2 bits per byte. Higher-end servers use special algorithms to correct full 8-bit errors. Registered memory includes registers where data is held for one clock cycle before being moved onto the motherboard. This very brief delay allows for more reliable high-speed data access.

Uninterruptible Power Supplies

In most every installation anywhere in the world, the uninterruptible power supply (UPS) is a standard part of the installation. In its simplest form, the UPS is an enclosure with batteries and some power outlets connected to the batteries. During normal operations, the UPS will keep the batteries fully charged and allow the server to pull its power from the commercial power. In the event of a power failure or even just a brownout, the batteries kicks in and keeps supplying power to the server.

We see a few things that people do wrong constantly. One of the biggest mistakes people make is that they do not plan for sufficient capacity. Consequently, the UPS is overloaded and cannot provide power to everything connected to the UPS. Here are a few tips:

◆ Always buy more UPS capacity than you think you are going to need.

◆ Plan for at least 15 minutes of battery capacity at maximum load.

◆ Don't forget other things that may end up on the UPS, such as monitors, external tape devices, and external storage systems.

◆ Make sure that network infrastructure hardware is protected by a UPS; this includes routers, switches, and SAN and NAS equipment.

◆ UPS batteries need to be replaced. Replace batteries based on the manufacturer's schedule.

INTERSERVER REDUNDANCY

Interserver redundancy is all about synchronizing a set of servers so that server failures result in no or little downtime. There are a number of third-party solutions that provide some synchronizing services, but Microsoft's Windows clustering does the most sophisticated and comprehensive job of cross-server synchronization. We're going to focus here on this product. We'll also spend a bit of time on redundant SMTP hosts using a simple DNS trick.

Mailbox Server Redundancy

To provide higher availability for mailbox access, you should consider implementing Exchange server clustering. The Enterprise and Datacenter editions of Windows Server 2003 include clustering capabilities. Interserver redundancy clustering is supported by the Microsoft Cluster Service (MSCS). MSCS supports clusters using up to eight servers or nodes. The servers present themselves to clients as a single server. A server in a cluster uses ultra-high-speed internode connections and very fast, hardware-based algorithms to determine if a fellow server has failed. If a server fails, another server in the cluster can take over for it with minimal interruption in user access. It takes between two and five minutes for a high-capacity Exchange server cluster with a heavy load (around 5,000 users) to recover from a failure. With resilient e-mail clients such as Outlook 2003 or Outlook 2007, client-server reconnections are transparent to users.

We will take a closer look at clustering Exchange servers later in this chapter.

Redundant Inbound Mail Routing

Larger organizations will want to provide some redundancy for their inbound mail from the Internet. Redundant inbound messaging starts with at least two SMTP servers. In Figure 15.2, we are showing two Exchange 2007 Edge Transport servers in the organization's perimeter (DMZ) network. This could just as easily be any type of SMTP mail system located in the perimeter network. If Edge Transport servers are not used, then these servers could be on the internal network and they could be Exchange 2007 Hub Transport servers.

FIGURE 15.2
Redundant inbound mail
routing

Server EDGE01 has an IP address of 192.168.254.10 and server EDGE2 has an IP address of 192.168.254.11. We will pretend that these are the public IP addresses. The most common way to provide redundancy for inbound mail is to use DNS and mail exchanger (MX) records. Here is a sample of the MX records that would provide inbound mail routing for a domain called somorita.com.

somorita.com	IN	MX	10	edge01.somorita.com
somorita.com	IN	MX	10	edge02.somorita.com
edge01	IN	A		192.168.254.10
edge02	IN	A		192.168.254.10

That number 10 in the MX record is called a priority value. Most mail servers will automatically load-balance between these two servers when they send mail. We could change one of the MX record's priorities to something higher and mail would always be routed to the lower-priority MX record. It doesn't matter what you set the higher value to as long as it is higher. You can have as many MX records for an Internet domain as you want. Just be sure each points to a different server.

Another method of providing higher redundancy and high availability for inbound SMTP servers is to use some type of load balancing. We'll talk more about that later in this chapter.

Neither network load balancing nor multiple MX records provides complete fault tolerance for inbound mail routing. They provide better availability, but if an Edge Transport server fails in the middle of a message being delivered to your organization, the message transfer will fail. However, the sending server will reestablish a connection and automatically use the other Edge Transport server either because of the additional MX records or because network load balancing directs the SMTP client to the other server.

Redundant Internal Mail Routing

Internal mail routing is handled by the Exchange 2007 Hub Transport server role. If the Hub Transport role is on a separate physical server from the Mailbox server role, then all mail delivery — whether on the local Mailbox server, another Mailbox server in the same Active Directory site, or a Mailbox server in a remote Active Directory site — must be routed through the Hub Transport server role. If the Mailbox server role and the Hub Transport server role are on the same physical machine, then the local Hub Transport server role takes care of messaging routing.

In a larger environment where server roles are all split, the best way to achieve redundancy in message routing is to install at least two servers that host the Hub Transport server role in each Active Directory site. Figure 15.3 shows a sample network with two Active Directory sites. Each Active Directory site has two servers with the Hub Transport role installed.

Exchange 2007 will automatically load-balance between the Hub Transport servers that it's using within your organization. If a server fails and an alternate Hub Transport server is available within the Active Directory site, Exchange will start using the other Hub Transport server.

Redundant Outbound Mail

Within your Exchange organization, all mail delivery is handled by the Hub Transport server role. This is also true for e-mail that is destined for outside sources, such as Internet domains. Outbound mail is delivered using Send connectors and/or using Edge Subscriptions to Edge Transport servers located in your perimeter network. Figure 15.3 includes two Edge Transport servers located in the perimeter network. To achieve redundancy in outbound mail routing, we would need to create Edge Subscriptions for the Edge Transport servers and define a Send connector that will deliver mail to the Edge Transport servers.

Again, this solution is not a completely fault-tolerant solution but rather a high-availability solution. If an Edge Transport or Hub Transport server fails during message routing or transmission, Exchange will attempt to deliver messages through an alternate path.

FIGURE 15.3
Improving redundancy with multiple Hub Transport servers

Client Access and Unified Messaging Redundancy

The Client Access server role and the Unified Messaging server role can both be made more available by implementing multiple servers supporting these roles in the same Active Directory site and then implementing some type of load-balancing solution.

Figure 15.4 shows an example of how you could provide higher availability for Client Access and Unified Messaging server roles. In this figure, the physical servers host both roles. Load balancing between the two physical servers will providing users with connectivity to the least busy server at the time that they need to connect. Load balancing will also direct users to the remaining server if the first server fails.

Notice in Figure 15.4 that we have included load-balanced ISA servers in the perimeter network. This allows you to securely publish Exchange 2007 web services such as Outlook Web Access, Outlook Anywhere, ActiveSync, and the Availability service. The ISA servers act as reverse proxy servers and handle the initial inbound HTTP/HTTPS connection from Internet clients.

Load-balancing a Client Access or Unified Messaging server provides higher availability, but it does not provide complete fault tolerance. If the Exchange server fails, any active connections on that server will be terminated and the user (or VOIP call) will be terminated and the connection will have to be reestablished.

Network Load Balancing

We have mentioned load balancing a few times in this chapter as a mechanism for improving availability for certain types of server roles or functions. Load balancing works well in situations where you have multiple servers (two or more) that can handle the same type of request. This includes web servers and SMTP mail servers. In the case of something like a web server, the assumption is that a copy of the website is located on all of the servers that are being load-balanced.

FIGURE 15.4
Implementing load balancing for Client Access and Unified Messaging servers

Mailbox Servers

Mailbox Servers

Load-Balanced Client Access/ Unified Messaging Servers

VOIP PBX or VOIP PBX Gateway

Internal firewall

Perimeter network

Load-balanced ISA Servers publishing Exchange Web services

External firewall

Internet

In the case of Exchange, we can use load balancing to help provide better availability to the following server roles:

◆ Client Access servers

◆ Hub Transport servers (for inbound e-mail from the Internet or POP3/IMAP4 clients)

◆ Edge Transport servers

◆ Unified Messaging servers

TIP

SMTP servers that provide inbound STMP connectivity from outside of your organization such as the Edge Transport or Hub Transport servers are best served by providing load balancing by creating multiple DNS mail exchanger (MX) records.

Load balancing does not work for mailbox servers because the mailbox is only accessible from one server at a time, even when the servers are clustered. If you provide load balancing for Hub

Transport, Unified Messaging, or Client Access servers, this only provides higher availability for the client access point; the actual mailbox data must still have a high availability solution such as clustering.

There are a number of solutions on the market for load balancing, including Cisco's Local Director appliance (www.cisco.com) and F5's BIG-IP (www.f5.com) appliance. Microsoft includes a built-in load-balancing tool with Windows Server 2003 called Network Load Balancing (NLB). You will often hear NLB people refer to NLB as a clustering technology; indeed, even the Microsoft Windows Server 2003 documentation refers to the feature as NLB clustering.

TIP

Prior to actually setting up load balancing for the first time, you always want to ensure that each node or host works independently before you put it into a load-balanced cluster. This will save you a lot of troubleshooting time.

Let's take a quick look at load balancing from a conceptual point of view and apply those concepts to an Exchange example. Figure 15.5 shows an example of load balancing where we want to provide higher availability for our Client Access servers. In this example, there are two Windows Server 2003 servers that are hosting the Exchange 2007 Client Access role and they are load-balanced using the Windows Network Load Balancing tool.

FIGURE 15.5
Implementing Network
Load Balancing

Each Windows server is assigned its own unique IP address, but all servers must be on the same IP subnet. These IP addresses are 192.168.254.38 and 192.168.254.39. The "cluster" IP address will be 192.168.254.40. We will create a DNS record called owa.somorita.com that will be mapped to 192.168.254.40. We will ask our Outlook Web Access, Outlook Anywhere, and ActiveSync clients to use this FQDN. The load-balanced IP address must be on the same IP subnet as the hosts.

As connections attempts are made to the IP address 192.168.254.40, the two hosts communicate with each other and decide which host should accept the connection. The connection will be accepted by one of the two hosts and that connection is maintained until the client disconnects or the host is shut down. The entire process is transparent to the end user.

DNS ROUND ROBIN FOR LOAD BALANCING

One option you will frequently hear people talk about when running more than one web server is to use DNS round robin. With DNS round robin, you configure a single hostname with multiple IP addresses. The DNS server rotates IP addresses it gives out. While this works reasonably well, the client may change IP addresses after the DNS cache lifetime expires and that will break an SSL session.

Setting up an NLB cluster using the Windows Server 2003 Network Load Balancing Manager is pretty straightforward. In our example, we are setting up two servers into an NLB cluster, so it is best to run the NLB Manager from the console of one of the two servers. Log on to the console of one of the servers as a member of the local Administrators group and then launch the Network Load Balancing Manager program from the Administrative Tools folder. The console should show no NLB clusters. From the Cluster menu, choose New to get to the Cluster Parameters screen (shown in Figure 15.6).

FIGURE 15.6
Creating a new NLB cluster

In the IP address and subnet mask fields, enter the "cluster" IP address and subnet mask, not the IP address and subnet mask of the individual node. In this example, we will use 192.168.254.40.

The Full Internet Name box is usually optional, but it is a good idea to enter the name here that the clients will be using when they connect to this NLB cluster.

Finally, in the Cluster Operation Mode section, depending on your network, either Unicast or Multicast should work, but we recommend using multicast mode. When you have finished with this screen, click the Next button. The following screen is the Cluster IP Addresses screen, which allows you to add additional cluster IP addresses. In most cases, this is not necessary, so you can click Next again.

The next screen is the Port Rules dialog box. Port rules allow you to configure the actual TCP or UDP ports to which the NLB cluster will respond. For example, you might configure a rule that says the cluster only services TCP port 80 or 443 if you wanted to provide Network Load Balancing clustering for just web applications. The default screen is shown in Figure 15.7.

FIGURE 15.7
Defining port rules for a Network Load Balancing cluster

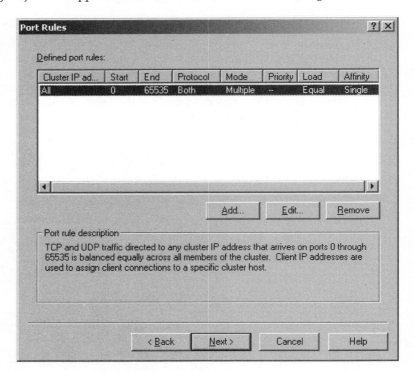

In the default configuration, all ports are used with the cluster, and for simplicity's sake you should leave it this way. Notice in Figure 15.7 that the protocol column is set to Both (meaning TCP and UDP) and the port range is 0 to 65535. Since you are not going to change anything on this screen, you can click Next.

The next screen is the Connect dialog box; when creating a new NLB cluster, there should be no interfaces or host information listed by default. In the Host box, you need to type the IP address of the first host that will be joining the cluster and click Connect. This will initiate a connection to the host you specify and list the network adapters that can be configured to join the cluster; this is shown in Figure 15.8.

FIGURE 15.8
Adding a host to the
Network Load Balancing
cluster

Select the network adapter to which you want to bind NLB and click Next. The following screen is the Host Parameters dialog box (shown in Figure 15.9). Here you specify a priority for the adapter (each host needs a unique priority), you confirm the IP address and subnet mask of the host you are adding to the NLB cluster, and you select the initial state of the host. We recommend that you always select Started as the default state so that you don't have to remember to start each node of the cluster manually after a reboot.

When you have finished configuring the host parameters, you can click the Finish button. The configuration change for this particular node of the NLB cluster will begin. If you are connected to the server via the Remote Desktop Connection client, you may be disconnected because the network will be stopped and restarted. In some instances, we have seen a situation in which configuring NLB leaves a node in an inconsistent state and you must manually reconfigure it from the console. While this is rare, if the server is remote, it is always a good idea to have someone available onsite that can log on to the server console and fix the problem. Or have some type of out-of-band server management tool available.

When you have configured the first node into the NLB cluster, you can add additional nodes. In the NLB Manager, connect to the existing cluster (if you are not already connected) and right-click on the cluster name. From the pop-up menu, select Add Host to Cluster. This takes you through another wizard that allows you to add a new node to the NLB cluster. When you have finally added all of the nodes, the NLB Manager (shown in Figure 15.10) will show you the status of the cluster and all of the nodes.

FIGURE 15.9
Confirming host parameters for a member of a Network Load Balancing cluster

FIGURE 15.10
Examining the status of the Network Load Balancing cluster

Network Redundancy

The concepts that apply to server redundancy also apply to network redundancy. There are network adapters, switches, bridges, and routers that support intradevice redundancy. Of course, as you learned with Exchange connectors, redundancy doesn't mean much if redundant devices are connected to the same physical network.

You can achieve network interface card (NIC) redundancy by using what is called *NIC teaming*. With teaming, two or more NICs are treated by your server and the outside world as a single adapter with a single IP address. For fault tolerance, you connect each NIC to a separate layer 2 MAC address–based switch. All switches must be able to physically communicate with each other; that is, they must be in the same layer 2 domain and they must support NIC teaming. All the network cards work together to send and receive data. If one NIC fails, the others keep on chugging away doing their job and you are notified of the failure. You need Windows Server 2003–based software from your NIC vendor to pull this off. Dell, HP, IBM, and others offer this software and compatible NICs.

Beyond the switch, you can use routers with redundant components. Cisco Systems (www.cisco.com) makes a number of these. Cisco also offers some nice interdevice redundancy routing options. They can get expensive, so if you want redundant physical connections to the Internet or other remote corporate sites, you need to factor in their cost.

If you use an ISP, you should pick one with more sophisticated networking capabilities. Maybe you can't afford multiple redundant links to the Internet, but your ISP should. Look for ISPs that use the kinds of routers discussed in the previous paragraph.

Supporting Infrastructure Redundancy

Exchange servers depend heavily on the ability to access domain controllers and global catalog servers. Exchange must locate these resources on the network using DNS. For this reason, it is imperative that any organization with more than one domain controller makes sure that more than one domain controller is configured as a global catalog server.

Microsoft's "formula" for determining how many domain controllers/global catalog (DC/GC) servers are required to support Exchange is one DC/GC CPU for each four Exchange CPUs. So an organization supporting 750 users on a single-dual processor Exchange server would require only a single DC/GC. This obviously would provide no redundancy. Plus, this formula is assuming dedicated DC/GCs for Exchange.

We recommend an alternate formula that is a little more complex, but more effective:

◆ Start with the minimum number of DC/GCs you require for basic directory services and authentication functions within your network. For an organization with 750 users, we would recommend two DC/GCs.

◆ Add additional DC/GCs based on Microsoft's formula for calculating the additional DC/GCs required to support Exchange.

Using this formula, our 750 user, single Exchange server network would have a minimum of three DC/GCs. You should follow this formula for any physical location that has an Exchange server. Any physical location that has an Exchange server should also have a minimum of two DC/GCs.

We also recommend using the Windows Server 2003 DNS server and ensuring that the Active Directory DNS zones are configured as Active Directory–integrated zones. All DC/GCs on the network should have the Windows Server 2003 DNS service installed. The DNS zone should be configured to replicate to all DNS servers in the entire forest (not just the domain).

All Exchange servers should be configured to use at least two DNS servers for name resolution. On networks with more than two DNS servers, you should configure a primary, secondary, and a tertiary DNS server. This can be done on the Advanced TCP/IP Settings property page (see Figure 15.11).

FIGURE 15.11
Configuring more than two DNS servers for a Windows server

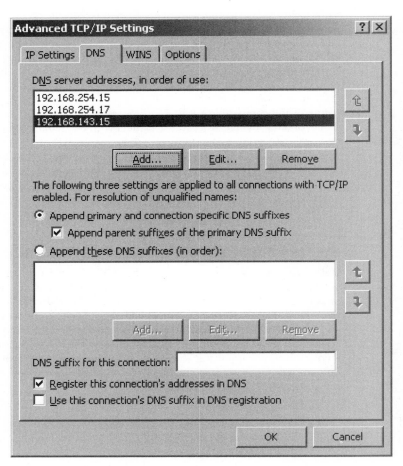

In the example in Figure 15.11, the server has been configured with a primary and a secondary DNS server; these are the DNS servers in the local Active Directory site. The third DNS server that is configured is a DNS server in a remote site. This would be queried only if the local DNS servers could not return a response to a query.

Introduction to Clustering

Conceptually, clustering is fairly simple to describe. A cluster is a collection of computers that work together to provide a single service. In some implementations of a cluster, multiple nodes all share the workload; the Windows Server 2003 Network Load Balancing feature is an example. In other implementations, one node provides the actual service (this is called the active node) and another node is waiting to take over that service if the first node fails (this is the passive node). An example of this is how Exchange 2007 mailbox servers are clustered.

Clustering is certainly nothing new. Microsoft has supported Exchange clustering since the Exchange 5.5 days, but other vendors, such as Digital Equipment Corporation (now part of HP), Tandem (now part of HP), IBM, and others, have supported clustering technologies for the last 25 years.

The purpose of clustering varies somewhat, but almost always one of the primary intentions is to have a mechanism to provide a higher level of availability. Network Load Balancing not only provides higher availability for the services it offers, it can also allow you to scale further and support more clients.

In the following sections, we want to introduce you to the clustering concepts supported by Exchange 2007 Mailbox server roles and familiarize you with some of the advantages and disadvantages of these types of clustering. If these technologies sound like "the next step" for your organization, then we encourage you to read further though the Microsoft website and white papers for implementation details. Full implementation details of mailbox clustering are beyond the scope of this book.

Is Clustering the Next Step?

When organizations are considering implementing Exchange clusters, the reason is that they want to achieve higher availability for their e-mail services. The most important question that should be asked, though, is whether clustering is the next step toward higher availability.

Carefully look at all of the reasons that you have had unscheduled downtime over the past year or two. Determine the root cause for each of these downtime incidents. For each of these, ask yourself if redundant hardware or redundant copies of the database would have spared you that downtime. You may be surprised at what you find. Many organizations find that clustering would solve almost none of their unscheduled downtime problems.

Next, examine the additional costs involved in implementing clusters. These costs include hardware, software, storage, consulting, and training. Will these additional costs be justified based on the amount of downtime that you have had versus the level of availability you require.

Clustering: The Good, the Bad, and the Ugly

We certainly don't want to discourage anyone from implementing Exchange clustering. If the technology is right for your organization and it will provide you with value, then certainly you should be seriously considering clustering your important Exchange 2007 mailbox servers. In the next sections, we give you our opinion of the good, bad, and ugly points of clustering.

THE GOOD

Many people that implement Exchange clustering become raving fans of the technology and would have the word *clustering* tattooed on their foreheads if their spouses or significant others would allow it. Let's look at a few of the high points and selling points for implementing a cluster.

- It increases availability by bringing failed mailbox servers back online sooner.
- It gives you the ability to meet service level agreements.
- It reduces scheduled downtime windows for mailbox servers.

◆ Clustered continuous replication allows for replicated copies of mailbox data.

◆ It provides automatic failover of Exchange mailbox services.

◆ Failover times are usually under five minutes in duration.

◆ Outlook in cached Exchange mode can make a failover invisible to desktop users.

THE BAD

Naturally, there are a few points that are going to count against clustering when you begin planning or implementing a clustered environment:

◆ Exchange 2007 only supports clustering the Mailbox role.

◆ There may be additional software costs (Windows and Exchange server licenses for passive node; Enterprise Edition of Windows and Exchange is required).

◆ Single copySingle copy clusters require shared storage such as storage area networks (SANs) regardless of whether iSCSI or Fibre Channel attached shared storage is used. This can significantly increase costs.

◆ Some third-party software (backup, message hygiene, and so on) is not supported on clustered nodes.

◆ Additional expertise is required to manage clustering technologies and shared storage.

◆ Some typical management functions (such as stopping and starting a service) are different on clusters than they are on typical Windows servers.

THE UGLY

Why the "ugly" category? Well, the "bad" category is all technology and cost. These are things that as information technology professionals, we can address through budgeting and training. However, "the ugly" rears its head at the management layer. Often clustering technologies are sold to senior management by salespeople. The technical implementation and requirements get a little fuzzy at this layer.

◆ When clustering is "sold" to management, expectations are often very high for what can be delivered. Management often views this as "magic" or the "answer to all our problems."

◆ Failover times are usually between two and five minutes, but possibly longer. The perception is often that failover is always instantaneous.

◆ Exchange clustering does not protect an organization from power failures, network infrastructure failures, Active Directory problems, DNS problems, and so on.

◆ Additional expertise and training are required to support the additional complexity. Often this is in the form of consultants and classes. This is a factor that management often does not hear about.

OVERCOMING THE BAD AND THE UGLY

Both the bad and ugly aspects of clustering can be overcome. The most important factor is to separate fact from fiction and hype in all of your management discussions, briefings, presentations, and documentation. Don't oversell the technology or feed the perception that Exchange clustering is actually "magic e-mail pixie dust." A lot of us get caught in the "gee it will be *so* great to have this new technology" frenzy that we are afraid to present all of the facts for fear we will lose our funding.

Balance and lessen the enthusiasm of salespeople, vendors, and senior management with by presenting a realistic view of clustering features, functions, and benefits.

THE INTIMIDATION FACTOR

One interesting factor of implementing a cluster is the intimidation factor. Junior or inexperienced administrators often look at clustering technology as a black box. Though they may have been trained to manage Windows servers, they are not trained in clustering.

Interestingly enough, this can function as a factor for improving availability. Quite a bit of downtime that we have come in contact with has been the result of junior administrators taking initiative (incorrectly) and making a situation worse. Frequently, though, with clusters, the junior administrator will leave them alone and wait for someone with more clustering experience.

Single Copy Clusters

In Exchange 2000/2003, we just referred to mailbox clusters as an Exchange cluster. However, in Exchange 2007, there are two different approaches to implementing clustering. The first is a single copy cluster (SCC); the SCC is identical to an Exchange 2000/2003 cluster. In this case, the "single copy" part of the name refers to the fact that there is only a single copy of each Exchange 2007 mailbox or public folder database. The database resides on some type of shared storage array.

With single copy clusters, there can be between two and eight nodes in a cluster. At any given time, there is always at least one node that is in the passive role and is ready to assume responsibility for a clustered mailbox server.

NOTE

Terminology update: If you used Exchange 2000/2003 in a clustered environment, then you are used to the term *Exchange virtual server*. This term has been replaced by *clustered mailbox server*.

Figure 15.12 shows a simple illustration of a two-node active-passive cluster. In this diagram, both the active node (NODE01) and the passive node (NODE02) are connected to the shared storage system. NODE01 owns the clustered mailbox server's name (EXCHANGE01), the clustered mailbox server's IP address (192.168.254.10), the shared disks (F:\ and G:\), and the other Exchange server resources such as the system attendant and the information store services.

Take note of the clustered mailbox server's name, EXCHANGE01. This name is part of a clustered resource and is not permanently assigned to any physical node in the cluster. This name, EXCHANGE01, is the name that Outlook clients use when connecting to the Exchange server.

All of the nodes in a single copy cluster are connected to both a public network and a private network. The private network is used for the cluster heartbeat. The heartbeat is what the nodes in the cluster use to determine if the other nodes are still alive and healthy. One of the two nodes will also own the cluster name and cluster IP address, though these are not shown in Figure 15.12. The same node that owns the generic cluster resources also owns the Q:\ drive resource, or the quorum disk. The quorum disk holds the cluster database and information about which node in the cluster owns each clustered resource. This helps to keep a passive node from taking over a resource that is owned (and in use) by an active node of the cluster.

FIGURE 15.12
Simple two-node
clustered mailbox server

If anything about physical NODE01 or the services running on it fails, this will initiate what is known as a failover. A failover occurs when the passive node in the cluster determines that something is not working properly on the active node. The resources necessary to bring the clustered mailbox server are taken over by the other node. So, in the case of Figure 15.12, NODE02 would assume control of the shared disks, the Exchange clustered mailbox server name, the clustered mailbox server IP address, and the Exchange services. The failover takes as long as necessary to mount the shared disks and then to start the Exchange services and mount the databases found on the shared disks. Depending on how busy the server was at failure, up to 20MB worth of outstanding transactions for each storage group may have to be committed to the database.

Clustered Continuous Replication Clusters

Clustered continuous replication (CCR) clusters is a new technology to Exchange 2007. CCR clusters use many of the same principals as single copy clusters but without the use of shared storage. Instead, as log files are filled up on the active node of the cluster, the passive node then copies those log files over and commits them to a backup copy of the database that resides on the passive node. CCR clusters are always two-node clusters. One node is always the active node and one node is always the passive node.

Figure 15.13 shows a simple CCR configuration. In this diagram, both the active and passive nodes have local storage. This storage could conceivably be on a SAN or iSCSI storage system, but the storage would not be shared between the two nodes. The only thing that is actually shared is a shared folder on a third server. The file share on the third server contains information that is used in the event that the two nodes cannot communicate over the private network. This helps to ensure that a failover does not occur due to the loss of the private network. This cluster type is called a majority node set. In Figure 15.13, the witness file share is a file server, but it could just as easily be one of the Client Access or Hub Transport server roles.

As transaction logs are filled and committed to the disk on the active node, they are copied to the passive node. A service on the passive node then commits those transactions to the backup copy of the databases.

FIGURE 15.13
Simple clustered
continuous replication
configuration

In the event of a failure of the active node, the passive node will mount the databases and roll forward any transaction logs that have not yet been committed. It will then assume the role of the production Exchange server (in this case EXCHANGE01).

Though we really like CCR clustering, there are a few positive and negative points you should be aware of when deciding to use this technology:

◆ The database on the passive node may not be completely synchronized with the active node. It might be a minute or two behind the active node (depending on activity levels). The transport dumpster on the Hub Transport servers help to minimize any data loss.

◆ The hardware on the active node and the passive node does not need to be identical, but it should be comparable with respect to CPU, memory, network, and disk capacity.

◆ Databases are replicated on a storage-group-by-storage-group basis and you can have only one database per storage group in CCR environment.

◆ CCR clusters reduce the complexity of Exchange mailbox server clustering somewhat because they do not require shared storage.

◆ CCR clusters can increase administrative complexity if the passive node of the cluster becomes out of sync with the active node. This may be because log files are not being copied to the passive node and thus the passive copy of the databases are out of sync.

◆ CCR clusters do not scale as well as SCC clusters. For example, a four-node SCC cluster could support three active Exchange nodes. To support three active clustered mailbox servers using CCR, you would need six servers.

Summary

In this chapter, we talked about some of the most important things you do as an Exchange administrator — that is, doing everything you can to provide higher availability for your messaging services.

An important part of providing higher availability is to ensure that you have the ability to perform proper and required maintenance during a time window that does not count against your availability numbers. Scheduled maintenance is important for ensuring the reliability and security of your Exchange environment. Don't sacrifice reliability for availability.

When looking at ways to improve your availability, you should look at the causes of any unscheduled downtime. Study what you need to do to eliminate or prevent those from happening in the future. This may include providing additional fault-tolerance components in your Exchange environment, such as redundant disks, redundant power supplies, and uninterruptible power supplies.

You can improve availability of services such as Client Access, Unified Messaging, Hub Transport, and Edge Transport server roles by implementing Network Load Balancing to balance the load between multiple servers that host the same server role and direct clients to a working server in the event one of the servers fail.

Clustering technologies can help you work toward higher availability for your mailbox servers. Single copy clusters work in much the same way as previous versions of Exchange did when cluster technology was implemented. Clustered continuous replication clusters are a new breed of clustered mailbox servers that provide redundancy not only for the physical server, but also for the databases.

In the next chapter, we will cover one of the other most important tasks that you perform as an Exchange administrator. This is a task that you must do daily: performing and verifying backups of your data and any other information necessary to recover a server in the event of a disaster.

Chapter 16

Backup and Disaster Recovery

In Chapter 15, "Reliability and Availability 101," we talked about some of the most important things an Exchange administrator does on a daily basis. At the top of the list (well, very nearly the top) is ensuring that you provide good availability to your user community. However, at the *very* top of the list is providing good recoverability.

If you do a Google search for "disaster recovery" or "backup software" for Exchange, you will end up with literally thousands of hits. Many of them will be discussing third-party software products, tools, utilities, and hardware technology that helps you to perform backups of your Exchange data.

While there are many good products on the market that can assist you in recovering from any number of problems with Exchange, we recommend that you evaluate these products against your recovery requirements rather than simply looking at the bells and whistles of the software.

There are far too many backup software packages for us to provide you with procedures for each, so we will be using the standard Windows Backup utility in our instructions. Many of the concepts and skills you learn simply using the Windows Backup utility will carry over to other backup products.

In this chapter, we will not only provide you with procedures for backing up and restoring Exchange databases, we will help you to develop backup procedures that are sufficient for your organization.

Topics in this chapter include the following:

◆ Planning for the best possible recoverability

◆ Using the Windows Backup utility to back up Exchange

◆ Restoring Exchange data to the recovery storage group

◆ Restoring a corrupted database

◆ Developing a disaster recovery strategy

Providing Good Recoverability

A wise technology curmudgeon once said, "Don't create a backup plan, create a restore plan." That is good advice. An administrator will typically look at the data on a server and select the data that they think they need to back up. A better approach is to back up the data that you need to restore and back it up frequently so you will not lose more data than you can afford to lose.

What Does Good Recoverability Mean?

Simply put, providing good recoverability means that you have available the information necessary to meet your organization's recovery objectives. This means that you are backing up everything you might need to restore and that you have procedures in place to ensure that you are you are able to restore the information that you need to restore. Here are some important requirements of a good recoverability plan:

◆ You have documentation necessary to recover every server role.

◆ You have analyzed the information necessary to perform a complete recovery of each Exchange server role.

◆ You perform regular backups of all data.

◆ Your backups allow you to meet your recovery point objectives.

◆ Your backups allow you to meet your recovery time objectives.

◆ You perform periodic verifications to ensure that you can restore data even if you are simply restoring to a recovery storage group.

◆ Your transaction logs are available if you need to restore the last full backup.

RECOVERY POINT OBJECTIVES

The term *recovery point objective (RPO)* defines the time to which you are able to recover data. The RPO could be the previous day's backup or it could be a specific number of hours. If you think about it in terms of a traditional tape backup solution being your only method of recovery, then the RPO can be a long period of time. If you specify that your RPO is the previous day's backup, then a catastrophic failure of your Exchange server's storage system could conceivably mean you could lose up to 24 hours worth of data. Depending on the type of data that you are backing up or restoring, that can be a lot of critical data, especially for an e-mail system that is being updated continually. If you specify that the RPO is a fixed number of hours (such as six hours), you must perform some type of backup ever six hours.

Determining your RPO and the maximum amount of acceptable data loss is important when it comes to planning your backup capacity and backup schedules. There are technologies that can help you to reduce the RPO for your organization by ensuring that you reduce the likelihood of a failure or that you keep your databases and transaction logs more highly available:

◆ Implementing local continuous replication (LCR) or clustered continuous replication (CCR)

◆ Storing databases and transaction logs on SAN- or iSCSI-based storage systems that are not affected by failure of an Exchange server

◆ Using SAN-based replication solutions that can keep replicated copies of databases and transaction logs

Of course, a simple solution to reduce your RPO is to simply perform more frequent backups of your data.

RECOVERY TIME OBJECTIVES

The *recovery time objective (RTO)* is the targeted amount of time it takes you to restore service for a particular application. Depending on the type of outage you experience, you may have different types of RTOs. An RTO for a single failed database might be one hour, while recovery of an entire failed server might be eight hours.

For Exchange, there are two types of recoveries that you should consider. The first type is called a dial-tone restore; messaging services are restored quickly, but actual Exchange data is restored at some point in the future (hopefully the very near future). The second type is restoring the entire messaging system (messaging services plus data) at the same time.

Defining and understanding your RTO can help you decide if your current processes, backup hardware, and backup software are sufficient.

INFORMATION NECESSARY TO RECOVERY

Probably the worst possible thing that can happen to an Exchange server is a complete server failure involving the operating system and data disks. This type of failure would require not only an operating system rebuild, but reinstallation of Exchange, reconfiguring any customizations that have been made to the system, and restoring the data. This type of recovery is called a bare metal restore.

If any one of your Exchange servers completely or partially failed, would you have the information necessary to rebuild it. First and foremost, the Active Directory data must be available since that is where much of the Exchange server configuration is located. Medium and large businesses should always have multiple Active Directory domain controllers, and the domain controllers and Exchange servers should run on separate hardware. Even a small businesses can simplify recovery by ensuring that Exchange Server is not installed on Active Directory domain controllers.

There is, of course, other important information that you will need in order to recover a server. Here is a list of the documentation that you should collect to simplify recovery:

◆ Server disk configuration (drive letters, capacity, LUN configuration if applicable)

◆ Backups of certificates uses for SSL (including private keys)

◆ OWA, Autodiscover, ActiveSync, and other web services virtual directory configurations

◆ Security customizations such as configuration files created by the Security Configuration Wizard

◆ Any custom scripts that you have created

BUILDING A CRASH CART

One of the first things that usually happens when even the most skilled IT department realizes that they have to do a server recovery is the "where is that?" syndrome. This naturally occurring phenomena is a result of no one knowing where to find things that are needed right away. Too frequently, CD-ROMs disappear, product keys get lost (or they are in a mailbox that is on the server that is down), and operating system setup CDs must be downloaded and burned again.

We recommend building a disaster recovery kit or a crash cart for each type of server that you support. This can be something as simple as a three-ring binder that contains the following:

◆ Escalation procedures such as who makes the decision to restore

◆ Contact list including cell phone numbers for IT management and a notification list of people that should be notified of an outage

◆ Server hardware, Windows, and Exchange documentation

◆ Product keys, activation codes, and license key disks

◆ Windows operating system and service pack CD-ROMs

◆ Hardware vendor CD-ROMs (such as a CD-ROM used to run setup for a particular piece of hardware)

◆ Exchange Server 2007 DVD

◆ CD or floppy with device drivers that is currently in use on the server

◆   Third-party CD-ROMs such as antivirus software and backup software

◆   Anything else that is critical to the server being rebuilt.

Once you have built this kit, set it aside and do not loan any of the contents to anyone. If you have a shrink-wrap machine, it might be a good idea to shrink-wrap the binder so that no one is tempted to borrow anything.

TESTING BACKUPS

Everyone who writes about backups always warns you to test your backups. Don't let the monotony of repetition lead you to ignore this warning. As many have said, a backup is useless if you can't restore from it. We recommend testing backups when you first set them up and then again whenever you change anything from server software and hardware to backup hardware and software. Try restore to hardware that is as much like the hardware on your real server as possible, though sometimes it is a good idea to restore to really different hardware just to be sure you can handle some diversity.

A number of system managers tell us that they just don't have the time to test backups. Actually, they usually use the past tense, as in, "I just didn't have time to test my backups." And this is usually in response to calls from clients in the middle of a resume producing event. These are usually administrators who have drifted far up the Exchange creek (crashed server) and now find themselves without a paddle (backup).

What can we say? If you really don't have time to test backups, tell your boss and ask for more resources or work with the boss to prioritize the tasks you have. While you're talking with the boss, be sure to add that without backup tests, you can't guarantee you'll be able to bring e-mail back up in case of a hardware or software failure. You can also use this argument when requesting the kinds of redundant hardware that we discussed in Chapter 15. If nothing else comes of these discussions, you will have at least set your boss's expectations at a more realistic level should all or part of all heck break loose.

Understanding Online Backups

The Exchange database file structure is a pretty complex thing. At the most basic level, the database is organized in a modified "b-tree" structure. All data is stored in 8KB pages; each page consists of a "next page" pointer, a "previous page" pointer, a checksum, and some data. If any of these pieces of the page of data becomes corrupted, the database itself could be in serious jeopardy.

> **NOTE**
>
> Which ever backup type you choose to use, it should be compatible with Exchange Server 2007.

There are essentially four methods of Exchange backups that you can perform against an Exchange database. The first method is a backup that is not Exchange aware. This backup type makes a backup of the actual file (or possibly the disk blocks in the case of some hardware solutions). If you use any method of standard tape backup software and attempt to back up the Exchange database files, you won't succeed unless you dismount the database files or stop the information store service. Some backup systems have open-file agents that can back up the Exchange database file even when it is in use. These should not be used with Exchange Server under any condition unless they have been approved by Microsoft for use with Exchange. These types of backups also do not purge the transaction log files once the backup is completed.

The second method uses the Exchange APIs to perform the backup. This method is called a streaming backup. This backup type does not back up the actual database file but rather requests the database a page at a time. As the Exchange database engine is reading each page of the database, it verifies the next page and previous page pointers as well as reads the data and checks to ensure that the checksum is correct. If the backup process detects corruption in the database, the backup halts. This is a feature of Exchange that is designed to help prevent you from continually making backups of corrupted data.

However, if the backup completes successfully, you know that the database has no problems with corrupted pages. Once the database has been successfully backed up, the transaction logs are backed up and then purged.

The third method of backup is a Volume Shadow Copy Service (VSS) backup; a VSS backup usually works in conjunction with third-party hardware and software and backs the data up at the disk level. The advantage of a VSS backup system is that it is much faster than streaming tape backups. If the VSS backup is compatible with Exchange, it will perform a verification to ensure that the database is not corrupted and purge the transaction logs just like a streaming backup.

The fourth method of Exchange backup is a mailbox-level backup. This type is more commonly referred to a *brick-level backup* and is supported by a number of third-party vendors. These backups use MAPI client software and back up each mailbox message by message and folder by folder. The advantage of these is that you can restore a single folder or single message without having to restore an entire database. However, with brick-level backups, there are often problems getting the backup client to work properly and they usually take at least three to four times longer to back up a mailbox database than a streaming backup takes. We do not recommend brick-level backups.

These are four basic types of Exchange backups. Undoubtedly, though, you will come across some specialized or vendor-specific solutions. While many of these solutions will have some merit, ultimately you should consider a solution that you know will allow you to recover the data you need to recover. If you choose a specialized backup and recovery solution, ensure that the vendor offers good support and that you are able to contact its support department when necessary.

What Can Go Wrong?

Anything that *can* go wrong *will* go wrong. Pessimists make good system administrators — at least pessimists that prepare for any possible contingency. When you are making plans for system backups, think about each type of restore, outage, or disaster that might occur within your organization and how you can mitigate those risks. While we are going to discuss most of these in more detail, here is list of possible issues that would require administrator intervention:

Deleted message or folder Users can recover their own deleted items or folders using the Recover Deleted Items feature of Outlook or Outlook Web Access. The only requirement is that the recover deleted items cache is enabled for the mailbox database. By default, deleted items and folders are retained for 14 days. If a message or folder cannot be retrieved, the administrator can always restore the database on which the mailbox resides to a recovery storage group.

Deleted mailboxes Accidents do sometimes happen; user accounts and mailboxes can accidentally be deleted. By default, a deleted mailbox can be reconnected to a user account (that does not have a mailbox) for 30 days after it was deleted.

Corrupted databases While a rare occurrence, an Exchange database can become corrupted. If you are using local continuous replication (LCR), you can swap out the production database for the LCR database. If you are using clustered continuous replication (CCR), you can move the clustered mailbox server to the passive node of the database and start using the CCR copy of the database. If you are not using either LCR or CCR, then you will need to restore the database from the last complete backup.

Server failure   The worst case failure situation is when the entire server fails. If you have not clustered the server (in the case of a Mailbox server role) or provided a high-availability solution such as network load balancing for Client Access, Hub Transport, Unified Messaging, or Edge Transport server roles, then you will need to rebuild the server (possibly from scratch) in order to restore the messaging services the server is providing.

Running Backups

In our opinion, the most important daily task that an Exchange administrator performs is running and verifying backups. Many administrators will probably take exception to this, but we firmly believe backups are essential. The ability to provide recoverability from alternate media (such as a tape) will be of paramount importance if you ever experience a complete server failure. We think your users will agree with us that a few hours of outage, queues backing up, or ActiveSync not working is minimal compared with the prospects of losing everything in their mailbox.

Exchange Backup Types

There are essentially four different types of backups that can run against an Exchange 2007 database. These backup types are all considered streaming backups and are performed against production databases, not against LCR or CCR copies of databases. You will pick one or more of these backup types based on the frequency of backup, backup capacity, and restoration requirements.

Full backup   The full backup is by far the simplest to perform, and it's the simplest to restore from. A full backup of an Exchange mailbox database, public folder database, or storage group backs up the entire database file and all transaction logs associated with the database and storage group. The database is requested page by page and each page is verified to ensure that the checksum and page pointers are correct. Once this backup is complete, the transaction logs that were backed up are purged by the information store. You should be running full backups at least once per week; if you have the backup capacity and backup windows available, then you should run full backups each night.

Differential backup   Differential backups back up only the transaction logs associated with a storage group. This means that the actual data that is being backed up consists of only the changes that have been performed against a database since the last full backup. The database file is not backed up, nor are the transaction logs purged after the backup is completed. If you performing incremental backups several days in a row, the amount of transaction logs backed up each time will continue to increase but the differential backup allows for simpler restoration.

Incremental backup   Incremental backups back up only the transaction logs associated with a storage group. Once the transaction logs have been backed up, they are purged. Incremental backups back up only the changes to the database since the last full backup or the last incremental backup was run. If you are performing a weekly full backup and then daily incremental backups, a full restore will require all of the incremental backups since the last full backup was performed.

Copy backups   Copy backups are almost identical to a full backup. The entire selected database is backed up as well as the transaction logs, but the transaction logs are not purged after the backup.

Backup Frequency, Schedules, and Rotation

Regardless of how much high-availability technology you have deployed, ultimately you need to have offline copies of your Exchange data. Redundant disks, clustering, and even replication solutions do not excuse you from performing regular backups.

Some organizations back up once per day and use the same tape media (or target backup destination) all the time. Some fairly common questions for organizations that are deploying Exchange are how often should we back up, when should we back up, and how long should we keep the backup media?

BACKUP FREQUENCY

The frequency of the backup will be determined partially on your backup capacity, partially on your system capacity, and partially on your recovery point objective. A recovery point objective of six hours means that you must perform some type of backup once every six hours.

Each time a backup is executed, a certain amount of system resources (CPU, network, disk, memory) is used to run the backup. This can be reduced by ensuring that backups that are run during normal work hours run as quickly as possible; you can do this by doing incremental or differential backups.

You can also lessen the overhead that a backup takes by using LCR to replicate the databases to an alternate disk drive and then perform VSS backups of the LCR databases.

BACKUP SCHEDULE

Backups should be scheduled during periods of reduced activity on the server. For a typical business that supports users within a single time zone, the server is most busy supporting user activity from 7:00 a.m. until approximately 6:00 p.m. You can schedule your backup operations outside of these hours. However, you should ensure that the online backup of each database does not interfere with the online maintenance period for that database. By default, this is daily from 1:00 a.m. until 5:00 a.m., but this can be modified on the General property page of each mailbox or pubic folder database. Figure 16.1 shows the General property page and the Maintenance Schedule drop-down list.

If an online backup of a databases starts while online maintenance is running, online maintenance will halt. Microsoft recommends that online maintenance complete on each database once every two weeks, but we recommend that it complete successfully every few days. Once a database gets behind in its maintenance tasks, it takes much longer to complete the maintenance tasks.

In general, we recommend starting online backups of Exchange database between 8:00 p.m. and 10:00 p.m. This gives the online backup time to complete so that online maintenance can be run. You can also reschedule online maintenance to run at another time.

If you have a tight recovery point objective, then you should consider running multiple backups each day. For example, if your recovery point objective is six hours, then you should consider running a full backup that completes at midnight and differential backups at 6:00 a.m., noon, and 6:00 p.m.

Backup Media Rotation

Having implemented a backup strategy that lets you rotate tapes off site, you should be sure the rotation happens. Also, you should buy a fireproof, magnetic-media storage safe and keep all other backups on site in that safe. A fireproof safe for paper does not protect magnetic media. Temperature and humidity control requirements for magnetic media are higher than for paper.

As we have implied throughout this chapter, you can make an initial backup to tape or disk. If you choose to do initial backups to disk, here are a few precautions you might want to consider.

First, don't back up to the disk that contains what you're backing up. You can't recover the disk if the backup is blown away when the disk is blown away. Second, immediately back up to tape whatever you backed up to disk. Even if your backup is on a different disk, it will do you no good if that disk fails. Third, rotate and store these tapes just as you would initial backups to tape. You can no more afford to lose these tapes than your initial backups to tape.

FIGURE 16.1
The default online maintenance time for a database is 1:00 a.m. until 5:00 a.m.

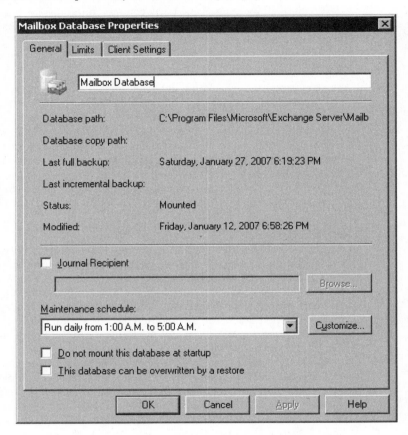

How long should you keep your backups? The ultimate answer to this question is whether or not you are compelled by either a law or company policy regarding data retention. Some organizations have policies or are compelled by law to be able to restore data from five or more years in the past, while other organizations may not wish to restore past two weeks.

Tape retention policies are, unfortunately, only partly related to technical issues. For legal reasons, some organizations must retain data, including e-mail data, for extended periods. Other organizations, to avoid the legal hassles associated with the subpoenaing of data, choose to dump their backups almost as quickly as they are created. For you, there is only one issue. Your users need to understand the implications for data recovery of whatever retention schedule is implemented. If legal niceties aren't an issue in your organization, we recommend that you retain daily backups for the last two weeks and one weekly full backup for up to a month or even up to a year, depending on your level of comfort.

In larger or publicly held organizations, you should consult with someone that is responsible for data retention and/or regulatory compliance. We have a basic tape rotation schedule we recommend that provides the operation for very good recoverability for a year's worth of historical data but as time passes by the exact date that you can recover is less specific. Table 16.1 shows the how you label a series of tapes for this rotation schedule.

TABLE 16.1:   Sample Exchange Backup Rotation Schedule

TAPE LABEL	PURPOSE OR USAGE
Monday - Even	Tape used on Monday if the day of the week is even
Monday - Odd	Tape used on Monday if the day of the week is odd
Tuesday - Even	Tape used on Tuesday if the day of the week is even
Tuesday - Odd	Tape used on Tuesday if the day of the week is odd
Wednesday - Even	Tape used on Wednesday if the day of the week is even
Wednesday - Odd	Tape used on Wednesday if the day of the week is odd
Thursday - Even	Tape used on Thursday if the day of the week is even
Thursday - Odd	Tape used on Thursday if the day of the week is odd
Friday - 1	Tape used on first Friday of the month
Friday - 2	Tape used on second Friday of the month
Friday - 3	Tape used on third Friday of the month
Friday - 4	Tape used on fourth Friday of the month
Friday - 5	Tape used on fifth Friday of the month
January–December	Create one tape for each month of the year. Use this tape on or about the first of the month as a long-term archive.

Naturally, this backup rotation is very simple and assumes that you perform full backups nightly and only Monday through Friday, but it can be adopted for your needs.

One backup method that is becoming popular is to use the Windows Backup utility and backing up to a BKF file rather than to tape and then keeping the two most recent backups on the server's local disk. The advantage of this method is that it is very quick to restore a recent backup file. However, if you use this method, you should save the BKF files on a separate Windows disk volume than the one on which the transaction logs or databases are located, and you should make backup copies of these BKF files to tape as part of your normal backup procedures.

Using Windows Backup to Run Exchange Backups

There are many third-party software utilities on the market that include an Exchange agent that is capable of performing online backups of Exchange databases. In our examples for this chapter, we are going to use the Windows Backup utility rather than one the third-party utilities. Let's go through an exercise of backing up the Exchange databases to a backup (BKF) file for a server.

First we launch the Windows Backup utility (`ntbackup.exe`), switch to the Backup tab, and navigate through the tree to the Microsoft Exchange Server container. An example of this is shown in Figure 16.2; in this example, we have selected the entire Microsoft Information Store object, which will include all storage groups and databases.

If you select a specific storage group in the tree, you can view the mailbox or public folder databases in that storage group in the right-hand pane of the Windows Backup utility. Notice also in Figure 6.2 that the backup media or filename that is in use is `C:\January27-Full-Backup`
`.bkf`; we are backing up to a disk file rather than to a tape. Do not select the System State selection in the directory listing tree if you are also backing up Exchange databases. System state backups should be performed separately.

When you click the Start Backup button, you are presented with the Backup Job Information dialog box. From this box, you must give the backup set a description and specify if you are overwriting the existing backup media. Be careful about appending to an existing backup file; if this is not what you intended to do, the backup file may grow until you run out of disk space. The description is important when you get ready to perform a restore of a database, so make sure the Backup Description and the If the Media Is Overwritten, Use This Label to Identify the Media boxes both include descriptive text.

If you click the Advanced button in the Backup Job Information dialog box, you will see the Advanced Backup Options dialog box. Almost everything on this dialog box is irrelevant for Exchange backups except for the Backup Type drop-down list. For Exchange backups, you can select Normal (Full), Copy, Incremental, or Differential. There is a Daily selection in this drop-down list, but it has no function for Exchange.

The Schedule button allows you to define a schedule for this backup to run. If you click the Schedule button, the first thing you have to do is to save the current backup selections to a backup selection script file (BKS). This file will be use when the `ntbackup.exe` program is executed by the Windows Task Scheduler service.

You must also provide a service account and password under which the scheduled job will run. The user account that you specify must have the right to log on as a service and it must have the rights to run backups on the Exchange server. Once you have specified a service account, you are prompted for the job name of the scheduled task.

By default, the job is scheduled to run immediately, but you can click the Properties button on the Schedule Data property page and view the Schedule settings. In the following example, we have scheduled this backup job to run every Friday evening at 8:00 p.m.

FIGURE 16.2
Selecting the Microsoft Information Store object for backup

This wizard will schedule a command to run at the time you specify and under the security context of the account you specified. Here is an example of the weekly backup job that we just scheduled:

```
C:\WINR2-64\system32\ntbackup.exe backup "@C:\Documents and
 Settings\Administrator.VOLCANOSURFB\Local Settings\Application
 Data\Microsoft\Windows NT\NTBackup\data\WeeklyFullBackup.bks" /n
 "Weekly Full Backup" /d "Weekly Full Backup" /n "Weekly Full Backup"
 /v:no /r:no /rs:no /hc:off /m normal /j "Weekly Full Backup" /l:s
 /f "c:\January27-Full-Backup.bkf"
```

Once you save the schedule task data, you can see the scheduled jobs in Control Panel ➤ Scheduled Tasks. An example is shown in Figure 16.3. From this dialog box, you can also right-click on any of these tasks and choose Run to start the job immediately.

FIGURE 16.3
Viewing properties of scheduled jobs

Verifying Exchange Backups

The best actual verification of a backup completion is to confirm that it restores properly. You certainly don't have time to do that every day, but we recommend that every few months you select a database and restore it to a recovery storage group just for practice.

However, there are some quick tasks that you should do as part of your daily operations. The first is to examine the backup program's log of the backup. This serves a couple of purposes, not the least of which is finding possible errors. Figure 16.4 shows the backup log from the Windows Backup utility for a backup of a mailbox and public folder store database.

There are a few things you should note from this backup report:

◆ The backup report contains no errors. This should help you to sleep better.

◆ The backup report indicates that what you wanted to back up (the mailbox database and the public folder database) was backed up.

◆ The amount of data that was backed up corresponds with the amount of data that you believe should be backed up.

◆ And finally, you can see the amount of time the backup took versus the amount of data. In this example, the mailbox database was 4GB and it took just over three minutes to back up. That is about 1.3GB per minute. That is not really great backup throughput, but this is a low-end test system.

The final place you should check for information about backups is the Windows Application event log. Figure 16.5 shows the Application event log immediately after an online backup.

The source column shows ntbackup-, ESE BACKUP–, and ESE-related events that are all part of the backup process.

FIGURE 16.4
Sample backup log

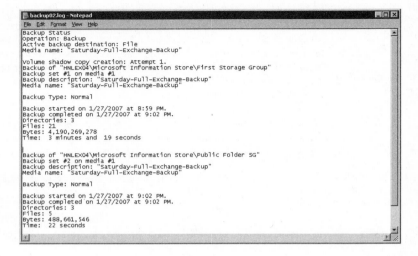

FIGURE 16.5
Event viewer showing backup-related events

As you scan through the log entries created by the backup process, you will find that many of these events are just informational, such as event that let you know the backup program is starting or has completed. Events from the source ntbackup are reports of this kind, while events from ESE and ESE BACKUP are reporting on the actual Exchange backup process being used.

There are two events, though, that you should watch for and you should see for each database that you are backing up. You will see these events for any streaming backup of an Exchange database regardless of which database you are using. These events are from the ESE source and are event ID 220 and 221. They are shown side by side in Figure 16.6. Event ID 220 indicates that the backup of a specific database (named in the Description field) is now beginning, while event ID 221 indicates that the backup of that specific database has completed. The actual text of the event says "Ending the backup of the file...," but it means that the backup was successful.

FIGURE 16.6
Important ESE backup
events

After all of the Exchange databases in a selected storage group are backed up, you will see events indicating that the transaction logs for a particular storage group are being backed up and then purged. This is another indication that all of the databases in a particular storage group have been backed up successfully. Figure 16.7 shows ESE events 223 and 224. Event ID 223 shows you the transaction logs that are being backed up for the storage group specified in the Description field.

FIGURE 16.7
ESE backup events
related to transaction
logs

Event ID 224 indicates that the backup logs have been backed up and they are now being purged. Both event ID 223 and 224 are good events. Table 16.2 shows the ESE and ESE BACKUP event IDs that you look for during an online backup. Usually to completely understand what is being backed up, you will need to read the Description field to see what database, transaction log, or storage group is affected.

You can also view the backup status of individual databases using the Exchange Management Console or the Exchange Management Shell. Previously, we showed you in Figure 16.1 that you can see the last time an incremental or differential backup was performed on a mailbox database. You can also use the EMs cmdlet `Get-MailboxDatabase` and the `-Status` option to retrieve database status information. Here is an example:

```
Get-MailboxDatabase "HNLEX04\Mailbox Database" -Status |
FL Name,Server,*backup*,Mounted

Name                           : Mailbox Database
Server                         : HNLEX04
BackupInProgress               : False
LastFullBackup                 : 1/27/2007 8:59:17 PM
LastIncrementalBackup          : 1/28/2007 1:06:22 PM
RetainDeletedItemsUntilBackup  : False
Mounted                        : True
```

TABLE 16.2:   Exchange Database Engine Backup Events

EVENT ID	SOURCE	DESCRIPTION
210	ESE	Indicates that a full backup of a specified storage group is beginning.
211	ESE	Indicates that an incremental or differential backup of the specified storage group is starting.
220	ESE	Indicates that a backup of a specified database is starting.
907	ESE BACKUP	Indicates that the backup data transfer method is shared memory.
221	ESE	Indicates that a backup of the specified database is completed.
223	ESE	Indicates that backup of specified transaction logs is starting.
224	ESE	Indicating that transaction logs for the specified storage group are being purged after successful backup.
213	ESE	Indicates that backup of specified storage group (databases and transaction logs) has completed.

Recovering Mailboxes and Items in Mailboxes

While a deleted item or a mailbox is not exactly a national emergency, the user that is being affected may think it is. Recovering quickly from even simple problems like a deleted message or a deleted mailbox is important for good relations with your user community.

Recovering Deleted Items

When a user deletes an item from their mailbox, the item is moved to the Deleted Items folder. When the item is deleted from the Deleted Items folder, it is moved into the deleted items cache where it is kept for the Keep Deleted Items retention period. By default, this is configured at 14 days for each mailbox database; this is configured for the entire mailbox database on the mailbox database's Limits property page (shown in Figure 16.8).

FIGURE 16.8
Limits property page for
a mailbox database

Once the Keep Deleted Items period has expired, the item is permanently deleted during the mailbox database's online maintenance process.

A user can retrieve something from the deleted item cache using Outlook by selecting the Deleted Items folder and then choosing Tools ➤ Recover Deleted Items. This will launch the Recover Deleted Items From dialog box (see Figure 16.9); from here you can select the item you want to recover and then click the Recover Selected Items button on the toolbar. This is the button that has an envelope icon with a small blue arrow on top of it.

Once the item is recovered, it will be restored to the Deleted Items folder. If the user is in Outlook cached Exchange mode, the item may not reappear locally for a minute or two, so the user should be patient.

There is also a type of delete called a *hard delete*; a hard delete occurs anytime a message bypasses the Deleted Items folder. This can happen when the user highlights the message and presses Shift+Delete. A hard delete can also occur if a user downloads messages using a POP3 or IMAP4 client and then deletes them from the server. So instead of being able to undelete the message from the Deleted Items folder, you have to undeleted it from the folder from which the message was deleted.

However, if the user hard-deleted the message from their Inbox, the Tools ➤ Recover Deleted Items menu choice is not available. To make it available, it requires a little Registry trick. On the

client computer, locate the following Registry key:
 HKLM\SOFTWARE\Microsoft\Exchange\Client\Options

FIGURE 16.9
Recovering a deleted
item

In this key, create a REG_DWORD value called DumpsterAlwaysOn and set it to 1. Restart
Outlook and the Tools ➢ Recover Deleted Items should now be available.

If the item cannot be recovered using one of these methods, then the only other choice available
to the administrator may be to perform a recovery to a recovery storage group and recover the
mail data that way.

Recovering Deleted Mailboxes

Occasionally after a mailbox is deleted, someone comes to the IT department and says that they
need it back. This might be because the user did not really leave or there might be something
important in the mailbox that must be recovered. By default, each mailbox database is configured
with a deleted mailbox recovery time of 30 days. This is configured on the Limits property page
(shown previously in Figure 16.8) in the Keep Deleted Mailboxes For (Days) property.

A mailbox can be recovered and reconnected to a user account, but it must be a user account
that does not have a mailbox assigned to it already. Mailboxes are reconnected using the Disconnected Mailbox subcontainer of the Recipient Configuration work center in the EMC. When you
select this container, you then click the Connect to Server task in the Actions pane to specify the
mailbox server on which the deleted mailbox exists.

Figure 16.10 shows the Disconnected Mailbox subcontainer and a list of deleted mailboxes
in the results pane. To reconnect a deleted mailbox, highlight the mailbox and then choose the
Connect task from the Actions pane.

When you choose Connect, you will be taken through the Connect Mailbox Wizard. This is very
similar to the wizard that runs when you create a mailbox. The Introduction screen asks if this is

FIGURE 16.10
Reconnecting a deleted
mailbox

a user, room, equipment, or linked mailbox. The Mailbox Settings page allows you to specify the user account to which you are reconnecting the mailbox as well as the Exchange alias, the managed folder mailbox policy, and the Exchange ActiveSync policy. This is shown in Figure 16.11.

FIGURE 16.11
Specifying the user
account to which
the mailbox will be
connected

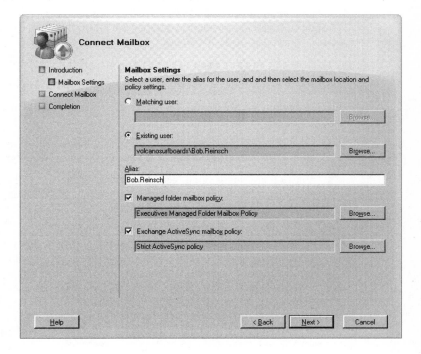

The mailbox reconnection could also have been done from the EMS using the `Connect-Mailbox` cmdlet. You need to retrieve the mailbox unique GUID, though. This can be retrieved using the

`Get-MailboxStatistics` cmdlet. Here is an example using the `Connect-Mailbox` cmdlet:

```
Connect-Mailbox -Identity 'e0b25cd9-b6b6-4214-9a1f-e0e1ddbea257'
-Database 'HNLEX03.volcanosurfboards.com\First Storage Group\Mailbox Database'
-User 'volcanosurfboards\Bob.Reinsch' -Alias 'Bob.Reinsch'
-ManagedFolderMailboxPolicy 'Executives Managed Folder Mailbox Policy'
-ActiveSyncMailboxPolicy 'Strict ActiveSync policy'
```

Restoring an Exchange Database

Restoring an Exchange Server 2007 database is not a terribly difficult process once you understand a few basic rules. In this section, we will go through the restoration process using the Windows Backup utility and restore the default mailbox database (called Mailbox Database). You might need to restore a database from backup if the production database had become corrupted, if the disk holding the database had become corrupted, or if the entire server failed.

Let's take as an example a situation in which a mailbox database needs to be restored. The first thing we need to know is what the backup schedule is and what tapes are available. In this example, we perform a nightly full backup and then an incremental backup at noon each day. The problem that requires the restoration occurs on Tuesday at 3:00 in the afternoon. In this example, we also will also assume that we have all of the transaction log files that have been created since the last incremental backup.

Let's put together a checklist of things we want to do prior to starting this restoration of the database named Mailbox Database.

1. Ensure that there is sufficient disk space for the database to be restored.

2. Ensure that there is sufficient disk space for the temporary files.

3. We will need the backup media for the Monday night full backup and the Tuesday noon incremental backup.

4. Dismount the mailbox store if mounted; if there is current database file in the database folder, we recommend that you rename it just in case you need it in the future.

5. Verify that there is not a recovery storage group somewhere in the organization that has this particular database configured. If there is, the database will be restored to the recovery storage group, not the production location.

Since, we are using the Windows Backup utility, we will run that program and then select the Restore and Manage Media tab. Then, in the left pane of the Backup utility, we must find the backup media and set we wish to restore. The first set we need to restore is the full backup set from Monday night. Figure 16.12 shows the Windows Backup utility and the selected information to be restored. Notice that we have chosen both the Mailbox Database and the Log Files selections from the Monday Night full backup set.

When we have finished selecting the mailbox database and transaction log files, we click the Start Restore button. This launches the Restoring Database Store dialog box, where we can direct the restore to an alternate server and specify the temporary file location for the restored log files. The transaction log files will not be restored to the production transaction log location. Take note of the temporary location for the log and patch files as we will need it again when we restore the incremental backup files.

Notice the check boxes on the bottom of the Restoring Database Store dialog box. These are the Last Restore Set (Log File Replay Will Start after This Restore Completes) and Mount Database after Restore check boxes. Since we have another restore set to go after this restore, we want to leave these check boxes cleared.

FIGURE 16.12
Restoring the database named Mailbox Database and associated log files

When we click the Start Restore button, we are presented with the Check Backup File Location dialog box since we are restoring from a BKF file instead of a tape. If the correct file is not specified, you can click the Browse button and locate the correct BKF file.

Once you have selected the correct file, click the OK button to start the restore. The restore process may take a while depending on the size of the database. Generally, restoring from tape will take twice as long as the backup took, so you should factor that in to your restore estimates.

During and after this restore, there will not be much of interest in either the Application event log or the backup log. The Windows Backup utility's log only has some information about the storage group name to which the restore was performed and the amount data. An example is shown here:

```
-----------------------------------------------

Restore Status
Operation: Restore

Backup of "HNLEX03\Microsoft Information Store\First Storage Group",
```

```
 Restored to"HNLEX03\Microsoft Information Store\First Storage Group"
Backup set #1 on media #1
Backup description: "Monday night - full backup"

Restore started on 1/28/2007 at 4:59 PM.
Restore completed on 1/28/2007 at 5:08 PM.
Directories: 3
Files: 20
Bytes: 3,648,996,564
Time:  8 minutes and  30 seconds


------------------------------------------------
```

Once this backup completes, we have to repeat the process. except this time, we select the incremental backup that was made on Tuesday at noon. This backup set will only have log files since it was an incremental backup.

When we click the Start Restore button, we will need to provide the same path to the log files and backup files, but we want to make sure that the Last Restore Set (Log File Replay Will Start after This Restore Completes) and the Mount Database after Restore check boxes are checked. This will automatically start the transaction log replay process.

When you click the OK button on the Restoring Database Store dialog box, you will once again be prompted for the proper location for the BKF file if restoring from a backup file set. When the restore process begins, it will run much quicker than the full restore did since all it will be doing is restoring all of the transaction logs since the previous night.

Once the restore is complete, the Application event log will begin to get interesting. Figure 16.13 shows event ID 204. This event indicates that the transaction log replay is beginning and that the process will start with the log files restored from tape (the log files from the full backup and then the incremental backup) that are found in the temporary restore directory.

FIGURE 16.13
Restore process starts
replaying log files

The log files found in the temporary restore folder will get the database restored up through the incremental backup that occurred at noon on Tuesday. However, in this example, we have all of the transactions that have occurred up through the time we had to restore the database. So the transaction replay (rolling forward) will continue in the production transaction log folder. Figure 16.14 shows event ID 201, which shows us the current transaction log that is being replayed. The figure shows that the most recent transaction log (E00.LOG) is being replayed.

FIGURE 16.14
Replaying a transaction log

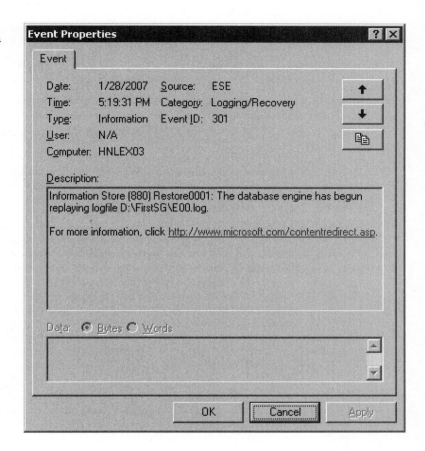

Using the Recovery Storage Group

One of the nicest additions to Exchange 2003 was the recovery storage group feature; this feature allows an administrator to create the recovery storage group (RSG) and add existing mailbox databases the list of mailbox databases that can be restored to the RSG. When an Exchange-aware backup utility attempts to restore one of the databases in the RSG, the database is restored to the RSG rather than to the production location. This feature is also supported on Exchange 2007 Mailbox servers, but there is not a graphical user interface for creating the RSG and adding mailbox databases to it.

NOTE

The recovery storage group can only be used when restoring mailbox databases, not public folder databases.

RSG management in the release-to-manufacturing version of Exchange 2007 is handled from within the EMS or from within the Exchange Database Recovery Management Wizard in the Toolbox work center. Here are some important points about RSGs to keep in mind:

◆ Restoring an RSG does not interfere with normal Exchange operations.

◆ An RSG can be restored to any Exchange 2007 Mailbox server, not just the server on which it originally existed.

◆ RSGs can be used to restore a mailbox from a previous backup so that a mailbox, folder, or item can be recovered.

◆ RSGs can be used to verify the integrity of backups without building a recovery system.

Preparing to Use a Recovery Storage Group

Before you use an RSG, there are a few things that you should consider or prepare. This includes ensuring that you have sufficient disk space and that you understand the limitations of the RSG.

You can create only one RSG on an Exchange 2007 Mailbox server. This RSG can contain Exchange 2007 mailbox databases from any storage group on any server in the entire organization, but at any one time an RSG can contain only mailbox databases from one original storage group. Exchange 2003 mailbox databases are not supported.

The Exchange 2007 Mailbox server on which you create the RSG must have a disk volume with sufficient disk space to support the database(s) to be restored and the transaction logs and to allow creation of temporary files that might be necessary during the restore. When you create the RSG, you must specify the path for the transaction logs and system files; these cannot be changed later.

A mailbox database that is restored to the RSG cannot be accessed by end users, from Outlook, or from Outlook Web Access. The mailbox data can be retrieved only by using the `Restore-Mailbox` cmdlet.

Databases in an RSG cannot be mounted automatically, they do not have online maintenance performed on them, message records management policies do not apply, neither LCR nor CCR applies to them, and they cannot be backed up.

Restoring a Mailbox Database to a Recovery Storage Group

Let's go through a sample recovery of a mailbox database using an RSG and the Exchange Database Recovery Management tool. In this example, a user has deleted something really important from their mailbox and they did so at 10:00 Tuesday morning. For whatever reason, we are unable to undelete the item. For this restore, we will use the previous night's (Monday's) full backup. We don't need the noon incremental backup since by that time the user had deleted the message. The LCR or CCR copies of the database would not do any good either because they are up-to-date copies of the production database. So we need to restore the Monday night backup to a recovery storage group.

The first step now is to create an RSG and put the mailbox database into it. While this can be done from the EMS, it is much simpler from the Exchange Database Recovery Management tool. From the Toolbox work center, we launch the Exchange Database Recovery Management tool and it will start through the Troubleshooting Assistant. Like most tools based on the Troubleshooting Assistant, we need to first go to the Welcome screen and provide a label to identify our activity, the Exchange server name, and a domain controller name.

The first screen that really tells us we are managing databases is the Select One of the following Tasks screen. Here we want to click on the Create a Recovery Storage Group link. From the Select the Storage Group to Link with the Recovery Storage Group, select the storage group that holds the database we want to restore. In this case, it will be the First Storage Group.

Select the Storage Group to Link with the Recovery Storage Group

Server name: hnlex03

First Storage Group
Public Folder SG

The recovery storage group is linked to an existing storage group. Only databases from the linked storage group can be mounted in the recovery storage group.

◄ Previous   ► Next

When we click Next, we are taken to the Create the Recovery Storage Group screen where we provide the name for the RSG as well as paths for the transaction logs, system path, and checkpoint file. We must click the Browse buttons to select a new location for the files, but for some reason, this screen does not show our intended paths When we're finished filling out this screen, we want to click the Create the Recovery Storage Group link.

Create the Recovery Storage Group

Server name: hnlex03
Linked storage group: First Storage Group

Recovery storage group name: Recovery Storage Group

Transaction log file folder

Original storage group (Enn.log) log path: D:\FirstSG   Browse...

System folder and checkpoint file folder

Original storage group (Enn.chk) path: C:\Program Files\Microsoft\Exchange Server\Mailbox\First Storage Group   Browse...

Database folders and file names

Database name: Mailbox Database   Browse...

◄ Previous   ► Create the recovery storage group

On the Create the Recovery Storage Group Result screen, we can verify that the RSG has been created and the database named Mailbox Database has been assigned to this RSG.

You can now move, copy or restore database and transaction log files to the recovery storage group paths. When you are ready to mount databases in the recovery storage group, go to the task center or start this analyzer again. If the domain controller you specified is different from the domain controller that the Exchange server is using, you may need to wait for the change to be replicated.

⌃ Hide Create Recovery Storage Group Information

Transaction log file folder
Original storage group (Enn.log) log path: D:\FirstSG
Recovery storage group (R00.log) log path: C:\RSG

System folder and checkpoint file folder
Original storage group (Enn.chk) path: C:\Program Files\Microsoft\Exchange Server\Mailbox\First Storage Group
Recovery storage group (R00.chk) path: C:\RSG

Database folders and file names
Original database name: Mailbox Database
Original database path: D:\FirstSG\Mailbox Database.edb
Recovery database path: D:\FirstSG\RSG20070128175527\Mailbox Database.edb

From the Tasks Center screen of the Troubleshooting Assistant, we can manage the RSG and the databases we have restored. Figure 16.15 shows the Select One of the Following Tasks screen.

Before we can do anything else, though, we need to restore the database to the RSG. The good news now is that the procedure is exactly the same for restoring to the RSG as it is if you are restoring to the production location of the database. The backup software does not have to be told anything new. We select the database we want to restore, and since there is an RSG that holds that database, the Exchange information store service will automatically put the database in the RSG. This means that we do not need to interfere with the production database at all.

FIGURE 16.15
Recovery storage group management tasks

We could have accomplished all of these tasks from the EMS. First we would need to create a storage group whose type is an RSG. Here is a sample:

```
New-StorageGroup -Name "Recovery Storage Group" -Server HNLEX03
-LogFolderPath C:\RSG -SystemFolderPath C:\RSG -Recovery
```

Next we need to assign the mailbox store to the RSG we have just created. We use the database name of the production database that we are restoring:

```
New-MailboxDatabase -MailboxDatabaseToRecover "Mailbox Database"
-StorageGroup "HNLEX03\Recovery Storage Group" -EDBFilePath C:\RSG
```

Next, we need to set this database so that we can allow the file to be restored. We would use this cmdlet:

```
Set-MailboxDatabase "HNLEX03\Recovery Storage Group\Mailbox Database"
-AllowFileRestore
```

Finally, after we restore the mailbox database, we will need to mount it. The command to do that would be as follows:

```
Mount-Database "HNLEX03\Recovery Storage Group\Mailbox Database"
```

Recovering Information from a Recovery Storage Group

As we mentioned earlier, you cannot accesses an RSG from either Outlook or Outlook Web Access, so you need to use either the `Recover-Mailbox` EMS cmdlet or the Disaster Recovery Management tool. We restored the appropriate backup to the Exchange server and now we can use the Mount or Dismount Databases in the Recovery Storage Group selection shown previously in Figure 16.15.

Once the database is mounted, we can copy or merge data back into the user's mailbox. From the Select One of the Following Tasks screen, we choose the Merge or Copy Mailbox Contents link and on the next page click the Gather Merge Information link. On the Select Merge Options page, we click the Show Advanced Options link so that we can see more detailed information about mailbox matching, date range filters, subject filter, and the start and end filter dates. An example is shown in Figure 16.16.

FIGURE 16.16

Selecting merge options

Notice that if we select the Match All Source Mailboxes to a Destination Mailbox check box, we can specify the alias of a mailbox to which we want all of the data copied. This is useful if we don't want to merge the data back into the original mailbox. When we have made our selections on the Select Merge Options screen, the next step is to click the Perform Pre-Merge Tasks link.

The next screen is the Select Mailboxes to Copy or Merge screen. From here, we can select the mailboxes that were found in the recovery storage group whose data we want copied or merged in to the target mailbox. In this example, we will select the user that deleted the important message and absolutely has to get it back.

Select Mailboxes to Copy or Merge

Server name: hnlex03
Recovery storage group name: Recovery Storage Group
Linked storage group name: First Storage Group
Selected database name: Mailbox Database
Linked database name: Mailbox Database

Matched mailboxes

Display Name	Mailbox GUID
☐ Dana Scully	1843121-6a4b-40d3-baf9-c882b7da98e0
☐ Jason Sherry	e0b25cd9-b6b6-4214-9a1f-e0e1ddbea257
☐ Jim McBee	ad903a00-0ab3-453d-925d-5218c5e8ad48
☐ Jim McBee - CTA Mail Backup	1fae0423-f371-45ae-82d8-a4dbd9b71412
☐ MergeMailbox	3dac64b8-6cc7-40dd-8e57-c8b8220db037
☑ Russ Kaufmann	dfafe65a-4dcf-45e8-812f-60736cd11216

[Save] [Select All] [Unselect All]

🔲 Previous   🔲 Perform merge actions

After selecting the mailboxes to merge or copy, we click the Perform Merge Actions link to start the merge.

We could also have accomplished the same thing with the `Restore-Mailbox` EMS cmdlet. Here is an example in which we are restoring a single mailbox and only items between 1/25/07 and 1/28/07. In this instance, we are restoring the data to a folder in the user's own mailbox, called Recovered Data:

```
[PS] D:\>Restore-Mailbox "Russ Kaufmann" -RSGDatabase "Recovery Storage
Group\Mailbox Database" -StartDate "01/25/07" -EndDate "01/28/07"
-TargetFolder "Recovered Data" -RSGMailbox "russ kaufmann"

Confirm
Are you sure you want to perform this action?
Recovering mailbox content from the mailbox 'Russ Kaufmann' in the recovery
database 'HNLEX03\Recovery Storage Group\Mailbox Database' into the mailbox for
 'Russ Kaufmann (Russ.Kaufmann\commatsomorita.com)'. The operation can take a long
time.
[Y] Yes  [A] Yes to All  [N] No  [L] No to All  [S] Suspend  [?] Help
(default is "Y"):y


Identity                       : volcanosurfboards.com/VolcanoSurfboards/
Russ Kaufmann
DistinguishedName              : CN=Russ Kaufmann,
OU=VolcanoSurfboards,DC=volcanosurfboards,DC=com
DisplayName                    : Russ Kaufmann
Alias                          : Russ.Kaufmann
LegacyExchangeDN               : /o=Volcano Surfboards/ou=Exchange
Administrative Group (FYDIBOHF23SPDLT)/cn=Recipients/cn=Russ.Kaufmann
PrimarySmtpAddress             : Russ.Kaufmann\commatsomorita.com
```

```
SourceServer                     : HNLEX03.volcanosurfboards.com
SourceDatabase                   : HNLEX03\Recovery Storage Group\Mailbox Database
SourceGlobalCatalog              : HNLDC01
SourceDomainController           :
TargetGlobalCatalog              : HNLDC01
TargetDomainController           :
TargetMailbox                    : volcanosurfboards.com/VolcanoSurfboards/
Russ Kaufmann
TargetServer                     : HNLEX03.volcanosurfboards.com
TargetDatabase                   : HNLEX03\First Storage Group\Mailbox Database
MailboxSize                      : 9868B
IsResourceMailbox                : False
SIDUsedInMatch                   :
SMTPProxies                      :
SourceManager                    :
SourceDirectReports              :
SourcePublicDelegates            :
SourcePublicDelegatesBL          :
SourceAltRecipient               :
SourceAltRecipientBL             :
SourceDeliverAndRedirect         :
MatchedTargetNTAccountDN         :
IsMatchedNTAccountMailboxEnabled :
MatchedContactsDNList            :
TargetNTAccountDNToCreate        :
TargetManager                    :
TargetDirectReports              :
TargetPublicDelegates            :
TargetPublicDelegatesBL          :
TargetAltRecipient               :
TargetAltRecipientBL             :
TargetDeliverAndRedirect         :
Options                          : Default
SourceForestCredential           :
TargetForestCredential           :
TargetFolder                     : \Recovered Data\Recovered Data
- Russ Kaufmann - 1/28/2007 10:02:34 PM
RsgMailboxGuid                   : dfafe65a-4dcf-45e8-812f-60736cd11216
RsgMailboxLegacyExchangeDN       : /O=VOLCANO SURFBOARDS/OU=EXCHANGE
 ADMINISTRATIVE GROUP (FYDIBOHF23SPDLT)/CN=RECIPIENTS/CN=RUSS.KAUFMANN
RsgMailboxDisplayName            : Russ Kaufmann
RsgDatabaseGuid                  : cde8e7e1-03f7-465b-a705-80a399c64e9a
MoveType                         : Restore
MoveStage                        : Completed
StartTime                        : 1/28/2007 10:02:39 PM
EndTime                          : 1/28/2007 10:02:42 PM
StatusCode                       : 0
StatusMessage                    : This mailbox in the recovery storage
 group database has been restored to the target usermailbox.
```

The result of this is that a folder is created in user Russ Kaufmann's mailbox that has everything from 1/25/07 through 1/28/07. This is shown in Figure 16.17. At this point, the help desk can now assist the user in copying back into the correct folder the very important message that got deleted.

FIGURE 16.17
The Recovered Data folder structure is created.

Recovering from Disasters

From a hardware and software perspective, we have already talked about at least 90 percent of the disaster recovery puzzle. If you're an Exchange system administrator and you've protected your servers with redundant hardware, especially interserver redundant hardware, or you can restore any crashed Exchange server under your management, you've pretty much got it made. If you also have to worry about Windows 2003 and you can bring a domain controller or stand-alone server back from the dead with VSS or Automatic Server Recovery (ASR) backups or even clunky, more traditional streaming backups, you're in a good place, too.

All too often the term *disaster recovery* is misused in our industry. It's used to mean something as simple as restoring a database. In the big picture, this is not a disaster for most organizations. In this section, we want to talk more about real disasters and disaster recovery.

Disaster recovery adds another dimension to the reliability and availability picture. You have to deal with simultaneous multisystem unavailability, up to and including the sudden disappearance of all or a major part of your server, storage, workstation, and networking systems. The cause of such a disaster can be anything from a terrorist attack to an earthquake, from a building fire to a major power outage or lightning strike.

Disaster recovery isn't fun to think about. There are so many variables, including the potential for astronomical costs, that it's easy to either go bonkers or avoid even thinking about the whole thing. The best way to calm yourself and your boss when disaster recovery rears its ugly head is by building and living by a set of best-possible, cost-realistic strategies that specify what you'll do to avoid disasters and the actions you'll take if disaster strikes.

Disaster Recovery Strategies

Shopping for a disaster recovery solution is a lot like buying a new car. Car salespeople will frequently urge you not to worry about price and just test-drive the car you really want. Before you know it, you have spent a lot of time looking at your ideal car even though you know you can't afford it.

Well, developing disaster recovery strategies can be like buying a car at a dealership. You call in a company that specializes in disaster recovery and before you know it, you've got a proposal for a multimillion-dollar solution. The solution, by the way, is usually quite impressive. If only you could afford it.

The first thing you need to consider when developing a disaster recovery strategy is what your organization does and how a disaster might affect what it does. If e-mail and related Exchange services are central to your organization's operation and bottom line, then you need a very aggressive disaster recovery strategy. If your organization could do without e-mail for a few days, then a less aggressive strategy should be acceptable.

In building your disaster recovery strategy, don't be driven by unrealistic assessments of the importance of e-mail. And don't take a seat on the curb in discussions about the role of e-mail in your organization. You live with Exchange. You know what users are doing with e-mail, and you hear user complaints when your Exchange system isn't available. Your goal must be to drive e-mail disaster recovery deliberation toward a solution that you are comfortable with — the checkbooks, egos, or misperceptions of your bosses notwithstanding. As strategies are considered, you need to make sure your management clearly understands the limits of each. This is not just to protect yourself, but to set realistic management expectations from the get-go.

PIGGYBACKING ON NON-E-MAIL DISASTER RECOVERY STRATEGIES

Unless e-mail is all your organization does, there should be a disaster recovery strategy for other IT functionality. Adding e-mail to an existing strategy can be a relatively inexpensive option. But don't piggyback if you know the non-e-mail strategy won't work for e-mail. We have been in situations where e-mail was both more and less important than other IT functions. Management loved it when we told them that e-mail required a less aggressive disaster recovery strategy. They hated it when we pressed for a more aggressive (more expensive) strategy for e-mail.

We are going to discuss five disaster recovery strategies, from the fanciest and most costly to the more mundane and reasonably priced. Remember that most of these strategies can be implemented in house or by a third party. Don't write off outsourcing for disaster recovery. For some organizations, it is a good, cost-effective option.

Here are the disaster recovery strategies that we will cover in this section:

◆ Offsite replication of an entire system, such as CCR solutions

◆ Offsite replication of servers, workstations, disk storage, backup hardware, software, and data

◆ Onsite replication of an entire system, such as CCR solutions

◆ Onsite replication of servers, disk storage, backup hardware, software, and data

◆ Onsite presence of spare server, disk storage, and backup hardware

For many organizations, a combination of these strategies makes the most sense. Disasters come in all flavors and intensities. Sometimes they require the aggressive solutions of offsite full-system replication. Sometimes a less aggressive strategy is all that's required. The key is to understand the various disaster recovery strategies and pick the ones that best serve your organization.

WARNING

Keep in mind as you read through the discussion of disaster recovery strategies that a strategy is not a plan. Once you've selected the strategy or strategies that work for your organization, you should develop a written plan that provides specifics. You need to specify your strategy in detail and provide step-by-step up-to-date instructions for recovering after a disaster. You also need clear and up-to-date documentation for your hardware systems and the software running on them. And, once you've completed your disaster recovery plan, make sure paper and electronic copies are available off site. The best-laid plans have no value if you can't find a copy when you need it.

BARRY GERBER ON OFFSITE REPLICATION OF AN ENTIRE SYSTEM

I live in Los Angeles. Any disaster recovery strategy I develop for my LaLaLand clients has to take into account the possibility of earthquake-related collapsing buildings and fractured WAN infrastructure. For those clients who need to operate without missing a beat and who can afford it, offsite replication of their entire system, including up-to-the-minute replication of data, is the right answer.

The idea is that the minute a production system takes a major hit, the offsite system becomes the production system. Appropriate IT and other staff go to the offsite location and begin doing their thing. While the transition is never going to be totally transparent, with networking switchovers and the loss of last-minute data to deal with, a total offsite strategy can get an organization up and running quickly.

One addendum to this strategy is to actually use the disaster site to conduct the organization's business. Staff at each site performs a portion of all or some of the IT and other business tasks of the organization. When disaster strikes, required personnel are already at the disaster recovery site and able to keep the organization running until reinforcements arrive.

As you can imagine, this sort of disaster recovery strategy is very, very expensive. It's for banks and other financial institutions, really big hospitals, and other corporate giants who both need this sort of quick recovery capability and can afford to put it in place.

None of my clients has placed their system in one of those bunkers built into a mountain in Colorado that you might have read about or seen in the movies. However, they have implemented less aggressive strategies where a replicated system is set up in a nearby structure and data is kept up-to-date, though not up to the minute, using tape backups. Often the offsite location is in a single-story building, which is less likely to be seriously damaged in an earthquake. They still have to worry about potential damage and loss of WAN infrastructure, but it's quite okay if these folks can back up within a day or so and not within minutes or hours of a disaster. So this strategy is fine for them.

OFFSITE REPLICATION OF SERVERS, WORKSTATIONS, DISK STORAGE, BACKUP HARDWARE, NETWORKS, RELATED SOFTWARE, AND DATA

The major difference between this strategy and offsite replication of data is that you don't replicate your entire production system off site. You replicate just enough of the system to get your organization back up and running in a reasonable time. In this disaster recovery scenario, you replicate hardware and operating system and applications software as required. However, you don't necessarily replicate data, being happy to recover data from backups shortly after a disaster strikes. You also don't necessarily replicate WAN links.

If you need to replicate data or even your entire disk storage system, consider the SAN systems that we discussed earlier in this chapter. Using capabilities built into SAN systems, the Windows Server 2003 cluster service, you can replicate the data on one SAN to another SAN. Such replication is fairly quick and well suited to disaster recovery strategies where data needs to be readily available after a disaster strikes.

Instead of going with a third-party product, you may choose to implement a Windows 2003 cluster and an Exchange Server 2007 clustered continuous replication solution. CCR does not require the same expenses for storage and third-party replication tools since the ability to replicate an Exchange database is built in to the product.

This disaster recovery strategy works if your organization can stand up to a few days of downtime. You and other IT staff need to be ready to scramble to get things running, but you don't have the staff expense and other costs associated with trying to build a full mirror of your production system.

ONSITE REPLICATION OF AN ENTIRE SYSTEM

This strategy is the same as offsite replication, except your replicated disaster recovery system exists in close physical proximity to your production system. This is a pretty fancy strategy, especially if you also have an offsite replication of your entire system. However, if you need to get up and running after a major system failure, onsite full-system replication might be the only answer.

Windows Server 2003 cluster services can play a major role here and in the next two strategies. Because your system is on site, you can use the very high-speed, server-to-server, server-to-storage, and server-to network links that make clustering such a great server and storage replication solution. It won't solve all of your replication problems, but it takes care of major components in the replication equation.

ONSITE REPLICATION OF SERVERS, DISK STORAGE, BACKUP HARDWARE, NETWORKS, RELATED SOFTWARE, AND DATA

As we are sure you've gathered, this strategy is an onsite version of the second disaster recovery strategy we discussed. It can provide the tools you need to meet the operating requirements of your organization. As we noted in the preceding section, Windows Server 2003 cluster services and clustered continuous replication can make this strategy much easier to implement.

ONSITE PRESENCE OF SPARE SERVER, DISK STORAGE, BACKUP AND NETWORK HARDWARE, SOFTWARE, AND DATA

Under this strategy, you have spares at hand, but they're not kept up-to-date by replication. Rather, you activate spares when a disaster requires.

Like so much of our discussion of disaster recovery strategies, this one brings to mind our earlier discussions of server recovery in nondisaster situations. We hope, as we come to the end of this relatively brief treatment of disaster recovery strategies, that you begin to synthesize the content of this chapter into a coherent view of the Exchange Server 2007 reliability and availability continuum.

BARRY GERBER: THE TAO OF DISASTER RECOVERY

A detailed discussion of actual disaster recovery operations is beyond the scope of this book. This whole chapter and the specific disaster recovery strategies that we've discussed provide detail and hints as to the how of disaster recovery. Your disaster recovery plan will provide the specific operational steps to be taken when a disaster occurs.

What I really need to talk about here is what might be called the Tao of disaster recovery. Taoism is a way of life that associates every aspect of existence with a kind of overarching spirituality. It mixes the right and left sides of the brain and, in so doing, can bring calm and understanding to even the most stressful experience.

I participated in disaster recovery operations after the September 11, 2001, tragedy in New York City. I wasn't on site and I didn't work for the biggies in the World Trade Center, but I was involved in a number of phone conversations with IT types in two buildings damaged but not destroyed by the airplane crashes. Most of what I talked about involved Exchange server recovery.

I'm a hands-on visual type, so I was especially nervous as I tried to provide help in a voice-only situation. I'm not a Taoist, but I've had enough exposure to the philosophy to know that going bonkers wasn't going to help. So I slapped myself in the face and began breathing in a consciously slow and regular manner before taking the first phone call.

It helped. I was relatively calm until I began talking to a bunch of people who had hours before seen two massive buildings collapse and kill thousands and who were worried about their own personal safety. Understandably, these folks were in a much worse state than I. My first suggestion to them was that they take a few minutes or even a few hours to relax — after, of course, clearing it with their bosses.

My clients agreed to try and called me back in 15 minutes to tell me that they had the go-ahead to wait for an hour. I strongly urged them to do anything but IT work during that hour. Given the mess that portion of New York was in, there wasn't a lot they could do. So they decided to see if they could help others in that hour.

Almost two hours later, my clients called back. It turned out that venturing out to help others made it very clear to them how lucky they were to be alive and still able to do their jobs. In spite of what they'd seen, my clients seemed calm and relaxed about the task ahead of us.

We took the recovery process in steps. After they got their power generator going, we started up their Exchange server, which had been pelted by a major portion of the ceiling and a bunch of heavy chairs from the floor above. Fortunately, they were able to shut off power to the server before its UPS had run out of battery power. Unfortunately, the server did not come back. Not only was their Exchange server dead, so were their two Windows 2000 domain controllers.

Not being major players in trade and finance, these folks didn't have any offsite disaster recovery setup. They also had no real onsite setup. Fortunately, they had backups that were stored both on site and off site. And, they had two standby servers in a closet that more or less survived the disaster. The servers both worked but didn't have current software on them.

So we set up a replacement Windows 2000 domain controller and recovered a backup of Active Directory to it. Then we set up a Windows 2000 server to support the Exchange server. At this point, I suggested we stop for 20 minutes and just talk about what was going on. I actually had a better view of things from Los Angeles by TV than they had in the still-smoky and dusty environment where they were working. This brief respite helped all of us relax, and we were able to recover the Exchange server fairly quickly.

The next day, employees were able to get some work done using internal e-mail. It took more than a week to get some sort of Internet connection running. It wasn't until several weeks later that they had their 1.5Mbps Internet connection back in place.

It took about four hours, including relaxation breaks, to get the job done. If we had pushed ourselves, I estimate it would have taken maybe 10 hours with all the mistakes we'd have made and had to correct. While these folks had a written plan for the recovery, they didn't have an easy-to-use checklist, which would have made things easier. They have one now.

The moral of this story is quite simple: Disasters are stressful. Don't try to recover from one when you're at your most stressed. And you can often make your job easier by involving someone who doesn't have the same emotional and job-related connection to your organization as you do. Don't call me. I'm disaster-recoveried out. However, you should try to get someone else involved in your recovery efforts, whether it's other Windows/Exchange system managers in your area or Microsoft or third-party consultants.

Summary

Providing users with reliable and available Exchange server services is a complex task. You have to combine redundant hardware with a whole range of backup and recovery strategies and, in case the unusual should happen, disaster recovery strategies.

Hardware redundancy and mastery of backup and recovery strategies takes you a long way down the path to high server reliability and availability. It also gives you a leg up as you enter the complex world of disaster recovery. Disaster recovery strategies depend significantly on hardware redundancy and Windows and Exchange server backup and recovery strategies.

Good disaster recovery strategies and plans are based on a careful balance between organizational needs and the resources required to meet those needs. E-mail disaster recovery needs might or might not be met by an organization's non-e-mail disaster recovery strategies. When disaster recovery strategies are considered, it's most important that bosses and managers understand the benefits and disadvantages of each strategy. Whatever strategy or set of strategies is chosen, bosses and managers must have a clear set of expectations regarding what can be recovered in what time frame.

Disaster recovery strategies can range from complex and costly offsite replications of entire systems to the onsite presence of spare pieces of hardware. The mechanics of a recovery after a disaster are the easiest things to specify and carry out. Maintaining the presence of mind required to pull off a disaster recovery is not so easy, but it's just as important.

Part 5

Outlook

In this section you will learn to:

Chapter 17

Supporting Outlook 2007

Though this book is about Exchange Server 2007, we want to talk a bit about the premier client for Exchange — Microsoft Outlook. Outlook Web Access as well as POP3 and IMAP4 clients may be popular in some places, but the Outlook client is king of the hill. This is because Outlook offers the widest range of features and takes advantage of most Exchange Server functions.

Outlook 2007 introduces a number of new features, including several that are of particular interest to Exchange administrators and that your users might ask you about, such as the To-Do Bar and RSS feeds. This chapter isn't intended to be a comprehensive review of Outlook 2007. For more in-depth information about Outlook 2007, you should see *Microsoft Outlook 2007 Bible* (Wiley, 2007).

Topics in this chapter include the following:

◆ Meeting the system requirements

◆ Installing Outlook

◆ Looking at the new interface

◆ Sending mail, using instant search, and synchronizing

◆ Using Outlook to manage your time and book appointments

System Requirements

Outlook 2007, like the rest of the Office 2007 suite, requires Windows XP Service Pack 2 or newer for the client operating system, with at least 256MB of RAM and at least 2GB of hard drive space. In reality, of course, running Windows XP, much less Office 2007, in 256MB of RAM is not a very satisfying way to work, so we recommend a bare minimum of 512MB of RAM; really, you should aim for 1GB or more if you can. Especially if you're running Vista you'll want the 1GB of RAM, and to get the benefits of Vista's Aero interface, you'll want a video card with at least 128MB of memory on board.

Since you're reading a book about Exchange 2007, it probably isn't necessary to mention that Outlook 2007 is not supported by Exchange versions prior to Exchange 2000. It's time to finally migrate off those old Exchange 5.5 servers if you still have any in use.

Installing Outlook 2007

The Office 2007 installation routine has been completely rewritten from the ground up. Now the Local Installation Source (LIS) is the standard method of installation; a fully compressed source is copied to the workstation on installation, and the installation is carried out from there. This makes the installation faster and more robust. When service packs or updates are issued in the future, there is no longer any need to provide the installation media (presuming you didn't remove the compressed LIS files after installation) because the full set of installation files are still right there on the workstation hard drive.

With previous versions, doing a customized deployment often meant either walking around and touching all of your workstations or using multiple tools to create customizations and "transforms" that you would apply to your installation.

Office 2007 has a single tool that lets you customize all of the settings in the product in one move. Its output is an XML file called `config.xml`, which you place in the \Updates folder and it will be automatically applied during setup.

We don't have time to go through every possible deployment scenario, so we'll go through the most basic one in this chapter to get you started.

Administrative Install

In Office 2003 you performed your base installation by running `setup /A` and actually doing an install to a share on a server that would serve as your base for client installs. In Office 2007, you simply copy the contents of the Office CD to a network share. Done.

> **NOTE**
>
> Why wouldn't you just share the CD instead of copying it to a network drive? Actually, you can. . .if you don't intend to do any customizations and you're okay with an "out of the box" install of Office, and your users being prompted for product keys and other installation information. Most deployments will want to enter that information for the users, however, and an install from the hard drive will perform better than an install from the CD.

Once you've completed that step, copy any product updates you might have into the \Updates folder of the installation share you've created.

Languages

Office 2007 is designed to be language neutral — that means that the core application files are not specific to any language and adding additional languages is as simple as copying any language packs you want to the installation point and answering no if asked to overwrite duplicate Setup files.

Being language independent has several advantages over previous versions:

◆ It's easy to add additional languages. Just copy in the language packs.

◆ You don't have to have any language you don't want, including English.

◆ Updates are much smaller. In past versions, the core files, and their related updates, were larger because they included the English (typically) language files. In 2007, updates to the core files don't have to include any language features.

◆ Installation files are much smaller. In previous versions, if you wanted to install English and Japanese you needed two complete sets of the installation files. In Outlook 2007, the language-neutral core files don't have to be duplicated, which can save a considerable amount of space.

Customization

In previous versions of Office, there were a number of different tools you needed to use to customize your installation. Those tools have all been rolled into a single tool for customizing Office and Outlook 2007 — the unimaginatively named Office Customization Tool (OCT).

The OCT lets you configure your office settings ahead of time and will create a setup customizations file called an MSP file that you simply place in the \Updates folder of your installation share. When you run Setup on the clients, it will automatically apply whatever changes and customizations you've made.

To run the OCT type setup /admin in the installation directory.

There are four sections to the OCT — setup, features, additional content, and Outlook — and each section has several pages of options.

SETUP

The setup section includes the primary options for setting up the application, including installation location, organization name, product key, and licensing. Outlook 2007 can't coexist with previous versions of Outlook and the setup routine will uninstall all previous versions of Office by default. The setup section gives you the option to tell Setup to leave certain installed applications (but not Outlook!) alone.

FEATURES

The features section lets you specify which Office features should be installed and which should not be installed and set options like which features should be installed on first use. Keep in mind that, thanks to the Local Installation Source, if you set a feature to install on first use, it will be available to install when the user needs it, even if the user doesn't have the original media or is disconnected from your network. The Local Installation Source provides the install files needed to complete the installation on demand.

ADDITIONAL CONTENT

The additional content section is where you can specify files you'd like to add or remove to the workstation or any custom Registry entries you'd like to create or remove. This section also lets you specify any shortcuts you'd like to create on the user's machine.

OUTLOOK

Outlook has its own section in the OCT. In the Outlook section you can customize the user's default profile, use an existing profile, or create a new one. If you lock down the computers so that the users don't have administrative rights, then the profile settings you make on install cannot be changed by the users. In this section, you can add additional accounts such as POP3 or IMAP accounts to the user's profile and even configure their send/receive groups if you like.

Client Deployment

At the client side, installation is as simple as initiating setup.exe from the workstation. That can be done manually by the end user or administrator, via a log-in script, or with any number of other utilities, such as Microsoft Systems Management Server, Altiris, and ScriptLogic. If you've used the OCT and correctly placed your MSP file, the setup routine will proceed without asking the end user for any input.

> **NOTE**
>
> Some organizations may have need to migrate data from mail clients other than Outlook. Outlook 2007 does include a number of converters, but they cannot be automatically run during installation. Each user will have to migrate their data individually.

If you want to install other Office products, you need only copy those files from the CD to the same installation point and be sure to answer no when prompted to overwrite duplicate Setup files.

Autodiscover

Configuring Outlook 2007 is easier than in any previous version. If you're logged into an authenticated domain account, Outlook 2007 can look up your user record in Active Directory and automatically enter your alias and e-mail server.

Outlook 2007 has the ability, under certain circumstances, to automatically configure itself to connect to an information service and set up the profile with little or no input from the user. In order to enable this capability for your clients, you have to enable Autodiscover on an Exchange 2007 server that has the Client Access (CAS) server role installed.

> **WARNING**
>
> If you have to enable Autodiscover on the server, you will have to use the Exchange Management Shell to do so — it can't be enabled from the Exchange Management Console.

For more information about configuring Autodiscover on the server, please see the section "Configuring Autodiscover" later in this chapter..

Autodiscover works for Outlook 2007 clients within your LAN as well as Outlook 2007 clients who will use RPC over HTTP, which Microsoft now calls Outlook Anywhere. Outlook Anywhere allows mobile users to connect Outlook 2007 to their Exchange server via regular HTTP protocol without having to connect to a virtual private network first. Essentially it tunnels RPC packets (the basic mechanism for Outlook/Exchange communication) over the HTTP protocol. Outlook 2007 can also usually autoconfigure your POP or IMAP account settings if you give it your e-mail address and password.

The 2007 User Interface

Outlook 2007's user interface is not dramatically different from Outlook 2003. Unlike the rest of the Office 2007 suite (except for OneNote and InfoPath), Outlook 2007 has not completely gone to the new Ribbon interface. The main Outlook window, known as the *explorer window*, still features the old menu bar/toolbar interface that you are familiar with. The *inspector windows*, those being the windows you get when you open a specific Outlook item, do have the new Ribbon.

One change to the Office 2007 user interface is the introduction of *skins*. Your users can choose between the traditional blue skin, a new clean silver one, or an ominous black one. To change the color scheme, click the New button as if to create a new item (or just start one of the Ribbon-enabled

Office applications like Word or Excel), click the Office button at the top left of the application, click the Options button for your application, and on the first screen of the Options setting you should see a list box for color scheme. Figure 17.1 shows us setting the color scheme to silver. Be aware that any change you make will change the color scheme for the entire Office 2007 suite. Once you've changed the scheme, you can close the new item inspector window without saving it.

FIGURE 17.1
Changing the color scheme in Office 2007

Inbox

The Inbox is the default delivery point for incoming communications. Traditionally this has meant e-mail, but increasingly firms are deploying *unified messaging*, which means that in addition to e-mail, your Inbox may contain voicemail and faxes.

Along the left side of the main Inbox screen you will see the now-familiar Navigation Pane, as shown in Figure 17.2. You use the Navigation Pane in Outlook 2007 to switch between the major categories such as Inbox, Calendar, or Contacts. At the top of the Navigation Pane you'll see the Favorite Folders section where the user can place folders they access frequently to make them easier to find.

To the right of the Navigation Pane is the item list, which is again essentially the same as the pane that you are familiar with in Outlook 2003. One major difference, however, is the search box at the top of the item list. This is your quick interface to Outlook 2007's Instant Search capability (see the section "Finding Items and More with Instant Search" later in this chapter for more information). Typing in that field will cause Outlook to initiate a search of the current folder.

On the far right side of the screen you'll see the most significant difference in the Outlook 2007 interface: the To-Do Bar. The To-Do Bar gives the user access to their upcoming appointments as well as their task list and e-mail messages flagged for follow-up. For a little more exploration of the To-Do Bar, see the section "Managing Your Time with Outlook" later in this chapter.

FIGURE 17.2
The Inbox in Outlook
2007

To maximize your screen real estate, you can minimize both the Navigation Pane and the To-Do Bar by clicking the double-arrows at the top of the respective window.

Editor

If you want to create or edit an item in Outlook, you'll need to use the editor. In Figure 17.3, we'll take a look at the new item editor, which, unlike the Outlook explorer screen, does get the new Ribbon interface. If it looks a lot like Word 2007 to you, there's a good reason for that — it is. The user can no longer choose between using the Outlook or Word editors — there is no more Outlook editor. All users will use the Word editor, and they have it even if they don't have Word installed because Outlook ships with a special stripped-down version of Word that comes as a DLL. This means that users will gain a number of advanced formatting features, including the ability to use WordArt, tables or charts, and the full set of Word styles.

Calendar

The Outlook calendar enables users to keep track of their schedules. The Calendar folder has undergone a few UI changes, as you can see in Figure 17.4, that your users will probably enjoy. You can open multiple calendars at the same time, as you could in Outlook 2003, simply by checking the appropriate box in the navigation pane. In the 2007 version, however, you can now overlay the calendars on top of each other by clicking the Overlay arrow that appears on the tab of the other calendars.

Adding the calendar of another user in your company is a simple matter. Simply click the Open a Shared Calendar link in the Navigation Pane and type the alias of the user whose calendar you want to open. Naturally that user will have to have granted you permissions to do so, but that hurdle cleared, this process will add that user to your Navigation Pane as an additional calendar. Viewing their calendar thereafter is a simple matter of checking the box next to their name.

One of the problems with the way the Tasks folder has traditionally been used is that users have wanted to display their tasks on the calendar day that they were due instead of in a separate list off to the side of the screen. To achieve that they have often entered their tasks right onto the calendar, either as appointment items or as all-day appointments. That isn't really the way the calendar was intended to be used, however, and it highlighted a weakness in the way task items were presented. In Outlook 2007, tasks are displayed in a bar located beneath the calendar so that the tasks due on a certain date line up nicely with the calendar date to make it easier to see which tasks are due when.

FIGURE 17.3
The Word editor is the only editor in Outlook 2007.

FIGURE 17.4
The calendar keeps you on schedule.

Contacts

The Contacts folder is where you can save contact information for the people you interact with most. The most notable difference in the Contacts folder of Outlook 2007 is the new Business Card view, as shown in Figure 17.5. You'll notice that the To-Do Bar persists in the Contacts folder as well.

FIGURE 17.5
The Business Card view of your Contacts folder

FIGURE 17.6
The Tasks folder helps you get things done.

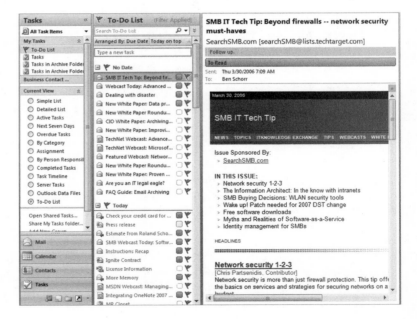

Tasks

The Tasks folder has some useful new views, perhaps the best of them being the To-Do List view, which gives you a rich view of your tasks and follow-up items complete with a reading pane that allows you to view an item without having to open it (see Figure 17.6).

New E-mail Features in Outlook 2007

E-mail has become perhaps the most ubiquitous computing task in business. We don't have to tell you it's mission critical — you know that. In fact, it's important enough that you bought a book about Exchange Server. We don't have enough pages in this book for a comprehensive review of e-mail, but the following sections highlight a few e-mail features of the Outlook 2007 client that we think are important.

Out-of-Office Assistant

Outlook 2007 has an improved Out-of-Office Assistant, which now lets you set distinct out-of-office messages for internal and external users. This is handy if you want to give a rich set of information to internal users but don't want to share all of that with users outside of your organization.

Also, your users can now schedule their out-of-office messages ahead of time so that they will start on a particular day and stop on another day. Gone are the days that they have to remember on the flight that they forgot to turn it on. Gone are the days that you have to remind them at noon that people are still getting out-of-office messages about their recently completed vacation.

Mailbox Full

If the user's mailbox fills up to the point where Exchange is going to prevent a send, the submission of a new message will now fail on the client side instead of the server side. That means that the message the user was trying to send will stay in their Outbox on the client side until the mailbox can be cleaned up enough to allow send.

Mailbox Cleanup

That brings us to mailbox cleanup. On the Tools menu, the users will find the Mailbox Cleanup tool, which gives them a single dialog box (shown in Figure 17.7) from which they can perform a number of useful cleanup tasks:

Mailbox Size   Gives the user an easy way to see how large their mailbox is and which folders are the largest.

Find   Purposely built find tools to help the user quickly find messages older than a certain age or larger than a certain size.

TIP

The Large Mail search folder is also a useful tool for keeping mailbox size down. We find that most users don't realize that they may have messages with gigantic attachments filling up their mailboxes. Either deleting the messages or moving the attachments to the file system and then removing the attachment from the message can dramatically reduce total mailbox size.

FIGURE 17.7
The Mailbox Cleanup tool helps keep your user mailboxes under quota.

AutoArchive   One button for the user to initiate an AutoArchive. This can be one of the easiest and most effective ways to reduce mailbox size.

Empty Deleted Items   How many users have you seen with thousands of items in their Deleted Items folder?

> **TIP**
>
> If you have users who can't seem to remember to empty their deleted items folders and who don't want Deleted Items emptied for them automatically on shutdown, consider turning AutoArchive on for the Deleted Items folder and setting it to permanently delete items older than a couple of weeks.

Delete Conflicts   When a synchronization error occurs, Outlook keeps a copy of items found in conflict. Over time those items can add up, and they do count against the mailbox quota. Here is a quick tool to see how big of a problem it is and a convenient way to clean them out quickly.

Recover Deleted Items

In Outlook 2003 with Exchange 2003, you could enable Deleted Items Recovery, which meant you could recover any items that you deleted and then emptied from your Deleted Items folder (within the specified time limit). A well-kept secret was that you could actually enable recovery from any folder with a registry hack. In Outlook 2007, Deleted Items Recovery is enabled from all folders by default. The user needs to only select the folder they want to recover and then click Tools ➤ Recover Deleted Items.

RSS Feeds

For more than a decade, various forms of "push" technology have been tried. The notion of being able to push content, especially time-sensitive content like breaking news, to end users is a powerful one. In the last couple of years, a new technology has evolved that is the most promising (and least proprietary) solution so far. Really Simple Syndication (RSS) specifies how a website or content provider can publish content to an Internet site. A software application, an RSS reader or newsreader, can connect to that site on a scheduled basis (hourly or sometimes even more often) and check for new or updated content. If there is some, the RSS reader will automatically download that content and present it to the end user. Think of it like a magazine, where new articles just appear as they are published. Not surprisingly, RSS is flourishing — nearly every site that updates content regularly, like news sites or blogs, is now publishing one or more RSS feeds.

Outlook 2007 integrates an RSS reader into the main product right out of the box. Now you can subscribe to your favorite RSS feeds, and even synchronize your feeds with Internet Explorer 7, and have those RSS items delivered to Outlook where they can appear right alongside your e-mail items.

> **TIP**
>
> A popular technique for dealing with multiple mail folders and RSS feeds is to create a Search folder that consolidates all messages received on a certain, including RSS articles. This gives the user a single view to deal with all new items.

To subscribe to an RSS feed in Outlook, simply copy the URL for the RSS feed, choose Tools ➤ Account Settings ➤ RSS Feeds in Outlook, click New, and paste the URL into the provided field as we have in Figure 17.8. Outlook will connect to that feed, get its default settings, and then start downloading articles from it. By default, Outlook will put that RSS feed into its own new folder under the RSS Feeds main folder.

FIGURE 17.8
Adding an RSS feed to
Outlook 2007

32KB Rules Limit Gone

The Rules Wizard is a useful tool that has evolved along with Outlook. With the wizard, users can create custom rules that automate message processing, automatically moving messages to subfolders or taking other actions based upon criteria they specify such as message sender or content. If your users extensively use the Rules Wizard, they've probably run into the problem of Outlook informing them that they've hit the limit on how many rules they can have. That limit was never really placed on the number of rules but rather on the total size of those rules, and since Exchange 5.0, it has been limited to 32KB. A single really enormous rule could trigger that limit, but more often it was several dozen large rules that did it.

> **NOTE**
>
> Why 32KB? Because the entire collection of a user's rules have to be able to fit within a remote procedure call (RPC) and the maximum allowable RPC buffer is 32KB.

Outlook 2003 was a little worse than its predecessors in this regard because Outlook 2003 rules were Unicode rules that required more space. Most users would hit the limit at around 20 rules in Outlook 2003. Since Outlook 2000, you could force all of your rules to be client-side rules, which got you around the limitation but required the Outlook client to be running in order for the rules to fire.

Exchange 2007 raises the limit to a default of 64KB, but the administrator can customize it up to 256KB for each individual mailbox. This can be changed using the Exchange 2007 Exchange Management Shell (EMS) cmdlet `Set-Mailbox`. For example, to set user Bob.Lawler's mailbox to a rule limit of 128KB, you would type the following EMS command:

```
Set-Mailbox Bob.Lawler -RulesQuota 128KB
```

You could use the EMS to set the rules quota for an entire department by using one cmdlet (`Get-DistributionGroupMember`) to retrieve the names in a particular department (such as the sales department) and piping the output of that cmdlet to the `Set-Mailbox` cmdlet. Here is an example:

```
Get-DistributionGroupMember "Sales Department" | Set-Mailbox -RulesQuota 128KB
```

Finding Items and More with Instant Search

If you used Outlook 2003 (or earlier), you probably had the experience of typing something in the search tool and then watching the little magnifying glass rotate around and around and around for quite a long time before finally bringing your results. With Outlook 2007, Microsoft has integrated the Windows Desktop Search (WDS) technology so that WDS is constantly indexing your Outlook items in the background. You'll be prompted to install WDS when you install Office 2007. This means when you type a search term in the new search box (see Figure 17.9), Outlook returns the results almost immediately. In fact, you can perform what we call a *type-ahead search* in which you start to type your search string and Outlook presents you with a list of results almost immediately. As you continue to type, the results list will narrow further until you complete the string.

FIGURE 17.9
Instant Search helps you find your items

You can search the current folder or perform an All Items search that will search across all the folders of a specified type. That means you can find contacts, notes, e-mail messages, and more that contain the term you're looking for in a matter of seconds.

If you're having problems with the index, such as content you know exists but doesn't get returned by a search, you may need to try rebuilding the index. Here are the steps to do so:

1. Right-click the Windows Desktop Search icon on the system tray.

2. Select Windows Desktop Search Options.

3. Click Advanced.

4. Click Rebuild.

Keep in mind that a full rebuild of the index can take quite a while. Depending upon how many items you have and how fast your computer is, it could be on the magnitude of hours to get the index fully rebuilt and usable.

Synchronizing with SharePoint

One of the strengths of technology in a corporate setting is in enabling collaboration between coworkers or departments. Microsoft's premier solution in collaboration technology today is called SharePoint, and it is a collection of technologies, built on Windows, that let administrators easily create browser-based portals for users to collaborate, share documents, create and maintain lists, and perform a number of other tasks. One of the strengths of SharePoint is that not only can it be used on an intranet, it can also be published to an extranet.

One of the significant frustrations that users and administrators had with previous versions of Outlook and SharePoint revolved around linking lists like contacts or calendars. You could access a SharePoint contacts list, for example, using Outlook 2003; you could even synchronize it and access it offline. What you couldn't do was edit any of those contact items in Outlook or have any additions synchronize back to the SharePoint server. The same was true for calendars as well, of course. Because it required extra steps to go back to the SharePoint site to make any edits, a lot of users simply skipped it and didn't make the best use of the SharePoint/Outlook connection.

With Outlook 2007 and SharePoint 2007, now you can do two-way synchronization so that you can edit those calendars, contacts, or other lists in Outlook and have the changes reflected in SharePoint. As an Exchange administrator, you should be aware of the capabilities that SharePoint 2007 brings to the table because, increasingly, things you are in the habit of doing with Exchange public folders can (and will) be done with SharePoint lists instead.

Managing Your Time with Outlook

Outlook 2007 makes some significant upgrades to the way users manage time and projects. One of the most noticeable new features is the To-Do Bar (shown on the right of Figure 17.10), which integrates the user's tasks, e-mails flagged for follow-up, and Calendar items into their Inbox. The To-Do Bar replaces the task pane that users of earlier versions of Outlook were familiar with. In previous versions, the Tasks folder tended to be underused because users didn't like having to switch to the Tasks folder (or use the task pane in Calendar) in order to view their To-Do list. The To-Do Bar gives you a quick and accessible view of your To-Do list and upcoming appointments right from within the Inbox or most of the other folders.

FIGURE 17.10

The To-Do Bar helps to keep you on task.

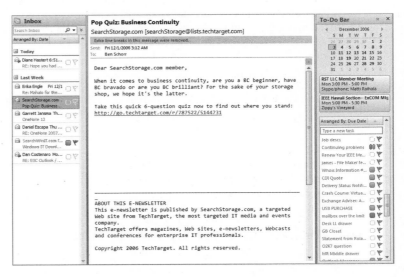

Adding a task is as simple as clicking the field at the top of the tasks list on the To-Do bar and typing the subject of your task there. When you press Enter, it will automatically be assigned to today's tasks. If you'd like to add more information to the task, change the due date or priority, or assign it to somebody else, just click on the task to open it from the To-Do Bar and the item inspector will open and let you make your edits.

When you complete the task, just single-click the flag on the right of the task item on the To-Do Bar and it will be marked complete and removed from the To-Do Bar (but it's still in your Tasks folder, just marked complete).

If you need to remove a task or other item from the To-Do Bar, just right-click the item and choose Delete from the pop-up menu that appears.

Categories and Follow-Up Settings

Outlook 2007 also changes the way that Quick Flags are used. In Outlook 2003, Quick Flags gave you seven user-definable colors that you could use to quickly and broadly categorize e-mail items for follow-up. Outlook 2007 removes the distinct colors and replaces them with the categories feature, which now assigns a color to each category. The result is one less form of categorization — no need for a follow-up flag *and* a category — and a great many more colors rather than just the seven in Outlook 2003. Outlook 2007 also adds the ability to specify when the item should be followed up and then places that for-follow-up item on the To-Do Bar as if it were a task. This blurring of e-mail items and tasks is a powerful tool for facilitating user productivity.

TIP

A lot of users don't realize that you can flag a contact item for follow-up. In Outlook 2007, that means it will appear on your To-Do Bar along with your tasks and other follow-up items. It's a handy way to be reminded that you need to contact a person. To flag a contact, while the contact item is open, click the Follow Up button on the Ribbon and select when you'd like to follow up. The flag isn't extremely obvious in the Contacts view (it just adds the "Follow Up: Tomorrow" field to the folder view), but this feature is best used with the To-Do Bar, which is a much more intuitive interface.

In Outlook 2003 and earlier versions, the categories were stored in the Registry, which made it difficult for users who used multiple computers and wanted consistent categories. With Outlook 2007, the categories (and their associated colors) are stored in the default data store, which means that they go wherever the user's data store does.

Calendaring and Scheduling

Outlook 2003 significantly improved the scheduling capabilities of the client, and Outlook 2007 builds upon those capabilities. Meeting organizers now cannot change the time or location of a meeting or cancel it without sending an update to all of the attendees. The organizer can change the notes or reminder time without an update going out, however.

NOTE

Don't expect to use Outlook 2007 to schedule NetMeeting events anymore. Neither NetMeeting nor Microsoft Exchange Conferencing is supported by Microsoft anymore. This functionality has moved to Microsoft Office Live Meeting.

Resource Booking

One of the most useful features of a groupware platform like Exchange is the ability to do scheduling and calendaring for your group. Exchange 2007 and Outlook 2007 significantly improve and increase your capabilities in the scheduling area.

Configuring Resource Mailboxes

If you have an Exchange server, you probably also have resources that you want to be able to schedule, such as conference rooms, audio/visual equipment, and maybe demonstration gear to take on the road. With Outlook and Exchange, you can create mailboxes for those resources; they will then have their own calendars that will accept reservation requests from your users and maintain a "free/busy" status that the users can use to determine whether they are available.

Exchange 2007's resource mailboxes are handled somewhat differently from the resource mailboxes in Exchange 2003 and earlier. In Exchange 2007, there are extensions made to the AD schema to uniquely identify resource mailboxes.

Creating a resource mailbox is not unlike creating any other kind of mailbox:

1. Start the Exchange Management Console.

2. Click Recipient Configuration.

3. In the Actions pane, click New Mailbox. The New Mailbox Wizard will start to walk you through the process.

4. On the Introduction page, select Room Mailbox and click Next.

5. On the User Type page, select New User and click Next.

The wizard will then prompt you for the standard account information, username, alias, and so forth.

> **TIP**
>
> We recommend creating a new organizational unit (OU) for resources so that regular users and resources don't get lumped together in the Active Directory.

After you've created the mailbox, you could stop there, but usually you'll want to configure the resource mailbox to automatically process meeting requests for your users. To do that, go to a workstation that has Outlook installed, log in with the resource account, and create an Outlook profile for that resource mailbox. Once you've logged into the resource mailbox with Outlook, choose Tools ➢ Calendar Options and click the Resource Scheduling button. On the resulting dialog box (see Figure 17.11) you can configure the resource scheduling options.

For more information about creating and managing resource mailboxes, see Chapter 10, "Managing Recipients."

FIGURE 17.11
Configure a resource
to accept scheduling
requests

Using Outlook 2007 and Autodiscover

Exchange 2007 introduces a new feature called Autodiscover that Outlook 2007 and later clients
can take advantage of. Autodiscover is a web service that resides on the Exchange 2007 Client
Access server role. The popular notion of Autodiscover is that it helps Outlook 2007 to automatically locate an Exchange 2007 server and that is correct. However, Autodiscover actually helps
Outlook locate a number of different types of Exchange resources, including these:

◆ User's home mailbox server

◆ Outlook Anywhere URL

◆ URL (internal or external) for the offline address book

◆ URL (internal or external) for Unified Messaging

◆ URL (internal or external) for Availability service

When a user launches Outlook 2007 for the first time, they are prompted for some basic
information (e-mail address or domain/username and password). Outlook 2007 contacts the
Autodiscover web service and looks up information such as the home mailbox server, display
name, and URLs for Outlook features such as free/busy information and the offline address book.
If this information is changed, then the Outlook client gets updated information (including the
home mailbox server name) from the Autodiscover service.

TIP

When the user specifies their e-mail address, they should use their default SMTP address. Autodiscover may not work for additional SMTP addresses.

Internal vs. External Autodiscover

Outlook 2007 uses two different approaches to locate an Autodiscover site and determine the necessary information. The first approach is used when the Windows computer is a member of the Active Directory forest in which the Exchange server exists. Figure 17.12 shows the process that Outlook uses to locate resources. In this example, the computer on which Outlook 2007 is installed is a member of the Active Directory forest. This is considered the service process for internal clients.

FIGURE 17.12
Autodiscover when a client is member of the Active Directory

Active Directory domain controller

Exchange 2007 Client Access server role

Exchange 2007 Mailbox server role

Outlook 2007 client
(Member of Active Directory)

In step 1 in Figure 17.12, Outlook is launched for the first time and there is not an Outlook profile for the user account. Outlook contacts the Active Directory to find a service connection point (SCP). A service connection point is an Active Directory object that can be used to publish and locate network services. The SCP object will provide Outlook with the fully qualified domain names of Client Access servers; Outlook contacts a Client Access servers in its local Active Directory site

In step 2, the Outlook 2007 client queries the Client Access server to retrieve the user's home server. The username and domain name are used to locate the user's home mailbox server. Outlook also retrieves information about the location of the Availability service and the distribution points for the offline address book. From this information, the Outlook profile is created.

In step 3, Outlook is able to connect to the user's home Exchange server.

If the desktop client is not a member of the Active Directory or is outside of the corporate network and cannot contact a domain controller, then Outlook 2007 uses a different approach. This is the Autodiscover service process for external access. In this approach, DNS is used to locate the Autodiscover service. Figure 17.13 shows an example of how the Autodiscover service is located for an external client. In this example, the user must provide their e-mail address since it cannot be provided for them using their Active Directory user account.

In step 1, Outlook tries to contact an Active Directory domain controller (if the client is a member of the Active Directory). If Active Directory cannot be located or the computer is not a member of the Active Directory, the user is presented with the Add New E-mail Account dialog box shown in Figure 17.14. From this dialog box, the user must enter their primary STMP address, their name, and their account password. The e-mail address is important because the STMP domain name is used in step 2.

FIGURE 17.13
External Autodiscover
location process

FIGURE 17.14
Providing Outlook
with your information
manually

In step 2, the Outlook 2007 client performs a DNS query and uses the SMTP domain name. In our example, the domain name is somorita.com. Outlook will use the following URLs to try to connect in order to locate the Autodiscover server:

```
https://somorita.com/autodiscover/autodiscover.xml
https://autodiscover.somorita.com/autodiscover/autodiscover.xml
```

These URLs will need to be resolvable in DNS and accessible from outside your network for external clients. If you will use the DNS approach for "external" clients on your inside network, you will want to make sure that one of these two URL's is resolvable using your internal DNS.

The Client Access server that hosts either the Autodiscover URL will then return the Outlook Anywhere information necessary to configure Outlook 2007 as well as external URL locations for the Availability service and the offline address book distribution point.

Configuring Autodiscover

When an Exchange 2007 Client Access server is installed, an SCP record is created in Active Directory for it. This includes the internal Outlook Anywhere settings, the internal internal URL for the offline address book, and the internal URL for Exchange web services. However, depending on your environment, there may be additional configuration settings that you need to perform, if, for example, you needed to enable Outlook Anywhere (formerly RPC over HTTP) or define external URLs for other web services.

CONFIGURING AUTODISCOVER VIRTUAL DIRECTORIES

An Autodiscover virtual directory is automatically created on each Exchange 2007 Client Access server. The only way to configure this is through the Exchange Management Shell. The `Get-AutoDiscoverVirtualDirectory` cmdlet can let you view the Autodiscover virtual directories. Here is an example:

```
[PS] C:\>Get-AutodiscoverVirtualDirectory
Name                          : Autodiscover (Default Web Site)
InternalAuthenticationMethods : {Basic, Ntlm}
ExternalAuthenticationMethods : {Basic, Ntlm}
BasicAuthentication           : True
DigestAuthentication          : False
WindowsAuthentication         : True
MetabasePath                  : IIS://HNLEX03.volcanosurfboards.com/W3SVC/1/
ROOT/Autodiscover
Path                          : C:\Program Files\Microsoft\Exchange Server
     \ClientAccess\
Autodiscover
Server                        : HNLEX03
InternalUrl                   :
ExternalUrl                   :
AdminDisplayName              :
ExchangeVersion               : 0.1 (8.0.535.0)
DistinguishedName             : CN=Autodiscover (Default Web Site),
CN=HTTP,CN=Protocols,CN=HNLEX03,CN=Servers,CN=Exchange Administrative
Group (FYDIBOHF23SPDLT),CN=Administrative Groups,CN=Volcano Surfboards,
CN=Microsoft Exchange,CN=Services,CN=Configuration,DC=volcanosurfboards,DC=com
Identity                      : HNLEX03\Autodiscover (Default Web Site)
Guid                          : 4ec07bc6-2e2a-4877-8d66-9626325a6666
ObjectCategory                : volcanosurfboards.com/Configuration/Schema
                                'ms-Exch-Auto-Discover-
```

```
Virtual-Directory
ObjectClass                   : {top, msExchVirtualDirectory,
 msExchAutoDiscoverVirtualDirectory}
WhenChanged                   : 12/22/2006 9:10:00 PM
WhenCreated                   : 12/22/2006 9:10:00 PM
OriginatingServer             : HNLDC01.volcanosurfboards.com
IsValid                       : True
```

If you want to set the external URL for Autodiscover, here is the command:

```
Set-AutodiscoverVirtualDirectory "HNLEX03\Autodiscover (Default Web Site)"
-ExternalUrl "https://owa.somorita.com"
```

CONFIGURING OUTLOOK ANYWHERE AND AUTODISCOVER

By default, Outlook Anywhere is not enabled on the Client Access servers. To enable Outlook Anywhere, locate each Client Access server in the Server Configuration work center in the Exchange Management Console (EMC) and select the Enable Outlook Anywhere task on the Actions pane. This launches a wizard that prompts you for the external hostname and the type of authentication and gives you the option to use SSL offloading.

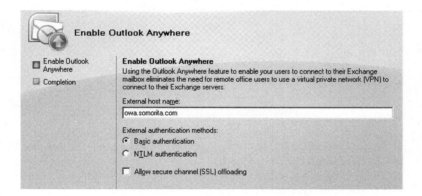

If you are using network load balancing, the external hostname will be the fully qualified domain name that the clients will use externally. When you have completed the information required by the wizard, you can click the Enable Outlook Anywhere button.

Optionally, you could enable Outlook Anywhere using the `Enable-OutlookAnywhere` cmdlet. Here is an example:

```
Enable-OutlookAnywhere -Server 'HNLEX03' -ExternalHostname 'owa.somorita.com'
-ExternalAuthenticationMethod 'Basic' -SSLOffloading $false
```

Once Outlook Anywhere is enabled, you can select the properties of the Client Access server and view the Outlook Anywhere properties of that particular Client Access server. An example is shown in Figure 17.15.

FIGURE 17.15
Configuring the external hostname for Outlook Anywhere

You can retrieve the same information (and more) using the Get-OutlookAnywhere cmdlet; here is an example:

```
Get-OutlookAnywhere

SSLOffloading             : False
ExternalHostname          : owa.somorita.com
ExternalAuthenticationMethod : Basic
MetabasePath              : IIS://HNLEX03.volcanosurfboards.com/
W3SVC/1/ROOT/Rpc
Path                      : C:\WINDOWS\System32\RpcProxy
Server                    : HNLEX03
AdminDisplayName          :
ExchangeVersion           : 0.1 (8.0.535.0)
Name                      : Rpc (Default Web Site)
DistinguishedName         : CN=Rpc (Default Web Site),CN=HTTP,
CN=Protocols,CN=HNLEX03,CN=Servers,CN=Exchange AdministrativeGroup
(FYDIBOHF23SPDLT),CN=Administrative Groups,CN=Volcano Surfboards,
CN=Microsoft Exchange,CN=Services,CN=Configuration,DC=volcanosurfboards,DC=com
```

```
Identity                    : HNLEX03\Rpc (Default Web Site)
Guid                        : 3f68d1ed-90ae-4778-aa23-88919b5a3284
ObjectCategory              : volcanosurfboards.com/Configuration/Schema/
ms-Exch-Rpc-Http-Virtual-Directory
ObjectClass                 : {top, msExchVirtualDirectory,
  msExchRpcHttpVirtualDirectory}
WhenChanged                 : 1/8/2007 6:24:32 PM
WhenCreated                 : 1/8/2007 6:24:32 PM
OriginatingServer           : HNLDC01.volcanosurfboards.com
IsValid                     : True
```

When configuring the external hostname for Outlook Anywhere, remember that this is the URL that will be referred to external Outlook 2007 clients when Autodiscover is used.

OFFLINE ADDRESS BOOKS AND AUTODISCOVER

The offline address book distribution points by default only contain the internal URL used to locate them. You can set these using the graphical user interface by selecting the properties of the offline address book virtual directory in the Exchange Management Console. The URLs property page of the default OAB virtual directory for a Client Access server is shown in Figure 17.16.

FIGURE 17.16
Setting the external URL for offline address book distribution

You can also set this parameter using the EMS cmdlet Set-OABVirtualDirectory. Here is an example:

```
Set-OABVirtualDirectory "hnlex03\OAB (Default Web Site)"
-ExternalURL https://owa.somorita.com/OAB -RequireSSL:$True
```

You can view the configuration of the offline address book virtual directory using the Get-OABVirtualDirectory cmdlet. Here is an example:

```
Get-OabVirtualDirectory | fl
```

```
Name                         : OAB (Default Web Site)
PollInterval                 : 480
OfflineAddressBooks          : {}
RequireSSL                   : True
MetabasePath                 : IIS://HNLEX03.volcanosurfboards.com/W3SVC/1/ROOT/
OAB
Path                         : C:\Program Files\
Microsoft\Exchange Server\ClientAccess\OAB
Server                       : HNLEX03
InternalUrl                  : http://hnlex03.volcanosurfboards.com/OAB
InternalAuthenticationMethods : {WindowsIntegrated}
ExternalUrl                  : https://owa.somorita.com/OAB
ExternalAuthenticationMethods : {WindowsIntegrated}
AdminDisplayName             :
ExchangeVersion              : 0.1 (8.0.535.0)
DistinguishedName            : CN=OAB (Default Web Site),
CN=HTTP,CN=Protocols, CN=HNLEX03,CN=Servers,CN=Exchange Administrative
Group (FYDIBOHF23SPDLT),CN=Administrative Groups,CN=Volcano Surfboards,
CN=Microsoft Exchange,CN=Services,CN=Configuration,DC=volcanosurfboards,DC=com
Identity                     : HNLEX03\OAB (Default Web Site)
Guid                         : f54b7b26-640e-4359-b845-02c2d995dd44
ObjectCategory               : volcanosurfboards.com/Configuration/Schema/
ms-Exch-OAB-Virtual-Directory
ObjectClass                  : {top, msExchVirtualDirectory,
msExchOABVirtualDirectory}
WhenChanged                  : 1/8/2007 7:17:58 PM
WhenCreated                  : 12/22/2006 9:09:56 PM
OriginatingServer            : HNLDC01.volcanosurfboards.com
IsValid                      : True
```

CONFIGURING WEB SERVICES AND AUTODISCOVER

If remote or external clients will need access to custom web services, you should configure the external URL for web services. This can only be done via the EMS. The following cmdlet is an example for setting the external URL for a Client Access server:

```
Set-WebServicesVirtualDirectory "hnlex03\EWS (Default web site)"
 -ExternalUrl https://owa.somorita.com/EWS/Exchange.asmx
 -BasicAuthentication:$True
```

To check the configuration of the Web Services virtual directory, you can use the `Get-WebServicesVirtualDirectory` cmdlet:

```
Get-WebServicesVirtualDirectory

Name                         : EWS (Default Web Site)
InternalAuthenticationMethods : {Basic, Ntlm}
ExternalAuthenticationMethods : {Basic, Ntlm}
BasicAuthentication          : True
DigestAuthentication         : False
WindowsAuthentication        : True
MetabasePath                 : IIS://HNLEX03.volcanosurfboards.com/W3SVC/1/
ROOT/EWS
Path                         : C:\Program Files\Microsoft\Exchange Server\
                                 ClientAccess\
exchweb\EWS
Server                       : HNLEX03
InternalUrl                  : https://hnlex03.volcanosurfboards.com/
EWS/Exchange.asmx
ExternalUrl                  : https://owa.somorita.com/EWS/Exchange.asmx
AdminDisplayName             :
ExchangeVersion              : 0.1 (8.0.535.0)
DistinguishedName            : CN=EWS (Default Web Site),CN=HTTP,
CN=Protocols, CN=HNLEX03,CN=Servers,CN=Exchange Administrative Group
(FYDIBOHF23SPDLT),CN=Administrative Groups,CN=Volcano Surfboards,
CN=Microsoft Exchange,CN=Services,CN=Configuration,DC=volcanosurfboards,DC=com
Identity                     : HNLEX03\EWS (Default Web Site)
Guid                         : b5cd3ea1-42c1-42b0-87db-35072316cf6a
ObjectCategory               : volcanosurfboards.com/Configuration/Schema/
ms-Exch-Web-Services-Virtual-Directory
ObjectClass                  : {top, msExchVirtualDirectory, msExchWebServices
                                 VirtualDirectory}
WhenChanged                  : 1/8/2007 7:07:25 PM
WhenCreated                  : 12/22/2006 9:10:12 PM
OriginatingServer            : HNLDC01.volcanosurfboards.com
IsValid                      : True
```

AUTODISCOVER AND SECURE SOCKETS LAYER

If you have tried to deploy both internal and external URLs already, then you are already wondering how Secure Sockets Layer is supposed to work if the FQDN of the internal location is different than the external FQDN. After all, if certificates are requested you usually only provide one name in the certificate signing request. There is a workaround, however, that allows you to have more than one DNS domain name for a Client Access server. To do this, you have to use the `New-ExchangeCertificate` cmdlet. The command line is fairly involved; here is an example:

```
New-ExchangeCertificate -generaterequest
-subjectname "dc=com,dc=volcanosurfboards,o=Volcano
Surfboards, cn=owa.somorita.com"
-domainname HNLEX03,HNLEX03.volcanosurfboards.com,owa.somorita.com,
autodiscover.somorita.com -path c:\certrequest-HNLEX03.txt
```

This cmdlet creates a certificate request with multiple hostnames. In this case, the hostnames include owa.somorita.com, autodiscover.somorita.com, hnlex03, and hnlex03.volcanosurfboards.com.

We can take the contents of this file and get a certificate signed and issued by a trusted certificate authority or we could sign it ourselves using Windows Certificate Server. The result will be a file that is returned to us from the certification authority (in this case, certnew.cer). Here is an example of using the `Import-ExchangeCertificate` cmdlet to import the signed certificate in to the certificate store:

```
Import-ExchangeCertificate -path c:\certnew.cer -friendlyname "HNLEX03 Cert"
```

If you are used to creating certificate requests using the Internet Information Services Manager console, then there is a new step you may not be familiar with. The `Import-ExchangeCertificate` cmdlet imports the certificate into the computer's personal certificate store, but it does not assign it to the default website. You will need to follow these steps to associate the certificate with the default website.

1. Run the Internet Information Server Manager console.

2. Open the Web Sites container, right-click Default Web Site, and select Properties.

3. Select the Directory Security property page.

4. Click the Server Certificate button and then click Next.

5. Select the Assign an Existing Certificate radio button and click Next.

6. In the Select a Certificate list, select the certificate you have just imported using the `Import-ExchangeCertificate` cmdlet. When you have selected the certificate, click Next.

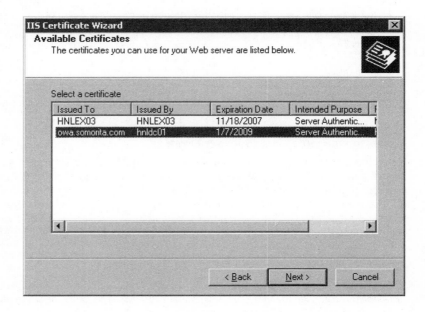

7. Confirm that port 443 is the SSL port. This is usually the case. Click Next.

8. On the Certificate Summary page, you can see some of the details of the certificate. When you are ready, click Next and then click Finish.

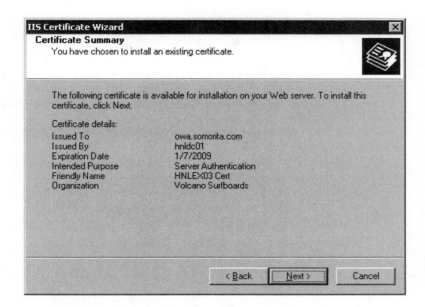

Congratulations. The certificate is now installed and associated with the default website. On the Directory Security property page, you can click the View Certificate button to see more details about the certificate. On the Details property page, if you scroll down to Subject Alternative Name in the Field column (see Figure 17.17), you will see the additional names you have specified for the certificate.

In the example we just showed you, the internal names of the server were HNLEX03 and HNLEX03.volcanosurfboards.com. The external names were owa.somorita.com and autodiscover.somorita.com.

Summary

Outlook 2007 is a pretty user-friendly electronic-messaging client with lots of bells and whistles, such as task and calendaring capabilities and contacts. When Outlook 2007 is installed properly on a server, a user can easily install Outlook on a workstation and begin using it without having to respond to a single installation query.

Creating, composing, and reading Outlook messages are very straightforward tasks. The Outlook address book, which can include Exchange mailboxes, distribution groups, contacts, and public folders, simplifies the e-mail addressing process. As with managing messages, basic public folder creation and management is an easy task, most of which can be done right in the Outlook client.

Among other things, Outlook profiles allow a single user to access a range of mail accounts with ease. Each user may have one or more Outlook profiles. When creating an Outlook profile, you can choose to access messaging services such as Exchange Server and Internet mail servers. You can also include personal folders and specific kinds of address books in a profile. By selecting a profile when Outlook 2007 starts, you choose which set of messaging services and other features will be available during your Outlook session.

The Outlook 2007 menu structure is complex, and unlike most of the other applications in the suite, it doesn't benefit much from the new Ribbon UI, but it's familiar to most users and easy to use when you're clear on what certain menu items do. Exchange Server 2007 brings several significant enhancements to the Outlook 2007 menu structure. One of these enables an Outlook user to recover items that were accidentally deleted (including items hard-deleted from folders).

The Exchange service Autodiscover should reduce the support burden for Outlook 2007 users by reducing the number of calls to the help desk and the confusion surrounding getting an initial Outlook profile configured when they first start using a new desktop computer.

Part 6

Connectivity

In this section you will learn to:

Chapter 18

Delivering E-mail

Exchange Server's primary purpose in life is to send, receive, and store messages. Sure, it stores contacts, calendar information, and tasks, but delivering e-mail messages is its life's purpose. In previous versions of Exchange, messages that were to be delivered locally (to a user whose mailbox was on your mailbox database or another database on the same server) never actually left that particular server. That all changes in Exchange Server 2007.

The new Hub Transport server role is now responsible for moving messages from one mailbox to another, and all messages must now pass through the Hub Transport server role. No matter where your messages come from, they have to travel through a Hub Transport server before delivery to your mailbox, even if the message comes from the same storage group, in the same Exchange database, or from the mailbox right next door. This lightens the load of transport from the Mailbox server and centralizes transport to a single server role. It also allows for specialized cluster servers that do not share a database, which is covered in another chapter.

The Hub Transport server role can be on a server with any other server role, except for clustered mailbox servers and Edge Transport servers. This means that if a Mailbox server does not also host the Hub Transport server, then the entire message is transferred to the Hub Transport server via Remote Procedure Calls (RPCs), then categorized, and finally routed to the appropriate location. This is true even if that location is the mailbox database on which the message originated. This is one of the reasons that it is so critical to have a Hub Transport server in each Active Directory site that contains a Mailbox server.

The Edge Transport server is separated from the rest of the Exchange server roles because it does not communicate directly with Active Directory but utilizes an ADAM directory database that is stored local to the server. The Edge Transport server role was designed to exist in a perimeter network/demilitarized zone (DMZ) segregated from the internal network. Both the Edge Transport and the Hub Transport servers facilitate transport in an Exchange organization.

Exchange 2007 lets you do a lot with a message while it is in transit. In Chapter 13, ''Managing Messages in Transit,'' you learned about transport rules that allow you to append disclaimers to messages, process messages based on sender or recipient, or apply corporate policies to e-mail. You can offload virus detection to Hub Transport servers. And you can even keep unwanted content (viruses, spam, or messages that violate corporate policies) from ever even reaching your Exchange servers by directing inbound mail to an Edge Transport server.

In this chapter, we will discuss message transfer from both the internal message routing perspective and the perspective of messages that are sent to/received from the Internet and how to reduce the amount of spam you receive.

Topics in this chapter include the following:

◆ Message routing within the organization

◆ Deploying an Edge Transport server

◆ Using a Hub Transport server for Internet mail

Messaging Routing within the Organization

We'll start with a bit of review about how Exchange 2007 delivers messages within a single organization. We covered this in Chapter 2, "Exchange Server 2007 Architecture," but we want to ensure that you properly understand it. The message routing architecture is significantly different enough from earlier versions of Exchange 2000/2003 that it deserves additional mention.

There are a couple of important points that you should understand about the basics of Exchange 2007 message routing:

◆ All messages must go through the Hub Transport server role.

◆ The Active Directory site architecture is used as a boundary for message routing.

◆ All Active Directory sites that contain a Mailbox server must also have a Hub Transport server as well as a Client Access server.

One of the nice features of Exchange Serve 2007 is that as long as your Active Directory site architecture has been properly configured, you will not need to worry about message routing architecture design.

Basics of Exchange Message Routing

In previous versions of Exchange, the message routing architecture was based on a structure that was defined by the administrator. For example, in Exchange 2000/2003, the message routing architecture was defined by a collection of servers separated by full-time and reasonably good available bandwidth. This collection of servers is called a *routing group*. Prior to Exchange 2000, all servers were grouped together in to a single collection of servers called a *site*.

In Exchange 2000/2003, the administrator could define the routing groups and move servers between routing groups based on their message routing requirements. Messages were then delivered between routing groups using some type of connector. The most common connector for routing groups is a connector called the *routing group connector (RGC)*, which uses SMTP to deliver messages.

Exchange 2007 changes this by relying on the Active Directory site architecture rather than requiring the administrator to create a separate routing infrastructure for their organization. Figure 18.1 shows a simple Active Directory site topology that consists of three Active Directory sites.

In Figure 18.1, each Active Directory site has a Mailbox server and a Hub Transport server. The Hub Transport server will always attempt a direct delivery of a message to a Hub Transport server in a remote Active Directory site even if that remote Active Directory site does not have an Active Directory site link directly to it. If you are still running any Exchange 2000/2003 servers, though, they retain their routing group architecture and have routing group connectors to the Exchange 2007 Hub Transport servers.

The Hub Transport server role is at the center of the message routing architecture for messages being delivered internally as well as messages leaving the organization. All messages are processed by the Hub Transport server role regardless of whether they are being delivered locally or remotely. Figure 18.2 shows an example of the Hub Transport setting at the center of the message delivery universe.

The Hub Transport server role handles categorization and delivery for mail that is intended for locally delivery and Mailbox servers in the same Active Directory site. The Hub Transport server uses the messaging API (MAPI) and RPCs to commute with the Mailbox server role. If a message is to be delivered to a Mailbox server in a remote Active Directory site, then the Hub Transport server delivers the message via SMTP; the remote Hub Transport server then delivers the message to the local Mailbox server via RPC.

FIGURE 18.1
Sample Active Directory
site infrastructure

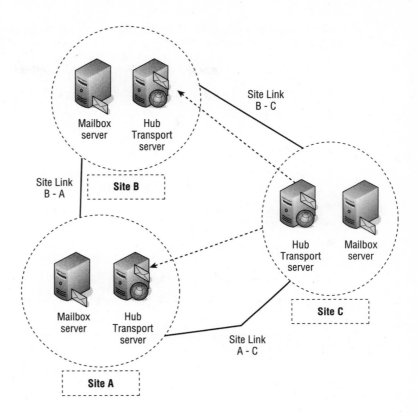

FIGURE 18.2
The Hub Transport is at
the center of all message
delivery.

The Exchange Server 2007 Hub Transport server handles the message categorization. Essentially, the Categorizer is the component that figures out where the message is going next. Messages arrive in the submission queue, and the Categorizer picks up the message and processes it. The following are some of the steps involved in message categorization:

◆ Expand any distribution lists, if applicable, by querying the global catalog.

◆ Resolve recipient addresses to determine which recipients are local, remote, or outside of the organization.

◆ Apply message transport rules to the message.

◆ Split the message into multiple parts if the message is going to local and has remote recipients; this process is called *bifurcation*.

◆ Examine the message sender, recipients, message header, body, and attachments and apply message transport rules that apply to that message.

◆ Convert the message the appropriate message format (Summary-TNEF, MIME, or UUENCODE) depending on the destination of the message.

◆ Determine the next "hop" for the message.

◆ Place the message in to appropriate local or remote delivery queue.

> **NOTE**
>
> With a few exceptions, such as application transport rules, the Categorizer function has not changed from Exchange 2000/2003.

As messages are moved within your organization's infrastructure, they are protected with different types of encryption. The encryption used is either RPC encryption or Transport Layer Security (TLS) encryption. Figure 18.3 shows different paths the message may take and how it is encrypted. We showed this in Chapter 2, but we wanted to review these here.

FIGURE 18.3
Messages are encrypted during transit.

As messages are transmitted via MAPI over RPC between Mailbox servers and Hub Transport servers, RPC encryption is automatically used. When a message is transmitted from one Hub Transport server to another, the Hub Transport servers transport the message using SMTP, they authenticate using Kerberos, and the data stream is encrypted using TLS. When messages are transmitted from a Hub Transport server to an Edge Transport server, SMTP is used for message transfer, mutual authentication using certificates is used for authentication, and messages can be encrypted using TLS. Optionally, an organization that is sending messages to another organization also using Edge Transport services can configure authenticated connections and TLS encryption to these remote organizations.

Send and Receive Connectors

In Exchange 2000/2003, each Exchange server had one or more SMTP virtual servers. These SMTP virtual servers received inbound mail from other servers, from outside of the organization, or from POP3/IMAP4 clients. The SMTP virtual server could be configured to host an SMTP connector for delivering messages to external SMTP hosts or it could host a routing group connector (RGC) for delivering messages to remote Exchange 2000/2003 routing groups.

Exchange Server 2007 has replaced the SMTP virtual servers and SMTP connectors with Send connectors and Receive connectors.

RECEIVE CONNECTORS

The Receive connector is the point where inbound SMTP mail is received on the Hub Transport server. Receive connectors do not deliver outbound mail (unlike the Exchange 2000/2003 SMTP virtual server). Each Hub Transport server automatically has two Receive connectors. These are the Default connector and the Client connector. Figure 18.4 shows the Exchange Management Console and the Server Configuration work center. In the Hub Transport subcontainer, you can see each server that hosts the Hub Transport role. The Receive connectors for server HNLEX03 are shown.

FIGURE 18.4
Receive connectors for an Exchange 2007 server

The properties of the Client HNLEX03 Receive connector are shown in Figure 18.4, specifically the Network property page of the Receive connector is shown. Notice that the Client Receive connector listens on port number 587, not port 25. The Client Receive connector is intended for receiving mail from non-MAPI client such as POP3 and IMAP4 clients. You would, of course, have to change the non-MAPI client's outbound SMTP port in order to use this connector.

The Default Receive connector is used to receive inbound SMTP mail from other Exchange 2007 Hub Transport servers in the organization. In Figure 18.5, the Permissions Groups properties of the Default HNLEX03 Receive connector are shown. These are the default permissions for the Default Receive connector.

FIGURE 18.5
Default Receive
connector permissions

The point we are making is that the Default Receive connector does not accept connections from anonymous users. This means that you cannot use it to receive e-mail from the Internet even though the Receive connector is listening on port 25. We will come back to this later when we cover receiving e-mail from the outside.

You can also view the properties of a Receive connector using the Get-ReceiveConnector cmdlet. Here is an example that receives all the properties of the Default HNLEX03

Receive connector:

```
C:\>Get-ReceiveConnector "Default HNLEX03" | FL

AuthMechanism                              : Tls, Integrated, BasicAuth,
 BasicAuthRequireTLS, ExchangeServer
Banner                                     :
BinaryMimeEnabled                          : True
Bindings                                   : {0.0.0.0:25}
ChunkingEnabled                            : True
DefaultDomain                              :
DeliveryStatusNotificationEnabled          : True
EightBitMimeEnabled                        : True
DomainSecureEnabled                        : False
EnhancedStatusCodesEnabled                 : True
Fqdn                                       : HNLEX03.volcanosurfboards.com
Comment                                    :
Enabled                                    : True
ConnectionTimeout                          : 00:10:00
ConnectionInactivityTimeout                : 00:05:00
MessageRateLimit                           : unlimited
MaxInboundConnection                       : 5000
MaxInboundConnectionPerSource              : unlimited
MaxInboundConnectionPercentagePerSource    : 100
MaxHeaderSize                              : 64KB
MaxHopCount                                : 30
MaxLocalHopCount                           : 3
MaxLogonFailures                           : 3
MaxMessageSize                             : 10MB
MaxProtocolErrors                          : 5
MaxRecipientsPerMessage                    : 5000
PermissionGroups                           : ExchangeUsers, ExchangeServers,
   ExchangeLegacyServers
PipeliningEnabled                          : True
ProtocolLoggingLevel                       : Verbose
RemoteIPRanges                             : {0.0.0.0-255.255.255.255}
RequireEHLODomain                          : False
RequireTLS                                 : False
Server                                     : HNLEX03
SizeEnabled                                : EnabledWithoutValue
TarpitInterval                             : 00:00:05
AdminDisplayName                           :
ExchangeVersion                            : 0.1 (8.0.535.0)
Name                                       : Default HNLEX03
DistinguishedName                          : CN=Default HNLEX03,CN=SMTP
 Receive Connectors,CN=Protocols,CN=HNLEX03,CN=Servers,CN=Exchange
Administrative Group (FYDIBOHF23SPDLT),CN=Administrative
Groups,CN=Volcano Surfboards,CN=Microsoft
```

```
Exchange,CN=Services,CN=Configuration,DC=volcanosurfboards,DC=com
Identity                          : HNLEX03\Default HNLEX03
Guid                              : 42364fae-4383-4eac-a6dd-2e8e7b2a2a08
ObjectCategory                    : volcanosurfboards.com/Configuration/
    Schema/ms-Exch-Smtp-Receive-Connector
ObjectClass                       : {top, msExchSmtpReceiveConnector}
WhenChanged                       : 12/27/2006 9:13:54 AM
WhenCreated                       : 11/18/2006 10:36:04 AM
OriginatingServer                 : HNLDC01.volcanosurfboards.com
IsValid                           : True
```

With few exceptions, you will usually not need to create additional Receive connectors, nor will you need to make many changes to the existing Receive connectors that are used internally.

SEND CONNECTORS

Although Receive connectors are configured for each server, Send connectors are organizational connectors that you can assign to a number of different Hub Transport servers. Each server also has an implicit Send connector, but that connector is used only for transferring mail to other Hub Transport servers. The implicit Send connector does not show up either in the Exchange Management Console (EMC) or when you use the Exchange Management Shell (EMS), and there are not properties that can be set for the implicit Send connector. Send connectors are managed in the EMC under the Hub Transport subcontainer of the Organization Configuration work center. Figure 18.6 shows the Send Connectors tab in the results pane.

FIGURE 18.6
Managing Send connectors

Figure 18.6 also shows the Source Server properties of a Send connector. The Source Server property page is where you designate which Hub Transport servers will deliver messages for this particular Send connector. When you assign more than one Hub Transport server as a source server, the outbound messaging load will be load-balanced between the source servers. You can

view the properties of this Send connector also using the EMS cmdlet `Get-SendConnector`; here is an example:

```
Get-SendConnector "E2K7 Send Connector to Internet" | FL

AddressSpaces               : {smtp:*;1}
AuthenticationCredential    :
Comment                     :
ConnectedDomains            : {}
ConnectionInactivityTimeOut : 00:10:00
DNSRoutingEnabled           : False
DomainSecureEnabled         : False
Enabled                     : True
ForceHELO                   : False
Fqdn                        : mail.somorita.com
HomeMTA                     : Microsoft MTA
HomeMtaServerId             : HNLEX03
Identity                    : E2K7 Send Connector to Internet
IgnoreSTARTTLS              : False
IsScopedConnector           : False
IsSmtpConnector             : True
LinkedReceiveConnector      :
MaxMessageSize              : 10MB
Name                        : E2K7 Send Connector to Internet
Port                        : 25
ProtocolLoggingLevel        : None
RequireTLS                  : False
SmartHostAuthMechanism      : None
SmartHosts                  : {smtp-server.hawaii.rr.com}
SmartHostsString            : smtp-server.hawaii.rr.com
SourceIPAddress             : 0.0.0.0
SourceRoutingGroup          : Exchange Routing Group (DWBGZMFD01QNBJR)
SourceTransportServers      : {HNLEX04, HNLEX03}
UseExternalDNSServersEnabled : False
```

Since Exchange Server 2007 does not have a default SMTP connector for outbound mail, you will need to create at least one Send connector. Most organizations will need to create only a single Send connector; this connector will be used to send mail to the Internet, to an Edge Transport server, or to an SMTP smarthost system that will deliver mail to the Internet on behalf of the Exchange server.

Now we'll go through an example of creating a Send connector that will be responsible for sending mail to the Internet. In the Hub Transport subcontainer of the Organization Configuration work center, make sure the Send Connectors tab is highlighted, and then click the New Send Connector task on the Actions pane. This launches the New SMTP Send Connector Wizard shown in Figure 18.7. On the Introduction page, you must provide the name of the connector and specify the intended use of the connector.

The wizard will allow you to create four types (intended use options) of Send connectors, but these are just predefined configurations and you can always change the properties of the connector you create later. The four types of Send connectors you can create are as follows:

- ◆ The Custom Send connector type allows you to manually configure all of the configuration settings at some point after the connector is created.

- ◆ The Internal Send connector type allows you to configure a connector that connects to other Hub Transport servers in your organization. Since all internal mail routing is automatic, you will usually not need to create an internal send connector.

- ◆ The Internet Send connector type is used to send mail to the Internet using DNS MX records.

- ◆ The Partner Send connector type creates a connector that will be used to send mail to specific Internet domains and will use certificate authentication and TLS encryption.

FIGURE 18.7
Introduction page of the New SMTP Send Connector Wizard

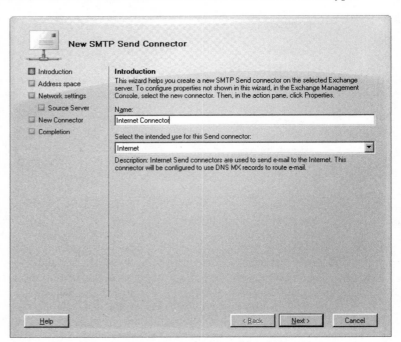

On the Address Space page of the wizard, you can specify the SMTP domains to which this Send connector will deliver e-mail. Since this connector is going to send mail to the Internet, we will use an address space of * in this example.

On the Network Settings property page, you can configure smarthost if you want mail to be delivered to another SMTP host for external delivery, such as with an Edge Transport server, or you can specify Use Domain Name System (DNS) "MX" Records to Route Mail Automatically. If you use DNS for mail delivery, then this Send connector will be responsible for all outbound mail delivery.

The Source Server page allows you to specify the Hub Transport servers that will deliver mail for this Send connector. If you have more than one Hub Transport server, we recommend you use additional Hub Transport servers for redundancy.

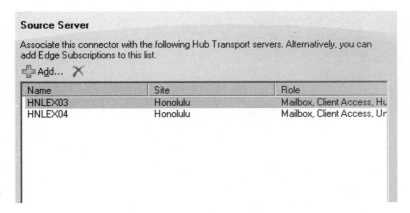

Once you click the New button on the New Connector page, the EMC will execute the command necessary to create the new Send connector. The following is the EMS command that was executed:

```
New-SendConnector -Name 'Internet Connector' -Usage 'Internet'
-AddressSpaces 'smtp:*;1' -DNSRoutingEnabled $true
-UseExternalDNSServersEnabled $false
-SourceTransportServers 'HNLEX03','HNLEX04'
```

Once you have created the connector, you should make one additional configuration option. On the General property page (shown in Figure 18.8) of the Send connector, enter the public name of the FQDN for this server, such as mail.somorita.com.

This name is the name that the Send connector uses in the EHLO or HELO command when it connects to a remote SMTP system. If you don't specify an FQDN for the connector to use, the connector will use the default FQDN for the server. Often this is an internal name that is not recognized on the Internet. Some Internet hosts will reject a connection if the name cannot be resolved.

FIGURE 18.8
General properties of a
Send connector

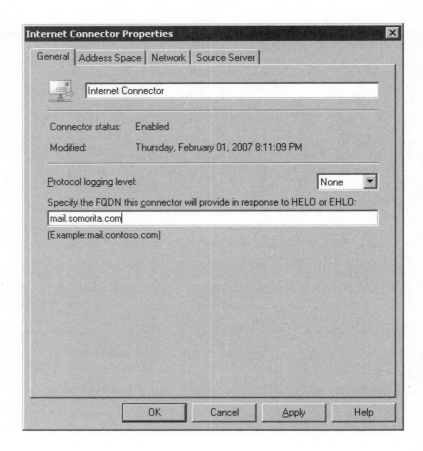

Connectivity to Exchange 2000/2003

When you install Exchange 2007 in an existing Exchange 2003 organization, to allow coexistence and facilitate routing, Setup creates an administrative group, a routing group, and a Windows security group for backward compatibility. These groups are as follows:

◆ Setup creates an administrative group for the Exchange 2007 servers to be housed in. This administrative group is called Exchange Administrative Group (FYDIBOHF23SPDLT). All Exchange 2007 servers will be in this administrative group; do not move them out of this administrative group.

◆ Setup creates a routing group called Exchange Routing Group (DWBGZMFD01QNBJR). All Exchange 2007 servers will be in this routing group and you must not move them out of this routing group.

◆ Setup creates an Active Directory universal security group called ExchangeLegacyInterop. The ExchangeLegacyInterop has permissions that allow Exchange 2003 and Exchange 2007 servers to send messages between each other.

The new administrative and routing groups are not visible within the Exchange 2007 Management Console, but you can see them using the Exchange 2000/2003 System Manager console (see Figure 18.9).

FIGURE 18.9
Viewing the Exchange 2007 administrative and routing group

If you are installing Exchange Server 2007 into an existing Exchange 2000/2003 environment, during the installation of the first Exchange 2007 Hub Transport server role, you are prompted for an Exchange 2000/2003 server to use as a bridgehead. The setup program will create a routing group connector from the Exchange Routing Group (DWBGZMFD01QNBJR) routing group to the specified server in the remote routing group.

For example, say an organization has two routing groups, the New York Routing Group and the San Francisco Routing group. Each routing group has two Exchange 2003 servers that function as bridgehead servers for the routing group connector that connects the New York and San Francisco routing groups, as illustrated in Figure 18.10.

When the first Exchange 2007 server is installed, the Exchange Routing Group (DWBGZMFD01QNBJR) routing group is created and the setup program prompts the installer for a remote Exchange 2003 server to use as a bridgehead. In this example, we are choosing one of the servers in the San Francisco routing group.

NOTE

In a native Exchange 2007 organization, routing group connectors are not used. They are necessary only when interoperating with Exchange 2000/2003.

The setup program creates a routing group connector from the Exchange 2007 routing group to the San Francisco routing group. A single local bridgehead and a single remote bridgehead are defined. An identical routing group connector is created from the San Francisco routing group to the Exchange 2007 routing group. Figure 18.11 shows the properties of one of these routing group connectors using the Exchange 2003 System Manager console.

FIGURE 18.10
Message routing between Exchange 2003 and Exchange 2007

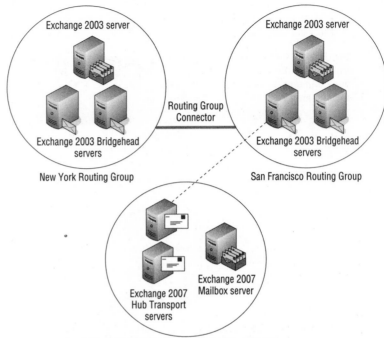

If you have multiple routing groups and multiple bridgehead servers, you will want to correct a couple of issues. First, there is no redundancy between the Exchange 2003 servers and the Exchange 2007 servers. If either the Hub Transport server or the Exchange 2003 bridgehead server that is being used for the routing group connector fails, then messaging between the Exchange 2003 and Exchange 2007 mailboxes will halt.

NOTE

Routing group connectors between Exchange 2007 and Exchange 2003 cannot be modified using the Exchange 2000/2003 System Manager console or the Exchange 2007 Exchange Management Console. You must use the Exchange Management Shell to edit the connector for Exchange 2007.

Second, you will want to verify that all messages from New York to the Exchange 2007 mailbox servers (and vice versa) will be sent through the San Francisco Exchange 2003 bridgehead servers.

You need to correct both of these issues using the Exchange Management Shell and the routing group cmdlets. The following are the cmdlets you can use for managing routing groups between Exchange 2000/2003 and Exchange 2007:

Cmdlet	Description
Get-RoutingGroupConnector	Retrieves the routing group connectors or properties of specified connectors
New-RoutingGroupConnector	Creates a new routing group connector
Remove-RoutingGroupConnector	Deletes a routing group connector
Set-RoutingGroupConnector	Sets the properties of a routing group connector

FIGURE 18.11
Properties of a routing group connector

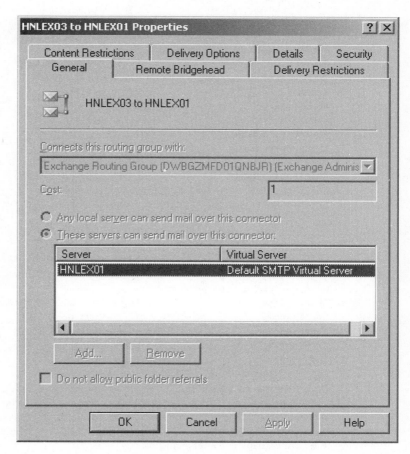

Let's start with some basics since this is all done from the EMS. First let's use the Get-RoutingGroupConnector with no parameters and retrieve a list of the routing group connectors. Here is an example:

```
Get-RoutingGroupConnector
```

Name	SourceRoutingGroup	TargetRoutingGroup
----	------------------	------------------
HNLEX03 to HNLEX01	Exchange Routing Group...	First Routing Group
HNLEX03 to HNLEX01	First Routing Group	Exchange Routing Group

The SourceRoutingGroup and TargetRoutingGroup columns have been truncated to fit better into the page in case you were wondering where the full name of the Exchange 2007 routing group is. Now let's retrieve all the properties of the HNLEX03:

```
Get-RoutingGroupConnector "HNLEX03 to HNLEX01" | FL

TargetRoutingGroup         : Exchange Routing Group (DWBGZMFD01QNBJR)
Cost                       : 1
TargetTransportServers     : {HNLEX03}
ExchangeLegacyDN           : /o=Volcano Surfboards/ou=First
Administrative Group/cn=Configuration/cn=Connections/cn=HNLEX03 to HNLEX01
PublicFolderReferralsEnabled : True
SourceRoutingGroup         : First Routing Group
SourceTransportServers     : {HNLEX01}
HomeMTA                    : Microsoft MTA
HomeMtaServerId            : HNLEX0
MinAdminVersion            : -2147453113
AdminDisplayName           :
ExchangeVersion            : 0.1 (8.0.535.0)
Name                       : HNLEX03 to HNLEX01
DistinguishedName          : CN=HNLEX03 to HNLEX01,
CN=Connections,CN=First Routing Group,CN=Routing
Groups,CN=First Administrative Group,CN=Administrative
Groups,CN=Volcano Surfboards,CN=Microsoft
Exchange,CN=Services,CN=Configuration,DC=volcanosurfboards,DC=com
Identity                   : HNLEX03 to HNLEX01
Guid                       : 4445126d-f275-4f5e-9934-d0048591a59a
ObjectCategory             : volcanosurfboards.com/Configuration/Schema/
ms-Exch-Routing-Group-Connector
ObjectClass                : {top, msExchConnector, msExchRoutingGroupConnector}
WhenChanged                : 11/19/2006 6:38:35 PM
WhenCreated                : 11/19/2006 6:38:35 PM
OriginatingServer          : HNLDC01.volcanosurfboards.com
IsValid                    : True
```

If you wanted to add HNLEX04 as an additional target bridgehead server, you would use the Set-RoutingGroupConnector cmdlet. But this is going to be a bit of a trick since the display names of the routing group connectors are identical, so you need to retrieve just the connector that connects from the Exchange 2000/2003 routing group to the Exchange 2007 routing group. Here is an example using the Where cmdlet:

```
Get-RoutingGroupConnector | Where {$_.TargetRoutingGroup -eq
"Exchange Routing Group (DWBGZMFD01QNBJR)"}

Name                 SourceRoutingGroup        TargetRoutingGroup
----                 ------------------        ------------------
HNLEX03 to HNLEX01   First Routing Group       Exchange Routing Group
```

You can pipe the results of that cmdlet to the `Set-RoutingGroupConnector` cmdlet. Here is an example:

```
Get-RoutingGroupConnector | Where {$_.TargetRoutingGroup -eq
"Exchange Routing Group (DWBGZMFD01QNBJR)"} | Set-RoutingGroupConnector
-TargetTransportServers HNLEX03,HNLEX04
```

Now you verify that this change has been made. Here a command that will list the relevant properties of that routing group connector:

```
Get-RoutingGroupConnector | Where {$_.TargetRoutingGroup -eq
"Exchange Routing Group (DWBGZMFD01QNBJR)"}
| FL Name,TargetRoutingGroup,SourceRoutingGroup,*transport*

Name                    : HNLEX03 to HNLEX01
TargetRoutingGroup      : Exchange Routing Group (DWBGZMFD01QNBJR)
SourceRoutingGroup      : First Routing Group
TargetTransportServers  : {HNLEX04, HNLEX03}
SourceTransportServers  : {HNLEX01}
```

Supporting Internet E-mail

Most all organizations have the ability to send and receive Internet mail. In this section, we'll cover configuring Exchange Server 2007 to send and receive Internet mail as well as implementing anti-spam protection. Outbound e-mail is actually pretty simple to configure and support because all you need to do is create a Send connector, which we discussed earlier in this chapter.

Inbound e-mail is another matter. You can choose from a number of different configurations or topologies to configure your Receive connectors based on security and message hygiene requirements. Depending on your needs and requirements, you can use one of the following:

◆ E-mail is sent directly to the Exchange 2007 Hub Transport server.

◆ E-mail is sent to the Edge Transport server, which performs anti-spam and antivirus inspections and then passes the message on to a Hub Transport server.

◆ E-mail is first sent to third-party software or a third-party appliance for message hygiene functions and then forwarded on to a Hub Transport server.

◆ E-mail is first sent to third-party software or a third-party appliance for message hygiene functions, then to an Edge Transport server for additional message hygiene functions, and then finally on the an Exchange 2007 Hub Transport server.

◆ E-mail is sent to a managed provider such as MessageOne or Microsoft Exchange Hosted Security where message hygiene, archival, and other security functions are performed. Then the e-mail is sent to the organization's Exchange 2007 Hub Transport servers.

We could actually come up with a number of additional permutations and possibilities for message security and message hygiene functions. Actually, we could fill up a couple of chapters of material on message hygiene, messaging security, and possible configurations. However, we'll keep this simple and explain the topic more conceptually.

First we will explain how to allow Exchange 2007 to receive e-mail directly from the Internet, and then we will talk about the use of the Edge Transport server.

Configuring Exchange to Receive Internet Mail

In this section, we will cover the fairly simple task of allowing one or more Exchange 2007 Hub Transport servers to receive mail from any Internet sender. Figure 18.12 illustrates this configuration. Both the external and internal firewalls allow SMTP traffic sent over TCP port 25 from any Internet host to be sent directly to the Exchange 2007 Hub Transport server.

FIGURE 18.12
E-mail delivered directly
to Hub Transport server

The Default Receive connector accepts the messages directly from Internet hosts once you have modified the Permissions Groups properties. Many organizations use this type of configuration successfully, but remember that this violates the concept of multilayer security because all content is delivered directly to the Hub Transport server role. You must employ some type of message hygiene function on the Hub Transport server to protect your organization from viruses and spam. Antivirus solutions are discussed in Chapter 20, "Securing Exchange Server."

By default, the Exchange 2007 anti-spam agents are not available on a Hub Transport server. However, you can enable the anti-spam agents on a Hub Transport server using the `Install-AntispamAgents.ps1` script in the `\Program Files\Microsoft\Exchange Server\Scripts` folder. Once the agents are installed, either reboot the Exchange server or restart the Microsoft Exchange Transport service. You can restart the service using the Exchange Management Shell with the following command:

```
Restart-Service msexchangetransport
```

Once the anti-spam agents are installed, management of the anti-spam agents on a Hub Transport is almost identical to managing them on an Edge Transport server. We will discuss these later in this chapter.

We mentioned this previously, but we want to make sure that you allow anonymous users to connect to the Receive connector that is exposed to the Internet. If you forget this step, you will end up spending a lot of time troubleshooting why your Exchange server is rejecting e-mail from the Internet. On the Permission Groups properties (shown in Figure 18.13) of the Default Receive connector, make sure that you have checked the Anonymous Users check box.

By default, your Exchange 2007 servers will only accept e-mail destined to the Windows Active Directory DNS domain that the server was a member of. In order to accept e-mail intended for your external SMTP domain, you will need to create a new accepted domain. We discussed this in Chapter 10, "Managing Recipients," but we thought it was important to reiterate this here.

FIGURE 18.13
Allowing a Receive
connector to receive
mail from the Internet

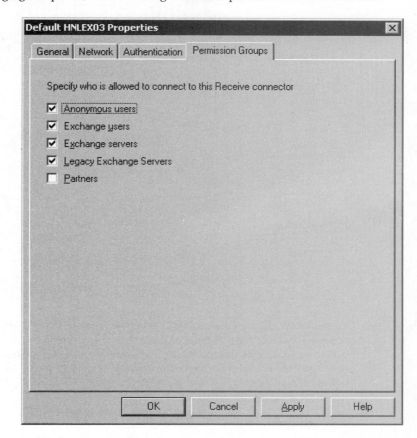

An accepted domain is a domain for which your Exchange organization can accept e-mail. You will need an accepted domain configuration for each domain for which your Exchange servers will accept e-mail. The accepted domain is the FQDN after the @ symbol in your e-mail address.

NOTE

If you fail to create an accepted domain for the e-mail domains for which you accept mail, people who send e-mail directly to your users will probably get an NDR with the error "550 5.7.1 Unable to relay."

We'll now go through a quick example. Accepted domains are created in the Hub Transport subcontainer of the Organization Configuration work center. You see the list of accepted domains on the Accepted Domains tab in the results pane. In this example, you support users whose e-mail domain is volcanocoffee.com, so you can to accept inbound mail for that domain. You should choose the New Accepted Domain task on the Actions pane to launch the New Accepted Domain Wizard (shown in Figure 18.14.)

FIGURE 18.14
Creating a new accepted domain

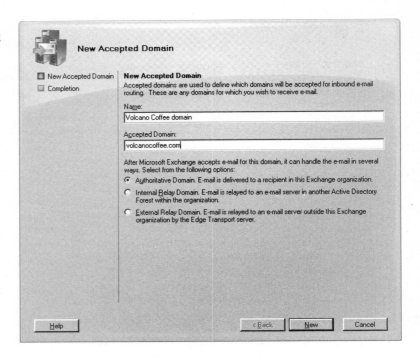

You must specify a name for the accepted domain along with the DNS domain name for the accepted domain. Since the e-mail addresses will all belong to internal mailboxes (this is the usual configuration), select the Authoritative Domain radio button, and then click New to create the new accepted domain. For more information on authoritative, internal relay, and external relay domains, see Chapter 10, "Managing Recipients."

Using Edge Transport Services

Implementing an additional layer of protection for your e-mail servers is always a good idea. This is certainly not a new concept for medium and large organizations. Even 10 years or more in the past, organizations frequently would put an SMTP server in their perimeter network and configure the SMTP in the perimeter network to accept their inbound mail and then relay the mail into an internal mail server. In the past, usually this was a hardened Unix system that performed only SMTP mail relay functions.

As viruses become more prevalent, these systems usually included virus-scanning functions. As spam has become more and more of a problem, these systems would also filter or quarantine messages suspected of being spam. This concept of inspecting mail before it arrives on the mail server has spawned a whole cottage industry of service providers, appliance vendors, and third-party software. Performing this initial inspection could be important for a number of reasons:

◆ It filters the unwanted content arriving on your network before it reaches internal mail servers.

◆ It reduces the load on mailbox and internal mail transport servers by keeping unwanted content off of them.

- ◆ It provides an additional layer of protection against spam or viruses.

- ◆ It filters the mail as closely as possible to the originating source.

- ◆ It prevents Internet hosts from directly accessing the internal Exchange servers.

Microsoft decided shortly after the release of Exchange Server 2003 that the Exchange server platform was not the best place for preliminary virus and spam inspection. Neither was it a good idea to put any Active Directory member server in the perimeter network. After all, an Exchange server is a member of the Active Directory and requires connectivity to other Exchange servers as well as the Active Directory domain controllers and global catalog servers. To build an Exchange 2000/2003 server that handles just message transfer, a number of unnecessary components had to be installed. The information store service even had to remain running. If this server is compromised, the entire network could be exposed.

The Edge Transport server was developed with minimal messaging functionality. Essentially, it is nothing more than a message transport engine that allows for the plug-in of additional components such as transport rules, anti-spam agents, and antivirus software. Edge Transport does not communicate or require Active Directory; instead, Edge Transport uses the Microsoft Active Directory Application Mode (ADAM) database for its configuration. The Hub Transport server runs a feature called Microsoft Exchange EdgeSync that pushes configuration data, recipient information, and safe/blocked senders lists. The EdgeSync process replicates the following data from the internal Active Directory to the ADAM database:

- ◆ A list of the valid SMTP addresses for the Active Directory, including mailbox-enabled users, mail-enabled users, mail-enabled contacts, mail-enabled groups, and mail-enabled public folders

- ◆ The list of internal accepted domains

- ◆ The list of remote domains

- ◆ Configured message classifications

- ◆ Safe and blocked sender lists for each user

- ◆ Internal send connector configuration

Edge Transport rules are based on SMTP addresses, not Active Directory objects — but you can use the SMTP addresses of mail-enabled groups. For the most part, the Edge Transport rules are a subset of hub rules — the exception is quarantine, which is only available on the edge as it is intended for spam.

As an added advantage, the Edge Transport server is managed using the same management tools (the Exchange Management Console, Exchange Management Shell, Queue Viewer, Best Practices Analyzer, and so on) you use to manage other Exchange 2007 server roles, so there is no steep learning curve associated with deploying the Edge Transport server role.

To maximize the security benefits, we recommend that the Edge Transport server be deployed in your perimeter network such as is shown in Figure 18.15. Figure 18.15 takes a slightly modified version of the implementation shown in Figure 18.12. The organization's DNS MX record directs inbound e-mail to the Edge Transport server that is located in the perimeter network.

The Edge Transport server performs anti-spam and antivirus functions and then passes messages on to an internal Hub Transport server. The firewall is configured such that TCP port 25 inbound from the Internet is allowed only to the Edge Transport server. The internal firewall only allows inbound TCP port 25 from the Edge Transport server in the perimeter network and only to the Hub Transport server on the internal network.

FIGURE 18.15
Deploying an Exchange
Edge Transport server

The Edge Transport server has specific anti-spam transport agents installed that handle different types of filtering, analysis, and transport rules. Table 18.1 shows the transport agents that are installed on an Edge Transport server.

TABLE 18.1:   Edge Transport Server Transport Agents

AGENT	DEFAULT STATE	FEATURES PROVIDED
Address Rewriting Inbound agent	Installed, Enabled	Messaging policy and compliance
Address Rewriting Outbound agent	Installed, Enabled	Messaging policy and compliance
Attachment Filter agent	Installed, Enabled	Anti-spam and antivirus
Connection Filter agent	Installed, Enabled	Anti-spam and antivirus
Content Filter agent	Installed, Enabled	Anti-spam and antivirus
Edge Rule agent	Installed, Enabled	Messaging policy and compliance
Protocol Analysis agent	Installed, Enabled	Anti-spam and antivirus
Recipient Filter agent	Installed, Enabled	Anti-spam and antivirus
Sender Filter agent	Installed, Enabled	Anti-spam and antivirus
Sender ID agent	Installed, Enabled	Anti-spam and antivirus

SETTING UP THE EDGE TRANSPORT

Now we'll go through a sample configuration of the Edge Transport server and the Hub Transport server, as illustrated in Figure 18.16. The internal firewall must first be configured to allow certain types of inbound and outbound connectivity between the internal network and the perimeter network. Specifically, connectivity is required between the Edge Transport server and the Hub Transport server. We have kept this example really simple; you would need to scale this for additional Hub Transport servers and Edge Transport servers.

FIGURE 18.16
Simple Edge Transport deployment

The Edge Transport server must be able to send SMTP (TCP port 25) to the Hub Transport server. The Hub Transport server should be able to send SMTP to the Edge Transport server if the Edge Transport server will be used for outbound mail. The Hub Transport server must also be able to communicate using the ports designated for LDAP synchronization to the ADAM database; these are either TCP port 50389 for regular LDAP or TCP port 50636 for secure LDAP. You will usually use port 50389 unless you have configured ADAM to use SSL.

You might need to open additional ports through the internal firewall and to the Edge Transport server if you want to use the Remote Desktop Connection (RDP) client to manage the Edge Transport server remotely. The RDP client uses TCP port 3389.

To configure simple mail flow between an Edge Transport server and a Hub Transport server, you could configure the necessary Send and Receive connectors, but you would not be reaching the full benefits of the Edge Transport. To receive the full benefits of the Edge Transport server role, you need to configure Edge Synchronization (EdgeSync). This process involves five basic steps:

1. Perform prerequisite checks and configuration settings.

2. Create an Edge Subscription file on the Edge Transport server.

3. Copy the Edge Subscription file to the Hub Transport server.

4. Import the Edge Subscription file and create a Send connector for the Edge Subscription.

5. Start the Microsoft Exchange EdgeSync service on the Hub Transport server (if it's not already started).

You should perform all of these steps within a fairly short period of time; this should be performed in under 24 hours because the bootstrap account that is created with the Edge Subscription file is only good for 24 hours from the time it was created.

The Edge Subscription that you are creating will work for all existing Hub Transport servers at the time you create it. However, if you add additional Hub Transport servers into the Active Directory site, you must create a new Edge Subscription.

Configuring EdgeSync

Let's go through the preconfiguration checklist and make sure you are ready to configure EdgeSync. Here is a list of tasks you should perform:

◆ Confirm that DNS name resolution between the Hub Transport and the Edge Transport works. In some cases, you may need to create HOSTS files for the two systems if the internal Hub Transport server is not resolvable in DNS by the Edge Transport server and vice versa.

◆ Ensure that the necessary ports on the firewall are opened.

◆ Configure the accepted domains and remote domains for your organization (on the internal Exchange 2007 servers).

◆ Define the internal SMTP servers so that Sender ID knows which servers are internal to your organization and so that connection filters know not to reject connections from your internal IP addresses.

The internal SMTP servers must be configured using the EMS cmdlet `Set-TransportConfig`. In the following example, we're defining internal mail servers as being the following IP addresses: 192.168.254.102, 192.168.254.19:

```
Set-TransportConfig -InternalSMTPServers 192.168.254.102,192.168.254.19
```

Next you need to switch to the console of the Edge Transport server and create the Edge Subscription file. The following command creates a new Edge Sync subscription file called EdgeSync.xml. Note that the confirmation message mentions a couple of the prerequisites:

```
New-EdgeSubscription -FileName "c:\EdgeSync.xml"
```

```
Confirm
Creating an Edge Subscription makes the configuration of this Edge
Transport server ready to be managed via EdgeSync. Any of the
following types of objects that were created manually will be deleted:
accepted domains; message classifications; remote domains; and Send
connectors. Also, the InternalSMTPServers list of the TransportConfig
object will be overwritten during the synchronization process. The
Exchange Management Shell tasks that manage those types of objects will
be locked out on this Edge Transport server. You must manage those
objects from inside the organization and allow EdgeSync to update the
```

Edge Transport server. EdgeSync requires that this Edge Transport
server is able to resolve the fully qualified domain names (FQDN) of
the Hub Transport servers in the Active Directory site to which the
Edge Transport server is being subscribed. Those Hub Transport servers
must be able to resolve the FQDN of this Edge Transport server. You
should complete the Edge Subscription inside the organization in the
next "1440" minutes before the bootstrap account expires.
[Y] Yes [A] Yes to All [N] No [L] No to All [S] Suspend [?] Help
(default is "Y"):y

The file that is created is shown in Figure 18.17. Take special note of the `EdgeServerFQDN`; this XML tag will be used by the Hub Transport server when it must transmit data (SMTP data or EdgeSync replication data) to the Edge Transport server, so this FQDN must be resolvable by the Hub Transport server.

FIGURE 18.17
The result of the New-
EdgeSubscription
command

Other content you will find in the EdgeSync subscription file includes the Edge server's certificate, the username, and password information that the Hub Transport server will use when authenticating to the Edge Transport server and vice versa.

You need to transport this `EdgeSync.xml` file to the Hub Transport server now. If all file sharing ports between the perimeter and the internal network are locked down, you may have to use a USB drive, CD-ROM, or, a floppy (oh, the horror). Once you have the EdgeSync subscription file on the Hub Transport server, you can import the file into the Exchange 2007 organization.

In the Organization Configuration work center of the Exchange Management Console, open the Hub Transport subcontainer and select the Edge Subscriptions tab. To import the new EdgeSync subscription file, choose the New Edge Subscription task from the Actions pane. This launches the New Edge Subscription Wizard (shown in Figure 18.18).

You must specify the Active Directory site that this Edge Transport server will be a member of. We recommend that you allow the New Edge Subscription Wizard to create the necessary Send connector to be used with the Edge Transport server. When you are ready, click the New button. The Completion page will remind you to verify firewall connectivity and name resolution.

Completion
The wizard completed successfully. Click Finish to close this wizard.
Elapsed time: 00:00:15
Summary: 1 item(s). 1 succeeded, 0 failed.

Edge Subscription   ⚠ Completed ⌃

Warning:
EdgeSync requires that the Hub Transport servers in Active Directory site Honolulu
must be able to resolve the IP address for EDGE.volcanosurfboards.com, and be able
to connect to that host on ports 50636.

Exchange Management Shell command completed:
new-EdgeSubscription -FileName 'C:\EdgeSync.xml' -Site 'Honolulu'
-CreateInternetSendConnector $true -CreateInboundSendConnector $true

Elapsed Time: 00:00:15

The Edge Synchronization process should start almost immediately and will synchronize configuration data once every hour afterward. Recipient information will be synchronized once every 4 hours. You can force the synchronization to run by running the EMS cmdlet `Start-EdgeSynchronization` with no parameters.

FIGURE 18.18
Creating a new Edge Subscription for the Hub Transport server

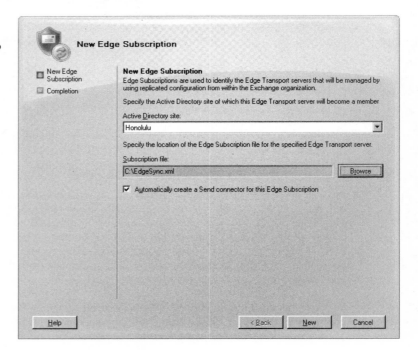

Confirming EdgeSync Is Running

Once you have started Edge Synchronization, you can perform a few tasks to confirm that the data is synchronizing to the ADAM database on the Edge Transport server. The first, of course, is to check the Application event log on the Hub Transport server that is running EdgeSync. Event ID 1000 from source MSExchange EdgeSync indicates that synchronization has completed successfully. Figure 18.19 shows this event.

FIGURE 18.19
Viewing successful
EdgeSync information

Annoyingly, if you look in the Description field of Event ID 1000, the times are in GMT time rather than in local time. The actual event time displays in local time, but the time in the description is different, so keep that in mind if you are troubleshooting.

In addition, you can verify that the configuration data has been transferred over to the Edge Transport server's ADAM database by looking in the Exchange Management Console on the Edge Transport server. Figure 18.20 shows the Exchange Management Console and the Edge Transport work center. In the Accepted Domains tab in the work pane for server EDGE, you can see the accepted domains that were transferred from the Exchange 2007 organization.

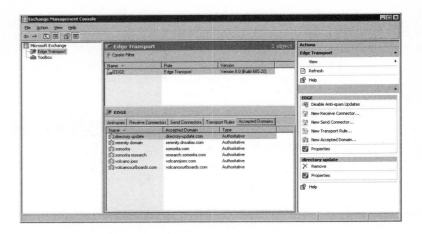

Any objects or properties that have synchronized from the internal Exchange Server 2007 organization (such as accepted domains, remote domains, Send connectors) should not be managed on the Edge Transport server. These objects and properties should be managed on the internal Exchange Server 2007 organization; they will be replicated to the Edge Transport server automatically.

NOTE

Note that Edge Transport servers cannot be managed remotely. You must manage them from their console or using Remote Desktop Connection.

CONFIGURING THE EDGE TRANSPORT SERVER TO FIGHT SPAM

You now have an Edge Transport server running and synchronizing with the internal Exchange Server 2007 system and the Active Directory. Out of the box, many of the anti-spam agents are enabled and configured; the configuration is usually targeted toward a typical organization. You can make some tweaks to ensure that your organization is effectively filtering spam. You can find the anti-spam features of the Edge Transport server on the Anti-spam tab, as shown in Figure 18.21.

You can see the different anti-spam configuration options you can configure for the Exchange 2007 Edge Transport server. It is also helpful to note that the same anti-spam configuration options will be available for your Exchange Server 2007 organization if you have run the Install-AntispamAgents.ps1 script on your Hub Transport servers.

Content Filtering

Content Filtering is the new feature in Exchange Server 2007 that was formerly known as the Intelligent Message Filter. The content filter examines the message's content based on keyword analysis, message size, and other factors and assigns the message a spam confidence level (SCL) ranking. This ranking is from 0 to 9. A message with a ranking of 0 is the least likely to be spam and a message with an SCL of 9 is very likely to be spam. Based on the SCL value of the message, you have a series of actions you can take (see Figure 18.22).

FIGURE 18.21
Customizing anti-spam features of an Edge Transport server

FIGURE 18.22
The Actions property page of the Content Filtering object

You can take three possible actions:

◆ Delete messages that meet or exceed a specific SCL threshold. This is the most drastic of actions because the sender does not know this has occurred and you can't later evaluate whether the message really was spam.

◆ Reject messages that meet or exceed a specific SCL threshold. The Exchange server analyzes the message and kicks it back to the sender with text indicating that the message was rejected because it looks like spam.

◆ Quarantine messages that meet or exceed a specific SCL threshold. Any messages with the specified SCL value or higher will be sent to an SMTP address where you can then analyze it to determine if it was truly spam or not.

You can take none, one, two, or all three of the actions, but the SCL values for each option must at the highest value and progress downward. For example, you could set a reject value of 8 and a quarantine value of 7. Any messages with a SCL value of 8 or 9 will be rejected; messages with an SCL value of 7 will be sent to the quarantine e-mail address. However, you could not set a quarantine value of 9 but then delete everything with an SCL value of 7.

On the inside of your Exchange organization, a global value called the SCL Junk Threshold is set to 8. This instructs the information stores to place any messages with a spam confidence level of 8 or higher into the user's Junk E-mail folder. The user can then review their Junk E-mail folder to determine whether a message was truly spam. However, if the quarantine value on the Edge Transport server is set to 7, then only messages with an SCL value of 6 or less will reach the Junk E-mail folder.

You can safely drop this value to 5 or 6. To lower the Junk E-mail threshold for all users, on one of the Exchange Server 2007 servers in your organization, type this command:

```
Set-OrganizationConfig -SCLJunkThreshold 6
```

You can view the organization configuration using the Get-OrganizationConfig cmdlet.

In some cases, a specific user may need a different set of SCL values than the Edge Transport server provides. The values the Edge Transport server provides can be overridden on a user-by-user basis. In the following command, we have disabled the quarantine and reject parameters for this particular user, and we have specified that this user's Junk E-mail threshold is 4:

```
Set-Mailbox "Matt Paleafei" -SCLRejectEnabled $False
-SCLQuarantineEnabled $False -SCLJunkThreshold 4
-SCLJunkEnabled $True
```

You can view the resulting configuration for the mailbox with the Get-Mailbox cmdlet. Here is an example:

```
Get-Mailbox "Matt Paleafei" | FL Name,*scl*

Name                  : Matt Paleafei
SCLDeleteThreshold    :
SCLDeleteEnabled      :
SCLRejectThreshold    : 7
SCLRejectEnabled      : False
```

```
SCLQuarantineThreshold : 9
SCLQuarantineEnabled   : False
SCLJunkThreshold       : 4
SCLJunkEnabled         : True
```

On the Exceptions property page of the Content Filtering properties, you can configure the SMTP addresses of the internal recipients to which you do not want to apply the content filter. This can be useful when managing a mailbox that is so important you never want a message to be filtered.

The Custom Words property page of the Content Filtering object enables some interesting features (see Figure 18.23). You can enable two types of word lists. If the message contains words in the first list, even if the message appears to be spam, the message is accepted. If the words in the second list are contained in a message, the message is blocked unless it contains words from the first list.

FIGURE 18.23
Configuring custom words for the content filter

The list with words and phrases that are always accepted can be particularly useful for organizations that know that legitimate messages to your company will frequently contain a particular word or phrase.

IP Block and Allow Lists

The IP Block List and IP Allow List features allow you to specify individual IP addresses, subnets, or entire ranges of IP addresses from which you will not accept or always accept mail, respectively. Figure 18.24 shows the interface for the IP Block List, but the interface for the IP Allow List is identical.

FIGURE 18.24
Configuring a IP Block List entry

In the foreground of Figure 18.24, you can see the interface for adding a single IP address. A nice feature of this interface is that you can specify that you always want to block an IP address, subnet, or address range or that you want to automatically unblock the address after a date and time.

IP Block and IP Allow Providers

An IP block list provider is better known as a *realtime block list (RBL)* provider. This is a service that keeps track of known sources of spam, open relays, open proxies, IP addresses used by dial-up connections, and IP addresses used by DHCP ranges. These are all frequent sources of spam. Conversely, an IP allow list provider is a service provider that maintains a list of IP addresses that are likely not to send spam.

The most common configuration is an IP block list provider. When an SMTP client connects to your Edge Transport server, the Edge Transport server issues a DNS query using the reverse format of the IP address along with the DNS suffix of the block list provider. For example, if an SMTP client at IP address 192.168.254.10 connects to an Edge Transport server, it will issue the DNS query 10.254.168.192.sbl-xbl.spamhaus.org if it is configured to use the Spamhaus SBL-XBL list.

If the IP address is not on the Spamhaus block list, then the DNS query will return a "host not found" message. However, if the entry is on a block list, the DNS query will return an IP address such as 127.0.0.1, 127.0.0.2, and so on. The different return codes have different meanings for different providers.

Figure 18.25 shows the IP Block List Providers properties; in this figure, three block list providers have been configured.

FIGURE 18.25
Viewing the current IP block list providers

If you click the Add button, you can add RBL providers (there are none configured by default). Figure 18.26 shows part of the Add IP Block List Provider dialog box and the custom error messages screen. The information that is required in the Add IP Block List Provider dialog box is a name for the provider and the DNS suffix or the lookup domain. You get the DNS suffix from the block list provider.

FIGURE 18.26
Adding a new IP block
list provider

When you add a new IP block list provider, you can also configure it so that it responds only to certain error codes. This could be useful, for example, if the provider returns different error codes for different types of hosts and you only want to block mail for certain error codes.

For each block list provider, you can configure a custom error message. This can be useful for administrators whose systems may be on a block list. We recommend configuring a message that would be helpful for the administrator of a system from which you are rejecting mail.

The Exceptions property page is useful if you want to specify SMTP addresses to which the RBL blocking should not apply.

A lot of RBL providers are available on the Internet, and almost all are free. Some of these providers are pretty accurate, and some are not. Some are more aggressive than others. The more aggressive RBLs will often block entire IP subnets or entire IP ranges from regions of the world. Other IP block lists make it difficult to remove your IP address if you get on their list. Table 18.2 lists some of the RBLs we recommend using. We usually recommend choosing two RBLs; in the table they are in order of preference. Our preference is to choose less aggressive RBLs and using other filtering technologies such as content filtering or sender reputation.

Recipient Filtering

When recipient filtering is enabled, the Edge Transport is configured to reject mail for any SMTP address that is not found in the Active Directory or to reject mail for specific SMTP addresses.

This will reduce a lot of the garbage messages that your Exchange server accepts and then has to issue a non-delivery report for. Figure 18.27 shows the Blocked Recipients list for the Recipient Filtering object.

TABLE 18.2:   Choosing an IP Block List Provider

PROVIDER	PROVIDER'S WEBSITE	PROVIDER'S DNS SUFFIX
Spamhaus	www.spamhaus.org	sbl-xbl.spamhaus.org
ABUSEAT CBL	cbl.abuseat.org	cbl.abuseat.org
SORBS	www.sorbs.net	dnsbl.sorbs.net
Spamcop	www.spamcop.net	bl.spamcop.net

FIGURE 18.27
Configuring recipient
filtering

We recommend that you check the Block Messages Sent to Recipients Not Listed in the Global Address List check box. This will help reduce the burden placed on your system by zombie networks of spammers. However, by recommending that you enable this check box, we are assuming that you have EdgeSync enabled and that all valid SMTP addresses are replicated to the Edge Transport server's local ADAM database.

If you are performing recipient filtering, newly created mailboxes may have their mail rejected by the Edge Transport server until the replication runs again. You can force the synchronization after new mailboxes are created by running the Start-EdgeSynchronization cmdlet. Or just make sure that the user does not give anyone their e-mail address for at least four hours after the account is created.

Sender Filtering

Sender filtering is one of the oldest anti-spam features in Exchange; it is probably also the least effective. The premise is that you provide a list of SMTP addresses or domains that should not be able to send your users e-mail. The problem is that most spammers don't use the same e-mail address twice, so this is less than completely effective. Figure 18.28 shows the Blocked Senders property page of the Sender Filtering object.

FIGURE 18.28
Configuring sender filtering

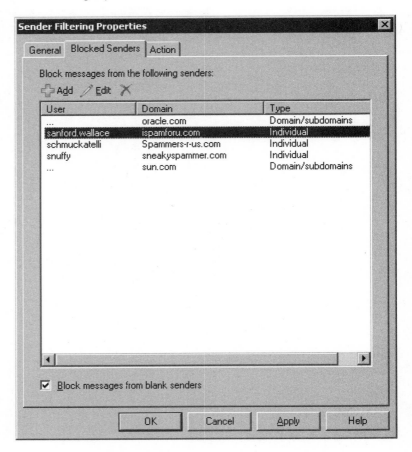

You can block individual senders and you can block all senders in a specific domain. One interesting anti-spam technique that some organization's employ is that they put their own domain in this list. This prevents those spam messages that claim to be from one of your own recipients. However, if you do that on an internal Hub Transport server, make sure that it is not being used for POP3, IMAP4, or other clients that use SMTP to send mail internally.

Another interesting anti-spam technique that blocks a few pieces of mail is the check box Block Messages from Blank Senders. If a message does not have a sender (and it should), then this rejects the message.

The interface is a little different than in previous versions of Exchange Server. When you add or edit blocked senders, you have the option of adding an individual user or an entire domain and subdomains.

On the Action property page of the Sender Filtering object, you can specify what action to take. You can either reject the message entirely or stamp the message with a blocked sender and allow it on through. If you stamp the message as being from a blocked sender, the content filter will rank it as spam.

Sender ID

Contrary to popular misconception, Sender ID is not an anti-spam technology but a anti-spoofing technology. Quite simply, each organization on the Internet that sends e-mail should register a sender protection framework (SPF) record in their public DNS server. This SPF record contains a list of the servers authorized to send mail on behalf of their domain.

When a server receives a message from a particular domain, it analyzes the message to determine the actual sender and determines which server sent it. If the message originated from an authorized server, it is probably not being spoofed. If it is accepted from a server who is not in the DNS SPF record, then the message might be from a spoofed sender.

On the Action property page of the Sender ID object, you can specify which action to take. Figure 18.29 shows the Action property page. You can reject the message, delete the message, or accept it for further processing by the content filter.

FIGURE 18.29
Configuring a Sender ID action

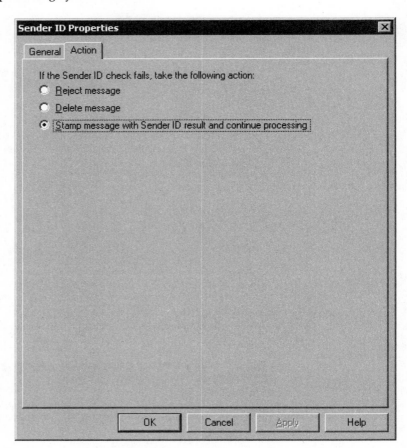

The problem with Sender ID is that fewer than 15 percent of all domains on the Internet have an SPF record. at least by our estimates. And frequently an organization's SPF records get out-of-date and are therefore wrong. The only thing worse than not having an SPF record is having one that is wrong. Therefore, it is impractical to reject or delete messages that fail the Sender ID test. You should keep this configured to Stamp Message with Sender ID Result and Continue Processing.

Sender Reputation

Sender reputation is the most promising feature of Exchange 2007 when it comes to reducing the amount of spam you receive. This is because much of the spam that is received today is sent by 'bot or zombie networks. Spammers have joined forces with virus writers; the virus writers have written malware that infects hundreds of thousands of users' computers. Periodically, these computers check with the spammer and download a new batch of spam. Blocking a single IP address becomes impractical because they have so many of these computers all over the Internet. However, these zombie networks are usually not using correct SMTP commands and are not RFC compliant. A lot of spammers also use SMTP proxies by sending messages through a proxy on the Internet.

Sender reputation allows Exchange to analyze the connections that are coming in to an Edge Transport server and look for things such as the number of protocol errors, invalid delivery attempts, and the number of messages from the same sender. These can be used to determine if a specific IP address is sending spam. On the Action property page of the Sender Reputation object (shown in Figure 18.30), you can specify the Sender Reputation Level (SRL) Block Threshold value; this is a value from 0 to 9 that is used to determine if a sender should be blocked if they exceed a certain "suspicious" threshold.

FIGURE 18.30
Configuring the sender reputation level block threshold

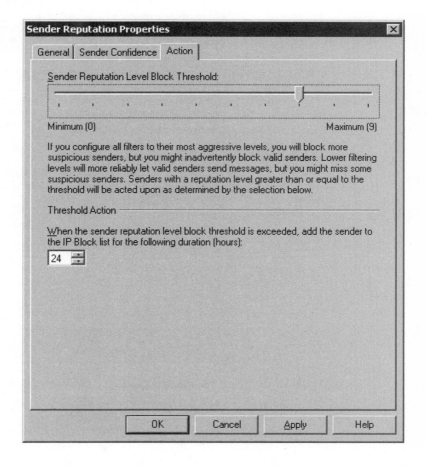

The default for the SRL block threshold is 9, but we recommend scaling it back to a slightly less aggressive value of 7 or 8 and then monitoring it to see if you still get a lot of spam.

If so, you can increase it slightly, but keep in mind that as you get more aggressive with this value, the possibility of valid connections getting rejected becomes higher.

The Threshold Action section allows you to specify how long a sender is retained on an IP block list once they have been determined to be suspicious. The default is 24 hours and we recommend that you keep that value.

Exchange can test for open proxies and determine if the source of a connection is an open proxy that is probably being used to send spam. On the Sender Confidence property page (Figure 18.31), you can enable the open proxy test. If a connecting SMTP client is determined to be an open proxy, they will be added to the IP block list for the time specified on the Action property page.

FIGURE 18.31
Configuring the sender reputation filter to perform an open proxy test

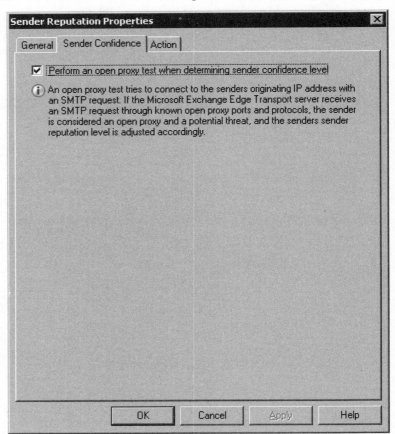

CONFIGURING THE EDGE TRANSPORT SERVER TO ENFORCE ORGANIZATION POLICIES

The Edge Transport server has a transport rules feature just as the Exchange 2007 Hub Transport server does. You may find this useful if there are certain types of organizational policies that you wish to enforce on messages that are arriving on the Edge Transport server and before they are delivered on to the Exchange 2007 Hub Transport server. We discussed transport rules in more detail in Chapter 13, "Managing Messages in Transit."

To illustrate the use of transport rules on the Edge Transport server, let's go through an example where to enforce a policy of blocking outbound messages that contain certain confidential words and phrases. Here are the requirements:

1. All messages being sent to a user outside of the organization should have this transport rule applied to them.

2. If the message subject or body contains the words *confidential*, *secret formula*, or *secret recipe*, we want to take action on the message.

3. If the message meets the criteria, an error should be recorded in the event log, the message should be dropped, and a copy of the message should be sent to the company audit alias.

For this example it is assumed that the Edge Transport server is used to relay outbound messages to the Internet as well as to accept inbound messages. This example could also apply to transport rules used inside the organization.

In the Actions pane, select the New Transport Rule task to launch the New Transport Rule Wizard. On the Introduction page (shown in Figure 18.32), provide a descriptive name for the policy as well as an accurate description of the function of the transport rule. When finished, click Next to move on to the next page of the wizard.

FIGURE 18.32
Introduction page of the New Transport Rule Wizard

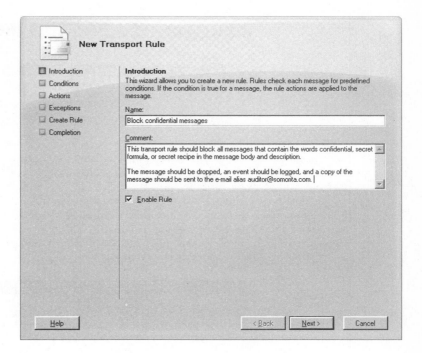

On the Conditions page, specify the conditions of the transport rule. For this rule, you have two conditions that must be met: the message must be from a user inside the organization and there must be specific words in the message body or subject. First check the condition When the Subject Field or the Message Body of the Message Contains Specific Words; this will add that condition to the Step 2 portion of the wizard page. From here you need to click the specific word's link so that you can use the Specify Words dialog box. In the Specify Words dialog box, you can add or remove words and phrases that are part of the condition.

When finished, click the OK button to close the Specify Words dialog box. You now need to select the second condition; select the From Users Inside or Outside the Organization check box. This adds that selection to the Step 2 portion of the wizard page. The default is from users inside the organization, but you could change this by clicking the Inside link to see the Select Scope dialog box.

The finished product for the Conditions page looks like Figure 18.33. You can see the conditions selected on the top part of the wizard page (the Step 1 section) and the additional information that was specified for the conditions, such as the words to search for and the fact that it applies to message sent by users inside the organization.

The next page of the wizard is the Actions page. On this page, you specify what you want to do if you find a message that meets the conditions you set on the Conditions page. First, you select the Log an Event with Message action; this adds a message link to the Step 2 section of the page. You click the message link to see the Specify Event Message dialog box. Here you enter the information you want entered in the event log.

FIGURE 18.33
Conditions page of the transport rule

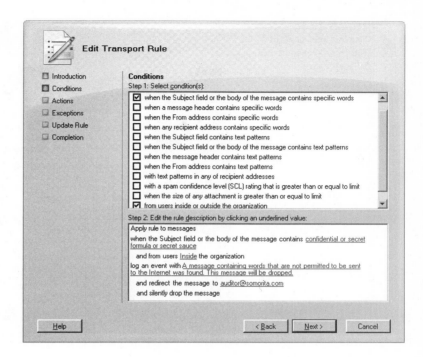

Next you select the Redirect the Message to Address check box and then click the addresses link that is now in Step 2 of the wizard page. This will display the Specify Recipients dialog box. Here you need to add the SMTP address auditor@somorita.com.

After you add the e-mail address to the Specify Recipients dialog box, click OK and then check the Silently Drop the Message check box. There is nothing else you need to do for this particular action. Figure 18.34 shows the finished product for the Actions property page.

You can now click Next to see the Exceptions page of the wizard. The Exceptions page allows you to add exceptions to this particular rule. In this example, there are none, so you can click Next to move on to the Create Rule configuration summary. From here, you can click the New button to create the new rule.

FIGURE 18.34
The Actions page of
the New Transport Rule
Wizard

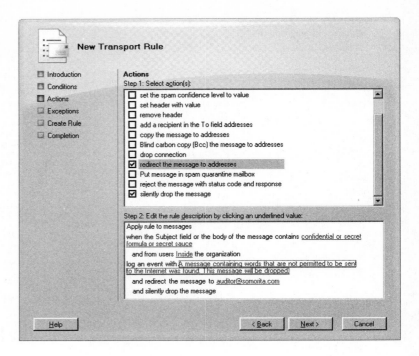

Summary

One of the primary functions of an Exchange server is to send and receive messages. That job is the
function of the Hub Transport server role. Once you start sending messages between more than
one Exchange server, you must understand how Exchange Server 2007 uses your existing Active
Directory infrastructure to route messages between Hub Transport and Mailbox servers.

Once you open your Exchange servers to receive e-mail from the Internet, you also have to con-
tend with spam and viruses. Exchange Server 2007 introduced the concept of the Edge Transport
server role, which helps in the fight against unwanted message content.

In the next few chapters, we will cover some additional topics that should be helpful to you
when managing your message routing infrastructure. Chapter 20, "Securing Exchange Server,"
discusses concepts that include providing multilayer virus protection and hardening the Windows Server platform. Chapter 21, "Logging, Auditing, and Monitoring," includes topics such
as enabling protocol logging for debugging and tracking purposes as well as using the Exchange
Server 2007 queue management features.

Chapter 19

Exchange Anywhere

E-mail has become what most businesses consider their most critical application, and as such, users demand access to their e-mail around the clock, whenever and wherever they may be. Throughout the various versions of Exchange, the remote access options have improved, with each version offering more. The remote capabilities of Exchange allow a user to have access to their mailbox from almost anywhere in the world and have allowed the hosting industry to expand rapidly. Users no longer need to be located with the e-mail server to have full access and the full functionality that Exchange can offer.

Traditionally, remote access to e-mail meant a basic Web interface or a complex virtual private network (VPN) deployment to provide the full Outlook client for remote staff.

Exchange 2003 changed all that. Outlook Web Access (OWA) became functional enough to use as a primary e-mail client. The introduction of RPC over HTTPS allowed administrators to provide the full Outlook and Exchange experience without a VPN. Then with the growth of mobile communications, Exchange ActiveSync (EAS) allowed e-mail to be available on the move, wherever you could get a mobile phone signal.

Exchange 2007 builds on the enhancements that Exchange 2003 introduced. There is a new Outlook Web Access that just gets better with every version of Exchange. RPC over HTTPS gets a new name (well overdue) and is now known as Outlook Anywhere. ActiveSync has also been enhanced, but some features will require the next version of Windows Mobile 6. Exchange 2007 also continues to provide access using more traditional methods, the old favorites POP3 and IMAP.

When considering what remote access options to offer your user community, you do need to consider security requirements as well. E-mail can often contain sensitive information and without a secure deployment can actually put your network at risk. Fortunately, it is possible to secure all of the remote access methods to e-mail, a process that protects your network without compromising functionality. Securing access to e-mail using Exchange is discussed in Chapter 20, "Securing Exchange Server," and all techniques discussed in this chapter should be considered along with the security needs of your organization.

Topics in this chapter include the following:

◆ Implementing Outlook Web Access

◆ Implementing ActiveSync and Windows Mobile devices

◆ Using Outlook Anywhere

◆ Supporting POP3 and IMAP4 clients

Using Outlook Web Access

Outlook Web Access (OWA) is one of the biggest selling points of Exchange, and it simply gets better with every new version. It is one of the most complex web applications available, and it offers significant levels of customization while retaining a familiar Outlook-like interface, allowing end users to quickly get to grips with it as an interface for their e-mail. From the very moment you access the forms-based login page, you know that you are using something very exceptional. Figure 19.1 shows the default forms-based authentication login page, which can be customized to your company look and feel if required

FIGURE 19.1
Outlook Web Access
logon form

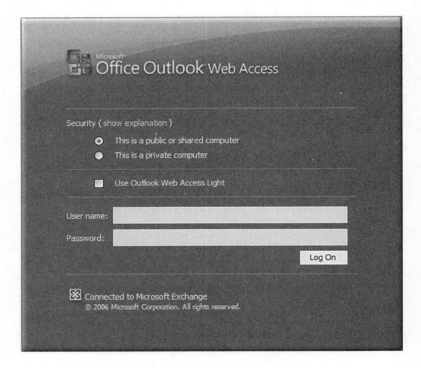

From the logon page, the user can select a radio button that indicates whether they are using a public or shared computer versus a private computer. If they are using a private computer, their inactivity time-out is 8 hours, but if they select the radio button that indicates they are using a public computer, the inactivity time-out is 15 minutes. This can help improve security by automatically disconnecting inactive users from their mailbox. The time-outs can be configured on a per-server basis via a Registry change.

The first time the end user logs in to OWA, they get the chance to set their location and language (see Figure 19.2). This avoids the problems with previous versions of OWA using the location information of the machine being used.

Once you have got logged in, the interface is very familiar. Anyone who has used Outlook or OWA on Exchange 2003 will feel comfortable quickly. You have full access to your mailbox, including all folders, contacts, tasks, and notes, as you would expect. Figure 19.3 shows the full OWA interface.

FIGURE 19.2
Setting the location and
language options

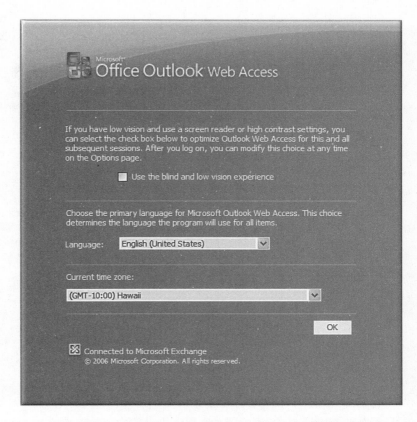

FIGURE 19.3
Exchange 2007 Outlook
Web Access interface

New in this version is the ability to open another Exchange 2007 mailbox directly from the interface simply by selecting the box in the upper-right corner where your name appears. You are prompted for the name of the other mailbox (provided you have permissions for it).

The list of options has grown considerably, giving you more control over how OWA works for you, displays messages, and works with other users. You can access options by clicking the Options button on the upper-right portion of the OWA interface. Figure 19.4 shows the Options pane and the message options.

FIGURE 19.4
Editing Outlook Web Access user options

There are also options that you're users control their Windows Mobile handheld. With a supported handset, they can wipe the device or recover their password. With Exchange Server 2003 this was only possible through the optional tool Mobile Admin. Administrators can disable this functionality if required and also have control over the device from the server.

Exchange 2007 introduced more control over your Out-of-Office message, allowing you to have one message for known people and another message for everyone else. Outlook Web Access provides an interface for the two messages types through the Options pane. Figure 19.5 shows the Out-of-Office Assistant features that a user can access through the OWA Options interface. Notice a few new Out-of-Office features, including the ability to schedule when the auto-replies are sent, an option for sending a separate Out-of-Office reply to external senders, and the ability to specify whether external senders must exist in your Contacts folder.

FIGURE 19.5
Setting Out-of-Office options through Outlook Web Access

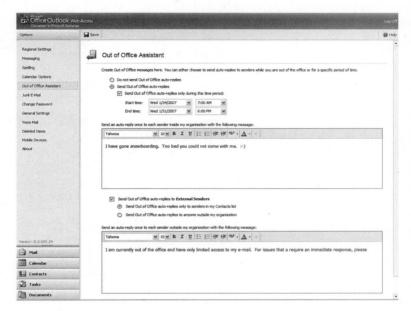

Changing your network password through OWA is also now built in rather than the manual configuration that it required with Exchange 2003. Network password control can be turned off as well, should that be required.

If you wish to support password changes for Exchange 2003 mailboxes, the virtual directories will need to be added to the Client Access servers as before. The built-in password change is for Exchange 2007 mailboxes only. Access to attached files has been improved, with a new WebReady feature that allows access to common file types such as Microsoft Word documents without that application needing to be installed on the machine being used to access OWA. This is also used with a new feature for OWA called document access. This allows access to SharePoint sites and documents libraries on your network through the OWA interface.

Regrettably, it is not all good news with the new version of OWA. With Microsoft's decision to deemphasize public folders, access to public folders on Exchange 2007 servers is not possible through OWA at all, though this feature is supposed to be included in Exchange Server 2007 Service Pack 1.

The ability to create and modify rules through OWA has also been removed, so if you want to work with rules, you will need to use the full Outlook client. Modifying and adding distribution groups have also been removed, along with support for S/MIME. Both of these features are supposed to be included in Exchange Server 2007 Service Pack 1.

As with Exchange 2003, the interface that you see for Outlook Web Access depends on the version of Exchange that your mailbox is located on. Therefore, although all users can see the new

Exchange 2007 login screen, if their mailbox is on Exchange 2003, they will get OWA for Exchange 2003, not Exchange 2007.

Outlook Web Access is handled by an Exchange 2007 server that has the Client Access server (CAS) role installed. The CAS role replaces the front-end server functionality from previous versions of Exchange.

One of the new features we find useful in Outlook Web Access is the enhanced address book access. If you click the small Address Book icon next to the Find Someone box, you are presented with the Address Book dialog box (shown in Figure 19.6) divided in to three columns.

FIGURE 19.6
Using the Outlook Web Access address book feature

The first column lets you select what type of addresses you can see. The second column lists the users in the global address list. The third column (which can be turned off) shows you their availability that day. Therefore, you could use this feature to see whether the person you want to call is in a meeting, out of the office, and so on.

Configuring Outlook Web Access

Outlook Web Access is enabled by default, so you don't have to do anything special to enable the feature. However, you do have control over what the end user can do with Outlook Web Access. Most of the Exchange 2007 Outlook Web Access options are enabled on a per-server basis.

PERFORMING CONFIGURATION VIA THE EXCHANGE MANAGEMENT CONSOLE

To configure the server via the Exchange Management Console (EMC), you need to select the server you want to configure in the Server Configuration work center. In the lower pane, you will see the directories configured on the server. Right-click OWA and choose Properties.

Authentication

The Authentication tab allows you to enable or disable Forms Based Authentication (FBA) and change how much information the end user needs to put in when using FBA. In a single-domain model, you can set a default domain so that the end user just needs to enter their username and password in the logon form. Figure 19.7 shows the Authentication property page of the OWA virtual directory.

FIGURE 19.7
Configuring
Outlook Web Access
authentication options

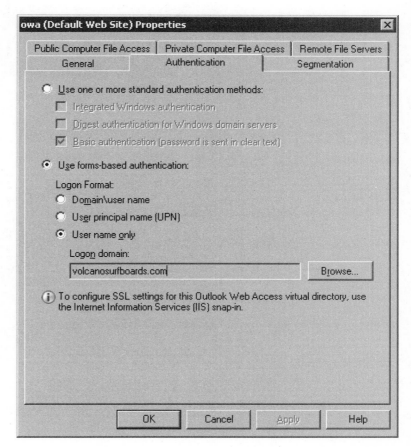

Segmentation

The Segmentation tab allows you to enable and disable features in OWA (see Figure 19.8). This can include user management of their handheld device, whether they can change their network password through OWA, access to folders, and other options.

By default, all options are enabled. The following options can be disabled:

◆ You can disable Exchange ActiveSync integration, which allows the user to manage their Windows Mobile– or ActiveSync-enabled devices.

◆ You can hide all address lists (by disabling All Address Lists) instead of just the global address lists.

FIGURE 19.8
Configuring
Outlook Web Access
segmentation

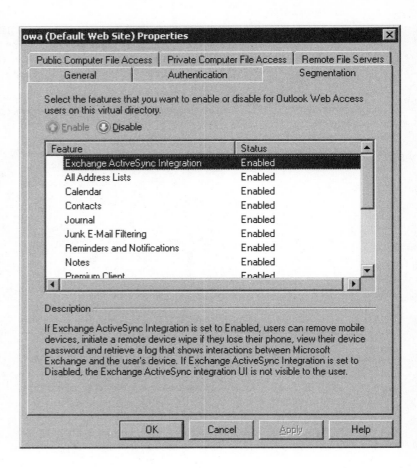

◆ You can hide the Calendar, Contacts, Journal, Tasks, and Search folders features.

◆ You can disable Junk E-mail filtering features.

◆ You can require that users use the basic client rather than the premium client.

◆ You can disable e-mail signatures.

◆ You can disable spell checking features.

◆ You can disable the ability to change themes.

◆ You can disable the change password feature.

◆ You can disable Unified Messaging integration.

Public and Private File Access

Public and private file access allows you to specify the types of files that a user can access if they have selected a public/shared computer (default) or private computer on the OWA logon page. These Public Computer File Access and Private Computer File Access tabs allow you to control access to files — either files attached to e-mail messages or files from Remote File Access — and are identical as far as the options that are available to you. This includes the new WebReady document viewing options, which allow users to view documents for common file types such as Microsoft Word without having the application installed on their machine. Figure 19.9 shows the Private Computer File Access property page.

FIGURE 19.9
Configuring private
computer file access

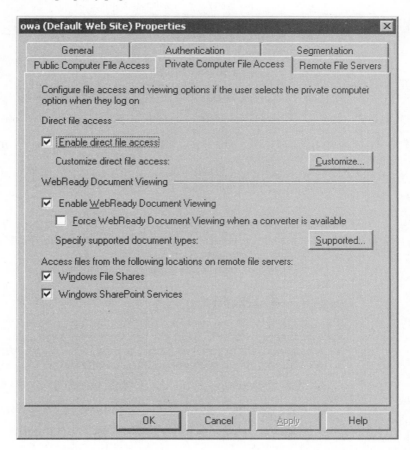

If you click the Customize button on the Private Computer File Access property page, you can configure direct file access, which allows you to force end users to save certain types of documents to the local machine before access is granted as well as block access to file types altogether. These options were previously available in the OWA Admin Tool for Exchange 2003 but now can be managed via the Exchange Management Console.

Remote File Servers

The Remote File Servers property page (shown in Figure 19.10) controls access to documents and SharePoint on remote servers through OWA.

We discuss remote file access later in this chapter.

SIMPLIFY THE OWA URL

If the server that the end users are accessing is a dedicated Exchange Client Access server, then you can simplify the URL to remove the need to put /owa at the end of the address. For example, the user can type https://owa.somorita.com rather than http://owa.somorita.com/owa. You do this via a simple change through Internet Information Server (IIS) Manager:

1. Open IIS Manager, and open the website that has OWA enabled on it.

2. Right-click the website container, and choose Properties.

3. Click the Home Directory property page. Select the option A Redirection to a URL. This will enable the option Redirect To. Enter in the box the URL to which you want to redirect users that connect to the default website. In Figure 19.11, we are redirecting the user to https://owa.somorita.com/owa.

4. Select the A Directory below URL Entered radio button.

5. Click OK.

Note that in a mixed environment, you should use the legacy /exchange virtual directory, as /owa will not allow access to Exchange 2003 mailboxes.

FIGURE 19.10
Configuring Outlook
Web Access for remote
file server support

Outlook Web Access and Larger Organizations

With the changes in Exchange routing in Exchange 2007, the location of the Client Access server becomes more important. The simple rule now is that in each Active Directory site that has a Mailbox server, there also needs to be a Client Access server. That means OWA, which is one of the functions of the Client Access server role. With the removal of Exchange's own routing capability (via routing groups in Exchange 2003 and 2000), Exchange 2007 now uses AD sites for routing.

However, you are not limited to a single Client Access server. You can have more than one. In some sites, where there is heavy remote access of the environment, you may want to look at having more than one CAS and then using load balancing and the Availability service to ensure that the servers are used to their fullest. We discuss the Availability service and network load balancing in Chapter 17, "Supporting Outlook 2007," and Chapter 15, "Reliability and Availability 101."

Enabling Document Access

Document Access is a new feature of Outlook Web Access that allows users of OWA to access Windows file shares and SharePoint Services sites through the OWA interface. Although the feature is enabled by default, no SharePoint sites or internal file shares are configured.

FIGURE 19.11
Redirecting the default
website to the OWA
virtual directory

Whether you want to enable this feature for your servers is something that needs to be carefully considered because the level of control over the access may not be enough for many sites. You should look at what can be accessed through this process before allowing it to be used by the end users.

The feature can be enabled on a per-server or per-user basis, allowing the administrator to control who can and cannot access the resources.

You can also control whether it is enabled depending on the selection of a public or private computer on the login screen. However, because you don't know where these computers are located, this level of control is limited as best. As soon as users figure out that choosing a different option allows the use of different features, they will select the option with the features they want to use wherever they are.

You can grant access to Windows file servers only on a per-server basis. Therefore, if a server hosts a number of shares, all of those shares will be available. However, one way around this limitation is to use a domain distributed file system (DFS) system. However, this involves adding domain.tld (where domain.tld is the DNS name of your Active Directory forest root domain) to the list of shares, which may expose or bring undue attention to other elements of the domain, such as the netlogon share.

CONFIGURING DOCUMENT ACCESS

You configure Document Access as part of the Outlook Web Access feature set, either via the Exchange Management Console or through the Set-OwaVirtualDirectory command.

> **NOTE**
>
> Changes to document access and segmentation take effect after 60 minutes of inactivity for users already logged in or when a user logs in. If you want to force the changes to take effect, you need to run the `iisreset /noforce` command on the Client Access server.

Exchange Management Console

You can also use the Exchange Management Console to configure the document access options. Because it is part of Outlook Web Access, you configure the options on the OWA virtual directory. Therefore, open EMC and then open the Server Configuration work center. Select the server you want to configure. In the list of directories in the lower pane, select the OWA directory that you want to change, and then choose Properties in the Actions pane to the right.

Access to remote file and SharePoint servers is enabled or disabled on the two file access tabs. In each one, you will see the options to enable access toward the bottom.

To grant or block access, select the tab Remote File Access. When configuring file server access, note that the block list overrides the allow list. When entering the server name, enter just the name — such as server1. Do not enter \server1.

You don't have to enter the fully qualified name for file servers because the list of domain suffixes controls that. However, if you do enter a server name with its fully qualified domain name (server.domain.tld), then domain.tld needs to be in the list of internal domain suffixes.

If you are granting access to a domain DFS, then you need to add the domain to the list of allowed servers and the list of internal DFS suffixes. You can define them in the list of suffixes that are treated internally (see Figure 19.12).

> **NOTE**
>
> If there is no dot in the URL, then the URL is treated as internal. If there is a dot in the URL, it is treated as internal only if the domain suffix is in the internal sites list.

Exchange Management Shell Commands

To use the Exchange Management shell to enable access to Windows file shares (UNC paths) for end users who have selected the Public Computer option on the login screen, use the following command:

```
Set-OwaVirtualDirectory -Identity "owa (default web site)"
-UNCAccessOnPublicComputersEnabled $true
```

For SharePoint access, the command is almost identical:

```
Set-OwaVirtualDirectory -Identity "owa (default web site)"
-WSSAccessOnPublicComputersEnabled $true
```

For private computers, the command is the same as except the word *Private* is used instead of *Public*:

```
Set-OwaVirtualDirectory -Identity "owa (default web site)"
-UNCAccessonPrivateComputersEnabled $true
```

FIGURE 19.12
Configuring internal
domain names

By default, all servers are blocked; therefore, to grant access you must add servers to the list. To allow access to servers server1 and server2, you would use the following command:

```
Set-OwaVirtualDirectory -Identity "owa (default web site)
-RemoteDocumentsAllowedServers server1,server2
```

To allow access to a DFS share, the command would be almost the same:

```
Set-OwaVirtualDirectory -Identity "owa (default web site)
-RemoteDocumentsAllowedServers domain.tld
```

When it comes to blocking servers, you have a number of options. The first option is to set all servers not listed as blocked, which is the default option. The second option is to allow access to all servers except the ones explicitly blocked. Depending on your environment, both options may be of benefit. However, remember that you have to set the options on each CAS server.

To block servers specifically, use the following command:

```
Set-OwaVirtualDirectory -Identity "owa (default web site)"
-RemoteDocumentsBlockedServers server1,server2
```

To set the default action for servers not listed, use the following command:

```
Set-OwaVirtualDirectory -Identity "owa (default web site)"
-RemoteDocumentsActionForUnknownServers Allow
```

Replace *Allow* with *Block* to block access, as in this example:

```
Set-OwaVirtualDirectory -Identity "owa (default web site)"
-RemoteDocumentsActionForUnknownServers Block
```

Using Outlook Anywhere

Outlook Anywhere is the new name for RPC over HTTP. Wrapping all the RPC traffic that Outlook requires in to a single HTTP traffic stream allows Outlook to connect to your Exchange server over the Internet, through your own firewall and any firewall on the client side, without having to open a large number of ports.

Ideally deployed with an SSL certificate, you only have to open a single port, 443. If you have deployed an SSL certificate to secure OWA and Exchange ActiveSync, you can use the same certificate for Outlook Anywhere.

With careful network configuration using a split DNS system, you can also use Outlook Anywhere inside your own firewall, allowing mobile clients to come and go from your network without having to reconfigure their machines. When successfully deployed, it should be totally transparent to the end user.

To use Outlook Anywhere, the client OS needs to be Windows XP Service Pack 2 or higher with Outlook 2003 or later installed. As with Outlook Web Access, Outlook Anywhere requires a server with the Client Access role installed.

TIP

When setting up Outlook Anywhere for the first time, if possible, configure your network so that the name on your SSL certificate works both inside and outside the firewall. Then get everything to work inside first. This ensures that any firewall problems are not causing a connection failure.

SPLIT DNS

Split DNS (aka Split Brain DNS) describes a configuration in which you have two DNS servers that deliver different results to a DNS query, depending on which server is used. You can use Split DNS to deploy a single name for Outlook Anywhere, Outlook Web Access, or any other web service that is accessible both internally and externally. Setting up a Split DNS system is very simple, but it does take some care:

1. Establish what services are being accessed externally using your external domain name. This will probably include your website and possibly an FTP site. If you have access to the domain name DNS records, take a look at what hosts are configured for your domain name. Make a note of any that are not configured to point to resources that are inside your network.

2. Create a new DNS zone on your internal DNS servers with a name that matches your external DNS domain name. You may already have one if your Active Directory domain uses your external domain name. In this new zone, add your external host with their external IP addresses.

3. Add your internal hosts to the DNS zone.

Once the zone has been set up, replicate it to other internal DNS zones. To test, drop in to a command prompt. If you ping www.yourdomain.com (where yourdomain is the external domain name), then you should get a response back from the external IP address where your website is hosted.

If you ping mail.yourdomain.com (where mail.yourdomain.com is an internal host — the Exchange server for example), you should get a response back from the Exchange server's internal IP address.

Any failures, such as the wrong IP address or unknown host errors, mean that the DNS zone isn't set correctly.

NOTE

Outlook Anywhere should be run over an SSL-secured connection. This ensures that the username and password information passes over the Internet encrypted. Although the dialog boxes in Outlook make it seem that you can run the feature without SSL, in practice, trying to get it to run without SSL is complex.

Configuring Exchange for Outlook Anywhere

Configuration of Outlook Anywhere is quite straightforward, which is a nice change from how it was configured in Exchange 2003, which required a number of Registry changes to the Exchange server and domain controller if you were not using a front-end/back-end scenario. It is enabled on a per-server basis.

Step 1: SSL certificate considerations   We discuss SSL certificate use in Chapter 20, "Securing Exchange Server." However, remember that for this feature to work correctly, the certificate needs to be trusted by the client. Outlook cannot cope with any SSL certificate prompts.

Step 2: Install the RPC Proxy component   Before you make any changes to Exchange, the RPC Proxy component needs to be installed. You will find this in Add/Remove Programs, Add/Remove Windows Components. The option is under Network Components. After the component is installed, a reboot should not be required.

Step 3: Enabling Outlook Anywhere on Exchange Server   As with all components in Exchange 2007, you can enable the Outlook Anywhere option using the Exchange Management Console or the Management Shell.

To configure Outlook Anywhere using the EMS, use a command similar to this one:

```
Enable-OutlookAnywhere -Server:'ServerName'
-ExternalHostName:'ExternalHostName'-ExternalAuthenticationMethod:'Basic'
-SSLOffloading:$false
```

In this command, *ServerName* is the real name of the server and *ExternalHostName* is the name by which the server is known on the Internet and the name used in your SSL certificate. For example, if your server is known as exchange01 and the certificate is in the name of mail.domain.com, then the command would be as follows:

```
Enable-OutlookAnywhere -Server:'exchange01' -ExternalHostName:'mail.domain.com'
-ExternalAuthenticationMethod:'Basic' -SSLOffloading:$false
```

> **NOTE**
>
> External authentication allows you to adjust the authentication type that is supported by the server. In a change from Exchange 2003, you can use either basic or integrated, but not both.

> **WARNING**
>
> SSL offloading is a process where the SSL certificate is held elsewhere — for example, on another proxy server or appliance. If you do not have SSL managed elsewhere, then having this option enabled will cause the feature to fail to work correctly.

If you want to configure Outlook Anywhere using the Exchange Management Console, follow these steps:

1. First, open the console, expand Server Configuration work center, and open the Client Access subcontainer.

2. Select the server on which you want to enable Outlook Anywhere. In the Actions pane on the right, select Enable Outlook Anywhere.

3. The Enable Outlook Anywhere Wizard (shown in Figure 19.13) appears. Enter the external name that the clients will be using to access the server — this should match your SSL certificate. Select your authentication method. We suggest starting with Basic.

4. Once configured, the options for Outlook Anywhere can be changed by selecting the server under Client Access and choosing Properties. An additional tab will be seen for Outlook Anywhere configuration (shown in Figure 19.14).

Configuring Outlook Client for Outlook Anywhere

On Outlook 2007, you can configure Outlook Anywhere via the Autodiscover service or manually. You must configure Outlook 2003 manually. Older versions of Outlook do not support Outlook Anywhere.

FIGURE 19.13
Enabling Outlook
Anywhere using the
Exchange Management
Console

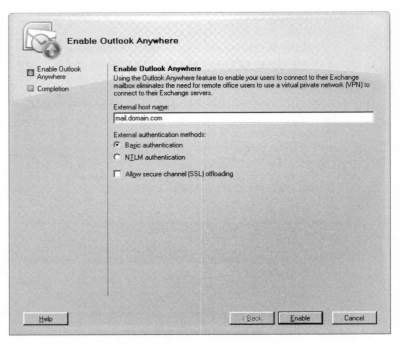

In all cases, you must have Outlook installed on Windows XP Service Pack 2 or higher. It can be any version of Windows XP, including Home and Media Center. For Vista, any version may be used, not just the business editions.

Where the host machine is not a member of the domain or forest that Exchange is installed in, you will need to take extra care with configuring the client.

AUTOMATICALLY CONFIGURING OUTLOOK CLIENT FOR OUTLOOK ANYWHERE (OUTLOOK 2007 ONLY)

You can carry out automatic configuration of Outlook Anywhere by using the Autodiscover service of Exchange 2007, which is available only with Outlook 2007. If you are using Outlook 2003, then you will need to manually configure the client.

However, if this is your first time with Outlook Anywhere, you should manually configure it to begin with, and then move to Autodiscover configuration once you have a working deployment. We discuss Autodiscover setup and configuration in Chapter 17, "Supporting Outlook 2007."

TIP

Test the SSL certificate before you try configuring any Outlook client. Open Internet Explorer, and browse to https://*mail.domain*.com/rpc (where `mail.domain.com` is the name on your SSL certificate). If you get an SSL certificate prompt, then the client will fail to connect correctly. Outlook cannot cope with any SSL certificate prompts.

FIGURE 19.14
Modifying the Outlook
Anywhere configuration

MANUALLY CONFIGURING THE OUTLOOK CLIENT FOR OUTLOOK ANYWHERE: LAN-BASED OR DOMAIN CLIENTS (OUTLOOK 2003 AND HIGHER)

If you just enabled Outlook Anywhere, we recommend that you carry out your initial testing and configuration of the client manually. This will allow you to troubleshoot the process and configuration. Once it is working correctly, you can use the settings with Autodiscover for Outlook 2007. Outlook 2003 users will need to use the manual setup process, which we will now describe. If you have configured Outlook 2003 to use RPC over HTTP with Exchange 2003 in the past, you'll see that the process is identical. Outlook 2007 changes some of the labels.

Carry out your first configuration inside the network using a machine that is part of the domain. By doing the initial setup inside, you can be sure that everything is working correctly. Once you have a working connection, you can move outside of your LAN and then your domain to confirm connectivity. Follow these steps:

1. Configure Outlook in the usual way, and confirm that it is connecting to the Exchange server correctly.

2. Open the property page for the account. This varies with the version of Outlook. In Outlook 2003, choose Tools ➤ Email Accounts ➤ View or Change Existing E-mail Accounts, and then click Next. Choose Change to access the account settings.

In Outlook 2007, choose Tools ➤ Account Settings, and on the E-mail tab select the Exchange account. Then choose Change.

3. Click the More Settings button, which is in the lower-right corner. Click the Connection tab.

4. Enable the option Connect to Microsoft Exchange using HTTP, which is under Outlook Anywhere (Outlook 2007) or Exchange over the Internet (Outlook 2003). Then click the Exchange Proxy Settings button.

5. Complete the boxes to match your environment. You use only the hostname when entering addresses; no directory name is required.

6. The first box, Use This URL to Connect to My Proxy Server for Exchange, should match the name on your SSL certificate.

7. Enable both Connect Using SSL Only and Only Connect to Proxy Servers That Have This Principal Name in Their Certificate (Outlook 2007) or Mutually Authenticate the Session When Connecting with SSL (Outlook 2003).

When it comes to the speed options, we find that you need to have both enabled for the feature to work reliably when the client machine is off site. Although in theory Outlook should be able to detect the speed of the connection to the server, with the growth of home networks, it gets easily confused and attempts to make a conventional TCP/IP connection to the Exchange server when that isn't possible. By forcing the connection to always use HTTP that is adverted. That does mean you need to ensure that the name entered under Use This URL to Connect to My Proxy Server for Exchange: box correctly resolves inside your network as well as outside.

8. Finally, set the authentication settings to match what you set on the Exchange server when enabling Outlook Anywhere.

9. Click Apply and OK to get out of each box, and restart Outlook.

You can confirm whether Outlook is making a connection to the Exchange server using HTTPS in one of two ways:

◆ Close Outlook completely; consider using Task Manager to ensure that it has closed because it isn't unusual for another application to keep the application running. Then choose Start ➢ Run, type **outlook.exe /rpcdiag**, and press Enter. Outlook will start normally, but it will also include an additional diagnostics box. This will show the connection method being used. All connections should show HTTPS.

◆ The diagnostics box can also be started once Outlook is running. While holding down the Ctrl key, right-click the Outlook icon in the system tray next to your clock. On the menu, you will see an additional item, Connection Status. Select that and the diagnostics box will open.

That Connection Status box is also useful if you are troubleshooting a conventional TCP/IP Outlook connection because it can show you which domain controller Outlook is connecting to.

MANUALLY CONFIGURING THE OUTLOOK CLIENT FOR OUTLOOK ANYWHERE: EXTERNAL CLIENTS THAT ARE NOT MEMBERS OF THE DOMAIN (OUTLOOK 2003 AND LATER)

Outlook Anywhere makes it possible for a client machine that is not part of your Windows domain to connect to Exchange and have the full feature set of an Exchange client available to them. This is what hosted Exchange companies do.

However, if Outlook is not on the same network as the Exchange server, getting it to use Outlook Anywhere can be a little fiddly. Ideally, your clients should be using Outlook 2007 because this allows you to use the Autodiscover service to configure Outlook automatically. However, if your end users are using Outlook 2003 as a client, then manual configuration is the only option.

Before you begin, make sure that the feature is working internally with a domain member by following the instructions earlier in this chapter for configuring a client on the domain and network. If you have not verified that the feature is working beforehand, then troubleshooting any problems becomes a lot more difficult.

The configuration process for machines that are outside of the firewall is almost identical to the process for those that are inside:

1. Configure Outlook as you would ordinarily, including entering the Exchange server's real name, not the external name from the certificate. However, *do not* click the Check Name button because the name check process will fail. Instead, click More Settings. You will get a prompt about the Exchange server being unavailable. Accept that. Then you will see another box prompting you to check the name again. Click Cancel to clear that message. That should open the More Settings dialog box. Click the Connection tab.

2. This stage is identical to being on the LAN. Enable the option Connect to Microsoft Exchange using HTTP, which is under Outlook Anywhere (Outlook 2007) or Exchange over the Internet (Outlook 2003). Then click the Exchange Proxy Settings button.

3. Again, fill in the boxes to match your environment. In this case, the speed options don't really apply because you want to always use HTTP, so enable both options. With the

authentication, choose the same one you selected when enabling the service on the Exchange server.

4. After configuring the settings, click OK or Apply to close the windows until you get back to the Check Name dialog box. Click Check Name. Outlook will now prompt you for credentials. Enter the credentials in the format of *domain\username* and then the password.

   For example, if your domain name was e2007 and your username was bob.smith, you would enter e2007\bob.smith. Don't bother with the Remember My Password option at this time. Once authentication is successful, the server name and username should be underlined. Click Next and Finish to close the Account Setup Wizard.

You can now start Outlook as usual. Because the computer is not a member of the domain, you will need to authenticate to the domain that Exchange is located in, so you will get a username and password prompt. This will happen each time Outlook is started and cannot be avoided.

For password maintenance of end users connecting to Exchange in this way, suggest that they change their password through Outlook Web Access.

After ensuring that Outlook Anywhere is working correctly, you need to ensure that the relevant port is open on your firewall. If you are using SSL, then only port 443 is required — no other special changes are required.

Refer to Chapter 20, "Securing Exchange Server," for full information on setting your firewall to work with Outlook Anywhere and other Exchange features.

Windows Mobile and ActiveSync

Currently two ActiveSync applications are available from Microsoft. First, the traditional ActiveSync is an application that is installed on to the desktop machine and allows synchronization through Outlook. Second, with Exchange 2003, Microsoft introduced Exchange ActiveSync (EAS), which allows synchronization directly to the Exchange server over a network or Internet connection. This was initially on-demand sync but Exchange 2003 service pack 2 enabled the "push mail" feature using HTTP or HTTPS. Push e-mail enables e-mail to be synchronized with the device as new messages arrive; when a message arrives in the user's Inbox, the Exchange server notifies connected mobile devices that a new message must be synchronized to the device.

Exchange 2007 takes EAS and has further enhanced it, although to take full advantage of the new features in EAS, you need to be using Windows Mobile 6.0 (aka Crossbow), which is still in development as this book is being written.

Exchange ActiveSync was available with Windows Mobile 2003 but really became popular only with Windows Mobile 2005. To use the push technology, you need to have a device with the Messaging and Security Feature Pack (MSFP) installed. This is not available as a separate download but will be part of a software update from the handset supplier.

TIP

Microsoft Messaging and Security Feature Pack updates for mobile devices or Windows Mobile 6 updates must be obtained from the device vendor or the cell phone provider, not Microsoft.

If you have purchased a device since approximately June 2006, it almost certainly will come with a version of Windows Mobile 5.0 with MSFP. Many devices that run Windows Mobile 5 can be upgraded to the MSFP version..

How Can You Tell Whether Your Device Has the MSFP?

You can identify whether your handset has the MSFP update in two ways. In both cases you need to look at the version information. This will be found in Settings ➢ System under the About applet.

You need to look at the version information. You will see a string that is something like OS 5.1.195 (Build 14847.2.0.0). With some handsets, the build number says Messaging and Security Feature Pack. If that is the case, you know for sure. If yours does not, then you need to look at the build number. The key element is the last three digits. To have the MSFP installed, it needs to be 2.0.0 or higher. Build 2.0.0 was the first build to have the MSFP update.

NOTE

We wrote this chapter using Windows Mobile 5.0 and are presuming that you are using a Windows Mobile–based device with at least that version of the software. You can find instructions for the older versions of Windows Mobile on Microsoft's website.

> **TIP**
>
> As an administrator, you will want to test Windows Mobile for yourself; however, getting a hold of a device with the relevant software may be difficult. Microsoft has released an emulator for Windows Mobile, which was originally designed for developer use but is now available as a stand-alone product. You can install this onto your workstation and connect to the Exchange server over your network. At the time of writing, you can download the emulator from `http://preview.tinyurl`
> `.com/otdx4`.

Configuring Exchange to Support ActiveSync

Exchange ActiveSync (EAS) should be enabled by default from the standard installation of the Client Access server role. You can confirm whether this is the case by checking for the presence of a number of elements in IIS Manager. In the IIS Manager under Default Web Site (see Figure 19.15), check to see whether the virtual directory Microsoft-Server-ActiveSync exists.

FIGURE 19.15
Viewing
Exchange-specific
virtual directories and
application pools

You can also check the Exchange-related application pools. For example, right-click the `MSExchangeSyncAppPool` application pool. If Start is available, then EAS is not running. Choose Start to enable the application pool.

You can do additional configuration of ActiveSync through the Exchange Management Console. Under Server Configuration, choose the Exchange ActiveSync tab. Right-click the virtual directory listed and choose Properties. You'll see three tabs. The first tab, General, allows you to set the internal and external URL for ActiveSync. The second tab, Authentication, allows you to control authentication, including whether to use client certificates. The third tab allows you to control remote file server access. This is identical in operation to remote file server access through Outlook Web Access but is not available with the current versions of Windows Mobile.

For Exchange Management Shell configuration, you use two cmdletss:

◆ The cmdlet `New-ActiveSyncVirtualDirectory` will allow you to create a new virtual directory for another website on the same server.

◆ The cmdlet `Set-ActiveSycVirtualDirectory` allows you to change settings for the ActiveSync virtual directory. This includes settings not available to you through Exchange Management Console. This command will enable basic authentication on a server named EXCHANGE01:

```
Set-ActiveSyncVirtualDirectory-Identity"EXCHANGE01\microsoft-server-activesync"
-BasicAuthEnabled:$true
```

Defining an ActiveSync Policy

An ActiveSync policy allows you to define certain settings for the devices. With Exchange 2003, the policy applied to all devices, or there were exceptions for certain users. The level of control was very low. You can now have different settings for different users, allowing you more control over the devices — possibly depending on their job function.

ActiveSync policies are Exchange organization wide, so they are set in the Organization Configuration work center in the Client Access subcontainer. The policy is divided in to two main areas: access and password.

The General property page is for access-related settings. You can define whether attachments are downloaded to the device, configure access to UNC and WSS servers, and choose whether nonprovisionable devices can be configured.

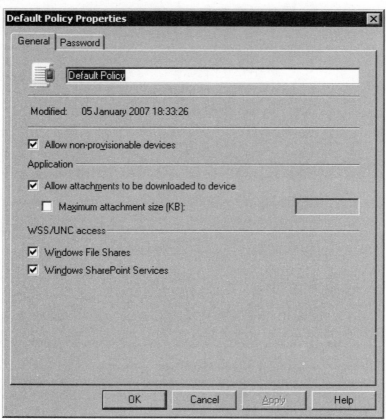

Nonprovisionable devices are devices that do not support the Autodiscover service. Most sites will need to enable non-provisionable devices, at least initially until their devices are all users are using a version of Windows Mobile that supports provisioning via Autodiscover.

The Password property page is for the password policy. The settings on this tab are fairly self-explanatory. If you want to be able to take advantage of the remote wipe features, you need to require a password. If you do not, when you attempt to wipe the device, the end user will be asked to allow enforcement of a password policy. By saying no, they can maintain access to the device. Allow Simple Password is a policy that allows the end user to set a password such as 1234. If you have policies regarding passwords, you may not want to enable that option.

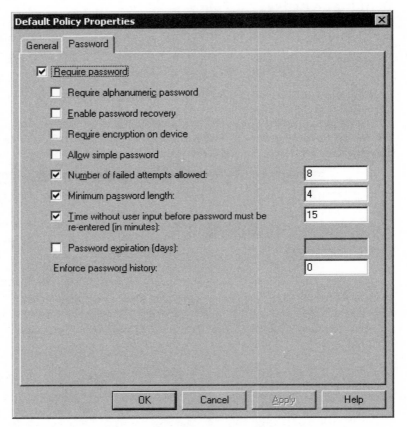

You can have more than one ActiveSync policy; to create another one, select New ActiveSync Policy from the Actions pane in Exchange Management Console, or run the cmdlet New-ActiveSyncPolicy with the required parameters.

This command will create a new policy called Sales, with Device Password enabled:

```
New-ActiveSyncMailboxPolicy -Name:"Sales" -DevicePasswordEnabled:$true
```

You can assign a policy to each user as required. To set a policy to a user through Exchange Management Console, open up the Recipient Configuration work center and select Mailbox. Find the user that you want to assign the policy to, and select Properties from the Actions pane.

Click the Mailbox Features tab and choose Exchange ActiveSync, and then click Properties. Enable the Apply an Exchange ActiveSync Policy option, and click Browse to choose the policy. Then click OK/Apply as required to close the user properties.

If you want to set multiple users at the same time, you need to use the Exchange Management Shell. To set the policy through the Exchange Management Shell, use the `Set-CASMailbox` command. For example, to set the policy Sales on user bsmith, you would run the following:

```
Set-CASMailbox David.Sengupta -ActiveSyncMailboxPolicy
(Get-ActiveSyncMailboxPolicy "Sales").Identity
```

If you want to set a policy to all users, which may be a good way to start off, you have to use a combination of commands. This command will set the policy Default Policy on all users:

```
Get-Mailbox | Set-CASMailbox -ActiveSyncMailboxPolicy
(Get-ActiveSyncMailboxPolicy "Default Policy").Identity
```

Configuring a Windows Mobile Device

This section guides you through configuring a Windows Mobile device. These instructions and screen shots were created using the Windows Mobile 5.0 emulator, which is running build 2.0.0. Therefore, you may find that a few screens look slightly different to what is shown here. The entries are identical, so it should be easy enough to adapt to the later versions of Windows Mobile that are released after this book is published.

To configure your device to sync with Exchange, follow these steps:

1. Select ActiveSync from Programs. If this is the first time you have configured ActiveSync, you should simply select the text "set up your device to sync with it." If you already have ActiveSync configured to synchronize with a desktop, then you can change the settings from the menu, or use ActiveSync on the desktop to configure synchronization with a server.

2. You will be asked for the server address. This needs to be the external name of the Exchange server — for example, mail.domain.com. If you are going to use SSL, then the name needs to match what is on the certificate. The certificate also needs to be trusted by the device (either because you are using a commercial certificate that has a root certificate in the device or because you have imported the root or client certificate into the device in advance).

3. Enter the username, password, and domain for the account that is being used. If you want to sync automatically, you will need to save the password.

WARNING

Saving your password is a security risk, but it could also cause your account to be locked out if you change your password. When changing your Windows password, remember to change the password on the device as well.

4. Whether you want to set the advanced settings is up to you. Advanced settings deal with item conflict (default is Replace the Item on My Device) and event logging (default is None).

5. On the last screen, you can set what is synchronized over the server connection. Most users will be configuring all four options (Inbox, Calendar, Contacts, and Tasks). You cannot sync the Notes folder over the air, so if you are using the Notes feature in Outlook, you will need to continue to use the desktop ActiveSync as well.

6. You can adjust how much is synchronized for some of the types, such as Calendar and E-mail. Select the type and then choose Settings to adjust. Calendar allows you to change how much of your calendar is synchronized. E-Mail allows you to change how much old e-mail is synchronized and whether attachments come across.

7. After you press Finish, the device will attempt to sync for the first time. If there is a lot of e-mail to come across, then you should have the device connected to the network via USB ActiveSync for that first sync.

TIP

Exchange ActiveSync will sync over a wireless network connection. However, the push technology for e-mail does not operate over wireless. That requires a mobile phone connection. Furthermore, if you have ActiveSync set to push, you will need to initiate a manual sync to sync over the wireless network.

Managing a Windows Mobile Device

At some point one of your users will lose their device, or you will need to wipe it. Management of the Windows Mobile devices is now built in to Exchange. You can manage the devices in three ways.

First, the end user can manage it through Outlook Web Access. The administrator can turn off this option if they want. However, if you have lots of remote users, you may want to enable this feature so that the users can wipe the devices as soon as they realize that they lost it. Mobile device management is within Options of OWA (shown in Figure 19.16) once the user has logged in.

FIGURE 19.16
Managing a mobile device through OWA

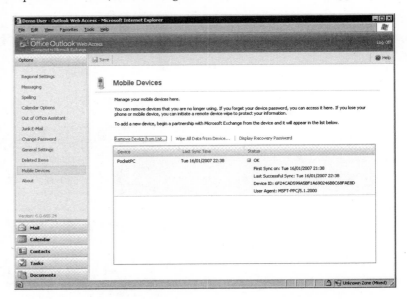

Second, you can manage the device through the Exchange Management Console. You can manage the device by right-clicking the user in Recipients Configuration work center and choosing Manage Mobile Device; this runs the Manage Mobile Device Wizard (shown in Figure 19.17).

> **TIP**
>
> The Manage Mobile Device task option appears only if there is a mobile device associated with a mailbox.

Change the action to Perform a Remote Wipe to Clear Mobile Device Data and then click Clear. You can go back in to this screen to confirm that the wipe has taken place.

Finally, you can manage the device through Exchange Management Shell. A series of command will allow you to wipe the device. To wipe the device through EMC, you need to perform two steps:

1. The first step is to get the identity of the device. To get the identity of the device that is used by user Chuck.Swanson, run the following command:

```
Get-ActiveSyncDeviceStatistics -Mailbox Chuck.Swanson | FL Identity
```

FIGURE 19.17
Managing a mobile
device

2. After you have the device ID, you can send the wipe command. To wipe a device with the
ID of WM_Chuck.Swanson11, use this command:

```
Clear-ActiveSyncDevice -Identity WM_chuck.swanson11
```

3. To confirm that the wipe was successful, use the following command:

```
Get-ActiveSyncDeviceStatistics -Mailbox Chuck.Swanson
```

Supporting POP3 and IMAP4 Clients

IMAP4 and POP3 are probably the most basic e-mail protocols in use. With SMTP, they are
the most straightforward of the e-mail delivery mechanisms, and virtually every e-mail server
available supports them. However, they do have their drawbacks, particularly when used with
Exchange.

For example, if you collect your e-mail with POP3 from your Exchange mailbox, all e-mail in
the mailbox will be marked as read whether or not the message has actually been read on
the client.

The other major issue with POP3 is that it is designed to remove the e-mail from the server and
store it locally. It is very easy to make an error in configuration and remove all of the e-mail from
the server. While there are options to leave e-mail on the server, it's easy to overlook them.

Things are a little better with IMAP4 because the e-mail is actually stored on the server.
However, you still are limited on the functionality from Exchange compared to the full Outlook
client or Outlook Web Access.

As such, POP3/IMAP4 access should be the last access protocol of choice, and where possible
you should not be supporting it. However, in some environments such as academic environments
POP3 and IMAP4 clients are very popular and must still be supported.

POP3 and IMAP4 are disabled by default in Exchange 2007, and there is no GUI configuration available through Exchange Management Console. You must configure the protocols using the Exchange Management Shell.

Configuration of SMTP for use by POP3/IMAP4 clients can be carried out using the Management Console. Although, you may want to look at deploying TLS/SMTP (see Chapter 20, "Securing Exchange Server") because the standard port 25 is often blocked for accessing remote SMTP servers from home user type connections, meaning the POP3/IMAP4 clients will be unable to send e-mail through your server.

Either way, because of the nature of the protocols, keeping a copy of the messages for compliance reasons is almost impossible. The end user could send the message through another SMTP server, so there will be no trace of the message on your server.

If you need to track e-mail messages for compliance reasons, you should look at using a MAPI connection such as Outlook Web Access or Outlook Anywhere.

Configuring Exchange to Support POP3 and IMAP4 Clients

Configuring Exchange Server 2007 to support POP3 or IMAP4 clients requires a couple of steps. These including enabling the services and configuring the Client Access servers to support these protocols.

ENABLING THE SERVICES

Before clients can connect to the POP3 or IMAP4 services, the services must be enabled and started because they are set to start manually. You can enable POP3 and IMAP4 in two ways. As with Exchange 2003, you can change the service in the Services console (shown in Figure 19.18) from Disabled to Automatic and then start the service.

You can also enable the services through Exchange Management Shell. To enable POP3, use the following command:

```
Set-service msExchangePOP3 -startuptype automatic
```

FIGURE 19.18
Configuring the POP3 service

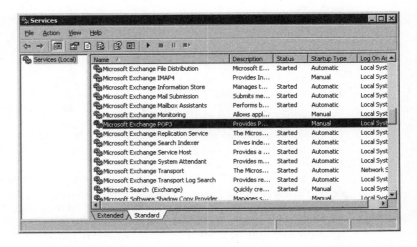

Once it's enabled, you need to start the service:

```
Start-service -service msExchangePOP3
```

For IMAP, the procedure is almost identical:

```
Set-service msExchangeIMAP4 -startuptype automatic
```

To start the service, use the following command:

```
Start-service msExchangeIMAP4
```

CONFIGURING POP3 AND IMAP4: SERVER

Once you have enabled the services, you can configure them. This must be carried out through the Exchange Management Shell. The default settings may be suitable for you. You can check the current settings using the following command:

POP3: `get-popsettings`

IMAP4: `get-imapsettings`

The only additional configuration that you may want to cover is enabling TLS/SSL support. Support of TLS is covered in Chapter 20, "Securing Exchange Server."

CONFIGURING POP3 AND IMAP4: MAILBOXES

By default, all user accounts are enabled for POP3 and IMAP4 access. Therefore, you may want to review the accounts and disable that functionality for those users who will not be accessing Exchange using POP3 or IMAP4. You do this using the `Set-CASMailbox` command.

For example, to disable POP3 for a user nick.gillott@somorita.com, use the following command:

```
Set-CASMailbox -identity nick.gillott@somorita.com -POPEnabled:$false
```

You can view the status of the mailboxes simply by entering the command `Get-CASMailbox`, which will display all mailboxes in the Exchange organization and whether they are enabled or not.

CONFIGURING A RECEIVE CONNECTOR FOR USE WITH POP3 AND IMAP4

POP3/IMAP clients need to have an SMTP connector to send their outbound e-mail through. For Exchange 2007, that means a Receive connector must be configured to accept their messages and allow them to be relayed through the server to the clients.

There should already be a Connector configured that is suitable for use, which is called Client *servername*. You can see this through Exchange Management Console or by the Exchange Management Shell command `Get-ReceiveConnector`.

Very little configuration of this default connector should be required. Note that this connector is configured to use port 587, which is the TLS port. It uses the certificate that is installed on the

Exchange server during installation. If you intend to have clients relay e-mail through the server on this port, then you need to either import the certificate to their machine so that it is trusted or replace the certificate with one from a trusted CA.

If you want to use the standard TCP port 25 to relay e-mail, you need to review the configuration of the server connector.

In all cases, basic authentication needs to be enabled on the connector because it is the only type of authentication that SMTP clients support. You can also use basic authentication, requiring TLS.

More information is available on Receive connectors in Chapter 18, "Delivering E-mail."

Configuring a POP3 or IMAP4 Client

You will no doubt be familiar with the configuration of POP3/IMAP clients and SMTP. For Exchange, it is almost the same as any Internet e-mail account you may have configured.

For the server address of the POP3, IMAP, and SMTP servers, you should use a hostname. Although you can use an IP address, if you ever need to change the IP address of the server, it is far easier to change a single DNS entry than to try to get many users to update their e-mail client configuration.

What you use for your hostnames is up to you — as long as they resolve correctly on the Internet. You may already have a hostname setup that points to your Exchange server used for MX records. If so, you could use the same hostname in the account settings. Alternatively, if you think that you might change the configuration in the future so that the servers are different, you may want to use pop3.domain.com, imap.domain.com, and smtp.domain.com, with them all pointing at the same IP address. If you need to change them later on, simply adjust the DNS records.

If you are using TLS/SSL for account access, ensure that you change the port setting in the e-mail client to use the alternative port. This is often found in the advanced settings.

Finally, you need to enter credentials. For Exchange, these credentials need to be in a specific format:

◆ For POP3 and IMAP access, it is in the format of *domain\username\alias*.

◆ For SMTP access, it is in the format of *domain\username*.

◆ In both cases, you can also use the UPN, *username@domain.local*.

The choice of authentication format is up to you and what you think will be easiest to support. We suggest deciding on one format and then sticking to it so that it is easier to write documentation and help guides while maintaining some consistency.

Summary

Access to e-mail away from the desktop is now very important to most users. Exchange 2007 provides more options than ever before for that access. The end user now has full access to their e-mail wherever and whenever they need it, and the security of the network is maintained.

Providing the necessary remote options for your users is important. In this chapter, we covered a couple of different ways that you can provide access to Exchange from anywhere.

Outlook Web Access provides much of the same functionality that you would get sitting at your desk and using regular Outlook, but through a Web browser. Exchange Server 2007 OWA has once again been improved to provide the user with more functionality than ever before.

For users that need a full-featured e-mail client even while traveling, Exchange Server 2007 provides Outlook Anywhere. Outlook Anywhere allows Outlook 2003 and Outlook 2007 clients to connect to their Exchange server using RPC over HTTP or RPC over HTTPS and synchronize their e-mail without the complexity involved in connecting multiple RPC ports through your company firewall. All that is necessary is port 80 or port 443 (recommended).

Windows Mobile and ActiveSync users can be provide with access to their mailbox from their mobile device. They can synchronize their mailbox from anywhere they can get a cell phone or WiFi signal.

Finally, while in some organizations POP3 and IMAP4 clients have been replaced completely by web-browser-based clients or Outlook, many organizations still use POP3 and IMAP. Exchange continues to support these clients.

In the next chapter, we will look at some of the considerations necessary to ensure that these services are provided to authorized Internet users while at the same time ensuring that the data and server resources are properly secured.

Part 7

Security and Tracking Activities

In this section you will learn to:

Chapter 20

Securing Exchange Server

Regardless of whether your Exchange servers are accessed by users on a local area network, whether your users receive e-mail from the Internet, or whether you are providing web services such as Outlook Web Access, ActiveSync, and Outlook Anywhere to Internet users, you need to keep security in mind. You'll be surprised how easy it is to make Exchange Server 2007 reasonably secure.

During setup, the person who installs Exchange server chooses the specific Exchange server roles that a particular server role will host. Only the software necessary to support the chosen roles is actually installed. This is in contrast to the installation process for Exchange 2000/2003; most Exchange services had to be installed and then the installer would later disable services that were not necessary. An Exchange Server 2007 server that is hosting only the Mailbox server role will not have unnecessary services installed and running.

In this chapter, we will cover many of the common steps you can easily perform to ensure that your Exchange server is as secure as possible without breaking your budget. We will also cover firewalls, perimeter networks, reverse proxies, and SMTP relays, all of which will help you to solidify your security and help you to sleep more soundly at night.

Topics in this chapter include the following:

◆ Security basics

◆ Using the Security Configuration Wizard

◆ Using Secure Sockets Layer (SSL) with Exchange

◆ Implementing message hygiene and multilayer security

◆ Using a reverse proxy to protect web services

Understanding Exchange Server Security Basics

When you are planning the procedures, technology, and precautions that you will implement to ensure better security for your Exchange server infrastructure, you should aim for a goal that we refer to as being "reasonably secure." This means you are taking precautions and implementing technology that is "at least" as good as the other companies in your own industry, and it will mean something entirely different to a small business that has no confidential or proprietary data in their mail system than it will to, for example, a health care provider.

Starting with the Obvious

Anyone experienced in fighting unauthorized intruders will tell you that malicious hackers usually attempt an attack by looking for the "low-hanging fruit." They look for known vulnerabilities and a weak defensive perimeter. So let's start with the more obvious security precautions and procedures. Many readers will look at this list and think it is painfully simple, but we find many organizations still miss the most basic points when securing their Exchange systems and even their networks.

◆ Your internal network should always be protected by a firewall. More on this later in this chapter.

◆ Physical server security is almost as important as firewall security. Ensure that servers are physically secured and in an environmentally controlled place. Backup media should be physically secured.

◆ No unnecessary Windows services, third-party software, or beta software should be installed on any Exchange server.

◆ Keep all operating systems and application software (Exchange included) up-to-date. You should plan to apply server-side critical security patches and updates within 4 to 6 weeks of release. In most situations, service packs should be applied within 8 to 12 weeks of release; this is dependent on verifying that no incompatibilities exist with current software or hardware.

◆ Administrator accounts (both local and domain) should be renamed and should have complex passwords assigned. The guest account should be disabled.

◆ Limit the membership the Administrators and Power Users groups to only absolutely necessary users. Limit the membership in Domain Admins, Enterprise Admins, and the domain's Administrators groups.

◆ Auditing and logging should be enabled on all Exchange servers. More information can be found on security logging and protocol logs in Chapter 21, "Logging, Auditing, and Monitoring."

◆ Administrative and operator accounts should not have mailboxes. Practice separation of administrative responsibilities from day-to-day tasks such as using e-mail, word processing applications, and so on.

◆ Do not install e-mail client software on your servers and do not use your servers to surf the Internet.

Thinking about Intruders

Almost all discussions of security, malicious hackers, and protecting your information infrastructure focus on protecting resources from being compromised from outside. While that will yield useful precautions and information for consideration, security violations do not always come from outside of your firewall. Employees and users from business partners may also be a source of data theft, data compromise, information leaks, and other security events. With that in mind, here are a few tips to consider:

◆ Enable mailbox logon diagnostic logging so that if necessary you can review who has accessed each mailbox.

◆ Network connections between business partners must be properly firewalled and audit. This not only protects your own information, it ensures accountability on the part of your own employees. Business partners should be provided with access to only the specific resources they require and nothing more. This is also true of resources that your own employees may need from your partner.

◆ Practice the principal of least permissions not only for administrators but also for users. Security group membership must be audited regularly to ensure that users do not have excessive rights and permissions.

Understanding Message Security Types

Messaging security can actually mean a lot of different things to different people. So let's quickly review the different types of security involved:

Operating system and Exchange Server software security Securing and protecting the operating system and the Exchange Server applications (services) is probably what most people think about when they think about Exchange Server security. And that is what much of this chapter discusses. This encompasses ensuring that the attack surface of the operating system and Exchange services has been minimized. We do this by employing firewalls, operating system/application updates, good physical security, and solid administrative procedures.

The security of e-mail data in transit Protecting e-mail data while the data is in transit usually involves some type of network encryption. This could be Secure Sockets Layer (SSL)/ Transport Layer Security (TLS) or IP security (IPSec). We protect data in transit if we are concerned about the physical layer of our network (or the networks on which e-mail traffic crosses) being compromised and allowing someone to perform protocol analysis. The Outlook client can implement built-in encryption and encrypt message traffic between the client and a Mailbox server. Implementing HTTPS on Client Access servers ensures that web clients (such as Outlook Web Access, Windows Mobile ActiveSync, or Outlook Anywhere) transmit data securely.

The security of e-mail data at rest Most of the time, e-mail data is at rest. E-mail is in the sender's Sent Items box, in a message queue, or in the recipient's Inbox. The message data may be moved in to an archival system or copied out to a personal store (PST) file. Protecting e-mail data at rest involves encrypting the data so that only authorized recipients can open a message. Technologies that can provide message encryption include Secure Multipurpose Internet Mail Extensions (S/MIME) and enterprise rights management (ERM) or digital rights management (DRM) technologies.

Protecting Your Firewall

The Internet can be a dangerous place: worms, 'bots, malicious hackers, script kiddies, and reality TV streaming video. Organizations that own public IP addresses often see dozens of attacks or probes against those IP addresses every day; these probes are often just someone (well an automated program) looking for a known vulnerability that they can exploit. Some organizations see attacks directed against their resources from a malicious hacker who is intentionally trying to do the organization or its data harm.

Something has to provide a layer of protection against these types of attacks. The firewall is a device that sits between an external network (an untrusted network) and a private or trusted network. In medium and larger organizations, actual management of the organization's firewall is outside of the e-mail administrator's area of responsibility. Oftentimes even in small organizations the firewall is managed by someone else. However, as an e-mail administrator, your servers are responsible for receiving SMTP mail from the Internet, sending SMTP mail to the Internet, and possibly receiving inbound traffic from HTTP/HTTPS clients. So you need to be able to converse effectively with the people who will provide the necessary access. If this is all "old hat" to you, then please skip on to the next section.

Figure 20.1 shows a simple Exchange 2007 deployment that is protected by a firewall. This organization is protected by an external firewall and an internal firewall. The network that sits between them is the perimeter network or the demilitarized zone (DMZ) network. The perimeter network is intended for servers that you must protect to some degree, but you do not want the traffic intended for those servers to be coming directly into your internal network. In this diagram, we are showing two separate firewalls, but this is a conceptual diagram. Some organizations will have both an internal firewall and an external firewall, while others will have a single firewall that provides internal, external, and perimeter network ports.

FIGURE 20.1
Typical firewall deployment protecting Exchange Server 2007

In this deployment, inbound SMTP (TCP port 25) mail from the Internet hits the firewall. The external firewall sees that TCP port 25 is permitted, but only for certain internal IP addresses. The inbound SMTP traffic is then directed to the internal firewall, where possibly a second set of restrictions or access lists (often called rules or an access control list) is consulted. The internal firewall allows inbound SMTP, but only to the Exchange 2007 Hub Transport server.

The same would happen for inbound HTTPS traffic (TCP port 443) that comes from Outlook Web Access, Windows Mobile ActiveSync clients, and Outlook Anywhere clients. The external and internal firewalls determine that TCP port 443 is permitted, but only to the internal Exchange 2007 Client Access server.

TIP

A very common question is whether or not the Exchange Client Access and Hub Transport server roles should be placed in the perimeter network. No, the Hub Transport and Client Access server roles should not be placed in the perimeter network. Neither Microsoft nor any reputable Exchange expert will advise you to do this. If you are advised to do this, get a second opinion.

Any other types of traffic that hits the firewall would not be allowed even to the perimeter network. Figure 20.1 showed a very simple example; most organizations' firewall configurations are far more complex. You may also be publishing more than one or two applications. Table 20.1 shows some of the typical ports that may be required on different Exchange server roles.

TABLE 20.1:   Typical Ports Required by Exchange Applications

APPLICATION	PORT	EXCHANGE SERVER ROLE
SMTP	25	Hub Transport server
SMTP w/TLS	25	Hub Transport server
HTTP	80	Client Access server
POP	110	Client Access server
IMAP4	143	Client Access server
HTTPS (HTTP with SSL)	443	Client Access server
POP3 with SSL	995	Client Access server
IMAP4 with SSL	993	Client Access server

While Table 20.1 does list some ports that are not encrypted (such as HTTP, POP3, and IMAP4), we do not recommend that these ports be opened. We recommend all Internet applications use SSL ports to protect logon credentials and data. We have intentionally left out LDAP ports since this would require that LDAP be opened to Active Directory domain controllers or global catalog servers; we do not recommend exposing any Active Directory services directly to the Internet.

Provided your Windows and Exchange servers are up-to-date on patches and you have taken reasonable measures to lock down your server configuration, the configuration shown in Figure 20.1 should provide reasonably good security. However, we will discuss the use of SMTP relay hosts (and the use of the Edge Transport server role) as well as reverse proxy servers to provide even better security for Exchange servers that are exposed to the Internet.

Using the Security Configuration Wizard

Microsoft includes a tool with Windows Server 2003 Service Pack 1 and Windows Server 2003 R2 called the Security Configuration Wizard (SCW). This tool includes templates for different types of server roles; the wizard asks you about the server roles, network security settings, and services that should be running on the server. The wizard then disables unnecessary services and helps to lock down or harden the server.

The SCW is a very powerful Windows tool that is helpful in ensuring that your servers are secured to the best point possible. However, if you do not configure the policy correctly or if you do not take into consideration the roles that the server is supporting or the software that the server is supporting, then you will break something.

You might have wondered if the SCW includes templates for Exchange 2007 roles. It does not, and you should not attempt to use the SCW with Exchange 2000/2003 templates. However, there is a procedure for updating a server's templates with Exchange 2007–ready templates.

The SCW has a "rollback" feature that will prove very useful when you're tuning your server's security configuration. If you have a plain-vanilla installation of Exchange with no additional software or options, the defaults will all work fine. In other situations, though, some fine-tuning may be required.

Preparing the Security Configuration Wizard for Exchange 2007

Exchange 2007 includes two files that you can use to register the necessary templates and settings for the SCW so that it recognizes Exchange Server 2007 roles and requirements:

◆ Exchange2007.xml includes the necessary configuration and extensions to register an Exchange Server 2007 Mailbox, Hub Transport, Client Access, Unified Messaging, or clustered mailbox server role with the Security Configuration Wizard.

◆ Exchange2007Edge.xml includes the necessary configuration and extensions to register an Exchange Server 2007 Edge Transport server role with the Security Configuration Wizard.

These files are found (by default) in the C:\Program Files\Microsoft\Exchange Server\ scripts folder. To register a Mailbox, Hub Transport, Client Access, Unified Messaging, or clustered mailbox server with the SCW, change to the scripts folder and use the following command:

```
scwcmd register /kbname:"Ex2007KB" /kbfile:"Exchange2007.xml"
```

To register the SCW extensions for an Exchange 2007 Edge Transport server role, change to the scripts folder and use this command:

```
scwcmd register /kbname:"Ex2007KB" /kbfile:"Exchange2007Edge.xml"
```

Using the Security Configuration Wizard

The Security Configuration Wizard is pretty simple to use. You can find a shortcut to the SCW in the Administrative Tools folder. Do not run this tool on an Exchange 2007 server until you have registered the Exchange 2007 extensions, though. In order to run the SCW, you must be a member

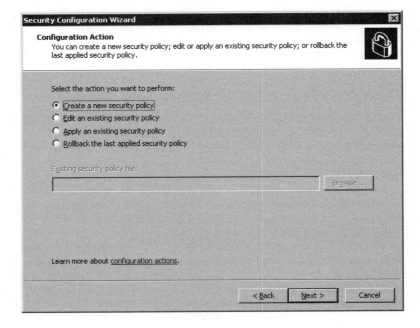

of the server's local Administrators group. When you launch the SCW, the first screen just introduces you to the SCW. Once you click Next, you are taken to the Configuration Action screen. Here you are prompted to select the action you want to perform.

There are four possible actions you can choose from the Configuration Action page of the wizard:

◆ Create a New Security Policy will walk you through the wizard and create a new set of security policy settings. This is the step you choose when you run the SCW for the first time.

◆ Edit an Existing Security Policy lets you make adjustments to a policy you have previously created.

◆ Apply an Existing Security Policy lets you apply or re-apply a policy you have previously created.

◆ Rollback the Last Applied Security Policy allows you to roll back security settings you have recently applied. This is very, very helpful if you have applied a policy that breaks something.

TIP

If you are not sure about a specific setting when running the SCW, it is best to take the defaults or recommended settings.

For this example, select Create a New Security Policy. On the next page of the wizard, you specify a server to use for defining the baseline of the security policy you are going to create.

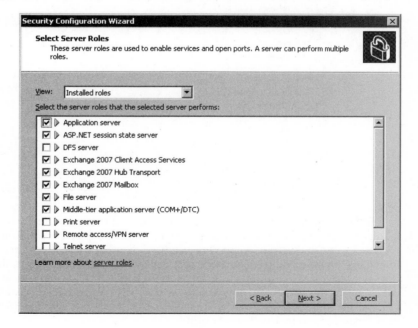

This can be another server on your network or it can be the local server. You must have administrative permissions on the server that you are selecting. When you click Next, the SCW will analyze the current security settings and it will give you an opportunity to view the configuration database. The configuration database will show you all of the options and server roles that are currently available and known to the SCW. You can view the configuration database to verify that it knows about Exchange 2007 server roles. Click Next until you come to the Select Server Roles page of the wizard. From this page, you can see the server roles that the SCW has detected.

If the View drop-down box shows that Installed Roles is selected, you will see the roles that the SCW detected on the server. From here, you can clear check boxes next to server roles that are unnecessary on this particular server. Notice in the screen shot that the Print Server server role was detected, but the check box is cleared. When the policy is applied, the Print Spooler service will be disabled. This means that this machine will not be able to use either locally installed printers or shared printers.

The next page of the wizard is the Select Client Features page. This page shows you the services and software that are used by client applications. From here you can see client-side services such as the DHCP client, the DNS registration client, the Automatic update client, and more.

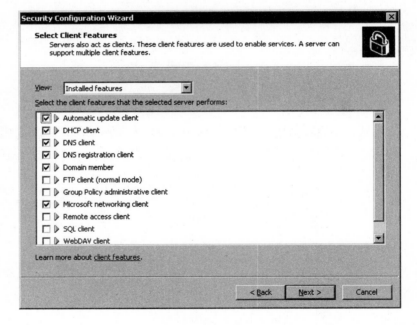

Take care not to disable a service that you may need to support Exchange. It is deceptively easy to break something important, such as domain membership or DNS lookups.

The Select Administration and Other Options page shows you the components that are used to manage a server and provide other networking services. For example, the Browser and the Browse Master services are in this list. For an Exchange 2007 server, these options will be cleared, which means this server will not participate in the My Network Places feature of Windows. While browser functionality is not required for Exchange server or Exchange clients, other software might require it, so review this list carefully.

The SCW determines which options are most likely required to administer an Exchange 2007 server, but it is important to realize that some fine-tuning may be necessary. The next screen of the wizard is the Select Additional Services page; here you can select additional software that is not defined in the SCW extensions. When you get to the Handling Unspecified Services page, you are presented with options to disable services that are not defined or leave them alone.

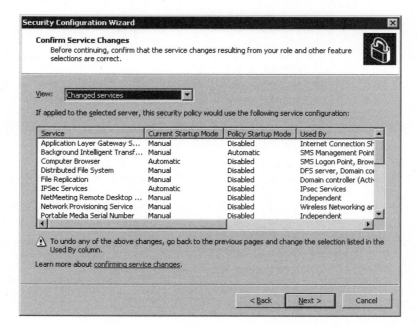

Unless you are sure you know that disabling services will not affect the required functionality of the Exchange server, we recommend you choose the Do Not Change the Startup Mode of the Service option.

The Confirm Service Changes page of the SCW allows you to view the current state of the service and what will be changed once you implement this particular SCW setting. By default, only the services that are affected by the SCW are listed.

Review the list of services that will be modified and ensure that no critical services that you require are going to be disabled. When you are sure that everything meets your requirements, click Next to move on to the network security section of the wizard. This section is optional, but you may want to consider running it if you want to tighten down the ports that being used on the network. On the first screen of the network security portion of the SCW, you can select the Skip. This Section check box and skip the network security section all together. When you have finished selecting the applications that are allowed to listen on network ports, you are asked to confirm the port changes.

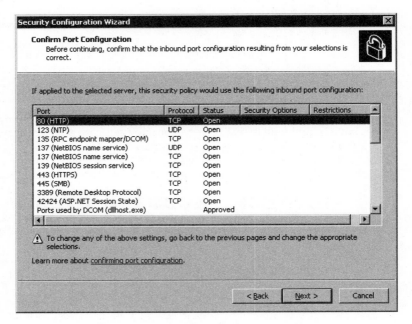

The next section is the Registry section of the SCW. This title is a little misleading since what it is configuring or locking down is specifically Windows configuration settings that can help reduce the possibility of attacks such as password cracking and protocol attacks. The actual Registry settings that are affected in this section are in the HKLM\System\CurrentControlSet\ LanManServer\Parameters key and the HKLM\System\CurrentcontrolSet\Control\LSA key. You can skip this section also.

The Require SMB Security Signatures property page allows you to specify that server message block (SMB) signing is required for all SMB traffic; this will generate slightly more CPU load and it will prevent clients older than Windows NT 4 SP6 from connecting to file or printer shares. However, this can reduce the possibility of a man-in-the-middle type of attack in which a user's session is hijacked.

The Outbound Authentication Methods wizard page allows you to configure the types of authentication that can be used when connecting to a remote server. By default, Domain Accounts authentication is the only method selected; this means that all computers to which you connect from this server must be domain members.

On the Outbound Authentication Using Domain Accounts wizard page, you can specify the types of operating systems you will be connecting to. The default is that all remote operating systems will be Windows NT 4 (or compatible) or later. Depending on the configuration on the Outbound Authentication using Local Accounts page, you may also see the Inbound Authentication Methods wizard page, which allows you to configure the LAN Manager/NTLM authentication level. Finally, on the Registry Settings Summary screen, you can verify the types of changes that are about to be made.

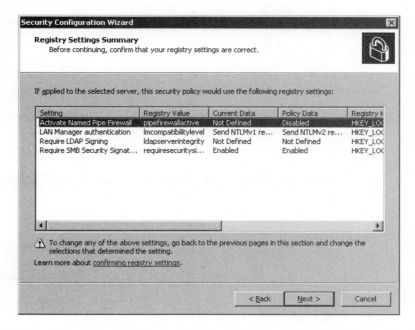

The next section is the System Audit Policy section, used to enable auditing settings. These are the same auditing settings that you can enable in the local security policy or via a group policy object (GPO). You can disable auditing, audit only successful events, or audit both success and failures. The Audit Policy Summary page of the wizard allows you to confirm which settings you are making.

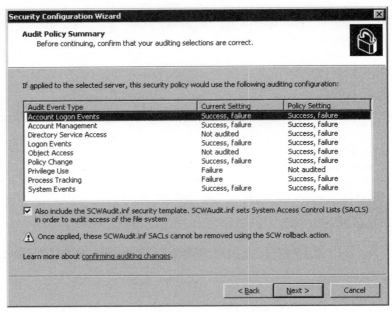

In the Internet Information Services section, you specify that web service extensions are enabled and which virtual directories will be allowed. Much of the configuration that you perform on the Internet Information Services section is similar to using the Microsoft IIS Lock Down tool. Unless you are running additional web applications on your Exchange servers, we recommend taking the defaults. The IIS Settings Summary page shows you the current settings and the changes that will be made.

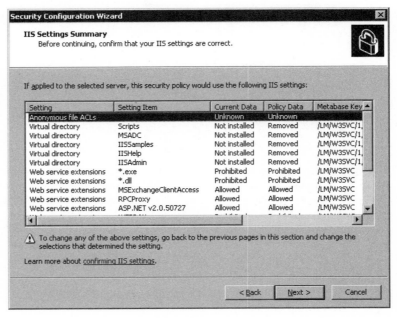

Finally, on the Security Policy File Name page, you are at the point that you are ready to save your security policy. Enter a name for your security policy file and provide a description. One of the really nice features of the SCW is that you can click the View Security Policy button and view all of the settings of your security policy. Figure 20.2 shows an example. The SCW Viewer will also let you print out the security policy if you like to keep hard copy records of your configuration.

FIGURE 20.2
Viewing your security policy

Once you save the policy, the next page of the wizard will ask you if you want to apply the security policy now or apply it later. You may also need to reboot the server after the policy changes have been applied. We recommend creating and testing a security policy prior to putting a server into production so that you don't have to worry about rebooting during working hours. You can always save your policy and apply it later, though.

Using Secure Sockets Layer (SSL) with Exchange

Secure Sockets Layer (SSL) is the foundation for almost all network-layer protection of Exchange data in Exchange Server 2007. SSL is a technology that allows a network client and a server to negotiate an encryption key that is used as a session key to encrypt data sent between the client and the server. The client requests the server's certificate (which will become important here shortly) and uses the server's public key to initially exchange an encryption key.

While the technology was designed for use with the HTTP protocol, it can be adapted to be used with almost any protocol, including SMTP, POP3, and IMAP4. It should be noted that the actual technology that is used with SMTP is Transport Layer Security (TLS), which is the Internet standardize version of SSL.

Using Self-Signed Certificates and Exchange 2007

A certificate is automatically installed on all Exchange Server 2007 Hub Transport and Client Access servers so they can use SSL or TLS. This certificate is a self-signed certificate that is generated automatically by the installation process. The self-signed certificate allows Outlook Web Access clients to use HTTPS web services and it allows Hub Transport servers to use TLS.

You might think this is all well and good, but self-signed certificates are problematic for a few reasons. First, when a user connects to an Outlook Web Access site that is using a self-signed certificate, they see a web browser error like the one shown in Figure 20.3.

FIGURE 20.3
Connecting to a website with an untrusted certificate

While the user can simply click Continue to This Website (Not Recommended) and proceed to Outlook Web Access and SSL will work, we strongly discourage any organization from allowing end users to do this. Getting users in the habit of ignoring security warnings is never a good thing.

The second problem will occur with Outlook 2007 when the client connects to the Autodiscover, Availability, and offline address book virtual directories. Figure 20.4 shows the error that may be displayed if the client does not trust the server's certificate.

FIGURE 20.4
A security warning of an untrusted certificate

Outlook Anywhere clients may not work if they don't trust the certificate authority that signed the certificate on the Hub Transport server. Remote SMTP servers that attempt to initiate TLS to

Exchange 2007 Hub Transport servers may also not transmit mail if they do not trust the Hub Transport server's certificate.

Requesting and Installing Certificates for Exchange Server 2007

When planning an Exchange deployment that includes the use of SSL or TLS, you need to ensure that certificates that are used by Hub Transport servers and Client Access servers are properly trusted. Let's look at the general properties of a self-signed certificate used for an Exchange server; this property page is shown in Figure 20.5.

FIGURE 20.5
Viewing a certificate's general properties

Trusted certificates have three characteristics:

- The date range for the certificate includes the current date. This is the Valid From information.

- The FQDN that the server was issued to matches the name that the client used to connect to the server. This is the Issued To information.

- The issuer of the certificate is a certificate authority that is trusted by the local computer. This is the Issued By information.

The reason the self-signed certificate is invalid is that the issuer is not one of the trusted certificate authorities. You need to get a certificate that has been issued by a trusted certificate authority. This can be one of many third-party certificate authorities or it could be your own internal certificate server. If you use an internal certificate server, you still have to distribute your certificate server's certificate to all clients that will use certificates issued by that server.

> **TIP**
>
> For a list of certificate authorities that are trusted by Windows by default, see the Microsoft Root Certificate Program Members list at `http://preview.tinyurl.com/2ktu9m`.

For simplicity's sake, we recommend using a third party's certificate server. Though an annual fee is usually involved, this is the simplest approach and ensures that clients do not receive security warnings or errors.

With simple websites and with Exchange 2000/2003, generating a certificate request was pretty simple since you all you needed to do was to generate the request and use the FQDN that the users would be using to connect to your site. Then you sent the certificate request to the certificate authority to be signed.

Exchange 2007 Client Access servers use different URLs for internal and external clients. This is not only because of Outlook Web Access, but also due to Autodiscover, the Availability service, offline address books, and other web services that may be associated with the default website in IIS. Let's take as an example a server that hosts the Hub Transport and Client Access server roles for an organization. It may be referred to by a number of different names under different circumstances. The server's name is HNLEX04, the Active Directory DNS name is volcanosurfboards.int, and the public domain name is somorita.com. The following hostnames and fully qualified domain names may be used against this server:

◆ hnlex04

◆ hnlex04.volcanosurfboards.int

◆ mail.somorita.com (by remote web clients)

◆ autodiscover.somorita.com (by remote Autodiscover clients

You might think that you need multiple virtual web servers in order to support all of these different names, but that is not the case thanks to a feature of X.509v3 certificates called a subject alternative name that allows for other hostnames and DNS domain names. However, you cannot use the Internet Information Services Manager to generate a certificate request. You must use the Exchange 2007 Exchange Management Shell (EMS) cmdlet `New-ExchangeCertificate` to generate the request. Let's do an example that requests a certificate with the following information:

Organization name	Somorita Surfboards
Organizational unit	IT Department
FQDN domain name	mail.somorita.com
Additional names	hnlex04, hnlex04.volcanosurfboards.int, autodiscover.somorita.com
Certificate request filename	`C:\CertReq.txt`

On the console of server hnlex04, you must type the following command to generate the certificate request file. Below the command is the output of the certificate request generation:

```
New-ExchangeCertificate -GenerateRequest -SubjectName
"ou=IT Department,o=Somorita Surfboards, cn=mail.somorita.com" -domainname hnlex04,
hnlex04.volcanosurfboards.int,autodiscover.somorita.com"
-path c:\CertReq.txt
```

Thumbprint	Services	Subject
5BDE878D6A6D34DE6462557F785B19D424642D42	.....	CN=mail.somorita.com, O...

The certificate request file (`CertReq.txt`) is not exactly a beauty-come-hither. As a matter of fact, it is a format that almost no one but a certification authority could love. Figure 20.6 shows the text of the certificate signing request.

FIGURE 20.6
The text of a certificate
signing request

The text that you see in Figure 20.6 is actually a base64 encoded request of the information that we created using the `New-ExchangeCertificate` cmdlet. We will need to take this text and give it to the certification authority; usually this is done by copying the CSR text and pasting it in to a text box on the certificate authority's website, as shown in Figure 20.7.

Depending on the certificate authority, you may get a signed certificate back immediately (especially if you have an account) or you may have to wait a few hours or even days for verification to take place. Ultimately, you will download a certificate file or the CA will e-mail the file to you. You need to save this to a file on to the server's local file system (hnlex04, in our case) and use the EMS cmdlet `Import-ExchangeCertificate` to import the certificate in to the machine's certificate store.

> **NOTE**
>
> At the time of this writing, the only 3rd party certificate authority we are aware of that will sign a certificate request containing subject alternate names is Entrust (www.entrust.com).

FIGURE 20.7
Pasting the certificate signing request into a text box on a certificate authority's website

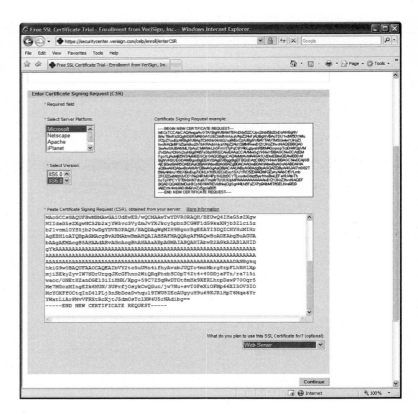

In the following example, we are importing a newly generated certificate into the machine's certificate store. The certificate file name is WebServices.cer and we will assign it the friendly name of HNLEX04 Web Services Certificate. Here is an example:

```
Import-ExchangeCertificate -path c:\WebServices.cer
-FriendlyName "HNLEX04 Web Services Certificate"
```

Thumbprint	Services	Subject
A171D0FA13E121AA553A83A4BDDC7BE830CB8034	.....	CN=mail.somorita.com, O...

This imports the certificate into the certificate store, but it does not enable the certificate. You now have to use the Enable-ExchangeCertificate cmdlet to associate the certificate with IIS (or other Internet services). Notice the thumbprint attribute; this will come in handy. Here is the command to enable the certificate for use with web services (IIS) as well as SMTP, POP3, and IMAP4:

```
Enable-ExchangeCertificate -Thumbprint
A171D0FA13E121AA553A83A4BDDC7BE830CB8034 -Services "IIS,POP,IMAP,SMTP"
```

If you don't remember the thumbprint, you can use the `Get-ExchangeCertificate` to retrieve it for you. Here is an example:

```
Get-ExchangeCertificate | where {$_.subject -like "*mail.somorita.com*"} | FL

AccessRules         : {System.Security.AccessControl.CryptoKeyAccessRule,
System.Security.AccessControl.CryptoKeyAccessRule}
CertificateDomains : {mail.somorita.com, hnlex04, hnlex04.volcanosurfboards.int,
autodiscover.somorita.com}
HasPrivateKey       : True
IsSelfSigned        : False
Issuer              : CN=hnldc01, DC=volcanosurfboards, DC=com
NotAfter            : 1/22/2009 7:08:17 PM
NotBefore           : 1/23/2007 7:08:17 PM
PublicKeySize       : 2048
SerialNumber        : 5334E5FC000000000009
Status              : Valid
Subject             : CN=mail.somorita.com, OU=IT Department,
O=Somorita Surfboards
Thumbprint          : A171D0FA13E121AA553A83A4BDDC7BE830CB8034
```

Implementing a Message Hygiene System

An important component of your overall Exchange design is properly implementing a message hygiene system. *Message hygiene* is an all-encompassing term that covers antivirus and anti-spam technology. The anti-spam components of Exchange 2007 are discussed in Chapter 18, "Delivering E-mail"; in this chapter we want to cover some of the best practices associated with the anti-spam components.

Choosing an Antivirus System

There are at least 10 antivirus software packages available on the market that work with Exchange 2007 or that are in development to work with Exchange 2007:

- Symantec Mail Security for Microsoft Exchange (`www.symantec.com`)
- Trend ScanMail for Microsoft Exchange (`www.trendmicro.com`)
- GFI MailSecurity for Exchange (`www.gfi.com`)
- eTrust InnoculateIT for Exchange (`www.ca.com`)
- F-Secure Antivirus for Exchange (`www.f-secure.com`)
- Proland Protector Plus Antivirus for Exchange (`www.pspl.com`)

◆ Kaspersky Security for Exchange Server (www.kapersky.com)

◆ McAfee GroupShield for Exchange (www.mcafee.com)

◆ Sophos PureMessage for Exchange (www.sophos.com)

◆ Microsoft Forefront Security for Exchange (www.microsoft.com)

If you have purchased Exchange Server Enterprise client access licenses and you have a Microsoft Software Assurance agreement, this includes licenses to use Microsoft Forefront Security for Exchange Server, so the decision as to which software package to use may have already been made for you. However, if you are in the process of evaluating Exchange-aware antivirus software, here are points to consider:

◆ The software should use the Exchange antivirus API's (AVAPI) when scanning the information store as well as scanning the messages in the message transport system.

◆ The software should use a different scanning engine technology and virus signature definitions than the client software on your perimeter network or client workstations uses.

◆ Consider software that uses more than one scanning engine technology and signature database.

◆ The software should be able to have updates scheduled at least once every hour. The updates should be applied automatically.

◆ In organizations with more than one Exchange server, look for software that can be centrally configured and managed.

◆ Consider software that can be configured with features such as file attachment blocking, customizable notification messages, and reporting features.

◆ The software should offer automatic mail database scanning, scheduled scanning, and manual scanning, as well as the ability to turn off automatic scanning altogether.

Blocking File Attachments

If you talk to any administrator that has ever survived a serious virus outbreak, you will hear several common causes of the virus or worm outbreak:

◆ E-mail was not being scanned for viruses.

◆ Viruses were downloaded to a user's desktop via an external mail system such as Yahoo! or Hotmail.

◆ Virus signatures were out-of-date or not yet available.

◆ Virus payload came into the network via a file attachment type that was not being blocked.

Hopefully you are planning to remedy the first bullet point by ensuring that all e-mail content is scanned as it enters your organization. The second bullet point can best be remedied by ensuring that all clients on your network have adequate virus protection installed. Virus signatures being out-of-date or not yet available as well as viruses arriving via attachments that were allowed (when they should not have been) are something you can do something about on the e-mail server. In this section, we want to review some potentially dangerous attachment types that you should consider blocking.

Table 20.2 shows a list of commonly suspected attachment types that many administrators block using their antivirus software.

TABLE 20.2:   Common Attachment Types That Might Be Dangerous

ATTACHMENT TYPES	ATTACHMENT DESCRIPTION
BAT	DOS/Windows batch file
CMD	Windows command file
COM	DOS command file
EXE	Executable program
JS	JavaScript file
MSI	Windows installer file
PIF	Program information file for 16-bit application
SCR	Screensaver executable
SHS	Shell scrap objects
VB	VBScript file
VBS	VBScript file
WSC	Windows script component file

Everyone knows about script files and executables, but there are a lot of other ways that hostile content can make its way onto your network. A long time ago, Microsoft published a list of attachments called Level-1 attachments that could conceivably transport a program or a script that could then be executed by a user or, even worse, executed automatically when a user opened a message. Outlook 2000 Service Pack 3 and later as well as Outlook Web Access won't even allow a user to open or save these file types, but remember that not all users use these applications. Many administrators still block Level-1 attachments so that they are stripped off of a message completely. The complete list of Microsoft Level-1 attachments is shown in Table 20.3.

TABLE 20.3:   Microsoft Level-1 Attachments Types

ATTACHMENT TYPES	ATTACHMENT DESCRIPTION
ADE	Microsoft Access project extension
ADP	Microsoft Access project

(CONTINUED)

TABLE 20.3: Microsoft Level-1 Attachments Types *(CONTINUED)*

ATTACHMENT TYPES	ATTACHMENT DESCRIPTION
APP	Microsoft Visual FoxPro application
ASP	Active server page
ASX	Windows media audio or video shortcut
BAS	Visual Basic class module or a BASIC program
BAT	DOS/Windows batch file
CER	Security certificate
CHM	Compiled HTML help file
CMD	Windows command files
COM	DOS command file
CPL	Control Panel extension
CRT	Security certificate
CSH	KornShell script file
EXE	Executable programs
FXP	Microsoft Visual FoxPro compiled program
HLP	Windows help file
HTA	HTML program
INF	Windows setup information file
INS	Internet naming service
ISP	Internet communication settings
JS	JavaScript
JS	JScript script file
JSE	JScript encoded script file
KSH	KornShell script file
LNK	Link or shortcut file
MDA	Microsoft Access add-in program

TABLE 20.3:   Microsoft Level-1 Attachments Types *(CONTINUED)*

ATTACHMENT TYPES	ATTACHMENT DESCRIPTION
MDB	Microsoft Access program
MDE	Microsoft Access MDE database
MDT	Microsoft Access workgroup
MDW	Microsoft Access workgroup
MDZ	Microsoft Access wizard program
MSC	Windows console definition
MSI	Windows installer files
MSI	Windows installer package
MSP	Windows installer patch
MST	Windows installer transform file
OPS	Office preferences file
PCD	Photo CD image
PIF	Program information file for 16-bit application
PIF	Shortcut to MS-DOS program
PRF	Microsoft Outlook profile setting
PRG	Microsoft Visual FoxPro program
PST	Microsoft Outlook Personal Folders file
REG	Registration entries
SCF	Windows Explorer command
SCR	Screensaver executables
SCT	Windows Script Component
SHB	Shell scrap object
SHS	Shell scrap object
TMP	Temporary file

(CONTINUED)

TABLE 20.3: Microsoft Level-1 Attachments Types *(CONTINUED)*

ATTACHMENT TYPES	ATTACHMENT DESCRIPTION
URL	Internet shortcut
VB	VBScript file
VBE	VBScript encoded script file
VBS	VBScript file
VBS	Visual Basic Script file
VSMACROS	Visual Studio .NET macro project file
VSS	Visio shapes and Visio stencils file
VST	Visio template file
VSW	Visio workspace
WS	Windows script file
WSC	Windows script component
WSC	Windows script Component
WSF	Windows script file
WSH	Windows script host settings file

Implementing Multiple Layers of Protection

A particular virus may sneak into your e-mail system because a signature has not yet been released for it. You can help mitigate this risk by checking for updates signatures hourly, but the time from which an antivirus software vendor learns about a new threat and when it actually releases signatures can be anywhere from a few hours to a few days.

The likelihood that you catch all viruses with a single scanning engine is pretty good, but additional scanning engines and additional layers of scanning can be even more effective. Multiple layers of protection are always a good precaution. Let's look at a couple of different approaches for doing this. In our definition of multiple layers of e-mail protection, there are certain things that should always be implemented:

◆ E-mail should be scanned in at least two different places.

◆ Multiple scanning engines, signature databases, or scanning technologies should be implemented. Don't be afraid to use more than one vendor.

◆ Clients should always have antivirus software installed.

Figure 20.8 shows a network with three layers of protection. Inbound e-mail is directed to an SMTP-based antivirus system located in the organization's perimeter network. The organization's

MX record directs inbound SMTP mail to the SMTP message hygiene system in the perimeter. The system in the perimeter network could be an Exchange 2007 Edge Transport server or it could be a third-party software package or mail security appliance. In the perimeter, the messages are inspected for viruses (and possibly also spam) and then directed to the Hub Transport server.

FIGURE 20.8
An example of a multilayer message hygiene system

The Hub Transport server inspects the message "in transit" and then passes it on to the Exchange 2007 Mailbox server. The Mailbox server may optionally also have antivirus software that inspects the message for viruses, though both store level and message transport level scanning is probably not necessary in the case of Exchange 2007. This is because all messages are sent through the Hub Transport server.

Clients can then download and view the message, where it may be inspected once again for a virus. In an ideal world, each step of the way a different scanning engine would be used. So the system in the perimeter network would use the vendor's scanning engine, the Hub Transport (and/or the Mailbox) server would use a different solution, and the clients would use a third vendor's solution. Some SMTP scanning systems and Exchange-aware solutions (such as Forefront Security for Exchange) already incorporate multiple scanning engines).

This approach may seem like overkill to some organizations, but it offers a few advantages:

◆ Hostile content can be blocked in the perimeter.

◆ There is an increased probability of detecting hostile content with multiple scanning engines.

◆ Corporate or security policies can be enforced at the perimeter by blocking undesirable file types (including multimedia files and compressed files).

◆ Internet IP addresses do not have direct access via SMTP to the Exchange Hub Transport system. The only SMTP system that can deliver e-mail to Exchange is the system in the perimeter network

Of course, you have to weigh these advantages with the added complexity and possibly managing more than one antivirus product. Another possible approach with many of the same advantages is to use a third-party managed provider to handle the initial message hygiene inspection.

Figure 20.9 shows how this might work. The organization's DNS MX records are configured to point to the managed provider's SMTP servers, not its own. The managed provider handles the initial message hygiene functions and then forwards the mail to the public IP address of the organization's Hub Transport servers. Then the internal virus scanning software can provide an additional layer of protection.

FIGURE 20.9
Using a third-party message hygiene solution

There are a few additional advantages to using a managed provider to provide this initial layer of protection besides just replacing software that you would have to manage:

◆ Managed providers are usually staffed 24 by 7 by 365 and can react very quickly to emerging threats.

◆ Managed providers usually use multiple scanning engines for both virus protection and spam detection.

◆ Both malware and spam can be blocked before it ever even reaches your network connection, thus eliminating a burden on your own Internet links.

◆ Your firewall can be configured to accept inbound SMTP only from the managed provider's IP addresses and thus provide better protection for your Hub Transport servers.

If you purchased Exchange 2007 Enterprise client access licenses and you have a Software Assurance agreement with Microsoft, this includes the ability to use Microsoft's Hosted Exchange Filtering service at no additional cost.

Using a Reverse Proxy to Protect Web Services

A lot of organizations expose their Client Access servers directly to the Internet. If the server is properly hardened and security updates are applied as needed, this scenario will work. However, many organizations have policies that state that no internal web server can have Internet connections directed to it. These organizations will often try to locate the Client Access server role in the perimeter network, which is not recommended. Other organizations are just concerned with improving security wherever possible.

In the previous section, we talked about preventing direct SMTP access to the Hub Transport role by using an SMTP relay located in the perimeter network. You can employ very similar protection by using a reverse proxy.

Figure 20.10 shows an organization that has implemented a reverse proxy in its perimeter network. A reverse proxy is similar to a regular proxy server. Inbound HTTPS is directed to the reverse proxy server instead of the Client Access server. Depending on the type of reverse proxy server, some additional security steps may be taken. The reverse proxy server then places the HTTP data back on the network (either as HTTP or HTTPS) and sends it on to the Client Access server. The internal firewall is configured so that the HTTPS data will be passed through the internal firewall only if it is sent from the reverse proxy server.

FIGURE 20.10
Implementing a reverse proxy in the perimeter network

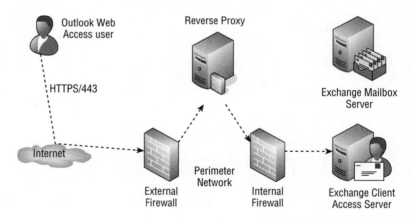

The Client Access server will accept the request, process it, and send the response back to the reverse proxy server. The reverse proxy server then sends the requested data back to the originating client. Depending on the reverse proxy server you are using, you may have some additional security benefits associated with using this solution:

◆ Improved security for all web services, including Outlook Web Access, ActiveSync, Outlook Anywhere, Autodiscover, Availability, and others

◆ Validation of URL path and sends to the Client Access server only valid virtual directories

◆ URLs examined for invalid HTTP requests such as directory traversal attacks or buffer overflow attacks

◆ Authentication offloaded so that the reverse proxy authenticates the client before ever allowing the client to connect to the Client Access server

◆ The overhead of SSL offloaded so that the reverse proxy rather than the Client Access server handles SSL encryption and decryption

There are a number of different reverse proxy solutions available that can help you improve the security of your published web applications. Microsoft's ISA Server (www.microsoft.com/isa), Blue Coat SG Appliances (www.bluecoat.com), and Squid Web Proxy (www.squid-cache.org) for Linux are just a few examples.

The example in Figure 20.10 shows one possible configuration that will work with most any reverse proxy solution. However, Microsoft ISA Server can also act as a complete firewall solution. Some organizations deploy ISA Server as their only firewall or they use it as an internal firewall. Figure 20.11 shows a configuration where ISA Server is acting as an internal firewall; in this configuration it can also act as a reverse proxy.

FIGURE 20.11
Using ISA Server as an internal firewall and reverse proxy

If you are using Microsoft ISA Server, the menus and wizards do not refer to this as a reverse proxy feature but rather mail-server publishing.

Summary

Any Exchange server that either receives e-mail from the Internet or is accessed by remote clients should be deployed with security in mind. The first and most critical step involved in securing an Exchange server is to ensure that the operating system and Exchange server software has recent security fixes and updates.

The Security Configuration Wizard can also be used to further harden an Exchange server by restricting the services that are running on the server as well as customizing the security settings in the Registry and the Windows firewall.

For Internet clients such as Outlook Web Access and Outlook Anywhere, implementing Secure Sockets Layer (SSL) ensures that data and authentication credentials transmitted over the network cannot be intercepted by someone using a protocol analyzer tool.

Protecting your users' mailboxes from malware (viruses, worms, Trojan horses) is the function of your message hygiene system. The Exchange server should be protected by Exchange Server–aware software. Implementing multiple layers of protection such as requiring that all clients have antivirus software and that inbound e-mail is first scanned in the perimeter network can help to ensure the security of the message transport system as well as prevent unwanted content from reaching a user's mailbox.

Finally, additional security can be provided for Client Access servers by putting a reverse proxy system between the users and the Client Access server. The reverse proxy intercepts inbound HTTPS requests and inspects them before passing them on to internal Client Access servers. The reverse proxy can also implement additional security measures.

Chapter 21

Logging, Auditing, and Monitoring

On a day-to-day basis, Exchange Server does not require a lot of direct attention. Once it's is set up and configured properly, the server itself can pretty much just sit on a corner of your computer room and run. You don't need to regularly reboot the server. You don't need to be performing maintenance on the databases. There are very few day-to-day tasks that require direct management on the Exchange server.

This brings us to the big question, What *do* you need to do to an Exchange server? We have broken down the "daily" tasks in to "the big five." The five most important daily management tasks for Exchange Server are as follows:

◆ Perform and verify daily backups of Exchange data.

◆ Check available disk space.

◆ Confirm that the message hygiene system (antivirus and anti-spam) are running and have up-to-date signatures.

◆ Review the event logs for errors and warnings.

◆ Check the message queues for stalled messages.

Did you notice something about this list? There is really nothing that you are doing directly to the Exchange server except running daily backups. Everything else falls in to the "monitoring" category. Once you have been managing an Exchange organization for a while, we think you will agree that the most critical tasks are simply related to watching Exchange and making sure it continues to perform as you expect and within the boundaries that you have set.

When we talk about boundaries, we are talking about defining the expected behavior your Exchange server system. These boundaries, such as the amount of disk space you are consuming (or expect to be consuming), will change over time. Also over time you may expect the CPU load or memory usage to increase as usage on the Exchange server increases.

Topics in this chapter include the following:

◆ Using the Exchange Best Practices Analyzer

◆ Auditing and logging

◆ Tracking messages

◆ Monitoring performance

◆ Removing content from users' mailboxes

Running the Exchange Best Practices Analyzer

The Exchange team has developed an excellent tool for helping you to find potential problems and check to see if you are following best practices in your Exchange environment. This tool is called the Exchange Best Practices Analyzer, or just the ExBPA. Originally, the ExBPA tool was a separate tool that you downloaded from Microsoft and then ran on your system. The ExBPA now comes as part of the Exchange Server 2007 software. You can find the ExBPA tool in the Exchange Management Console (EMC) toolbox work center (see Figure 21.1).

FIGURE 21.1
Exchange Server 2007
Tools work center

The Exchange 2007 ExBPA has been completely rewritten to take advantage of the new Windows PowerShell and the Exchange Management Shell extensions to the PowerShell.

Exchange programmers, support engineers, consultants, and other specialists have all collaborated on what is the best possible configuration for Exchange Server in different environments. From this collaboration, a consensus of the best configuration is developed and added to the ExBPA database. As new best practices are developed, the database is updated. The ExBPA downloads the most current "best practices" definitions from Microsoft so that each time you run it you are using the most up-to-date information possible.

The ExBPA uses these recommendations and best practices in its database to gather performance and configuration data about your Exchange organization, perform specific tests in your environment, and make recommendations about what might need to be changed.

A Sample Best Practices Run

Let's start with an example of what a typical ExBPA run looks like. We can either run the Best Practices Analyzer link in the Toolbox work center or we can run it manually: `C:\program files \Microsoft\Exchange Server\Bin\exbpa.exe`. Anytime you start the ExBPA, it will check to see if there are any updates to the ExBPA database. You can also check for updates once you have launched the ExBPA. Naturally, this requires Internet access.

Checking for Updates...

Please wait while we check for updates.

▮▮▮▮▮   13%

Estimated time to complete: 0 minutes, 52 seconds

Once the ExBPA is updated, the next step is to go to the Welcome screen (by clicking the Go To Welcome Screen link). Since we are running a new ExBPA scan, choose the Select Options for a New Scan option on the Welcome screen. The Select Options for a New Scan option takes you to the Connect to Active Directory page (shown in Figure 21.2). Figure 21.2 shows the Connect to Active Directory page along with the advanced login options. From this page, you specify the name of the domain controller that you will use for discovery of Exchange- and Active Directory–related information.

FIGURE 21.2
Connect to Active
Directory options

The Connect to Active Directory page also has options for providing alternate credentials for accessing Active Directory and Exchange. In many organizations, your administrative account will have all of the permissions necessary to perform the scan, but in other organizations the administration roles between Exchange Server and Active Directory are separated.

In order to successfully run the ExBPA against Active Directory, the user account you are using must be a member of each global catalog server's local Administrators group. The ExBPA must confirm configuration values on the global catalogs and will need to connect as an administrator.

For each Exchange server, the account that the ExBPA uses must be a member of that server's local Administrators group and it must have at least View Only administrator permissions to the Exchange organization.

As long as the account you are using has the necessary permissions, you can just click the Connect to the Active Directory link to continue.

The next page in the wizard is the Start a New Best Practices Scan page; this page is shown in Figure 21.3. The first thing to do is specify a descriptive name for this scan because you will probably want to refer back to it in the future. Next, in the Specify the Scope for This Scan box, select the Exchange servers that you want to run the scan against. Figure 21.3 shows a mixed Exchange 2003/Exchange 2007 organization, so we will scan against both of them.

FIGURE 21.3
Selecting the options for the ExBPA scan

The Select the Type of Scan to Perform options allow you to specify the types of things that will be checked during this particular scan. Depending on what you want to check, you will choose different options, but the most common is the health check. Here is a list of the options available and what they perform:

ExBPA Option	Function
Health Check	The health check runs a complete scan against the selected servers to look for possible incorrect configuration settings, changes, warnings, and errors.
Permission Check	The permission check verifies that you have the Exchange, Active Directory, and Windows permissions necessary to run the scan you are about to run.
Connectivity Test	The connectivity test checks each of the selected servers and confirms that the permissions are valid to run the ExBPA and that the servers have the necessary connectivity (such as opened ports) between them to function. This test also verifies connectivity to the Active Directory.
Baseline	The baseline scan allows you to run a configuration scan against the selected servers to confirm that they are still configured the same as they were when you originally set baseline values.
Exchange 2007 Readiness Check	The readiness check validates that the Exchange organization is ready for Exchange 2007 to be installed.

If you select Health Check, there is a Health Check Options check box available for running a performance baseline. This runs for two hours and monitors common Exchange performance counters on the selected Exchange servers. The other scan options do not have additional options.

The LAN speed selection allows you to specify your estimated connectivity to the selected servers. This value is merely used to give you an estimate of how long the scan will take and does not affect any of the scan parameters.

Finally, you can click the Start Scanning link or the Schedule a Scan link. You might want to schedule the scan for an off-hour period of time if you are concerned about network bandwidth or affecting your production environment.

In this example, we are going to run a health check and run it immediately. Now comes the part that requires some patience. In the scan we are running, both servers are on the same LAN and will scan much more quickly than if some of them were on the other side of a WAN link. The progress bar will indicate the estimated time left in the scan, and you can also see which servers have completed and which are still pending.

Scanning In Progress...

Please wait while the Exchange Best Practices Analyzer creates a Best Practices report by gathering data from the specified servers and analyzing it.

∎∎∎   6%

Estimated Time Remaining: 5 minutes, 34 seconds

➡ Stop Scanning

Server scanning details:

Total servers: 2 pending

Exchange Administrative Group (FYDIBOHF2

   HNLEX03   Pending

First Administrative Group

   HNLEX01   Pending

In a larger environment, though, you will notice some servers completing before others. This is due to not only link speeds, but the servers' performance and Exchange roles. When the scan is complete, you'll see a "Scanning Completed" message and a View a Report of This Best Practices Scan link.

Scanning Completed

Scanning has completed successfully.

➡ View a report of this Best Practices scan

Server scanning summary:

Total servers: 2 completed

Exchange Administrative Group (FYDIBOHF2

   HNLEX03

   UM

The real meat of the ExBPA is on the View Best Practices Report page. From here you can view the report as a tree view (based on category of listing) or you can view the report based on the ranking of the issues. The List Reports report type offers several report property pages and options for viewing the report. The Critical Issues property page shows the things that the ExBPA thinks are the most important. Figure 21.4 shows the Critical Issues page of the list report. Notice that the report has two critical issues listed.

FIGURE 21.4
Viewing the critical
issues

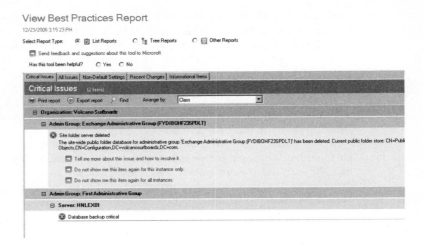

FIGURE 21.4
Viewing the critical
issues

One of the critical issues listed in Figure 21.4 is that one of the Exchange servers shown has not had a recent backup. The other issue reports that a site-wide public folder database has been deleted. In this figure, we clicked the Site Folder Server Deleted link and it expanded the information about the problem and provided some additional information.

Note that in the additional information in Figure 21.4 there are three links. These links are the same for all issues:

◆ The Tell Me More about This Issue and How to Resolve It link opens an external web browser window. The web browser is directed to a link at Microsoft that provides more information about the issue and how to resolve it (if necessary). The resolution to the site folder issue reported by the ExBPA is shown in Figure 21.5.

FIGURE 21.5
Getting advice on
problem resolution from
the Best Pratices
Analyzer

◆ The Do Not Show Me This Item Again for This Instance Only link tells the ExBPA not to report this particular issue the next time it runs. This might be useful if you know that the configuration property or if item that is being reported is not really relevant to your configuration.

◆ The Do Not Show Me This Item Again for All Instances link tells the ExBPA that it should ignore this issue anytime it is reported for any server or administrative group.

TIP

The links in the ExBPA to learn more about particular settings or best practices will give you excellent information about fine-tuning Exchange. Microsoft has done a good job of writing and presenting some in-depth technical about Exchange, and we urge you to take advantage of this resource.

We can expand this report and delve more deeply into the findings and recommendations of the ExBPA by selecting the All Issues tab on the View Best Practices Report page. Despite the fact that the tab is labeled All Issues, it is not "all the information" that the ExBPA has collected. All Issues finds anything that the ExBPA finds to be out of the ordinary, not a best practice, or things that are potentially a problem.

Figure 21.6 shows an example of the All Issues page. This page has been arranged by the issue severity. You can still see the two critical issues at the top of the page. Below the critical issues are the warnings. Finally, below that are the recommendations based on best practices.

FIGURE 21.6
Viewing the Best Practices All Issues report

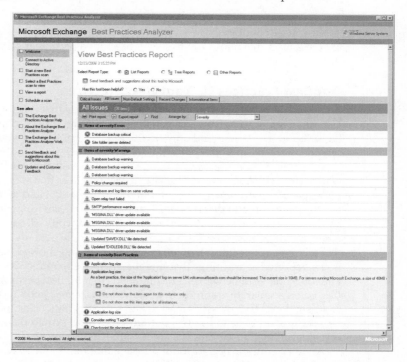

You can export the report to an HTML, CSV, or XML file. However, the report is saved to your local user profile directory so you can view it again if you want to. You can find it in the \Application Data\Microsoft\ExBPA folder within your user profile.

If we had chosen to include a performance baseline when we started the scan, then the Best Practices Report would include an additional tab called Baseline. A sample is shown in Figure 21.7. This part of the report includes the maximum and averaged values for some of the critical performance counters. When you first configure your Exchange server, you can run a performance baseline report and then periodically run the report again as you start adding mailboxes.

FIGURE 21.7
Including a performance baseline in the Best Practices Report

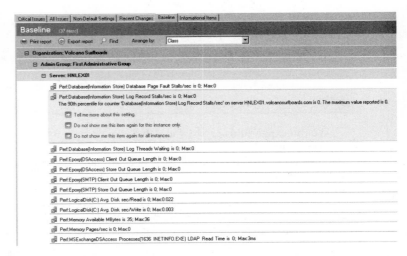

As you can in other parts of a ExBPA report, you can expand any of the items in the report to access links that allow you to see more about a particular setting or to exclude a setting from future reports.

Our Best Practices vs. Your Best Practices

A common misconception when using the ExBPA is that it is the Exchange team's magic wand. You run it and it will give you a list of recommendations and potential problems. Once you follow these recommendations and address the potential problems, you are on your way to Exchange nirvana.

While the ExBPA may *help* you on the road to Exchange nirvana, it is certainly not a magic wand. The ExBPA is using a database of best practices that were developed without knowledge of your specific environment. You cannot follow it blindly, and therefore you must review each recommendation and determine if it applies to your environment and how following it might affect your configuration. A recommendation that would dramatically help performance, recoverability, or stability for one environment might actually break something in another.

Let's look at the report that we ran previously and showed in Figure 21.6. There are a couple of issues reported as warnings that might actually be required. For example, the Database and Log Files on Same Volume warning recommends that for best performance and reliability, the database files be on a separate volumes. In general that is a very good recommendation, but if this server has a single RAID 1 or RAID 5 array and supports only 50 or 100 mailboxes, then this would not be as critical an issue to resolve. Certainly 100 users would usually not overtax a well-configured server, even if all of the files are on the same disk volume.

Another example of a warning message that might not be relevant is Open Relay Test Failed. The ExBPA attempts to relay mail through each of the SMTP servers that it finds in the organization. This particular SMTP virtual server (on an Exchange 2003 server) is configured to allow relay for certain internal IP addresses only. The warning is worth looking into, but it does not mean that it is something that must be changed.

There are a number of other issues like this that the ExBPA will report to you. It is your job as the Exchange server administrator to research each of them and decide if it is something that must be fixed or changed for your organization.

Auditing and Logging

Both Windows and Exchange Server present you with a lot of options for recording activity that occur on an Exchange server. Some auditing and logging options are on by default, while others must be enabled manually. We will break these up in to two broad categories. The first is Windows auditing, which reports on security- and operational-related events that affect the Windows operating system. The second is auditing and logs related to Exchange; within this category we can break these up further in to audit events relating to security and operations and events relating to message transport.

TIP

You never know when you are going to need historical information from logs. Plan to have a few weeks' worth when configuring logs and designing the capacity of your Exchange servers.

We are going to examine a number of different types of logging and auditing. We will often recommend that you turn on logging and auditing that is not turned on by default. Our reasoning behind this is that when you must start troubleshooting a problem or looking in to a possible security issue, you will need these logs available to you.

However, keep in mind that each time you increase the amount of logging or auditing that a system is doing, you increase the system overhead (CPU, disk, and memory).

Windows Auditing

Windows auditing can be applied to each server by using the Local Security Policy Editor or by applying the settings centrally using a group policy object (GPO) via Active Directory. In our example, we will use the Local Security Policy Editor. By default, Windows 2003 enables success auditing for some event logging categories, but we recommend enabling additional auditing of both success and failures.

When choosing to enable success, failure, or both types of auditing, there are two different philosophies at work. Those that recommend enabling mostly success auditing are usually interested in auditing things that actually happened or things that were successfully done by authorized users. This seems to be the mindset of the people that set the original Windows default auditing values.

Those that recommend enabling mostly failure auditing are usually interested in auditing things that were attempted but failed, such as logon failures or someone trying to run a program that they do not have permissions to run.

Finally, there is the third category of event logging that can best be described as logging done by paranoid control freaks. That is the category into which we place ourselves. We not only want an audit history of successful events, we also want to be able to audit failures that might help us track down intrusion or unauthorized access attempts.

As you increase the amount of logging that you are doing on any server, you will increase the load that is placed on it. The larger the event logs grow, the more challenging it will become to disseminate any useful information from them. So keep this in mind. Security-minded organizations with more than a few servers and a few hundred users should consider investing in an event log management system that can collect and analyze event logs centrally.

INCREASING THE SIZE OF EVENT LOGS

If you plan on keeping more than a few hours worth of information in your security and application logs, you will probably need to increase the overall size of the logs. The default event log file sizes are not sufficient for larger servers. You can configure the size of the event log sizes using the Event Viewer (right-click on each event log and select Properties from the pop-up menu). The Application event log properties are shown in Figure 21.8. The size of the event log is set in the Maximum Log Size box and must be in multiples of 64KB.

TIP

Event log sizes and overwrite behavior can be set centrally using a group policy object (GPO).

FIGURE 21.8
Changing the Application event log properties

We recommend that you increase the size of your event logs on both your Exchange servers and your domain controllers. Table 21.1 shows the recommended event logs sizes for Exchange servers and domain controllers.

TABLE 21.1:   Recommended Maximum Event Log Sizes

EVENT LOG	EXCHANGE SERVER	DOMAIN CONTROLLER
Application	147,456KB	49,152KB
Security	49,152KB	147,456KB
System	49,152KB	49,152KB
PowerShell	16,384KB	N/A
Directory Service	N/A	16,384KB
File Replication Service	N/A	16,384KB
DNS Server	N/A	16,384KB

The recommended sizes shown in Table 21.1 are just estimates and you can tweak them in whatever direction you see necessary. However, for the best performance and accuracy with event logs, we recommend that the combined size of all event logs not exceed 300MB.

TIP

Event log sizes and overwrite settings can be configured using Event Viewer on a server-by-server basis or by using an Active Directory group policy object. If you have more than one or two servers, using a GPO is much simpler.

Notice also in Figure 21.8 that there is a setting for controlling the behavior of event logging when the maximum log size is reached. The default is Overwrite Events as Needed. In a security-conscious environment, you may want to set this to either Overwrite Events Older Than 7 Days (you can change the number of days) or Do Not Overwrite Events (Clear Log Manually). If you set either of these two settings and the event log fills up before it is either cleared or the maximum number of days is reached, then event logging will stop. That is considered a feature and is designed to prevent an intruder or evildoer from covering their tracks by generating additional event logging and thus removing evidence of their evil deed.

DEFINING AN AUDIT POLICY

Defining an auditing policy for a member server is really simple. Open the Local Security Policy management console program and drill down to the Local Policies ➤ Audit Policies container (shown in Figure 21.9).

FIGURE 21.9
Configuring events to be audited

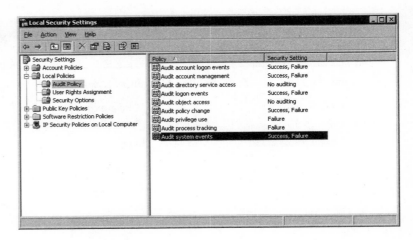

FIGURE 21.9
Configuring events to be audited

Table 21.2 shows the audit settings that we recommend enabling for a Windows 2003 machine that is functioning as a member server. Anything that is logged by these settings will be logged to the Security event log.

TABLE 21.2:   Auditing Levels for an Exchange 2007 Member Server

POLICY	SETTINGS
Audit Account Logon Events	Success and Failure
Audit Account Management	Success and Failure
Audit Directory Service Access	No auditing
Audit Logon Events	Success and Failure
Audit Object Access	No auditing
Audit Policy Change	Success and Failure
Audit Privilege Use	Success and Failure
Audit Process Tracking	Failure
Audit System Events	Success and Failure

To select an audit level, double-click on the policy to see the dialog box that allows you to select whether to audit the success or failure of events.

Exchange Diagnostics Logging

Exchange Server has a lot of possible categories for diagnostics logging and troubleshooting. Most of this report information is much more advanced and detailed than we typically need on a day-to-day basis when monitoring Exchange, but there are some diagnostics logging events that we recommend you enable. They help you to monitor some of the common events that you might need to be aware of for either security reasons or operational purposes. Figure 21.10 shows an example of one of these events; in this event we see that a user is logging on to their own mailbox.

> **NOTE**
>
> Exchange diagnostics logging information appears in the Application event log.

Table 21.3 lists event log services and categories that you should consider enabling.

If you are familiar with Exchange 2000/2003, then you probably already know that diagnostics logging was set using the Exchange System Manager. However, Exchange 2007 does not include a graphical user interface for managing diagnostics logging. These must be enabled using the Exchange Management Shell (EMS). There are two EMS cmdlets that are used to retrieve event logging levels and to set them. They are as follows:

Get-EventLogLevel   Reports on the level of logging of the specified event category or all categories if no category is specified

Set-EventLogLevel   Configures the diagnostics logging level of the specified logging category

FIGURE 21.10
An application event indicating that a user is logging in to their own mailbox

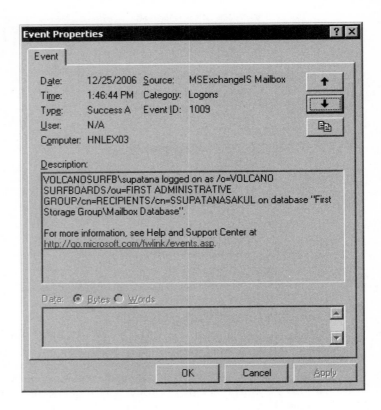

TABLE 21.3: Recommended Exchange Diagnostics Logging Categories

EVENT CATEGORY	DESCRIPTION
MSExchangeIS\9000 Private\Logons	Audit events relating to mailbox access
MSExchangeIS\9000 Private\Send As	Audit events relating to the use of the Send As permission
MSExchangeIS\9000 Private\Send On Behalf Of	Audit events relating to a user using the Send on Behalf Of permission
MSExchangeIS\9000 Private\Storage Limits	Audit events indicating that mailboxes are exceeding storage limits
MSExchangeIS\9002 System\Move Mailbox	Audit events indicating that a mailbox has been moved
MSExchangeIS\9002 System\Virus Scanning	Audit events relating to virus scanning
MSExchangeMailboxAssistants\Email _Lifecyle_Assistants	Audit events relating to processing message records management settings
MSExchangeMailboxAssistants\Resource Booking Assistant	Audit events relating to the use of the resource booking assistant

If you use the `Get-EventLogLevel` cmdlet with no parameters, the output will show you all of the diagnostics logging levels relating to Exchange. The following is the output of the `Get-EventLogLevel` cmdlet. We are listing these here as a reference.

```
Get-EventLogLevel
```

Identity	EventLevel
MSExchange ActiveSync\Requests	Lowest
MSExchange ActiveSync\Configuration	Lowest
MSExchange Antispam\General	Lowest
MSExchange Autodiscover\Core	Lowest
MSExchange Autodiscover\Web	Lowest
MSExchange Autodiscover\Provider	Lowest
MSExchange Availability\Availability Service	Lowest
MSExchange Availability\Availability Service General	Lowest
MSExchange Availability\Availability Service Authentication	Lowest
MSExchange Availability\Availability Service Authorization	Lowest
MSExchange Cluster\Move	Lowest
MSExchange Cluster\Upgrade	Lowest
MSExchange Cluster\Action	Lowest
MSExchange Common\General	Lowest
MSExchange Common\Configuration	Lowest
MSExchange Common\Logging	Lowest
MSExchange Extensibility\Transport Address Book	Lowest
MSExchange Extensibility\MExRuntime	Lowest
MSExchange EdgeSync\Synchronization	Lowest
MSExchange EdgeSync\Topology	Lowest
MSExchange EdgeSync\SyncNow	Lowest
MSExchange TransportService\TransportService	Lowest
MSExchange Web Services\Core	Lowest
MSExchange IMAP4\General	Lowest
MSExchange Messaging Policies\Journaling	Lowest
MSExchange Messaging Policies\AttachFilter	Lowest
MSExchange Messaging Policies\AddressRewrite	Lowest
MSExchange Messaging Policies\Rules	Lowest
MSExchange Messaging Policies\Prelicensing	Lowest
MSExchange Anti-spam Update\HygieneUpdate	Lowest
MSExchange Management Application\Shell	Lowest
MSExchange Management Application\Console	Lowest
MSExchange OWA\FormsRegistry	Lowest
MSExchange OWA\Core	Lowest
MSExchange OWA\Configuration	Lowest
MSExchange OWA\Themes	Lowest
MSExchange OWA\SmallIcons	Lowest
MSExchange OWA\Proxy	Lowest
MSExchange OWA\Transcoding	Lowest
MSExchange OWA\ADNotifications	Lowest
MSExchange POP3\General	Lowest
MSExchange Process Manager\ProcessManager	Lowest
MSExchange Repl\Service	Lowest

MSExchange Repl\Exchange VSS Writer	Lowest
MSExchange System Attendant Mailbox\General	Lowest
MSExchange ADAccess\General	Lowest
MSExchange ADAccess\Cache	Lowest
MSExchange ADAccess\Topology	Low
MSExchange ADAccess\Configuration	Lowest
MSExchange ADAccess\LDAP	Lowest
MSExchange ADAccess\Validation	Low
MSExchange ADAccess\Recipient Update Service	Lowest
MSExchange ADAccess\Site Update	Lowest
MSExchangeAL\Ldap Operations	Lowest
MSExchangeAL\Service Control	Lowest
MSExchangeAL\Attribute Mapping	Lowest
MSExchangeAL\Account Management	Lowest
MSExchangeAL\Address List Synchronization	Lowest
MSExchangeIS\9000 Private\Transport General	Lowest
MSExchangeIS\9000 Private\General	Lowest
MSExchangeIS\9000 Private\Transport Sending	Lowest
MSExchangeIS\9000 Private\Transport Delivering	Lowest
MSExchangeIS\9000 Private\Transfer Into Gateway	Lowest
MSExchangeIS\9000 Private\Transfer Out Of Gateway	Lowest
MSExchangeIS\9000 Private\MTA Connections	Lowest
MSExchangeIS\9000 Private\Logons	Low
MSExchangeIS\9000 Private\Access Control	Lowest
MSExchangeIS\9000 Private\Send On Behalf Of	Lowest
MSExchangeIS\9000 Private\Send As	Lowest
MSExchangeIS\9000 Private\Rules	Lowest
MSExchangeIS\9000 Private\Storage Limits	Lowest
MSExchangeIS\9000 Private\Background Cleanup	Lowest
MSExchangeIS\9000 Private\DS Synchronization	Lowest
MSExchangeIS\9000 Private\Views	Lowest
MSExchangeIS\9000 Private\Download	Lowest
MSExchangeIS\9000 Private\Local Replication	Lowest
MSExchangeIS\9001 Public\Transport General	Lowest
MSExchangeIS\9001 Public\General	Lowest
MSExchangeIS\9001 Public\Replication DS Updates	Lowest
MSExchangeIS\9001 Public\Replication Incoming Messages	Lowest
MSExchangeIS\9001 Public\Replication Outgoing Messages	Lowest
MSExchangeIS\9001 Public\Replication NDRs	Lowest
MSExchangeIS\9001 Public\Transport Sending	Lowest
MSExchangeIS\9001 Public\Transport Delivering	Lowest
MSExchangeIS\9001 Public\MTA Connections	Lowest
MSExchangeIS\9001 Public\Logons	Lowest
MSExchangeIS\9001 Public\Access Control	Lowest
MSExchangeIS\9001 Public\Send On Behalf Of	Lowest
MSExchangeIS\9001 Public\Send As	Lowest
MSExchangeIS\9001 Public\Rules	Lowest

```
MSExchangeIS\9001 Public\Storage Limits                        Lowest
MSExchangeIS\9001 Public\Replication Site Folders              Lowest
MSExchangeIS\9001 Public\Replication Expiry                    Lowest
MSExchangeIS\9001 Public\Replication Conflicts                 Lowest
MSExchangeIS\9001 Public\Replication Backfill                  Lowest
MSExchangeIS\9001 Public\Background Cleanup                    Lowest
MSExchangeIS\9001 Public\Replication Errors                    Lowest
MSExchangeIS\9001 Public\DS Synchronization                    Lowest
MSExchangeIS\9001 Public\Views                                 Lowest
MSExchangeIS\9001 Public\Replication General                   Lowest
MSExchangeIS\9001 Public\Download                              Lowest
MSExchangeIS\9001 Public\Local Replication                     Lowest
MSExchangeIS\9002 System\Recovery                              Lowest
MSExchangeIS\9002 System\General                               Lowest
MSExchangeIS\9002 System\Connections                           Lowest
MSExchangeIS\9002 System\Table Cache                           Lowest
MSExchangeIS\9002 System\Content Engine                        Lowest
MSExchangeIS\9002 System\Performance Monitor                   Lowest
MSExchangeIS\9002 System\Move Mailbox                          Lowest
MSExchangeIS\9002 System\Download                              Lowest
MSExchangeIS\9002 System\Virus Scanning                        Lowest
MSExchangeIS\9002 System\Exchange Writer                       Lowest
MSExchangeIS\9002 System\Backup Restore                        Lowest
MSExchangeIS\9002 System\Client Monitoring                     Lowest
MSExchangeIS\9002 System\Event History                         Lowest
MSExchangeIS\9002 System\Database Storage Engine               Lowest
MSExchangeMailboxAssistants\Service                            Lowest
MSExchangeMailboxAssistants\OOF Assistant                      Lowest
MSExchangeMailboxAssistants\OOF Library                        Lowest
MSExchangeMailboxAssistants\Resource Booking Attendant         Lowest
MSExchangeMailboxAssistants\Email_Lifecycle_Assistant          Low
MSExchangeMailSubmission\General                               Lowest
MSExchangeMU\General                                           Lowest
MSExchangeSA\Clean Mailbox                                     Lowest
MSExchangeSA\NSPI Proxy                                        Lowest
MSExchangeSA\RFR Interface                                     Lowest
MSExchangeSA\OAL Generator                                     Lowest
MSExchangeSA\Proxy Generation                                  Lowest
MSExchangeSA\RPC Calls                                         Lowest
MSExchangeSA\RPC-HTTP Management                               Lowest
MSExchangeTransport\SmtpReceive                                Lowest
MSExchangeTransport\SmtpSend                                   Lowest
MSExchangeTransport\DSN                                        Lowest
MSExchangeTransport\Routing                                    Lowest
MSExchangeTransport\Logging                                    Lowest
MSExchangeTransport\Components                                 Lowest
MSExchangeTransport\RemoteDelivery                             Lowest
```

```
MSExchangeTransport\Pickup                  Lowest
MSExchangeTransport\Categorizer             Lowest
MSExchangeTransport\PoisonMessage           Lowest
MSExchangeTransport\MessageSecurity         Lowest
MSExchangeTransport\TransportService        Lowest
MSExchangeTransport\Exch50                  Lowest
MSExchangeTransport\Process                 Lowest
MSExchangeTransport\ResourceManager         Lowest
MSExchangeTransport\Configuration           Lowest
MSExchangeTransport\Storage                 Lowest
MSExchangeTransport\Agents                  Lowest
MSExchangeFDS\General                       Lowest
MSExchangeFDS\FileReplication               Lowest
```

Each diagnostics logging category can be set to one of five levels. Each of the levels will log progressively more information. The levels are as follows:

Lowest (0)   Lowest is the default level for most categories of Exchange diagnostics logging. When a category is set at this level, you will only see the default information. Depending on the category, that may be no events at all, some informational events, warnings, or only errors.

Low (1)   Low-level logging reports generic warning and errors but does not report a significant amount of detail. You should always start logging at the Low level.

Medium (3)   Medium-level logging reports slightly more detailed information than Low logging.

High (5)   High-level logging reports detailed support information.

Expert (7)   Expert-level logging reports information that is usually only useful to Microsoft Customer Support Services. Not all components or programs will report additional information if you set the logging level to Expert.

Any type of ongoing logging should be set to Low. Increase logging levels only if the Low level does not provide you with the information you require to monitor a component or troubleshoot a problem. The level of information you get depends entirely on how much logging the program or component that you are monitoring was designed to report.

To adjust the logging level for a particular component (such as information store logons), you use the EMS. Here is an example that would work if you were on the console of the Exchange server in question:

```
Set-EventLogLevel "MSExchangeIS\9000 Private\Logons" -Level Low
```

You can also include the server name as part of the service or component that you are logging such, as this example:

```
Set-EventLogLevel "HNLEX03\MSExchangeIS\9000 Private\Logons" -Level Low
```

Using Message Tracking

All versions of Exchange have had a message tracking facility and Exchange 2007 is no exception. The message tracking features have been nicely expanded in Exchange 2007 and give you access to more details of the message tracking log from the graphical user interface as well as the EMS.

If you have not used the message tracking facility before, you are missing out on a powerful diagnostics tool. When message tracking is enabled, each Exchange component that processes or moves a message within an Exchange organization logs an event that will include information about that message to the current server's message tracking logs.

Information is logged about message submission (SUBMIT), message transmission (SEND), message receipt (RECEIVE), distribution list expansion (EXPAND), and local delivery (DELIVER). From these events, you can track the progress of a message as it moves within your organization. You can track the progress of a message right up until the point that it leaves your organization, but you cannot track it once it is outside of your organization.

Introducing Message Tracking Logs

Let's first talk about the message tracking logs themselves. Administrators of earlier versions will recall that they had to enable message tracking for each server in their organization. In Exchange 2007, message tracking is configured for each Hub Transport server (since that is the server role that actually moves messages around). Message tracking is enabled by default and messages are retained for a maximum of 30 days. We can retrieve information about the message tracking log configuration for each server using the EMS cmdlet `Get-TransportServer`. The following is an example of retrieving the properties relating to message tracking for server HNLEX03. There are quite a few more properties for the transport server, but we are just interested in those relating to message tracking:

```
Get-TransportServer "HNLEX03" | fl name,*track*

Name                                   : HNLEX03
MessageTrackingLogEnabled              : True
MessageTrackingLogMaxAge               : 30.00:00:00
MessageTrackingLogMaxDirectorySize     : 250MB
MessageTrackingLogMaxFileSize          : 10MB
MessageTrackingLogPath                 : C:\Program Files\Microsoft\
Exchange Server\TransportRoles\Logs\MessageTracking
MessageTrackingLogSubjectLoggingEnabled : True
```

There are a couple of important pieces of information in the output of `Get-TransportServer`. Most important is that it is enabled (`MessageTrackingLogEnabled = True`) by default and that the message tracking logs include subject logging (`MessageTrackingLogSubjectLoggingEnabled = True`), but also the following is true:

◆ Message tracking logs are found in the `C:\Program Files\Microsoft\Exchange Server\TransportRoles\Logs\MessageTracking` folder.

◆ Message tracking logs are retained for 30 days. After 30 days they are automatically deleted.

◆ The maximum size of a message tracking log is 10MB

◆ The maximum amount of space the message tracking logs can consume is 250MB

For servers with fewer than 500 average users, this is probably sufficient. However, for servers supporting larger numbers of users, you will want to increase the maximum log file size and the maximum amount of space the logs can consume. These can all be changed using the `Set-TransportServer` cmdlet. The following cmdlet will change the maximum log file size to 25MB, change the maximum directory size to 500MB, and change the tracking log folder to `C:\TrackingLogs`.

```
Set-TransportServer "hnlex03" -MessageTrackingLogPath "C:\TrackingLogs"
  -MessageTrackingLogMaxFileSize:25MB -MessageTrackingLogMaxDirectorySize:500MB
```

Once you have executed this command, Exchange should automatically start using the new tracking log folder. However, the existing files will not be moved.

If you want to implement these settings for all Hub Transport servers, you can use the `Get-TransportServer` and `Set-TransportServer` cmdlets in the same command. The following command will set these settings for all transport servers:

```
Get-TransportServer | Set-TransportServer -MessageTrackingLogPath "C:\TrackingLogs"
  -MessageTrackingLogMaxFileSize:25MB -MessageTrackingLogMaxDirectorySize:500MB
```

Tracking a Message

Let's look at the actual message tracking feature. The graphical interface for the message tracking facility is part of the new Exchange Troubleshooting Assistant (shown in Figure 21.11).

FIGURE 21.11
Exchange
Troubleshooting
Assistant

You can launch the Exchange Troubleshooting Assistant and run either the Message Tracking or the Mail Flow Tools or you can run them separately from the Toolbox work center. The Message Tracking portion of the Exchange Troubleshooting Assistant is wizard driven. The first screen in the wizard is the Message Tracking Parameters screen, where you can narrow down the criteria of the message for which you are searching (see Figure 21.12).

FIGURE 21.12
Specifying the criteria for a particular message

Message Tracking Parameters

Select checkboxes to include criteria in the message tracking search.

Recipients	☑ JMcBee@directory-update.com	Resolve Recipient
Sender	☑ supatana@somorita.com	Resolve Sender
Server	☑ HNLEX03	Server from Sender
EventID	☐ SEND	
MessageID	☐ <C27B18ED17ABBB4CBFC6346F93820D1B26C9CA54DA@	
InternalMessageID	☐ 17	
Subject	☐ Aloha and testing	
Reference	☐	
Start	☑ Monday , December 25, 2006 9:00 AM	
End	☑ Monday , December 25, 2006 10:30 AM	

Exchange management shell command

```
get-messagetrackinglog -Recipients:JMcBee@directory-update.com -Sender "supatana@somorita.com" -Server "HNLEX03" -Start "12/25/2006 9:00:00 AM" -End "12/25/2006 10:30:00 AM"
```

⬅ Go Back   ➡ Next

Criteria for searching for a message include the sender, recipient, message ID, and subject. You can narrow the focus of the type of message using the EventID field, which allows you to designate the type of event you are looking for, such as Send, Receive, Submit, Transfer, Expand, DSN, and so on. Finally, you can narrow the focus even further by looking for messages sent only during a specific date and time range.

Once you have specified the criteria you want to use to search for a specific message, click Next and the wizard will search the messages that meet those criteria. Depending on the size of the message tracking logs and the number of servers that the messages will cross, the results might take a minute or two to generate. In a single-server environment, results are generated pretty quickly. A sample output is shown in Figure 21.13.

FIGURE 21.13
Viewing the message tracking results

Message Tracking Results

Selected row will populate parameters for next message tracking search.

Timestamp	EventId	Source	SourceConte	MessageId	MessageSubj	Sender	Recipients	InternalMess
▶ 2006/12/26 09:19:13	RECEIVE	STOREDRIV		<C27B18ED1	Aloha and tes	supatana@so	JMcBee@cta	16
2006/12/26 09:19:13	SUBMIT	STOREDRIV	MDB:7cd0b6	<C27B18ED1	Aloha and tes	supatana@so		
2006/12/26 09:19:14	TRANSFER	ROUTING	ContentConv	<C27B18ED1	Aloha and tes	supatana@so	JMcBee@cta	17
2006/12/26 09:19:20	SEND	SMTP	08C8F6B8CB	<C27B18ED1	Aloha and tes	supatana@so	JMcBee@cta	17

One thing that is a bit annoying about this interface is that the results are not always sorted based on when they occurred. A quick solution to this is to click on the Timestamp column to get it to resort; the events may still not sort correctly if two events occur during the same second. The events you are seeing in Figure 21.3 illustrate that the following actions occurred:

1. A message was submitted to the information store.

2. The transport system received the message from the STOREDRIV (store driver).

3. The message went through the message routing system.

4. The messages was transmitted via SMTP.

If you click on one of the events in the message tracking results list and then click Next, the Message Tracking Parameters screen reappears with the specific criteria to track that particular message. Figure 21.14 shows a modified Message Tracking Parameters screen from which we could track that specific message. We can do so because this screen now includes the message ID.

FIGURE 21.14
Tracking a specific event

Notice at the bottom of the page the EMS command necessary to perform the message tracking using the `Get-MessageTrackingLog` cmdlet. If you select the EventID check box and include SEND in the criteria, you can look for one part of the message trace. In the following example, we have taken this search criteria and used the EMS to track the specific event in which the message was transmitted from the Hub Transport server to a remote server on the Internet:

```
get-messagetrackinglog -Server "HNLEX03" -EventID "SEND" -MessageID
"<C27B18ED17ABBB4CBFC6346F93820D1B26C8CA54DA@HNLEX03.volcanosurfboards.com>"
-Start  "12/26/2006 9:09:00 AM" -End "12/26/2006 9:29:00 AM" | FL


Timestamp              : 12/26/2006 9:19:20 AM
ClientIp               : 192.168.254.19
ClientHostname         : HNLEX03
ServerIp               : 66.75.160.20
ServerHostname         :
SourceContext          : 08C8F6B8CBFD8A6F
ConnectorId            : E2K7 SMTP to Internet
Source                 : SMTP
EventId                : SEND
InternalMessageId      : 17
MessageId              : <C27B18ED17ABBB4CBFC6346F93820D1B26C8CA54DA@HNLEX03.
volcanosurfboards.com>
Recipients             : {JMcBee@cta.net}
```

```
RecipientStatus           : {250 2.1.5 <JMcBee@cta.net> ... Recipient ok}
TotalBytes                : 3611
RecipientCount            : 1
RelatedRecipientAddress   :
Reference                 :
MessageSubject            : Aloha and testing
Sender                    : supatana@somorita.com
ReturnPath                : supatana@somorita.com
MessageInfo               : 12/26/2006 9:20:00 AM
```

Probably the two most relevant properties of this particular event are the `ServerIp` property and the `RecipientStatus` property. The `ServerIp` property tells you the IP address of the remote server to which the message was sent. The `RecipientStatus` property tells you that the message recipient was accepted by the remote server.

Introducing Protocol and Connectivity Logs

Exchange 2007 provides a lot of options for logging and troubleshooting connectivity problems. Each Hub Transport server can be configured to track all connectivity to and from it and each Send connector or Receive connector can be configured to log inbound or outbound connections. The resulting logs are comma-delimited text files that can be read using any text editor or even imported into a database.

Configuring Connectivity Logging

Each Hub Transport server can be configured with connectivity logging. The connectivity log contains a record of all communications a particular Hub Transport server handled. This includes inbound and outbound SMTP communication as well as MAPI connections from Mailbox servers. Figure 21.15 shows a sample connectivity log. Connectivity log files all start with CONNECTLOG followed by the current date.

FIGURE 21.15
Sample connectivity log

In this log, you can see the outbound sessions and you can see the MAPI sessions to and from the Mailbox server (named hnlex03.volcanosurfboards.com in this log file). One column of interest in this log file is the direction column. There are four different characters that you may see in the direction column that indicate connections or direction of message flow. They are as follows:

+   Indicates a connection is being established either to a remote SMTP system or to a mailbox server.

-      Indicates a connection has been completed or disconnected.

>   A message is being sent outbound to a remote SMTP system.

<   A message is being received from a remote SMTP system.

Another interesting column to know about is the session-id column. The session ID is a globally unique identifier that will be the same for an entire SMTP session (it is blank for MAPI sessions). The cool thing about this is that the session ID corresponds to the session column in the Send and Receive logs.

Connectivity logging is disabled by default and must be enabled for any Hub Transport server on which you want to view the logs. To enable connectivity logging, you use the Set-TransportServer cmdlet. The following is an example for setting connectivity logging on server HNLEX03:

```
Set-TransportServer "HNLEX03" -ConnectivityLogEnabled $True
```

You could use the Get-TransportServer and Set-TransportServer cmdlets to enable connectivity on all Hub Transport servers as shown here:

```
GetTransportServer | Set-TransportServer "HNLEX03" -ConnectivityLogEnabled $True
```

As with message tracking logs, the logs are retained for 30 days, the maximum size of the log file directory is 250MB, and a maximum log file size is 10MB. The log files are found in the C:\Program Files\Microsoft\Exchange Server\TransportRoles\Logs\Connectivity folder.

You can view the connectivity log configuration using the Get-TransportServer cmdlet. The following is an example:

```
Get-TransportServer hnlex03 | FL Name,*connectivity*

Name                               : HNLEX03
ConnectivityLogEnabled             : True
ConnectivityLogMaxAge              : 30.00:00:00
ConnectivityLogMaxDirectorySize    : 250MB
ConnectivityLogMaxFileSize         : 10MB
ConnectivityLogPath                : C:\Program Files\Microsoft\Exchange Server\
TransportRoles\Logs\Connectivity
```

You update or change this information using the Set-TransportServer cmdlet.

Configuring Send and Receive Logging

One big improvement with Exchange 2007 is the ability to narrow the scope of protocol logging to an individual connector only. With Exchange 2000/2003, if you were troubleshooting an SMTP connectivity problem, you enabled protocol logging for the SMTP virtual server. The protocol logs would contain all inbound and outbound SMTP information for all connectors that used that SMTP virtual server.

In Exchange 2007, each Hub Transport server has Send and Receive protocol logs, but these are enabled for each Send and Receive connector, not for the entire Hub Transport server. Let's start by looking at the properties of the Send and Receive logs using the `Get-TransportServer` cmdlet. By now, you are going to be familiar with the properties of these logs since they are almost identical to the properties of the connectivity and message tracking logs.

```
C:\>Get-TransportServer "HNLEX03" |
FL Name,*sendprotocol*,*receiveprotocol*,*intraorg*

Name                              : HNLEX03
SendProtocolLogMaxAge             : 30.00:00:00
SendProtocolLogMaxDirectorySize   : 250MB
SendProtocolLogMaxFileSize        : 10MB
SendProtocolLogPath               : C:\Program Files\
Microsoft\Exchange Server \TransportRoles\Logs\ProtocolLog\SmtpSend
ReceiveProtocolLogMaxAge          : 30.00:00:00
ReceiveProtocolLogMaxDirectorySize : 250MB
ReceiveProtocolLogMaxFileSize     : 10MB
ReceiveProtocolLogPath            : C:\Program Files\
Microsoft\Exchange Server\TransportRoles\Logs\ProtocolLog\SmtpReceive
IntraOrgConnectorProtocolLoggingLevel : None
```

These logs are kept for a maximum of 30 days, the maximum log file size is 10MB, and the maximum size of the log file directory is 250MB. The logs are found in separate directories in the `C:\Program Files\Microsoft\Exchange Server\TransportRoles\Logs\ProtocolLog` folder.

The one thing that you may notice is that there is not a parameter for enabling or disabling the Send and Receive logs. This is because the actual logging is enabled and disabled on a per-connector basis. For example, we have created a Send connector that delivers mail to the Internet called E2K7 SMTP to Internet; on the General property page (shown in Figure 21.16) of that connector, we can enable logging in the Protocol Logging Level drop-down list.

There are two choices for protocol logging on both Send and Receive connectors. The choices are None and Verbose. You can also set the logging level for Send and Receive connectors using the `Set-SendConnector` and `Set-ReceiveConnector` cmdlets. Let's first look at an example where the E2K7 SMTP to Internet Send connector has logging enabled:

```
Get-SendConnector "E2K7 SMTP to Internet" | FL Name,*log*

Name                : E2K7 SMTP to Internet
ProtocolLoggingLevel : None
```

FIGURE 21.16
Enabling protocol
logging for a Send
connector

You can use the `Set-SendConnector` cmdlet to enable this connector to supporting logging.

```
Set-SendConnector "E2K7 SMTP to Internet" -ProtocolLoggingLevel Verbose
```

The same format of logging can be used to enable protocol logging for a Receive connector. One thing you do have to watch out for is whether you have more than one source server configured for the Send connector. When you configure a Send connector, you can configure more than one Hub Transport server to be a source server for the connector. This is done on the Source Server property page of the connector, shown in Figure 21.17.

If you have more than one source server defined, an outbound SMTP message may be processed by any of them. This means that if you are troubleshooting a particular outbound message, you will need to check the Send protocol logs on all of these servers.

Another important point to note when reviewing protocol logs and debugging connectivity problems is that not all communication is logged to the Send protocol logs. All Hub Transport servers have a Send connector that is automatically created but is not visible. This implicit Send connector is used for internal delivery of e-mail between Hub Transport servers, Edge Transport servers, and Exchange 2003 servers. If you want the Hub Transport servers to log internal connectivity, you need to enable this on each Hub Transport server. This is the

`IntraOrgConnectorProtocolLoggingLevel` property found on the Hub Transport server's properties page. Here is an example of enabling this type of logging for Hub Transport server HNLEX03:

```
Set-TransportServer "HNLEX03" -IntraOrgConnectorProtocolLoggingLevel Verbose
```

FIGURE 21.17
Defining source servers for a Send connector

Alternatively, if you want to enable intra-organization logging for all Hub Transport servers, you could use this cmdlet:

```
Get-TransportServer | Set-TransportServer
-IntraOrgConnectorProtocolLoggingLevel Verbose
```

While the intra-organization logging may be useful for troubleshooting, you might not want to keep this type of logging enabled all the time. If you need to globally disable intra-organization logging, here is a command that should do the trick:

```
Get-TransportServer | Set-TransportServer
-IntraOrgConnectorProtocolLoggingLevel None
```

Now that you know how to enable and disable Send and Receive protocol logs, let's take a look at an actual log file. The text would not fit nicely here in the book, so Figure 21.18 shows an example of a Send protocol log.

FIGURE 21.18

Sample Send protocol
log

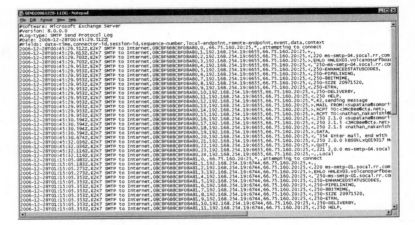

A lot of the space in both the Send and Receive logs is taken up by the `date-time`, `connector-id`, `session-id`, and `local-endpoint` columns. The real meat of the logs (from a troubleshooting perspective at least) is the information found in the `remote-endpoint` (the IP address of the remote system), `event`, and `data` columns. The `data` column contains the actual data that was sent to the remote system or that was received from the remote system. The `event` column contains a character that helps you to identify what is occurring or the direction of the data. The following information is found in the `event` column:

+   A connection has been established.

-      A connection has been closed.

\>   Information is being sent to a remote SMTP system.

<   Information is being received from a remote SMTP system.

*   An informational event has occured.

We realize that we have probably tossed a lot of minutia and detail to you on message tracking, connectivity, and protocol logs, but we think that you will find this information useful.

Monitoring

In Chapter 6, "Scaling Upward and Outward," we talked about monitoring your system. Most of the examples and performance monitor counters we discussed were really targeted toward determining whether it is time to expand the capacity of your system and to help you find bottlenecks. There is certainly overlap between "insufficient capacity" and a "healthy Exchange server," though.

In this section, we'll look at some Exchange and Windows tools that you can use to determine whether your server is healthy and processing messages.

Checking Queues

Confirming that e-mail message are being delivered is one of the most basic and important things that you do when managing an Exchange environment. The Queue Viewer tool is usually your front-line monitoring and troubleshooting tool. Queue Viewer is found in the Toolbox work center of the Exchange Management Console. Figure 21.19 shows the Queue Viewer interface.

FIGURE 21.19

Managing queues on a Hub Transport server

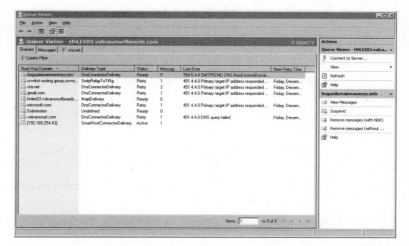

The first thing you need to know about the Queue Viewer is that it communicates with servers that have the Hub Transport role. Since queues are only maintained only on the Hub Transport server, there is no reason for it to communicate with another server role. Figure 21.19 shows the Queue Viewer being used to view the queues on server hnlex03.volcanosurfboards.com; the Microsoft Exchange Transport service must be running on the Hub Transport server. You can use the Connect to Server task in the Actions pane to connect to a different Hub Transport server.

Looking at the queues in Figure 21.19, we can tell a little about the messages that are waiting to be delivered. In this particular environment, server hnlex03 hosts a Send connector and is responsible for delivery to the Internet. It is also a bridgehead server for a legacy Exchange routing group connector to an Exchange 2000/2003 routing group.

The first column in the Queues listing is the Next Hop Domain column; it shows the destination Internet domain, remote smarthost, remote Hub Transport server, or legacy routing group. The Delivery Type column also shows some interesting information about a particular queue:

SmtpRelayToTiRg   is shorthand for SMTP relay to a Titanium routing group. Titanium is the code name for Exchange 2003, but this queue could be a queue to either Exchange 2000/2003 routing groups.

DNSConnectorDelivery   is a queue for messages that will be sent directly out to the Internet by using DNS to look up the remote domain's MX records.

Undefined   is an internal queue that is used to hold messages that have been submitted to the Submission queue but have not been placed in a link queue for delivery to a remote domain, relay, or server.

SmartHostConnectoDelivery   is a queue that is used to hold messages that are to be delivered to a specific smarthost. The smarthost to be used is specified in the Next Hop Domain column.

SMTPRelayWithinAdSite is the queue that is used to hold messages that must be delivered to another Hub Transport in the same Active Directory site. This other server might be a server that hosts an SMTP connector or an Edge Transport connection.

STMPRelaytoRemoteAdSite is the queue that is used to hold messages that are being delivered to a Hub Transport server in another Active Directory site.

NonSmtpGatewayDelivery is a queue that holds messages that are queued for delivery to a local, non-SMTP gateway. An example of this type of gateway is the Lotus Notes connector.

SmtpRelayWithinAdSiteToEdge is a queue that holds messages that are queued for delivery to an Edge Transport server.

MapiDelivery is a queue that holds messages queued up for Mailbox servers in the local Active Directory site.

Unreachable is a queue that holds message for which a route to the recipient can not be established.

The Status column of the Queue Viewer gives you some indication of what the queue is currently doing. There are four possible status values in the Exchange 2007 Queue viewer:

Active means that the message transport system is currently servicing this queue and delivering (or attempting to deliver) messages.

Suspended means that the administrator has placed the queue on hold so that no messages in the queue will be delivered.

Retry means that there has been a problem delivering the messages in this particular queue and that the message transport system will try to deliver the messages again.

Ready means that the queue is currently not servicing any requests but is awaiting the submission of any messages that need to be delivered.

Notice the Last Error column in the Queue Viewer; this column can usually give you some helpful troubleshooting information about why the messages are not being delivered. We have staged a couple of different potential errors in Figure 21.19 that represent some typical problems. We moved the Last Error column over further to the left and widened it some in this screen capture so that you could see it more clearly. In the default Queue Viewer interface, you may need to scroll to the right to see the Last Error column.

◆ 451 4.4.0 Primary target IP address responded with: "421 4.2.1 Unable to connect." Attempted failover to alternate host, but the attempted failover did not succeed. Either there are no alternate hosts or delivery failed to all alternate hosts. This message indicates that the remote host did not respond. This could be a connectivity problem or it could be that all of a remote domain's servers are down.

◆ 554 5.4.4 SMTPSEND.DNS.NonExistentDomain. This error indicates that a user has sent a message to a remote SMTP domain that cannot be resolved in DNS. This may be because it does not exist or it could be the result of DNS problems. Unlike previous versions of Exchange, within a few minutes Exchange 2007 will issue a non-delivery report to the user.

◆ 451 4.4.0 DNS query failed. This error indicates that the domain exists but that mail exchanger (MX) or address records (A) could not be resolved. Exchange will continue to try to look up address records and deliver the message until the time-out period ends (two days by default).

A common complaint about the Queue Viewer interface is that the Last Error column is difficult to read if there is much text in the column. You can move the mouse pointer over the text and you will the text in that column expand in much the same way that "fly over" or "mouse over" help works. That still may not be of much help if you need to get a copy of the actual message. That is one place that the EMS cmdlet `Get-Queue` comes in really handy. Here is a example of using the `Get-Queue` cmdlet with no parameters:

```
Get-Queue

Identity            DeliveryType Status MessageCount NextHopDomain
--------            ------------ ------ ------------ -------------
HNLEX03\95          DnsConnec... Retry  2            cta.net
HNLEX03\96          DnsConnec... Retry  1            microsoft.com
HNLEX03\98          SmartHost... Active 1            [192.168.254.43]
HNLEX03\100         DnsConnec... Retry  1            volcanosurf.com
HNLEX03\101         DnsConnec... Retry  1            gmail.com
HNLEX03\102         SmtpRelay... Retry  3            cn=first routing..
HNLEX03\Submission  Undefined    Ready  0            Submission
```

The `Get-Queue` cmdlet outputs the queue identity; that will prove to be really useful in troubleshooting. You can use this queue identity as input for the `Get-Queue` parameter; here is an example for getting all of the information for a particular queue:

```
Get-Queue "hnlex03\95"
Identity            DeliveryType Status MessageCount NextHopDomain
--------            ------------ ------ ------------ -------------
HNLEX03\95          DnsConnec... Retry  2            cta.net
```

You can pipe the output of the `Get-Queue` cmdlet to the `Format-List` cmdlet and get the details of the specified queue:

```
Get-Queue "hnlex03\95" | FL

Identity         : HNLEX03\95
DeliveryType     : DnsConnectorDelivery
NextHopDomain    : cta.net
NextHopConnector : 3fa8724f-689b-4b88-a91c-42b69c77d1f0
Status           : Retry
MessageCount     : 2
LastError        : 451 4.4.0 Primary target IP address responded with:
 "421 4.2.1 Unable to connect." Attempted failover to alternate host,
 that did not succeed. Either there are no alternate host, or delivery
 failed to all alternate hosts.
LastRetryTime    : 12/30/2006 11:47:03 AM
NextRetryTime    : 12/30/2006 11:57:24 AM
IsValid          : True
ObjectState      : Unchanged
```

When you highlight a particular queue in the Queue Viewer, the Actions menu gives you a number of different options for managing it. These are shown in this screen shot.

The following tasks appear in the Actions pane when you select a particular queue:

View Messages allows you to open a new tab in the Queue Viewer. This is the default behavior if you double-click a queue. The View Messages option creates a tab similar to the one shown in Figure 21.20.

FIGURE 21.20
Viewing the messages queued up in a specific queue

Suspend allows you to stop any messages in the specified queue from being delivered. This option will show by default if the queue is not already suspended.

Resume allows you to resume delivery of messages in a queue that has been suspended. This option will appear only if a queue has been suspended.

Retry forces the message transport system to immediately try to deliver the messages in a particular queue.

Remove Messages (With NDR) will delete all of the messages in a particular queue and send the message originator a non-delivery report (NDR) message. This is a nice new capability in Exchange 2007; in previous versions you had to delete messages one at a time.

Remove Messages (Without Sending NDRs) will delete all of the messages in a particular queue but not send a non-delivery report (NDR). As with the preceding task, this is a new capability in Exchange 2007; in previous versions you had to delete messages one at a time.

Notice that a filter is automatically created that filters the messages in a specific queue ID.

The Queue Viewer's Messages tab allows you to see all of the messages that are queued for delivery as well as additional information such as the message size, message subject, and the Queue ID and Last Error columns. The Messages tab also allows you to specify a filter based on the sender, Queue ID, spam confidence level (SCL), Size (KB), date received, expiration time, status, or subject. Figure 21.21 shows the Messages property page with a specific sender filter (From Address) applied.

FIGURE 21.21
Viewing and filtering all queued messages

From the Messages tab, you can select one or more messages and suspend, resume, or remove them. There are two remove options; you can remove the message and send an NDR or you can remove the message without sending an NDR. The Properties task on the Actions pane allows you to view more detailed information about the message. The General property page for one of these messages is shown in Figure 21.22.

FIGURE 21.22
General properties of a queued message

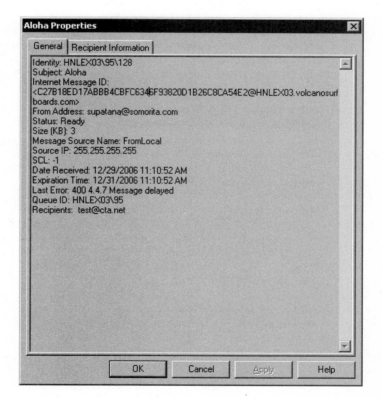

On the General property page, you can see detailed property information about the selected message. This includes the full text of the Last Error message as well as the identity of the message. The identity of the message can be used with the EMS queue management cmdlets Get-Message, Export-Message, Suspend-Message, Resume-Message, and Remove-Message. Here is an example of retrieving queued messages using the Get-Message cmdlet:

```
Get-Message

Identity          FromAddress      Status   Queue         Subject
--------          -----------      ------   -----         -------
HNLEX03\95\128    supatana@som...  Ready    HNLEX03\95    Aloha
HNLEX03\95\131    supatana@som...  Ready    HNLEX03\95    R&D budget f...
HNLEX03\96\134    supatana@som...  Ready    HNLEX03\96    Outbound mai...
HNLEX03\98\140    supatana@som...  Ready    HNLEX03\98    Product test...
HNLEX03\100\143   supatana@som...  Ready    HNLEX03\100   Can you send...
HNLEX03\101\146   supatana@som...  Ready    HNLEX03\101   More informa...
```

From this listing, you can get the identity of the message you are interested in viewing more information about. If the listing is larger (dozens or hundreds of messages), you could use the Where cmdlet to narrow the search. For example, if you know that the subject includes the word *Aloha*, you could use a search such as this:

```
Get-Message | where {$_.subject -like "Aloha"}

Identity          FromAddress      Status   Queue         Subject
--------          -----------      ------   -----         -------
HNLEX03\95\128    supatana@som...  Ready    HNLEX03\95    Aloha
```

Once you have the message identity, you can use the following command to retrieve more information about the queued message:

```
Get-Message "hnlex03\95\128" -IncludeRecipientInfo | FL

Identity          : HNLEX03\95\128
Subject           : Aloha
InternetMessageId :
<C27B18ED17ABBB4CBFC6346F93820D1B26C8CA54E2@HNLEX03.volcanosurfboards.com>
FromAddress       : supatana@somorita.com
Status            : Ready
Size              : 3284B
MessageSourceName : FromLocal
SourceIP          : 255.255.255.255
SCL               : -1
DateReceived      : 12/29/2006 11:10:52 AM
ExpirationTime    : 12/31/2006 11:10:52 AM
```

```
LastError        : 400 4.4.7 Message delayed
RetryCount       : 0
Queue            : HNLEX03\95
Recipients       : {test@cta.net}
IsValid          : True
ObjectState      : Unchanged
```

Note that this example includes the `-IncludeRecipientInfo` parameter; if this parameter was not included, the Recipients information would be blank.

Monitoring Health

Performance monitoring is one of the more important tasks that administrators need to do for their mail systems. A clear picture of your server's performance may help you to find bottlenecks or performance problems before they affect your users. Yet performance monitoring is something that most Exchange administrators seem to avoid like the plague.

Performance monitoring is not rocket science; it is not even nearly as difficult as most people think (or fear) it is. Often, the challenge to performance monitoring is in knowing which counters and thresholds indicate a possible performance problem. We hope to remedy that in this chapter, but at the very least we hope to get you started.

If you have not read Chapter 6, you should go back and review the section on performance monitoring. There is quite a bit of overlap between these two chapters, though in that chapter we focused on counters that might indicate the need to scale additional servers or add additional hardware resources. In this chapter, we are going to focus more on counters that indicate performance problems and server health.

Using Performance Monitoring Counters

Let's now look at some of the counters that you may find useful when monitoring performance problems or looking for bottlenecks. Before we jump into this discussion, though, here's a review of a few tips for performance monitoring:

◆ Don't sweat spikes in activity. You are interested in average activity over a typical period of time.

◆ Monitor over a few hours rather than a few minutes.

◆ Pick periods of typical activity. If most of your user community arrives at work at 8:00 in the morning and leaves for lunch at 11:30, then monitor during that period of time.

◆ Record performance monitor counter logs. You can analyze them later and refer back to them for historical information.

◆ Avoid performance monitoring immediately after restarting the server. On a mailbox server, a freshly restarted server is in what is called a cold state operation; this is when the Exchange server is just beginning to cache frequently used data. The disk I/O profile and CPU usage will be higher than normal.

◆ Performance monitoring is one part science and one part art. Take every counter value that you measure and think about what factors could cause that particular value to be too high (or too low).

MEMORY COUNTERS

Provided you have sufficient memory in your server, it won't usually be a bottleneck for Exchange 2007. We recommend that you have more than just the minimum amount of RAM in your servers. If you suspect memory problems, there are some counters that will prove to be very useful when making this determination. Table 21.4 shows some common performance monitor counters and some recommended values to watch for.

TABLE 21.4:   Counters That May Indicate a Shortage of Physical Memory

OBJECT/COUNTER	EXPLANATION\RECOMMENDATION
Memory/Pages/sec	This is the number of pages per second that Windows had to either retrieve from the page file or write to the page file due to a shortage of physical memory. This value should not exceed an average of 10 pages per second during typical activity.
Memory/Available Mbytes	This is the total amount of physical memory that is available to Windows. This value should be greater than 10 percent of the total amount of physical memory in the server.
Process/Working Set	The Working Set counter for each instance of the process running on Windows can be viewed and this can give you an idea of how much memory each of the processes running in Windows are allocating.

PROCESSOR COUNTERS

In most cases, the processor subsystem of a server is not usually the bottleneck or the cause of performance problems. Table 21.5 shows some of the common counters that you can use to determine if you need additional CPU capacity.

TABLE 21.5:   Counters That May Indicate Insufficient Processor Capacity

OBJECT/COUNTER	EXPLANATION\RECOMMENDATION
Processor/% Processor Time	This is the total percentage of time that the processors are doing useful work (as opposed to running idle threads). You want this to be below 70 percent on a sustained basis. If this value is higher than 70 percent, you may need to add additional processor capacity or split some workload off to another server.
Processor/% Processor Time	The Processor object allows you to select individual programs running under Windows and determine the resources that a particular process is using. In this case, you can isolate the percentage of the CPU that each process is using. An example of a performance monitor chart that is analyzing Exchange-related processes is shown in Figure 21.3.

We mentioned in Table 21.5 that the Process object lets you view the usage of specific processes running under Windows. This can be useful if you want to watch the usage of a particular or Exchange process. You can add an instance of each Exchange process to a performance monitor chart and see what percentage of the processor each of these processes is using.

FIGURE 21.23
Monitoring the
CPU usage of
Exchange-related
processes

FIGURE 21.23
Monitoring the
CPU usage of
Exchange-related
processes

DISK COUNTERS

Monitoring disk activity can also help you in determining where possible bottlenecks are within your system. For servers that supported more than a thousand mailboxes in Exchange 2003, disk bottlenecks were a frequent problem as often the disk subsystem did not have sufficient I/O capacity to support the number of reads and writes to the disk. While Exchange 2007's additional memory capacity has addressed this by allowing for better caching and more efficient disk I/O, if you do not have sufficient memory, a low memory situation may manifest itself as a disk performance problem. This is due to the fact that when an Exchange server does not have enough RAM to cache frequently used data, it must rely on the disk more frequently.

When monitoring disk counters, there are two disk counter objects that you can select: PhysicalDisk and LogicalDisk. Their names are pretty self-explanatory and make it easy to figure out which types of counters they provide. Depending on your system configuration, one or both might be disabled. You can use the `diskperf.exe` command to determine if the counters are available. Here is an example:

```
C:\>diskperf

Both Logical and Physical Disk Performance counters on this system
are automatically enabled on demand.
For legacy applications using IOCTL_DISK_PERFORMANCE to retrieve raw
  counters, you can use -Y or -N to forcibly enable or disable. No
  reboot is required.
```

In this case, both the physical and logical disk counters are available.

The physical disk counters are useful when determining which particular physical disks have the greatest load on them, while the logical disk counters are useful if you need to monitor a specific logical disk drive. In a perfect world, each logical disk is on a separate physical disk and the counters will report the same information. When you add performance counters to a chart or report, the physical disk object presents you with instances of the physical disk numbers while the logical disk object presents you with just the logical drive letters. Figure 21.24 shows the Add

Counters dialog box and the subtle difference between the physical disk instances and the logical disk instances. The physical disk instances include the disk number as well as the logical disks that are found on particular physical disks. The logical disk instances just include the individual drive letters.

FIGURE 21.24
Choosing instances of a physical disk versus a logical disk

Table 21.6 shows some common disk counters and what to watch out for. We are using just the logical disk counters in this table.

TABLE 21.6: Common Disk Counters That May Be Useful in Determining Disk Bottlenecks

OBJECT/COUNTER	EXPLANATION\RECOMMENDATION
LogicalDisk/% Disk Time	This is the total percentage of time that the disk is spending performing read and write operations. This value should usually be below 50 to 60 percent on a sustained basis. If this value is excessive, you want to look at the LogicalDisk %Read Time and the LogicalDisk % Write Time values to see if you can determine if the majority of the activity consists of reads or writes.
LogicalDisk/Avg. Disk Queue Length	This is the total number of read and write operations that are currently queued up and waiting for the disk subsystem to perform. This value should not exceed three or four on a sustained basis.
LogicalDisk/Split IO/Sec	This is the number of times per second that a single I/O operation was split into multiple I/O operations. While we don't have a specific number to watch for, a high value may indicate that the disk is fragmented. Ideally, Exchange database and transaction logs are on separate spindles and are less prone to fragmentation.

NETWORK COUNTERS

The network is usually not a performance bottleneck for Exchange and Outlook clients if the Exchange server is on a 100Mb/s, full-duplexed, switched network and the network usually has sufficient capacity. Networking problems usually result from improperly configured switches, routers, or virtual LAN components. In some situations, the network adapter or switch port may be misconfigured and either cause network problems or cause the network to function at the lowest possible speed. Table 21.7 shows some counters that are useful in evaluating your network connectivity and determining if there are problems. When selecting counters to monitor, make sure that you select the correct network adapter instance; in some cases the MS TCP Loopback Interface is selected by default.

TABLE 21.7:   Common Network Counters That Are Useful for Troubleshooting

OBJECT/COUNTER	EXPLANATION\RECOMMENDATION
Network Interface/Current Bandwidth	This counter will show you the network bandwidth at which the network adapter is configured to operate. The value is in bits, so it might be hard to read.
Network Interface/Bytes Total/sec	This is the total bytes sent and received per second. If you convert this to bits per second and then compare it to the Current Bandwidth counter, it will give you an idea of whether the network or network adapter is nearing its capacity.
Network Interface/Packets Outbound Errors and Network Interface/ Packets Received Errors	These counters show the total number or packets that could not be received or transmitted due to errors. These values should be fairly low and should not be rising while you are looking at them. If these values seem excessive, update the network adapter driver, check for network switch configuration problems, or even possibly replace the cable.
TCPv4/Segments Retransmitted/sec	This counter shows the number of TCP segments that had to be retransmitted because they were not properly received by the remote host. This value should be a very low percentage (less than two to three percent) of the total Segments/sec counter. If this value is excessive, it usually indicates problems with the network infrastructure such as routers or switches dropping packets.

EXCHANGE-SPECIFIC COUNTERS

Now that we have looked at some generic Windows counters for performance monitoring and troubleshooting, let's look at a few counters that Exchange server provides that might indicate a bottleneck. Table 21.8 shows some counters that may be useful in determining if there are bottlenecks in your environment that affect Exchange servers or users.

Finding the Right Elixir

Depending on your findings when you use performance monitor, there may be solutions that let you address performance problems without adding additional hardware. Usually, however, at least some additional hardware needs to be thrown into the mix to improve performance. Let's look at some of the major dependencies of Exchange and how we would address bottlenecks related to Exchange.

PHYSICAL MEMORY

With older versions of Exchange, adding additional memory to an Exchange server was something of a cure-all recommendation. This was true until you reached around 4GB of physical memory. At that point, unless the Windows server was supporting more applications that just Exchange components, adding more than 4GB of RAM was just a waste of money. The Exchange

TABLE 21.8: Exchange-Specific Counters That Are Helpful in Troubleshooting Problems and Monitoring Performance

OBJECT/COUNTER	EXPLANATION\RECOMMENDATION
MSExchangeIS/RPC Averaged Latency	This counter represents the average latency (in milliseconds) of the last 1,024 RPC packets. This value should be below 50 milliseconds. Higher values indicate that the server is not responding to requests quickly enough or that there are network problems.
Database/Database Cache % Hit	Selecting the Information Store instance of this counter will tell you the percentage of database file page requests that were serviced from memory rather than having to generate read requests to the disk. A low Database Cache % Hit value will also cause the disk usage to be higher than it should be. We recommend that this value be above 95 percent. If it is not, then consider adding more memory.
MSExchange ADAccess Domain Controllers /LDAP Read Time	This is the time (in milliseconds) that it takes to successfully perform an LDAP search. This value should not be more than 50 milliseconds. Higher values indicate that the selected domain controller is not responding quickly enough due to either performance issues of its own or network problems.

2000/2003 information store service (`store.exe`) could access a maximum of about 1.7GB of physical memory; the other Exchange components together might use another 1GB of memory. Anything over 4GB of RAM was wasted.

With Exchange 2007, though, adding more memory is once again a cure-all for what ails you. Since Exchange Server 2007 is a 64-bit application, you will find that it has the ability to access far more memory than previous versions of Exchange. Adding additional memory can also reduce demands on the disk subsystem.

As of the release date for Exchange 2007, the maximum amount of memory that Exchange can efficiently access and use is 32GB. Beyond this 32GB, Exchange reaches a point of diminishing returns where additional memory will not yield much additional performance when calculating the amount of money necessary to build a server with more than 32GB of RAM.

PHYSICAL AND LOGICAL DISKS

If you are finding performance problems relating to your disk subsystem, there are a couple of options available to you. It will depend on the problem you are experiencing, of course, but you should have some low-cost options as well as more expensive options.

◆ If the problem is related to Exchange database reads/writes or transaction log writes, try increasing the amount of physical memory.

◆ If the problem is specific to one physical disk, try distributing the disk I/O to other physical disks. Transaction log writes and database reads/writes should always be split to separate physical disks when possible.

◆ If you're using RAID 5 or RAID 0+1 arrays, add additional disks to the array to allow for additional I/O capacity.

◆ Move one or more server roles to additional hardware. If you have already split server roles on to dedicated server hardware, you may need additional servers handling a specific role.

PROCESSOR CAPACITY

In Chapter 2, "Exchange Server 2007 Architecture," we talked about having sufficient processor capacity for your servers. The number of processors recommended varies based on the server's roles and, of course, the user profile. Table 21.9 shows the processor recommendations for Exchange 2007.

TABLE 21.9:   Processor Recommendations for Exchange 2007

SERVER ROLE	MINIMUM	RECOMMENDED	MAXIMUM
Client Access	1 x processor core	4 x processor cores	4 x processor core
Combined role	1 x processor core	4 x processor cores	4 x processor core
Hub Transport	1 x processor core	4 x processor cores	8 x processor core
Mailbox	1 x processor core	4 x processor cores	8 x processor core
Unified Messaging	1 x processor core	4 x processor cores	4 x processor core
Edge Transport	1 x processor core	2 x processor cores	4 x processor core

Table 21.9 takes into consideration single-core processors, but based on the price and performance of dual-core processors, a dual-core processor can be a good option if you need additional processor capacity.

Note also that Table 21.9 does not take in to consideration additional applications that may be running on a particular Exchange server. For example, on a heavily loaded Exchange server, antivirus software can consume quite a bit of both CPU and memory resources. Another good example is a Hub Transport server that must process dozens or hundreds of transport rules for each message that it handles.

You may also have noticed in Table 21.9 that for the combined role server (a server that handles more than one role, such as a server with the Mailbox, Hub Transport, and Client Access server roles), the maximum recommended processors is four. The logic behind this (we are assuming) is that once a combined function server gets to the point that it requires more than four processors, it should probably be split into more than one physical machine rather than adding more hardware.

Cleaning Up Unwanted Content

We were not quite sure where to put this section of the book since it did not fit well into any particular chapter. So here is where you find information on how to export data out of a mailbox. In the past, we used tools such as ExMerge to remove mail from a mailbox if it was no longer necessary (such as old mail that's archived) or if we had to remove a message that contained a virus.

Exchange 2007 introduces a new Exchange Management Shell cmdlet called `Export-Mailbox` that you can use to remove content from a mailbox or a whole group of mailboxes. `Export-Mailbox` is a lot more efficient and flexible than ExMerge is too.

The `Export-Mailbox` wizard allows you to search through one or more mailboxes, and when message content is found, it is copied to an alternate mailbox. Optionally, you can specify a parameter that allows you to delete the message from the original location. You can specify a number of different criteria to narrow the scope of the messages for which you are searching. Table 21.10 lists the `Export-Mailbox` parameters along with a description and an example of using each one.

TABLE 21.10:   Search Parameters That Can Be Used with the Export-Mailbox Cmdlet

PARAMETER	DESCRIPTION AND EXAMPLE
AllContentKeywords	When all AllContentKeywords is used, the command will find the keywords you specify in the message subject, body, and attachments. This parameter should not be used in conjunction with the ContentKeywords and SubjectKeywords parameters. Here is an example of this parameter's formatting: -AllContentKeywords "ILOVEYOU"
AttachmentFilenames	Locates messages with a specific filename or when using wildcards. Here are two examples: -AttachmentFilenames "*.txt" and -AttachmentFilenames "iloveyou.vbs"
ContentKeywords	Content keywords allow you search for content in the message body and attachment content. If you use ContentKeywords and SubjectKeywords in the same command, the content must match both. Here is an example: -ContentKeywords "secret formula"
EndDate	EndDate specifies the last date that will be used when copying or moving messages out of a mailbox. If a message is dated after the end date but it meets the criteria, it will not be copied or moved. You can optionally use a time with the date if you want to search only to a certain point during a day. Here are some examples: -EndDate "02/01/2007" and -EndDate "02/02/2007 11:30:00"
ExcludeFolders	If you have specific folders that you do not want to include in the search, you can use the ExcludeFolders parameter. Here is an example where we can exclude the Sent Items folder: -ExcludeFolders "\Sent Items"
IncludeFolders	If you have only specific folders that you want to include in your search, you can use the IncludeFolders parameter. For example, if you want to search in only the Inbox folder, here is an example: -IncludeFolders "\Inbox"
StartDate	StartDate allows you to specify a starting date for your search. When it's used in conjunction with the EndDate parameter, you can narrow the scope of time you are using to search for messages. You can optionally use a time with the date if you want to search only to a certain point during a day. Here are some examples: -StartDate "01/31/2007" and -StartDate"1/31/2007 11:30:00"
SubjectKeywords	Subject keywords are words found in the subject of a message. Here is an example: -SubjectKeywords "I quit"

When using the Export-Mailbox cmdlet, you must specify a target mailbox and a target folder to which you want to copy or move the messages. The -TargetMailbox parameter is used to specify the name of an existing mailbox; the mailbox must exist. The -TargetFolder parameter specifies the name of a folder in the root of the target mailbox. If this folder does not exist, it will be created.

Mail is copied (or moved) to the target folder in the specified target mailbox. A folder structure is created under the specified target folder that includes the recovered data, the mailbox name, and the date of the recovery. An example of this is shown in Figure 21.25. One thing that you may find annoying is that all folders from the source mailbox are created even if there are no messages that meet the search criteria in a particular folder.

FIGURE 21.25
Example of the folder structure created by the Export-Mailbox cmdlet.

The Export-Mailbox cmdlet takes as input the identity of the mailbox to be searched; this can be in the form of the Exchange alias, the SMTP address, or the display name of the mailbox. Export-Mailbox will also accept as input mail-enabled objects piped from cmdlets such as Get-Mailbox and Get-DistributionGroupMember. Let's start out with a really simple example and look at the output. In this example, we want to export (copy) everything in a mailbox called supatana over the date range 01/01/2006 through 12/31/2006. The target mailbox is called MergeMailbox and the target folder is Jan2007Archive. Here is the cmdlet that will perform this operation:

```
Export-Mailbox supatana -TargetMailbox MergeMailbox -TargetFolder Jan2007Archive
-StartDate "01/01/2006" -EndDate "12/31/06"
```

When you kick off the command, you will see a progress bar on the top of the management shell window.

The actual text output of this operation is as follows:

```
C:\>Export-Mailbox supatana -TargetMailbox MergeMailbox
-TargetFolder Jan2007Archive

Confirm
Are you sure you want to perform this action?
Exporting mailbox content from the mailbox 'Matt Suriya' into the mailbox for
'MergeMailbox (MergeMailbox@somorita.com)' inside folder
'\Jan2007Archive\Recovered Data - Matt Suriya - 1/1/2007 5:40:33 PM'.
 This operation may take a long time to complete.
[Y] Yes  [A] Yes to All  [N] No  [L] No to All  [S] Suspend  [?] Help
(default is "Y"):y


Identity                            : volcanosurfboards.com/Somorita Surfboards/
Matt Suriya
DistinguishedName                   : CN=Matt Suriya,OU=Somorita Surfboards,
DC=volcanosurfboards,DC=com
DisplayName                         : Matt Suriya
Alias                               : supatana
LegacyExchangeDN                    : /o=VOLCANO SURFBOARDS/ou=FIRST
ADMINISTRATIVE GROUP/cn=RECIPIENTS/cn=SSUPATANASAKUL
PrimarySmtpAddress                  : supatana@somorita.com
SourceServer                        : HNLEX03.volcanosurfboards.com
SourceDatabase                      : HNLEX03\First Storage Group\Mailbox Database
SourceGlobalCatalog                 : HNLDC01
SourceDomainController              :
TargetGlobalCatalog                 : HNLDC01
TargetDomainController              :
```

```
TargetMailbox                   : volcanosurfboards.com/Users/MergeMailbox
TargetServer                    : HNLEX03.volcanosurfboards.com
TargetDatabase                  : HNLEX03\First Storage Group\Mailbox Database
MailboxSize                     : 198655KB
IsResourceMailbox               : False
SIDUsedInMatch                  :
SMTPProxies                     :
SourceManager                   :
SourceDirectReports             :
SourcePublicDelegates           :
SourcePublicDelegatesBL         :
SourceAltRecipient              :
SourceAltRecipientBL            :
SourceDeliverAndRedirect        :
MatchedTargetNTAccountDN        :
IsMatchedNTAccountMailboxEnabled :
MatchedContactsDNList           :
TargetNTAccountDNToCreate       :
TargetManager                   :
TargetDirectReports             :
TargetPublicDelegates           :
TargetPublicDelegatesBL         :
TargetAltRecipient              :
TargetAltRecipientBL            :
TargetDeliverAndRedirect        :
Options                         : Default
SourceForestCredential          :
TargetForestCredential          :
TargetFolder                    : \Jan2007Archive\Recovered Data -
Matt Suriya - 1/1/2007 5:40:33 PM
RsgMailboxGuid                  :
RsgMailboxLegacyExchangeDN      :
RsgMailboxDisplayName           :
RsgDatabaseGuid                 :
MoveType                        : Export
MoveStage                       : Completed
StartTime                       : 1/1/2007 5:40:36 PM
EndTime                         : 1/1/2007 5:48:28 PM
StatusCode                      : 0
StatusMessage                   : This mailbox has been exported to the target
user mailbox.
```

The report says that the mailbox was "exported," but that is actually a little misleading. It would be better to say that the mailbox was "copied" since the command did not delete any of the original content from the mailbox. To remove the content after it was copied, we could have used the `-DeleteContent` parameter in the command.

You may also wonder about all of the properties that don't seem to have values in this output. The `Export-Mailbox` cmdlet can also be used to move mailboxes from other Exchange organizations and into Exchange 2007, so many of these options are used with migrations from other organizations.

Let's look at a more useful example. What if a user had sent a message with the subject Executive Compensation to everyone in the Viper Pilots group? We can use a combination of two cmdlets to completely remove any message with that subject:

```
Get-DistributionGroupMember "Viper Pilots" | Export-Mailbox
-TargetMailbox MergeMailbox -TargetFolder ExecCompMessage
-SubjectKeyWords "Executive Compensation" -DeleteContent
```

Summary

Administrators that run healthy Exchange organizations and provide their users with good availability have something in common. They're attentive to their Exchange server's needs without overadministering the server. We have a list of the "big five" tasks that we recommend administrators perform daily:

◆ Perform and verify daily Exchange database backups.

◆ Verify that a sufficient amount of disk (and approximately the expected amount of disk space) is available.

◆ Check the Hub Transport server queues to verify that outbound messages are not stalled and queuing up.

◆ Review the event logs for unexpected errors or warnings.

◆ Confirm that your message hygiene software is up-to-date.

Granted these guidelines are just an overview of some basic tasks, but they give you an idea of the types of things you should do on a regular basis. These tasks have a few things in common. Most important, they are more focused on monitoring Exchange and checking to make sure things are done (like daily backups) than on performing any sort of direct action against the Exchange server. Contrary to popular belief, a stable, well-configured Exchange server does not need to be rebooted regularly, nor do databases need any sort of offline maintenance.

There are some basic auditing and diagnostics logging categories that should be enabled to allow the server to be audited or to get information about daily activity. Periodically, you may need to increase diagnostics logging on other components for troubleshooting and diagnostics. If more in-depth troubleshooting and diagnostics logging are used, they should be disabled or set back to their default values after you are through.

To know what normal behavior is for your server, though, you should do some basic performance monitoring periodically on your Exchange servers. It does not need to be done weekly or even monthly. Perhaps once every three to four months should be sufficient.

Look at some of the common Windows and Exchange performance monitor counters to make sure you have not developed any bottlenecks.

Finally, Exchange administrators periodically find themselves faced with the need to remove content from users' mailboxes. This may be viruses, messages with unauthorized content, or just data that needs to be archived. Exchange 2007 provides a powerful new cmdlet called `Export-Mailbox` that serves this purpose.

Appendix: Cool Third-Party Applications for Exchange Server and Outlook Clients

We never appreciated the meaning of *cool* until we started playing with Exchange Server and its clients and some of the fantastic applications that third-party vendors have created to extend the reach of an already great set of products. Here we will tell you about some of our favorite products.

Products are listed by category, along with information on how you can contact the vendors. Some vendors provide live demos or even trial versions of their products that you can download over the Internet.

While we have tried hard to keep this list of tools and vendors accurate, it is by no means complete and may not even be completely accurate by the time you read it. There is continual change in vendors and ownership of products in our industry.

Most of the vendors listed here either have begun shipping or are committed to shipping Exchange 2007 versions of their products, though as this book is being written, many vendors are still shipping only Exchange 2000/2003 versions. Contact the vendor for more information.

WARNING

Remember, we can't be responsibile for the performance for these products in your Exchange Server and organizational environments. We recommend that you install and test each product in a lab environment prior to putting it into production.

Administration and Management

Exchange administration and management covers a wide area. The products listed here do the same. Some monitor Exchange servers and connectors, reporting on such things as e-mail loads and network availability. Other products assist in migrating mailboxes and other Exchange objects within an Exchange organization or between Exchange organizations. Still other products help you automate the resource-draining creation of Outlook profiles for Exchange server. And one product in this section is a substitute for Windows clustered servers.

Availability Manager for Exchange   Quest Availability Manager for Exchange ensures business continuity by providing the ability to detect when an e-mail outage has occurred, and rapidly failover users to a predefined Exchange database where they will continue to have uninterrupted e-mail capabilities. Clients including Outlook, Outlook Web Access, ActiveSync and BlackBerry users can continue to access their e-mail including access to historical information. Contact Quest Software (www.quest.com)

ChooseFrom for Microsoft Exchange   ChooseFrom allows a user to choose an alternate address for a message to be from rather than their default address. This is useful, for example, when a group of users receive a message sent to the Sales alias and a user wants to reply to that message but have the Sales e-mail address rather than their own address be in the From field. At press time, ChooseFrom has been announced for Exchange 2007. Contact: IVASoft (www.ivasoft.com)

Directory Update   Directory Update is a Web-based administration tool that allows an end user to update their own information in the Active Directory and thus the Exchange address lists. The administrator specifies which attributes the user can update. Contact: ITCS Hawaii (www.directory-update.com)

EmpowerID Suite   The EmpowerID Suite is a web-based account provisioning that works against Active Directory and ADAM directories. EmpowerID can join attributes from multiple directories. Contact: The Dot Net Factory (www.thedotnetfactory.com)

Exchange Administrator   Exchange Administrator is a nice front end for managing the Active Directory side of Exchange server. It supports the automation of administrative tasks such as mailbox creation. The product is an add-on to NetIQ's Directory and Resource Administrator. Contact: NetIQ (www.netiq.com)

Exchange Migration Wizard   The Exchange Migration Wizard is a comprehensive migration tool that will allow you to perform migrations from Exchange 5.5 to Exchange 2007 with minimal disruption to your user community. This tool is part of a fairly comprehensive offering of migration tools from Quest Software. Contact: Quest Software (www.quest.com)

Exchange Migrator   Another product from NetIQ, Exchange Migrator simplifies the migration of Exchange objects from one Exchange organization to another. As this book goes to press, we are not sure if NetIQ will release a migrator for Exchange 2007 or not. Contact: NetIQ (www.netiq.com)

Exchange POP3   Exchange POP is a gateway that downloads messages from non-Exchange POP3 and IMAP4 mailboxes to Exchange mailboxes. This product is useful for users who receive all or some of their e-mail outside of Exchange, for example, at an ISP. Exchange POP includes antivirus and anti-spam screening. See also the product Mail Essentials for Exchange/SMTP in the section "Virus, Spam, and Content Control" later in this appendix. Contact: Kinesphere Corporation (www.exchangepop3.com)

MailShadow   MailShadow is one of the truly unique products on the market for Exchange server. It allows the administrator to select mailboxes and have the content replicated and then synchronized to another server. If the user's mailbox server fails, they can be switched over to their backup mailbox. Contact: Cemaphore Systems (www.cemaphore.com)

Message Classification   Titus Labs Message Classification is the classification and policy enforcement tool for Outlook and Outlook Web Access that allows customers to manage the classification, distribution, and retention of valuable corporate e-mail. It includes the ability to enforce users to assign e-mail classification labels at the desktop before messages are sent, restricting the distribution of sensitive e-mail to authorized recipients only. In addition, it allows users to categorize e-mail for easy storage, search, and retrieval. Designed for large enterprises, Message Classification allows users to assign categorization properties to e-mail messages. Contact: Titus Labs (www.titus-labs.com)

Message Manager   Message Manager can scan e-mail databases for specific content to find information leaks, track specific messages, and investigate e-mail related to specific employees or subjects. Contact: Intellireach Corp. (www.intellireach.com)

Migration Manager for Exchange   Migration Manager for Exchange is comprehensive solution for seamless, transparent inter-org migrations from Exchange 2000/2003 to Exchange Server 2007. It supports multiple Exchange migration scenarios; one- or two-way synchronization of directory objects; mailboxes and public folders; address updating on migrated messages; and comprehensive coexistence capabilities. Contact: Quest Software (www.quest.com)

Network E-mail Examiner   Network E-mail Examiner is a tool that allows you to search and analyze an Exchange Server database for words and phrases that you may need to look for when searching for content that is not permitted within your organization or performing a legal discovery. At press time, an Exchange 2007 version of this tool has not been announced, but check with the vendor. Contact: Paraben Forensics Tools (www.paraben-forensics.com)

Notes Migrator for Exchange   Quest Notes Migrator for Exchange enables organizations to migrate direct from Lotus Notes to Microsoft Exchange Server 2007 with complete project management and reporting while minimizing impact to users. Contact: Quest Software (www.quest.com)

Profile Maker   Profile Maker helps Exchange managers build and support common Outlook/Exchange Server profiles. It allows for configuration of local file paths, message retention settings, addressing, delivery, and folder options. If a user changes their profile, that profile is replaced with their Profile Maker profile the next time they log in to the network. These tools are especially helpful for older versions of Outlook that may not have full GPO templates or the Autodiscover features of Outlook 2007. Contact: Desktop Standard (www.desktopstandard.com)

Profiler   Profiler is a web-based tool that allows a user to update some of their Active Directory/global address list information via a web page. This includes mailbox forwarding. Profiler also allows designated account managers to manage user accounts through a web interface. Contact: Directory Wizards (www.dirwiz.com)

PST Policy Administrator   PST Policy Administrator is software that allows you to keep your users' PST usage in check. The software can also manage PST file content and delete attachments from PST files. Contact: Sherpa Software (www.sherpasoftware.com)

Public Folder Migrator for SharePoint   Public Folder Migrator for SharePoint is a new tool from Quest Software that allows you to perform assessments of migration requirements and to migrate the public folder hierarchy and data into SharePoint sites. It is no secret that public folders are going to be less important in the future. Organizations that get a head start toward moving their public folder content to another platform will be much better off with future versions of Exchange. Contact: Quest Software (www.quest.com)

SimpleSync   SimpleSync is a directory synchronization tool that allows you to synchronize user and contact information between multiple directory sources, including Active Directory, Exchange 5.5, and others. Contact: CPS Systems (www.cps-systems.com)

WebDir   WebDir is a complete web-based account provisioning system that includes delegated administration, Exchange mailbox management, and self-service directory management options. Contact: Imanami (www.imanami.com)

ZANTAZ EAS Discovery   ZANTAS EAS Discovery enables an administrator to perform keyword searches against Exchange databases and other e-mail locations such as PST files or archival systems. Contact: ZANTAZ (www.zantaz.com)

Monitoring and Reporting

Let's face it, our bosses love reports. Especially if those reports have colors and graphics! Systems people love monitoring systems that will help them be more proactive in the monitoring of their servers. In this section, we will introduce you to a few monitoring and reporting packages that will make your life easier and let you send the boss those spiffy reports.

AppManager for Microsoft Exchange   AppManager for Exchange lets you monitor the health and performance of an entire distributed Exchange system. It can tell you such things as the time it takes to deliver e-mail, where Internet e-mail is being sent, what is making some mailboxes as large as they are, and where offensive e-mail resides on your server. Contact: NetIQ (www.netiq.com)

Argent Exchange Monitor   Argent Exchange Monitor is for small to very large Exchange environments (up to 2,000 Exchange servers). Monitoring includes response-time tracking, SMTP connectivity, top senders and receivers of messages, and mailboxes over storage limits. Contact: Argent Software (www.argent.com)

Control Suite for Exchange   Control Suite for Exchange is a monitoring, alerting, and reporting tool for Exchange. It includes two products: MessageInsight for Exchange (usage reporting with histories) and ExRay for Exchange (monitoring, alerting, and reporting). Contact: Intellireach Corp. (www.intellireach.com)

Promodag Reports   Promodag Reports is an agent-less reporting tool that uses existing Exchange log files such as the message tracking logs to provide extensive usage reports of your Exchange servers. Contac: Promodag (www.promodag.com)

MessageStats   MessageStats is a comprehensive reporting tool for Exchange Server that reports on mailbox usage, top senders, most commonly used domains, and more. Contact: Quest Software (www.quest.com)

OmniAnalyser   OmniAnalyser provides monitoring and reporting solutions for Exchange as well as service metrics that can be used for service level agreement management. Contact: Hypersoft (www.hypersoft.com)

Power GUI   PowerGUI is an extensible graphical administrative console for managing systems based on Windows PowerShell. These include Windows OS (XP, 2003, Vista), Exchange 2007, Operations Manager 2007 and other new systems from Microsoft. The tool allows administrators to access and use the rich capabilities of Windows PowerShell in a familiar and intuitive GUI console. Contact Quest Software (www.quest.com)

Spotlight on Exchange   Spotlight on Exchange and its companion product Spotlight on Active Directory are two of the slickest and most "Star Trek"–looking server monitoring tools on the market. These tools monitor server health and report server problems, bottlenecks, and performance in a very slick graphical user interface. Contact: Quest Software (www.quest.com)

Smarts Application Discovery Manager   EMC Smarts Application Discovery Manager is powered by EMC nLayers technology and provides the infrastructure for real-time hands-off dependency-driven change, configuration, incident, and problem management. It works with

Exchange, SQL, and Active Directory among other applications. Contact: EMC Corporation (`www.emc.com`)

Zenprise   Zenprise is a not really a monitoring or reporting tool in the traditional sense but rather a proactive monitoring and diagnostics tool for Exchange. Zenprise scans your Exchange server's configuration, event logs, and services and analyzes Exchange in real time. A knowledge base of common problems and solutions is used and can provide administrators with knowledge of an impending problem before it affects users. Contact: Zenprise (`www.zenprise.com`)

Backup, Recovery, and Archiving Software

The key here is support for Exchange Server. Windows Server 2003's own backup program backs up the Exchange mailbox and public information stores while they're open and in use. That's really nice, but Windows Server 2003's Backup utility isn't the most full-featured backup product around. For example, it doesn't back up individual Exchange mailboxes and its disaster recovery capabilities aren't all that sophisticated. Still, the Windows 2003 backup program can work well for small networks, especially if each server is backed up locally. For more features, turn to third-party backup solutions that include such features as Windows Server 2003's ability to do volume shadow copy backups of Exchange databases.

Organizational requirements, governmental regulations, or just plain diminishing disk-storage resources might require that e-mail be archived. Whether it's to protect employee pension information, to meet the financial requirements of agencies such as the Securities Exchange Commission, or to free up space on Exchange Server disks, e-mail archiving is becoming an important function in IT shops. You can do some archiving with tools built into Exchange Server and Outlook, but third-party add-ons make archiving much easier.

Archive Manager   Archive Manager captures, indexes and stores messaging data for the purpose of mailbox management, compliance archiving and knowledge sharing. Powerful search tools allow for retrieval from the archive to support e-discovery. Features mobile access for BlackBerry and Windows Mobile 5 devices as well. Contact: Quest Software (`www.quest.com`)

Brightstor ARCserve Backup   ARCserve has been around for a long time and is a good package. Under the enterprise-oriented hand of Computer Associates, the Brightstore ARCserve Backup suite has become a very strong contender in large system backup. Contact: Computer Associates (`www.cai.com`)

Backup Exec   Like ARCserve, Backup Exec has been around for eons and is a good backup product with nice backup-scheduling capabilities. Also check out Symantec's Remote Storage for Exchange, which archives message attachments to a secondary storage device such as tape and then seamlessly returns the attachment when a user tries to access it. Contact: Symantec (`www.symantec.com`)

Exchange Archive Solution   Exchange Archive Solution archives Exchange messages so that they can be managed and retrieved as needed. This is a high-powered product that allows for centralized backup while leaving room for local control and end-user recovery of archived messages. Contact: ZANTAZ. (`www.zantaz.com`)

Galaxy Backup and Recovery for Microsoft Exchange   Galaxy Backup and Recovery for Microsoft Exchange is a very nice product. It has a fine user interface and it allows individual recovery of messages and other Exchange items. Contact: CommVault Systems (`www.commvault.com`)

EmailXtender   EmailXtender is an e-mail archiving application. It runs on a separate server and can archive mail in a variety of server environments, including Exchange, Lotus Notes, and Unix Sendmail. Data is stored in Microsoft SQL Server. Administration includes the ability to set retention parameters and policies for categorization of messages. Contact: EMC Corporation (www.emc.com)

Enterprise Vault   Enterprise Vault is one of the industry leaders in Exchange archiving. It runs on a dedicated server and supports Exchange 5.5–2007, Lotus Notes, File Server Archiving, SharePoint Archiving, PST migrations, and many third party add-ins such as instant messaging, Bloomberg, and fax archiving. Contact: Symantec (www.symantec.com)

NetWorker   Well known for the excellence of its storage products and Unix backup products, EMC also supports the Windows NT 4 and Windows 200x Server environments with its NetWorker backup product. An optional module extends support to Exchange Server. Contact: EMC Corporation (www.emc.com)

NetBackup   NetBackup is the industrial-strength enterprise backup product from Symantec, makers of Backup Exec. The product provides centralized control of the backup process and comes in three flavors for different-sized organizations and backup needs. Contact: Symantec (www.symantec.com)

Recovery Manager for Exchange   Recovery Manager for Exchange allows administrators to restore, search and export individual message-level items, including e-mails, appointments, tasks, contacts, and attachments from backups, un-mounted edb files and PST files without setting up multiple dedicated Exchange recovery servers. Contact: Quest Software (www.quest.com)

Replication Manager   EMC Replication Manager manages EMC replication technologies and coordinates the entire replication process, from discovery and configuration to the operation of multiple disk-based replicas. Put the right data in the right place at the right time, on demand or based on user-defined schedules and policies. With Replication Manager, you can automate the discovery of storage arrays, applications, replication technologies, and hosts in the environment; record and catalog all information and activities for replicas; and enable point-and-click copies of information. Contact: EMC Corporation (www.emc.com)

UltraBac   UltraBac Software's backup entry sports very nice backup setup and scheduling interfaces. An optional Exchange information store backup module is available. Contact: UltraBac Software (www.ultrabac.com)

Fax Servers

Though Exchange Server 2007 provides good integration for inbound faxing with the Unified Messaging server role, you may have other needs, such as outbound faxing. The cost to implement a full unified messaging solution may also be too high for your organization. Generally, fax servers enable users to send and receive faxes through a central server instead of their own workstations or traditional fax machines. Fax servers that integrate with Exchange Server add a new address type for faxing. To send a message to an e-mail user, you select the user's e-mail address from an Exchange address book. To send a message to a fax user, you select the fax address from an Exchange address book.

FACSys Fax Connector 2000   FACSys Fax Connector 2000 operates pretty much like any other connector on an Exchange server, but it sends faxes. The product is managed right inside Exchange System Manager. Contact: FACSys (www.facsys.com)

Faxcom for Exchange   Faxcom for Exchange runs as a Windows service. It integrates Exchange recipient information so users can send faxes using their Outlook contacts. Contact: Biscom, Inc. (www.biscom.com)

Faxination Server for Microsoft Exchange   Faxination Server for Microsoft Exchange provides full Exchange Server integration and supports a range of languages. It allows for off-hours scheduling and least-cost routing. Contact: Fenestrae, Inc. (www.fenestrae.com)

FAXmaker for Exchange   FAXmaker for Exchange runs as a Windows service and allows faxes and GSM phone service SMS messages to be sent from an Outlook client with seamless Exchange Server integration. It includes call cost accounting. Contact: GFI (www.gfi.com)

DM Fax Server   DM Fax Server installs and works as a Windows service. It can function as a high-traffic fax server and it can support a range of e-document distribution functions, such as automated faxback. Contact: IMECOM Group (www.imecominc.com)

Genifax   Genifax is a sophisticated fax server that works with a wide range of high-end messaging platforms, including Lotus Notes and Exchange Server. Omtool, the product's manufacturer, specializes in the legal and health care industries. Genifax can be expanded to include e-document distribution functionality. Contact: Omtool (www.omtool.com)

MsXfax XP for Exchange   MsXfax XP for Exchange can be installed on an Exchange or Windows server. It integrates with Active Directory without modifying the schema. Contact: BSN Group (www.bnsgroup.com.au)

RightFax   RightFax is an enterprise-level product focusing on e-document delivery. The product is tightly coupled with application solutions from SAP AG. Contact: Captaris, Inc. (www.captaris.com/rightfax)

Replication and High-Availability Software

Exchange Services are now required in many instances to be highly available or recoverable in alternate locations. With these rigorous requirements, organizations are adopting tools to supplement the backup technologies in place and the built-in replication mechanisms available. The goal of these vendors is to provide flexibility and control in how Exchange databases are replicated and how they will be available during a disaster.

MailShadow   MailShadow is one of the truly unique products on the market for Exchange server. This product allows the administrator to select mailboxes and have the content replicated and then synchronized to another server. If the user's mailbox server fails, they can be switched over their backup mailbox. Contact: Cemaphore Systems (www.cemaphore.com)

NearPoint   Mimosa NearPoint for Microsoft Exchange Server is the industry's most comprehensive information management solution for Microsoft Exchange. It unifies archival, eDiscovery or e-mail discovery, fine-grained and immediate recovery, user self-service access to all historical e-mail, and storage management. The NearPoint software solution comprises Information Management (ILM), e-mail archiving, disaster recovery, data protection, and mailbox extension functions. Contact: Mimosa Systems, Inc. (www.mimosasystems.com)

EMC RepliStor   EMC RepliStor is an easy-to-use, out-of-the-box software technology that provides data recovery and protection for Microsoft Windows. RepliStor increases the availability of your data by delivering real-time replicas to one or many locations. You can use data for offline backup protection, disaster recovery, data distribution, and application testing. Contact: EMC Corporation (www.emc.com)

RecoverPoint   EMC RecoverPoint (formerly Kashya) is an intelligent data protection and recovery solution that runs on out-of-band appliances located on the network. RecoverPoint provides comprehensive data recovery for storage area network (SAN)–attached devices across the entire data center, including heterogeneous, continuous remote replication and local continuous data protection. You can protect your organization from data loss due to common issues such as server failures, data corruption, software errors, viruses, and end user errors as well as from catastrophic events that can bring entire data centers to a standstill. Contact: EMC Corporation (`www.emc.com`)

SRDF Family   The SRDF family of software is a powerful suite of remote storage replication solutions available for disaster recovery and business continuity. It leverages high-end Symmetrix storage architecture to offer unmatched deployment flexibility and massive scalability — so you can meet mixed service level requirements with minimal operational impact. Regardless of the application and RTO/RPO requirements, SRDF has the capability to meet your needs. Contact: EMC Corporation (`www.emc.com`)

Network Security Monitors, Scanners, and Intrusion Detectors

We talked about network security monitors and scanners in Chapter 20, "Securing Exchange Server." Scanner products plow through network nodes on an IP-by-IP basis looking for such things as missing service packs and hotfixes, open ports, weak passwords, and potentially dangerous assignments of security privileges as well as services, applications, and Registry key entries that might threaten security. Security monitors examine system logs for potential security holes and breaches.

Intrusion detectors are sort of intelligent firewalls for networks, servers, and workstations. They can find and thwart internal and external attempts to access resources far beyond the port and protocol level.

LANGuard Security Event Log Monitor   LANGuard Monitor combs Windows event logs looking for evidence of internal and external security violations. It provides real-time notifications and reports to system managers. LANGuard also supports systemwide log management, including automated archiving and clearing of event logs. Contact: GFI Software (`www.gfi.com`)

LANGuard Network Security Scanner   LANGuard Scanner looks at network nodes for known security problems. It's fast, and we have found it to be quite accurate. It produces very nice reports in HTTP format. LANGuard can remotely install service packs and hotfixes. Contact: GFI (`www.gfi.com`)

Monitor Magic   Monitor Magic stores its findings in Microsoft SQL Server or Access databases. It comes with a range of very useful preconfigured security and other reports. A web interface is also included. Contact: Advanced Toolware (`www.advtoolware.com`)

Network Monitoring Suite   Network Monitoring Suite includes features similar to LANGuard Monitor. The product also includes performance monitoring based on Windows performance logs and Windows service monitoring with auto restarts. Contact: LANWare, Inc. (`www.lanware.net`)

RealSecure Network Protection Components   The RealSecure Network Protection Components suite includes modules for networks, gateways, servers, and workstations. The modules detect attempted internal and external intrusions and stop them in real time. Contact: Internet Security Systems (www.iss.net)

RealSecure Vulnerability Assessment   The RealSecure Vulnerability Assessment suite includes components for the Internet, servers, databases, and 802.11b wireless networks. These components scan their targets looking for a range of security threats. This product offers the most comprehensive approach to system security. Contact: Internet Security Systems (www.iss.net)

RETINA Network Security Scanner   Like LANGuard, RETINA scans network nodes for known security problems. The program includes an interesting if not easy-to-validate artificial intelligence component that tries to get into a network as a hacker might. In our experience, RETINA is fast and quite accurate. Contact: eEye Digital Security (www.eeye.com)

SecureIIS   SecureIIS is designed to protect Microsoft's Internet Information Server from external and internal attacks. The product examines traffic coming into IIS and stops packets that pose a threat. It can protect IIS servers with security problems for which Microsoft has not yet issued fixes. Contact: eEye Digital Security (www.eeye.com)

Unified Messaging

Unified messaging, the linking of a variety of messaging tools — pagers, telephones, e-mail clients, fax — has long been a dream of forward-looking communications types. As these products indicate, the tools for accomplishing unified messaging have emerged.

Mitel Networks 6510 Unified Messaging   Mitel Networks 6510 Unified Messaging brings together voice, incoming fax, and e-mail messaging. It also supports text-to-speech conversion and is scheduled to support speech-to-text in the near future. Wireless PDAs are supported. Contact: Mitel Networks Corporation (www.mitel.com)

PageMaster/ex   PageMaster/ex allows Exchange Server users to send pages and text messages to pagers. Page recipients appear on Exchange and can be selected from global or personal address lists. Messages can be sent in pager alphanumeric or GMS SMS format. It has a companion product called PageMaster/ol, which will send text messages for Outlook reminders. Contact: OmniTrend Software, Inc. (www.omnitrend.com)

Unified Messenger   Unified Messenger is a high-end product that integrates with Exchange Server. It stores voicemail messages inside users' Exchange mailboxes. You can reply to voicemail with e-mail and vice versa. More real coolness! Contact: Avaya, Inc. (www.avaya.com)

Virus, Spam, and Content Control

What scares users more than the boss? Viruses, junk mail, and outgoing messages containing confidential information! These products let you catch mail-borne viruses, spam messages, and messages with sensitive content in their natural habitat: your Exchange server. They automatically download and install virus updates. Most also scan for viruses in real time as messages pass through your Exchange server and can perform scheduled and on-demand scans of information stores for viruses.

Forefront Security for Exchange Server   Forefront Security for Exchange Server (formerly Sybari Antigen) does real-time virus scans and repairs of inbound and outbound messages. It also does scheduled scans and fixes. Antigen supports third-party virus-scan engines for better virus coverage, especially with new viruses. Contact: Microsoft Corporation (www.microsoft.com/forefront)

Clearswift MIMESweeper   MIMESweeper is a suite of content security products that integrate with Exchange. MIMESweeper has been used since the Exchange 5.5 version of the product and continues to be reliable. Contact: Clearswift Ltd. (www.clearswift.com)

iHateSpam Server Edition   iHateSpam is server-based anti-spam software. It allows for extensive customization according to individual user needs. This overcomes one of the real weaknesses of server-based anti-spam solutions. There is a desktop version of iHateSpam that is not integrated with the server version. Contact: Sunbelt Software (www.sunbelt-software.com)

Mail Essentials for Exchange/SMTP   Mail Essentials for Exchange/SMTP is a multifeatured package that does spam control with keyword and black and white lists, addition of disclaimers to outgoing messages, mail archiving, mail monitoring, and automatic replies. It also can download mail from POP3 mailboxes into Exchange mailboxes. Contact: GFI (www.gfi.com)

Mail Security for Exchange/SMTP   Mail Security for Exchange/SMTP is a comprehensive virus-control package that supports multiple virus-scanning engines. It also does content checking and HTML script checking and blocking. Contact: GFI (www.gfi.com)

Mail Security for Microsoft Exchange   Mail Security for Microsoft Exchange provides full-service virus scanning and cleaning. It also includes spam control features. Contact: Symantec Corporation (www.symantec.com)

MailWise   MailWise isn't a product that's installed on servers or workstations. Rather, it's a third-party service set up to receive mail destined for an SMTP server and quarantine it if it contains viruses or spam. Administrators can then either delete quarantined mail or send it along to its recipient. Contact: MailWise (www.mailwise.com)

MessageScreen   MessageScreen supports virus and spam control as well as detection and prevention of information leaks. Contact: Intellireach Corp. (www.intellireach.com)

Panda Anti-Virus for Exchange Server   Panda Anti-Virus for Exchange Server does most of the Exchange Server–based virus scanning and cleaning tricks performed by its competitors. Contact: Panda Software (www.pandasoftware.com)

Power Tools for Exchange   Power Tools monitors messages and attachments for violations of corporate policy, offensive language, viruses, and spam content. The product also adds signatures to outgoing Internet messages, enabling the insertion of corporate disclaimers in all messages. Contact: NEMX Software (www.nemx.com)

Praetor for Microsoft Exchange Server   Praetor for Microsoft Exchange Server includes both antivirus and anti-spam functions. The product includes proprietary technology developed through the analysis of techniques used by spammers. Contact: Computer Mail Services, Inc. (www.cmsconnect.com)

ScanMail   Trend ScanMail looks for viruses on an Exchange server, even in encoded and compressed items. The product also does limited spam control. Contact: Trend Micro Inc. (www.antivirus.com)

SecurExchange Anti-Virus   SecurExchange Anti-Virus, like most of its competitors, scans e-mail and attachments, including zipped files on an Exchange server, for viruses. Contact: Nemx Software (www.nemx.com)

SurfControl E-Mail Filter for SMTP   SurfControl E-Mail Filter for SMTP is a comprehensive package that includes multi-engine virus scanning, high-powered anti-spam control, and very sophisticated content-checking functionality. At press time, SurfControl is the only product that can check images for textual and other indicators of spam. Contact: SurfControl (`www.surfcontrol.com`)

Outlook and Outlook Web Access Add-Ins

There are a huge number of Outlook add-ins available out there in the third-party world. Here are a few extensions and add-ins from third parties that we found particularly useful.

EasyRecovery EmailRepair   EasyRecovery EmailRepair is a software utility that allows you to repair damaged Outlook PST and OST files. Contact: Kroll Ontrack (`www.krollontrack.com`)

MaX Compression   MaX Compression integrates with Outlook, Outlook Web Access, Exchange Server, and SMTP gateways to automatically compress (and optionally decompress) e-mail messages with attachments. If the client has MaX Compression installed, the compression and decompression process is transparent to the end user. Contact: C2C Systems (`www.c2c.com`)

Outlook Web Access for PDA/Outlook Web Access for WAP   Outlook Web Access for PDA and Outlook Web Access for WAP are two extensions for Outlook Web Access that provide a significantly better OWA interface for small screens such as PDA screens or for WAP browser-enabled cell phones. Outlook Web Access for WAP is a nice addition to Exchange Server 2007 since the Outlook Mobile Access feature is no longer supported. Contact: Lee Derbyshire (`www.leederbyshire.com`)

PKZIP for Windows   PKZIP for Windows includes an extension for Outlook that will automatically compress e-mail attachments larger than a certain size. This can dramatically reduce your mail storage requirements and bandwidth necessary to transmit e-mail messages. Contact: PKWare (`www.pkware.com`)

Workflow

The great promise of electronic messaging systems such as Exchange Server lies in their capability to help manage the flow of documents to complete a specific task among the various persons who need to be involved in the task. The products listed here add to Exchange Server's already wide-ranging capabilities in the workflow arena.

80-20 Document Manager   80-20 Document Manager works with Exchange, IBM DB2, and Microsoft SQL Server databases. It enables users to share files with full document-level security, version control, check-in/check-out, and full-text indexing. This product enables serious Exchange-based groupware applications. Contact: 80-20 Software (`www.80-20.com`)

KnowledgeMail   KnowledgeMail scans corporate e-mail looking for topic areas and connections based on senders and recipients. It seeks to find sources of organizational expertise and activity. Users can then access the KnowledgeMail database when embarking on new projects or to enhance ongoing projects. Contact: Tacit Knowledge Systems, Inc. (`www.tacit.com`)

Transform Response   Transform Response is a tool for developing group inbox applications. The product can be used to support such applications as a customer service center for a website, an e-mail extension to a call center, or a corporate or customer help desk. Contact: Transform Research (`www.transres.com`)

Index

Symbols and Numbers